Made
From
This
Earth

# Gender & American Culture

# Made

*American Women and Nature*

# From

*VERA NORWOOD*

# This

*The University of North Carolina Press*

# Earth

*Chapel Hill & London*

© 1993 The University of North Carolina Press

All rights reserved

Manufactured in the United States of America

Library of Congress Cataloging-in-Publication Data

Norwood, Vera.

   Made from this earth : American women and nature / Vera
Norwood.

     p.   cm. — (Gender and American Culture)

   Includes bibliographical references and index.

   ISBN 0-8078-2062-8 (cloth : alk. paper).

   —ISBN 0-8078-4396-2 (pbk.: alk. paper)

   1. Women naturalists—United States—History.   2. Women
conservationists—United States—History.   3. Ecofeminism.
I. Title.

QH26.N67   1993        92-22562

508.73'082—dc20        CIP

The author is grateful for permission to quote several lines
from "Come Into Animal Presence," by Denise Levertov. The
complete poem is from *Poems, 1960–1967*. Copyright © 1961
by Denise Levertov Goodman. Reprinted with permission of
New Directions Publishing Corporation.

97  96  95  94  93     5  4  3  2  1

*For* AGATHA *and* MIKE

# Contents

# Illustrations

# Preface

*Watch this, gents. Watch the lady act like a woman. For that's
what she did. The well-behaved, quiet, pretty, serene, domestic
creature peaceably yielding herself to the uses of man all of a sudden said NO. And she spat dirt and smoke and steam . . . She
swore and belched and farted, threatened and shook and swelled,
and then she spoke. They heard her voice two hundred miles away.
Here I go, she said. I'm doing my thing now. Old Nobodaddy you
better JUMP.*

—Ursula Le Guin, *"A Very Warm Mountain"*

WHEN MOUNT SAINT HELENS blew her top, Ursula
Le Guin used the occasion to meditate on the usual portrayal of nature as
female, arguing that Saint Helens reminded us of the destructive but potentially cleansing meanings of such a metaphor. Le Guin also considered the
divergent messages the volcanic explosion sent to men and to women, stem-
ming from gender-based differences in conceptions of the feminine. Le Guin's
allegory raises two issues central to the concerns of this book. First, how have
American women found meaning in, and ascribed meaning onto, the biophysical landscape? Do they speak of nature as mother, sister, friend, lover?
If so, what do such metaphors imply? What aspects of the natural world have
attracted the notice of American women—small, enclosed gardens; domesticated fields and pastures; forests; oceans; deserts—and how do they integrate
such disparate landscapes? Second, what is the context for American women's
responses to nature? To what extent have gender roles influenced what women
have valued in nature? How have women used gender differences to distinguish their environmental values from men's? Further, how have education,

class, ethnicity and race, and the period in which a woman lives informed the responses she might make to a phenomenon like the eruption of Mount Saint Helens?

In his preface to the new edition (1990) of *Back to Nature: The Arcadian Myth in Urban America*, Peter J. Schmitt comments on the contemporary impression that American women have come only lately to nature writing: "Have we lost track? What of . . . Anna Comstock or Gene Stratton Porter, Katharine Pinkerton or Sally Carrighar?"[1] Originally published in 1969, *Back to Nature* included many such women, marking it as a singular history of American environmental values. Although classic studies like Hans Huth's *Nature and the American* (1957), Roderick Nash's *Wilderness and the American Mind* (1967), and Joseph Petulla's *American Environmental History* (1977) mention a few women, the thrust of their narrative is carried by male voices, male agendas. More recent histories, such as Paul Brooks's *Speaking for Nature* (1980), Thomas Dunlap's *Saving America's Wildlife* (1988), and Stephen Fox's *John Muir and His Legacy: The American Conservation Movement* (1981), provide somewhat more detailed discussions of women's work. Even in these studies, however, women appear as significant actors only sporadically, and then in roles meshing perfectly with gender stereotypes. Excepting Rachel Carson, who achieved solitary fame as one of the founders of the environmental movement, women have received most attention for their work in bird protection campaigns, city sanitation and beautification efforts, and the antivivisectionist and antihunting movements.

Women's marginalization stems in part from men's very real dominance in nature study. From the earliest work in natural history—the general investigation of plants, animals, and the physical environment—to its nineteenth- and twentieth-century growth and division into specialized disciplines like botany, ornithology, and geology, men have defined the subjects and methods of study. Environmental historians have reflected this structure of both subject matter and modes of inquiry. As a result, we know a great deal about the men who framed America's environmental agenda, and we know something about how men—naturalists and historians—have viewed women's contributions to nature study and the environmental movement. But we have very little information on the nature study and preservation work that women actually performed or the meanings such activities held for them.

This book centers around women in order to explore the question of how they perceive and act within the natural world. Obviously, American women who took part in nature study recognized that they entered terrain controlled by men. The male narrative defining the meaning of nature has formed a significant aspect of the context for their own efforts. I depart from traditional approaches to environmental history, however, in situating that male narrative as a backdrop to women's efforts, and in questioning the extent to which women have found their nature values mirrored in those of their male colleagues. Although probing the differences between male and female visions of nature, I have chosen not to include detailed analyses of important men in American natural history. Historians of the American environmental movement have well described the nature values of the likes of William Bartram, Henry David Thoreau, John Burroughs, John Muir, Aldo Leopold, Edwin Way Teale, Roger Tory Peterson, Barry Commoner, Loren Eiseley, John Hay, and Barry Lopez. I focus my attention on a large group of influential women who were key players in the study and preservation of nature. Given the masculine context in which they often worked, I am interested in the interpretations women have made of the nature values of their male colleagues. In American women's comments on the similarities and differences between their view of nature and men's lie many clues suggesting that there is a distinctly female tradition in American nature study.

That women have often played supporting roles in environmental history does not mean that they lack a separate tradition. Feminist revisions of the history of science demonstrate that women working in male-dominated fields do not necessarily view their work or practice their science from the same perspective as men. Margaret Rossiter, Sandra Harding, Evelyn Fox Keller, and others argue that gender-role expectations have informed both women's choice of scientific fields and the nature of their work within those fields.[2] And, in fact, women have been more heavily represented in botany and ornithology than in zoology and geology because, during the nineteenth century, they and their male colleagues constructed a match between the study of plants and birds and women's social roles. Whenever a woman has committed herself to nature study, she has done so with some consideration of the propriety of the endeavor. My analysis looks at two aspects of that awareness: women's perceptions of male/female roles within a particular field and their use of gender dichotomies to describe and analyze the natural world.

Surprisingly, feminist historians of science have given scant attention to the broader question of how men and women might hold different concepts of nature. My initial interest in this project grew in part from questions about the extent to which female scientists shared with other women a particular way of understanding nature. This book represents a first step toward delineating what I see as a significant, continuous tradition in the interactions of women with nature. My study of their experiences observing and recording nature, of their work designing and cultivating gardens and wildlife sanctuaries, and of the utopias they have imagined suggests some common ground in American women's sense of their ethical relationship with the biophysical environment. Throughout, I analyze how gender roles have informed women's involvement in and descriptions of the environment.

One feminist historian of science has served as a pioneer in raising some of these issues. In *The Death of Nature: Women, Ecology, and the Scientific Revolution* (1980), Carolyn Merchant probes the consequences of the scientific revolution of the sixteenth and seventeenth centuries for women's relationship to nature. In *Ecological Revolutions: Nature, Gender, and Science in New England* (1989), she extends her analysis to consider the impact of European ideas about nature on American Indians and the land they inhabited. Merchant documents the horticultural knowledge and skills of precolonial southern New England Indian women and outlines the collapse of native agricultural practices with the arrival of Europeans. She also argues that early European farming communities evidenced a knowledge of nature that in some ways was similar to the understanding of agricultural American Indians. Rural Euro-American women of the eighteenth century themselves knew a good deal about the plants and animals that were key to subsistence agriculture. Their knowledge and skills also were reduced and limited with the emergence of the market economy and industrialized farming. Although she briefly discusses Euro-American women's shift into nature study and preservation by the mid-nineteenth century, Merchant does not address the new roles women would play over the next century as Americans expanded their knowledge of the natural landscapes of North America.[3]

The study of nature by American women began in the eighteenth century with scattered accounts by botanists, agriculturists, and travelers. It blossomed in the nineteenth century as women educated the public about nature and worked to preserve and conserve plants and animals. In the twentieth century it came to fruition when women became major voices in nature writing and artistic depiction, in gardening and landscape design, in wildlife conservation, and in the development of environmental philosophy. This study, therefore, concentrates on the nineteenth and twentieth centuries. During the course of the nineteenth century, natural history became a popular hobby as well as a scientific endeavor in America, succeeding a similar rage in England. The nineteenth century, of course, also witnessed many changes in women's roles as America industrialized. Reflecting broad societal concern with defining women's place, specific arenas of nature study and conservation became identified as peculiarly suited to women's domestic responsibilities.

During the nineteenth and twentieth centuries, mainly well-educated, urban, middle-class, Euro-American men and women have engaged in interests commonly thought of as "nature appreciation." Poorer residents of urban areas have had little access to the parks and wilderness areas that figure so heavily in both nature study and conservation circles, while rural farming communities have often been dismissed as blights on an otherwise beautiful view.[4] Further, stereotypes among the Euro-American middle class have depicted most racial and ethnic minorities and lower-class peoples as insensitive to nature. Intellectual elites, defining privileged American flora and fauna, have displayed little interest in other groups' folklore, gardens, or material arts. While my study concentrates on the values expressed by middle- and upper-class Euro-Americans, I recognize the diversity in women's appreciation of nature.

Not all Euro-American women who tended gardens and sketched plants were wealthy; many found nature study a way to make a living as well as to serve a passion. The chapters on illustration and gardening consider some of the class issues reflected in women's work in these areas. Although I briefly cover African American women's gardening preferences, very few minority women have participated in environmental history as nature writers, illustrators, or wildlife observers. I found that the bounds of natural history, the fields in which the traditions of naturism and environmentalism have developed, made integrating the experiences of women of color throughout the book problematic. In designing this study, however, I thought it was critical to consider the reasons for the exclusion of women of color from elite activities and to explore their depictions of plants and animals. I found rich documentation forcefully revealed in fiction and poetry. The chapter on nature imagery in American women's fiction unfolds from stories written by American Indian, African American, and Euro-American women. Here, as women of color name the sources of their isolation from Euro-American environmental traditions and give voice to their own nature lore, I consider in detail race and ethnicity as major determinants of difference in women's responses to nature.

The book falls into two parts. The first four chapters deal with women who located their nature appreciation and work within approved gender codes. The next four chapters chronicle women who experienced tension between their efforts and the social expectations of proper female behavior.

Although the chapters flow in a roughly chronological sequence, my goal was not an exhaustive history of all aspects of women's nature study and work. I chose to highlight arenas in which women have created a niche for themselves and located specifically gendered meaning in the work they have done. When I first began to study women naturalists, it seemed to me that their history was made up of singular, individual heros. The more I probed, however, the more I discovered that these individuals reflected the history of many women who dedicated their lives to the study and protection of nature. While considering the contributions made by key individuals, each chapter surveys the efforts and traditions of a set of women engaged in a similar endeavor. The intent of this strategy is to shift singular women away from their subordination within the male-dominated stream of environmental history and situate women's group achievements within female culture.

For a good many women, teaching children about butterflies, botanizing and birding on leisurely Sundays, sketching wildflowers collected in local terrain, and making an old-fashioned flower bed exemplify appropriate female behavior. Focusing on the environment, making it one's familiar and home, has been key to woman's appreciation of nature. During the early nineteenth century, influential European and American women encouraged botanical study as a particularly suitable endeavor for women. Chapter 1 examines this history, arguing that the blend of sentimental and scientific approaches espoused by these tastemakers provided a significant entry point for middle-class American women's domestication of the natural landscapes of home and neighborhood. Chapter 2 documents women's earliest efforts at nature writing, showing how Susan Fenimore Cooper's 1850 seasonal journal, *Rural Hours*, established a tradition carried on by botanists, entomologists, birders, and other nature lovers throughout the nineteenth century. That tradition culminated in the twentieth century with the work of such contemporary essayists as Ann Zwinger and Josephine Johnson.

As well as writing natural history, women have represented the flora and fauna of America in drawing, painting, and photography. Chapter 3 considers why women came to dominate the field of scientific illustration in the late twentieth century. I construct a history of their artistic endeavors, beginning with the little-known shell illustrators working in the 1830s in Philadelphia, then moving to botanical artists who worked later in the century for the federal government and to bird photographers who turned a home-based hobby to the service of science. An enclosed flower garden filled with beautiful women at their ease remains a classic image of woman's proper role in nature.

In Chapter 4, I move beyond this passive image to explore how early garden writers like Celia Thaxter and landscape designers like Beatrix Farrand managed to maintain societal expectations about women's relegation to the enclosed gardens of home while encouraging women's expansion into the public arenas of city beautification and urban landscape design. Women's preferences in selecting ornamental plants often crossed class boundaries. Indeed, I found a surprising amount of consensus among nineteenth- and twentieth-century American women on the subject of a beautiful flower bed.

For the most part, in each of the areas considered in the first four chapters, women smoothly integrated their own developing interests in nature with broad-based gender-role expectations. The next four chapters study women whose activities and values part company with the dominant expectations of "proper" female relationships to nature. Some of these women—biologist Rachel Carson and anthropologist Dian Fossey—were surprised to discover themselves at odds with the conservation establishment. Others, such as contemporary American Indian writer Leslie Marmon Silko and ecofeminist Ynestra King, clearly expect tension and, in fact, emphasize in their relationship with nature their differences with the dominant culture. Chapter 5 is a study of the network of women conservationists supporting Rachel Carson's battle in the 1950s and 1960s with chemical companies, government agencies, and entomologists to stem the flood of pesticides poisoning the environment. Male critics of Carson's *Silent Spring* used her gender to discredit her ecological warnings. This period provided some of the most public signs that women's sense of their responsibilities to nature could differ from men's.

Women novelists and poets have plumbed the ideologies of Western patriarchal culture, which treat women and the rest of nature as objects of both male domination and exploitation. Women of color have long been aware of racist images of themselves as more animalistic than human; contemporary writers use fiction to bring such stereotypes to wider consciousness and to move beyond them. Chapter 6 analyzes literature by American Indian, African American, and Euro-American women to reveal the symbols underlying the increased tensions between men and women that surfaced in the public arena in the 1950s and 1960s. American Indian, African American, and Euro-American women also have different histories of life on the land. As well as gender splits, this chapter considers the differences among cultural groups as they have articulated their nature lore.

Following this study of women's fiction, Chapter 7 reviews women's actual work with wildlife. I trace the historical tensions in their partnerships with early trophy hunters and scientific collectors and their own tradition as intimates of wild animals studied in the field. Dian Fossey was a principal contemporary representative of these women. I argue, however, that her work was part of a continuum, including early twentieth-century zoologist Theodora Stanwell-Fletcher and mid-century field observers Sally Carrighar and Lois Crisler.

Finally, Chapter 8 examines the emerging philosophy of ecological feminism and places this newest expression of women's collective environmental effort within female traditions in nature appreciation and protection. Directly confronting the Euro-American biases of traditional environmentalism, ecofeminists hope to forge a coalition among women of various classes and races. The literature of the movement portrays American Indian, African American, and Euro-American women engaged in collective political struggle. Rejecting the patriarchal meanings placed upon a female nature, ecofeminists assert their own ability to change the future in much the same way as the explosion of Mount Saint Helens changed the landscape. While acknowledging the potential contributions of the ecofeminist movement to contemporary environmental problems, I show that its utopian focus has at times masked the heritage of women naturalists, conservationists, and environmentalists of the nineteenth and twentieth centuries. Failing to recognize their debt to these forebears, ecofeminists also lose the opportunity to call on women's long-standing traditions in their own movement for change.

In writing this book, I had to choose between many equally important individual women, areas of endeavor, and aspects of nature. For example, there is a chapter on gardening but not on farming. The selection here was informed by my sense that, by the mid-nineteenth century, women's work in landscape architecture and ornamental gardening offered more information on the values driving popular ideas about nature than did the lives of farm women. To get at my broad interest in women's perceptions about nature, I also included activities somewhat less obviously connected to nature study. This is the case especially in the chapter on fiction, but women's imaginative narratives of heros' adventures in the wilderness offer rich information on their symbolic connections to animals and plants. Finally, my choice of chapter topics was fueled by my own interests in nature and reflects personal favorites among many deserving women. These essays are only a beginning; a good deal remains to be done—by environmental historians, in particular—in considering the nature perceptions of women not included within the

Euro-American, urban middle class. I hope my initial attempt spurs the discovery of more unsung heros and engenders critical analysis of the pluralistic strands of, and the continuity in, Americans' responses to nature.

My introduction to the depth of women's commitment to the study and preservation of nature came as I sifted through boxes of Rachel Carson's correspondence in the rare book and manuscript collection at Yale University's Beinecke Library. This book could not have been written without the assistance of knowledgeable staffs of the Beinecke and other libraries and archival collections. I am particularly indebted to Carol Spawn at the American Academy of Natural Sciences of Philadelphia and James White at the Hunt Institute for Botanical Documentation of Carnegie Mellon University. Also, the interlibrary loan staff at the University of New Mexico helped immeasurably in locating sources for even the most arcane material. Research for this book was supported by a summer fellowship from the American Council of Learned Societies and by several Research Allocation awards from the University of New Mexico. These grants were critical to the background research of the book; I am deeply grateful to the funding sources.

Many individuals generously gave of their time to critique portions of the manuscript. Patricia Clark Smith and M. Jane Young, my friends and colleagues at the University of New Mexico, provided good conversation about the issues, as well as support and encouragement through the lengthy process of seeing a research project of this scope to completion. I also am indebted to Minrose Gwin, Jane Lancaster, Ruth Salvaggio, Pat Turner, and Blanche Linden Ward for helpful readings of specific chapters. Finally, I want to thank my editors at the University of North Carolina Press for their support of this project. Iris Tillman Hill encouraged my first efforts at outlining a broad, interdisciplinary study of American women's perceptions about nature. Kate Torrey's firm but generous guidance helped me throughout the writing process. Kate read several drafts of the manuscript and gave me excellent advice (and a good bit of courage) as I moved through the revisions.

There really is no sufficient way to express my gratitude to my husband and daughter. Mike has been my best friend, my intellectual sounding board, and my emotional mainstay for over twenty-five years. He encouraged my early enthusiasm for this project, took on parenting and housekeeping duties while I was on research expeditions, and sympathized with my struggles to finish the manuscript. Agatha traipsed endlessly through the library with me, wrote off-limits signs for the study door to protect my writing time, and occasionally served as an editorial assistant. My family is most happy that the book is finished, because now we can get back to exploring our favorite rivers, forests, mountains, and deserts together. To them this book is lovingly dedicated.

# Made
# From
# This
# Earth

*And she wrote, when I let this bird fly to her own purpose, when this bird flies in the path of his own will, the light from this bird enters my body, and when I see the beautiful arc of her flight, I love this bird, when I see, the arc of her flight, I fly with her, enter her with my mind, leave myself, die for an instant, live in the body of this bird whom I cannot live without, as part of the body of the bird will enter my daughter's body, because I know I am made from this earth, as my mother's hands were made from this earth, as her dreams came from this earth and all that I know, I know in this earth, the body of the bird, this pen, this paper, these hands this tongue speaking, all that I know speaks to me through this earth and I long to tell you, you who are earth too, and listen* as we speak to each other of what we know: the light is in us.

—*Susan Griffin*, Woman and Nature:

The Roaring Inside Her

# I

Sources for
American Women's
Nature Study *The
English Tradition,
Sentimental Flower
Books, and Botany*

*It is recorded that Adam gave names to all the beasts of the field,
and the fowls of the air; and Milton imagines, that to Eve was assigned the pleasant
task of giving names to flowers, and numbering the tribes of plants. When our first
parents, as a punishment for their disobedience, are about to leave their delightful
Eden, Eve, in the language of the poet, with bitter regret, exclaims:*

> *Must I thus leave thee, Paradise? * **
>
> *   *   *   *   ×   *   Oh flowers*
>
> *That never will in other climate grow,*
>
> *   *   which I bred up with tender hand,*
>
> *From the first opening bud, and gave ye names;*
>
> *Who now shall rear ye to the sun, or rank*
>
> *Your tribes?*

> —*Almira Phelps*, Familiar Lectures on Botany

ALMIRA HART LINCOLN PHELPS was one of the first American proponents of scientific education for women. In the early decades of the nineteenth century she and her sister, Emma Willard, founded female seminaries, where scientific education played an important part in the curriculum. Phelps also wrote popular textbooks on science for a largely female audience. From her, American women learned—and went on to teach their students across the country—not only how to conduct scientific study, but also how such knowledge fit into their roles as women.[1] In *Familiar Lectures on Botany* Phelps begins her lecture on the "History of Botany, from the Creation of the World to the Present" noting that although Botany was "nursed in the same cradle" as Natural Philosophy and Chemistry, she may be considered "the elder sister."[2] Biblical history, such as Moses' account of God's gift of the living world to Adam, explains man's work as shepherd of nature, but Phelps must resort to Milton's tale of Adam and Eve's complementary roles in naming the world to locate space for women's connection to the green world. After this literary excursion, the narrative returns to more approved historical sources—the Bible and Homer. Phelps's difficulty finding a historical precedent for associating botany with women encapsulates early American women's struggles to claim their place in nature study and appreciation.

Phelps's lament for Eve's loss of an active role in nature uncannily mirrors radical changes taking place in a significant segment of nineteenth-century American society. In *Ecological Revolutions: Nature, Gender, and Science in New England*, Carolyn Merchant argues that the capitalist revolution of the seventeenth century shifted Euro-American women out of work as equal producers in subsistence agriculture to "reproducers of daily life" in the home. With the arrival of large-scale industrialized agriculture, women's contact with and assumed expertise in the plant world shrank. Merchant observes that as capitalist modes of production replaced the small farm, women lost their traditional voice in naming and molding plants. Increased emphasis on women's duties setting up a household and socializing children and husbands compensated for such constriction. Home should serve as a refuge from the competition, amorality, and artificiality of the urban marketplace. Women's role was to remind husbands and children of the republican virtues increasingly at risk in industrialized America. Ironically, idealized farms were offered as model households, in part because on small farms the family seemed closer to romanticized nature. Women instructed their children in the morals taught by nature study carried out in the domesticated fields and woods on the family grounds.

Such duty required that nineteenth-century women become better educated, particularly in the burgeoning science of botany.[3]

These shifts in women's contact with nature were, of course, more apparent in some regions of the country than in others. In the South, for example, poor white women and slaves continued to work on the land as integral contributors to the production process and identified themselves through this work. Slaveholding women had a mixed relationship with nature. They oversaw the gardens and flower beds close to home, but the actual work in these spaces was done by servants. Further, their fathers and husbands rarely consulted them in agricultural management decisions affecting the moneymaking aspects of the plantation. Elizabeth Fox-Genovese persuasively argues that southern women of the slaveholding class interpreted the meaning of true womanhood differently from their northern sisters. In their relegation to private spheres (and perhaps in the obsession with keeping a delicate, pale skin tone), however, they experienced some of the same disconnection from nature. Euro-American women along the moving frontier often maintained close ties with homestead gardens, viewing their carefully tended plots as literal hedges against the loss that Eve expresses in Milton's tale of the first woman in strange terrain. Migrants from the East also encoded the new divisions of farm labor into their travel narratives and novels and constructed an image of the frontier Eve making a new paradise within the bounds of the domestic landscape of home, thus encouraging the constraints that Merchant describes in the New England experience.[4]

One key to sorting out regional responses to national trends is education. Almira Phelps and her sister Emma Willard were most influential in the Northeast. This region spawned most of the amateur and professional female botanists in the nineteenth century. Teachers who had trained in Willard's Troy Female Seminary and other women's schools carried the new education in natural history to the South and West. Although the Northeast housed the elite institutions of scientific study, important nature study centers sprang up early in the 1800s in both the South and the West. Charleston, South Carolina, and San Francisco, California, had active naturalist organizations before the Civil War and included women in their educational programs and as plant collectors. New England and the Middle Atlantic states nurtured women's shift into the study of natural history, but nationwide interest in nature study and women's education buttressed the spread of such activities to other regions.[5]

Education did not automatically grant Eve equal status with Adam in nature study. As Phelps well knew, the answer to Eve's question about who would now name and rank the plants in the world outside the garden was the scientist. In the eighteenth and nineteenth centuries, men newly trained in European science, dedicated to exploring the wilds of the New World and to collecting, drawing, and classifying new species, controlled natural history. Although women worked as collaborators in this effort, they were almost invisible (and often sought invisibility) as namers of the New World.[6] Yet, for women to claim the public, moral voice supposedly engendered out of their nature study, they had to develop some new rhetoric connecting botany to the domestic round. In stories like that of Eve's anguished loss of the plants she had nurtured in Eden, Phelps and her compatriots acknowledged that many women's contact with nature was changing in the early nineteenth century. As women struggled to find biblical and literary sources offering them a tradition for nature study, they articulated a code for women's contribution to American nature values. The early nineteenth century, then, provided the entry point for American women's conscious, public enunciation of their responsibilities to the plants and animals of the New World.

One model for proper female nature study was available in the journals and narratives of European women travelers. The heyday of natural history in Europe began about 1820 and peaked in the 1870s. British and European women were enthusiastic naturalists throughout this period. Their travel narratives of the journey through America reveal the rising interest in the study of flowers, ferns, mosses, shells, birds, and marine life.[7] This surge of nature enthusiasts from across the ocean, bringing with them their scientific knowledge, romantic aesthetic, and gender-based behavior codes, provided a backdrop against which American women developed their own voices for describing, valuing, and protecting the plants and animals they discovered.[8]

By the time Phelps published *Familiar Lectures on Botany* in 1846, however, American women had a reputation among British and other European visitors as isolated from nature. Europeans often noted the protected lives that American women led. The seeming lack of public gardens or places suitable for taking walks reflected women's lives in private, enclosed spaces.[9] Fredrika Bremer, a widely known Swedish writer well-trained in Linnaeus, devoted a good deal of her 1850s' travel narrative to exploring the meaning of seclusion. Initially, Bremer witnessed an example of female retirement that she found enthralling. Greeted on her arrival in the East by Andrew Jackson Downing, the influential landscape architect, she spent some of her first days in America in his home. Enthusiastically describing the residence as perfectly melding nature and culture, she portrayed Mrs. Downing as a bird living in a beautiful villa.[10] Later, in St. Louis, she discovered a more negative aspect of such seclusion at a wedding party:

> The bride . . . struck me like a rare hot-house plant, scarcely able to endure the free winds of the open air . . . When I left that perfumed apartment, with its hot-house atmosphere and its half-daylight, in which was carefully tended a beautiful human flower, I was met by a heaven as blue as that of spring, and by a fresh, vernal air, by sunshine and the song of birds among the whispering trees . . . Ah, said I to myself, this is a different life! After all, it is not good; no, it is not good, it has not the freshness of Nature, that life which so many ladies lead in this country; that life of twilight in comfortable rooms, rocking themselves by the fireside from one year's end to another, that life of effeminate warmth and inactivity, by which means they exclude themselves from the fresh air, from fresh invigorating life!

Bremer's tour through America and her experiences with such sheltered women led her to conclude that women were shut out of public life in America, a view with which Harriet Martineau agreed.[11]

Bremer also alleged that the physical weakness of these Americans was at base attributable to their "effeminate education." The British explorer Isabella Bird, on her first American tour in the 1850s, concurred, noting that education was a waste among these "extremely domestic" women. In the 1820s an early English traveler, Mrs. Trollope, had reported that the schools gave women science and math but expected little beyond a superficial understanding of such subjects.[12] In judgments such as these, European women implied that American women were unfit to engage in the kind of naturalizing done by the Europeans, leading to the Americans' unfortunate lack of familiarity with the flora and fauna of their own land.[13]

When these tourists generalized about women's roles and their problems, they were addressing middle-class, mostly urban women.[14] Of course, Europeans did not only make observations about genteel women of their own sort. They also commented on agriculturists, settlers of many classes going west, and American Indian and African American women. Yet, when they ran across women of other classes or races who did engage in outdoor activities as gardeners, field-workers, migrants, and such, they did not celebrate them for the health and knowledge they might gain by such lives. In the first place, many of the women they saw in these occupations were at the mercy of the elements. Mrs. Trollope's (probably apocryphal) account of a woman and her children who were eaten by alligators because the husband built their cabin over a nest suggests that nature was not always kind to women who ventured forth from the cities. Second, women on the prairies and the frontier seemed to be isolated from the culture that gave context to their lives. Isabella Bird did not paint one positive picture of American women settlers in Colorado: middle-class women struggled to maintain a genteel life in rude cabins, and lower-class women lost whatever vestige of respectability they might have hoped to attain in living so close to nature but so far from civilization.[15]

Distanced from many of the women they encountered, Europeans relied only on what they saw in passing, or what they had read, to describe the real people they met. African American women, for example, apparently had little sensitivity to the natural world with which they often lived in close contact. In fact, one commentator had difficulty placing African American women in the environment at all. Harriet Martineau found them at odds with the beautiful surroundings in which they lived, leaving unreconciled the contradictions in her description of a plantation as a "perfect Eden": "There were black women ploughing in the field, with their ugly, scanty, dingy dresses, their walloping gait, and vacant countenance. There were scarlet and blue birds flitting over the dark fallows. There was a persimmon sprouting in the woods." Whereas Martineau had trouble locating African American women within nature, Fredrika Bremer could not imagine American Indian women outside nature—particularly wild nature. At one point, in describing an Indian woman who had married a white man, she noted that such women vanish from home "when the birds warble of spring and the forest . . . This wild life must assuredly have a great fascination." In both cases, Europeans denied such women any of the reflective responses to nature experienced by white women. Obviously, visitors relied heavily on preconceived notions based on what they had read or heard prior to visiting America.[16]

Ironically, Martineau later corresponded briefly with an African American woman for whom contemplating nature carried great meaning. Charlotte Forten Grimké came of a free, middle-class family in Philadelphia. In the 1850s her family sent her to school in Salem, Massachusetts, where she attended classes with white students. Her education provided her much opportunity for nature study. Charlotte Forten yearned for a career as a writer. Steeped in the romantic poets of England and America, she looked to nature for inspiration. Her diaries reveal her conviction that women should take healthful exercise in natural settings, educate themselves about the flora of the country, and collect and preserve the most beautiful flowers they found on their rambles. Class and education opened the door to nature study for Forten as surely as for her white classmates.

Nature study held for Forten much more ambiguity than for white Americans or Europeans. She was separated from nature—not by some inherent defect in her race, but by a society living under slavery. Inspired by an illustrated lecture on the wonders of the Mammoth Caves, Forten lamented in her diary that she could not see the caves until slavery's end. She felt guilty for enjoying nature's charms in the face of the suffering of so many of her people: "How strange it is that in a world so beautiful, there can be so much wickedness." [17] Bound by the constrictions of their class, European travelers assumed that America's female naturalists could come solely of European stock. As Forten's struggle to read nature appreciatively reveals, the Europeans were right in assuming that women of color might have difficulty stepping into the naturalist mode, but they had no understanding of the underlying reasons for such peoples' silence.

Europeans came to America with the New World metaphor firmly in mind and on occasion did manage to find the perfect Eve for the garden. Trollope and Martineau saw her in the 1850s and she reappeared in the English painter Constance Gordon Cumming's narrative in the 1870s. Significantly, Trollope did not see Eve until she found the garden, sighted in the Alleghenies during the last stage of her travels. Here she met an enchanting and enterprising young woman who "told us . . . that wild strawberries were profusely abundant, and very fine; that their cows found for themselves, during the summer, plenty of flowery food, which produced a copious supply of milk; that their spring gave them the purest water, of icy coldness in the warmest seasons; and that the climate was the most delicious in the world . . . My eloquent mountaineer gave me some specimens of ground plants, far unlike anything I had ever seen." Harriet Martineau was inspired by an old woman in Virginia Springs who lived on an isolated farm in a lovely setting, had never traveled eight miles beyond her own doorstep, and did not need to—she inhabited paradise. Years later, Cumming came across a "California maiden" who was the "lady" of a "rock-girt lake"; she was taking care of brothers, sisters, horses, and cattle "and withal, finding time to carry on her own studies unaided, and intensely interested in working at Euclid and Algebra! These still waters run deep!" [18] Each of these Eves was embedded in the domestic round, but not the sort of isolated, artificial homelife Bremer meant when she described the hothouse flower. Rather, they lived on an idealized farm landscape that for Europeans and Americans symbolized virtuous space.

Further supporting the importance of correctly conceived domesticity, none of these Eves was wild. Each displayed enough distance from nature to appreciate her environment in a scientific or aesthetic way. Fredrika Bremer was perhaps the most adamant about what American women should be doing in the luxuriant wonderland they inhabited. Entranced by a biophysical landscape she portrayed in her narrative as wild, fecund, and decidedly female, Bremer was careful not to extend this metaphoric wildness to humans. In fact, she went out of her way to criticize some young southern women she found too free in their manner: "If nature is left to itself, it becomes a wilderness, and wildernesses of human nature are very much less beautiful than those of the primal forest—nor would even these be good to live in." [19] Correct appreciation of nature was a civilizing experience. When Bremer and her compatriots chastised American women for their lack of botanical skills, they were calling into question the Americans' ability to function as civilized women.

Civilized women were necessary to the healthy functioning of American society. Values arising from the domestic sphere reminded Americans of their republican roots, balanced the threat that material wealth would overcome moral character. Proper understanding of and receptivity to nature could help forestall not only women's but also society's fall from grace. Two examples from Bremer make the point and introduce what the Europeans did find American women accomplishing in nature study. Near the end of her journey, crowds of tourists disturbed Bremer's stay at a hotel in the mountains. Such men and women merely brought urban values out to the country. She contrasted these tourists with a father and daughter botanizing in the woods, true "worshippers of the great goddess." Although Bremer found very few women in America who shared her passion for nature study, in Charleston she met Mrs. John Edwards Holbrook, with whom she could both botanize and philosophize. Mrs. Holbrook was a leading light among a group of southern women who collected plants. [20]

For Bremer, this meeting rivaled her visits with the New England elite: "We were alone, we two, the whole day; we wandered in myrtle-groves—we botanized—we read . . . Mrs. Holbrook was like a perpetually fresh-welling fountain . . . that day, in the fragrant myrtle-groves of Belmont, on the banks of the Ashley River, is one of my most beautiful days in the New World, and one which I shall never forget." It was no accident that Bremer walked with her new friend through myrtle groves, for this was a highly civilized, cultivated kind of nature study, the sort that led one to ponder the symbolic meaning of the lush environment of the New World: "Mrs. H. is a Platonic thinker, who can see (which is rare in this world) system in all things, and dissimilar radii having all relationship to one common centre." The meeting concluded with Bremer's critique of the major weakness in women's education: "Women acquire many kinds of knowledge, but there is no systematizing of it . . . no application of the life in this to life itself, and no opportunity afforded, after leaving school, of applying this knowledge to a living purpose. Hence, it falls away out of the soul, like flowers that have no root."[21] When the Europeans met a woman who used her knowledge, they lauded her accomplishment and made specific mention of her in their narratives. Until the late 1870s such women were a rare breed in European chronicles.

Female American naturalists were not so scarce, however, as the Europeans feared. Colored by their initial sense that the Americans were a hothouse variety of flower, that they rarely ventured outdoors and so never engaged in botanizing, European narratives overemphasized these limitations. Read closely, the European narratives are self-contradictory. For example, Mrs. Trollope, some pages after reporting that there were no public gardens in Cincinnati, described a public garden "where people go to eat ices, and to look at roses." Harriet Martineau met a young girl in a New England farmhouse who was "fond of flowers, and had learned a great deal about them. She was skillful in drying them, and could direct to the places in the woods and meadows where they grew." Amelia Murray, after meeting a couple of young women in Newport, Rhode Island, who "sympathize with me about flowers and stones," continued in almost the same breath: "I find American ladies are at this moment so little informed with regard to natural productions, and so unfitted for country pursuits, that their ignorance of these matters is at once the evidence and cause of their lack of physical strength."[22] Nor did she ever revise her opinion of Americans, even after meetings with Mrs. Holbrook in Charleston and other female naturalists at the American Scientific Association.

Initially, Constance Gordon Cumming's narrative looks as though it will continue in the same vein. Touring San Francisco in the 1870s, she went out to view the sea lions, complimenting Americans on their efforts to make sanctuaries for these animals. She voiced her opinion to some "town-bred" ladies, who "looked at me with pitying wonder. They were in the constant habit of driving to the Cliff House, but not for the love of the sea-lions!" But at Yosemite, she discovered that some American women had developed nature sensibilities comparable to, and in some ways, surpassing hers. Cumming tells of American women who spent the summer in cabins with their children, riding horseback through the valley. Such women "start on . . . prolonged picnics, with or without a 'help,' fully prepared to rough it, making sport of all difficulties; and these gather up stores of health and strength to carry back to their homes in the great cities." Especially impressive were campers who braved the dreaded rattlesnake, a feat she dared not try. Her last excursion in California was a horseback adventure with two American girls traveling alone from Boston and Detroit to see the Sequoia.[23]

From their early narratives these European authors, who read each other's published travelogues as they set out on their journeys, constructed a common narrative about American women. As the story went, on one hand, American women of the "right sort" for nature study were not able to botanize and collect because their domestic round was limited to the artificial interior spaces of middle-class homes. On the other hand, direct contact with nature coarsened or destroyed settlers, slaves, and American Indians. Until Cumming's report, this was the explanation for American women's lack of participation in the task of naming the plants and animals of the New World. A running subtext, however, suggested more activity than the writers implied. Every early account mentions at least one or two indigenous naturalists until Cumming finally witnessed sufficient numbers to change the tale altogether.[24] These laudable women rejected hothouse seclusion and seriously studied the native plants of home and neighborhood. Sheltered from the wild, they were not denied contact with nature. Such contact garnered them virtue and a moral voice in the public sphere.

My reading raises the question of why the Europeans failed for so long to note what the Americans were doing. Here Bremer, Murray, and Bird offer some clues. These three saw themselves as women engaged in a public sphere controlled by men: Bremer as a writer, Murray as a botanist/geologist, and Bird as an explorer. Although each evinced some interest in women's achievements in America, they aligned themselves more closely with men, even when they discussed women's proper role. Bremer, for example, was well aware of the women writers of the period. After assessing their relative merits, she commented: "but I have not as yet heard among these minstrels either the rich, inspiriting song of the lark, or the full inspiration of the nightingale; and I do not know whether this rich artistic inspiration belongs to the womanly nature. I have not, in general, much belief in the ability of woman as a creative artist. Unwritten lyrics, as Emerson once said when he spoke on this subject, should be her forte." Such a judgment did not apply to herself—an accomplished authoress. With specific reference to nature study, Andrew Jackson

Downing referred Bremer to Susan Fenimore Cooper's *Rural Hours*, but she either never read it or did not find it noteworthy.[25] Amelia Murray's opening tribute of a case of plant specimens to Asa Gray clearly indicates that she came to meet the natural history lions of America—all of whom were male. Even though Murray spent a good deal of time botanizing with the Grays, she never mentions Asa Gray's wife's interest in nature study. And Isabella Bird, though she carefully bowed in her writings to Victorian gender codes, spent all the time she could outdoors among men who hunted, ranched, and climbed the Colorado peaks. Trapped in such unexamined contradictions, the visitors did not recognize American women's increasing interest in the sentimental appreciation and systematic study of American flora.

When, in the 1840s, Almira Phelps poised her imaginary Eve on the edge of the garden, looking back with regret at a lost connection with nature, she did so to remind American women caught in a similar disenfranchisement that they had a historical right to name and nurture the flora of their new homeland. If, upon laying down the role of agriculturist, American women were to take on the mantle of botanist, then botany had to have a longer history than that constructed by the leading male naturalists of the previous century. Botany had to be in some way female and connected to the domesticity of the nineteenth century. So Phelps's image of Eve is as a mother—gently nurturing plant life. Within this sentimental context, Eve also served the cause of science—naming and ranking her plants. Phelps's mixture of science and sentiment formed the context for American women's increasingly public interest in nineteenth-century nature study.

Ironically, another group of European women imported the first keys to a naturalist's education. Europeans wrote books that were studied by their compatriots, teaching the Americans new systems of botanical and zoological classification, and establishing codes for appropriate natural philosophy among women of the nineteenth century. Mrs. Matilda Charlotte Houstoun, yachting along the Texas coast in the 1840s, noticed the passion with which American women were consuming books from across the ocean: "I have laid in a stock of new books for the voyage [home], for at no place can a temporary library be procured at a less outlay than in the United States . . . A work published in England comes out almost simultaneously in the United States; and English works of standard authors are eagerly bought, and read— I suspect—mostly by the ladies."[26] This observation was particularly true of books written specifically for women.

Historians of science have discussed the importance of popular science books during the eighteenth and nineteenth centuries in England and on the Continent and have documented their increasing availability in America after the turn of the nineteenth century. Although, as Margaret Rossiter has noted, such books "legitimized [women's] having some elementary knowledge of science," what that knowledge meant to them in their broader role as women has not been addressed.[27] Such study is crucial to understanding why women, when they began to engage in nature writing and nature illustrating, chose the forms and subjects they did. One of the clues to their careers is hidden in the asides, sentiments, philosophy, and structure of books purportedly about the scientific study of plants and animals. A genre neglected by historians of science offers a second important clue. Sentimental books of poetry and drawings taught women to read in nature symbols of their female roles in life, and to locate socially important moral values in their new knowledge. As authors sought ways to make botany (to some, a dead endeavor) come alive to women who might not enjoy it, they often included lessons from sentimental literature. As sentimental literature developed over the nineteenth century, it included the systematic study of plants and animals begun by Linnaeus. Both scientific and sentimental books by and for women opened new worlds of activity to their readers, but they often did so cautiously, beginning, if not always ending, with women's self-image as domestic beings more emotional than analytical.[28]

The sentimental approach to nature arose in France and focused appropriately enough on botany—the study of the sexual relations of the plant kingdom. One early representative, Charlotte de La Tour's *Le Langage des Fleurs* (1819), spawned a series of such books in both England and America.[29] In these books women learned a little botany, but most of all a tasteful set of symbols through which to communicate their feelings. A gaudy example of the genre was *Les Fleurs Animées*, a French production appearing in English in 1847 as *The Flowers Personified*. *The Flowers Personified* was a collaborative book by the artist J. J. Grandville, writers Taxile Delord and Alphonse Karr, and botanist Comte Foelix (a pseudonym for L. F. Raban).[30] Grandville provided portraits of flowers personified as women, and the authors composed complementary texts, partly serious but sometimes ridiculing the excesses of the sentimental tradition. Reminding women of their responsibility for the death of many flowers (killed in tribute by eager lovers), the authors encouraged them to cultivate plants. There follows a set of stories based on the decision of the flowers to leave the "Court of Flora" and live in the world as women.

Grandville's plates set the tone for these witty tales filled with the lore of flowers (Figure 1). A botany for ladies concludes the book.

To the modern reader, the tone is patronizing, jocular, and irritating in the authors' assumption that women will find the scientific study of plants a dry, difficult, and boring subject. One of Grandville's plates even suggests that the scientific study of plants is deadly to both flora and women. The Periwinkle appears as at once a dried botanical specimen and a female corpse laid out for viewing (Figure 2). Expanding on the idea that botany is a "forbidden fruit" to women, Raban promises to avoid the use of scientific terms as much as possible since such terms "have no other effect than to distort pretty mouths into ugly grimaces." The sentimental association of flowers and women intermingles with botanical information: "Flowers . . . are the appointed organs in the great work of reproduction. Attractive colors—sweet odors—elegant forms—delicate tissues—the charms of opening beauty and graceful bearing—all the attributes of liveliness, lavished, as they are on even the most ordinary flowers—render the season of bloom a season of display and triumph." Later, readers are told: "Not only is the corolla . . . always arrayed in beautiful colors, but these colors sometimes change. Some coquettish corollas vary their dress three times in a single day." For all this personifying, however, Raban sidesteps the "fecundation of plants," noting only that Linnaeus says that flowers "love—and, daring fellow that he is, he proves it, too!"[31]

One must be careful not to dismiss the science offered in this book for, like the moralizing stories about women-flowers, the point is to encourage women's appreciation of flowers as more than decorative.[32] Thus, the author introduces the reader not only to the artificial system of Linnaeus but also to the natural system of Antoine Laurent de Jussieu. In Linnaeus one learns how to identify individual plants, but a study of Jussieu teaches "floral structure, affinities, and whole natural history." For all the teasing and stereotyping of women's responses to the highly structured study of plants, *The Flowers Personified* assumes that women should and could understand what was at the time felt to be a most complex method for studying plants.[33] Such willingness to tackle the natural system, even in such a humorous work as this, indicates more the seriousness with which women's education in science was taken than the minor reluctance to discuss Linnaeus and his "men and ladies" in their various monogamous (or nonmonogamous) relationships.

In America, sentimental books engendered by writings like La Tour's and Grandville's contained similar mixtures of literature, science, and illus-

FLÈCHE-D'EAU

FIGURE 1. *In a typical example of the symbolism of flowers, this Water Arum represents an enchantress whose early morning fragrance lures a fisherman away from his work. (J. J. Grandville, "Flèche-D'Eau" [Water Arum], in* The Flowers Personified *[1847]. Reproduced in* The Court of Flora *[1981]. Reprinted by permission of George Braziller, Inc.)*

14    *Made From This Earth*

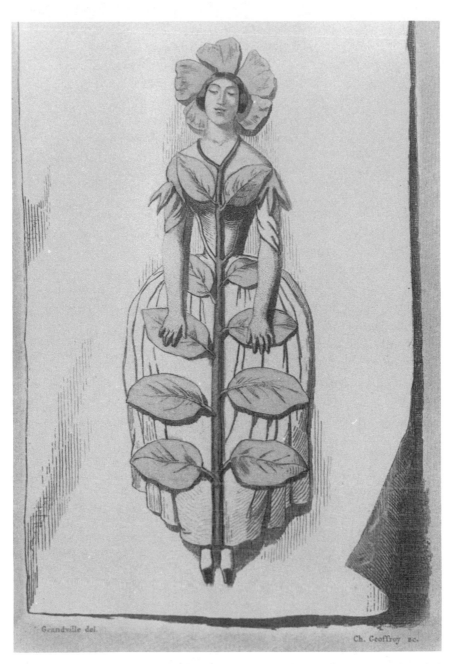

FIGURE 2. *This Periwinkle illustrates a more troubling image of woman as a botanical specimen. (J. J. Grandville, "Pervenche Desséchée" [Periwinkle], in* The Flowers Personified *[1847]. Reproduced in* The Court of Flora *[1981]. Reprinted by permission of George Braziller, Inc.)*

*Sources for American Women's Nature Study* 15

tration but were interesting as well for their self-conscious celebration of American flora. At about the same time that Trollope, Martineau, and Bremer took American women to task for not appreciating the paradise in which they lived, leading American tastemakers produced works focused on the unique plants of the New World. Sarah Hale's *Flora's Interpreter: or, The American Book of Flowers and Sentiments* (1832), a popular compendium of poetry on flowers, was written to answer foreign critics' disparagement of native American flowers: "And it is not without pride, as well as pleasure, that I have found so many fair specimens . . . flourishing in a land that has been stigmatized as producing nothing but corn and cotton, the tobacco and potato. If we shelter and cherish our flowers, they will soon beautify our Republic." The American Starwort is celebrated in a poem by Mrs. Lydia Howard Sigourney explaining the sentiment engendered by the sight of an American flower: "They feed no worm, and they hide no thorn, / But revel and grow in our balmy air; / They are flowers which *Freedom* hath planted there."[34] In addition to such sentiment, Hale offered information on each flower's class, order, range, and scientific name.

While Sarah Hale concentrated on poetry to evoke the sentiments stirred by flowers, her compatriot Lucy Hooper took a more wide-ranging approach. Hooper's *The Lady's Book of Flowers and Poetry, to which Are Added a Botanical Introduction, a Complete Floral Dictionary; and a Chapter on Plants in Rooms* suggests her approach in its title. The opening chapter concerns the cultivation of plants indoors—thus providing a clue to the intended audience and its interests. Hooper included beautiful illustrations of real flowers (not flower-women). When unable to find poetry illustrating the feelings associated with a particular flower, she wrote it herself. And unlike Hale, she provided extended information on each flower. A good example is the selection on the Peruvian Heliotrope. She began with a description of its looks and behavior when grown in the hothouse and went on to recount Oriental folklore of the heliotrope, a romantic story from Denmark involving a heliotrope, Jussieu's discovery of the plant in the Cordilleras, the genesis of its name, and its meaning as a flower symbolizing both love and flattery.[35] Hooper added an introduction to botany, in which she discussed her preferences for Linnaeus over Jussieu. Obviously, scientific knowledge did not exist separately from a variety of other types of knowledge or associations that humans had with the natural world. For these authors, and the women reading their works, the sight of a flower called forth a mixture of science and sentiment, as well as practical questions about how such a plant might be cultivated.

Such literature brought science into the drawing room. When Hale used her botanical knowledge to argue for America's native virtues, she moved the values of domesticity into the public sphere as well. Posing no challenge to woman's role as domesticator and cultivator of sentiment, these books suggested, rather, that appropriate study and cultivation of the plant kingdom would enhance female capacities. Their authors did not promote knowledge for its own sake, but for moral improvement. They occasionally criticized botanists for their unwillingness to attach moral lessons to their findings, offering women's view of nature as a meritorious compliment to men's.[36] They encouraged women to see themselves symbolically connected to nature through their identification with flowers. If nature could be improved by cultivation, so could woman: "Culture does for flowers, what education does for young ladies. It saves them from many dangers; it augments their charms, by the peculiar graces which it imparts; and, more than anything else, it gives durability to those charms."[37]

In addition to sentimental flower books, American women benefited from books offering a more scientific approach. A variety of texts on botany, chemistry, geology, and natural philosophy were available from the turn of the century. Particularly influential was the Englishwoman Jane Haldiman Marcet's *Conversations on Vegetable Physiology; Comprehending the Elements of Botany, with Their Application to Agriculture*.[38] An older woman (Mrs. B.) instructs two girls, Emily and Caroline, in the principles of botany as she had learned them from Augustin Pyramus De Candolle (a proponent of the natural system). The youngsters represent two stages of intellectual development—one interested in objects and therefore ready for Linnaeus, the other in relationships and so Jussieu.

The book begins with the girls' misgivings about studying botany. Mrs. B. convinces them that it need not be a dry study if approached correctly and criticizes those (apparently scientists and possibly followers of Linnaeus over Jussieu) more interested in models than in nature's vagaries: "If people will attend more to the frame than to the picture which it contains, and if they will even cut and disfigure the picture, in order to make it fit into the frame they have prepared for it, no wonder that the subject should lose its interest." Following her own instructor, De Candolle, she notes that she will teach her two young pupils botany through agriculture.[39]

Although the bulk of her text is a highly detailed account of how plants grow, beginning (much to the girls' chagrin) with the root system, interspersed throughout are comments on nature and women's proper understanding of their relationship to plants. Mrs. B. argues that one must start with the roots because the flower is so complex, but when she does reach the flower, a rather different story surfaces: "If I have allowed the most beautiful part of the vegetable creation to remain so long unnoticed, it was in order that, when I described it, your interest might be excited, not merely by the brilliancy of its colours, the elegance of its form, or the sweetness of its perfume, but that, having acquired some previous knowledge of the economy of vegetation . . . you would take a deeper and more rational interest both in the blossom and the seed."[40] Thus, she structures her lessons with an eye to weaning women away from mere aesthetic appreciation, educating them as well in the economy of nature.

Sentimental flower books sometimes reduced aspects of the natural world to simplified codes for love, flattery, jealousy, motherhood, and nationalism. Marcet wanted to teach women to see the whole interactive system that the new botany was discovering. While God may have fathered the universe, the creation was best described by a symbolic female sustaining all life. When Mrs. B. discusses the pollination of flowers that have no pistils, she appeals to the feminine, noting "she" (Nature) has made such flowers as a "provision" for the profligate bees, "and they thus unconsciously labour for those plants, which afford them food. Every insect, however ephemeral, every weed, however insignificant, has its part assigned, in the great system of the universe."[41] Although such a statement harks back to the mechanically designed and ordered world that was beginning to come apart with new findings in geology and biology, it also points to a new approach to nature interested in the interactions of a complex system.[42] Marcet here offers women a way to continue their own naming of the natural world; this approach contains potential power in a redefined female principle—one identified with a good deal more than flowers.

The little work done on women's role in the American debate on natural versus artificial methods of classification implies that women tended to support Linnaeus because he was easier for the amateur to follow.[43] Yet these women did not feel too intimidated to participate in the debates, or to offer their readers information on competing theories. They saw themselves as popular educators—of both sentiment and science—and tried to provide their readers with a complete yet accessible study. Marcet displayed some of the pedagogical consciousness in acknowledging that a person's age in part determined what concepts she could grasp. When teaching young women science, one must start with the capabilities of the student. Marcet, however, couched her new information in a rather old-fashioned instructional format. Other scientific popularizers in England and America were offering their readers not only the most up-to-date knowledge, but also a new method of teaching. This new pedagogy spread rapidly throughout America, thanks primarily to a group of men and women devoted to providing natural history lessons in the schools.

Much of the educational literature in the early nineteenth century made a bow to the Pestalozzian method of instruction. First championed in America by Amos Eaton and furthered in the middle of the century by Louis Agassiz when he settled in America, this approach gained much favor in female seminaries, in large part because of the efforts of one of Eaton's students—Almira Phelps.[44] When Phelps determined that women needed better education in the sciences, she surveyed the existing textbooks and found them lacking. In 1829 she published *Familiar Lectures on Botany* with the aim of providing an alternate method to the dry, technical approach then available for the men's schools. Her work was very popular, going through various editions and selling more than 275,000 copies during the next forty years. From her, American women learned not only botany but also a specific method for studying nature.[45]

Johann Heinrich Pestalozzi emphasized an inductive approach, beginning with concrete objects rather than abstract theories. As Phelps explains it in her book's preface for teachers, the first day of botany class begins with a flower—preferably one of simple structure such as the lily or tulip. By dissecting the flower and viewing its parts, students are drawn into the classification system—always aware that observable details account for the flower's place in the system: "The advantage in this kind of explanation, over that of any abstract idea, is, that it is manifested to the senses of the pupils by the object before them." Anne Scott has argued that in such an approach, Phelps not only challenged the conventional wisdom of the time, which held that women's brains simply could not cope with mathematics or Greek, but also "inaugurated laboratory science for undergraduates and led the way in introducing modern languages." Scott also suggests that such education succeeded better than the rote lessons that young men were still learning.[46] Students in the female seminaries of Almira Phelps and Emma Willard, as well as the women at Louis Agassiz's Anderson School later in the century, spread out across the country, carrying with them the seeds of a new way for the educated woman to spend her time—in pursuit of a better knowledge of her natural environment.[47]

Phelps's work offered much more than an introduction to the methods of botanical classification. She provided a thorough introduction to the sciences, to flower parts, to the whole plant, to competing methods of classification, and to the seasons of plants and botanical geography, as well as a history of botany from "the Creation of the World" to the present. Although unconvinced by Jussieu and favoring Linnaeus, she framed her later editions in keeping with the natural system. Phelps did not hesitate to give women an accounting of Jussieu's method, even though she considered the natural system an approach for the "more experienced botanist" and found Linnaeus more widely popularized.[48] Finally, her text includes some practical advice on naturalizing plants and a chapter covering the "language of flowers." It is easy to see why *Familiar Lectures* became a handbook: it provides folklore, history, scientific knowledge, practical skill, and encouragement to become at least an amateur botanist.

While lauding her contributions to women's scientific education, historians have considered Phelps conservative in her goals. She viewed learning as a way of fostering religious contemplation, as a boon to mothers' roles as children's first teachers, and as an alternative to trivial pursuits that women might otherwise entertain.[49] Whereas the original Eve may have turned to face a howling wilderness on her expulsion from Eden, many a mid-nineteenth-century American Eve faced the enervating life of a pampered hothouse flower. Phelps agreed with the European travelers that not only did American women need to pursue more scientific education, they also needed to spend more time outdoors. She blended the pleasures of scientific study with a sentimental appeal to botany's particular mesh with women's emotional makeup in order to move women out of the parlor and into the gardens, fields, and woods of their homeland. According to Phelps, "the study of Botany seems peculiarly adapted to females; the objects of its investigation are beautiful and delicate; its pursuits, leading to exercise in the open air, are conducive to health and cheerfulness." She counseled such study in contrast to zoology, which elicited "painful emotions" in the dissecting room.[50]

Phelps's idea of exercise was not limited to walks around the garden collecting familiar flowers. In the 1846 edition of her text, she expanded her earlier focus on common neighborhood plants of the Northeast to include descriptions of southern and western plants. Further, after describing the healthfulness of botanical study, she suggested where women should do such work: "It is not a sedentary study which can be acquired in the library, but the objects of the science are scattered over the surface of the earth, along the banks of winding brooks, on the borders of precipices, the sides of mountains, and the depths of the forest." She reiterated this adventurous stance near the end of her history of botany, noting that the best botanizer was one who "explored the plains, valleys, and mountains." Of all the writers mentioned in this chapter, only Phelps offers in American Indians a model for how the middle-class woman might pursue socially useful nature study. Aware that the New World had yielded various medicinal plants, she reminded her readers of the Indian women herbalists preceding them whose knowledge was lost and must be reconstructed.[51]

Although Margaret Rossiter may be correct in asserting that Phelps did not urge women to see themselves as anything but popularizers and educators, she did open a door to serious, specialized, extended nature study.[52] Phelps knew who created scientific knowledge:

> It is well for mankind that there are philosophers, whom the enthusiasm of scientific pursuits will lead to spend years, even a whole life, in searching into the fructification of a moss, or mushroom, or in examining into the natural history of a gnat or a spider; and thus, discoveries are continually brought forward, which add to the general stock of knowledge. This is a kind of martyrdom in the cause of science, to which but few seem called by the powerful impulses of their own minds. Females, in particular, are not expected to enter into the recesses of the temple of science; it is but of late that they have been encouraged to approach even to its portals, and to venture a glance upon the mysteries within.

If Phelps here acknowledged the difficulties of the endeavor, she also could not think of any reason women might not enter the "temple" into which they now peeped. And her next comment required that they should, if they were even to teach effectively: "It is in natural as in civil history,—general remarks upon the beauty and utility of the vegetable world, or the curious structure of plants, make but slight impressions. But by contemplating the peculiarities of some one tribe, genus, or species, the mind seizes upon something definite, and reason, imagination, and feeling are easily awakened; thus, the impression made is permanent."[53] If as mothers and teachers women wanted to inspire an understanding of nature in their children and students, they must become deeply familiar with specific aspects of the environment. If changes in nineteenth-century agriculture had denied many women daily contact with nature, the new rage for natural history offered them a way back to such experience. By closely observing the mosses, mushrooms, and spiders of

America, women nurtured both their reason and their emotion. In so doing, they achieved at once private moral character and the potential for expanding their public role.

Nowhere in *Familiar Lectures on Botany*, however, do we witness Almira Phelps in any direct communion with nature. Rather, she sticks to the knowledge gleaned from her studies with Professor Eaton, relies heavily on his *Manual of Botany*, and describes plants as a series of parts making up a rather mechanical whole. Although Phelps may have given her students and readers clues to how to write and draw vibrantly the New World plants and animals they saw, she did not herself engage in such a task. Thus, although we know that she cared about the native plants of America and helped nurture the first generation of scientifically trained women able to conduct nature study as competently as their English sisters, we have not yet met an American who actually studied and wrote about the plants and animals of her country.

There was such a woman. Amelia Murray met her, but true to her adulation of male scientists, Murray only mentions her as the professor's wife. Elizabeth Cabot, Louis Agassiz's second wife, was familiar with Pestalozzi. In the 1840s Louis Agassiz came to America championing the method and here met with strong support from a variety of groups.[54] What the visiting European women—who were themselves taken with the professor—did not see was that his wife, Elizabeth Cabot Agassiz, also was a devoted observer of the natural world. In 1859 she published, under the pseudonym "Actaea," a little, unpretentious book for children in which she combined the Pestalozzian method with a strong grounding in science (garnered from her husband) and, most important, the nature essayist's sensibility. In her book poetic and scientific influences come together, yielding a fitting capstone to this early period when American women worked as educators about nature for each other, for children, and for their country.

Elizabeth Agassiz addressed her writing to her nieces. Her book, she notes at the beginning, owed much to "the direction of Prof. Agassiz." *First Lesson in Natural History* focuses on the marine life of the Nahant shore, where she and Agassiz often naturalized. At the time, conchology and the study of marine life in aquaria were popular in both America and England. Women could now go bathing (appropriately dressed) and while at the shore, they could learn about this particular field of zoology.[55] The book's structure is pure Pestalozzi, beginning with common sea anemones and corals, proceeding to coral reefs, then jellyfish, starfish, and sea urchins. Only when children are familiar with the details of these creatures' lives are they introduced to their classification as "Radiates." As Phelps had counseled, Agassiz centered her study around one small aspect of marine life.

What makes her text more lively than Phelps's *Familiar Lectures* is its grounding in her own work with marine life. Agassiz uses her rambles around the Nahant coastline to encourage the nieces to collect animals for their aquaria. As she knew from experience, the first task in any nature study is finding a good specimen. Discussing starfish, she notes: "there is scarcely a puddle of sea-weedy rock along any part of the Nahant shore where they are not to be found in numbers, and if you ever have an opportunity of rowing in a boat around Egg Rock at low tide, you may see them by the hundreds."[56] (She herself lovingly gathered starfish, sea urchins, and sea anemones to take home and watch in her aquarium.) And, mirroring Phelps's suggestions, she encourages the girls to at least think about what they might learn by traveling beyond their neighborhood and exploring more exotic coastlines. Again based on her own investigations, she describes the coral reefs on the coast of Florida and the fossils of distant relatives of the starfish found in the West Indies. In this way, she hoped to engender a curiosity about the world beyond her nieces' garden and to provide a sense of the deep time that geologists were beginning to trace in America's history.

There is a new language in Agassiz's book, one that Phelps did not contemplate. Rather than finding value in nature study as a way to develop reverence for the Creator, Agassiz reveres the magical world itself for its surprises as well as its familiarity. In the writing of Elizabeth Agassiz, we begin to see nature brought to life, not with a stylized list of canned emotions gleaned from poets' projections onto flowers or a set of labels learned from a male biology professor, but from immersion into concrete details. Agassiz loved the marine life of Nahant because she had made it hers through patient attention; that was her most important message to her nieces. From that attention, and with sensitive language, she described a jellyfish: "a little, fairy-like, transparent thing, so slight and delicate indeed that it seems almost as if some drops of the water had taken form and shape, and that this strange little being, that is darting about in it, were but a part of the element in which it floats . . . It is perfectly transparent; a drop of water, a bubble of air, a spider's web, a fly's wing, anything that has form and shape at all, can hardly be more slight in texture than this little creature."[57]

With Agassiz's personal, immediate voice, the various pieces that go into making the women's tradition in American nature study fall into place. As Almira Phelps recognized, American women of the early nineteenth century experienced a sort of disenfranchisement from participation in the naming and claiming of their environment. Some of this feeling may have been a function of their comparatively new tenancy on the land and their sense of a break with older, familiar landscapes; some of it grew out of male scientists' control of the language of natural description, and some of it was a result of their indoor, domestic lives. As Phelps also knew, however, American women were addressing these constrictions. Historians of science have lamented nineteenth-century women's exclusion from the professional study of biology, zoology, and chemistry and have concentrated on their work as disseminators through textbooks. But the message that women were receiving from those textbooks, the sentimental literature addressed to them, and the published accounts of the amateur naturalist travelers from across the ocean was to meld intellect with emotion. The lessons they learned from closely observing America's plants and animals validated their domestic round while opening the public sphere to their influence. Nineteenth-century women made their first contributions in natural history not with a paper given before a professional society but in the nature essay and the nature drawing. In these genre we discover Eve in the act of naming and ranking the flowers, fruits, spiders, jellyfish, hummingbirds, and horned toads of the New World.

# 2

## Pleasures of the Country Life
### Susan Fenimore Cooper and the Seasonal Tradition

*We are none of us very knowing about the birds in this country, unless it be those scientific gentlemen who have devoted their attention especially to such subjects. The same remark applies in some measure to our native trees and plants; to our butterflies and insects. But little attention has yet been given by our people generally, to these subjects . . . Had works of this kind been as common in America as they are in England, the volume now in the reader's hands would not have been printed . . . But such as it is, written by a learner only, the book is offered to those whose interest in rural objects has been awakened, a sort of rustic primer, which may lead them, if they choose, to something higher.*
—*Susan Fenimore Cooper*, Rural Hours

WITH THE PUBLICATION of her seasonal journal—*Rural Hours*—in 1850, Susan Fenimore Cooper stepped into the charmed circle of American writers who created and popularized the nature essay. Although there were a few precedents, such as William Bartram's late eighteenth-century *Travels*, not until the early nineteenth century did American writers and artists give voice to the beauties of the American landscape. William Cullen Bryant and Susan's father, James Fenimore Cooper, had written nature poems and novels based on the American country landscape for only a little more than twenty-five years. Ralph Waldo Emerson's *Nature* appeared in 1835. Henry David Thoreau had published his first essay only four years earlier and was still four years away from the introduction of *Walden*. John Burroughs's popular essays on birds would not appear for another fifteen years.[1] Obviously, all of these writers were men, although their adult reading public consisted of both men and women. Susan Cooper was the first woman to enter this company.[2] Her appearance not only sets the stage for women nature essayists, but also raises the question of how she and the men whose world she entered handled this new woman's public voice. For she also grew to womanhood during a very restrictive period in American women's history, when many northeastern, middle-class, Euro-American women were confined to the home and domesticity. Her life mirrored the picture of proper womanhood touted in ladies magazines and sentimental novels of the time.[3]

James Fenimore Cooper believed that members of the female sex were most suited to the privacies of home and needed the thoughtful protection of their men. Discouraged by both parents from marrying, Susan, the oldest daughter, never left the family home. Early in life she took on the role of assistant to her father's writing career.[4] Her parental fidelity was also instrumental to her education. Her family taught her to love the plants and animals of her native New York and exposed her to some of the premier naturalists and tastemakers of her day. In "Small Family Memories," an autobiographical essay, she fondly remembers a flower garden kept by her Grandmother Cooper. Her maternal grandfather first introduced her to botanizing as he took her on drives throughout his property. Her father was an avid gardener and followed the new American landscape aesthetic espoused by Andrew Jackson Downing. Susan often rode with him around their Otsego properties, consulting with him on landscape design. James Fenimore Cooper's father, Judge William Cooper, had written one of the first American texts on the agricultural potential of the wilderness. His son retained an interest in the natural history of the region. Not only did father and daughter read widely in natural history; they had as visitors to their home such luminaries as Downing and Dr. James De Kay, author of an early New York zoology.[5] By the mid-nineteenth century such interest in nature was a socially condoned way for middle-class American women to display their civility. Susan received her training within the approved bounds of home under a watchful paternal eye. The effort signified her rejection of the frivolous materialism so much a threat to city women.

Cooper's writing career further demonstrates the importance of gender-role expectations in her life. Before the publication of *Rural Hours*, she had tried her hand at the domestic novel, a genre that was popular among female writers by mid-century. In 1846, under the pseudonym Amabel Penfeather, she published *Elinor Wyllys; or, The Young Folks of Longbridge* with her father's blessing and help. When the manuscript of *Rural Hours* was complete, James took on the public role of choosing a publisher and negotiating the financial deal. Susan remained secluded in the country, safe from the potentially coarsening impact of such city doings. The anonymity of *Rural Hours* attested to a fitting modesty. The mechanisms behind the publication of Susan Cooper's works mirror strategies of the women writers of the time, women Mary Kelley has dubbed "literary domestics." The content of her writing also fits the mold. Literary domestics brought the scenes and values of middle-class homes to a wide readership. They handled the tensions involved in such an effort by "disparaging and dismissing" their talent and by couching their literary role as an expansion of their domestic duty.[6]

Although her own domestic novel did not garner Cooper the kind of fame others achieved, *Rural Hours* did place her on the public stage. William Cullen Bryant and Washington Irving both knew of the book; Bryant wrote a favorable review. Downing encouraged Fredrika Bremer to read it as an example of American women's nature writing. And Henry David Thoreau cited her comments on loons in his journals.[7] Prefacing *Rural Hours* with a disclaimer, Cooper alerted the reader that she had written a "simple record" of the "little events" of her life that have slight "merit of their own" and "make no claim to scientific knowledge" (v). With such language, she carefully maintained female propriety. As the literary domestics centered around home, so she focused her nature essay on the family grounds. Such tactics upheld the social codes bounding Susan Cooper's public voice.

*Rural Hours* also benefited from changing ideas about the value of the native American landscape. Hans Huth has shown how the development of a strong set of nationalistic ideas in early nineteenth-century America altered artists' and writers' portrayal of the natural landscape. Exemplifying this trend, the landscape painter, Thomas Cole, in 1835 wrote about the importance of familiarity with the "home" scene. Responding to Europeans' image of Americans living in a wilderness that contained no civilized history,

Cole urged his countrymen and countrywomen to adopt the American landscape as a true and worthwhile domicile. James Fenimore Cooper was himself one of the early proponents of the value of sparsely settled, rural America over European cities. Encouraged to locate their homes in nature, Americans incorporated images of that landscape into their homes. Huth documents the rise of landscape painting and the frequent appearance of regional landscapes on such domestic appurtenances as glassware and wallpaper. Further, as the century progressed, the value of rural life increased as an antidote to America's own increasingly urban character. Country traditions in the old homestead—in touch with the seasons, the birds, and the trees—were inherently more moral than a life dominated by the artificial environment of the city.[8]

Who could better tell the story of America domestica than an individual whose own life mirrored what was most valuable in the national character? Secluded from urban corruption, often situated in the suburbs or the country, women like Susan Cooper lived in households within the larger home that was nature. Collecting and identifying the common flowers of their gardens and local woods, studying natural history in order to adequately educate their children as well as nurture their own moral character, women were primed to participate in the burgeoning celebration of the American environment. Unique though it was, *Rural Hours* was actually a predictable occurrence. Conjoining women's roles as domesticator and the American landscape's new image as home, Susan Cooper found a space in which to write a classic naturalist's essay. In so doing, she framed the context in which many American women have produced such works from her day to the present.

*Rural Hours* grew out of the perfectly centered Cooper family home in Otsego. From her ancestral base, Susan Cooper describes the changing, seasonal landscape in an area within walking distance, or occasionally a day's carriage ride from this spot. All the important elements of the biophysical environment exist in this space. Her book, though written over a two-year period, recounts one year in her life roaming the gardens, fields, and woods of her region of New York. Divided by the four seasons, beginning with spring and ending in winter, the text takes the form of a diary that documents how the details of her own domestic life are embedded in the natural round. Although the restriction of her rambles to home and environs, and of her voice to that of the common woman's diary, marks this as a female genre, precedents existed among male naturalists for just this approach.

Two of Cooper's favorite authors, and two men who influenced the circle of American nature writers, were the Englishmen Gilbert White and John

Leonard Knapp. White inaugurated the natural history essay with the appearance in 1789 of his *Natural History of Selborne*. Knapp looked to him as a mentor when in the early nineteenth century he published *Country Rambles*. Susan Cooper served as the American editor of Knapp's text when it was reprinted in America in 1853; her introduction praises both Knapp and White for their work.[9] These Englishmen focused their nature study on the landscape of their homes. White's text consists of letters sent to colleagues. Although not as tightly structured around the seasons as Cooper's *Rural Hours*, both books cover the seasonal round. Such harmonies between her role as a nineteenth-century female writer and the traditional nature essay style enhanced Cooper's ability to appeal to a broad readership.

In *Rural Hours*, Cooper speaks to a mixed-sex public in the voice of a woman with an interest in the national issues of her day. Although her identity was meant to be a secret, her gender was not. On the title page is the descriptor "By a Lady." References to the utility of a parasol in a lady's adventurous walks around local terrain reinforce her status. Throughout, Cooper's lady is very clear on appropriate behavior for women. Observing women laboring in a hayfield or behind a plow in her neighborhood, she imagined them newly arrived from Europe, for American men would never expect such work of their wives and daughters (171–72). Although she bemoaned the harsh life of these poor rural women, she did not celebrate the ease of more middle-class village dwellers. Concerned that young village girls were too materialistic—"these are often wildly extravagant in their dress"—she offered farm wives of a certain class as better models. Making their own domestic goods kept farmers in their proper domain: "it is certainly pleasant to see the women busy in this way, beneath the family roof, and one is much disposed to believe that the home system is healthier and safer for the individual, in every way. Home, we may rest assured, will always be, as a rule, the best place for a woman; her labors and interests, should all centre there, whatever be her sphere of life" (161–62).

Cooper stated here a set of conservative values that she clung to for the rest of her life. Unlike some women of her time, she never shifted from her commitment to the woman's sphere to argue for women's rights. Cooper resisted feminism, preferring to end her days performing the sort of charitable work common to women's maternal associations. Unlike some of her literary sisters, she did not doubt that the dominant culture paid serious attention to the values of home. This did not mean, however, that the domestic round offered no corrective to American public life. On the contrary, women's different voice in *Rural Hours* serves just the purpose it should in recalling her readers to their republican roots in the unassuming country life.[10]

Although well read in the naturalists of her day, not all Susan Cooper learned met with her approval. She found the new specialists somewhat too willing to take over knowledge of nature from the common folk. *Rural Hours* contains a long discussion of the perils of the Latinate system for naming plants. Its author bemoaned the loss of common names for wildflowers. She felt that many American plants never had a chance of receiving a common English name, discovered as they were by traveling naturalists who proceeded to dub them "Batschia, Schoberia, Buchnera, Goodyeara," and the like. Such practices denied nature its poetry (and female muses): "Can you picture to yourself . . . maidens, weaving in their golden tresses, *Symphoricarpus vulgaris, Tricochloa, Tradescantia, Calopogon*?" (138–40). Further, scientific naming removed nature study from the home: "if we wish those who come after us to take a natural, unaffected pleasure in flowers, we should have names for the blossoms that mothers and nurses can teach children" (141).

Expanding on women's duty to use nature study for moral education throughout her text, Cooper used plants and animals she saw in nature as a springboard for religious meditation and moral instruction.[11] Critical of scientists' tendency to forget the moral aspect of their studies, she reminded her readers that "every new science introduced into the school-room brings with it an additional weight of moral responsibility" (366). So, parasol in hand, Susan Cooper sallied forth from her domestic hearth to the gardens and woods of her home to speak to all Americans about their native land, in a voice blending lessons from the woman's sphere with knowledge garnered from the scientist-naturalists whose company she kept and books she read.

The home-dwelling, semirural women among whom Cooper counted herself shared in the national effort to define America and Americans. She counseled her compatriots to cherish the rural life and native plants and animals of their locale, rather than looking back to Europe for models of landscape beauty. This emphasis on the virtues of the bucolic American scene continued throughout Cooper's writing career. In her sentimental novel *Elinor Wyllys*, the female protagonist is a country dweller whom her male counterpart comes to love only after rejecting the lures of Europe; one of the other sympathetic characters is an American landscape painter. Her appendix to Knapp's *Country Rambles* mostly distinguishes American flora and fauna from that described by Knapp. In her preface to the same volume, she states that many Americans, through their familiarity with English writers, have more knowledge of the British outdoors than their own. She exhorts readers to "open [your] eyes to the beautiful and wonderful realities of the world we live in . . . Americans are peculiarly placed in this respect; . . . their native soil being endued with the . . . deeper interest of home affections." [12]

Cooper knew that English literature, particularly that penned by the romantics, relied on images from nature for its effect. British flora and fauna provided most nature symbolism for English and American writers. Yet America, she argued, could now provide the stage for new achievements in literature about nature. If the English bard James Thomson had established the standard for poetry of this type in "Seasons," American poets could create their own national literature writing about the unique seasonal round of their new homeland. [13] Cooper envisioned that ultimately Americans would surpass the English in nature writing, making her country the standard-bearer of romantic nature poetry (335). At the heart of this new writing was the rural landscape in the fall, seen in *Rural Hours* as the essential American homescape: "At this very moment, . . . the annual labors of the husbandman are drawing to a close, . . . the first light frosts ripen the wild grapes in the woods, and open the husks of the hickory-nuts, bringing the latest fruits of the year to maturity . . . [these] are the heralds which announce the approach of a brilliant pageant—the moment chosen by Autumn to keep the great harvest-home of America is at hand" (337–38).

As a rural woman, Cooper conserved traditional American country life because the gardens and woods of Otsego were an extension of her domestic sphere. As a public figure, and as the daughter and granddaughter of men who helped define what it meant to be an American, she wanted to protect America domestica—those aspects of nature widely perceived by mid-century as the American heritage. Throughout her descriptions of the plants and animals of her home, these two positions—as native daughter and as member of the new breed of American nature writer—intermingle to create a text that speaks from the personal experience of a rural lady in a voice tinged with the public duty of a well-educated scion of an influential family and class. [14]

By the middle 1800s the Northeast had been settled and cultivated by many generations of Euro-Americans. As James Fenimore Cooper well knew, the location for the classic American tale of confrontation with the wilderness was shifting further west along a moving frontier. To describe America as home, however, required something more than awesome accounts of newly discovered terrain. In striking contrast to the frontier tales of families who kept moving west over the course of the century, and to her father's parallel motion of Leatherstocking's escape to the same wilderness terrain, Susan Cooper and other native nature writers wrote stories of a landscape in which they had deep roots. Because generations of Euro-Americans had lived in the same spot for many years, they could experience American history in a way that more mobile Americans and visitors from Europe could not. As Europeans were reminded of the history of their civilization upon viewing their cathedrals, so Americans could now find a record of their achievements in the land they had domesticated.[15]

On seeing flowering thorn trees while out for an afternoon drive, Susan was reminded of the Revolution: "during the war . . . the long spines of the thorn were occasionally used by the American women for pins . . . probably it was the cockspur variety, which bears the longest and most slender spines, and is now in flower" (121). She went on to note that though there was no longer any need for such improvisation, the thorn tree still was useful to rural women for storing yarn (122). Americans did not have to build monuments, or constantly seek new territory, to create a national identity. As Cooper knew, they read their history in the common, everyday plants around and in their towns and villages. As she shows here, knowledge of natural history—of the difference between one kind of tree from another—is integral to the construction of national history. One gathers knowledge by settling in one place, becoming familiar with its native flora and fauna.

A mixture of wild and tame plants constituted a chief virtue in Cooper's rural landscape. Domesticating the wilderness did not necessarily eradicate it. For Cooper, the original natural landscape before Euro-American settlement remained an integral part of the country's heritage and appeared in the terrain around her home. A stand of forest pines at the top of a hill overlooking her village represented a crucial aspect of American history as surely as a ruined castle contained symbolic meaning for an Englishwoman. In describing such a stand of aged trees, Cooper labored to give them an exact and unique past similar to the history found in buildings. This specific pine grove could not be cut down and replanted with young trees to grow back over time. Rather, like a historic monument, the forest pines were creatures of a particular time and place. Losing them meant losing American history: "no other younger wood can ever claim the same connection as this, with a state of things now passed away forever; they cannot have that wild, stern character of the aged forest pines" (194). As the thorn tree reminded her of the Revolution, the pine stand contained memories of the "tenants of the wilderness"—the "wild creatures" and the "red man" (190). In taming the land, Cooper asserted, Americans had a responsibility to preserve as historic monuments those features of its original face, for without them her country would be in danger of losing its knowledge of the past. In this way, wilderness became part of a homescape rather than some far and fearsome frontier threatening civilization.

In Susan Cooper's time and place, wilderness had been, at least for her, subsumed under a new class—the native. Used to define a distinctive American character, the native usually was elevated over the imported.[16] Original American forest was not so much wild as it was indigenous; in this lay its merit. Cooper realized that she and her compatriots were most knowledgeable about the plants and animals of England. She also knew a good deal about their importation to America. Although appreciating many of the changes wrought by these foreigners, she consistently encouraged her readers to value the bounty of their own land. Much of her journal celebrates patches of native growth surprised among recently cultivated fields around home. Following a path through a meadow, she led her readers into a hidden runnel "filled with native plants; on one side stands a thorn-tree, whose morning shadow falls upon grasses and clovers brought from beyond the seas, while in the afternoon, it lies on gyromias and moose-flowers, sarsaparillas and cahoshes, which bloomed here for ages, when the eye of the red man alone beheld them. Even within the limits of the village spots may still be found on the bank of the river, which are yet unbroken by the plough, where the trailing arbutus, and squirrel-cups, and May-wings tell us so every spring" (148–49).

With the negative connotations of wilderness controlled in the celebration of the native, Cooper offered her audience a bountiful nature functioning as the mid-nineteenth-century home was meant to function—as a place of harmony where citizens found security, contentment, and civility. This domestic haven arose not only from the tended crops, but equally from the native plants and animals of the region. On her daily walks, Cooper often gathered food from wild-growing plants—various berries were a particular source of pleasure. Other plants, such as the pumpkin, transplanted easily into the country garden. In fact, the whole landscape appears to have been incredibly fecund, created as a sort of Eden for the new settlers: "Year after year, from the early history of the country, the land has yielded her increase in cheerful abundance; the fields have been filled with the finest of wheat, and maize, and rice, and sugar; the orchards and gardens, aye, the very woods and wastes, have yielded all their harvest of grateful fruits . . . like the ancient people of God, we may say, that fountains of milk and honey have flowed in upon us" (392). In a landscape revealing little difference between tilled fields and the "woods and wastes," where terrain served the same purpose as another room in their household, settlers rightly preserved all aspects of nature.

Finally, American readers discovered that, for all the blessings peculiar to their new home, their land was really but one room in the greater household of earth: "The mandrakes, or May-apples, are in flower . . . This common showy plant growing along our fences, and in many meadows, is said also to be found under a different variety in the hilly countries of Central Asia. One likes to trace these links, connecting lands and races, so far apart, reminding us, as they do, that the earth is the common home of all" (91). With language culled from religious texts, and from the emerging ecological understanding of the naturalists, Cooper constructed an all-encompassing household, placing a heavy duty on its human tenants to make their individual homes in keeping with the terms of the environment.

Cooper encouraged her readers to change their confrontational attitude toward their home. For all her glowing reports of the fecundity of the American landscape, *Rural Hours* also documents declining populations. Animal life suffered the most obvious loss. Cooper wrote little about animals until the winter, when she had less to say about the plant world. Spending more time indoors, writing from her reading, she reported on the decline in fish and game birds; on the disappearance of deer, bear, and beaver from her region; and on rare sightings of otter, of whom she could only report that "it is said that they actually slide down hill on the snow, merely for amusement . . . One would like to see them at their play" (499). She called for the enactment of laws to protect certain animals before hunting and settlements eradicated them from the area (306, 376).

In the plant kingdom, her major concern was the devastation of the forests, and here the home imagery came to the fore. Arguing for the preservation of native forests, Cooper appealed to a variety of interests—some pragmatic, some aesthetic, some moral and religious. All centered, however, on the understanding that Euro-Americans could no longer behave as though they were just passing through, on their way back to the old home across the ocean or to the new on the western frontier. First, she counseled those who profited from the land to remember that trees constituted a large part of the country's current and future wealth (214). Then, moving on to the moral value of trees (conjoining the good with the beautiful here), she declared that preservation of trees around the home signified advanced civilization and looked better than expensive coats of paint on the walls or columns around the porch (items often purchased with funds earned by cutting down native timber) (215).

She argued that the wanton cutting of trees displayed "careless indifference to any good gift of our gracious Maker, shows a want of thankfulness, . . . betrays a reckless spirit of evil" (217). If we are to live here, it is our responsibility to act with restraint and nurturance toward the woods: "thinning woods and not blasting them; clearing such ground as is marked for immediate tillage; preserving the wood on the hill-tops and rough side-hills; . . . permitting bushes and young trees to grow at will along the brooks and water courses; sowing, if need be, a grove on the bank of the pool" (216). Much of creation could be lost with the devastation of the forest. Understanding that "the dullest insect crawling about these roots lives by the power of the Almighty; and the discolored shreds of last year's leaves wither away upon the lowly herbs in a blessing of fertility" (203) obligated citizens to protect all of the forest and its denizens as it would its own family.

Her religious belief in a divinely created, static nature, in which humanity's responsibility was to preserve an assumed status quo, informed Cooper's understanding of a rudimentary sort of ecology. Yet, in her arguments for the conservation of nature, hers was one of the early voices warning Americans about the dangers of their profligate use of resources. Certainly, some of her insight sprang from her father's tutoring and from her reading of the naturalists. But *Rural Hours* remains one of the few popular texts of the time containing a holistic comprehension of nature, calling for the protection not only of certain plants and animals, but also of the household in which these individuals flourished.[17] Her father sensed the uniqueness of her work when he observed that he had "very little doubt of its ultimate success, though at first the American world will hesitate to decide."[18] Actually, her words were perfectly timed. The journal sold well, reflecting increasing interest in such conservation activities as Arbor Day and the rise of the popular essay celebrating amateur birding.[19]

In the public arena, Cooper's linkage of America and home served broad political purposes. Home also meant a private, secluded space for which she, as a woman of her time, had special responsibility. But seclusion did not mean a life restricted to domestic interiors. Protected from the physical and psychic threats of the city, the proper country home allowed women spatial freedom to seek outdoor pleasures and nature studies. An idealized version of the country house and grounds appears in the home of Cooper's hero in *Elinor*

*Wyllys*: "The grounds were of the simplest kind. The lawn which surrounded the house was merely a better sort of meadow, from which the stones and briars had been removed with more care than usual, and which, on account of its position, received the attention of one additional mowing in the course of the summer. A fine wood, of a natural growth, approached quite near to the house on the northern side, partially sheltering it in that direction, while an avenue of weeping elms led from the gate to the principal entrance."[20] For urban apartments or the new suburban houses on modest lots, the dividing line between private and public began at either the family's front door or the edge of the lot. Country houses had the luxury of more expansive surroundings. The yard and local woods and fields of Otsego were merely extensions of Cooper's (and her imaginary hero's) domestic round.[21] Thus, in describing her personal circumstances in *Rural Hours*, she made no distinction between the supposedly secluded domain of her father's house and the natural world outside her door. Her life exemplified the interconnections and interdependencies between humans and the rest of the natural world that she espoused in her book.[22]

Confined to the house on a blustery day, longing for early spring flowers, she consoled herself by surveying the nature imagery in the wallpaper, rugs, furniture, and glassware of her home:

> here, winter as well as summer, we find traces enough of the existence of that beautiful part of creation, the vegetation; winter and summer, the most familiar objects with which we are surrounded, which hourly contribute to our convenience and comfort, bear the impress of the plants and flowers in their varied forms and colors. We seldom remember, indeed, how large a portion of our ideas of grace and beauty are derived from the plants, how constantly we turn to them for models . . . Branches and stems, leaves and tendrils, flowers and fruits, nuts and berries, are everywhere models (504–5).

Cooper was a proponent of Andrew Jackson Downing's rustic style. Her sense of oneness with nature's aspects, however, was not merely a fashionable fancy. Generally unconcerned in *Rural Hours* with the interior of her home, she mentions it only at this point, when it serves as a surrogate for the outdoors. As the flowers on the wallpaper were reflections of nature's model, so her house and its domesticity mirrored the lives of plants and animals living on the Cooper grounds. Their nests and dens, their responses to various forms of domestication, offered corollaries to her own experience as a female in a very traditional household.[23]

Excepting the coldest part of winter, Cooper usually took one and sometimes two daily walks or drives around Otsego. On these excursions she surveyed the state of agriculture and engaged in amateur naturalizing—seeking flowers or birds new to her. She often considered how other forms of life provide models or cautions for human behavior. She was consumed with understanding what nature suggests about female roles and family responsibilities, and how gender definitions and familial arrangements help people comprehend what they see in nature. Birds specifically interested Cooper, as she, and apparently many of her generation, subscribed to Alexander Wilson's contention that humans and birds share common habits and emotions.[24] Her comments about birds exemplify the influence of gender roles on her ideas about nature.

Cooper felt a strong sense of fellowship with her bird neighbors. On one chilly fall day she hoped that they would come in her windows for "they would be very welcome to warm themselves and fly away at will" (320–21). Equally as willing to open her house to their view as they were to display theirs for her, she spent long hours watching their domestic round:

> late evening hours are not the most musical moments with the birds; family cares have begun, and there was a good deal of the nursery about the grove of evergreens in the rear of the house, to-night. It was amusing to watch the parents flying home, and listen to the family talk going on; there was a vast deal of twittering and fluttering before settling down in the nest, husband and wife seemed to have various items of household information to impart to each other, and the young nestlings made themselves heard very plainly; one gathered a little scolding, too, on the part of some mother robins (77).

Anthropomorphizing at will, she gave the birds' home a domestic arrangement similar to her own, breathing individuality into the creatures with her tale of domestic dissent.

Sometimes birds serve as models of excellent behavior; rather than our equals, they then become our betters. A mother on the nest offered one exemplar. Her "voluntary imprisonment" "hour after hour, day after day, upon her unhatched brood, warming them with her breast—carefully turning them— that all may share the heat equally, and so fearful lest they should be chilled, that she will rather suffer hunger herself than leave them long exposed" is "a striking instance of that generous enduring patience which is a noble attribute of parental affection" (39–40). Of course, not all birds merit such high praise. Cooper was quick to distinguish between the more reliably "domestic" ones and such animals as the "cow-pen black-bird." A terrible mother, she laid her eggs in other birds' nests, abandoning her young to their care (408). Wherever possible, however, Cooper urged her readers to view the domestic arrangements of birds as comparable to and part of nature's great, enveloping household.

Birds were not the only creatures subject to this sort of empathetic regard for their maternal doings. Almost any other creature she observed or about which she had read enough to have a sense of its family arrangements received similar treatment. Her discussion in *Rural Hours* of the "upholsterer bee" she had seen in England provides a case in point. The bee was associated with a red poppy, whose leaves the animal used in constructing a nest. Cooper provided an extravagant vision of the "careful mother" cutting a bit of "the scarlet flower" for her nest, where she "spreads it on the floor like a carpet" and makes "handsome hangings" for the "brilliant cradle" of "one little bee" (199). As with the birds, such an encapsulated domestic scene gives the insect a moral character comparable to that of a human mother. John Leonard Knapp, who also wrote about these bees, took little notice of the insect's domesticity. Knapp and Cooper also parted company in describing the English hedgehog. Both saw it as a harmless animal subjected to much mistreatment by humans. But whereas Knapp described a generic hedgehog, focusing on its physical features and habits, Cooper, in her addition to his text, tells a touching tale of a mother hedgehog's fidelity, even unto death, to her young.[25] For Susan Cooper, gender and the family responsibilities of females in particular were significant aspects of hedgehog, bee, and bird character.

One commentator on *Rural Hours* has argued that, as a woman of her time, Cooper had to "dispense moral precepts and display a set of principles," whereas Knapp and Gilbert White could freely engage in "spontaneous" nature description.[26] Although Cooper admired White, as did most of the budding nature essayists in England and America from the 1830s on, she and Knapp wrote about nature in rather different circumstances than White. As Donald Worster has shown, for White, nature study was an "integral part of the curate's life." White's work became important fifty years after its publication, when the pressures of industrialization engendered a search for the old pastoral landscape of White's Selborne.[27] Writers like Knapp and Cooper described nature with an eye to morally improving a people who were sorely threatened by the materialism of the city, thus taking a more principled tone than White. The more basic, gender-coded difference between Cooper and her male predecessors is Cooper's focused interest in family life and female behavior in plants and animals. That many important moral lessons sprang from nature's domestic affairs obviously supported the valuable contribution women (who viewed themselves as most attuned to family life) could make to nature study and appreciation.

Knapp and White gave little thought to what nature, or nature/human interactions, had to say about gender roles. On one occasion Knapp chided his countrymen for killing hedgehogs to prove their manhood, but on the whole his moralizing took a more general tone.[28] Nor was nature thought of as home in the same way in the men's writings. Knapp and White open their texts with a loving description of their home regions but present themselves primarily as researchers into nature's secrets. They collected plants and animals, experimented with them, and corresponded with scientific colleagues about their findings. Nature's household was not commensurate with their own. Neither pondered what their findings suggested about their roles as fathers and husbands.

Susan Cooper always considered what her knowledge and her actions had to say about her womanly role, particularly as keeper of the home. Although she might join in pronouncements with men when public concerns mirrored domestic affairs, she was conscious of her status as a lady. In *Rural Hours*, we never see Cooper engaged in collecting specimens for the microscope. She collected flowers for ornament and berries for dinner. When, as in her comments on bird families, bees, and hedgehogs, she addressed her audience as a private woman describing her feeling for nature, rather than as an American converting the landscape from wilderness to household, Cooper spoke specifically to a female readership about the particular interests of women.

The plant kingdom also provided opportunities for commenting on human gender divisions and sexual differences. Aware of the language of flowers and schooled enough in botany to distinguish among plant types, Cooper showed her female readers how a close observation of flowering plants taught the proper female virtues of modesty, constancy, and sisterhood. When she observed the birds, she found her family; when she looked at flowers, she saw images of the female sex. Laying to rest men's fears that Linnaean botany, with its emphasis on sexual characteristics of plants, was too coarse a subject for female sensibilities, Cooper emphasized the emotional connotations of femininity that flowers called forth. In the spring, she found violets "growing in little sisterhoods" in the fields and forests (78). The regular appearance of these violets as well as arbutus, squirrel cups, and ground laurels offered a lesson in constancy: "How pleasant it is to meet the same flowers year after year! If the blossoms were liable to change—if they were to become capricious and irregular—they might excite more surprise, more curiosity, but we should love them less" (48). She found all of these flowers in her walks. They were not hothouse plants secluded in an artificial environment. Such hardiness was a positive attribute in both plants and women thriving freely and openly in the healthy rural atmosphere of Otsego.

While Cooper celebrated indigenous plants as part of her encouragement to Americans to make their home among the natives of the continent, she also believed that such plants were important sources of virtuous lessons to American women. Echoing Fredrika Bremer's fear of pampering, Cooper counseled her sisters to resist overcultivation—both in themselves and in their flowers. The wild rose was much lovelier than the grafted tree roses popular in some gardens. Grafted roses lacked modesty: "[they] remind one of the painful difference between the gentle, healthy-hearted daughter of home, the light of the house, and the meretricious dancer, tricked out upon the stage to dazzle and bewilder, and be stared at by the mob. The rose has so long been an emblem of womanly loveliness, that we do not like to see her shorn of one feminine attribute; and modesty in every true-hearted woman is, like affection, a growth of her very nature, whose roots are fed with her life's blood" (123). If women were like roses, then it was their duty to protect the roselike quality of their nature as well as the nature of the rose.

Mirroring her public concern for the loss of morality in science, Cooper, speaking from the domestic sphere in a voice consciously female, reminded her readers that women, as conservators of tradition, had a responsibility to resist ambitious manipulation of God's creation.[29] Like the families who sold their native pines to buy ostentatious paint for their houses, women who bought such artificial plants as the grafted rose forgot their republican roots.[30] Such behavior endangered nature, American society, and women's status as moral standard-bearers. Linking woman's nature to the indigenous plants of America, Cooper framed women's appreciation, nurturance, and protection of such plants and their environments as a function of gender. By the late nineteenth century many women had picked up on her suggestion and were writing books grounded in their sense of the particular bond between themselves and nature.

Among the many traits these later texts share with Cooper's, the most striking is their emphasis on the gender of the writer. All are self-consciously nature studies by a woman who writes from within the domestic confines of her home about the seasonal round of plant and animal life. Among the earliest to follow Cooper were investigators who added to our knowledge of American flora and fauna. Often connected to the scientific community, these women saw themselves marking out a bit of experimental territory peculiarly suited to their gender. They included Mary Treat (*Home Studies in Nature*), Olive Thorne Miller (*In Nesting Time*), and Florence Merriam (*A-Birding on a Bronco*), all of whom published before the turn of the twentieth century. They lived middle-class, intellectual lives in much the same domestic circumstances as Susan Cooper. Nature study fulfilled their obligation to use their leisure in a productive, nonfrivolous manner that would be beneficial to society.

In *Rural Hours* Cooper encouraged Americans to learn more about insects, a neglected and misunderstood category of animal life. Mary Treat, of Vineland, New Jersey, took her up on the suggestion. In the 1880s she began publishing accounts of her experiments with spiders in her self-constructed "insect menagerie" at home. Whereas Susan Fenimore Cooper had a rank amateur's understanding of science and never proposed to conduct experiments, Treat—enjoying women's increasing involvement in science—worked at her research.[31] She provided detailed studies of birds, spiders, ants, wasps, and insectivorous plants, referring the reader to her articles in various scientific and popular journals, quoting from her correspondence with Asa Gray and Charles Darwin, and pointing out her own contributions in the field. She viewed nature as much less static than did Cooper. Aware of the explosion in theory attendant upon the publication of Darwin's *On the Origin of Species* (1859), Treat argued against human supremacy in a hierarchical natural world created in one stroke by God. She urged her readers to marvel instead at the constantly changing environment in which they lived. Along with others of this early generation of Darwinists, she saw evidence of evolution all around her.[32]

Mary Treat was, however, much more Susan Cooper's soul mate than she was Charles Darwin's colleague. Most of her experiments and her work centered around the domestic landscapes of her home in Vineland, with the rest resulting from winter excursions to Florida. In her most comprehensive work, *Home Studies in Nature*, she argued that to the true nature lover, "the smallest area around a well-chosen home will furnish sufficient material to satisfy all thirst of knowledge through the longest life" (6). Throughout the text she commented on the virtues of observations and experiments made in this more restricted sphere. If most women could not (and perhaps should not) join male naturalists on heroic journeys of exploration, they could make another sort of journey traveling the familiar round of home, garden, and local neighborhood. In this round, too, one could contribute to the public effort to understand the natural world.

For all its scientific voice, *Home Studies in Nature* is clearly a woman's book. Beginning, as had Cooper, with a description of her home and gardens, Treat highlighted the domestic life of animals. Her studies of birds emphasize family habits and read gender-coded meaning into nesting behavior. Treat's most fulsome consideration of animal life concerns an unlikely specimen—the spider. The spider habitat she built served as both a scientific laboratory and a domestic garden, surrounded by an arborvitae hedge, with a centered maple tree, "ornamental plants," and a couple of bird baths (113). Particularly interested, as she was with birds, in spider architecture, she offered lyric observations of the maternal instincts of various specimens/pets. One ground spider, whose carefully contrived home tower Treat described in some detail, evinces model domesticity in caring for her young. In one session, the babies crawl over the mother and she picks them up, holding them in front of her and "perhaps giving them a homily on manners. Soon she gently releases them" (105). Shedding their skins, the children dispose of their "baby dresses" (107). When the little ones are old enough to leave the nest, the mother "behaves much in the same way that the higher animals do in weaning their young" (107). Treat stressed not only her status as a woman at home engaging in nature study, but also how nature functions as a home akin to the human home.

Like Cooper, Treat found little difference between outdoors and indoors, or wild and domestic. As well as building a garden for watching wild spiders, she brought them into her study, housed in glass cases, where she could observe them throughout the seasons. Domesticating an animal meant accommodating it to her presence. In her terminology, wild birds were domesticated when they used her bird bath while she sat quietly watching. Although she was aware of the importance of struggle and competition in Darwin's model of evolution, she chose not to dwell on this aspect of life. Treat saw all of nature as a household, with each plant and animal playing a cooperative, harmonious part.[33] Nature "red in tooth and claw" receives short shrift in her work, whereas images of cooperative behavior predominate. This is particularly true in her comments on preserving bird populations. Aware that many agriculturists held deep prejudices against certain birds, she underlined their dependence on the birds for insect control (41–42). More sophisticated in her ecological understanding than Susan Cooper, she explained in more detail how the organic system operates.

Mary Treat's nature studies provide a missing link in accounting for the explosion of women naturalists studying birds in the late nineteenth century. In most nineteenth-century histories, women appear as individualized voices only once—as participants in these late-century bird preservation movements. During this period, a group of women writers produced many books on birds. Some were scientific studies of bird behavior, some were amateur naturalist accounts of birding, and some were children's books written to encourage the next generation to preserve bird populations. Trying to account for this phenomenon, historians have noted that by this time women had a long tradition of working on social issues through voluntary organizations. Much of the impetus for the "bird ladies" came from the rise of the Audubon clubs, often headed by men but whose members were primarily female amateurs trained in women's colleges.[34] Although such reasoning explains the mechanism by which women came to speak publicly for birds, it does not tell us much about the value they placed on these animals or about the nature of their interest. As the language of flowers provided early nineteenth-century women with entrée into botany, so the image of birds as microcosms of human domesticity offered women later in the century a rationale for their study.

Two of the most prolific bird authors, who were also political activists in the fight to save birds from their commercial use in women's hats and from hunters, were Olive Thorne Miller and Florence Merriam. Their works are typical of the sort of book produced by women during this period. Miller (born in 1831) upheld traditional gender-role expectations. She began publishing her bird books only after raising four children and then wrote under a pseudonym. Merriam (born in 1863) was of the next generation, contributing both to the more humanistic nature writing of the time and to the burgeoning science of ornithology. She was the first woman to win the Brewster Medal (for *Birds of New Mexico*), awarded for original work in ornithology. Merriam has received praise as well for her courage and stamina, when, in 1899, after marrying the naturalist Vernon Bailey, she traveled with him throughout the West surveying birds. Regardless of these differences, Miller and Merriam were close friends. Merriam's library contained inscribed copies of Miller's books, and Merriam occasionally mentions Miller in her own work. Their texts reveal a common language of birds, one concerned with female metaphors of domesticity.[35]

Both women wrote books featuring local birds. Miller's *In Nesting Time* details her efforts to make her home a home to birds. She kept one room in the house separate for her bird studies. In this room she housed birds in cages, but she also encouraged them to roam free. Thus, the room became a large aviary and she just one of the tenants. Generally, the birds were not house pets. After a brief season indoors, they were freed in her yard or the surrounding woods. Whereas Susan Fenimore Cooper, stranded inside in the winter, could locate nature only in the patterns on her rug, Miller entertained herself by watching a brown thrush peel the wallpaper in the bird room: "First came a little tear, then a leap one side, another small rent, another panic; and so he went on til he had torn off a large piece which dropped to the floor, while I sat too much interested in the performance to think of saving the paper. (The room and its contents are always secondary to the birds' comfort and pleasure, in my thoughts)." [36] Befitting her book's title, *In Nesting Time*, Miller concentrates on the mating and nesting habits of birds she kept indoors and those she spied on outdoors. As usual, the primary metaphors for describing behaviors come from her own female duties: "I discovered very soon that mocking-bird babies are brought up on hygienic principles, and have their meals with great regularity" (46). Bird mothers, like human mothers, subscribed to the newest trends in domestic science.

Not only did she write as a woman, she exhorted women readers to enter the field of ornithology. Noting that the old days of killing, dissecting, nest robbing, and mounting were over, that "all that can be learned with violence" has been learned, she asserted that the next phase of bird study required field observation of their habits, "infinite patience, perseverance, untiring devotion, and . . . a quick eye and ear, and a sympathetic heart" (16). Who among her readers shared these qualities better than women? "This is the pleasant path opening now, and in some ways it is particularly suited to woman with her great patience and quiet manners" (18). Florence Merriam, arriving a generation later, shared some of the qualities of the so-called New Woman, who had a much more visible and diverse public role and was less likely to marry and have children. Yet Merriam couched her interest in birds in exactly the gendered terms that Miller envisioned.[37]

Although Merriam wrote standard handbooks on western birds, full of straight, scientific information, in these texts and in more personal publications about her life among the birds, her tone differs little from that of Miller, Treat, or Cooper. Merriam patiently watched her subjects, with no more threatening weapons than a parasol and a consuming interest in courtship and family behavior. A good companion book to Miller's *In Nesting Time* is Merriam's *A-Birding on a Bronco*, written while the author was in California recuperating from tuberculosis.[38] For all the title suggests a woman escaping the confines of home for adventure in the rugged West, Merriam stays close to home, rambling around on her trusty horse until she knows the ranch as well as her own home back east. *A-Birding on a Bronco*'s precursor is not the high adventure of a John James Audubon lost in unknown territory, but Susan Cooper's *Rural Hours*.

The center of Merriam's interest was the home—the nest—which made nature worth studying. Riding through a eucalyptus grove, she commented on the importance of the domestic scene: "How one little home does make a place habitable! From bare silent woods it becomes a dwelling place. Everything seemed to centre around this little nest, then the only one in the grove; the tiny pinch of down became the most important thing in the woods."[39] Merriam regarded birds as persons, with rights to tenancy on her land and deserving of the same respect due human neighbors (65). As persons, they were interesting in their domestic arrangements. She spent much time speculating about the meaning of their family life. Occasionally, the questions that the women of her time were raising about gender roles informed her descriptions of bird life. Reflecting the New Woman's challenge to some of the constraints of patriarchy, Merriam lamented the classification system that science applied to birds. Female birds had to "bear their husband's names, however inappropriate . . . Here an innocent creature with an olive-green back and yellowish breast has to go about all her days known as the black throated warbler, just because that happens to describe the dress of her spouse."[40] Such a comment suggests somewhat more awareness of women's rights issues than either Cooper or Miller demonstrated. It does not, however, call into question the valuable lessons learned when female naturalists turn their gendered interest on the study of nature. Like Cooper, Merriam found within woman's different culture a source for correcting a form of scientific hubris and drawing a social lesson from nature's domestic arrangements.

Her interest in male/female roles created some difficulties when a bird's sex was not so easily determined by its plumage. Trying to figure which of a pair of gnatcatchers was the female, she realized that certain nesting behaviors could, using the human model, be attributed to either gender (51). Nevertheless, such questions did not lead her to violent methods. Unable to identify an elusive bird family, she was advised to shoot a specimen and send it to "the wise men." But her familiarity with their domestic scene made this impossible: "after knowing the little family in their home it would have been like raising my hand against familiar friends. Could I take their lives to gratify my curiosity about a name?"(141). *A-Birding on a Bronco* studies a natural world that is home, not a foreign terrain from which the explorer feels he has a right and an obligation to bring back plunder. As Miller had encouraged, Merriam found in the branch of ornithology emphasizing observational fieldwork a space appropriate to women's conservationist role.

The works of Treat, Miller, and Merriam share one other similarity with the earlier generation's study of the language of flowers. Just as botany was proper only insofar as plant sexuality camouflaged behind a mask of gentility, bird behavior had one taboo arena. With all the emphasis on mating and nesting, the reader might expect occasional descriptions of sexuality. Each author provides some details—describing, for example, a male bird's showy courting dance—but all avoid any mention of the sexual act. Female birds always act modestly as they are being wooed, and a pair invariably retreats to the cover of a handy tree at the point of mating, reemerging ready to build their nest and get on with family affairs. As the struggle to survive is touched upon lightly, so too is the procreative act. Birds, like their female observers, have too much taste to reveal such matters to the public eye.[41]

The reticence and gentle quality of the bird books produced by women in the latter part of the century no doubt contribute to their contemporary critical reputation. While women are acknowledged to have had an important impact on wildlife preservation during the period for educating the popular readership in the virtues of birds, they have been dismissed by at least one historian from a secure place in the literary naturalist canon in part because of this emphasis on domesticity: "the special perceptions they brought to the study of birds were more valuable in giving instruction than in providing inspiration; they bestowed the gift of sight rather than insight."[42] Of course, the question such a comment raises is to whom, and in what context, these women were writing.

Between the publication of Susan Fenimore Cooper's *Rural Hours* in 1850 and Florence Merriam's *A-Birding on a Bronco* in 1896, the nature essay had become standard fare in many popular magazines. Specialized journals for nature lovers were common. With the appearance of Henry David Thoreau's *Walden* and John Burroughs' *Wake-Robin*, literary writing about nature entered the mainstream.[43] Thoreau and Burroughs developed the same theme Susan Cooper mined in writing about the American environment as home. These men and women shared a preference for the rural life, an antimaterialist bias, a strong sense of the respect due to all life, and more interest in the ecological system than in tales of struggle and dominance. The men's images of home, however, are less focused on the domestic round than the representations of Cooper and the other women considered here.

Men and women developed somewhat different voices for writing about nature, but one wonders if, to the readership of the time, one voice was any less inspirational than the other. Certainly, the women were successful: they published a great deal and their texts enjoyed many printings. There is little in male naturalists' comments of the period to suggest that they found women less capable; in fact, in certain instances men cited women's works to settle public debates.[44] The reason for women's tenuous rank in the canon of literary nature writers probably lies in particular trends in the literary world and the scientific establishment during the late nineteenth and early twentieth centuries.

As Ann Douglas has shown, Victorian literary fashion was in many ways defined by the combined forces of middle-class women and the clergy. Disturbed by the feminization of culture, some writers criticized what they saw as excessive sentimentalism in women's literature, while more popular male novelists turned to producing works supportive of a burgeoning "crusade for masculinity."[45] As Margaret Rossiter has shown, the newly emerging scientific establishment was grappling with a concurrent explosion of women seeking and finding training in various fields. Certain areas, such as botany, appeared completely feminized. Reflecting this incursion of women into previously male domains was their membership in naturalist groups like the Audubon societies. As well as their work in these activist organizations, women sought entrance into scientific societies and edited scientific journals. The scientific establishment began a series of efforts to limit control and predominant membership in such institutions to men. For example, Florence Merriam became the first female member of the American Ornithological Union in 1885, but she was listed only as an associate.[46]

For the nature essayists, such a climate produced predictable results. On the literary side, the home-based tradition established by Gilbert White and carried on in America by Susan Fenimore Cooper, Henry David Thoreau, John Burroughs, Olive Thorne Miller, and Florence Merriam was eclipsed by more virile tales of the wilderness challenge popularized by Teddy Roosevelt, Jack London, and Edgar Rice Burroughs. Thrilling stories of wild animal hunting expeditions (with either gun or camera) held more interest than women's domestic tales of patient watching by the nest of a common yard bird. Although men and women had written the first nature essays, the privilege granted heroic exploration effectively silenced women's voices, while prominent men in the home-based tradition were rehabilitated and lauded for those aspects of their work that fit the new mold.[47] In the developing hierarchy of the scientific professions, women's names disappeared from the leadership; assigned associate roles, they appeared less influential—capable of "sight but not insight." Thus, the disappearance of women's voices from the canon was more a function of the end-of-the-century effort to reestablish masculine control of scientific and literary culture than any generalized defect in their ability as observers and writers.

Nothing in the accounts of women nature writers during this period suggests that they either repudiated their traditional form or recognized the threats to their status. In fact, the tradition begun by Cooper, Treat, Miller, Merriam, and others continued into the twentieth century and flourishes today. Throughout this century, writers have produced books in which their individual round as women in a country setting exemplifies a mode of living in keeping with the natural environment. Around the turn of the century, women more directly connected to agricultural or backcountry life began to publish. The narratives of these women continue Susan Cooper's belief that rural life avoids the excesses of materialism. Cooper looked to farm women as models of modesty and frugality; the chronicles of twentieth-century farm women repeat her theme. Martha McCulloch-Williams's *Next to the Ground* (1902), Louise Rich's *We Took to the Woods* (1942), Sue Hubbell's *A Country Year* (1986), and Maxine Kumin's *In Deep* (1987) all echo Cooper's practical interest in what the environment yields for human survival and how women may use and preserve nature's bounty.

These authors also reiterate the conservationist role that Cooper and Miller saw as women's responsibility, including pointed messages about women's duty to preserve and protect the plants and animals of home. McCulloch-Williams's protagonist in 1902 was given the task of nursing injured birds brought in from the field while her brother and father went shooting. Eighty years later Kumin argues that women, because of gender socialization, are more successful than men at working with problem horses.[48] Like Cooper, the twentieth-century writers believe that the city and, later, the suburbs trivialize women's lives. Both Rich in 1942 and Hubbell in 1986 argue that scraping out a living in the backcountry is preferable to the consumerist existence each had led as urban women.[49] And, finally, although these books from the farmlands speak consciously from within a woman's round, that sphere also offers a corrective to the public excesses of the day—be they the terrors of world war in Rich's 1942 narrative or the problems of "survival, of hunger and genocide" in Kumin's account.[50] As did Susan Cooper in 1850, the contemporary nature essayists have found room to write from within the private domestic spaces of their lives about public, political issues facing Americans.

By the turn of the century, women were also immersed in conservation and preservation efforts developing out of the Progressive Era's reformist agenda. Reflecting the broadening national interest in safeguarding America's wilderness landscapes, key figures in this movement came from all over the country. During the first three decades of the twentieth century, Mary Hunter Austin, a midwesterner transplanted to the deserts of the Southwest, served as a leading female voice in the effort to protect arid regions from over-development. Inspired in part by John Muir's call to preserve natural land-scapes, Austin worked on political campaigns to conserve and appropriately use water in the West. Her talent as a nature writer, however, made more impact on American environmental values. Following in Cooper's tradition, Austin tracked seasonal variations in the flora and fauna around her homes in the California and Nevada deserts and the mountains of New Mexico. She earned her reputation as the most famous female nature writer of the period from such books as *The Land of Little Rain* (1903), *The Flock* (1906), and *The Land of Journey's Ending* (1924). Austin forms a link between the nineteenth-century birders and the women nature essayists who published in the 1960s and 1970s.[51]

Mary Austin and her literary daughters champion ways of living holis-tically in keeping with nature, seeking a way back into the endangered wild landscape. In Austin's *Land of Little Rain*, Helen Hoover's *The Gift of the Deer* (1965), Josephine Johnson's *The Inland Island* (1969), and Ann Zwinger's *Be-yond the Aspen Grove* (1970), women naturalists have picked up the thread Cooper began in her pleas for the preservation of native forests and their plants and animals. The late twentieth-century reader of *Rural Hours* is struck by the devastation of animal populations more than one hundred years ago, particularly when Cooper recounts the sad death of one of the last deer in the area or the almost mythical sightings of an elusive "panther" near Otsego (240–44, 422). In the century since publication of Cooper's work, public concern for the preservation of wilderness areas has blossomed; with that con-cern has come an interest in living in the shadow of the forest (or, in Austin's case, on the edge of the desert).[52] Whereas Cooper and her family retired to a semidomesticated, rural landscape, this more contemporary group of female writers locates itself beyond the agricultural fringe, in the last pockets of American wilderness. Here its members seek an experience, however, much akin to that of Cooper, Treat, Miller, Merriam, and their more recent agricultural sisters. They establish a domestic life that makes room for the native plants and animals of the land.

Although twentieth-century writers do not share the nineteenth-century burden of constantly demonstrating the propriety of their work on the public stage by emphasizing their ties to home, their voices are clearly female. Sometimes being female in the twentieth century mirrors the nineteenth-century experience; at other times it does not. Hoover presents "Pretty," a female deer of the herd, in proper women's makeup. Zwinger writes about flora as though they are children and her daughters as though they are fauna. Johnson finds herself engrossed in a female passion to "tidy, tidy, tidy, tidy—lives . . . leaves . . . trees . . . emotions . . . house . . . endless sweeping, clipping, washing, arranging."[53] Whereas Cooper replaced the wild with the native in order to make indigenous plants preferable to the fancy hothouse flower, modern writers reinvest the native with connotations of the wild. Links between natural women and native landscape remain, but they have begun to reflect less gentility and more ambiguity than in Cooper's day.

While she struggled in her own life with early twentieth-century feminism, Austin created a free, sensuous female landscape and desert women invigorated by contact with the wilderness. Austin was of the same generation as Florence Merriam. Like Merriam and the other female nature writers of her day, the message she heard in nature reinforced her understanding of women's proper role. But Austin also spoke in the voice of the second wave of New Women who more openly questioned the meaning of women's sexuality. Her sensitivity to emerging women's issues rendered hers a lone female voice among the nature essayists in the early twentieth century when she suggested that there were connections between male domination of nature and women's oppression. Wilderness offered a clear lesson of the true freedom at the heart of both the natural world and women's nature: "If the desert were a woman, I know well what like she would be: deep breasted, broad in the hips, tawny . . . eyes sane and steady as the polished jewel of her skies . . . passionate, but not necessitous, patient—and you could not move her, not if you had all the earth to give, so much as one tawny hair's breadth beyond her own desires. If you cut very deeply into the soul that has the mark of the land on it, you find such qualities as these."[54]

Austin's sensitivity to female oppression was not picked up in women's nature essays until much later in the twentieth century. As inheritors of the feminist movement of the 1960s and 1970s, contemporary writers often question some of the constraints in their domestic inheritance. Reminding her readers of the distance of middle-class nineteenth-century women from the sexual content of nature, Maxine Kumin finds her own delicate aversion to intimate knowledge of horse foaling offensive and proudly celebrates her initiation into "a hardy band, a secret cell" of those able to attend such a birth.[55] Nineteenth-century women located positive reinforcement for their domesticity in images of middle-class animal families; Josephine Johnson performs an ironic twist on that tradition when she describes her meeting with a female fox. Recognizing that few female animals, whether fox or human, lead a life of ease and tranquility, she faced a vixen whose imagined life symbolized freedom to Johnson and discovered "her as she really was—small, thin, harried, heavily burdened—not really free at all. Bound by instinct as I am bound by custom and concern."[56] In such imagery, twentieth-century naturalists reinvest native plants and animals with a wildness suppressed by the domestic cults of the nineteenth century. However, as nineteenth-century women located messages about human gender codes in the nesting habits of birds, so twentieth-century women continue to find models of their own female lives in the other animals with whom they live.

Over time, female nature writers have continually resisted constraints on women's round that artificially separated them from nature. The definition of appropriate limits has, of course, changed from 1850 to the present. As women's sphere has broadened, so too has their understanding of nature's domestic round and their image of the landscape of home. Throughout, however, women nature writers have warned against forces that would diminish or falsify the moral quotient of woman's sphere. If Susan Cooper located the threat in women's relegation to the hothouse and Maxine Kumin saw it in their exclusion from the barn, both did so in the belief that the domestic life, fully experienced, offered a necessary corrective to the social dislocations of their time.

In twentieth-century authors' identification of their own nature with the natural round, they too find a reason to act as conservators and protectors of the environment. In *The Land of Little Rain*, Mary Austin criticized the arrogant development of arid landscapes. Her home and its surrounding fields appear literally at the center of her book, critiquing by example domination of the land. She contrasts her attempt to coax various wild plants and animals into her yard from a neglected field next door with her neighbor's plan to turn the field into town lots. Austin, better acquainted with the field than he, argues: "though the field may serve a good turn in those days it will hardly be happier. No, certainly not happier."[57] *The Land of Little Rain* served as a cautionary tale to twentieth-century settlers in the Southwest, and the narrator achieved the right to speak as a result of her own adaptation to the place. Ann Zwinger built a cabin in the rugged Colorado mountains so she might learn how to fit her life into the ecology of the terrain, teach her daughters to do the same, and write books in support of public appreciation of the web of life. Similar to the bird writers before her, Helen Hoover became a spokesperson for the rights of deer, using as her weapon highly charged accounts of their family life in the forest around her Minnesota cabin.

Josephine Johnson, whose *Inland Island* is one of the finest nature essays ever written, captures perfectly (and with some humor) the role of female protector each of these twentieth-century writers embodies. Johnson and her husband lived outside Cincinnati on farmland that they encouraged the native plants and animals to reclaim: "This place, with all its layers of life, from the eggs of snails to the eyes of buzzards, is my home, as surely as it is the wild bird's or the woodchuck's home. I'll defend it if I have to patrol it with a bow and arrow—an old lady, like a big woodchuck in a brown coat, booting up and down these knife-cut hills, shouting at the dogs and hunters, making a path through that encroaching ecology we were told would come inevitably as the tides, and faster."[58] It may seem a long way from Susan Fenimore Cooper, planning for the salvation of old stands of pine as she strolls through the countryside of Otsego, to Josephine Johnson, angrily defending her island from destructive humans. However, the urge to preserve a native landscape contains the same appeal to women's special responsibility as wives, mothers, and teachers of the moral lessons derived from the domestic round. The most basic thread running from Susan Cooper's *Rural Hours* in 1850 to Ann Zwinger's *Beyond the Aspen Grove* in 1970 is the act of homing in on one spot, living with it through the seasons until the rocks, flowers, trees, insects, birds, deer, panthers, and coyotes are family. Enfolded within women's family, carrying the emotional weight of home, American flora and fauna are due the same consideration as human members of the household.

Having established a continuous, coherent tradition in women's writing on nature, I wondered why the century-old story these women composed has gone for so long unnoticed. Ann Zwinger provided one answer in a speech to the Thoreau Society in 1983. Her talk responded to a comment Thoreau made about a young woman's attempt to live alone in a cabin in the woods. In Thoreau's opinion, "her own sex, so tamely bred, only jeer at her for entertaining such an idea."[59] Based on this and other disparaging remarks about women in Thoreau's *Journals*, Zwinger concluded that he believed women were incapable of writing well about nature. She then refuted his finding by pairing quotations from various women naturalists with similar writings by men, proving that the women were as skilled as the men.

Zwinger is singular among nature writers in suggesting that, almost from the beginning, male writers subordinated women's work to their own and did not (contrary to Susan Cooper's hope) listen with equal attention to women. Although female nature essayists consistently pose women's images of nature as a critique of certain male behaviors, they have done so in the full confidence that they and their male compatriots ultimately share the same public stage and often have the same goals. Their history of joint endeavors suggests a large degree of overlap in nature study and appreciation. Cooper helped popularize Knapp, Treat did the same with Darwin, Florence Merriam worked companionably alongside her husband Vernon Bailey, Mary Austin supported John Muir's preservationist agenda, and Ann Zwinger returned to Thoreau's rivers in the company of Edwin Way Teale.[60] The happy congruence of Gilbert White's seasonal journal with Susan Cooper's daily diary set the stage for such male-female collaboration and for a flourishing nature writing tradition among American women. But the genre was White's to begin with; it developed out of the male-controlled naturalist tradition. As the history of women's disappearance from the literary naturalist canon after the turn of the century suggests, men have continued to control the field. It is as though a door of opportunity opened with the ornithologists in the nineteenth century and quickly closed again as the pantheon of nature essayists firmly cohered around a select group of men. Signifying the effectiveness of that canon, not only men but also women have neglected the work of writers like Susan Fenimore Cooper, Mary Treat, Florence Merriam Bailey, and Josephine Johnson.[61] Ann Zwinger is the first female nature writer to recognize the loss and speak for those who have been silenced. With her encouragement, the door once more opens and we discover that, in fact, the natural round has provided much inspiration to women who "recorded for their own or another's pleasure the tilt of the earth and the slant of the sky."[62]

# 3

# The Illustrators
## *Women's Drawings of*
## *Nature's Artifacts*

*His daughter Jennie is a Florist and Botanist, she has discovered*

*a great number of Plants never before described and has given*

*their Properties and Virtues, many of which are found useful in*

*Medecine, and she draws and colours them with great beauty . . .*

*N.B. She makes the best cheese I ever ate in America.*

—*A description of Jane Colden by a Scottish friend*

THE NOVEMBER 1893 issue of *Contributions from the U.S. National Herbarium* published a report on the 1891 botanical survey of Death Valley, California. Included in the report are twenty-one drawings of plants collected, seventeen of them signed by R. Cowing (Figure 3). Roberta Cowing was one of many female artists employed by the U.S. Department of Agriculture in the nineteenth and twentieth centuries. Government-sponsored publications such as *Contributions* and the *Yearbook of the United States Department of Agriculture* contain a treasure trove of women's nature art.[1] As the ornithologists of the late nineteenth century represent women's traditions in the nature essay, so these botanical artists typify women's place in drawing America's flora and fauna. Women have also made important contributions in shell, insect, and bird documentation. To some extent, the subjects of these illustrators have varied in response to trends in scientific nature study. Jane ("Jennie") Colden—mistress of the Linnaean system and maker of the best cheese in eighteenth-century New York—was a singularly early botanical illustrator.[2] Women came to the scientific depiction of flora in significant numbers only after the 1850s. Their earliest sustained subject matter was shell

FIGURE 3. *Roberta Cowing's 1893 illustration of* Aquilegia pubescens *(columbine), one of the plants collected on Frederick Vernon Coville's Death Valley expedition. (Hunt Institute for Botanical Documentation, Carnegie Mellon University, Pittsburgh, Pa.)*

illustrating, begun by Lucy Say in the 1820s. By the turn of the twentieth century, women artists and photographers were documenting shells, plants, insects, and birds. Whether they did such work at home or in institutions like the National Herbarium was driven in part by changing concepts of proper female behavior during the nineteenth and twentieth centuries. In the late twentieth century, women have continued to work as scientific illustrators to such an extent that they now dominate the field.

The popularity of art depicting native flora and fauna throughout the nineteenth century provides another proof of Americans' interest in defining the landscape as home. Such imagery appeared in many forms. Landscape painting increasingly included accurate renderings of plants and animals. Still-life painters first drew fruits from local gardens, then shifted into flowers, including wildflowers, arranged out of doors in gardenlike settings. Government surveyors of the West hired artists to depict flora and fauna as well as topography. Ornithologist-artists Alexander Wilson and John James Audubon established an American tradition for zoological studies. Artists' works appeared in ladies flower books, gardening manuals, magazines like *Scribners*, and lithographs and chromolithographs published by Currier and Ives and Prang.[3]

Women appear as minor participants in all these efforts except landscape painting and government survey work. The Peale sisters worked as still-life painters. Garden and wildflower delineators Maria Oakey Dewing, Ellen Robbins, and Fidelia Bridges represented the flower painting tradition (Figure 4). Art historians sometimes include Bridges among the bird art as well, but most often the only woman noted in this genre is Maria Martin. Martin drew botanical backgrounds for John Audubon and did a few bird paintings of her own. In the popular market of magazines and prints, women appeared more regularly. Bridges, Ellen Fisher, and Frances Bond Palmer sketched for the mass audience. The overall impression, however, is that women were present but not particularly significant.[4]

There are several reasons for women's sparse appearance in histories of nineteenth-century nature art. Art history covering nature painting in America emphasizes the influence of government surveys on the form. We know a great deal about art produced by the men who went on these surveys but very little about the works of women and men who, like Roberta Cowing, stayed home and drew the plants brought back to the herbarium. The history of the opening of the frontier holds a strong, continuing interest in studies of American culture. Only recently have questions about what it

FIGURE 4. "Untitled" (1876), painted by Fidelia Bridges (1824–1923). Bridges made
her mark as a professional artist specializing in the birds and wildflowers of Connecticut's
meadows and coastal flats. (National Museum of American Art, Smithsonian Institution,
Washington, D.C., given in memory of Charles Downing Lay and Laura Gill Lay by their
children)

meant to domesticate the frontier, to make the West a home, surfaced in historical accounts. One could argue that such domestication was precisely what Cowing was doing when, from the safety of the National Herbarium in Washington, D.C., she drew plants collected in Death Valley and published her work in an educational journal. Landscape painting receives attention because it embodies nineteenth-century American attitudes regarding the biophysical environment. But landscape painting is, again, a male-dominated tradition, partly due to its close ties to western exploration. Most nineteenth-century women continued drawing close-up, detailed studies of flowers and birds, studies that the men drew as well. Men, however, then incorporated detailed work into large-scale, often heroic murals.[5]

Understanding women's contribution to the art of natural history requires redrawing the boundaries of standard scholarship to include genre and subject matter traditionally open to females. Art that is close up, detailed, and created from collected specimens as well as field observation can be found in the herbaria and zoological collections of natural history museums and other such institutions. Such art appears in standard reference texts on plants or animals, field guides, scientific journals, and special interest popular magazines like *Bird-Lore*. Here, ironically in the heart of the scientific establishment, women have found a niche and made a significant contribution to the way we see the plants and animals of America. From secluded, suffocating rooms full of dried flowers and mummified beasts, they have moved into the field, drawing and photographing living plants and animals. Their audience has included scientists and the amateur public interested in the history, identification, and preservation of plants and animals. Again, their work melds national environmental agendas with the continuous tradition of women as conservators of home.

From the beginning women produced their illustrations of nature within the confines of a social institution, under the watchful eye of a man. First, they worked at home, where fathers and husbands taught them to draw plants and animals. Later, they worked in museums and government agencies. Women were very much interested in what they illustrated and in perfecting their skill as artists. They shared a passion for rendering nature as deep as the desire driving men to a lifelong artistic pursuit. Although most of the women discussed here did some sort of floral sketching during their lives, they also depicted shells, insects, birds, and various plants. Usually, each honed in on one particular subject, becoming its familiar and exhausting its types as male illustrators did. Unlike the nature essayists of the preceding chapter, their subject matter extended well beyond the common plants of home and neighborhood. However, they knew a plant or animal so well that it became an old friend and contained a shared history. Their illustrations often served the national effort to describe America domestica.

In any history of women's scientific illustration, the first person of any prominence is Jane Colden. Her father, Cadwallader Colden, was a Scottish emigrant to America, first living in Philadelphia, then in New York. In 1728, when Jane was about four, he moved the family to a country home in rural New York where he could pursue his botanical interests. Here he produced one of the first local floras of the region, based on the plants that grew around his home. Jane's parents provided her education. When she was in her twenties, her father began teaching her botany. She had had no Latin, so he wrote out a text of the Linnaean system in English. Because the family did not have access to botanical gardens, he acquired Tournefort's *Herbal and the History of Plants* and several other illustrated texts. Jane then set out to sketch and describe the plants around her home; by 1757 her catalog had three hundred entries. Her proud father presented her to American and European scholars with whom he worked. She met the famous Philadelphia naturalists, John and William Bartram. Correspondents began exchanging seeds and specimens with her, commenting that her work was "extremely accurate."[6]

Jane Colden was an interesting rarity; the English naturalist Peter Collinson said she was "perhaps the only lady that makes profession of the Linnaean system." Cadwallader apparently had no fears about his daughter's education in the sexual classification of plants. To him, women's culture suited them well for botanical work: "I thought that botany is an amusement which may be made agreeable to the ladies, who are often at a loss to fill up their time. Their natural curiosity, and the pleasure they take in the beauty and variety of dress, seems to fit them for it."[7] Botanical study was not yet linked to women's domestic responsibility; this connection came later during the high point of true womanhood in the mid-nineteenth century. Rather, Cadwallader was referring to the new leisure afforded upper-class women of the late eighteenth century.[8] Either Jane had little leisure time after her marriage in 1759 to Dr. William Farquhar, or her new household had different ideas about filling such time, for her botanical work apparently ended when she left her father's home. In 1766, at the age of forty-one, she died, along with her only child.

Her *Botanic Manuscript* reveals an excellent observer of nature. Contemporary opinion confirms the accuracy of her work and its significance to eighteenth-century botany. Jane Colden was, however, a more skilled writer than artist. Her narrative forms the basis of her standing in botanical circles. She did not execute her drawings well and confined her work to leaves and stems; flowers are not in evidence. One commentator has noted that the drawings are "of no use for the identification of the species."[9] In any case, the actual drawings were not as important as the act of making them. Jane Colden's work shows how the art of floral reproduction became a fitting female occupation. Not only were women encouraged by educators like Almira Phelps to study botany, but also, by the turn of the nineteenth century, they were receiving more sophisticated instruction in the art of illustration. Typical of the drawing books gaining popularity was Henrietta Maria Moriarty's 1807 edition of *Fifty Plates of Green-House Plants, Drawn and Coloured From Nature. With Concise Descriptions, and Rules for Their Culture. Intended Also for the Improvement of Young Ladies in the Art of Drawing*.[10] Women could combine their female interest in decoration with worthwhile nature study. For many, botanizing provided an opportunity to mingle art with science in a genteel manner.

Women's early floral art has received little attention in studies of scientific illustration because much of it concerns local flora, often common flowers already illustrated elsewhere. Like Jane Colden's illustrations, it is often more decorative than accurate. Some historians believe that the high period of botanical illustration ended around 1840.[11] Between the time of Colden's studies and the mid-nineteenth century, few women seriously pursued science.[12] At the point when women were beginning to find a way back into the scientific study of plants as a result of increased educational opportunities encouraged by such women as Emma Willard and Almira Phelps, the interest in illustrated botanical works had waned. During the hundred-year interval between Colden's *Botanic Manuscript* and the reappearance of female illustrators of scientifically significant botanical subjects, the decorative arts maintained the link between women and flowers. Women still-life painters such as the Peale sisters led the way for many floral artists enrolled in drawing courses at female academies. By mid-century women had established themselves among the ranks of flower artists.[13] That connection to floral study as a proper female role would prove important to some of the finest scientific illustrators of the late nineteenth century. Until then, however, women—encouraged by family based engraving businesses supporting America's increased printing capacity—put their illustrative skills to other uses.

Scientific illustrations were crucial in the identification and classification of the flora and fauna discovered in North and South America during the eighteenth and nineteenth centuries. As American printing capabilities increased so did the production of books for professionals and amateurs. These texts helped identify and popularize the plants and animals of home. The bird books of Alexander Wilson and John James Audubon have received the most attention in this field, but the first half of the nineteenth century yielded many works on natural history. The production of such books was not an individual task. Audubon's *Birds of America* required several other artists to help with the drawings, as well as an engraving firm to copy Audubon's illustrations onto plates. Artistic firms in Europe and America served a critical function in making the new illustrations available to the public. Often such firms were family businesses. Wives and children assisted husbands and fathers with drawings, engravings, and etchings for books. When the naturalist artist was himself trained in etching, he and his family might take on the whole process, drawing birds from specimens, then etching the plates.[14] Thus, the production of illustrations for natural history books was a collaborative, loosely organized process. Women frequently played major roles as artists, making the initial drawings, following up with engravings and etchings, or hand-painting the final images.

American women were less involved in the production of bird books, partly because Audubon had to go to England for printers, but their work pervaded other books of natural history. The women whose art helped identify and classify the mollusks of the continent provide a fulsome example of these early illustrators and the tradition they engendered. Philadelphia has a long history as the home of many famous conchologists (later called malacologists).[15] Thomas Say, one of the founding members in 1812 of the American Academy of Natural Sciences of Philadelphia, published an early illustrated text on shells, *American Conchology* (1830–34). In late 1880 the academy received the extensive collection of George Tyron, an affluent Philadelphian who began the massive, illustrated *Manual of Conchology*, then passed the task on to Henry Pilsbry. Pilsbry labored at the academy until his death in 1957 trying to complete a comprehensive guide to shells. Outside the academy, S. S. Haldeman, an instructor from 1851 to 1880 at the University of Pennsylvania, and Amos Binney, a Boston contemporary of Say, round out the pantheon of men whose work on shells made up the primary illustrated texts of the nineteenth century.[16] Female artists provided the bulk of the illustrations in every one of these books. Between 1830 and 1957 women made some of the best drawings of mollusks known, yet their exquisitely detailed art has received little recognition.

Shell collecting is another of those nineteenth-century occupations benefiting the potentially idle hands of the female leisure class. English women were much involved in early efforts to learn more about ocean life by combing the beaches for shells and seaweed.[17] American women were not slow to catch on. As shown in Elizabeth Agassiz's *First Lesson in Natural History*, a day at the shore could be both edifying and recreational. When tired of botanizing or birding in the fields and woods, women could attend to their shell collection. Throughout the nineteenth century and into the twentieth, the study of mollusks has been open to amateurs.[18]

In two early journals, *Conchologists' Exchange* and *Nautilus*, women regularly appeared as collectors. In 1887, for example, the *Exchange* reported: "Mrs. Mary B. A. King, of Rochester, N.Y. is an enthusiastic collector of shells, although in her eighty-ninth year, and received great encouragement from the late Isaac Lea, L.L.D., who named the Unios and Anondontas in her collection upwards of forty years ago."[19] Women joined conchological clubs like the Isaac Lea chapters of the Agassiz Association and reported their research in *Nautilus*. Through the years their reports gain in scientific sophistication, if not liveliness. Lorraine Frierson, a Louisiana amateur, published in *Nautilus* from 1897 to 1933. Her later pieces are more objective, but the 1898 description of how to catch the elusive Unio is a delight: "Did any of my fellow Unio 'cranks' ever catch Unio during the winter months by means of a long slender switch? You go to a bed of mussels in clear water, and standing on the shore you gently poke the end of your switch into the gaping hole of the unsuspecting unio. As soon as it feels the stick it closes the shell tightly on it; then you gently pull the mussel out and put it in your game bag."[20] Women also drew the shells in their collection. The Academy of Natural Sciences of Philadelphia holds an amateur conchology by Julia Planton, probably made in the 1830s or 1840s, filled with watercolors of various shells as well as notes on the Linnaean system for classifying animals.[21] Interest in collecting and illustrating shells and their inhabitants continues to the present time. In a 1974 register of professional and amateur malacologists and private shell collectors, women represented 20 percent of the total biographies and over half of those listing themselves as illustrators.[22]

The first female shell delineator of prominence was Thomas Say's wife, Lucy Way Sistare. Thomas, a well-respected entomologist, had worked in Peale's Museum in Philadelphia before becoming the first conservator at the Academy of Natural Sciences of Philadelphia. His *American Entomology* appeared in three volumes from 1824 to 1828, and his *American Conchology* was printed in seven parts between 1830 and 1834. Sixty-eight plates illustrated the *Conchology*, all but two drawn by his wife. Lucy Say did not make the engravings of her drawings but, with the help of other artists, she hand-colored the plates. Illustrations were crucial in such texts, as Linnaeus had discovered when he published *Systema Naturae* without them.[23] Shell collectors had a difficult time identifying their finds with only verbal descriptions. Thomas Say recognized this problem and determined to "fix the species of our Molluscous animals, by accurate delineations in their approximate colours, so that they may be readily recognized even by those who have not extensive cabinets for comparison."[24] Thomas collected and classified the shells; Lucy made scientifically accurate illustrations of them.

Little is known about Lucy Way Sistare before her marriage to Thomas Say on January 4, 1827. She was born on October 14, 1801, in New London, Connecticut, one of five children. By 1824 Lucy and her two younger sisters were attending a boarding school for girls in Philadelphia run by a Frenchwoman, Madame Marie Duclos Fretageot. Established in 1806 by the Scottish geologist William Maclure, the experimental school taught students science emphasizing the Pestalozzian style of close, detailed observation of natural artifacts. In 1824 Madam Fretageot met Robert Owen, a British cotton manufacturer who had bought the town of New Harmony, Indiana, to try a communitarian experiment. Madam Fretageot became interested in the project and encouraged Maclure to invest in it. On December 8, 1825, Maclure and Fretageot organized a keelboat that sailed out of Pittsburgh bound for New Harmony carrying a host of Philadelphia scientists and educators. On board were Lucy Sistare, her sisters, and Maclure's colleague, Thomas Say. Lucy married Say and took charge of the schoolchildren in New Harmony. In the first year of their marriage, Thomas advertised for subscribers to his illustrated book on the shells of North America.[25]

Publishing an illustrated text in New Harmony was a time-consuming task. William Maclure provided the community with a printing press, primarily for publishing a newspaper, the *Disseminator of Useful Knowledge*, but several books were also printed. *American Conchology* was planned to cover all the mollusks of North America, beginning with the United States. As in the case of most illustrated books, this was a collaborative effort. Lucy Say made all but two of the drawings for the plates (Figure 5). Most of the plates were engraved by Cornelius Tiebout; two other men did some of the work. The engravings were then hand-colored by Lucy Say and two of Tiebout's children. In 1832 Thomas Say's letters noted that "Lucy has colored 2450 impressions with the help of Henry Tiebout this winter." In the midst of the publication

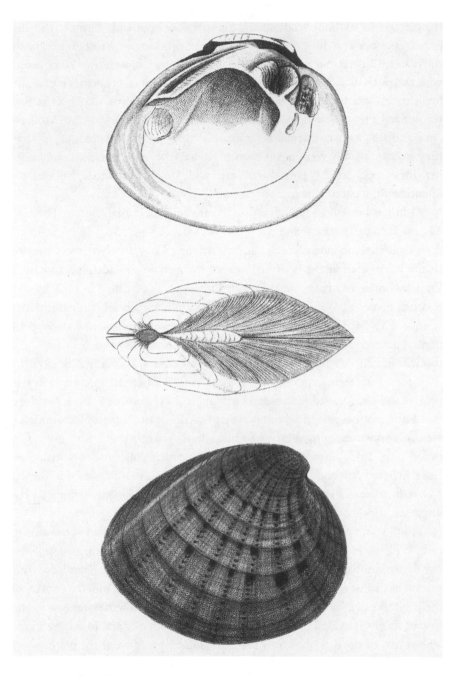

FIGURE 5. *Lucy Say (1801–86) drew the illustrations for her husband's books on American mollusks. Shown here is* Unio lineolatus raf., *the original plate for Thomas Say's* American Conchology *(1830). (Library, Academy of Natural Sciences of Philadelphia)*

64   *Made From This Earth*

Cornelius Tiebout and another engraver died. Thomas Say lived to see the publication of the first six numbers before his own death in 1834.[26]

Lucy Say was not fond of the domestic round—indeed, Madam Fretageot's letters criticize her attempts to avoid household responsibilities. Nor was she particularly happy with New Harmony's isolation; several letters mention that she encouraged Thomas to return to Philadelphia. Apparently, she worked diligently on the illustrations. No doubt she had some interest in geology and shells when she met her husband, and probably she was also skilled in drawing. The illustrations in the *American Conchology* are well done, revealing an eye for fine detail and design. A note written on the back of an etching indicates that she considered herself a competent artist. The image is inscribed: "First attempt, August 1834." In her note, Say comments: "I could have learned etching very soon—but an engraver was procured." This experience remained a frustrating memory for her. In a letter written in 1835, after her husband's death, she remembered the incident again: "I am looked upon as being very singular, particularly since I have commenced Engraving—a gentleman remarks 'Well! at what, do you think the ladies will stop!' I replyed, I hoped at nothing, short of breaking up the Monopoly so long held by the Gentlemen—that we were tired of cramping our genius over the needle and distaff."[27]

Say did not see her art as an extension of the woman's round, but as a potentially liberating device. The fact remains, however, that gender codes informed the illustrations she produced and the circumstances of her work. She remained at home while Thomas went off on shell-collecting expeditions. Her professional career began with her marriage, and her husband directed her art. Significantly, her work ended after Thomas's death—not by her own choice. In 1835 she wrote to a scientist who was interested in Thomas's work: "My greatest desire is, to be able to contribute to the continuation of the 'Conchology' by drawing and engraving."[28] Lucy published some of Thomas's papers and corresponded with his colleagues about his shell collection, but her talent was not used in subsequent illustrated books. Her failure to continue with another scientist the collaborative work begun with her husband left her bitter and disappointed.[29] In 1841 she was the first woman elected as an associate member of the Academy of Natural Sciences of Philadelphia, primarily in recognition of her donation of her husband's collections to the institution.[30] When she died in 1886, her claim to any sort of fame rested on being Mrs. Thomas Say.

Yet her drawings endured and with them her own contribution to the field. The Says' illustrated *American Conchology* heralded a series of massive texts documenting American mollusks. In 1842 and 1845, S. S. Haldeman, another Philadelphian, published *A Monograph of the Freshwater Univalve Mollusca of the United States, Including Notices of Species in Other Parts of North America.* Between 1851 and 1878 Amos Binney's *The Terrestrial Air-Breathing Mollusks of the United States, and the Adjacent Territories of North America* appeared in five volumes. The third volume of Binney's study (1857) has been called one of the "most splendidly illustrated works" of the nineteenth century.[31] Fueled by exponentially increasing descriptions of species, and by the rising interest in shell collecting, texts aiding scientists and amateurs alike were in demand.[32] With increased knowledge and funds, shell illustrating in America became a fine art; well-known illustrators and engravers joined in the effort. By the mid-nineteenth century, Philadelphia was home to many of the most prestigious printing firms in the country.[33] Both Haldeman and Binney hired a Philadelphian, Alexander Lawson, already famous for the engravings he had done for Alexander Wilson's *American Ornithology.* Lawson made engravings for the Haldeman and Binney books but left the bulk of the shell drawing to his son Oscar and daughter Helen.

Alexander Lawson emigrated from Scotland in 1794 and worked in America as an engraver all his life. Wilson, a fellow Scot, hired him to work on his *Ornithology* in 1808. Lawson produced engravings from Wilson's drawings and from live and stuffed specimens. According to his daughter Malvina, "with History and Science he was well acquainted, and found time to instruct the intellect, and the hearts of his children." In addition to natural history, he taught at least two of his children drawing, engraving, and etching. Apparently, Lawson did not make a fortune in his profession, for Malvina also reports that "Mr. Lawson never took any pupil except his own son, although . . . offered large fees as an inducement. He felt that for many years to come in this country; his would be an unprofitable profession, and he declined receiving them, not satisfied that the youths presented to him, [shared] his own self-denial, and enthusiasm, without which qualities, he knew, they would eventually, regret the career they had chosen."[34] In Malvina's mind, her sister Helen was not preparing for a career when she learned scientific illustration from her father. Helen simply contributed to the family business, as had numerous other daughters and wives. Her work appears in books that her father engraved, ending shortly after his death in 1846.[35]

Scant information exists on Helen Lawson. Malvina's biography tells nothing about the family except that Helen was Alexander's second daughter.

Like her father, she drew, etched, and engraved a variety of subjects including birds and insects. She was a highly skilled illustrator. Her engraved, hand-colored female rice bunting posed in standard fashion on a piece of branch looks drawn from a specimen, but the work is finely detailed with intricate feather delineation (Figure 6). Her major contribution, however, was the mollusk drawings for the Haldeman and Binney books. For these texts, she served as a key artist, drawing many sketches that her father and brother engraved. She reappeared, as did Lucy Say, to hand-color the plates. Although apparently she was in charge of the engraving for the Binney book, she probably did not make the engravings or etchings for this work or the Haldeman text.[36] Her role, like Lucy Say's, was to produce the original drawing.

Shells, like flowers, have a long history as decorative artifacts. Helen Lawson's illustrations are impressive in their delicate beauty. Each is a marvel of graceful form and exquisite coloration. Variations among similar species, among specimens of different ages within a species, and among individuals give each drawing a character of its own. Shells also offer interesting opportunities for design in composition. Scientists need to know how the creature looks from different angles and how the shell changes over the animal's life history. In illustrating these facts, artists, like shell collectors in their cabinets, organize the shells in groupings both informative and ornamental. Further, the patterns on shells call for skills in detailing rivaled only by bird illustrations (Figure 7). That Helen Lawson was especially skilled at shell drawing is clear in a comparison of her illustrations to Lucy Say's. Say worked at her craft in isolation, depending on the amateur instruction in art provided at Madam Fretageot's school. Lawson was trained by one of the finest scientific illustrators of the period. Her achievement reflects that schooling.[37]

However wonderful her art, Lawson's career ended with the publication of Binney's opus. Mirroring Lucy Say's experience, Helen Lawson's life as an artist took place within the confines of family and home. Later in the nineteenth century, women began working outside the family as scientific illustrators. Male scientists employed in natural history museums replaced husband and father. In shell illustration, the male collaborator was Henry Pilsbry, curator of the Conchological Section of the Academy of Natural Sciences in Philadelphia. Pilsbry took on the ambitious task set by his predecessor, George Washington Tyron, to produce a comprehensive guide on the Mollusca. Tyron died in 1888, having partially completed the task. Pilsbry worked on the *Manual of Conchology* until 1935, when the project was abandoned; forty-five volumes had been published.[38] Henry Pilsbry knew fine art when he

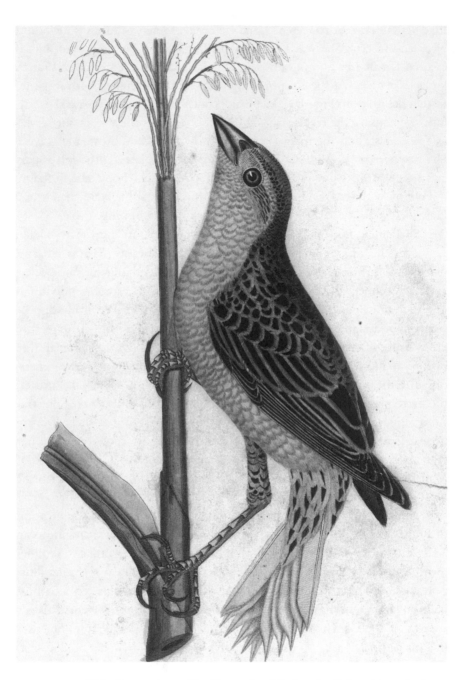

FIGURE 6. *Helen Lawson learned her illustrating skills from her father, Alexander Lawson. This engraving, entitled* Female Rice Bunting, *appeared in the* Port Folio *(July 1827). (Library, Academy of Natural Sciences of Philadelphia)*

FIGURE 7. *Helen Lawson spent most of her artistic career producing shell illustrations for Amos Binney's study of American mollusks. This depiction of* A. dissimilis say *is a sample of her fine illustrating skills. (Library, Academy of Natural Sciences of Philadelphia)*

saw it; he felt that Binney's book contained the "finest series of shell engravings ever made."[39] Pilsbry hired as his assistant Helen Winchester, the last in this history of fine shell illustrators affiliated with the academy in Philadelphia.

Helen Winchester worked as an illustrator at the academy during the first half of the twentieth century. As well as helping with the *Manual*, in the early 1900s she made many drawings for an unpublished monograph on "New York Land and Fresh-Water Mollusks" and for Pilsbry's articles on a scientific expedition to the Belgian Congo. Pilsbry apparently learned shell illustrating from Winchester. Their work appears together in both these efforts.[40] Winchester's association with the academy continued at least until 1946, when her original watercolor drawings of *Liguus* shells formed the frontispiece of a monograph series on North American land mollusks prepared by Pilsbry.[41] In addition to making fine drawings, she also photographed shells. Many of her plates include both drawings and photographs. The twentieth century brought an increased demand for precision in illustration. Where Lucy Say would have drawn three views of a shell and Helen Lawson six or more, Helen Winchester produced many more. Although each drawing retains the pristine beauty of the earlier women's work, shells are arranged on the page with more interest in scientific information and with more economical use of space.

The turn of the century witnessed a rise in the number of professionally trained female scientists, particularly in geology and botany, fields linked to the naturalist tradition. Many played secondary roles, working as assistants to men at tasks generally more open to their sex.[42] Helen Winchester's position at the academy fit this pattern. She was not, by any means, the institution's only female employee. Other women worked there as amateur malacologists; some even went on expeditions. None, however, rose to the prominence of a Henry Pilsbry.[43] Winchester's long collaboration with Pilsbry was not much different, at a professional level, than Lucy Say's with her husband and Helen Lawson's with her father. Winchester must have been Pilsbry's junior by fifteen to twenty years, yet her work at the academy was tied to his. The academy, mirroring patriarchal domestic arrangements, became a second home, one in which women, for all their vaunted release from the domestic strictures of the nineteenth century, continued to play the role of helpmate. Unless one carefully reads the prefaces to published works or studies the caption of individual illustrations, women's role in making available new scientific knowledge about the plants and animals of the continent remains invisible.[44]

Drawings of shells and the creatures inhabiting them embody the cultural contexts driving women's work as scientific illustrators. Illustration required little advanced training in science, although some background was useful. Once America had the technological resources to print its own illustrated books, these texts appeared in volume. Early on such publishing ventures were financially risky, often taken on by men of modest circumstances. Under such conditions, the entire family became involved in production. With increased centralization of research around museum collections after the turn of the century, women worked outside their homes but the roles they played for their employers mirrored their lives with husbands and fathers. For many, work outside the home was temporary, ending when they married or when their collaborator retired or died.[45] Because they were assistants to men pushing back the frontiers of knowledge, their contribution easily disappears from the record.

Nevertheless, the illustrations of these women were crucial to the ongoing attempt to identify and classify the flora and fauna of America. In their patient, persistent efforts to delineate each shell and its occupant accurately, Say, Lawson, and Winchester complemented women writers whose dedicated observations saved many bird populations. Both groups contributed to the country's increasing awareness of the bountiful plant and animal life of the continent. Historians have credited the birders for their conservation efforts. Yet the unsung illustrators helped inspire wide-flung regional networks of mollusk specialists engaged in education and preservation.[46] In doing so, the artists participated in the tradition—first consciously articulated by Susan Fenimore Cooper—of women working within the strictures of gender roles to expand the bounds of home until the domestic round included a spider's tower, a thrush's nest, and a Unio's shell.

By the mid-nineteenth century, woman's task as illustrator had spread across various subjects while remaining consistent with socially acceptable gender roles. With increased opportunities for advanced training, women reappeared as botanical illustrators. Mirroring the nature essayists' interest in birds, women entered the field of ornithological photography. As the subject delineated broadened, so too did the institutions in which women worked. Some women continued to work at home, recording the local plants or animals of the landscapes of their childhood. Others gradually moved, as the shell illustrators had done, into more public institutions—museums, universities, and government agencies. Whether remaining within the confines of home, or moving out into more public endeavors, each connected her nature study to woman's role as conservator of domestic space.

Botanist Kate Furbish, ornithologist Cordelia Stanwood, and bird and insect photographer Gene Stratton Porter achieved fame while working at home. Kate Furbish, born in 1834, grew up in Brunswick, Maine, where she first studied local plants with her father. After briefly training in drawing and botany in Portland and Boston, she returned to Brunswick to devote herself to collecting, classifying, and illustrating Maine's flora. Her watercolors earned a reputation for accuracy and beauty among such scientists as Asa Gray (Figure 8).[47] Botanical study took her into rugged, largely uninhabited regions of the state. Her accounts emphasize not so much the dangers of wilderness as the hard work collecting in such terrain entails. Describing a remote swamp, she notes that she had heard stories of men going into such places and never coming out again, but

> I found no skeletons, had no misgivings, and always enjoyed surmounting every obstacle which presented itself. Few men or women care to endure the fatigue which usually attends such excursions, but a true botanist . . . feels richly repaid for it in every way. Strange to say, the inhabitants of these sacred silent places scarcely flutter at your approach, the squirrel sits and gazes at you, scolds perhaps, but does not scamper away; and the cedar-partridge hardly notices your movements at all. The dew drops on your hat and shoulders all the day, and in hot July when everything outside is dry and parched, and the sand burns your feet, there is no more delightful retreat than one of these damp cool swamps.[48]

Thus cleansed of any hint of wilderness, the landscape is an appropriate place for a woman studying the native plants of her home state.

The summer 1915 issue of *Bird-Lore* ran an article by Emma L. Turner of Cambridge, England, entitled "Bird Photography for Women," in which she described her methods for studying birds in the field while maintaining womanly decorum. Landowners, she argued, provided women more access to their holdings, secure in their knowledge that, unlike men, women would not collect the birds they photographed. The same issue included a poem suggesting that young men preferred young women who photographed birds over those who hunted. Such public pronouncements reinforced gender-based distinctions in men's and women's modes of bird study articulated a generation earlier by Olive Thorne Miller.[49] The camera provided an excellent vehicle for documenting bird activity. Unlike the gun, it carried few masculine connotations. Turner, for example, felt that she did not need to describe her photographic equipment because "the scientific outfit is the same for either sex, and information with regard to that is easily obtained from any bird photogra-

FIGURE 8. *Kate Furbish (1834–1931) botanized in Maine and painted the local wild-flowers she encountered. This plant,* Pedicularis furbishiae, *was one of her own discoveries and was named for her. (Furbish Collection, Bowdoin College, Brunswick, Maine. Photograph by John McKee.)*

FIGURE 9. *Cordelia Stanwood (1865–1958) made exhaustive photographic studies of the birds around her home in Ellsworth, Maine. She gained the most fame for her studies of chicks, such as this image of "Six Little Chickadees." (Stanwood Wildlife Sanctuary, Ellsworth, Maine)*

pher."[50] While in the early nineteenth century American women had played a small role in drawing birds, Cordelia Stanwood and Gene Stratton Porter typified their later contributions in photographic illustrations of animal life.

Cordelia Stanwood shared Turner's logic that the camera was a proper tool for documenting the habits of birds while preserving their lives. Born in 1865, Stanwood had a more extensive education than Kate Furbish. She worked for seventeen years outside Maine as a schoolteacher, returning home after a nervous breakdown. Home was a forty-acre family estate in Ellsworth, Maine. In 1905 she began keeping extensive field notebooks on local bird populations, publishing her first article in *Bird-Lore* in 1910.[51] By 1920 she was photographing her subjects, eventually producing more than nine hundred plates that beautifully documented the family life of birds (Figures 9, 10). Her work on nesting behavior and nest building earned her an international reputation, but she remained at home, carrying on her research with other ornithologists through correspondence. As it had for so many nineteenth-century women, nature study meant a life of spartan pleasures and being in

FIGURE 10. *"Immature Broad Winged Hawk," photographed by Cordelia Stanwood.*
*(Stanwood Wildlife Sanctuary, Ellsworth, Maine)*

touch with higher truths than the latest fashions. Stanwood wrote: "When the thrush speaks to me, it seems as if the rags and tatters that enshroud my soul fall away and leave it naked. Then I must be simple and true or I cannot feel the message the small voice brings to me. When the thrush sings, I desire to live in a small, scrupulously neat camp, open to the sun and the wind and the voices of birds."[52]

As the author of the popular children's books, *Freckles* and *A Girl of the Limberlost*, Gene Stratton Porter earned a good deal more fame (and money) than her contemporary, Cordelia Stanwood. Porter alternated these fictional writings with classic nature studies of birds and moths, for which she contributed photographic illustrations.[53] As with Furbish and Stanwood, all her writing and illustrating centered around her home near Limberlost Swamp in rural Indiana. In such books as *Moths of the Limberlost* and *Homing with the Birds*, Porter combined field observation with autobiography, offering insights into the challenge of photographing live specimens in the open. Cecropia moths particularly fascinated her. Such a moth was one of her first finds as a child but eluded her adulthood. Lucky enough to be given a pair of intertwined cocoons, she detailed the problems in documenting the moths' emergence, particularly working with the slow camera equipment of the day. Calling on her family (the "Deacon," her husband, and Molly-Cotton, her daughter) for assistance, she laboriously changed the heavy photographic plates: "Quickly as possible I changed the plates again . . . The male was trying to creep up the wall, and the increase in the length and expansion of the female's wings could be seen. The colours of both were exquisite, but they grew a trifle less brilliant as the moths became dry. Again I turned to the business of plate changing. The heat was intense, and perspiration was streaming from my face. I called to Molly-Cotton to shield the moths while I made the change. 'Drat the moths!' cried the Deacon. 'Shade your mother!'"[54] (Figure 11). Throughout her illustrating career, Porter struggled with the scientist's need for accuracy and the aesthetic's love of pattern and form. In contrast to her documentary efforts, for example, she posed moths indoors on such furnishings as a bit of "Brussels lace" in memory of the first such moth she had collected as a child.[55]

Furbish, Stanwood, and Porter, although working in different media with somewhat different goals, represent a continuation of Jane Colden's, Lucy Say's, and Helen Lawson's tradition. Each contributed to scientific illustration by staying firmly within the bounds of home. At roughly the same time, however, other women were becoming somewhat more adventurous.

FIGURE 11. *In addition to popular novels, Gene Stratton Porter (1863–1924) wrote naturalist accounts of American birds and moths and illustrated them with her own photographs. "Cecropia Moths," shown here, appeared in* Homing with the Birds *(1919). (Indiana State Museum and Historic Sites, Indianapolis, Ind.)*

In addition to venturing into the fields and forests of home, they risked the terrain of urban museums and universities to work with the premier scientists of their day. While Kate Furbish tramped the Maine woods, Graceanna Lewis studied in the Academy of Natural Sciences of Philadelphia with John Cassin, a leading bird authority. While Gene Porter photographed the moths and birds around her rural estate, Anna Botsford Comstock assisted her husband in the study of insects at Cornell University. Each regarded her work as representative of women's role as conservators of home. But home now included nature's artifacts housed in museums and research laboratories.

Graceanna Lewis was born in 1821 to Quaker farmers near Kimbertown, Pennsylvania. Lewis credited her mother with engendering her love of nature. Quakers played a central role in the study of natural history in America, in part accounting for Philadelphia's preeminence among early naturalists. They also encouraged women in this study. Graceanna was no exception. She studied botany under Abigail Kimber, who achieved some fame as a plant collector. Lewis began teaching natural history herself in 1840. To illustrate her lectures and to aid other teachers, she prepared charts outlining everything from the vegetable kingdom to the "races of men" (Figure 12). Her most concentrated artistic work was a series of trees for the commissioners of forestry of Pennsylvania. The Chicago and St. Louis World's Fairs of 1893 and 1904 exhibited some of these paintings. Wide-ranging in her interests and her art, Lewis gained her reputation as an ornithologist through her work with Cassin. With his guidance, she produced a pamphlet showing the relationship of birds in the animal kingdom. Lewis was voted membership in the Academy of Natural Sciences of Philadelphia (after first being rejected) in 1870.

Her work flourished in the self-described "leisure of a country home," where she studied books by Thomas Nuttall, Spencer Baird, and Cassin: "My studies seldom interfered with household avocations. Gardening, walks, or rides connected with business or pleasure afforded me occasion for after-study . . . At the time I was ripe for it, I think in 1862, a friend procured me an introduction to John Cassin . . . I had found a MASTER . . . The Academy of Natural Sciences was opened to me. My table there was filled to overflowing with books of his selection; the museum, with its thousands of specimens, could be referred to." With the organic reference—"at the time I was ripe for it"—Lewis artfully included the libraries and specimen collections of the academy in her domestic round, rendering these public, urban institutions no less domesticated than her kitchen garden or neighborhood park.[56]

Graceanna Lewis's educational illustrations encouraged the public (particularly young women) to study nature. In the early twentieth century, another Quaker woman, Anna Botsford, helped design an influential nature study curriculum adopted by many American schools. Her achievements developed from her work as illustrator and assistant to her husband, the entomologist John Henry Comstock. Botsford arrived at Cornell University as a student in 1874, two years after the institution began admitting women. She married her entomology professor in 1878. Although she had little training in drawing, at the encouragement of her husband, Comstock learned the art of woodcutting and began illustrating insects to aid her husband's research. Her artful drawings, which appeared in his textbooks, earned her an international reputation.

In 1898 Cornell's Extension Division (with some reluctance from the trustees) appointed Anna Comstock assistant professor of "Nature Study." The Nature Study movement blossomed in the early twentieth century out

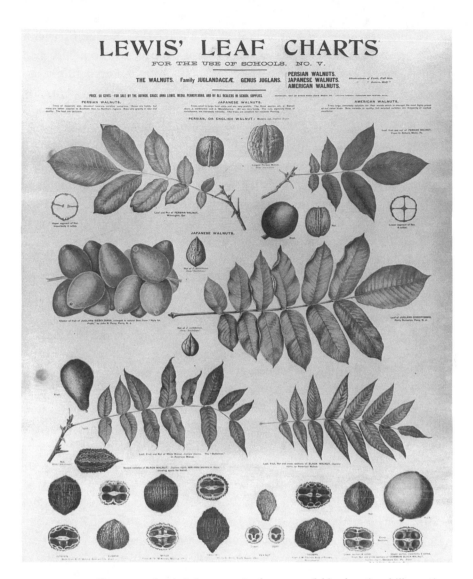

FIGURE 12 *Graceanna Lewis (1821–1912), the creator of this educational illustration, was an early woman scientist who worked in both botany and ornithology. (Friends Historical Library of Swarthmore College, Swarthmore, Pa.)*

of late nineteenth-century fears that urban life denied children contact with nature. The fruits of this interest in popularizing America domestica had ripened into a nationwide belief that children out of touch with nature could not grow into responsible American citizens. Comstock was involved in early experimental instruction in Nature Study, which led to her appointment at Cornell. Between 1880 and 1930, many Nature Study guides for public school-teachers were published. In 1911 Comstock wrote the *Handbook of Nature Study*, a guide instructing schoolteachers in methods for instilling an understanding of natural history in their students. Even though he thought the book would lose at least five thousand dollars, her husband John supported her effort. Surprisingly, the *Handbook* sold well. Anna reported that it became "the Bible" for Nature Study education in the United States and abroad.

Anna Botsford Comstock was a pioneer among women holding faculty positions in colleges. Her career illustrates as well, however, how the subtle connections between women's modes of nature study and their female role continued into the twentieth century. According to Anna's autobiography, John supported her absolutely in her education and her work. Her first set of drawing tools came as a surprise gift from John. He directed her into entomological illustration, encouraging her to finish her degree so as to improve her work.[57] Even though she had as much training in entomology as her husband, she used that knowledge to assist her husband as his illustrator. When she achieved her own career, she focused on the moral improvement of children. Neither John nor Anna questioned the different paths their careers took because each fit accepted gender roles, meshing harmoniously to create a productive working relationship.

Although Gene Porter was more "forward" in seeking publishers for her photography than the reclusive Cordelia Stanwood, and although Anna Comstock entered more nontraditional terrain as a faculty member at Cornell than did Graceanna Lewis at the academy, these four women shared an image of themselves as engaged in work that was suitable to women's role. Porter was only photographing the familiar birds of her home and Comstock was following Almira Phelps's educational model. Even though Porter earned a significant income from her work, she joined the others in also serving as a model of the middle-class woman who rejected frivolous consumerism in the serious pursuit of learning. By the late nineteenth century, this genteel, middle-class tradition shifted somewhat as women who earned their own living took up scientific illustration.

Between 1890 and 1920 women's participation in the labor market increased dramatically. Women of both the middle and lower classes entered the work force, many after taking advantage of burgeoning educational opportunities at the secondary and college levels. Anna Botsford Comstock's lifework represents one career path chosen by women with the financial security to attend college; unlike many of her middle-class contemporaries, however, she was not compelled to give up her profession after marriage.[58] Others, apparently finding too many barriers to the married career woman and requiring some means of earning their living, chose a career over marriage. Involved in "celibate careerism" and "social motherhood," many working women of these decades devoted themselves to paid employment contributing to the public welfare in some way. They were teachers, home economists, and employees in government health agencies, holding themselves—as women—responsible for preserving humane values in an increasingly competitive society. Their careers mirrored their service in volunteer organizations—such as the Woman's Christian Temperance Union—whose memberships influenced local and national leaders to aid the poor and the weak. In place of husband and children they created families of close friends, sometimes fulfilling an interest in nurturing children by serving as godmothers.[59]

Such working women performed many of the same tasks in the public round that they had accomplished at home, their low salaries reflecting societal ambivalence to their presence in the work force. Women scientists carried out tasks that were thought to be consistent with woman's genteel, nurturing role, their supposedly limited intellectual capabilities, and the (largely mistaken) belief that most only worked for "pin money." For example, the U.S. Department of Agriculture was by the 1920s the single largest employer of women scientists in the country. However, its female employees had limited options. Until 1919 women could try out for jobs studying human and plant diseases, but not animal diseases; they could work on potato diseases, but not tobacco crop diseases.[60]

Many a career woman in the scientific establishment sacrificed much—both in her personal life and professional life—to contribute to the national welfare. At the core of the group of female scientific illustrators working for the Department of Agriculture during this period was a woman whose life exemplifies the experience of celibate careerism. In 1960 Mary Agnes Merrill Chase, an international authority on grasses, wrote to her goddaughter that "it is no fun to be 91 and have enough work for several years laid out to do in the herbarium and a great pile of mss on S. Amer. Paspalum, about ¾ finished and typed—but unable to get at it because of the *piles* of work—the

FIGURE 13. *Agnes Chase (1869–1963), who began her career in science as an illustrator for the U.S. Department of Agriculture in 1903. (Hunt Institute for Botanical Documentation, Carnegie Mellon University, Pittsburgh, Pa.)*

best young agrostologist left for twice as much salary elsewhere though he loved grasses and liked the work—but has a family . . . If I had any sense I'd quit the herbarium and grasses, but it would be easier to stop breathing."[61] Agnes Chase spent more than fifty years illustrating, collecting, and classifying grasses, first for Agriculture and after her retirement, in 1939, as a volunteer in the Division of Plants, U.S. National Museum, at the Smithsonian Institution (Figure 13). As her letter says, grasses were her life, but both the subject and the life she lived pursuing it meshed with gender-role expectations of the early twentieth century.

Agnes Merrill was born in Illinois in 1869, attending elementary and secondary school in Chicago. Her father died when she was three. Apparently the family had little money, to which Agnes later attributed her inability to attend high school and college. At eighteen, she married William Ingraham Chase. Following his death in the first year of their marriage, she spent a summer with his relatives in a rural area of Chicago, where she began botanizing in earnest. Her marriage had not given her any financial security, so she had to combine paid work with her passionate pursuit of botanical knowledge. From 1901 to 1903 she took night jobs in Chicago to free her days for her studies. She worked as an assistant in botany (apparently on a volunteer basis) at the Field Museum of Natural History, where she prepared illustrations for Charles Frederick Millspaugh's "Plantae Yucatanae." In 1903 she passed the examination to become a botanical illustrator in the Department of Agriculture. Dedicated to learning more botany, she spent her free time working in the grass herbarium. By 1907 she had been appointed a scientific assistant in systematic agrostology. For the next twenty-odd years she worked with Professor A. S. Hitchcock, the head of agrostology, on his studies of North and South American grasses. On his death, she took over his post, retiring at the mandatory age of seventy in 1939. Until her death at ninety-four, she worked as a volunteer at the Smithsonian Institution revising Hitchcock's *Manual of the Grasses of the United States* and compiling a massive index to grass species. Throughout her career, her skills as an illustrator were important to her research. Her artwork appeared in Hitchcock's publications, in her own articles, and in *The First Book of Grasses*, an introductory text she wrote.[62]

Hitchcock became her mentor at Agriculture, promoting her work in the herbarium and the field. Chase was known for her dedication to the department and to her work; never taking time off for lunch, she also worked almost every Saturday. After Hitchcock died, she took on the task of revising and updating his manual, maintaining her previous role as his assistant. She never remarried but built a close-knit family among friends, their children, and young scientists (particularly women botanists). She also supported many of the progressive reform movements of her day—joining with other single, childless women in the new role of social mother. A militant suffragette, Chase was jailed in 1918 and again in 1919 while protesting. One of her goddaughters remembered that she always encouraged younger women to believe in their own abilities. She contributed a good deal of her salary to such worthy groups as the Quakers, the National Wildlife Federation, and the Columbia Lighthouse for the Blind.[63]

In her own mind, the love of grasses grew from an interest in flowers. She remembered playing as a child in her grandmother's backyard, which had no ornamental flowers. One day she picked a bouquet of grass flowers and brought them to her grandmother, who pointed out that grasses did not flower. Agnes encouraged her to look more closely at the minute blooms in each spike, reporting that she knew she was right about the flowers.[64] As

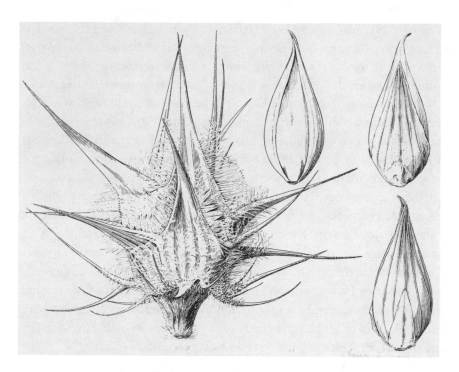

FIGURE 14. Cenchrus tribuloides *(bur grass), illustrated by Agnes Chase. (Hunt Institute for Botanical Documentation, Carnegie Mellon University, Pittsburgh, Pa., indefinite loan from Smithsonian Institution)*

Chase often pointed out, the spikelets of grass plants, in which the minute flowers grow, are the most important features used in classifying the plants (Figures 14, 15).[65] Studying grasses, she engaged in an appreciation of the beauties of plants and in progressive knowledge promoting human welfare. Grasses were of interest to the Department of Agriculture for their importance in feeding both humans and range animals. Much of Hitchcock's and Chase's work aimed at improving—through a better understanding of wild or native grasses and the importation and breeding of new grasses—the country's agricultural resources. Chase's commitment to these goals sent her much farther afield than most. She gained some fame for her collecting trips in South America, supporting increasing American dominance in the knowledge of plants worldwide. Press reports of her adventures in such expansionist endeavors also emphasized her womanly modesty.[66] As a botanist, Chase demonstrated women's ability to give their nature study a seriousness beyond the leisure-time hobby that Cadwallader Colden had predicted. Collecting, classi-

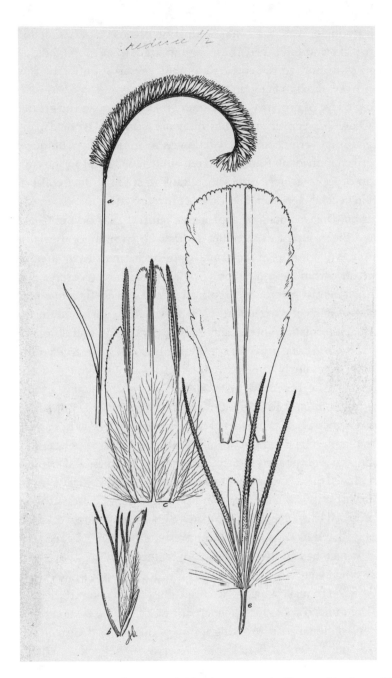

FIGURE 15. Bouteloua scorpioides *(grama grass)*, *illustrated by Agnes Chase. (Hunt Institute for Botanical Documentation, Carnegie Mellon University, Pittsburgh, Pa., indefinite loan from Smithsonian Institution)*

fying, and illustrating grasses was a vital occupation because, as Chase stated in her book, "of all plants grasses are the most important to man."[67] Her life's passion was to contribute to the conservation and preservation of the tiny flowers she once presented to her grandmother.

In merging a love of flowers with the desire to contribute to the greater good, Agnes Chase—as a government illustrator and scientist—typified many women engaged in government work. Chase was in some ways a uniquely talented and driven individual. Rather than remaining an illustrator, she educated herself in order to achieve professional rank as scientist. Her collaboration with Hitchcock helped her develop her expertise and gain some individual recognition while maintaining appropriate female behavior. But Chase also represented the group of women illustrators who spent a good part of their lives simply as delineators of the plants in the herbarium. Their circumstances differed little from Helen Lawson's or Helen Winchester's except that the father or the scientist-mentor was replaced by the equally directive personnel system of the federal government. They provided scientists and the lay public with visual information about the flora of America (and useful flora of other parts of the world) as part of the continuing national effort to identify, expand, use, and (increasingly) preserve natural resources.

The 1935 edition of Hitchcock's *Manual of the Grasses* contains a footnote crediting its hundreds of illustrations to Mary Wright Gill, Edna May Whitehorn, and Agnes Chase.[68] Not apparent in Hitchcock's brief note were the friendships that developed among women doing such work. For example, Chase once adopted an orphaned squirrel, named him Toodles, and wrote a children's story based on his escapades in and around her home. Mary Wright Gill drew the illustrations for the book and photographed Chase with her little pet. In her story, Chase mentions the many single women who worked in government and shared living quarters in the Washington area.[69] By the turn of the century women had created a niche in government service. Like Agnes Chase, these women were not seeking substitutes for a life of middle-class leisure. They worked to make a living. Scientific illustration allowed them to labor among like-minded colleagues at an artistic task fulfilling their creative drive and serving national goals. Working for many divisions of Agriculture, women drew a wide variety of flora as the need arose. They left a heritage of thousands of illustrations gracing government publications on everything from the discovery of a new cactus to the agricultural potential of an imported grape variety.

By the 1890s women's study of botany and art had come to fruition. For

the *Yearbook of the United States Department of Agriculture* Deborah G. Passmore, Bertha Heiges, Amanda Newton, Mary D. Arnold, and Ellen Schutt
were beginning to produce detailed drawings and watercolors. When, between 1902 and 1913, the *Yearbook* ran a regular series on "Promising New
Fruits," these women, particularly Passmore, could claim credit for the bulk
of the watercolor illustrations (Figures 16, 17). Historians have noted that
these illustrations are both beautiful and technically accurate; some also may
be "the only illustrations of the cultivars they represent."[70] Although little
biographical material on these women has been located, one hint from Passmore's materials indicates that her work was done as much for pleasure as for
money, that she considered herself an artist as well as an illustrator.

Born in 1840 in Delaware County, Pennsylvania, of Quaker parents,
Deborah Passmore studied art in Philadelphia and Europe. Apparently never
married, she tried to support herself with her own art studio in Washington,
D.C. After the studio venture failed, she began working for the Department
of Agriculture in 1892. In addition to her government work, she produced an
unpublished folio of watercolors of the "Wildflowers of America."[71] Reminiscent of Susan Cooper's admiration for the cultivated lands of America and
love of its native plants, Passmore divided her time between illustrating agricultural domestics and the native flowers she, and so many other women of
her generation, hoped to preserve.[72]

Women accomplished a prodigious amount of illustrating for Agriculture. Roberta Cowing, whose work introduced this chapter, provided fine
illustrations for the *Contributions from the U.S. National Herbarium*, along with
Agnes Chase, Mary D. Baker, Blanche Ames, Mary Wright Gill, Katherine
Mayo, and Juliet C. Patten.[73] Patten's work also appeared in publications
of the U.S. Forest Service, along with that of Mrs N.W. Brenizer, Annie
Elizabeth Hoyle, and Leta Hughey (Figure 18). Leta Hughey's drawings in
the Forest Service Collection are well done. She contributed an extensive
set of illustrations for many publications, covering a variety of plant forms
(Figure 19).[74] The purpose of these illustrated government publications was
to educate a broad audience (scientists, government employees, farmers and
ranchers, suburbanites, and tourists) about the flora of the continent and
to encourage appropriate conservation of existing plants and cultivation of
introduced species. Such objectives supported the national effort to define
Americans through their relationship with a land containing their history in
its flora and fauna.[75] Using their talents as botanical artists, women illustrators
played a key role in this effort.

FIGURE 16. *"Stayman Winesap Apple," made by Bertha Heiges for the "Promising New Fruits" series published in the* Yearbook of the U.S. Department of Agriculture *(1902). (National Agricultural Library, U.S. Department of Agriculture, Beltsville, Md. Photograph by L'Imagerie.)*

FIGURE 17. *"Eulalia Loquat," by Deborah Passmore (1840–1911), which appeared in* *"Promising New Fruits,"* Yearbook of the U.S. Department of Agriculture *(1905).* *(National Agricultural Library, U.S. Department of Agriculture, Beltsville, Md. Photograph* *by L'Imagerie.)*

FIGURE 18. *Annie Elizabeth Hoyle also worked as an illustrator for the U.S. Department of Agriculture in the early twentieth century. Abies grandis (giant fir), depicted here, represents the type of illustration such women made for the U.S. Forest Service. (U.S. Department of Agriculture Forest Service Collection, Hunt Institute for Botanical Documentation, Carnegie Mellon University, Pittsburgh, Pa.)*

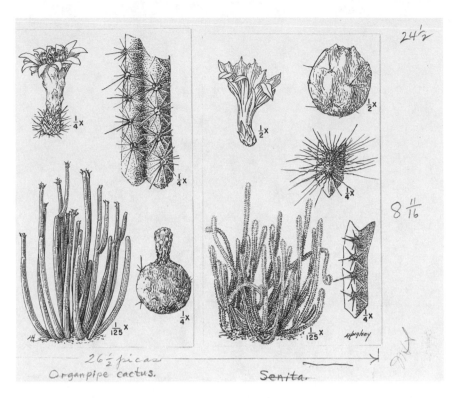

FIGURE 19. *Leta Hughey's drawings of cacti, which illustrated Elbert L. Little, Jr.'s* Southwestern Trees: A Guide to the Native Species of New Mexico and Arizona *(1950). (Hunt Institute for Botanical Documentation, Carnegie Mellon University, Pittsburgh, Pa.)*

Women have continued to serve as governmental illustrators throughout the twentieth century. Elaine Hodges has worked as an entomological illustrator at the Smithsonian Institution since 1965 (Figure 20). She also does free-lance work and is one of the founding members of the Guild of Natural Science Illustrators.[76] This organization, begun in 1968 by Smithsonian illustrators, brings together artists working for the government, universities, herbaria, zoological museums, botanical gardens, and as free-lancers. Women constitute a majority of its membership; of the ten presidents elected to 1989, eight have been women. In a 1986 exhibit of members' works at the National Museum of Natural History, more than 70 of 101 illustrations were by women.[77] Nor are women still limited to botanical and entomological subjects. They now work in all areas of science, including zoology and

FIGURE 20. "Pseudaugochloropsis graminea *[bee]* on Senecio *Flower,*" *by Elaine R. S. Hodges, a contemporary illustrator at the Smithsonian Institution. (Courtesy of the artist)*

human anatomy.[78] Among the fine contemporary scientific illustrators, Nancy Halliday and Biruta Galdikas Hansen, for example, illustrate plants, insects, vertebrates, fish, mammals, and birds as well as paleontological specimens (Figure 21).[79] The doors to botanical and zoological collections, to universities and government agencies, which opened to women in the late nineteenth century, have continued to provide an avenue into nature study for many women illustrators.

Many have taken the final step and struck out on their own, doing contract work for authors/scientists much as their fathers and husbands had done early in the nineteenth century. Some produce their own books. Among the free-lancers are women whose work, while sharing characteristics of scien-

FIGURE 21. *"Japanese White-eye (*Zosterops japonica*) on Indian Golden Shower Tree (Cassia fistula)," by Nancy Halliday. (Hunt Institute for Botanical Documentation, Carnegie Mellon University, Pittsburgh, Pa., gift from Dr. and Mrs. Alan R. Katritzky of Gainesville, Fla., in memory of Frederick Charles Katritzky)*

tific illustration, has other ends besides the documentation of flora and fauna. Americans have retained an interest in nature imagery, particularly that of native plants and animals. Although the general trend in the fine arts has been away from the still lifes and garden paintings of the nineteenth century, there remains a healthy market for superior nature studies. Some of the best-known artists in this field are women. Until her death in 1985 at age ninety-five years, Grace Albee was a highly successful painter and wood engraver who concentrated on close studies of plants (Figure 22).[80] Anne Ophelia Dowden has published many books for a general audience. In works like *Wild Green Things in the City: A Book of Weeds*, she encourages urbanites to take a new look at the nature surrounding them. She and many other illustrators publish their work in popular scientific journals such as *Audubon* and *Natural History* and in domestic magazines like *House Beautiful* and *Life*.[81] Their images grace the calendars, date books, and framed prints found in many middle-class homes.

Anne Ophelia Dowden's career encapsulates women's work illustrating nature. Growing up in Colorado drawing insects and plants, she studied art at Carnegie-Mellon University during the depression. Unable to make a living as a book illustrator, she taught art in New York at the Pratt Institute and at Manhattanville College. She also helped found a group of young designers that fashioned wallpapers and drapery fabrics. After using plant forms and flowers in her patterns for almost twenty years, she realized that her real interest was in illustrating plants. While on sabbatical, she produced a set of drawings of "edible wild plants" and began her career as a botanical illustrator. For the past thirty-five years, she has worked as a free-lance botanical artist and author, her goal being "to raise botanical art above mere mechanical reporting."[82] (Figure 23) Dowden is passionately interested in depicting the beauty of nature's forms. Her art is accessible and meaningful to both the scientific community and the general public; many advocates are women who share her interest in bringing nature's designs into their homes, much as Susan Fenimore Cooper did when she admired the organic forms in her rugs and furniture on a cold winter's day in the 1850s.

Thanks to the diligent research of feminist historians, we know that women were shut out of many careers in science because of stereotypes about their sex and because their entry posed a threat to the male establishment. What I have suggested here is that, in emphasizing such constrictions, we may have overlooked a major contribution that female scientific illustrators have made both to science and to public appreciation of the plants and animals of the continent. From early in the nation's history, American women

FIGURE 22. *Grace Albee (1890–1985) earned a national reputation for her fine wood engravings such as this* Demonstration Block, New York World's Fair *(caterpillar). (Hunt Institute for Botanical Documentation, Carnegie Mellon University, Pittsburgh, Pa.)*

FIGURE 23. Watercolor Research Painting, Curly Dock *(Rumex crispus)*, *by Anne Ophelia Dowden. Photograph by D. James Dee. (Courtesy of the artist)*

have influenced the way we look at nature. Without the exquisite shell drawings of Helen Lawson, the bird photographs of Cordelia Stanwood, the grass illustrations of Agnes Chase, and the flower and insect compositions of Anne Dowden, Americans' knowledge about and care for nature would be diminished. Without their path-breaking commitment to patient, detailed, technically accurate work, many other women might not have found a way to perform creative tasks while earning a living for themselves and their families.

Socially defined gender roles are a significant factor in determining the artistic genre in which women have worked. Steered away from heroic landscape painting and into still lifes and small-scale, detailed illustrations of delicate flowers and shells, women cultivated talents placing them at the heart of scientific illustration. Accustomed to pursuing their art under the guidance of fathers and husbands, they adapted to working for male supervisors in the scientific establishment. Told repeatedly by both male and female tastemakers that the middle-class woman's salvation from a life of aimless leisure was in the study of nature, such study took on a moral value. Progressive Era women who eschewed traditional roles as wives or mothers, and who often had to work to support themselves, benefited from such genteel stereotypes. Their labors as unsung government artists suggest that nature appreciation was not limited to the leisured and wealthy, that women with few resources made many sacrifices to pursue their passion for plants and animals.

The connection between women's homes and America domestica made scientific illustration appear to be an organic outgrowth of women's role as conservators of both households: by drawing the flora and fauna of America, women at once fulfilled their roles as private women and as public citizens. Women of the late twentieth century may not be as bound by such stereotypes as were their grandmothers and mothers. They certainly have covered a great deal more terrain. That they now have a major voice in all branches of nature art is due, however, in great measure to women like Agnes Chase, who at ninety-one could not "quit the herbarium and grasses, . . . it would be easier to stop breathing."[83]

# 4

## Designing Nature
### *Gardeners and Their Gardens*

*I never did have the fennel, and the clematis seed you sent are larger than any I have seen . . . I do hope to get some up. I love to work with flowers, advertise, and get letters from people . . . I turn my flower money back into more flowers. I have a friend in Texas that swaps plants with me, and a pen pal in Indiana that sends me peonies and lilies. As long as I can, I'll work with my flowers, but I am about to get disabled to work much in them like I used to, so I want bulbs and perennials that will stay there. I must stop now, or I won't have room to enclose some seed. I love to give as well as receive.*

—Lucy (Mrs. Grady) Stamps

LUCY STAMPS of Bogue Chitto, Mississippi, dealt in seeds and plants raised in her rural flower beds. She shared her plants and garden lore with Elizabeth Lawrence, one of America's best contemporary garden authors. In the 1950s Lawrence was introduced by the novelist Eudora Welty to farmer's market bulletins published in several southern states. The bulletins served as advertising devices for rural families with most anything to sell—livestock, farm implements, hunting dogs, and garden plants. Most of the dealers in flowers were women. Lawrence, the child of a middle-class Raleigh, North Carolina, home, well educated in literature at Barnard College and in landscape design at North Carolina State College, had little in common with the farm women advertising in the bulletins.[1] They shared, however, a passion for plants, for growing the "old" ones first seen in their mother's and grandmother's gardens, for trying out new varieties listed in plant catalogs, and for adapting local wildflowers to their beds. Lawrence developed long-term relationships with women who bought, sold, and traded their favorites around the regional network of gardeners. Working in her garden in Raleigh, Elizabeth Lawrence nurtured plants that reminded her of Lucy Stamps, her friend in rural Mississippi. In return, Lucy thought fondly of Elizabeth as the clematis vine twined around her farm porch.

Women's gardens have figured in the history of American plant culture since the eighteenth century. A Mrs. Grant, a resident of Albany, New York, in the 1750s and 1760s, admired the well-tended gardens of Dutch women in the town. South Carolina's Eliza Lucas Pinckney planted the first indigo in the 1740s and created beautiful gardens of ornamental natives and exotics. The most famous woman gardener of the early period was Martha Logan, another South Carolinian, who advertised plants and seeds for sale through the *South Carolina Gazette*. Logan traded plants and advice with John Bartram and wrote an early American book on gardening, *The Gardener's Kalendar* (1755).[2]

In the early nineteenth century, class divisions developed around what sort of work women did in the garden. Increasing urbanization led some commentators to bemoan the loss of women's traditions as gardeners. In *Rural Hours*, Susan Fenimore Cooper noted that many young women of her class did not take part in the gardening activities still prevalent among rural wives (132). Echoing the English lady travelers' impression that middle- and upper-class women spent too much time indoors, Americans like Cooper and Andrew Jackson Downing lamented their compatriots' withdrawal from the garden. The proprieties of class lines were marked, however, in their suggestions for addressing the problem. Cooper did not want American women behind the plow; rather, they were to tend the flower garden.

Prodding the ladies out into the garden, Downing wrote persuasive articles for *The Horticulturalist* and edited a famous Englishwoman's garden book for his American audience. In the 1840s American women purchased Jane Loudon's *Gardening for Ladies*, where they discovered such amenities as ladies' gardening gloves and wheelbarrows and learned how "a lady, with a small light spade, may, by repeatedly digging over the same line, and taking out only a little earth at a time, succeed in doing, with her own hands, all the digging that can be required in a small garden."[3] Catharine Beecher, the

FIGURE 24. *Illustrating the popular nineteenth-century concept of gardening as a middle-class family endeavor, this image of "Springtime in the Country—Gardening" appeared in* Harper's Weekly, *May 9, 1869. (Photograph courtesy of Winterthur Library: Printed Book and Periodical Collection, Winterthur, Del.)*

influential American delineator of middle-class women's responsibilities, also preached the virtues of the garden to suburban wives. By 1869 Beecher and Harriet Beecher Stowe's *The American Woman's Home* included in its frontispiece a prominent illustration of the genteel woman gardener (appropriately sheltered from the sun by a servant holding a parasol) and three chapters on gardening. Beecher assumed that the middle-class wife would master not only the spade but also complex instructions for the grafting of trees.[4] Popular magazines like *Harper's Weekly* both reflected and promoted women's status as gardeners with idealized images of family harmony expressed in home horticulture (Figure 24).[5] Such celebration of the genteel joys of gardening originated in the northeastern states among influential tastemakers, but the values spread along the frontier. Mid-nineteenth-century promotional literature encouraging families to move to the prairies portrayed middle-class women making domestic garden spaces. Such literature mingled descriptions of vegetable gardens with ornamental plantings. Whatever the plant material, frontier women used it to decorate (and domesticate) the spaces immediately surrounding their cabins.[6]

Following the 1872 publication of Anna Warner's *Gardening By Myself*, women's gardening books dominated the market. As the title suggests, *Gardening By Myself* urged American women to take part in making and maintaining flower beds and responded to upper- and middle-class women's desire for practical advice in fulfilling their role as domestic gardeners.[7] The explosion of gardening books for American women on the heels of Loudon's publication indicates that women of these classes really never quit their flower beds except, perhaps, in the imaginations of the intellectual elite.[8]

Women's garden literature (both in America and Great Britain) is heavily class-coded to this day. People who own property and have the leisure and education to write about the design of their own or others' domestic surroundings produce the bulk of gardening books. Lavish garden books designed by influential women tout the large estates of the very rich. Books of garden photographs like Louise Shelton's *Beautiful Gardens in America* document the spread of upper-class garden styles from Long Island to Los Angeles. National standards influenced middle-class residential landscape design as well. Upper-class women wrote gardening manuals for more middle-class suburbanites, suggesting how they might adapt garden styles of wealthy country places to their smaller plots on the urban fringe. Finally, believing that a woman who gardened demonstrated feminine civility, influential garden writers wrote books showing how to accommodate the dominant style to the cramped outdoor spaces of suburban and urban working-class homes.

Because the garden literature produced by influential elites provides a wealth of information on women's work with plants, this chapter centers on the garden values of educated, landed women. The garden books, landscape designs, and plant preferences of such women mirror writers' and illustrators' contributions to popular definitions of America and Americans deriving from our relationships with local flora and fauna. In part because of the influence of nineteenth-century tastemakers like Susan Cooper and Andrew Downing, the stereotypical lady gardener appears as a wealthy dowager with an excess of leisure time.[9] Actually, women from many stations of life garden. As the correspondence between Elizabeth Lawrence of Raleigh, North Carolina, and Lucy Stamps of Bogue Chitto, Mississippi, shows, women with little else in common easily may share a love of plants.

Many of the writers and artists covered in previous chapters kept gardens. Mary Treat not only designed a garden for her friends the spiders, but also wrote a book about the control of insect pests for amateur horticulturists. Among the birders, Mabel Osgood Wright had a famous garden and penned garden books herself. Friends remembered Agnes Chase as an avid gardener who packed plants into her modest suburban yard.[10] Assuming that each of these women expressed upper-class values in the act of gardening simplifies the sources of their passion for plants. Chase, for example, grew up in reduced circumstances and first developed her love of flowers in the unpromising garden of her grandmother's yard. That she achieved middle-class status through government employment may not be as critical to her planting preferences as what she learned about gardening from her mother and grandmother. Two issues became apparent as I surveyed what women have done in gardening. First, not every garden writer speaks solely in the voice of the upper class. Second, women gardeners share some plant preferences crossing class lines. Thus, in examining the role of influential women in American gardening history and their participation in elite culture, I also give some consideration to their interactions with women from different classes and cultural backgrounds.

The best garden autobiography of the late nineteenth century was Celia Thaxter's *An Island Garden*. Thaxter shared with Agnes Chase the discovery of her love of plants in an unpromising setting of sparse vegetation. It is ironic that such an influential garden book sprang from a childhood on a small, rocky island along the harsh New England coast. In the preface, Thaxter recalled her first flower garden: "Ever since I could remember anything, flowers have been like dear friends to me, comforters, inspirers, powers to uplift and to cheer. A lonely child, living on the lighthouse island ten miles away from the mainland, every blade of grass that sprang out of the ground, every humblest weed, was precious in my sight, and I began a little garden when not more than five years old. From this, year after year, the larger one, which has given so much pleasure to so many people, has grown."[11]

In 1839, when she was about four, Celia Laighton's father became the lighthouse keeper at White Island, part of the chain called the Isles of Shoals off the coast of Portsmouth, New Hampshire. Celia and her family lived on the tiny, three-acre island until she was twelve, when they moved to Appledore, the largest of the Isles. Laighton owned this and several other of the islands. Here he and his partner, Levi Lincoln Thaxter, built a summer hotel, Appledore House. Appledore House opened its doors in 1848, quickly gaining fame as the favorite haunt of many New England writers and artists. Levi Thaxter, the Harvard-educated son of a wealthy, intellectual Boston family, found himself unsuited to the task of running the hotel but stayed on as the children's tutor.[12] Celia Laighton's childhood on White Island and Appledore bred her landscape preferences. Her first publication, *Among the Isles of Shoals*, portrayed a rugged, storm-swept terrain somehow sheltering the most beautiful of plants. The small size of the islands ensured that she was ever conscious of the surrounding ocean, making her home an oasis. Her first loves were native flowers and imports gone wild.[13] The islands were Celia's whole life. Before her marriage to Levi Thaxter at age fifteen, she had only spent a part of one year away from home.

In 1855, disenchanted with the austerity of year-round life on Appledore, Levi Thaxter moved his wife and two young sons to Newtonville, Massachusetts. Celia began writing poetry about her life on the islands, partly to lessen her longing to return and as intellectual relief from the rigors of raising three young sons when barely in her twenties. Boston's literary circle embraced the young poet. John Greenleaf Whittier became a lifelong friend and mentor. Nevertheless, she maintained close ties with her family and friends on the island.

Wherever she lived on the mainland, Thaxter kept a garden. Her garden invariably included common plants of the region.[14] After the 1860s, because of her husband's dislike of the islands as well as his ill health, Celia and Levi experienced a series of long separations as she spent more and more time on Appledore. She summered on the island, helping her brothers run the hotel, and wintered in Boston or Portsmouth. During these summer sojourns she worked on the garden that became the source of much of her celebrity. Published in 1894, the year of her death, *An Island Garden* tells the story of how Celia Thaxter made the garden and what it meant to her.

Part of the garden's fame can be attributed to the artists who visited Thaxter and Appledore House. They came to paint the landscape. The garden offered a vibrant addition to the rocky, ocean vistas surrounding it. One of the most famous paintings of an American garden (and the woman in it) is Childe Hassam's 1892 rendition of *Celia Thaxter in Her Garden* (Figure 25). Influenced by John Ruskin's romantic visions of naturalized gardens and Monet's impressionistic garden paintings, Hassam and other American painters offered American versions of the centuries-old image of the lady in the garden.[15] Paintings like Hassam's reveal how the wilderness landscape was transformed into the domesticated home. In this painting, Celia Thaxter stands at the edge of the gate separating her garden from the surrounding untamed coast. Hollyhocks and Shirley poppies in the garden spill outside the fence, mingling with native wildflowers. Rather than a formal cultivation, the garden itself typifies the naturalized design valued during the period. Thaxter, dressed in elegant white, appears as a simply taller flower, cultivated for her

FIGURE 25. Celia Thaxter in Her Garden, *by Frederick Childe Hassam. (National Museum of American Art, Smithsonian Institution, Washington, D.C.)*

plain style, her native civility. Such blurring of boundaries extends Thaxter's range as well, making the world outside the gate suitable for a proper Victorian woman.[16] *Celia Thaxter in Her Garden* suggests that wilderness is merely a valued aspect of the domesticated, country home. As with Susan Cooper, domestication does not signal rigid formality, but an easy, native gracefulness celebrated as the true character of the American woman and the American landscape.

In the mid-nineteenth and early twentieth centuries, garden design and landscape painting were closely intertwined. This period witnessed the rise, in men like Andrew Jackson Downing and Frederick Law Olmsted, of the landscape architect. These influential men envisioned American estates and parks echoing scenes depicted by the country's landscape painters: deep vistas moving from lush, close-up details of native plants through framing trees, often over a lake or river, to a far horizon. Consumers of such spaces strolled along artfully winding paths, taking advantage of judiciously placed, rustic benches, to rest and view the scenery. In *Celia Thaxter in Her Garden*, Hassam depicted a late nineteenth-century version of America's ideal terrain. The work's dominant landscape aesthetic of the period partially accounts for its continuing popularity in the canon of American painting.[17]

The naturalistic style could, however, render the landscape designer's work almost invisible. In Hassam's painting of Thaxter, the pure white of her dress, the ability of the plants to amble gracefully out of the garden and down to the sea, bespeak a garden in need of no guidance and a passive woman observing, rather than making, the landscape. Such an image was driven not only by painting and landscape traditions of the time, but also by unresolved tensions in the effort to get the American woman into the garden. Cooper and Downing set the making of a flower bed into a more genteel context than farmland. Images of women planting young seedlings (like the *Harper's Weekly* engraving) masked the fact that raising flowers often required hard work under trying conditions. Similarly, when he painted Thaxter's portrait, Hassam created an American woman of the leisured class in an idealized landscape. Like the populace strolling through Central Park little appreciating the extent to which the park was made land, viewers of the painting could easily miss Thaxter's labor to make the garden.

In fact, Celia Thaxter rarely had the opportunity to linger at her garden gate in thoughtful appreciation of the landscape. She was too busy digging beds, transplanting flowers, and fending off weeds. She designed and worked the garden with her own hands partly out of necessity. Evidence suggests that Levi Thaxter was not a particularly successful provider. Celia earned a significant portion of the family income from her writing; indeed, she published *An Island Garden* for that purpose. She also earned money painting flowers and seascapes on porcelain. Thaxter's father had little wealth as well; through the garden she helped his finances along. The garden on Appledore served at once as a part of Thaxter's home and as a scenic addition to the hotel. This hotel, and another the family managed on Star Island, served as another source of sometimes chancy income. For both businesses, Celia took on the strenuous task of making suitable gardens to draw more tourists to the islands.[18]

Educated by and married to a member of Boston's intellectual elite, then befriended and celebrated by this group, Thaxter occasionally offered romanticized views of women gardeners in her garden autobiography. Constrained, however, by limited financial resources, she also challenged the leisured passivity implicit in images of women in gardens. Thaxter addressed *An Island Garden* to friends who had asked her how to make a flowering paradise like her own. She tried to be scrupulously honest about her methods, her successes, and her failures, knowing that others would follow her lead. *An Island Garden* supports the image of private gardens as suitable backdrops to the genteel round of middle- and upper-class women. But it also suggests that gardening drew Thaxter into physically demanding work requiring specialized knowledge not usually expected of the lady in the garden.

Like Susan Fenimore Cooper before her and Agnes Chase after, Thaxter believed that one of women's most important roles was as exemplar of moral values. Her friends remembered her always dressed in a plain style, in black, gray, or white dresses, with seashells around her neck and wrists and a flower at her waist.[19] Though never a church member, she was deeply religious and believed that gardening engendered spiritual emotions, an awareness of the "exhaustless power of the great Inventor" (77). Thaxter integrated her garden seamlessly into her domestic round, reading the flowers symbolically and using them ornamentally.

She made few distinctions between indoors and outdoors at her home on Appledore. The music room doors opened onto a piazza, with steps leading into the garden. She grew flowers as much for their use in this room as for their beauty in the sunlight. In summer, she filled the room with garden plants, arranged with an eye to complementary colors and forms. Thaxter had two special display spaces—the "altar" and the "shrine." On the altar, the top of a bookshelf, she designed a display of color running from "the dazzling white single Poppy, the Bride, to lead the sweet procession" to the pale rose tints, "delicate as the palm of a baby's hand," culminating in "the deeper tones to clear, rich cherry, and on to glowing crimson" (95–96). The shrine, a table below the shelf, held "a few of the fairest flowers" (96). Flowers filled every nook, creating an indoor garden comparable to the one guests viewed through the windows just below the piazza. Vases also held wildflowers and grasses found outside the bounds of her garden, making slight distinction between cultivated and wild.[20] Nor was much difference noted between nature and culture. Flower guests, as much as human visitors, thrilled to the beautiful music played in the room and the wild bird's tune blended with the sonata (102). Most significant, female guests complemented the flowers: "lovely women in colors that seem to have copied the flowers in the garden" (103). Thus, both the actual setting Thaxter created and the verbal picture of it she painted reflect the graceful Victorian hostess portrayed by Hassam.

Further, *An Island Garden* shares the predominant landscape values of the nineteenth century's intellectual elite. In designing gardens for the wealthy, landscape architects working in the naturalistic tradition kept flower beds, domestic shrubs, and formal designs (which most bespoke the cultivating hand of humans) close to the residence, gradually making the spaces farther from the house more naturalistic, with winding drives through groves of native trees leading to expansive vistas of old stands of forest or the sea beyond.[21] Thaxter's cottage at Appledore, by virtue of its placement on the small island, mirrored this landscape aesthetic even though she was not a wealthy woman. Although the piazza looked out to the ocean, the viewer's gaze first fell on the orderly beds of cultivated flowers at the bottom of the steps. Succeeding the formal beds were less controlled banks of similar flowers, providing a transition between the cultivated garden and the native plants growing wild on the island. Throughout her book, Thaxter emphasized the delight she found in this view from the porch. The garden expressed for her exactly what Hassam envisioned in his painting—a proper setting for the not overly civilized, but appropriately cultivated American woman.

Yet the garden symbolized much more than that static moment on the piazza. Celia Thaxter called upon a good deal of specialized knowledge and skill in making her flower beds into the perfect setting for her womanly presence. Further, many of her design and plant preferences sprang from her humble background as the lighthouse keeper's daughter and from her financially strained adult life of genteel poverty. The garden was a 15 by 50-foot rectangle off the piazza running the length of her private cottage (Figure 26). As the plan shows, the garden was laid out in a simple pattern of formal beds with paths in between, reached through the steps off the piazza. Two gates led out from it—one to the sea on the south. The whole was fenced, with banks of less formally organized flower plantings bordering the outside of the enclosure. The flowers included an informal mix of native plants and imports, annuals and perennials. Her main interest was the same as that ex-

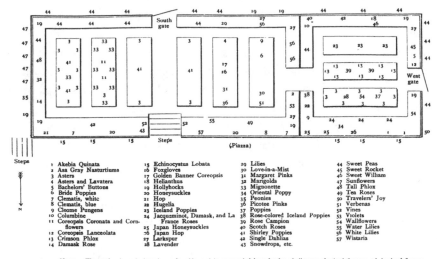

Steps

| 1 Akebia Quinata | 15 Echinocystis Lobata | 29 Lilies | 44 Sweet Peas |
| 2 Asa Gray Nasturtiums | 16 Foxgloves | 30 Love-in-a-Mist | 45 Sweet Rocket |
| 3 Asters | 17 Golden Banner Coreopsis | 31 Margaret Pinks | 46 Sweet William |
| 4 Asters and Lavatera | 18 Helianthus | 32 Marigolds | 47 Sunflowers |
| 5 Bachelors' Buttons | 19 Hollyhocks | 33 Mignonette | 48 Tall Phlox |
| 6 Bride Poppies | 20 Honeysuckles | 34 Oriental Poppy | 49 Tea Roses |
| 7 Clematis, white | 21 Hop | 35 Peonies | 50 Travelers' Joy |
| 8 Clematis, blue | 22 Hugelia | 36 Picotee Pinks | 51 Verbenas |
| 9 Cleome Pungens | 23 Iceland Poppies | 37 Poppies | 52 Violets |
| 10 Columbine | 24 Jacqueminot, Damask, and La | 38 Rose-colored Iceland Poppies | 53 Vines |
| 11 Coreopsis Coronata and Corn- | France Roses | 39 Rose Campion | 54 Wallflowers |
| flowers | 25 Japan Honeysuckles | 40 Scotch Roses | 55 Water Lilies |
| 12 Coreopsis Lanceolata | 26 Japan Hop | 41 Shirley Poppies | 56 White Lilies |
| 13 Crimson Phlox | 27 Larkspur | 42 Single Dahlias | 57 Wistaria |
| 14 Damask Rose | 28 Lavender | 43 Snowdrops, etc. | |

NOTE.—The garden is 50 ft. long by 15 ft. wide, and is surrounded by a border of all sorts of mixed flowers. A bank of flowers at the southwest corner slopes from the garden fence.

FIGURE 26. *Celia Thaxter (1835–94) published this plan of her garden in* An Island Garden *(Boston: Houghton Mifflin, 1894).*

pressed in her indoor floral arrangements—to display each flower's unique form in complementary color groupings.

Thaxter knew that her garden violated certain fashionable gardening trends. In *An Island Garden* she dismissed the craze for "bedding out" annuals, partly because such gardens looked artificial: "I have not room to experiment with rockworks and ribbon-borders and the like, nor should I do it even if I had all the room in the world. For mine is just a little old-fashioned garden where the flowers come together to praise the Lord and teach all who look upon them to do likewise" (71). The key words in her description are "little" and "old-fashioned." Reflecting her middle-class status, the garden was neither large nor ostentatious. Thaxter was well aware of how much more money and work went into bedding out annuals each season. The necessity of working the garden herself determined its size and plant material. An "old-fashioned" garden implied vernacular values and knowledge shared between generations and among nonelite groups.[22] Celia's work in the garden raised fond memories of plant lore learned from her mother. The flowers contained stories of Celia's life and the lives of those before her. Moreover, these old-fashioned flowers were often the hardiest and the most easily transplanted to the gardens of relatives, friends, and neighbors—a task Thaxter loved performing. They were plants suitable for the humble flower gardens of seamen's wives and daughters.[23] The garden existed, then, not only as a scenic addition to the rugged landscapes of the Isles of Shoals, but also as a piece of personal and local history whose specific plants reminded a network of ordinary women of their lives and friendships.

Thaxter supplied her readers with copious lists of the plants she used and a diagram of her garden, but she knew that this information told nothing about how to make plants bloom. The major portion of *An Island Garden* is taken up with the daily round of the horticulturist. When Celia Thaxter detailed the work that went into creating a landscape suitable for meditative moments on the piazza, the little plot took on larger proportions and the passive female in Hassam's painting emerged a much livelier figure. Except for the initial spading, Thaxter did all the work in her garden. Her book begins with a major problem in plant cultivation—pests and what to do about them: "The cutworm, the wire-worm, the pansy-worm, the thrip, the rose-beetle, the aphis, the mildew, and many more, but worst of all the loathsome slug, a slimy, shapeless creature that devours every fair and exquisite thing in the garden,—the flower lover must seek all these with unflagging energy, and if possible, exterminate the whole" (6). Thaxter opposed the fashionable use of bird feathers in women's finery, criticized her husband's ornithological hunting expeditions, and refused to kill birds that were devouring young plants in her garden. But her regard for birds did not extend to other species. Thaxter rigorously controlled any other supposed threat to her perfect flower beds.[24]

Familiar with Darwin's theories of natural selection, she used such concepts to justify any lingering guilt she had about slaughtering slugs or ruthlessly thinning the weakest of her painstakingly raised seedlings. In *An Island Garden* Downing's genteel lady, querulously trying to figure out the uses of lime in the garden, is transformed into a dealer in death, mistress of a shed full of "deadly powders" she expertly applies to save her plants from the insect onslaught.[25] Thaxter provides graphic descriptions of the work involved in, for example, dusting the underside of rose leaves with hellebore or fighting slugs with salt and lime (6–7). Although she loved all the plants on the island, she did not enjoy them in her garden. A proponent of thorough weeding, Thaxter spent whole days in the hottest part of the summer performing that task. Andrew Downing had no such exhausting, dirty business in mind when he encouraged women to get out in the garden for a little healthy exercise (in the morning hours only, before the sun became too strong) and to enliven parlor conversations.

Celia Thaxter and her gardening compatriots of the late nineteenth and early twentieth century established American women as caretakers among the flora and fauna. The writers and illustrators discussed in previous chapters may have themselves gardened but their primary mode of interacting with nature was as observers and reporters. A woman whose life is gardening takes a direct hand in creating her environment. Although Thaxter enjoyed her quiet moments on the porch drinking in the beauty of her flowers, she preferred to nurture the plants. In her autobiography she waxes enthusiastic on the rewards of working the soil with one's own hands (24–25, 59). The gardener earns moments of complete immersion in nature, not by pondering the symbolic connections between women and flowers, but by hard labor among her plants. Making a virtue of necessity, Thaxter argues that to the garden laborer comes the truest understanding of nature. Setting herself off a bit from the intellectual naturists, she posits: "It takes Thoreau and Emerson and their kind to enjoy a walk for a walk's sake, and the wealth they glean with eyes and ears. I cannot enjoy the glimpses Nature gives me half as well, when I go deliberately seeking them, as when they flash on me in some pause of work. It is like the pursuit of happiness: you don't get it when you go after it, but let it alone and it comes to you."[26] The painting *Celia Thaxter in Her Garden* captures the brief moments when she paused in the garden, a classic contemplative feminine presence in an Edenic setting, but it does not tell us what she was really about in her little, old-fashioned patch of flowers. To Thaxter, the garden represented the opportunity to create a world, to engage in meaningful work, to bring her own talents to bear on nature's canvas.

The match between the garden setting on Appledore and landscape values of the period, coupled with Thaxter's ability to write in the voice of the intellectual elite, masked the class differences between herself and many of her admirers. Thaxter looked the part of a Victorian woman of leisure whose gardening activities supported her civility. Her success creating a domestic retreat, which resonated with the national attempt to design the essential American landscape, also suggested that women's expertise as cultivators of home gardens could serve more public purposes. Such blurring of the lines between home and business, hobby and profession helped a woman of the next generation launch a profitable career as a member of the new professional class of landscape architects.[27] With Beatrix Jones Farrand, women's amateur hobby of designing flower beds shifted into the professional world of the urban-based architectural firm. From an upper-class Philadelphia family, Farrand designed gardens for some of the wealthiest American households. Her work was done in close consultation with the women who were responsible for decorating the home and its grounds. Architects like Farrand and her wealthy clients, in turn, hired another group of entrepreneurial women to photograph the gardens they designed. Thus, by the turn of the century the business of greening America domestica offered new career paths for women.

Beatrix Jones Farrand was born in 1872 in New York City to wealthy, well-educated, and much-traveled parents. They were divorced before she was twelve. Schooled at home, she made many trips abroad with her mother and her paternal aunt, Edith Wharton, a skilled reader of the architectural landscape. Author of *Italian Villas and Their Gardens* (1910), which fed the American mania for gardens designed in this style, Wharton influenced her niece's later garden designs. Although a member of the social elite, Farrand's mother worked part-time as a literary agent for Wharton to earn some income. Beatrix was a strong-willed child who showed an early interest in landscape gardening and a determination to have a career. In 1892 she met Charles Sprague Sargent and his wife. Sargent was the founder and director of the Arnold Arboretum in Boston and an important figure in American horticulture. He encouraged Farrand to study landscape gardening.[28]

For the next several years Beatrix divided her time between botany at the arboretum and travel on the Continent. While in Boston, she stayed with the Sargents at their suburban estate, a typical country place famous for its naturalized grounds. During her trips abroad, she studied gardens and met with the English horticulturist, Gertrude Jekyll. Jekyll popularized the return of native materials and informal landscaping to the British garden, a style she adapted from vernacular cottage gardens. In 1895 Beatrix opened her first office on the top floor of her mother's house and began making landscape designs on commission. Initial work came from wealthy friends of the family, but as she became more prominent, her commissions spread to other rich families outside of her social circle. Marriage in 1913 to Max Farrand seemed not to interfere with her work. Beatrix Farrand had a long, profitable career, continuing her early residential projects and preparing landscape designs for private schools, universities, and churches. At the time of her death in 1959, she was one of the country's best-known landscape architects.[29]

Gender codes concerning women's appropriate role in the public sphere influenced Farrand's progress as a landscape designer and the careers of

FIGURE 27. *Gray Gardens, East Hampton, N.Y., the estate of Robert C. and Anna Gilman Hill. (Photograph by Mattie Edwards Hewitt (1929), Nassau County Museum, Hempstead, N.Y.)*

women who followed her into the profession. The symbolism binding women to a love and cultivation of plants was well established in the America of her youth. She once reported herself to be "the product of five generations of garden lovers," including a grandmother who owned an early espaliered fruit garden.[30] The last decade of the century saw the rise of the country place. Wealthy families retired to areas outside cities, some of a decidedly rural character, others in new, spacious suburban developments platted in lots of several acres. They hired architects to design houses based on a hodgepodge of styles viewed on their travels to the Continent. After decorating the interior and the grounds, the women of these upper-class homes wrote books about their adventures in the garden and had their gardens photographed. The photographs appeared in magazines like *House Beautiful* and in early coffee table books such as Louise Shelton's *Beautiful Gardens in America*.

Published first in 1914 and in an enlarged edition in 1924, Shelton's book included a cross section of country places. *Beautiful Gardens in America* documents the landscape tastes of the period and their spread across the country. It

FIGURE 28. *The Creeks, East Hampton, N.Y., the estate of Albert and Adele Herter.* (*Photograph by Frances Benjamin Johnston, Library of Congress, Washington, D.C.*)

also reveals women's key role in determining the garden aesthetic of the time. The "four garden experts" with whom Shelton consulted in the preparation of her book were female members of local garden clubs. Two had written gardening texts, one painted flowers, and one was a landscape architect.[31] Included among the book's showplaces were two Long Island estates, The Creeks, the home of artists Adele and Albert Herter, and Gray Gardens, the residence of Anna and Robert Hill (Figures 27, 28).

Adele Herter oversaw the planting of the acre of radiating flower beds lying in front of the house, as well as several other large flower beds on the property. Anna Hill detailed her involvement in the making of Gray Gardens in her own book of garden memoirs, *Forty Years of Gardening*, which includes a chapter on the family collection of garden books, begun by her grandmother, continued by her mother, and handed down to her. Hill noted that "in America we have many good men amateur gardeners who write, but for the most part it is the women who have worked in and loved their own gardens who have given us the greater number of the charming and practical garden books which are now on every library table."[32] Turn-of-the-century upper-class women clearly had taken up the challenge laid down fifty years earlier by Andrew Jackson Downing. They were the horticulturists of their estates, and they formed networks with others of their station to create a design standard for large country homes.

Although Downing, Olmsted, and Calvert Vaux were practicing the profession of landscape architecture in the nineteenth century, no schools offered training in the field until Harvard College and the Massachusetts Institute of Technology began the first degree programs in 1900, a year after the founding of the American Society of Landscape Architects. The combined history of women's roles as horticulturists and their surge into employment in the 1890s naturally raised the question of their suitability as members of this new profession. Beatrix Farrand seems to have been the early example whose success opened the profession to other women. Farrand matured as a landscape designer in the decade in which she was singular. Among the ten founding members of the Society of Landscape Architects, she was the only woman.

Her entrée into this masculine domain came through the expected role of a woman of her class. She began by designing private gardens for family friends. In the context of college-trained women's increased participation in certain professions (such as scientific illustration or home economics), Farrand's foray into landscape architecture was not particularly revolutionary. In fact, within a year of the opening of the landscape programs at Harvard and MIT, Mrs. Edward G. Low founded the Lowthorpe School of Landscape Architecture and Horticulture for Women in Groton, Massachusetts. By 1915 two other women's schools had opened, the Pennsylvania School of Horticulture for Women and the Cambridge School of Architectural and Landscape Design for Women. Each of these institutions emphasized women's strengths designing residential properties, particularly in making planting plans and working with plant material.[33] Female students were encouraged to view their careers through gender filters. A popular periodical of 1908 quoted a professor at MIT on women's horticultural talents: "A woman will *fuss* with a garden . . . in a way that no man will ever have the patience to do." Beatrix Farrand, the fingerpost for the next generation, believed "that for some time to come women's work will be almost entirely limited to that of a domestic character."[34]

Of the work done by women professionals in the early decades of the century, Farrand's has been studied the most. Her designs exemplify the match between certain aspects of women's role and aesthetic values expressed in the gardens of the period. In the country place, meant to seclude the family from the hustle and bustle of urban life, gardens were extensions of the interior of the house. Not only did designers check the view from windows, seeking to meld indoors and outdoors as Celia Thaxter did at Appledore, but they also conceived of the gardens closest to the house as outdoor rooms. Farrand built such rooms for her clients. One famous project, Dumbarton Oaks in Washington, D.C., home to the U.S. ambassador to Sweden, Robert Bliss, and his wife Mildred, was constructed as a series of increasingly less formal garden rooms, each with a gateway into the next, gradually leading away from the house and into larger, unwalled, naturalized spaces (Figure 29). As extensions of the house, such rooms were designed for use of the family and guests. Reminiscent of Thaxter's pleasure in the way her flowers complemented her guests' apparel, the Green Garden at Dumbarton Oaks was planted to serve as "background to the colors of dresses at the outdoor entertainments." The wives of Farrand's clients consulted closely with her. Mildred Bliss involved herself in every decision on the Dumbarton Oaks gardens and participated in planning the planting arrangement. The Abby Aldrich Rockefeller garden in Seal Harbor, Maine, was created to house Abby Rockefeller's collection of oriental sculpture. She made many suggestions on the color schemes and assumed full direction of the ongoing design from 1935 to 1945.[35]

Beyond such obvious conjunctions between woman's role as domesticator and the design of home gardens, other aspects of Farrand's approach reveal the mesh between expectations of her sex and landscape values of the period. Sargent had advised her to work within the constraints of the land in designing her plantings; this became one of Farrand's particular strengths. She was known as well for using only plants with which she was familiar, many of which were native. She preferred less showy types—her taste in roses, for example, tended toward the simpler varieties. A central theme in women's writings and illustrations of nature is just this regard for the more modest, least disruptive forms of landscape crafting. Farrand's interest in indigenous plants and natural materials was in part sparked by Gertrude Jekyll's celebration of simple cottage gardens. One of British and American women's major contributions to the landscape aesthetic of the period was their advocacy of the rustic over the sophisticated, the common over the exotic, the traditional over the modern.[36]

Although an excellent landscape architect, Farrand preferred being called a "landscape gardener." Successful garden designers, she wrote, "must know intimately the form and texture as well as the color of the plants" used. Unlike

FIGURE 29. *Dumbarton Oaks, Washington, D.C., the estate of Robert and Mildred Bliss (1932), designed by Beatrix Farrand. (Photograph courtesy of Dumbarton Oaks, Trustees for Harvard University)*

the architect who designed the house, oversaw its building, then went on to a new project, Farrand's sort of gardener stayed on to "fuss" with the organic designs she created. Farrand worked on Dumbarton Oaks for twenty years and at Seal Harbor for twenty-four; several other of her projects also entailed such extended commitment to the living canvases she created.[37] She concen-

FIGURE 30. *Landscape architect Marian Cruger Coffin (1876–1957), who designed gardens for wealthy eastern clients like the Fricks, Vanderbilts, and Du Ponts during the 1920s. (Winterthur Library: Winterthur Archives, Winterthur, Del.)*

trated on the spaces she created, finding more personal gratification in their nurture than her image as a career woman might suggest.

Following Farrand's lead, women landscape architects began to make their mark on the domestic horticultural tastes of the elites at the turn of the century. Their work appeared in popular periodicals like *House Beautiful*. Several produced popular books on landscape design. Ruth Dean's *The Livable House* (1917) and Martha Brookes Hutcheson's *The Spirit of the Garden* (1923) introduced amateurs to such technicalities as planning the grounds along an axis with the house, selecting hedges and foundation plantings, and designing an adequate turnaround for that new commuter's luxury item—the motor car. In Dean's book, photographs of various country places included the name of the landscape architect, advertising the work of these professionals and placing women on an even basis with men. By 1933 women had achieved prominence as garden designers; six members of the "Hall of Fame" listed in *House and Garden* were female (Figure 30).[38]

One could not, of course, rely on verbal descriptions to make the point about the design and placement of a pergola or a gate; visual evidence was much more effective. With the increase in women garden writers and architects, there also developed a cadre of women photographers who earned a portion of their income documenting famous gardens. Two of the most successful were Frances Benjamin Johnston and Mattie Edwards Hewitt. Johnston was a well-known documentary and portrait photographer before joining forces with Hewitt in 1909 to run a New York–based studio specializing in garden and architectural photography. From 1909 until 1917, when the partnership was dissolved, this studio produced numerous images of the homes and gardens of the very rich (see Figures 27, 28 above, and 31 below). A member of the Progressive Era reform-minded generation, Johnston used her camera to advocate better education and work and living conditions for the poor. She obtained her livelihood from her art. Johnston knew that more wealth in the country meant increased opportunities for women photographers. In an 1897 article on "What a Woman Can Do with a Camera," she advised taking up a photographic specialty. One of the specialties she had in mind required a wealthy clientele interested in documenting their possessions—as, for instance, in "outdoor pictures of babies, children, dogs and horses, and . . . country houses."[39] Women photographers earned a good living during the country place era doing just this kind of work. Others who figured prominently in garden photography were Jessie Tarbox Beals, Clara Sipprell, and Antoinette Perrett.[40]

These documentary photographers helped broadcast the new garden standards among members of the rising middle class who read popular magazines and books lauding the beauties of gardens on country estates.[41] Johnston's and Hewitt's photographs, along with those by Jessie Tarbox Beals, figure prominently in Louise Shelton's *Beautiful Gardens in America*. In perusing Shelton's book, the reader learns how to look at gardens. Although representing various styles—from very formal, Italianate places to remodeled farms grounded in a naturalistic landscape—the basic design principles are familiar. Revealing the Italian influence, the photographs emphasize the importance of the play of light and shadow over the garden. Also stressed are the proper placement of paths, flower beds, gates, and arches along well-designed and terminated axes; materials (both plants and garden architecture) that are compatible with the garden's design; and the complementary use of colors and textures, including Gertrude Jekyll's principles for modulated floral borders.[42] Overall, gardens are depicted as enclosed, private spaces evoking the seclu-

FIGURE 31. *Garden of the Misses Pyrne, East Hampton, N.Y., designed by Ellen Shipman. (Photograph by Mattie Edwards Hewitt (1924), Nassau County Museum, Hempstead, N.Y.)*

sion and intimacy of home (Figure 31). Such photographs not only document design, but also interpret the garden's meaning to the viewer.

These images appeared during a period of urban retreat by the upper and middle classes. Country estates and suburban properties reinforced the sense that the American character was sustained by immersion in nature. The country's moral fiber depended on having the time and space to cultivate a garden.[43] Marks of status accrued around large gardens displaying labor-intensive formal styles, including exotic plant material imported from Europe and from botanical surveys in the North American West and South America. Such gardens moved beyond Susan Cooper's simple celebration of native American plants over imports to suggest expanding dominance of the continent and the country's ability to re-create historical landscapes of Europe.[44]

For female gardeners, this public display of American imperialism was balanced by the private meaning of their gardens as landscapes defining traditional womanhood. The idealized garden of the respectable farm wife, filled with old-fashioned flowers, served as an especially attractive focal point in

FIGURE 32. *Frances Benjamin Johnston (1864–1952) photographed the grand country estates of wealthy clients, but this picture of her own house and garden in Washington, D.C., illustrates the constraints posed by the spaces of middle-class suburbs (ca. 1900). (Library of Congress, Washington, D.C.)*

many elite gardens, particularly when supported by the American embrace of Gertrude Jekyll's cottage garden style. When designers considered the appropriate garden for middle- and lower-class families, cottage gardens made of common imports and native plants suggested solutions to the cramped spaces of less affluent suburbanites.

Unlike Beatrix Farrand, who also lived in the sorts of country places she designed, Frances Benjamin Johnston came of more middle-class origins and resided in a comparatively unpretentious house. The garden of her home exemplified the problems faced by landscape designers when confronted with the dwellings of middle- and working-class people (Figure 32). Constrained by a small lot, the garden contained bits of the grand design in its rose beds with walks in between, arched side gate, and stretch of lawn. The long views of tall trees in the distance, so entrancing in the homes of the rich, were replaced by a scraggly specimen in the neighbor's yard. From this garden, and the small courtyard she made after retiring to her final home in New Orleans, Johnston sallied forth at the end of her career to give popular illustrated lectures on gardens and gardening. In 1920 she characterized her talks given during a western tour from Ohio to California: "My lectures appeal not only to garden clubs, but also to organizations fostering civic improvement, art and literary study, in that I endeavor to present the best sources of information on a wide range of subjects relating to gardens and flowers."[45]

In addition to their increased participation in the work force after 1890, women had also escalated their efforts to serve as caretakers of the poor and the weak through voluntary associations and clubs. Many gardeners viewed the new middle- and lower-class suburban developments with dismay, convinced that families living in flat, desolate, cramped spaces would lose their moral character. They also turned their attention to the living conditions of immigrants in the cities, tackling problems of insufficient sanitation, poor ventilation, and the lack of decent streets and parks. These were the audiences for Johnston's garden talks—women in garden clubs and city beautiful organizations who believed it was their domestic responsibility to improve the homes (and by extension, the character) of all classes of Americans through the development of plans for small gardens, well-laid out suburbs, and city parks.[46]

Designers of gardens for the middle class recognized that some of the most cherished landscapes of the day could not be transplanted to a backyard the size of Frances Benjamin Johnston's. Specifically, the gradual, outward progression from enclosed formal spaces, to a naturalized garden, to old woods or the ocean simply was not possible. The solution was to keep the sense of space through a stretch of lawn, and of enclosure through fencing, an arbor, shrubbery, and a rim of flower beds. Beatrix Farrand tried her hand at a plan for the middle-class suburban cottage in 1910 (Figure 33). Noting that the winding paths and informal plantings of the large estates would not work in a small lot, she designed a fairly formal yard for year-round use. In this case, the owners could create and maintain their garden at reasonable expense and effort. For the apartment-dwelling couple escaping the city to a house in a new development at the end of a streetcar line, plans such as Farrand's provided advice on what to do with their bare lot.[47] In addition to a general design, the new owners also received directions on plant selection and nurture. Dozens of popular books advised neophyte gardeners on the selection of trees, shrubs, and flowers for a successful outdoor room. Women were major contributors to this literature, directing their comments to other women. They understood that middle-class wives shouldered much of the

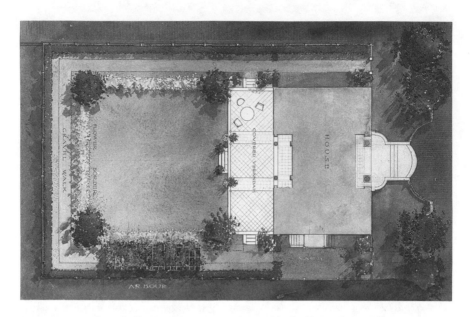

FIGURE 33. *Beatrix Farrand (1872–1959) attempted a design befitting the small yard in this "Plan for a Suburban Garden" (1910). (Documents Collection, College of Environmental Design, University of California, Berkeley)*

day-to-day responsibility for designing and maintaining ornamental gardens. In responding to requests from new suburban settlers for simple directions for cultivating ordinary, inexpensive gardens, garden writers couched their advice in explicitly gender-coded terms.[48]

Lena May McCauley's *The Joy of Gardens* (1911) describes the idealized audience for such garden books: "Woman first saw the light of day in a garden, and could she cherish the faith that 'in paradise a garden lies' what comfort could be hers! The suburban bride, settled in her new home, goes to town at the first sign that spring is on the way, bent upon investing in garden tools. The last snowbank has not retreated before the March sunshine, and you may see her going forth one of these fair mornings equipped with garden gloves, a hoe, and a rake."[49] McCauley imagined this modern woman, riding the streetcar confidently into town for tools, as a true daughter of Eve. Throughout her gardening book, she scattered images of a folk heritage behind the suburban woman's activities. Dandelions in the lawn reminded the gardener of colonial farm women gathering such plants for salads. McCauley assumed that suburban women tended old-fashioned gardens full of flowers. Reminiscent of Celia Thaxter's defense of the moral virtues attendant upon her necessarily humble garden, her modern suburbanite defends her modest garden from the elite fashions of the day. Resisting the sophistications of pergolas and sunken gardens, as well as the opinions of professional landscape designers and her husband, "the woman gardener, with a strain of feeling of the dandelion gatherer, takes her genuine comfort in the border of old-fashioned flowers. The flowers themselves are as curious and wayward as the folk of a country village, and their outlook on life just as illogical" (49).

Finally, just as the bird lovers of the late nineteenth century located lessons about gender roles in bird behavior, so the woman gardener cared for her garden as she cared for her family. The state of her garden mirrored the state of her home as a whole: "Many a floral tragedy is created, many a domestic failure precipitated, by putting off the day of preparation. Who blames flowers for giving up the ghost when they have been invited into the world to meet beds unready and to suffer for nutriment and water? Who wonders that household bliss fades away where there is neither cheer nor welcome?" (37) Although the new arrival on the fringes of the city may have been ignorant of nature, by applying her domestic heritage to the care of her grounds, she not only extended her field of endeavor but also remained true to woman's oldest history—as Eve in a newly created garden.

Louisa Yeomans King also encouraged middle-class women to resist impractical advice unsuited to the demands of their home life. King was one of the most prolific and well respected of the garden authors of the 1910s and 1920s. Having taken up ornamental gardening under the guiding hand of her mother-in-law, who had designed a famous garden in a Chicago suburb, King wrote many articles and books about her own two-acre grounds in Alma, Michigan. Although she wrote for the upper middle class from the rural seclusion of her country place, her books included garden plans for the middle and lower classes as well, those families lucky to have even a twenty-foot-wide, seventy-foot-deep lot. In *The Little Garden*, she offered specific suggestions for creating the secluded nook so favored by suburbanites of the period.

King deplored the landscapes fashioned by real estate developers, agreeing with Grace Tabor, another garden authority, that developers destroyed the privacies of home. "Commercial designers" tore down walls and fences to make expanses of open yard visible to potential buyers. King encouraged new suburbanites to enclose their backyards, keeping only gates.[50] This idea that a fine garden began in an enclosed space appeared throughout women's garden literature and was implemented in intimate, walled gardens on the expansive estates of the wealthy. In arguing for the return to such layouts in middle-class homes, King appealed not only to design aesthetics but also to the needs of mothers: "fancy the freedom from care of the mother of young children, whose garden is enclosed by a wall. What freedom, as compared with the present, when children spill over the landscape in a way both inconsequent and dangerous" (27).

In planning for the suburban landscape, garden writers had to grapple with setting in a way completely different from what Celia Thaxter experienced on her undeveloped island or Beatrix Farrand encountered in designing a country place. Until books like King's, American gardening was assumed to be done in a semirural space in which a primary concern was to plan for the long view through formal gardens and out to an old native landscape of timber or rocky cliffs. With the development of the suburban lot, the design had to concentrate on enclosure, on fooling the eye into believing that a lot seventy feet deep contained the long vista. Walls served many functions; against them one could plant tall trees and shrubs, mimicking the old woods surrounding Susan Cooper's residence. A lawn leading to a view of these plantings gave the feeling of space found in the rolling greens of the country estate. Fruits and vegetables reminded one that indeed this was the country, that on the urban fringe one returned to rural life. Flower beds bespoke leisure and merged indoors with outdoors. Finally, the plant material itself should consist mostly of common flora, much of it available in low-cost seed packets, inexpensive to maintain, and often conveying an old-fashioned image.[51]

Families moved to the fringes of cities and beyond seeking connection to that expansive landscape at the edges of the country place photographs. Farrand's watercolor of her garden plan for a 1910 middle-class home provides a good example of the typical image of suburban life. The lot might be small, but nature, not other homes, surrounded it (Figure 34).[52] In reality, as the photograph of Frances Benjamin Johnston's home shows, such lots rapidly took on a residential character (Figure 32). This did not mean, however, that the garden lost its connection to the native landscape so valued by Susan Cooper. Those lucky enough to live close to untouched stretches of woods collected wildflowers and shrubs for transplanting.[53] Others relied on their local nurseries or seed catalogs for native materials. Through such sources, women located both native plants and imported varieties adapted to their climate. Louise Wilder, for example, wrote of her success with newly available wildflowers from the Rocky Mountains, and Louisa King lauded a garden in southern California designed around plants native to New Mexico.[54]

The architect of the San Diegan garden praised by King was one of the

FIGURE 34. *Beatrix Farrand's watercolor of her "Plan for a Suburban Garden," which exemplifies the romantic view of the open spaces supposedly surrounding the middle-class suburban home. (Documents Collection, College of Environmental Design, University of California, Berkeley)*

most famous nurserywomen of the early twentieth century. Kate Olivia Sessions represented the horticultural professional who was available to assist the middle-class, suburban gardener of the time. Families moving into rapidly developing residential areas across the country looked not to landscape architects as much as to the local nursery owner to help them design and plant their grounds. While some women were breaking into the field of landscape architecture, others were opening floral shops and plant outlets. Sessions earned fame through her commitment to gardening within terms established by the regional environment, creating landscapes from plants adapted to the southern California climate, as in the Aloe Garden designed in her honor in Balboa Park (Figure 35). She collected and popularized California natives like the Matilija poppy (*Romneya coulteri*) and the San Diego lilac (*Ceanothus cyaneus*) and tested eucalyptus, bougainvillea, aloe, and other succulents, encouraging her patrons to try these plants in their gardens. Sessions was the leading plant dealer in San Diego during the city's explosive growth at the turn of the century; her biographers report that hardly any home owner landscaped her yard without the advice and plants of Kate Sessions.[55]

A member of the same generation as Agnes Chase and Anna Comstock, Kate Sessions never married, earned a Ph.D. in science at the University

FIGURE 35. *The Kate O. Sessions Agave and Aloe Garden in Balboa Park, San Diego, Calif., which was established in 1935 to honor her for the many plants she introduced to southern California. (San Diego Historical Society, Ticor Collection, San Diego, Calif.)*

of California, Berkeley, in 1881 and devoted her life to the propagation of plants suitable for the southern California landscape. Although formal portraits present her as a properly attired, passive lady, residents of San Diego knew her as shabbily dressed, energetic, aggressive, and deeply involved in designing both the private and public gardens of San Diego (Figure 36). Early in her career, she gave up the attire of the middle-class woman for men's boots and practical gardening clothes, preferring to be driven around town in a truck. Reportedly, she never learned to drive because she wanted her eyes free to monitor the gardens of the city.[56] Sessions played a very public role in San Diego. For many years she published a regular gardening column in the local newspaper and in the journal *California Garden*. Serving as official "City Gardener," she yearly planted one hundred trees in Balboa Park, transforming it from a piece of urban fringe land into a fine park that is now one of San Diego's scenic attractions. She was also one of the founding members of the San Diego Floral Association and initiated Arbor Day celebrations in the city.

Sessions cherished her friendships with other women interested in horticulture and native plants. At the turn of the century, California boasted many women whose work created the contemporary landscape of the state. As well as their contribution to residential ornamental gardening, they were leaders in fruit farming and in botanizing among the native plants of the region. One of Sessions's close friends was Alice Eastwood, another single career woman, who served for many years as curator of botany at the California Academy of Sciences. Sessions once wrote to Eastwood that "our friendship developed through flowers—our children, which I am growing and you are naming."[57] Interested in preserving the wealth of native plants and in encouraging the importation of new species suitable to the region, such women were the gardening counterpart of the botanical illustrators in Washington, D.C., whose drawings of wildflowers and promising fruits helped create the green landscapes of twentieth-century America.

Early in the century, American women established a nationwide gardening network. Such collaboration explains Louisa King's familiarity with Kate Sessions's work. Louise Shelton's book emphasized the gardens of the Northeast, but she also offered glimpses of those in the South, Midwest, and West, concluding with a brief section on new gardens in Alaska. The garden club movement began in 1891 with the formation of the Ladies Garden Club of Athens, Georgia. By 1913 the burgeoning popularity of regionally based groups resulted in a national organization, the Garden Club of America. In 1929 the National Council of State Garden Clubs was founded.[58] Women

FIGURE 36. *Kate O. Sessions (1857–1940).*
*(San Diego Historical Society, Ticor Collection, San Diego, Calif.)*

in any reasonably sized town, in the suburbs ringing large cities, and on farms found a common bond in their love of gardens and their interest in sharing knowledge and plant material. Arbor Day was a favorite holiday for women's clubs; members turned out to plant trees along streets in both new and old communities. The Mesquite Club of Las Vegas, Nevada, for instance, earned a place in history by arranging the planting of more than two thousand shade trees in one day. Membership in such clubs, particularly those in remote suburban areas and small towns, included both city-based and farming representatives.[59] This national network, interested in both native plants and introduced species, helped expand the varieties of plants women grew in their gardens. Flower beds contained natives from all over the continent, as well as newly imported or hybridized exotics from Europe and Asia.

That their gardens contained the world suggests one reason for the ease with which women of these decades involved themselves in decisions about the public green spaces of the suburban train station, the city park, and the housing project. As Susan Fenimore Cooper had flung the net of home widely across the native landscape of Otsego, so too women gardeners felt a domestic responsibility for ensuring that their green world was protected and extended throughout the country. Middle-class women retiring to the outskirts of town often found their landscape rapidly encircled by the city. Lena McCauley perfectly described the force driving suburbanites into activist, progressive reform movements centered around control of urban expansion. Finding that she has begun gardening a bit too early in the season, McCauley's "suburban bride" "leans on her rake . . . and looks abroad up and down the road to find what the rest of the world is about . . . Far down the road a cock crows lustily . . . Led by his call, the woman looks in the distance. What is it that hides the grove since last she looked that way . . . The woman sighs; she might have known that the billboard fiend had made his plans and stolen a march on suburban beauty" (20–21). Local garden clubs wielded group power as suburban wives organized to beautify the roadways, train stations, and shopping centers of emerging residential areas.

Women of the Progressive Era were not alone in their interest in improved plans for landscape development; men's civic organizations also committed time and money to the beautification movement engendered by J. Horace McFarland at the end of the nineteenth century. But men recognized that women could build local consensus for civic improvement projects and encouraged their participation. While nineteenth-century female volunteer associations played a role in many women's shift from passive observers to concerned activists, another key was their sense of responsibility for protecting and developing green spaces of home and neighborhood. McCauley's suburbanite defended the roadside from "billboard fiends" as she defended her garden plants from slugs, pursuing both tasks with equal vigor.[60]

Although they escaped the city, middle-class suburban women of the period did not shed the tenets of domestic feminism. Women's organizations worked to improve living conditions for all families, including those unable to leave the urban core. Women took on the job of creating green landscapes in the city as part of their role as "municipal housekeepers." Agreeing with the Olmsteds and McFarlands of their time that green spaces were the lungs of the city and supported the moral virtue of its residents, women worked assiduously to make gardens in urban areas. Much current thinking on the Progressive Era addresses the top-down approach taken by many middle-class reformers, who believed that a rational restructuring of lower-class life could create a homogeneous American population. Some of the push to create well-designed gardens and parks in the inner city was a product of such thinking.[61] Louisa King's prescriptions for a well-organized suburban yard, based as they were on upper-class landscape preferences, sometimes smack of the reformist approach. The gardening elite's belief that every American woman, no matter what her status, naturally enjoyed plants masked these class divisions. By the turn of the century, amateur gardening had become popular, supporting garden tastemakers' impression that the entire population wanted a little plot to beautify. Such widespread interest in plants was linked to the elevating experience of democracy. One of the best handbooks for urbanites of moderate means was Frances Duncan's *The Joyous Art of Gardening*. Duncan expressed a generally agreed-upon assumption when she asserted: "No passion is more democratic than that of love for a garden . . . The passion for a garden . . . and the joy of making one may exist alike in millionaire and washer-woman."[62]

In her book Duncan included practical suggestions for creating privacy in small yards, for gardening on the roofs of city houses, and for making easily maintained gardens. Recognizing that the woman of the household would most likely design and nurture the garden, she discussed female needs for certain spaces, spending a good deal of time on such issues as screening the clothesline and creating cool arbors in which to do the weekly wash (Figure 37). Citing Celia Thaxter throughout her work, Duncan preferred the vernacular, the old-fashioned garden. Its primary qualities were enclosure; hints of the kitchen-garden tradition in herbs, vegetables, and fruits; a mixture of common imports and native plants easily grown from seed; and design sim-

FIGURE 37. *"A Shaded Walk from the Kitchen to the Vegetable Garden,"* *illustrated for Frances Duncan's* The Joyous Art of Gardening *(1917). (Reprinted by permission of Charles Scribner's Sons, an imprint of Macmillan Publishing Co.)*

plicity. The virtue of such an aesthetic was its applicability across the classes. Such gardens could be developed in one of the outdoor rooms on a wealthy estate, in the rustic seclusion of a middle-class suburb bordering on the country, on small lots in streetcar suburbs, or in cramped spaces outside urban row houses. By the turn of the century, this garden bore the same symbolic meaning among garden tastemakers as the mingled wild and agricultural landscape had for Susan Cooper and her compatriots. The old-fashioned garden typified the mix of native and cultivated flora seen as the essential American landscape.[63]

Such belief in the universal efficacy of plants and plant care in supporting the American character led to the extension of private garden values into civic spaces. Progressive Era women created small parks and playgrounds for use by women and children living in tenements.[64] Such efforts by garden club members were matched by at least one professional landscape architect of the 1920s and 1930s. Marjorie Sewell Cautley worked with Clarence Stein and Henry Wright on the plans for Phipps Garden Apartments, Sunnyside Gardens, and Radburn in New Jersey. Inheritors of the English Garden City tradition, this team designed low-cost urban housing with room for suburb-like green spaces, aiming to re-create the sense of privacy and enclosure found in upper- and middle-class homes of the suburbs and the country.

The Garden City movement has been criticized for its authoritarian approach and class bias. Like Progressive Era garden writers, its proponents were convinced that all Americans, regardless of their station, wanted to live close to nature. Although plans for the projects reflected dominant landscape design values, they also left much room for tenants to express their own planting preferences. Cautley devised a landscape suggesting the sense of space and freedom of movement found in turn-of-the-century photographs of country places.[65] In an article on her planting designs for Radburn, she encouraged visitors to see the place through a walking tour. From the living room, a guest stepped out onto a small lawn and garden "with tall growing shrubs for privacy between porches and windows, with hedges staggered along property lines so each owner might enjoy his share of blossoms, with trees that will give shade when mature, and with vines for shady and sunny locations."[66] Although these private spaces were partially planted for the owners, there were no restrictions on what might be grown. Cautley reported that residents enjoyed maintaining their private yards (29). Her imaginary visitor looked across this personalized outdoor room to a sweeping park inviting a saunter along winding paths among "clumps of birch, viburnum, shrubby dogwood, wild azalea, sweetfern, and highbush blueberry . . . [transplanted] from the neighboring woods" (24).

Although Cautley was a professionally trained landscape architect who designed spaces for the masses in keeping with elite values, her comments on Radburn suggest that she believed in the average person's attachment to American flora and ability to work out her own plant designs. This conviction informed *Garden Design*, her popular guide to the basic principles of good gardening practice. The book includes much information for the urban resident who shared a bit of green space with apartment-dwelling neighbors, including layouts and plantings tolerant of city conditions. Cautley implicitly regarded gardening as women's work. In *Garden Design* she reminded her readers that, as one would not select the buttons before the dress pattern, neither should the gardener buy flowers before deciding the style of the garden.[67] Thus, women who worked on city gardens often depicted the outdoors as an extension of home, encompassing, as it had for Susan Cooper, a green landscape of familiar native and imported plants. Distinct from expansive city parks, which served as the poor family's weekend escape from home, landscapes like Cautley's were intended for daily use, supporting the centering of family life in the environment but near the front door.

Unlike the Rockefellers, the Hills, and the Herters, women of the lower classes were not often pictured in their gardens describing the aesthetic informing their activity. Critics of Progressive Era reforms suggest that upperclass elites denied less affluent classes the right to determine their own culture. Certainly, the landscape architects and garden designers considered here never report consulting middle- and lower-class clientele about their plant preferences. No doubt, discouraging remarks about the unsuitability of an Italian garden to a small suburban lot serve as class markers for the elite. While not disagreeing with such interpretations, I have argued that changing tastes in garden styles, coupled with women's tendency to read gender codes into plant preferences, led influential garden designers to favor the vernacular garden. Female regard for the old-fashioned garden appears in influential garden literature as a common bond among all women. Such reading raises questions about the gardens of the "common" class of women. Only recently, through the efforts of folklorists and a new breed of landscape architects and urban historians, are the plant preferences of nonelites entering garden history. Although this material is still preliminary, it suggests that there is some truth to Duncan's assertion that a love of gardening pervades women's culture.

Susan Fenimore Cooper assumed that rural farm women had valuable botanical knowledge. Among such women, she located the understanding of both simple flowers and native plants so important to rising American culture. Elizabeth Lawrence's correspondence with rural southern gardeners one hundred years after Cooper's visits to New York farmsteads supports Cooper's perception. Rural women conserved the old gardens and old values of mothers, grandmothers, and great-grandmothers. While many upper-class women remade the American landscape in the style of Italian gardens, they also valued vernacular gardens and formed bonds with the less wealthy women who made them.

In women like Lucy Stamps, whose letter to Elizabeth Lawrence introduced this chapter, Lawrence found a representative of her favorite sort of gardener: "I like to think about the hard-working farm women who are never too tired, when their farm work is done, to cultivate their flower gardens. They always find time to gather seeds, to dig and pack plants, and to send them off with friendly letters . . . Reading the flower lists is like reading poetry, for the flowers are called by their sweet country names, many of them belonging to Shakespeare and the Bible" (36). As she read southern market bulletins and corresponded with individuals offering local plants for sale or trade, Lawrence realized that she had struck a vein of women's culture. *Gardening for Love*, her description of the correspondence, richly documents the meaning of plants to rural American women and the power these individuals held in making the landscapes of their homes and of a region (Figure 38).

Lawrence's correspondents dealt in "old timey" plants, which were not available in the fancy, often expensive, garden catalogs of the mid-twentieth century.[68] Shrubs and flowers of mother's and grandmother's gardens represented continuing family history. Miss Bessie Bloodworth, of Currie, East (North) Carolina, sold various plants, including one called "turkey-gobbler beads" that came from her grandmother's garden. Lawrence, who was well-trained in botany, identified the plant as Indian currant (*Symphoricarpos orbiculatus*), an American native. Other plants established connections among women of different regions in the South, creating letter-writing friendships that continued over the years. As Lawrence participated in this network, she became involved in the women's family life, hearing of illness, economic difficulties, and children's triumphs; she worried when a correspondent stopped advertising or writing (76).

Interested in tracing regional variations in the naming of popular plants, Lawrence cataloged women's confident christenings: "Love-entangled is an old name for nigella or love-in-a-mist, but as often happens when old names linger, the farm women have transferred it to another plant. Love-tangle vine is their name for Kenilworth ivy, an old favorite for hanging baskets" (76). In addition to the personal and local history contained in the rural gardens, Lawrence found that the oral tradition had preserved plant lore abandoned when medieval herbal knowledge was replaced by scientific plant classification: "In the sixteenth century Paracelsus praised lemon balm (*Melissa officinalis*) as a renewer or restorer of youth. Some of the women who advertise it in the market bulletins make the same claim exactly, causing me to wonder by what precise chain the old herbal wisdom has passed down to the rural South. If it does not renew my youth, at least for the moment it lifts my spirits" (67).

Lawrence's correspondence reveals how networks developed among gardening women of differing classes. In her comments on what she learned from her correspondents, Lawrence stressed the value of their knowledge and their work. By the 1960s and 1970s, such women had become a major source of native wildflowers that were rapidly disappearing from the regional land-

FIGURE 38. *Elizabeth Lawrence (1904–85) in her Raleigh, North Carolina, garden. (Archives, Northwestern State University of Louisiana, Natchitoches. Courtesy of Warren W. Way III.)*

scape. Influential gardeners like Lawrence and her Louisiana colleague, Caroline Dormon, encouraged the preservation and propagation of such plants.[69] Rural women in isolated areas of the South taught them much about the natives. One of Lawrence's favorite correspondents was Rosa Violet Hicks, who lived deep in the mountains on the North Carolina–Tennessee border. Hicks supplied Lawrence with many native plants and appears in *Gardening for Love* as an authority on the wildflowers of the region (97–98). She and the other rural women were Lawrence's colleagues, partners, and friends, sharing a common set of values about what plants should be grown on the land. Possessing her correspondents' appreciation of vernacular gardens that reflected local and family history, Lawrence passed on these values to a wider audience through a regular column in the *Charlotte Observer* and through her gardening books. Eminently practical and modest in her own garden values, Lawrence once wrote: "I am not interested in having something no one else can grow. I am not writing for those who want to be told how to grow rare and difficult plants, but for those who want to grow a variety of plants in an average garden, giving them a reasonable amount of care and spending a reasonable amount of intelligence upon them."[70]

Lawrence described the rural South. The current literature indicates that African Americans and Euro-Americans in the South share some gardening preferences. Women—black and white—often are responsible for designing and maintaining the yard and its ornamental garden. Richard Westmacott's study of traditional black gardens in rural Georgia, for example, identifies such similar styles as dependence on home-grown plants rather than store-bought specimens and maintenance of swept yards. African Americans also make distinctive gardens, preferring self-seeding, ornamental flowers over the shrubs they say are more commonly found in white, middle-class yards. Slave women had scant opportunity to make their own gardens, but Westmacott's study suggests that by the turn of the century, African Americans were using the yard as an outdoor room. By the 1930s, when Farm Security Administration photographers began to document rural life-styles, black women engaged in ornamental gardening, defining a folk style that continues to the present (Figure 39). Ellen Bolton, of Oglethorpe County, Georgia, describes both the design and her love of the traditional garden: "Always we had a big area to sweep. We had a whole big area, two big beautiful oak trees. And on around the trees we put rocks, make beds. Had all these flowers around the sides. Zinnias, marigolds, four-o'clocks."[71] Rural African American women, in the

FIGURE 39. *"General Took's Old Home," near Montezuma, Ga. (Farm Security Admin-istration photograph by Marion Post Walcott, May 1939, Library of Congress, Washington, D.C.)*

tradition of their mothers and grandmothers, make their yards into outdoor spaces for carrying on family and community life.

The vernacular gardens of home carry meanings that refute much of the top-down literature on the need for green spaces in urban areas. This material, written by landscape professionals, focuses heavily on design while slighting plant material. For Lawrence and her network of plant-trading correspondents, a garden was not about passive viewing or even recreational use—the two primary goals of urban park planners. American park planning has emphasized the necessity of a professional landscape architect to set the terms upon which humans and land will interact.[72] Like Childe Hassam, who depicted Celia Thaxter as a passive observer in her own garden, park planners often have assumed that the consumer will be uninvolved in either the design or the planting of the public spaces she visits.

Although American cities began reserving space for community vegetable gardens in the nineteenth century, such space was usually planned and controlled by bureaucratic elites for inner city dwellers. As Sam Bass Warner and others have shown, a new type of "garden politics" arose out of the civil rights movement of the 1960s with the availability of vacant urban land. Interracial coalitions of long-term inner city residents and newcomers from the suburbs formed to take control of these abandoned places and build community-designed public gardens.[73] While many of these gardens are used to grow vegetables for local consumption, others contain ornamental plants. Warner's interviews with the founders of community gardens in Boston reveal that the meanings of these urban gardens are much the same as those communicated by Lawrence's southern correspondents and Westmacott's rural Georgia African American informants: a sense of connection with family history and traditions and the creation of a network of friends who develop the land together.[74] Plants in the urban vegetable gardens of African American, Anglo-Irish, Italian, Chinese, and Hispanic families tell a cultural history as surely as the plants southern rural women traded in the market bulletins. Community-designed recreational space stresses indigenous and recycled materials and flexible patterns of use, rather than the overcontrolled, formal spaces of classic contemporary park design.[75] Urban community gardeners look at their handiwork and see land they have nurtured and marked with their own history: "We've left something of ourselves here. When you've planted a garden, you've left something permanent. They can't take that away from you—no matter what, short of digging up the land . . . even if nobody tended this garden for years, something would remain here, something would still be growing here that we had something to do with. And you could come back here and look at it and smile"[76] (Figure 40).

Women's role in the making of community gardens crosses boundaries of class, race, and ethnicity. Progressive Era garden club reformers may have been primarily white women of the upper and middle classes, but the wave of urban activists of the 1960s, 1970s, and 1980s included a significant proportion of African American and Hispanic women. Social histories of the move to reclaim urban space for garden use by inner city residents have documented women's crucial role. In addition to actually remaking the land, women often have led politically powerful community groups that negotiated with city governments, federal funding agencies, and private land developers for the control of vacant lands and neighborhood parks.[77] Reflecting the legacy of the city beautification movements of the twenties and thirties, middle-class women have continued to work on the preservation and creation of urban green spaces. One of the most visible inheritors of Progressive women's gardening

FIGURE 40. *Mattie Davenport and Rose Braud, urban gardeners in Boston, Mass. (Photograph by Hansi Durlach, courtesy of the artist)*

traditions is Lady Bird Johnson, who in the 1960s revived the city beautification movement in Washington, D.C., and across the country. Through her efforts, not only were the public parks of the nation's capital expanded and renovated, but also community groups in the black areas of Washington began to develop residential gardens in the inner city.[78] Some inner city women involved in such old-style beautification programs have become leaders in new efforts to gain local control of garden and park spaces.[79]

In the 1990s, women continue to produce garden autobiographies and gardening handbooks, to join garden clubs working for civic improvement, and to operate nurseries and catalog businesses, including those dealing in native plant propagation.[80] A visit to the annual plant sale of a local garden club reveals the vitality of women's continued interest in working with plant material. Following the decline of the country place, women landscape architects lost their prominence as professional designers. The women's schools closed in the 1940s and, after World War II, landscape architecture was taken over by government contracts and large corporate offices. Such institutions tended to exclude women except at the clerical level. Although some, like Elizabeth Lawrence, earned a living by taking on middle-class residential design work in addition to writing newspaper columns and books, landscape architecture became for a time a male-dominated profession.[81]

One historian of the modern, or international, period of landscape design describes it as "efficient, top down, power oriented, big, specialized, clean-edged, inflexible, impersonal and anonymous." A foremost practitioner and historian of this style once dismissed Gertrude Jekyll's innovations in modulated color as the feeble attempts of an "amateur artist," skilled at plant knowledge but not design. Gardens, he opined, would have been better served without this attention to color and with more emphasis on form. In fact, he suggested that Monet was a better gardener than Jekyll. Thus, he returned woman to her proper place as the passive lady posing for the active (male) painter.[82]

Women garden makers brought a set of values—many of them connected to the domestic role—to their work as professionals. When those values meshed, as they did during the Progressive Era, with broad social trends, women worked in the mainstream. When the gap between women's plant preferences and elite garden styles widened, as it did between 1930 and 1970, their influence shifted to the periphery. The gender codes initially opening the door to professional landscape work for women also led to their specialization in areas stressing familiarity with plant material and collaborative projects. Beatrix Farrand sensed this when she insisted on the professional title of "designer" rather than "architect," a distinction later echoed by Elizabeth Lawrence in her own dislike of the appellation "landscape architect."[83] The gardens that women professionals made for specific people or groups were meant to express individual preferences and the unique qualities of the physical and biophysical geography of local sites. Materials were not universal but regional; twenty-year commitments to an ever-changing, flexible plan certainly were not efficient.

By the 1970s, partially in response to the return of women to many areas of professional training and partially in response to increased interest in community-responsive landscape planning and the conservation of natural resources, female landscape architects reappeared as important voices in a new school of landscape architecture.[84] Anne Whiston Spirn is an authority on the redesign of cities based on new knowledge about the ecology of urban spaces. Her *The Granite Garden: Urban Nature and Human Design* offers a design for healthy city environments with sufficient plant material for clean air, water, and soil. *The Granite Garden* is very much a postmodernist book emphasizing regional designs, acknowledging the physical limitations of the land on which a city is built, and encouraging cultivation of plant material adapted to the particular place. Suitable plants include both native species and the imported "urban weeds" sprouting on abandoned land in the inner city.

Combining both a conservationist and a community-based aesthetic, Spirn argues for the direct involvement of local residents in designing and maintaining public and private green spaces in the city.[85] Rejecting abstract, aesthetic principles, and respecting the requirements of the green world, she contends: "The city must be recognized as part of nature and designed accordingly. The city, the suburbs, and the countryside must be viewed as a single, evolving system within nature, as must every individual park and building within that larger whole. The social value of nature must be recognized and its power harnessed, rather than resisted. Nature in a city must be cultivated, like a garden, rather than ignored or subdued."[86] Using garden imagery to paint an ecological picture of interdependence, Spirn states a fact long recognized by women gardeners: the little enclosure by the side of the farmstead, in the swept yard, at the rear of the suburban lot, or on the roof of the urban apartment is a model of the whole landscape. The woman who knows how to create a successful green space within those garden walls has a powerful knowledge and the responsibility to use her skills in making the wider landscape an appropriate home.

By the time Celia Thaxter published *An Island Garden* in 1894, American women had made significant contributions to the literature and art of nature appreciation and conservation. They were not, however, given much credence as creators of the landscape. Childe Hassam's painting of a meditative Thaxter in an Edenic garden mirrored Andrew Jackson Downing's image of American women as consumers rather than producers of the floral environment. Thaxter's garden autobiography revised the passive image to suggest that, as well as making the interior of the home restful and healthy, women should create domestic spaces outdoors. Given the 1890–1920 surge of women into employment sectors focusing on the improvement of homes, it was not surprising that a network of residential landscape designers was established, or that the municipal housekeepers working to reform city environments included the design of neighborhood green spaces in their efforts. When Lena McCauley's suburban bride noticed a billboard encroaching on her rural seclusion, it fit the conservationist image for her to organize the local garden club to control the spread of such urban blight into the landscapes of home.

In all these cases, women's contributions went unnoticed as creative modes of shaping the land because they were conservative, centered around home and family, and consistent with broad-based visions of women's proper role. One can read the cumulative history of such activities as a record of failure: these women applied restrictive gender codes to their gardening efforts and continued to locate the virtues of America in an outdated image of rural seclusion, disappearing even as Susan Fenimore Cooper was composing *Rural Hours*. Yet such a reading denies the accomplishments of women gardeners working within the terms of the landscape and the meanings they located in the act of gardening. Because turn-of-the-century women garden writers celebrated the green landscape did not mean they shared the city antipathies of many nineteenth-century women. Much of what they missed in city spaces was the family history contained in vernacular gardens. When suburban writers like Frances Duncan faced the challenge of city garden design, they urged urban residents to make green spaces suit their lives. As Anne Spirn wisely notes, the point is to cultivate nature in whatever space and under whatever conditions are available.

Because so much of women gardeners' publicly recognized work in urban and suburban areas was associated with the upper-class country place and city beautification movements, it has been trivialized as mere icing, leaving a myriad of problems that remain unaddressed. William Whyte is one of the few contemporary commentators to note the implicit sexism in much commentary on garden clubs: "if 'garden-club ladies' are cited, the reference is clearly pejorative."[87] Although women's contribution to the making of green landscapes in America meshed with domestic roles, by the late twentieth century many of the values consistent with such gender codes have taken on renewed relevance in the broader culture. Urban planning is now based on the local, participatory model, and landscape history searches for continuing traditions in ethnically diverse folk gardens. Women's work as gardeners, conserving the green spaces of private homes and public landscapes through an exertion of will, paved the way for their aggressive involvement in the environmental movements of today.

# 5

## Nature's Advocates
### *Rachel Carson and Her Colleagues*

*There was a strange stillness. The birds, for example—where had they gone? Many people spoke of them, puzzled and disturbed. The feeding stations in the backyards were deserted. The few birds seen anywhere were moribund; they trembled violently and could not fly. It was a spring without voices. On the mornings that had once throbbed with the dawn chorus of robins, catbirds, doves, jays, wrens, and scores of other bird voices there was now no sound; only silence lay over the fields and woods and marsh.*

—Rachel Carson, Silent Spring

I N *Forty Years of Gardening*, Anna Hill described the formation of one of the early garden clubs of Philadelphia; its aims were "to study gardening as a fine art, to protect birds and wildflowers and to encourage civic planting."[1] Many nineteenth- and twentieth-century garden writers emphasized the importance of planting native flowers and attracting local birds into suburban gardens; they also worked to preserve public spaces for wildflowers and wildlife. Carolyn Merchant has documented the broad mix of women's clubs coalescing during the Progressive Era to protect forests, waterways, and birds.[2] In addition to such traditional preservationist activities, some women of the late nineteenth and early twentieth centuries advocated decent treatment for domestic and wild animals. Women who worked for the passage of bird protection laws battled their sisters' predilection for wearing feathers on their hats and decried the death and disruption of bird families by unprincipled hunters.[3] During this period, women were influential in the founding and spread of animal rights movements in both England and America. Although initially focused on laboratory animals, American advocates also fought for humane treatment in zoos and wildlife sanctuaries.[4]

These efforts meshed seamlessly with women's social roles. Merchant locates Progressive Era women's commitment to conservation in their image as conservators of home and family. Yet, for all their visible leadership in conservation circles in the late 1800s, women's influence on national initiatives dwindled in the early 1900s. During these decades, the progressive movement spawned a new generation of technical professionals who were trained to manage nature efficiently. Emerging careers in forestry and waterpower engineering were controlled by men. Women came to be viewed as amateur enthusiasts and propagandists while men carried on the work of wilderness and wildlife administration. Although some regional club women spoke in favor of increasingly popular schemes for managing natural resources, most women's organizations supported old-style naturalists, like John Muir, who were themselves at odds with the narrowing goals of early twentieth-century conservation. As women landscape architects lost ground between 1930 and 1960, so did women's leadership of the national conservation agenda.[5]

The middle decades of the twentieth century have been described as some of the most rabidly restrictive in American women's history. From the depression to the 1960s, the ideological separation of roles was perhaps more rigid than that of the mid-nineteenth century. Men dominated the public sphere, the stage where intellect and rationality constructed society. Home was a place of retreat from activity, a static zone in a landscape of endless change: "Woman's home function was 'expressive' in nature; it called forth her aptitude for divining personal needs, supplying emotional support, and monitoring interpersonal relationships. The new family system dictated that women socialize children but leave their education to schools, and soothe weary husbands but never interfere in their business affairs."[6] Though more women than ever worked during these years, their jobs were perceived to be secondary to their role as homemaker. Ideology also affected the work women could do. Reflecting ideas about women's crucial role in the home, their participation in the professions declined relative to the turn of the century. Most were pigeonholed into such traditional female vocations as teaching, librarianship, and home economics.[7]

Although still a space separate from urban battles, home no longer settled on the edge of the native landscape that had allowed Susan Fenimore Cooper so much freedom. Trapped in burgeoning suburbs, middle-class women planted symbolic pansies in yards where squirrels and robins made up the wildlife. Such women appeared to have nothing very important to say about the redesign of cities or the preservation of game on nature preserves. In environmental history, the 1930s to the 1950s were dominated by wildlife management efforts, with sporting interests controlling the political agenda. Although sporthunting was dwindling, the connection between conservation and commercial hunting interests made some women uncomfortable.[8] Coupled with the conservationist emphasis on scientific game management, the City Beautiful movements of the early Progressive Era were replaced by the "city practical," whose design lay in the hands of professionally trained architects and engineers. Garden club appeals for the preservation of local plants and birds were described as nothing more than trivial concerns with "frills and furbelows."[9]

The record of Lady Bird Johnson's city beautification campaigns during the 1960s demonstrates the ideological climate. Johnson had a long-standing love of gardening and shared many garden club women's concerns about some forms of environmental pollution. She found an ally in Secretary of the Interior Stuart Udall, whose 1963 book, *The Quiet Crisis*, documented widespread environmental blight. In addition to their fears about the pollution of air and water, Udall, Johnson, and other conservationists were appalled by the trashing of the landscape with superhighways, billboards, and litter.[10] With the encouragement of his wife and Udall, Lyndon Johnson formed the Task Force on Natural Beauty in July 1964. Following the task force's recommendation that the government act to preserve and develop the "natural beauty" of America, Lady Bird launched a national City Beautiful agenda. Recognizing the negative feminine undertones of a "beautification" campaign, she cast about for the right image. Noting that beautification sounded "cosmetic and trivial and it's prissy," she echoed her male supporters' reluctance to involve themselves in something that had a "feminine aura" to it. In his study of Lady Bird Johnson's environmental work, Lewis Gould probes the masculine discomfort with the close ties between women's culture and the preservation of natural beauty. For example, Charles Haar, who served on the Task Force on Natural Beauty, was relieved when the president came out in support of his wife's initiatives, for "it became a much more masculine approach, and it became much more talking of natural parks and society. It became much more acceptable."[11]

Lady Bird Johnson understood how women's image as homemakers excluded from policy-making threatened the work that she had in mind. Her apprehension about the symbolic ties of beautification to feminine impracticality stymied her collaboration with key women in the state Roadside Councils, who could have provided valuable support for her campaigns for billboard control and native plant preservation along the highways. Nevertheless, Johnson publicly argued for women's right and responsibility to influence environmental policies. The gap between her broad-based interest in improving the quality of life in cities and her tag as the Johnson administration's "beauty queen" reflected the discrepancy between women's actual contributions to public life and their supposed relegation to an isolated home.[12]

Part of Johnson's difficulty lay in the fact that neither she nor her supporters in the administration coined a descriptive metaphor expressive of more than aesthetic degradation of the landscape. When Rachel Carson published *Silent Spring* in 1962, she defined the threat more precisely. Appealing to the same upper- and middle-class experience as Johnson, Carson opened *Silent Spring* in the heart of the suburbs. Superhighways made commuting easier but they produced chemical spraying campaigns that killed the native flora and fauna so important in defining the American landscape and American character. *Silent Spring*'s influence rests in part on Carson's brilliance in reaching into the supposed sanctuary of suburban homes and showing the cycles of death on which they were constructed.

Nevertheless, such inspired writing did not exempt Carson from the same gender constrictions that Lady Bird Johnson faced. For all their differences in background, training, and environmental agendas, Carson and Johnson were dismissed by influential men who used gender stereotypes to discredit their work.[13] After the publication of *Silent Spring*, critics attacked Carson as a hysterical female, declaring that she was out of her league among professional scientists. Both women expressed their environmental concerns in images resonating with women's historical role as nurturers of the home, but gender stereotypes of the 1950s and 1960s also informed attempts to constrain and trivialize their contributions to the public debate on environmental issues.

Although much was known about the dangers posed by chemical pesticides before the appearance of *Silent Spring*, the book apprised the lay public of this knowledge. Believing that environmental devastation reflected a loss of respect for nature, Carson offered a comprehensive critique of Americans' unthinking surge to manipulate and control all life. Samuel P. Hays's study of the contemporary environmental movement shows how interwoven were concerns about urban and suburban pollution, human health, and threats to wilderness and wildlife habitat.[14] Though individual activists and local and national groups may have pursued one or more of these issues, *Silent Spring* provided the platform from which each effort proceeded.[15] Carson's debt to scientific knowledge of her time and her critique of professional entomology are well known.[16] But her role as a trained zoologist working from within the scientific community has served to isolate her from other women of her generation. While establishing her as a hero of sorts, such isolation continues to trivialize women's environmental work in the mid-twentieth century.

Comprehensive environmental histories of this period often suggest that more could be made of women's contributions. That Rachel Carson might have received as much critical sustenance from within female culture as she received from sympathetic male scientists, however, has not been considered.[17] Unlike Lady Bird Johnson, who sometimes separated herself from potentially useful women's groups, Carson aligned herself with women as well as with men. She understood and responded to the powerful women's networks of the 1950s. Equally important to her career as a scientist and nature writer were professional relationships, friendships, and public support developed among female government employees, journalists, nature writers, conservationists and naturalists, and women's clubs and organizations. A close study of Carson and her female colleagues opens up the history of women's environmentalism in the mid-twentieth century and reveals the difficulties women faced in garnering respect for a political agenda arising from the congruencies between human homes and nature's household.

With the huge success of *The Sea Around Us* in the 1950s, Carson became the country's most famous female naturalist. Many of the women who defended her during the *Silent Spring* controversy had come to know her through her earlier evocations of sea life. They wrote to her for advice on nature writing, obtained her backing on specific environmentalist issues, and honored her with awards from their organizations. She expressed many of their own beliefs and values about nature. As the controversy over *Silent Spring* grew, women's voices were as instrumental in building support as the male scientists and politicians who defended Carson's findings. National organizations like the American Association of University Women (AAUW), National Council of Women, and Garden Club of America recognized Carson's achievements and heeded her call to involve themselves in the environmental debates of the 1960s. Women in such conservation groups as the local Audubon societies shared Carson's concern for wildlife preservation and worked to spread *Silent Spring*'s message. Presswomen provided her with up-to-date information on local battles against chemical spraying and encouraged her interest in animal welfare issues. A study of Carson's dialogues with her less famous colleagues confirms what Susan Cooper, Celia Thaxter, and Lady Bird Johnson all knew: American women played an active role in preserving the natural landscape. By the mid-twentieth century a national network of female environmentalists, with influential positions in powerful public interest organizations and in publishing, operated in support of Carson's groundbreaking work.

Her eloquent writings suggest how these modern women's ideas about home fed into their sense of personal responsibility as teachers of a proper reverence for nature. Historically, one of American women's primary metaphors for describing plant and animal life has been as a home. Domestic metaphors have been important to the ways women regard plants. Susan Cooper, for example, delighted in the native rosebush over her "meretriciously" tricked out hothouse sister. Observations of animals have yielded the richest evocations of nature as our home. Florence Merriam could look on a eucalyptus grove and see the whole scene domesticated by the presence of one small bird's nest. In studying the mating and child-rearing practices of birds, fish, and wolves, women have used models from their own homes to encode meaning onto what they see, and to test the differences between humans and other species. Trained in zoology, committed to closely observing nature's round, and devoted to nature writing, Carson focused her attention on how animals create homes in nature and what meanings those homes might hold for humans.

Rachel Carson was born on May 27, 1907, in Springdale, Pennsylvania. She credited her mother, Maria, for her childhood interest in nature and her youthful efforts as a writer. Pursuing her education at the Pennsylvania College for Women (now Chatham College), she was torn between majors in English and zoology, finally graduating in science under the wing of her major professor, Mary Scott Skinker. After earning an M.A. in zoology at Johns Hopkins University, she taught part-time at Hopkins and the University of Maryland. When her father died in 1935, she took on the support of her mother. In 1936, following her sister Marian's death, Carson and her mother cared for Marian's two daughters. Having assumed financial responsibility for the family, Carson sought full-time work in government. During the 1940s she made her way up the professional ranks in the U.S. Fish and Wildlife Service, writing and editing publications aimed at a broad readership (Figure 41).[18]

In addition to her government work, Carson returned to her childhood

FIGURE 41. *Rachel Carson (1907–64). (Rachel Carson Council, Inc., Chevy Chase, Md. Photograph by Erich Hartmann.)*

interest in writing and began producing naturalist essays. In 1937 *Atlantic* printed "Undersea," a sensitive account of the patterns of life in the ocean. The piece caught the attention of an editor at Simon and Schuster, leading to the publication in 1941 of *Under the Sea Wind*. Carson described her first book as "a series of descriptive narratives unfolding successively the life of the shore, the open sea, and the sea bottom."[19] Although not a commercial success, it earned her recognition from other naturalists and led to a more comprehensive study of the oceans. In 1951 Oxford Press published *The Sea Around Us*. The book made Carson famous; its sales freed her from government work. *The Sea Around Us* sold over a quarter of a million copies in the first year of publication. Much to Carson's satisfaction, her book topped Thor Heyerdahl's *Kon-Tiki* for a number of weeks as a national best-seller. Highly praised in reviews, *The Sea Around Us* earned the National Book Award. Carson received many honors, including honorary doctorates from the Pennsylvania College for Women and Oberlin College, the John Burroughs Medal, and the Frances K. Hutchinson Medal for conservation work from the Garden Club of America.[20]

Carson was struck by the widely divergent backgrounds of those who appreciated *The Sea Around Us*—"hairdressers and fishermen and musicians; . . . and classical scholars and scientists." She was surprised and amused by some male readers' "reluctance to acknowledge that a woman could have dealt with a scientific subject" and their attempt to rationalize the problem by addressing her as "Sir," assuming she was "grey haired and venerable" or "a very large and forbidding woman."[21] Carson commented on the reactions of her male readers at the 1954 meeting of Theta Sigma Phi, a national fraternity of women journalists. In contrast to the men, the women in her audiences responded to her work as a validation of female contributions to the public good. By the 1955 publication of *The Edge of the Sea*, the last in her trilogy of ocean studies, Carson had touched the lives of a broad base of women readers. Her influence was apparent in awards from such organizations as the American Association of University Women and the National Council of Women of the United States. Professional women recognized the restrictions placed on their careers during the 1950s. Reflecting this concern, the National Council of Women instituted its annual book award because it felt that women were passed over for such prizes as the Nobel and Pulitzer. Announcing the annual award to *The Edge of the Sea*, the council stressed Carson's ability to work in a stereotypically male profession while maintaining woman's appropriate role:

"Miss Carson has successfully invaded a man's field and with a poet's eye, a scientific mind and a woman's intuition, has taught the world to wonder."[22]

What message in Carson's ocean books appealed so powerfully to the women of her generation? One clue lies in twentieth-century trends in biology. Carson trained in ecology, a science whose central metaphor for describing nature is as a household or home.[23] When she wrote about the oceans, she focused on the daily round of interdependent communities, emphasizing the life cycles of the animals described. One particularly important question concerned shelter. What constituted the home of a marine animal apparently adrift in the wide seas? Ocean homes offered excellent lessons in interdependence. Chronicling the life cycle of a barnacle, for example, Carson noted how its death bequeaths an inheritance of life: "When, through the attacks of fish, predatory worms, or snails, or through natural causes, the barnacle's life comes to an end, the shells remain attached to the rocks. These become shelter for many of the minute beings of the shore. Besides the baby periwinkles that regularly live there, the little tide-pool insects often hurry into these shelters if caught by the rising tide. And lower on the shore, or in the tide pools, the empty shells are likely to house young anemones, tube worms, or even new generations of barnacles."[24] This emphasis on the house as a haven from a threatening world must have appealed to a generation of women raised to attach a great deal of importance to their homes as similar places of shelter. In this way, lessons about the web of life learned in scientific ecology meshed with women's knowledge of the web of life they nurtured in their homes.

Ecologists' appeal to home had a more expansive meaning than the appeal to individual homeplaces. To Carson and her scientific colleagues, earth is a shelter where humans live in intimacy with other creatures as members of a household.[25] Describing the "intricate fabric of life by which one creature is linked with another, and each with its surroundings," *The Edge of the Sea* offers a brief glimpse inside a favorite tide pool:

> Under water that was clear as glass the pool was carpeted with green sponge. Gray patches of sea squirts glistened on the ceiling and colonies of soft coral were a pale apricot color. In the moment when I looked into the cave a little elfin starfish hung down, suspended by the merest thread, perhaps by only a single tube foot. It reached down to touch its own reflection, so perfectly delineated that there might have been, not one starfish, but two. The beauty of the reflected images and of the limpid

pool itself was the poignant beauty of things that are ephemeral, existing only until the sea should return to fill the little cave.[26]

Accurate science, such description also calls upon images of home—we peer through glass windows at a comfortable carpet, a lovely ceiling, and a tenant regarding herself in the mirror. Yet this is a tenuous household at best, existing strictly on terms set by the ocean. Such images capture the endless change marking the household, denying any separation of individual homeplaces from the environment. Metaphors of home extended beyond the insulated, domestic round of 1950s' culture to include all of nature, while individual human homes took on meanings linking them to their environment.

Carson's voice in the sea books was that of a tantalized watcher. Her scientist's understanding of the unity of life engendered in her a respect for other creatures shown in her approach to nature study. Carson believed it to be the duty of humans to live cooperatively with other life. Her discoveries were not couched in heroic battles of confrontation, but in surprises attendant on one who waits. Uninterested in revealing her command of nature through the mastery of scientific facts, she encouraged her readers to understand the lives of creatures rather than master scientific nomenclature. The study of animal life did not have to entail death and disruption. Offering herself as a model, she reported that "one night when the tide was ebbing I went down to the low-tide world to return a large starfish I had taken on the morning tide. The starfish was at home at the lowest level of these tides of the August moon, and to that level it must be returned."[27] Such an approach to understanding nature appealed to American women. Following the Audubon bird campaigns and building on women's long-standing interest in strolling through native woods, collecting shells along the shoreline, and working in the garden, Carson's sea books further encouraged women's observation, appreciation, and preservation of nature.

Although never a club woman herself, Carson understood the power in women's common bonds. The 1954 speech to Theta Sigma Phi articulated a theme she often repeated when speaking to women's organizations: women's responsibilities in the domestic sphere attuned them to the health of the earth: "I believe it is important for women to realize that the world of today threatens to destroy much of that beauty that has immense power to bring us a healing release from tension. Women have a greater intuitive understanding of such things. They want for their children not only physical health but mental and spiritual health as well. I bring these things to your attention because I think your awareness of them will help, whether you are practicing journalists, or teachers, or librarians, or housewives and mothers."[28] Her warning echoed much that had worried preceding generations of birders, wildflower illustrators, and gardeners—the sacrifice of woodlands and waterways to superhighways, suburbs, and urban blight in a "perilously artificial world."[29] An inheritor of the nineteenth-century belief in the restorative powers of direct contact with nature, a member of the generation witnessing the birth of the Atomic Age, and already aware of the destructive potential of chemicals like DDT, Carson concluded her speech with a statement of one of her deepest fears and strongest hopes: "Mankind has gone very far into an artificial world of his own creation . . . But I believe that the more clearly we can focus our attention on the wonders and realities of the universe about us, the less taste we shall have for destruction."[30] When the time came to bring out *Silent Spring*, her sense that women's role contained the seeds for environmental activism and that she could rely on the support of a broad base of powerful women's groups did not fail her.

In early 1962, prior to the publication later in the year of *Silent Spring*, Carson corresponded with the cochair of the Food Safety Committee of the Swarthmore, Pennsylvania, League of Women Voters. She wanted an extra copy of the group's leaflet on the environmental dangers posed by chemical contamination of foods. The Swarthmore league hoped to place the issue of chemical threats to humans, domestic animals, and wildlife on the organization's national agenda. The thoroughly researched leaflet pointed to scientific studies of chemical pollutants and offered a plan for political action at the local and national levels aimed at protecting the home. A drawing of a suburban shopper, her grocery cart full of bread, milk, lettuce, and a skull and crossbones exemplified the group's focus on domestic pollution. Carson wrote to request a second copy of the leaflet because she had lent her original to a friend acquainted with members of the National Board of the league. The friend wanted ammunition to encourage the board's support of the issue at the national convention.

Carson was pleased to hear that her Swarthmore correspondent had read and enjoyed *The Sea Around Us* but advised that her next book might prove somewhat surprising to her earlier audiences. Although the problem of chemical pollution did not make the league's national agenda in 1962, Carson offered to continue her backing of the Swarthmore group.[31] Clearly, social pressure on middle-class women to confine their concerns to the home did not prevent work in the public arena to determine the fate of that home.[32] Further, although the League of Women Voters' leaflet emphasized the rights of human consumers, it also contained information on threats to wildlife. Animals shared some of the same rights to a safe home life and needed activist women to help protect their domestic terrain.

Carson and her editors at Houghton Mifflin were well aware of the highly controversial message of *Silent Spring* and she urged them to exercise caution in announcing and advertising the book.[33] Proof copies were sent to prominent scientists and nature writers, to environmental groups that had endorsed Carson's earlier work, and to politically powerful women and women's groups. Congresswomen Maurine Neuberger, Leonor Sullivan, and Edith Green received proofs, as did the heads of the Children's Bureau, National Council of Jewish Women, National Federation of Women's Clubs, Garden Club of America, and American Association of University Women. Like the League of Women Voters, many of these groups had consumer study committees offering ready audiences for *Silent Spring*. The book fell on fertile ground. For example, after receiving proof copies of *Silent Spring*, the Social and Economic Issues Committee of the AAUW invited Carson to speak to the group.[34]

Of course, not every club woman worried about the effect of chemicals on the environment or immediately agreed with Carson's contentions. However, in the process of collecting information for *Silent Spring*, Carson had made enough contacts with influential club members to receive the support of the majority. The national network of garden clubs provides an excellent example of the way in which her work served as a lightning rod for change. As the chemical companies well knew, home gardeners were major consumers of their products. Garden clubs were the targets of much advertising from herbicide and insecticide producers and of much proselytizing by agricultural agents, highway officials, and at least one influential female garden expert.[35] Although many garden club women no doubt continued using chemicals on their lawns after the appearance of *Silent Spring*, Carson's connections with concerned members, and their work educating others, assured endorsement of her message by local and national garden clubs.

Enough crossover existed between Audubon societies and garden clubs that some garden club members were aware of the chemical threat to birds. Countering chemical sales campaigns, such women provided other club members with information on the dangers of uncontrolled use of pesticides. Carson especially respected Ruth Scott, who first wrote to her in June 1961. Scott was the state bird chair of the Garden Club Federation of Pennsylvania. Committed to enlightening her colleagues about the dangers that insecticides and herbicides posed to birds and wildflowers, she asked Carson for advice on how to increase environmental awareness among the membership. A warm collaboration continued for the next several years.[36] Scott felt that women were potentially a powerful lobby for conservation issues and Carson agreed. They developed a network of supporters in Pennsylvania, drawing in other garden club groups and broadening the effort to include the Pennsylvania State Federation of Women's Clubs. Carson shared her research materials with Scott, who in turn used them to good effect among the local gardeners. The Garden Club of America awarded Carson a special commendation in 1963. In her acceptance speech, she lauded the Pennsylvania State Federation of Women's Clubs' program of environmentally responsive education and legislation.[37] Rachel Carson consciously supported and drew upon women's interest in protecting their families, neighborhoods, and the country from threats posed by the "artificial world" of post–World War II America. Part of Silent Spring's enormous success was due to her connections with highly visible groups representing the concerns of large numbers of women.

Interconnections between home and environment, so celebrated in the household metaphors of the sea books, took on new urgency as the unity of all life became a nightmare in Silent Spring. Dangerous chemicals pervaded the environment: "They have been found in fish in remote mountain lakes, in earthworms burrowing in soil, in the eggs of birds—and in man himself. For these chemicals are now stored in the bodies of the vast majority of human beings, regardless of age. They occur in the mother's milk, and probably in the tissues of the unborn child."[38] In her collaboration with environmentalists like Ruth Scott, Carson recognized the extent to which pollution was of concern to women. Silent Spring appealed to that interest and confirmed women's right to work on public policies for controlling such threats to the home. As Carson described the webs of contamination resulting from overreliance on chemicals, home offered no haven from the world. Government agents sprayed pesticides over flower beds and bird baths and did not adequately regulate residues in heads of lettuce and gallons of milk. Pest eradication campaigns of public agencies invaded the private spaces of home, destroying domestic pets and wildlife, harming children, and poisoning gardens. Moreover, advertising prompted individual consumers to buy chemicals for waging similar battles against their crabgrass and household crickets. In imagery encouraging families to view such products as harmless, industry took little responsibility for the user's safety.[39] Silent Spring's documentation of pollution in the home both supported existing initiatives by groups like the Swarthmore League of Women Voters and provided ammunition for other women's organizations concerned with the safety of products invading the home.[40]

In their evocative descriptions of the communities that gathered on such homeplaces as tide pools and ospreys' nests, Carson's sea books painted memorable pictures of developing embryonic life, of the processes by which one generation led to another. *Silent Spring* returned to these themes, addressing what the prevalence of pesticides in the web of life means to humans. Rapid advances in genetic research led Carson to describe another type of interconnection: "There is an ecology of the world within our bodies. In this unseen world minute causes produce mighty effects." Detailing increased knowledge of the processes of fertilization and growth in embryos and threats posed to the "fires of life" by radiation and pesticides, she asked whether observations of death in frogs' eggs, sea urchins, and eagles' nests did not raise the question of hazards to human reproduction. Recognizing that similar growth processes occur in a "frog or a bird or a human infant," Carson warned her readers that this new understanding of our shared heritage with all life carries new responsibilities to future generations: "For mankind as a whole, a possession infinitely more valuable than individual life is our genetic heritage, our link with past and future. Shaped through long eons of evolution, our genes not only make us what we are but hold in their minute beings the future—be it one of promise or threat. Yet genetic deterioration through man-made agents is the menace of our time."[41] Emphasizing reproduction and children's health, Carson's message appealed to the many women who believed it was their task to nurture the children of the future.

In June 1963 Carson received the first "Woman of Conscience" award from the National Council of Women. In her acceptance speech, she considered the meaning of the title:

> I have been thinking about what it means to be a woman of conscience, and I have concluded that—if indeed I am such a person—then I am in the midst of kindred spirits tonight. For surely all of you, who are gathered from far places, are here because you, too, are women of conscience. The work of your organization is founded on concern for human welfare—for the future of mankind—and as such it is the translation of conscience into action. The thought I would like to leave you with tonight is that there has never been a time . . . when the very existence of future generations depended to so great an extent on what we do, in

this day and hour . . . We have . . . acquired the power to change the hereditary materials of the future. Unless this power is tempered with wisdom and with a deep sense of personal responsibility, the outlook will be grave indeed. I am honored by this happy association with so many responsible leaders among women.[42]

Carson understood how women's perception of their roles as protectors and educators of the next generation generated not only the values they taught to children but also a desire to translate those values into action. Women's organizations helped the causes she believed vital. She appreciated their support even though she was not herself a club woman.

Closer to her heart were the various preservationist and nature study groups with which she had long-standing connections.[43] Members of these groups formed another strand in the web of female colleagues sharing Carson's concern for the environment. While women's clubs showed more interest in the human welfare aspects of her environmental agenda, colleagues in the Audubon societies touched her lifelong commitment to wildlife protection. Ruth Scott, state bird chair of the Garden Club Federation of Pennsylvania, was also active in the local Audubon society. Like a good many of her nineteenth-century predecessors, Scott created a green space attractive to birds around her home and lobbied to preserve native bird habitats. She wrote "Conservation Reports" for the Audubon Society of Western Pennsylvania in which she encouraged the collaboration of Audubon members and the garden clubs to restrict brush control spraying campaigns by the highway department.[44] Carson shared Scott's pleasure in bird-watching. Rachel and her mother Maria enjoyed the birds around their homes in Silver Spring, Maryland, and Maine. Rachel and Shirley Briggs, a colleague and friend from Fish and Wildlife, did a good deal of Audubon-sponsored birding together, as well as collaborating on Fish and Wildlife publications.[45] Carson included nicely detailed descriptions of bird life in the "Conservation in Action" booklets she wrote for Fish and Wildlife.[46]

Between 1920 and 1950 environmental politics emphasized the protection of wildlife, a concern raised in the nineteenth-century Audubon defense of plume birds and game birds. After their early dominance of these campaigns, women lost their prominence in the Audubon organizations; indeed, their leadership roles in many such groups declined. The woman who gained most publicity in defending wildlife denounced the ties between the National Audubon Society and hunting organizations and argued for the preservation of wildlife for observation. In the arena of preservation politics, Rosalie Edge, a suffragette who used her training in the fight for the vote to take on the Audubon establishment, appears a solitary female in this period. Throughout the thirties, she educated the membership about alliances with hunting interests and lobbied for changes in the goals of the organization.[47] Although Edge was the most visible, a few other women also achieved some status within national groups at this time. Lucy Furman, for example, was named a vice-president in the Anti-Steel Trap League in recognition of her work in Kentucky to develop humane traps. Aware that calls to abolish hunting would be futile, she and others in the humane movement did what they could to reduce the pain of the animals killed.[48]

Rachel Carson was sympathetic to humane concerns in wildlife protection. Her membership in local Audubon groups and her interest in birdwatching reflected a deep-seated empathy with the lives of all animals. She had little regard for blood sports, arguing that "until we have courage to recognize cruelty for what it is—whether its victim is human or animal—we cannot expect things to be much better in the world. There can be no double standard. We cannot have peace among men whose hearts find delight in killing any living creature. By every act that glorifies or even tolerates such moronic delight in killing, we set back the progress of humanity."[49] In her first book, *Under the Sea Wind*, Carson expressed her outrage at such activities. *Silent Spring* castigated sportsmen who poisoned lakes in order to "improve fishing" and linked nineteenth-century wildlife carnage with campaigns in the twentieth century to eradicate insect pests: "The history of the recent centuries has its black passages—the slaughter of the buffalo on the western plains, the massacre of the shorebirds by the market gunners, the near extermination of the egrets for their plumage. Now, to these and others like them, we are adding a new chapter and a new kind of havoc—the direct killing of birds, mammals, fishes, and indeed practically every form of wildlife by chemical pesticides indiscriminately sprayed on the land . . . nothing must get in the way of the man with the spray gun."[50] Clothing the local extension agent in hunting garb, she reminded her readers of battles they had fought in the past and encouraged them to view the new generation of men with spray guns with the same jaundiced eye they had turned on hunters and plume merchants.

Carson summarized the feelings of a good many women whose private gardens had become battlegrounds of dead birds. In January 1958 Olga Owens Huckins wrote to the editor of the *Boston Herald* deploring the aerial spraying campaigns in her region and sent Carson a copy of her letter. An avid bird-watcher who had made a bird sanctuary of her yard, Huckins reported that "the 'harmless' shower bath killed seven of our lovely songbirds outright. We picked up three dead bodies the next morning by the door. They were birds that had lived close to us, trusted us, and built their nests in our trees year after year. The next day three were scattered around the bird bath. (I had emptied and scrubbed it after the spraying but YOU CAN NEVER KILL DDT.)"[51] Huckins and Carson were old friends and Huckins knew that Carson might have some ideas about how to stop such wildlife kills. This letter, which expressed one woman's anguish at the destruction of the wildlife in her yard, helped inspire *Silent Spring*.[52] In the book, Carson acknowledged her debt to such women.

Much of *Silent Spring* drew on Carson's synthesis of scientific evidence on the harm caused by chemicals. In counterpoint to the primarily male voices cited in such evidence, Carson included a chorus of women who expressed the same sense of outrage, loss, and call to action as Huckins in her letter to the *Herald*. Women were often the ones who wrote to newspapers and appeared at public hearings asking sensitive questions about wildlife kills and stressing the value of intimate contact with native plants and animals. At one point in *Silent Spring* Carson touched on the male/female division in attitudes toward nature: "Justice [William O.] Douglas tells of attending a meeting of federal field men who were discussing protests by citizens against plans for the spraying of sagebrush . . . These men considered it hilariously funny that an old lady had opposed the plan because the wildflowers would be destroyed." Citing Douglas's perception in asserting the woman's right to "search out a . . . tiger lily," Carson pointed out the place of native vegetation in the "economy of nature," thus validating the serious content to the woman's concern.[53]

Carson knew that some men also understood the threats posed by environmental degradation; she was not suggesting that only women cared about such issues. She did argue, however, that the key decision makers—from powerful elites—were male. Men who shared Justice Douglas's sensitivity were "not the men who order the wholesale drenching of the landscape with chemicals."[54] When a room full of professionally trained government employees, all of whom were male, dismissed the concerns of a female citizen out of hand, Carson recognized that gender stereotypes played a role in that denial. *Silent Spring* builds a strong case for the rights of any citizen to know and have a say in public policy, but it also suggests that female citizens in particular have difficulty getting such a hearing. By including the letters and statements of ordinary women as part of her documentation in *Silent Spring*, Carson supported their credibility in shaping public policy.

In addition to their interest in protecting birds, Carson and Olga Huckins shared beliefs about what it meant to be an animal and the nature of human society's moral duty to other creatures. Huckins's letter to the *Boston Herald* described the suffering that DDT caused wild birds: "All of these birds died horribly, and in the same way. Their bills were gaping open, and their splayed claws were drawn up to their breasts in agony."[55] The late nineteenth century's fascination with watching birds in their habitat provided one stimulus for movements to protect animals from torment at human hands. Women who condemned hunting did so partly because they sympathized with the painful death of animals whose home life seemed so like their own, whose observation by adults and children developed moral understanding.[56]

Rachel Carson's generation inherited the fruits of sweeping public campaigns against cruelty to animals during the Victorian period and early twentieth century, campaigns in which women played a prominent part. Distress over scientific experiments on animals, the treatment of animals in circuses and zoos, the living conditions of some domestic pets, and the gruesome deaths of wildlife at the hands of hunters caused influential Victorian women to lead public groups in support of animal rights. They aimed to reduce the pain that humans inflicted on particular animals. During the antiplumage battles in the late nineteenth and early twentieth centuries, women combined such animal rights activities with conservation goals. Many American leaders of the Society for the Prevention of Cruelty to Animals (SPCA) were also prominent in Audubon circles.[57] By the turn of the century compassion for animal suffering was common to large segments of the English and American public.

Sympathy for animals, springing from post-Darwinian efforts to cope with humanity's new place as a part of (rather than dominant over) nature, was further inspired by ecological visions of a mutually interdependent web of life. James Turner has studied the process by which such relatively value-free explanatory models of nature were used to support moral visions of humanity's proper responsibility to other animals, creating a widely shared ethic of reverent treatment of all species.[58] When Huckins argued that spraying birds with DDT was inhuman, she appealed to this set of values concerning animal rights and human duties. Rachel Carson shared Huckins's belief that people had a responsibility to grant to other animals the same relief from human cruelty that we grant to our own species.

Much of Carson's reputation rests on her ability to place the meanings of scientific ecology within an ideology of species preservation. In her beautiful descriptions of the daily round of animal communities, she stressed the importance of each species to the survival of the whole. Such knowledge demanded respect for all life and, Carson hoped, more restraint in dealing with animal populations. Her angry outburst against hunting sprang in part from her concern for the potential extinction of valuable species, but it also evoked the pain caused to a single animal. This interest in the rights of individual animals as well as endangered species formed a critical part of Carson's message. The painful deaths of particular birds in Olga Huckins's garden and Huckins's grief at their loss was as important a force behind the writing of *Silent Spring* as the threat posed by DDT to entire species.

In a letter to her close friend Dorothy Freeman on completing the manuscript of *Silent Spring*, Carson mentioned how much her love of animals drove the effort: "I think I let you see last summer what my deeper feelings are about this when I said I could never again listen happily to a thrush song if I had not done all I could. And last night the thoughts of all the birds and other creatures and all the loveliness that is in nature came to me with such a surge of deep happiness, that now I had done what I could."[59] Not only did pesticides like DDT imperil populations of grebes and grouse, they created much suffering in the individual animals who died. Citing studies of the death throes of meadowlarks and ground squirrels after massive spraying operations around Sheldon, Illinois, Carson reiterated her stance against such cruelty. A pesticide "poisons all life with which it comes into contact: the cat beloved of some family, the farmer's cattle, the rabbit in the field, and the horned lark out of the sky. These creatures are innocent of any harm to man. Indeed, by their very existence they and their fellows make his life more pleasant. Yet he rewards them with a death that is not only sudden but horrible."[60]

In 1959 Rachel Carson had sent a letter to the *Washington Post* outlining some of the material she was then collecting for *Silent Spring*, including the danger that pesticides posed for local birds. She painted a picture of human-bird interaction, appealing not so much to scientific ecology as to the ordinary citizen's appreciation of common animals: "To many of us this sudden silencing of the song of birds, this obliteration of the color and beauty and interest of bird life, is sufficient cause for sharp regret." The letter sparked the interest of Christine Stevens, who encouraged Carson to look into the use of poisons on predators and rodents, a topic on the agenda of the Animal Welfare Institute, a humane organization that Stevens headed. Some of the more conservative goals of humane groups had been accomplished by the turn of the century. However, their radical critique of scientific experimentation on animals had been defused by a tide of support for science between the two world wars. Antivivisectionists, for example, were regarded as the lunatic fringe by mainstream animal protection groups like the SPCA. During the late 1940s and early 1950s, the rapid infusion of government support for research increased the demand for animals. To obtain them, some communities passed laws requiring pounds to turn over strays for experimental research. Such legislation spurred a new wave of activism among animal rights groups. In keeping with the Victorian tradition, women played a key role in the new push for animal rights. Exemplifying women's involvement was Christine Stevens, whose effective leadership made the Animal Welfare Institute an important advocacy group for animal rights in the 1950s and 1960s.[61]

Much as she had with Ruth Scott, Carson continued to work with Stevens throughout the rest of her life. Carson became a member of the advisory board of the Animal Welfare Institute and encouraged other women colleagues to become active in the organization. In the aftermath of *Silent Spring*'s publication, Stevens used her connections with various congressional representatives to inform them of Carson's work and lobby for legislative controls on the chemical industry. In the last years of her life, Carson supported the development of federal standards to protect research animals; wrote a moving foreword to Ruth Harrison's *Animal Machines*, a British study of the inhumane conditions in factory farming operations; and joined the board of directors of the Defenders of Wildlife.[62] In accepting the Animal Welfare Institute's Albert Schweitzer Medal in 1963, Carson eloquently argued that an ecological respect for life grew out of personal contact with animals: "the truest understanding of Reverence for Life comes . . . from some personal experience, perhaps the sudden, unexpected sight of a wild creature, perhaps some experience of a pet. Whatever it may be, it is something that takes us out of ourselves, that makes us aware of other life."[63]

In associations like the Animal Welfare Institute and Defenders of Wildlife, Carson met women with similar goals who worked to change public policy. She and her female colleagues in both the animal rights and wildlife protection movements felt little contradiction between protection of species and humane treatment of individual animals; these were complementary goals equally necessary to a holistic ethic of human-animal relations. Nor was there any hierarchy of concern for domestic over wild animals. Like women of previous generations, twentieth-century preservationists defended wildlife as an extension of the home, marking few boundaries in their role as protectors of the natural American landscape.

The 1964 recipient of the Schweitzer Medal was Ann Cottrell Free, a Washington, D.C., journalist who had written articles on the treatment of research animals and who, with her husband James, covered the progress of various local efforts to block pesticide-spraying campaigns. Free's association with Carson and the Animal Welfare Institute exemplifies the final network of women among whom Carson found support. Carson's work as a writer—both in government and as a free-lancer—had put her in touch with a wide range of professional women in publishing, including journalists. Her early friendship with Shirley Briggs continued past their days as government employees. Briggs became the editor of the *Atlantic Naturalist*, a publication of the Washington, D.C., chapter of the Audubon Society. As Carson gathered materials for *Silent Spring*, she sent items to Briggs for publication in the *Naturalist*.[64] In 1959, when Ann Free and her husband began a series of articles and columns on pesticides, she contacted Carson. Free already had questions about the treatment of research animals, particularly in Food and Drug Administration (FDA) laboratories. She and Christine Stevens had lobbied Congress together for policies providing decent living conditions among test animals. In Carson, Free found a sympathetic and well-connected ally. Carson and Free exchanged information on both animal rights issues and pesticides. When Carson received the Swarthmore League of Women Voters' leaflet on pesticide dangers, she sent it to Free, who wrote a story about the league's work.[65]

Another presswoman who shared Carson's concern for the welfare of wildlife was Agnes (Mrs. Eugene) Meyer, the owner of the *Washington Post*. After reading Carson's 1959 letter to the *Post* on the dangers of massive pesticide use, Meyer wrote to express her support for Carson's warning. Threats to local birds caught Meyer's attention: "I am sure you started all the nature lovers on an important campaign. At this moment the ginkgo trees in front of my house all have a sign to motorists to beware because the trees are going to be sprayed within a few days. I wish the birds could read!"[66] When the first installment of *Silent Spring* appeared in the *New Yorker* in June 1962, Meyer wrote to congratulate her on the book. Meyer had put Carson in touch with some of the women's organizations supporting *Silent Spring* and noted in her letter her pleasure that the National Council of Women had invited Carson to speak at its conference, as "these women will really get to work in any way that you can suggest." When the Women's National Press Club invited Carson to speak at its December meeting, Meyer promised that the *Post* would give the speech good coverage.[67] With Agnes Meyer, the web of women supporting Carson's career is defined. Although club women, conservationists, and professional journalists might seem to travel in different circles, in fact, their common commitment to environmental protection brought them together in fruitful alliances not immediately apparent in histories focusing only on major players on the national scene. In Carson, her female colleagues found a spokesperson for some of their most deeply held convictions. Her symbolic power was increased by her gender. As important as Carson's message was the fact that a woman was the messenger.

Sensitivity to the gender of female naturalists is nothing new. Susan Fenimore Cooper's father and male friends felt that in writing about nature, she posed an excellent model for other mid-nineteenth century women. Cordelia Stanwood's photographic studies of the birds around her home offered women a new arena for nature exploration, one in keeping with gender-role proscriptions against hunting. Beatrix Farrand's residential landscape designs provided a suitable niche in architecture for women to make a contribution. Each woman added to the general appreciation of American flora and fauna while conforming to expectations of women's place as keepers of the home. Only garden diaries like Celia Thaxter's suggested that women's modes of interacting with nature contained more than the passive meanings assigned to the domestic round. Although female gardeners offered more active images, continuing stereotypes of passive ladies among the flowers did not reflect women's changing role. Rachel Carson wrote during a period in American culture when the home, and women's place therein, had much symbolic meaning. Women indeed worked for wages in the public arena, but such work was decidedly secondary to their contributions within the separate, private sphere of household. Like the tensions in the vision of the lady gardener, the contradictions between women wage earners and this celebration of the homemaker usually were invisible. When, however, an event like the popular success of *The Sea Around Us* displayed a woman's skill in the public world of science, the disparity between the actual content of women's lives and domestic ideology had to be addressed.

In 1958 *Life* magazine published an article on underwater salvage operations. The author credited *The Sea Around Us* for the increasing popularity of underwater recreation. A Vitalis hair-grooming advertisement facing the story showed a handsome diver plagued with "wild" hair—presumably caused by too much time in a diving helmet. Imaging a woman in a similar predicament would have been unthinkable.[68] Yet women participated in the expansion of recreational diving, which had been prompted by technologies coming out of the war years. During the 1950s stories about lady scuba divers began to complement coverage of rugged underwater frogmen. In 1957 *Life* carried a photographic essay on Clare Boothe Luce's first dive off Bermuda; she said she felt like "a bird lighting on a bough." *McCalls* magazine did a similar story on Jacques Cousteau's wife, Simone, describing her as a "deep water sailor with the figure of a fashion model." *Recreation*, a magazine covering changes in leisure activities, underscored the unexamined contradictions in diving stories by first noting that the ocean "presents the ultimate for the man seeking excitement," then commenting that "family groups . . . will enjoy joint recreation activity for years to come in which *each member of the family can participate*."[69] Clearly, when women went into the ocean, they carried with them the responsibilities of home. They were not explorers, but wives and mothers who kept their priorities straight even under water. Contradictions between the ocean as a place of challenge and a family playground were not apparent because the separate spheres' model carried over into the depths. A parting image of Simone Cousteau skin-diving on the surface of the clear Mediterranean Sea, peering down at her husband and sons exploring the bottom, effectively captured the assumed compatibility between male and female terrain.[70]

Women in the late nineteenth century had been encouraged to study marine biology, particularly in the summer schools run by Louis and Elizabeth Agassiz. They had also helped establish one of the country's premier institutions for marine research, the Marine Biological Laboratory at Woods Hole, Massachusetts. Reflecting their diminished role in marine science in the twentieth century, by the 1930s and 1940s they were all but invisible among research scientists in the field.[71] Eugenie Clark appears as the only notable woman of Carson's generation who worked in oceanography. Famous for her shark studies, Clark had difficulty getting her research done in the heavily masculinized discipline. For example, she was not allowed on overnight research cruises while working at the Scripps Institute of Oceanography in 1946 and 1947 because she was the only woman on the ship.[72] In 1949 Carson faced a similar handicap. When a Fish and Wildlife assignment sent her on a scientific voyage aboard the service's research vessel, the *Albatross*, she took along a female chaperon, her friend and agent Marie Rodell: "No woman had ever been in the *Albatross*. Tradition is important in the government, but fortunately I had conspirators who were willing to help me shatter precedent. But among my male colleagues who had to sign the papers, the thought of one woman on a ship with some fifty men was unthinkable. After much soul searching, it was decided that maybe *two* women would be all right, so I arranged with a friend, who was also a writer to go with me." Carson went into the ocean's depths only once, making a brief expedition at the suggestion of her mentor, William Beebe, who declared that she could not write a book about the ocean if she had not been below its surface.[73]

In their government work Carson and her few female colleagues found a niche fitting with expected gender roles. Like the scientific illustrators, women in Fish and Wildlife reported on progress in knowledge and served as conduits between government and the public for explaining and encouraging support of various conservation efforts.[74] What made Carson unique in the eyes of her male colleagues was the extension of her work into a comprehensive, scientifically up-to-date book on the oceans. Men who knew the oceans well found *The Sea Around Us* a good read. Carson's step into a subject popularized by explorers like Thor Heyerdahl led some male readers to place Carson outside the domestic realm—to address her as "Sir" or imagine her as a sea goddess. The dominant ideology, expressed in articles on women's amateur, ladylike diving excursions, offered no room for a typical woman to write such an authoritative work as *The Sea Around Us*. In her book Carson challenged the separation of the spheres as she symbolically donned a diving helmet and explored male terrain.

By contrast, her female colleagues did not find her books (or herself) in the least unwomanly. Unlike Heyerdahl's *Kon-Tiki*, which told an exciting story of man against the elements, Carson's sea books were based on the art of patient watching. Reflecting rising interest in recreational hikes along a local beach or scuba dives in coastal waters, her writings supported many women's mode of ocean study. The books stressed cooperation rather than confrontation with nature. Experiencing marine settings as Clare Boothe Luce had— like "a bird lighting on a bough"—conformed with women's perceptions of correct dealings with all life. So in 1954, when Carson spoke to Theta Sigma Phi, she confidently appealed to gender roles to encourage the women in her audience into environmental activism. Women who listened to her speeches and knew her work both recognized her unique place as a female marine biologist and found it "natural" for her to act as a spokesperson for the rights of the planet.

Until *Silent Spring*, the difficulty some men had reconciling her authoritative books with her sex was mainly a source of humor for Carson, her women colleagues, and the men who supported her work. The publication of *Silent Spring* brought to a head men's and women's differing readings of Carson's status as a woman with a voice in the public sphere. *Silent Spring* served to rally a wide variety of women who questioned the safety of the chemicals used in their homes, gardens, and woodlands. Women figured prominently in many of the lawsuits filed to stop local spraying. Carson corresponded with many of these women while developing materials for her book and after its publication.[75]

Reporters emphasized the apparent preponderance of women voicing their displeasure with pesticide use at city and state government meetings. For example, in January 1963 the Virginia Department of Agriculture planned a spray campaign in the Norfolk area to destroy the white-fringed beetle, an insect that allegedly threatened a wide variety of crops. After the local newspaper ran a story on the plan, a delegation of concerned citizens appeared at both the Norfolk City Council and the governor's office to protest the widespread spraying over their homes and surrounding wetlands. During the meetings, passages of *Silent Spring* were read aloud to public officials. The protesters, organized by Mrs. C. Dodson Morrisette, consisted of fifteen women and one man representing local garden clubs. National and local newspapers made note of women's key role in the outcry. At least one woman believed that the battle lines were drawn along gender-role divisions. In a letter to the editor of the *Virginia Pilot*, Mrs. Ida H. Swarts noted that government representatives had cast themselves in "father knows best" garb: "'Papa' does not always know best. In this instance it seems that 'papa' is taking an arbitrary stand, and we, the people are just supposed to take it, and count the dead animals and birds, and whatever other casualties there may be."[76] Men were prominent in many of the protests and lawsuits filed; Mrs. Morrisette's husband, a lawyer, handled the suit in Norfolk. Yet, when a contingent of women met with public officials and faced a table of men, both groups couched their differences in gender-loaded terms.

Recognition that *Silent Spring* had uncovered some basic differences between men and women was widespread. Press stories linked Carson to Dr. Frances Kelsey, the FDA physician whose questions helped ban thalidomide in America. The appearance of *Silent Spring* in the same year as Kelsey's findings led one newspaper editor to assert: "men may dominate the sciences but women are making the headlines." One of Carson's male readers told her that *Silent Spring* offered a voice of womanly compassion in a world of men entranced by cold technology. Not all gender-based commentary was complimentary, however. Although many male scientists and politicians supported her book, those who did not often used her sex to discredit her message. John Leonard, science editor for *Time* magazine, wrote a scathing review of *Silent Spring*, accusing its author of being "hysterically overemphatic." In a later speech before the National Agricultural Chemicals Association, Leonard noted that his review invited a flood of letters defending Carson, not all from "faddists and hysterical women." But this did not alter his opinion. In his uncomplimentary report on the book for the *Archives of Internal Medicine*, Dr. William B. Bean appealed to his professional audience's domestic experience: "*Silent Spring*, which I read word for word with some trauma, kept reminding me of trying to win an argument with a woman. It cannot be done."[77] Carson was distressed by personal attacks suggesting that her devotion to her mother, her affection for birds and cats, and her sensitive and gentle prose somehow invalidated her findings. Men like Leonard and Bean reminded Carson and her female colleagues that their freedom to work and involve themselves in public life stretched only so far and did not include the right to criticize the professional male establishment.[78]

While writing *Silent Spring*, Carson had known that she must be wary of some of her colleagues' positivist attitudes and she recognized the gender implications in her critique of their work. Outlining the book to her editor, Paul Brooks, she commented: "I am convinced there is a psychological angle in all this: that people, especially professional men, are uncomfortable about coming out against something, especially if they haven't absolute proof the 'something' is wrong, but only a good suspicion. So they will go along with a program about which they privately have acute misgivings. So I think it is most important [in the book, that is] to build up the positive alternatives."[79] Carson carefully noted in *Silent Spring* that some men were working to change the futile reliance on chemicals to eradicate insect pests and noxious weeds. Nevertheless, such men constituted a minority among their colleagues.[80]

Carson did not make any direct correlation between masculine dominance of entomology and limitations of the field's methods—these connections have been raised more recently in the feminist critique of science.[81] She did, however, criticize the absolutist values she saw informing the science of her times. Appearing in the same year as Thomas Kuhn's *The Structure of Scientific Revolutions*, *Silent Spring* provided a case study of Kuhn's contention that "normal" science is "predicated on the assumption that the scientific community knows what the world is like" and is "tradition-bound," yielding up that tradition only under the pressure of new evidence.[82] Carson argued that the model biology applied to nature was erroneous in positing the earth as a passive subject for man's probing and controlling mind. The new ecology offered a competing paradigm that defined nature as active and responsive: "we are dealing with life—with living populations and all their pressures and counterpressures, their surges and repressions. Only by taking account of such life forces and by cautiously seeking to guide them into channels favorable to ourselves can we hope to achieve a reasonable accommodation between the insect hordes and ourselves."[83] *Silent Spring*'s concluding chapter on biological methods of insect control was meant to provide the positive alternatives that Carson mentioned in her letter to Brooks.[84]

*Silent Spring* was not like a paper presented within the scientific community. Aimed at a general audience and previewed in mass-circulation magazines, the book alerted readers to the dangers of DDT and other pesticides and urged them to question the course of research. Carson's presentation of a scientific debate in a context critical not only of the chemicals but also of science itself sparked many of the fires around *Silent Spring*.[85] By granting status to the worries of ordinary citizens, many of whom were women, Carson empowered people to question the authority of scientific figures in government and industry. Making complex new knowledge of genetics and chemistry available to laypeople, and encouraging them to make connections between this knowledge and their daily lives, Carson helped deflate the worship of science prevalent in post–World War II America. To some men, that a woman not only entered their profession but also criticized it was unthinkable. They responded by appealing to the stereotype of women as incapable of true scientific understanding. Reading *Silent Spring* was akin to having an argument with the wife—and about as important in the affairs of the world.

By contrast, women readers found that *Silent Spring* validated their sense that home management required educating oneself about the products used in home and community. Flooded with goods and services aimed at the home, women consumers tried to stay abreast of developments in industry in order to maintain healthy living conditions for their families. Their lack of professional training did not make them incapable of intelligently evaluating scientific studies. Further, home was most assuredly not limited to one's suburban ranch house. When women in Carson's circles talked about responsibility to protect the home, they referred, as had their mothers and grandmothers, to their community, their country, and, in their most expansive moments, the whole earth. When they saw potential dangers to their individual homes or the earth/household, they felt comfortable raising their voices in protest.

The gender divisions in male and female responses to *Silent Spring* are reflected in Carson's speeches to women's organizations after 1962. In her 1954 address to Theta Sigma Phi, Carson had linked women's work on environmental issues to their role as mothers of the next generation. She did not delve too deeply into what the task of homemaker meant. In speeches following *Silent Spring*, she located women's concern for the environment not only in emotional ties to the family home, but also in their informed, efficient management of a household. Her 1962 address to an international conference organized by the National Council of Women, entitled "Tomorrow's Spring," opened with the traditional image of women as caretakers of the family. Carson went on to note that the apparent security of contemporary, middle-class home life posed new, complex problems for women: "The achievement of comfort and ease and pleasure may bring in its wake many problems, for these things are often bought at a price. In the relaxation and enjoyment of a cigarette, perhaps we pay dearly in disease. For the balm of sleep conferred on the mother by a pill, thousands of babies have suffered tragic deformity." The rest of her speech covered the kind of knowledge women needed to ensure that the world remained a fit place for children to grow. Describing in technical detail the potential for genetic damage that chemical pollution posed, she encouraged women to take "positive action" for controlling and redirecting the research agendas of government, science, and industry. Directly addressing attempts to discredit her findings by aspersions on her sex, she argued that "there is something more than mere feminine intuition behind my concern about the possibility that our freewheeling use of pesticides may endanger generations yet unborn. There is stark handwriting on the wall that justifies the greatest possible caution."[86] Carson did not deny women's emotional ties to family life; rather, she included the intellectual requirements of homemaking. Contending that women's fears for the future of the planet were informed by knowledge as well as passion, she validated their critique of environmentally destructive public policy—giving her audience the tools to continue the fight in the political arena.

At bottom, speeches like "Tomorrow's Spring" were informed by Carson's scientific understanding of ecology and by her grasp of humanity's moral obligation to live in harmony with the rest of nature. With many of the women in her audience, she felt that an ideology separating "home" from "industry" or "science" was wrongheaded. Home had a much deeper meaning, based on Carson's own family life as well as her training in ecology. When she wrote about nature, her imagery centered on how animals made their homes and on the interlocking connections among all life that made of the earth a household. She shared this focus with a number of female colleagues who, like Rachel Carson, found in their domestic round a metaphor for human responsibility to nature.

In contrast to previous generations, however, women of the mid-twentieth century found themselves at cross-purposes with the male professional elite when they worked for the rights of all animals to a safe home and a secure future. Women of the 1950s and 1960s increasingly recognized how popular images of "little old lady bird-watchers" were used by professional men to trivialize their environmental goals. Rather than criticizing women's ties to home, these women articulated a more expansive view of the interconnections between the domestic sphere and the world of science and industry. Grounding their ties to nature in the flora and fauna of their yard and community, they did not repudiate the metaphor of nature as home. In the fortuitous appearance of a woman trained in the new science of ecology—who described nature as a household—female environmentalists of the mid-twentieth century found a stronghold allowing them to transform the restricted sphere of suburban homes into holistic nurturance of all earth's creatures. Rachel Carson formed the center of a web of women from various walks of life who shared among themselves not only a moral understanding of their relationship to nature but also a political commitment to assuring that male professionals incorporated their values into environmental policy. That preservation of the health and diversity of the natural landscape gained national prominence in the 1960s and 1970s was due in large measure to their effort.

# 6

## Writing Animal Presence *Nature* in Euro-American, African American, and American Indian Fiction

*What is this joy? That no animal*

*falters, but knows what it must do?*

*That the snake has no blemish,*

*that the rabbit inspects his strange surroundings*

*in white star-silence? The llama*

*rests in dignity, the armadillo*

*has some intention to pursue in the palm-forest.*

*Those who were sacred have remained so,*

*holiness does not dissolve, it is a presence*

*of bronze, only the sight that saw it*

*faltered and turned from it.*

*An old joy returns in holy presence.*

—*Denise Levertov, "Come Into Animal Presence"*

DISAGREEMENTS ENGENDERED BY the publication of Rachel Carson's *Silent Spring* revealed conflicts between female conservationists and key men shaping environmental policy in America. Those conflicts were not superficial but reflected deep-seated arguments among middle-class white men and women over the meaning and value of gender roles. Since the Victorian period, Euro-American women's confinement to the landscape of home has been symbolic of their "nature." Biological models of women's reproductive functions have been used to tie them more closely to animals and "explain" their perceived lack of rationality and heightened emotionalism. Women's dangerous links to nature seemingly justified bounding middle-class females within the domestic sphere.[1] Home provided a safe haven, protecting women at once from the wilderness in themselves and in nature. One important effect of such relegation to home has been to distance women both from their own animal being and from contact with certain classes of animals in nature.

Women have grappled most clearly with their placement on the boundary between nature and culture in their expressive writings. In this genre, freed from the naturalist's observing eye, they explore their feelings about their status among the other animals. Women's literature not only reflects social codes but also sometimes imaginatively reconstructs them to open new terrain to their gaze. The issues for them are twofold: how to describe their responsibility within the community of all animal life, and how to come into the animal presence at the heart of their being.[2]

More important, women's expressive writings provide a place to consider the values of women of color. Most standard histories of naturalists, conservationists, and environmentalists simply note the extent to which such activities have been the ken of the white middle class. Historians of conservation and environmentalism in America have posited class as a critical determinant in the rise of these movements. Americans turned to the preservation of nature only after achieving comfortable standards of living. Because Euro-Americans dominated the middle and upper classes, they defined the environmental movement. Recently, some environmental groups have begun to address the underrepresentation of people of color in their memberships by expanding preservationist agendas to include issues of concern to poor, inner city residents.[3] But, as the free black woman, Charlotte Forten Grimké, realized over one hundred years ago, inequalities rooted in centuries of racism have made it difficult for people of color to look at nature in the same way as Euro-Americans, or for Euro-Americans to see racial minorities as equally sensitive to America's flora and fauna.

In the mid-twentieth century, at least one African American woman—Zora Neale Hurston—echoed Charlotte Forten's earlier understanding that race, more than class, was the bar used by whites to deny her people rights to nature appreciation. Supporting the positioning of women as closer to nature than men, the nineteenth century's popular image of the chain of life ranked nature lower than culture, other species lower than humans, and all African Americans and American Indians lower than white women. In her essay, "What White Publishers Won't Print," Hurston described the continuing power of such racist divisions into the 1950s. This black novelist, folklorist, and anthropologist castigated the white press for refusing to print stories about the "higher emotions" of anyone except the WASP middle class. The reasons for "this indifference, not to say skepticism, to the internal life of educated minorities," she asserted, were displayed in "THE AMERICAN MUSEUM OF UNNATURAL HISTORY." The museum represented "typical" American Indians, American Negroes, Orientals, Jews, and other ethnic groups. Focusing on African Americans, Hurston argued that the dominant culture continued to believe in genetic differences in blacks, differences making them incapable of sharing in the community of beliefs and feelings making up Western culture. Euro-Americans harbored doubts that educating blacks resulted in any more than "an aping of our culture . . . Turn him loose, and he will revert at once to the jungle. He is still a savage, and no amount of translating Virgil and Ovid is going to change him." Until such ideas disappeared, "it [would] remain impossible for the majority to conceive of a Negro experiencing a deep and abiding love and not just the passion of sex. That a great mass of Negroes can be stirred by the pageants of Spring and Fall; the extravaganza of summer, and the majesty of winter . . . is ruled out."[4]

Hurston assumed that the major themes in Western culture have been love of another person and love of nature and that both spring from elite values. She also knew that racial stereotypes continued in the twentieth century to place blacks, American Indians, and various ethnic groups within nature, whereas Euro-Americans seemed to exist outside nature as observers and appreciators of the green world. Thus, African Americans could never move outside because they were, by their "nature," presumed to be trapped within—within an ape's skin and within the jungle. Hurston criticized such ideas as unnatural to encourage the publication of literature by and about middle-class blacks who were deeply in love with both other humans and the natural world.[5]

Links between uncontrolled sexuality and a "wild nature" were crucial to the relegation of certain groups outside culture. White, middle-class women were protected from a fall from culture into nature only by the stringent bounds of domesticity. Those bounds were reinforced by images of women of color as the wild "other" whom white women could become. Recent studies of Victorian conceptions of black and American Indian women show the burden they bore under such stereotyping. Assumed to be more passionate than their white sisters, women of color became the model, in the most extreme readings of their "animal nature," of deviant sexual behavior. Images of perversion appeared in references to "wild" emotions and "primitive" sexual parts. Black women, in particular, were used as a standard for measuring white women's status as humans. Sander Gilman, for example, has shown how, in nineteenth-century Europe, images of Hottentot women's physical features were applied to white prostitutes to explain their fall from culture into nature.[6] Zora Neale Hurston was not alone among women of color in recognizing the continuing prevalence of such stereotypes into the contemporary period and in understanding how these icons served to bar any but white voices from classic nature writing; these issues are woven throughout nineteenth- and twentieth-century narratives by African American and American Indian women.

African American and American Indian women have responded to the plants and animals of their yards and neighborhoods in ways learned from their own people. As in the case of women's gardening activities, much work remains to be done on the nature perceptions of those outside the dominant elites. My emphasis on the problematic relationships these writers have located in their response to nature in no way implies that such images cover the full range of feelings about well-loved plants and animals expressed in the literature by women of color. I find compelling, however, Hazel Carby's argument that one key to understanding American black women's narratives is as in dialogue with the "dominant discourse of white female sexuality."[7] Extending Carby's thesis, I argue that, for many women of color, the specific choice to write about their feelings for familiar animals brings to the surface problematic visions of uncontrolled sexuality. Their personal memoirs and fictional tales spanning the last hundred years show African American and American Indian women to be aware of the pressures of the dominant ideology, yet successfully subverting that imagery and, more important, formulating their own visions of the sensual desire and spiritual meaning that connect their lives and the lives of other animals. Such women's invisibility in the canon of nature lore and nature conservation reflects the dominant culture's resistance to the alternative nature values expressed by women of color.

Euro-American women's writings in the same period also contend with issues of sexuality and spirituality in themselves and other animals, but their status within the dominant culture produces different conflicts. Victorian domesticity sanitized women's sexuality and tamed the animals (human and non-human) of home. Euro-American women writers since the late nineteenth century have struggled to reinvest themselves and their animal familiars with a wildness at the center of nature. For all their differences, American Indian, African American, and Euro-American women finally have come to share the joy that Denise Levertov describes. The expressive literature of each group ultimately returns women to the sacred heart of animal presence, both in themselves and in other beings.

I

In 1932 Frank Linderman published *Red Mother*, the life story of a Crow woman born in the 1850s. The book was reprinted in 1972 under the title *Pretty-shield: Medicine Woman of the Crows*. Linderman interviewed Pretty-shield when she was in her seventies, working through sign language and a Crow woman interpreter. He asked her to tell the story of a woman's life. For all the interpretive difficulties posed by such a text, *Pretty-shield* yields a good deal of information about Crow women's images of the plains environment.

Linderman knew that a good starting point in his conversations with Pretty-shield was to ask about a specific plant or animal. Seeing some chickadees as he walked to the interview, he began with these birds since "every tribe of Indians in the Northwest respects the chickadee."[8] At first Pretty-shield did not grasp what bird he was describing. When at last he hit upon whistling the call of the chickadee, she excitedly asked him if he knew the bird well. He replied that he was something of an expert, having written many stories about the creatures. But Pretty-shield provided Linderman with a new piece of information when she informed him that the bird has one tongue in the fall that gradually develops into seven tongues by spring: "It is by the chickadee's tongue that we tell what moon of the winter we are in . . . In the first moon the chickadee shows *two* tongues, then *three*, then *four*, then *five*, then *six*, and finally *seven* . . . And then . . . the chickadee says 'summer's near, summer's near,' and goes back to *one* tongue" (153). Pretty-shield assured him that "we do not harm the chickadee when we look at his tongue to see what moon of the winter we are in . . . We catch them, look quickly at their tongues, and then let them go again" (154). She told him several tales in which the chickadee provided warnings and predictions to humans, revealing it to have much power in Crow belief.

Linderman spent little time wrestling with the meaning of her stories, but he found the fact of the ever-splitting tongue fascinating and verified its accuracy. Capturing two chickadees, "with the aid of a jeweler's glass I discovered that their tongues were not alike, one having four sharp points resembling the spines on the cactus plant, two on the right, and two on the left of the tongue's center; the other, seven thread-like strands resembling a raveled edge of cloth . . . The tongue of the chickadee is phenomenal and a careful examination of it late in February or early in March may prove Pretty-shield's contention to be correct" (154). While thinking about the chicka-dee led Pretty-shield into stories of human-animal reciprocity, it led Linder-man into scientific verification. When Pretty-shield asked him if he knew the chickadee, she had in mind a different familiarity than he.

To Linderman the chickadee remained an artifact of nature, whereas to her the chickadee provided an integral link to the beliefs and history of her people. Further, to him Pretty-shield herself was grounded in nature, closer to the animals of nature than to Linderman's Euro-American culture. At one point he compared her to a chickadee (97). In the introduction to his book, he noted that it was often difficult to separate dreams from real experience in Indian oral narratives: "Trying to determine exactly where the dream begins and ends is precisely like looking into a case in a museum of natural history where a group of beautiful birds are mounted against a painted background blended so cunningly into reality that one cannot tell where the natural melts to meet the artificial" (11). He viewed the Indians as much closer to animals and as objects for similar scientific study.

Much has been written—particularly since the environmental move-ments of the 1960s and 1970s—about American Indian belief systems as models of appropriate conservationist approaches to the environment. Some Euro-American scholars have agreed with Ake Hultkrantz's assertion that "the harmonious combination of nature and religion that they have impresses every outsider." Others have suggested that Euro-Americans' reading of a preservationist urge in Indian naturism is more a function of feelings of fail-ure in their own management of the environment than an accurate assessment of American Indians' actual relationship with the land.[9] My aim here is not to argue the merits of either reading. Regardless of its accuracy, the Euro-American notion that North American tribes are more in tune with, or im-mersed in, nature has also served to place such people outside the ranks of human culture. American Indian women have attempted to counter the con-straints posed by such stereotyping.

In 1932, when Pretty-shield told Linderman her life history, she chose not to dwell on her experiences after white contact. Most of the narration depicts a girl's free life on the plains unencumbered by white projections of what it meant to be an Indian woman in the early twentieth century. Pretty-shield narrated both what she wanted to remember and what Linderman wanted to hear—a tale of precontact freedom.[10] We cannot judge from Linderman's mode of presentation what she thought of his version of her life or of his interest in her as a representative of nature. By the turn of the century, however, other American Indian women were beginning to publish their own tales of the postcontact period. Their narratives addressed the problems inherent in viewing Indian women as kin of the animals with whom they drew so many parallels in their stories of life on the land. One of the most important of these women was Pauline Johnson, born in 1861 near Brantford, Ontario, of an English mother and a Mohawk father.

Johnson published poetry and short fiction, as well as many traditional tales, before her death in 1913. Her work chronicled the experiences of mixed-blood American Indians—particularly women. Ernest Thompson Seton once quoted her as commenting, "there are those who think they pay me a compliment by saying I am just like a white woman. I am Indian, and my aim, my joy and my pride is to sing the glories of my own people."[11] A part of being Indian was her connection with the lands of the Mohawk, but what did such a heritage mean to her white readers? A hint is provided in Sir Gilbert Parker's introduction to the 1913 edition of her collection of tales, *The Moccasin Maker*. Parker felt that "she could not be impersonal enough, and therefore could not be great; but she could get very near to human sympathies, to domestic natures, to those who care for pleasant, happy things, to the lovers of the wild."[12] Implicit in Parker's assessment is the standard image of the tribal person bound by subjective ties to the natural world, ties preventing rationality.

Johnson was aware of such stereotyping, particularly as it related to Indian women. Some of her stories deal with the ramifications of such attitudes. "As It Was in the Beginning," from *The Moccasin Maker*, begins with the line, "They account for it by the fact that I am a Redskin, but I am something else, too—I am a woman" (163). In this story a young Indian girl is given to a Christian missionary so she can be educated. Impressed by the missionary's images of damnation, her father lets the preacher take the child to "save her from hell" (165). Unhappy in her new situation, she longs for the time when she may return home, ignoring the whites' admonitions that she can never go back: "they told each other that if I returned to the prairies, the tepees, I would degenerate, slip back to paganism, as other girls had done" (167). Her determination to return home continues until she reaches woman-hood, falls in love with the missionary's nephew, and agrees to marry him. At this point she says farewell to her old life and prays to his "great white God" (169). Johnson's tale suggests no inherent difficulty in assimilation—the young woman appears ready to shift to the whites' world.

When the missionary is told of the engagement, he explains why assimi-lation is merely a figment of her imagination. He informs his blond nephew that he must marry yellow-haired Ida McIntosh, not the Indian woman. Over-hearing his reasons, the Indian learns what the whites mean when they say she is of nature, not outside it. The uncle begins by cautioning the nephew: "you can never tell what lurks in *a caged animal that has once been wild*" (172). Then he asks: "what would you do with a wife who might any day break from you to return to her prairies and her buckskins? *You can't trust her*" (173). Finally, he gives the reason she cannot be trusted: "Think of her silent ways, her noise-less step; the girl glides about like an apparition; her quick fingers, her wild longings—I don't know why, but with all my fondness for her, she reminds me sometimes of a strange—*snake*" (174). Struck by this image, the nephew agrees to give her up. Overhearing the conversation, the young woman re-solves to return to the wilds, delaying just long enough to kill her lover with an arrow tipped with snake venom given her by her mother. She murders out of jealousy, determined that the yellow-haired Ida shall not have him. The image that begins the story closes it: people say she killed him because she is a "Redskin," but they forget she is a woman (177).

Denying stereotypes about Indians' wild nature, Johnson slipped into similar stereotypes of women. The point, however, is that Johnson was "im-personal" enough to recognize the fallacies in reducing the Indian to nature. In fact, in this story she turned the tables on such imagery, picturing the missionary as a voracious hawk (172) and a snake (174–75). Johnson linked women and men, Indians and whites, to the animal kingdom. She recog-nized the difficulty created for American Indian women if they told white audiences tales of their deep connections with nature. Such tales were used to deny these women a measure of humanity extended to the lowest, most reprehensible white.

The point at which the young woman becomes a snake in the missionary's eyes is the point at which she poses a sexual threat to his nephew. Euphe-mistic descriptions of Indian women as wildflowers, panthers, or snakes in white literature are really means for describing their wildness as potential sexual license. Johnson's early twentieth-century narrative provides an eerie introduction to Leslie Silko's short story, "Storyteller." Johnson locates great power in her protagonist (and in the traditions handed to her from her mother) but ultimately reduces its impact by leaving her trapped in Christian religion and Victorian gender codes. Silko releases her character in "Storyteller" from the dominant culture; in so doing, she creates one of the truly powerful nature heros in contemporary fiction. Silko's hero uses white men's connection of female sexuality with animal nature to her own advantage.

"Storyteller" forms the title piece for a collection of Silko's writings. Several tales and poems recount the escapades of Yellow Woman, a character based on traditional Laguna oral narratives. Pat Smith and Paula Gunn Allen argue that Yellow Woman serves as a role model for Laguna women's sexuality, a sexuality expressed in liaisons with nature gods like Whirlwind man.[13] The Yellow Woman stories generally take place within the confines of Laguna land in western New Mexico, in a landscape where precontact legends are as important as the history following contact. The Yellow Woman cycle has received much critical attention partly because it offers an alternative, positive reading of white visions of American Indian women as sexually licentious beings. That these tales have garnered attention reflects contemporary critics' continued romanticization of American Indian environmentalism: the Indian woman as a passionate herbalist replaces the older image of Indian men as a noble savage. Neither provides much power to effect change in dominant stereotypes. Silko, well aware of the difficulties in presenting such tales of sexual freedom to a primarily white readership, balances the Yellow Woman cycle with stories offering a more problematic bite, recalling the venom-tipped arrow of Pauline Johnson's hero.

In "Storyteller," a Tlingit woman lures a white store owner to his death on a frozen river in retribution for his murder of her parents by trading them tainted alcohol. Paralleling her account is the story that a dying old man, mate to her grandmother, tells of a hunter pursuing a polar bear across the tundra. In the end, the bear kills the hunter. Stalking through these two tales is a narrative of the coming Arctic winter, moving like a bear across the land; it is perhaps the last winter ever, the ultimate cold freezing the sun in the sky so that it moves "like a wounded caribou running on strength which only dying animals find, leaping and running on bullet-shattered lungs" (32). The Tlingit woman's plans to kill the store owner deepen with the ever-encroaching winter and the hunter's stalking of the bear; thus, her story, the tale from the old man, and the narrative unfolding in the seasonal cycle mirror one another.

Whites, or Gussucks as they are called in the story, appear as rapists of the land and the people. The old man says "they only come when there is something to steal. The fur animals are too difficult for them to get now, and the seals and fish are hard to find. Now they come for oil deep in the earth" (22). Only men come, bringing their dogs. Much to the Indians' disgust, they keep the dogs indoors with them. The old man notes: "they tell us we are dirty for the food we eat—raw fish and fermented meat. But we do not live with dogs" (22). Symbolic of their arrival are red tin barrels of fuel for their machines, which the tribal people scavenge and use for shelters. To the narrator this red tin disrupts the continuities of the landscape and reminds her of the red spilled in the snow where her parents died. It is "something not swallowed up by the heavy white belly of the sky or caught in the folds of the frozen earth" (28).

She continues to live with her grandmother's lover after the old woman dies but grows curious about the Gussucks and goes to their village bent on finding "something different from the old man" (21). The old man knows when she has been with one of these men because she returns smelling of their dogs. Connections between the Gussucks and their domestic pets culminate in her discovery that the man she has sex with places a picture above the bed each time they sleep together, using it to reach his climax. It is of "a woman with a big dog on top of her" (24). Imagining tribal women as participants in his fantasy, the white man reveals to the Tlingit woman the connections he makes between herself and a tamed beast. But Silko uses the story to turn the tables on the man, demonstrating that bestiality is a weakness of the whites. Later, when the hero goes to the store to lure the owner out onto the ice to his death, he follows easily, for he is "like a dog tied up all winter, watching while the others got fed" (29). Whites become domesticated animals; as such, they have less sacred power than both the Tlingit people and other animals.

Silko does not allow her hero to become trapped in the white man's illusion. Once she has discovered the Gussucks for what they are, the woman uses that knowledge to destroy them. She is connected with animals in the tale, but they are not dogs of the hearth. Rather, she is the polar bear of the old man's story, stalking the hunter. Much of the story is of her dawning recognition of her power and the power of the glacier bear. Her grandmother shows her how women truly are immersed in nature. The grandmother is linked to winter and to the bear: "The predawn light would be the color of an old woman. An old woman sky full of snow" (27). Given her grandmother's wolfskin parka, she remembers "when the old lady had walked across the tundra in the winter, she was invisible in the snow" (20). The bear stalks as does the northern cold, merging into the terrain as her grandmother had: "when the boundaries were gone the polar ice would range across the land into the sky . . . She would watch for its approach in the stars, and hear it come with the wind. These preparations were unfamiliar, but gradually she recognized them as she did her own footprints in the snow" (27).

As her grandmother had prepared her to merge with the bear, so she had prepared her for life in that polar winter—a winter silencing the engines of the Gussuck machines. With all evidence of technological society disabled by the ice, the hero finds the whale oil lamp that her grandmother left, realizing "the old woman had saved everything they would need when the time came" (24). By the end of the story, she has been identified with a host of powerful animals. In addition to the connections with Arctic wolves and bears, she is identified with the fish on which the tribe lives. Readying for the death she will bring and for the winter that attends it, in the summer the woman helps her grandfather smoke fish. Like the fish, she feels "herself growing wide and thin in the sun as if she had been split from belly to throat and strung on the willow pole in preparation for the winter to come" (26). Set against the Gussucks' attempts to reduce the woman to some equation with the domesticated dog, such imagery redeems this woman's sense of her connection with nature and reveals the power intrinsic in her identification with animal life.

## II

When Zora Neale Hurston called for the publication of African American literature appreciative of the natural world, she was, perhaps, defining nature in a rather generalized way—writings about beautiful flowers, graceful creatures, awesome thunderstorms. But the classic nature essay springs from immersion in a specific landscape and evocation of its variety. Euro-American appreciation of American Indian environmental values is based in part on the ability to speak from long tenancy in North America. American Indian stories often have the environmental specificity valued in the Euro-American nature writing tradition; this is true even in statements of loss and dispossession.[14]

To African American writers the North American landscape offers radically different meanings. One illustrative story appearing occasionally in the literature provides a good starting point. My favorite telling is in Paule Marshall's *Praisesong for the Widow*. In this novel, the hero visits her great-aunt in Tatum, South Carolina. Each summer the aunt takes her on a hike through farmed-out cotton fields to Ibo Landing. At this landing a ship once docked with a full load of Ibo slaves. The people stand on the shore seeing not only the land for the first time, but also the whole history of what will happen in that place up to the time that the aunt and niece stand there generations later. Then they turn, walk back onto the water, and trek across the ocean home to Africa.[15]

The Ibo foresaw how difficult it would be for slaves to take possession of that landscape. As Alice Walker has so poignantly written, "if it is true that land does not belong to anyone until they have buried a body in it, then the land of my birthplace belongs to me, dozens of times over. Yet the history of my family, like that of all black Southerners, is a history of dispossession. We loved the land and worked the land, but we never owned it."[16] Many of Walker's essays deal with the problems of being a southern writer exiled from the region giving birth to much of her fiction. Her work specifically explores the reasons that blacks might evidence little appreciation of "nature's nation." Returning to Mississippi in the 1970s, she remembered her arrest in the 1960s for swimming in the "Ross Barnett Reservoir, this area's largest recreational body of water" (167). This memory makes it difficult for her to share in American rituals of renewal through holidays in the outdoors.

Walker refines Hurston's call to publish the nature writing of middle-class blacks. She separates the class problems in Hurston's statement from the right of all blacks to express their connections with nature and through nature with basic life-affirming principles. Walker argues that it was difficult in the 1960s and 1970s for politically aware African Americans to write anything about their love of nature. Discussing her colleagues' assessment of Sammy Lou, the hero of Walker's poem "Revolutionary Petunias," as "incorrect," she posits that the most incorrect thing about Sammy Lou is her love of flowers: "I have heard it said by one of our cultural visionaries that whenever you hear a black person talking about the beauties of nature, that person is not a black person at all, but a Negro. This is meant as a put-down, and it is. It puts down all of the black folks in Georgia, Alabama, Mississippi, Texas, Louisiana—in fact, it covers just about everybody's mama" (267).

Realizing how often Euro-Americans have used nature appreciation as a litmus test of class and civility, Walker remains committed to locating sources within African American traditions for immersion in the green world, identifying spirit in trees, plants, birds, and apple blossoms (252). On this point of seeing the world as inspirited, contemporary black writers are finding connections with contemporary American Indian writing. Walker uses this affinity to distinguish her nature values from those of the dominant culture: "If there is one thing African-Americans and Native Americans have retained of their African and ancient American heritage, it is probably the belief that everything is inhabited by spirit. This belief encourages knowledge perceived intuitively" (252). She writes of African American concepts of nature not to prove some sort of participation in middle-class taste, but to reveal links to stories with African roots fortified by life in North America.

Alice Walker has written fine examples of the sort of literature she espouses, but one of the most fulsome narratives exploring the gender issues involved in being a black woman mediating between white culture's stereotypes and her own history in nature is Toni Morrison's *Beloved*.[17] *Beloved* begins with the dual vision every southern place engenders in Morrison's major characters. Sethe, the hero of the novel, recalls Sweet Home in Kentucky, the landscape of her slavery, with both longing and disgust: "suddenly there was Sweet Home rolling, rolling, rolling out before her eyes, and although there was not a leaf on that farm that did not make her want to scream, it rolled itself out before her in shameless beauty. It never looked as terrible as it was and it made her wonder if hell was a pretty place too."[18] Sweet Home's hellishness was due in part to the master's equation of his slaves with animals. Sethe fled north so her children would never experience that comparison.

Morrison proposes that slavery forms an important quotient in black attitudes toward nature. She partly derived *Beloved* from stories of slaves' lives. Nineteenth-century slave narratives have offered a key point of reference for contemporary writers' attempts to tell how African American women may come into animal presence. One of the most interesting original slave narratives providing both a woman's view and information about nature is Harriet Jacobs's *Incidents in the Life of a Slavegirl*, published in 1861 under the pseudonym Linda Brent. Recently shown to have come primarily from the pen of Jacobs rather than her abolitionist editor Lydia Maria Child, the text tells of her life in North Carolina until her escape to the North in 1842, when she was about thirty-seven.[19] Sprinkled throughout the story are references to whites' images of blacks as animals, or even as less than animals. Her brother escaped north after telling her: "we are dogs here; foot-balls, cattle, and every thing that's mean."[20] Jacobs herself acknowledged that black women "are considered of no value, unless they continually increase their owner's stock. They are put on a par with animals" (49). In fact, some masters considered dogs more civilized than slaves. Jacobs tells of the death of a slave woman who was forced to eat the family dog's mush after the animal had died from it. Her master assumed that her "stomach was stronger than the dog's" (11).

In a context of such inhumanity, Jacobs found little to value in the green landscapes of the South. She contrasted the life of slave girls to that of their white counterparts, using garden imagery to place the whites: "the fair child grew up to be a still fairer woman. From childhood to womanhood her pathway was blooming with flowers, and overarched by a sunny sky . . . [The black child] was very beautiful; but the flowers and sunshine of love were not for her" (28–29). Forced, on the day of her father's death, to "[gather] flowers and [weave] them into festoons [for my mistress' party], while the dead body of my father was lying within a mile from me" (8), Jacobs received scant comfort in the garden. Susan Willis has shown that for slaves in the cultivated lands of the Caribbean, "the garden is . . . not a natural phenomenon to be shared, enjoyed or destroyed, but a piece of capital."[21] Similarly, the gardens of southern slaveholders represented little more than a place of hard labor for slaves like Jacobs.

Jacobs also suggests that female slaves experienced the additional burden of seeing in the garden their exclusion from the ranks of domestic womanhood. The white mistress in the garden symbolized female nature tamed, civilized, the true woman. Neither their masters nor their mistresses desired that slaves should step into this terrain. Hazel Carby has outlined the historical image of African American women as carriers of a "rampant sexuality," in whom any pretense of virtue and purity posed a threat—both economically in their role as "breeders" and psychically in their role as the release valve for white masters' sexuality.[22] To portray a slave at her ease among the cultivated flowers of the ornamental garden would violate the stereotype of black women as, by their nature, incapable of purity.

Outside the bounds of the household, only one place had some value for Jacobs as a refuge. The graveyard in the woods where her parents were buried functioned as the only sacred spot in her landscape. While Melvin Dixon, reading mostly male slave narratives, has located "salvation and liberation" in the wild lands bordering the plantation, Jacobs's account does not confirm such feelings.[23] On her first attempt to escape, she prayed to God to guide her through the wilderness but received no answer (58). During her later, successful flight, she entered a natural world of darkness, with swamps, snakes, and mosquitoes threatening her life at every turn. At one point she was bitten by a poisonous snake. Yet, however bad her situation, the sight of a white man was worse: "I passed a wretched night; for the heat of the swamp, the mosquitos, and the constant terror of snakes, had brought on a burning fever . . . But even those large, venomous snakes were less dreadful to my imagination than the white men in that community called civilized" (116). For Jacobs, God was not located in either the garden or the wilds because, in terms of her personal safety, there was no difference between the plantation and the swamp; white men could reach her anywhere. The traditional image of nature as a place of escape simply did not hold for her.[24]

The most important aspect of her nature attitudes in the book is contained in her comments on whites. Rejecting their application of animalistic characteristics to herself, she applied them to white society. At one point she called her master a tiger, at another she referred to the plantation as a "cage of obscene birds" (53). Finally, seemingly free of the South, she commented that northern summers made her nervous because "hot weather brings out snakes and slaveholders, and I like one class of the venomous creatures as little as I do the other. What a comfort it is, to be free to *say* so!" (179). The memory of the South that Jacobs carried north with her was of a land infested with "snakes and slaveholders" on the one hand and decorated with Edenic gardens filled with demanding white mistresses on the other.[25]

I chose to focus my comments regarding the nineteenth-century text on Jacobs because she clearly states the sense of dispossession that writers like Alice Walker, Toni Morrison, and Paule Marshall have expressed in their own writings about the South over one hundred years later. It is also important to notice what goes unsaid in Jacobs's narrative. She makes no references to tribal beliefs that slaves brought with them, connections between those African traditions and Western European folk beliefs; physical and biological similarities between their homeland and the South, which meant that knowledge brought from home was useful in the new place; or new knowledge they gained as they lived on the land. Elizabeth Fox-Genovese argues that, in fact, slavery served to negate many West African beliefs about the sacred in women and nature, denying slaves a "vital part of the basis for gender solidarity and identification." Slave narratives may not always contain accurate information about continuities with African traditions. Barbara Christian suggests that nineteenth-century writers like Harriet Jacobs might have suppressed non-Christian references in their works anyway, aware as they were of the destructive stereotypes that might "terrify their [white] readers."[26]

Yet occasionally slave narratives show that blacks felt they had the edge on understanding nature. Lawrence Levine quotes one black informant who believed she had a more informed understanding of local flora and fauna than the master: "white folks just go through de woods and don't know nothin.'"[27] Research into the postbellum gardens of southern blacks shows that freed people took control of their landscape, designing intricate swept yards and ornamental flower gardens that expressed strong feelings for nature. As African Americans in the twentieth century began a similar reappropriation of their oral history, they located in African traditions and nineteenth-century folklore an ideology for appropriate relations with the land.

Early in the twentieth century, Zora Neale Hurston's collections of black folklore brought that sense of spiritual connection with nature to fruition in literature as well as on the landscape.[28] Hurston was well aware of stories like Harriet Jacobs recounts. She embedded an example in *Their Eyes Were Watching God*. Janie Wood's grandmother remembers her escape, when Janie's mother was a baby, from her white mistress. She runs to the swamps: "De noise uh de owls skeered me; de limbs of dem cypress trees took to crawlin' and movin' round after dark, and two three times Ah heered panthers prowlin' round."[29] Snakes may be better than whites, but there is still very little security in the wilds. Janie's mother is later raped in the woods (36).

Even more potent than general descriptions of wilderness is Hurston's use of animal imagery. Her grandmother explains to Janie that black women are the mules of the world (29). Janie's first husband, Logan Killicks, tries to work her as a mule (52), and her second, Joe Starks, encourages her to "look on herself as the bell-cow" to other women of his town (66). Black men, internalizing the slave master's images of women as animals, themselves use such metaphors to justify various types of abuse. As Pauline Johnson had done before her, Hurston turns these images back on men. In trying to make Janie a mule, Logan Killicks becomes a bear (52). Mirroring his assignment of Janie to a rank above the other women, Joe Starks confounds the town with his middle-class pretensions. He metamorphoses into an alligator: "It was bad enough for white people, but when one of your color could be so different it put you into a wonder. It was like seeing your sister turn into a 'gator. A familiar strangeness. You keep seeing your sister in the 'gator and the 'gator in your sister, and you'd rather not" (76). Later, when even Tea Cake, her true love, falls prey to the drive for ownership of Janie, he too becomes animal—the mad dog she must kill to survive.[30]

Given such negative connotations of the natural world and women's place in it, how does Hurston create in Janie a bountiful, fecund, flowering hero? Only twice in the novel is Janie compared favorably to an animal—when her grandmother states that she wants to protect her "feathers" from being "crumpled" by men (37) and when Tea Cake tells her that her hair reminds him of a dove's wing (157). Otherwise, the source of Janie's power comes from her connection with the green world of plants. Her sexuality is connected not with animals, but with the blooming, blossoming world of a pear tree. In contrast to the negative imagery of black women as beasts of burden, Janie becomes the "rose of the world" (23–25). Her power arises from the physical landscape as well—the earth, the moon. Like Lawrence Levine's black informant who knew more about nature than any white folks, she is credited with a sacred knowledge of the world's constant creation and destruction: "She knew things that nobody had ever told her . . . She knew that God tore down the old world every evening and built a new one by sun-up. It was wonderful to see it take form with the sun and emerge from the gray mist of its making" (44).

It makes sense in the end that the hurricane threatens Janie less than the dead animals and the animals displaced by the flood. The terrified cow and rabid dog, like Logan Killicks, Joe Starks, and Tea Cake in his weaker moments, damage her dreams of cyclic renewal. Animals have potency in this novel as a counterforce to Janie's sensual green world. They represent nature in need of guidance—a wilderness of women and other animals dominated by men, always on the verge of chaos. Hurston was mindful that such stereotypes of animalistic women prevailed in American society. She saved her hero from dismissal as the mule of the world by investing her and the landscape in which she lived with a competing metaphor. In the end, what Janie brings back of Tea Cake are seeds. His spirit will return in the plants that have nurtured Janie and her dream of a way of being part of nature, yet outside the animalistic stereotypes limiting black peoples' full connection with the environment.

Such divisions are problematic: they deny a holistic embrace of the world at the heart of animistic religions. The difficulty is similar to Pauline Johnson's in her story of the young Indian woman who discovers that she is thought of as second cousin to the snake—it is not a snake anyone would mistake for a relative. The animal is being read through the filter of dominant cultural values—as are the mules, gators, and dogs of *Their Eyes Were Watching God*. If the world is inspirited, then animals must have spirit as well. There must be a measure of value in their lives that cannot be dismissed. This is the problem Toni Morrison approaches in *Beloved*, where she provides a hero who knows what it means to talk about the earth as a home for all life.

Like Janie, Morrison's Sethe in *Beloved* takes a good deal of pleasure in plants around Sweet Home. Morrison imagines her admiring "pretty, growing things" and carrying flower sprigs with her as she goes about her labors. Her few moments of sexual pleasure with her husband Halle are compared to the sensual stripping of corn husks (27). Plants also serve as metaphors of the birth of Sethe's youngest child. Spores of blue fern fall around her and the white girl who helps her during her labor: "On a riverbank in the cool of a summer evening two women struggled under a shower of silvery blue. They never expected to see each other again in this world and at the moment couldn't care less. But there on a summer night surrounded by bluefern they did something together appropriately and well" (84). Morrison's novels contain some of the most beautiful nature writing in contemporary fiction. She invests the green world with a sacred quality and shows African American people deeply in touch with the land.

But the green world cannot save Sethe from the violence of slavery. Though Morrison never denies the beauties of nature, she pointedly rejects any romantic notion that Sethe's connection with plants provides her power: "As though a handful of myrtle stuck in the handle of a pressing iron propped against the door in a whitewoman's kitchen could make it hers" (23). Like Janie, Sethe is identified with a tree. Amy Denver, a white girl who helps her during her escape, sees it first: "See, here's the trunk—it's red and split wide open, full of sap, and this here's the parting for the branches . . . Tiny little cherry blossoms, just as white. Your back got a whole tree on it. In bloom" (79). But Amy Denver is wrong. Sethe's back is not inscribed with nature's tree, but with the "decorative work of an ironsmith" (17). Sores and scars from a vicious beating make the tree on Sethe's back. Amy Denver makes the same mistake most whites do in reading signs from nature: they use imagery from the natural world to cover up or justify evidence of their own inhumanity to fellow beings. This is why Sethe is so angry with herself for remembering the beautiful landscapes of Sweet Home, because such memory conflicts with the actual use whites made of the land. Whenever Sethe fondly remembers the trees around Sweet Home, she forces herself to remember as well the feet of hanged slaves (including her mother) dangling below their branches.

Morrison recognizes that the most damaging misreading of nature's artifacts is not with plants but with animals. She lays open ways that racist images of blacks as animals are used to justify slavery, rape, and murder. She expands her critique to show how such domination of slaves is only one reflection of a general lack of respect for all of nature. Like Silko, Morrison also finds a way to reinvest both animals and African Americans' supposed animal nature with power and spirit. Turning white stereotypes back on themselves, she locates Sethe's strength in her shared status with other animals.

Sethe's master, the "Schoolteacher," studies the blacks on his plantation as representatives of the links between apes and humans. He teaches his nephews to see slaves as animals. Specifically, blacks are cast as domestic beasts of labor. Halle and Sethe are allowed to consummate their marriage in a cornfield among a "crop animals could use as well as humans" (26). Literally playing out the imagery, the nephews trap Sethe in the barn and take milk from her breasts. Schoolteacher punishes them only when they beat her. He is angry for the same reasons he would be angry at such treatment of any other domestic animal: "Suppose you beat the hounds past that point thataway. Never again could you trust them in the woods or anywhere else. You'd be feeding them maybe, holding out a piece of rabbit in your hand, and the animal would revert—bite your hand clean off" (149–50). Following her violation in the barn and vicious beating, Sethe escapes north. In Schoolteacher's mind, he lost a breeder, one young enough to produce more stock.

Northerners display similar stereotypes, if in somewhat different fashion. Cincinnati, where Sethe settles after her escape, functions as a sacrifice area for thousands of animals that go to feed easterners. The slaughter is carried out by former slaves. In the North, as in the South, African Americans create beautiful landscapes for whites by doing the labor the upper classes do not want to see. Deemed closer to nature, better suited to handle direct contact with domestic animals, their toil allows whites to deny the mutilation and death on which their lives are built: "Cincinnati's stench had traveled to the country: from the canal, from hanging meat; . . . from small animals dead in the fields, town sewers and factories . . . They could be seen going to . . . scrape hog skin, press lard, case-pack sausage or hide in tavern kitchens so white-people didn't have to see them handle their food" (257–58). Morrison is not suggesting that humans are separate from animals and that the whites' only error is in conjoining blacks to a "lower" species. Rather, she critiques whites' dealings with all other life forms as though they were only meat for the table, beasts of burden, or, in the case of Schoolteacher, data for his theories.

Poised against these images of slaughter, rape, and mutilation are the slaves' memories of Africa. Morrison imagines African tales offering a different narrative about human connections with animals. The memories she gives Sethe are not about domestic beasts, but about native, wild animals that are sacred. Remembering the stories links Sethe to these totems.[31] Sethe, on the run to the North, is six months pregnant. On the verge of death, she thinks of the child in her belly as an antelope who stirs uneasily when she threatens to give up. She knows she has never seen an antelope and surmises that she imagines the child as this animal from a memory of her childhood, a memory of slaves direct from Africa dancing, "and sometimes they danced the antelope. The men as well as the ma'ams . . . They shifted shapes and became something other. Some unchained, demanding other whose feet knew her pulse better than she did. Just like this one in her stomach" (31). On the point of remembering this ability to become one with other beings, she hears what she thinks must be a white boy following her in the woods. Assuming he will rape, then kill her, she shifts into the shape of a snake. Unlike the reptile in Pauline Johnson's story, this snake is not connected with treachery but with truth: "Down in the grass, like the snake she believed she was, Sethe opened her mouth, and instead of fangs and a split tongue, out shot the truth" (32).

Schoolteacher was right on one count: Sethe's violation did change her from domestic beast to wild animal. Her connection with the green world offered her no protection, but her dawning understanding of what it means to come into animal presence gives her a terrible power. When Schoolteacher comes north to reclaim her after she has run away, she gathers her children together and tries to kill them, succeeding with the next youngest. Seeing it as nothing but the loss of good stock, Schoolteacher offers the perverted view that she has reverted to her "cannibal" heritage. Rather than denying that Sethe is evincing animal-like behavior, Morrison casts her wildness in a different context. One of the black men watching sees her for who she really is: "how she flew, snatching up her children like a hawk on the wing . . . how her face beaked, how her hands worked like claws, how she collected them every which way" (157). Comparing her to a mother hawk, tragically killing her young to protect them from capture, Morrison shows that the domination and violence delivered upon Sethe by slavery represents the real perversion of nature. Sethe, like other animals, responds with the best defense she can muster under the circumstances.

In contrast to Janie's fear of the mad dog, Sethe's embrace of animal presence makes her fearless: she "will never run from another thing on this earth" (15). She is "the one who never looked away, who when a man got stomped to death by a mare right in front of Sawyer's restaurant did not look away; and when a sow began eating her own litter did not look away then either" (12). When her lover, Paul D., horrified to learn that she has killed her own child, reminds her that she is not an animal, he makes a grave error, the sort of error that whites make in separating themselves from all of creation. The issue is not easily resolved by some appeal to the moral responsibilities of two-leggeds over four-leggeds. Such dualities themselves buy into the hierarchies that whites used to justify enslaving African peoples. Rather, the answer is found in tribal beliefs investing the whole world—plant, animal, human—with spirit.

Included in that tribal heritage is Sethe's conviction that nothing ever disappears from the world—that death is only a shifting of shapes. This, of course, forms the premise of *Beloved*. The child Sethe killed to keep her from having to go back to the South continues to haunt her home and her life. Sethe and many of her friends know why Beloved returns; African traditions include in the natural world space for the "dangerous ghosts of men who have been lost, or drowned or burnt alive." [32] But in America such aspects of nature take on new meaning, in large part because there are so many ghosts of people killed by slavery. The spirit of Beloved moving around Sethe's house is one voice in the "mumbling of the black and angry dead" (198). This child ghost emerges from the stream at the edge of Sethe's property. She is always on the verge of melting back into the natural world. Understood to be "wild game," she lives outside the rules of culture (242). To look upon her is to face the heart of animal life. Sethe gains great power in the novel as the one person willing to accept communion with the spirit world in her embrace of Beloved.

My study suggests a shared tradition of organicism in African American and American Indian writing, as well as a shared difficulty in describing that holism in the face of the dominant culture's stereotypes about people of color, particularly women. Nineteenth- and twentieth-century writers have struggled to find a way to express their feelings for animal life without being dismissed as sexually licentious creatures. Pauline Johnson and Harriet Jacobs wrote mainly for white audiences that were threatened by the thought that women of color could take on the mantle of the cultured domesticity reserved for Euro-American women. They made the best of the situation by suggesting that whites were themselves as animalistic in their desires as they believed people of color to be. Neither, however, was able to construct a positive tale of their own culture's understanding of nature. Zora Neale Hurston tried to counter racist stereotypes about African American's closeness to nature by investing her hero with values deriving from the green world. Well aware of the Euro-American tradition connecting appropriately domesticated women with flowers, Hurston created a character whose sexuality, by virtue of its expression through plant reproduction, was cleansed of disturbing connections with animal behavior. Janie's sensitive reading of the plants in her landscape also articulated African American plant lore and the importance of gardens in black women's lives. Hurston's revelations of the values her people invested in the green world have proven inspirational for contemporary writers like Alice Walker. Yet emphasis on the "rose of the world" essentially dodges the troublesome issues of women's supposed animal nature and their ethical relations with animals.[33]

Both Toni Morrison and Leslie Silko use their fiction to dispel simplistic connections of woman with a fecund, treacherous, lower form of life classified as animal. They do not do so as Hurston supposed they might, by proving they can write of the "higher" joys of nature love. Rather, each redefines animal—placing humanity's animal nature within the cycles connecting birth with death, summer with winter, earth with sky, plant with animal, spirit with body—within a sensate universe in which no part is more or less filled with consciousness than any other. Understanding that female sexuality has been used as a key determinant in the dominant culture's efforts to define women's place in the ranks of human and animal, they probe the ways in which Euro-American versions of sexuality are unnatural. They show the links between perversions of sexuality and the dominance of all nature, suggesting that abuse of women of color reflects as well the lack of respect for and destruction of the natural world. Rather than observing nature as outsider, they pull white folks into the world, denying the attempt at objectivity.

III

She swaggers in. They are terrifying in their white hairlessness. She waits. She watches. She does not move. She is measuring their moves. And they are measuring her. Cautiously one takes a bit of her fur. He cuts it free from her. He examines it . . . They announce she is alive . . . She backs her way toward the closed doorway and then roars . . . "Why does she roar?" they ask. The roaring must be inside her, they conclude. They decide they must see the roaring inside her . . . They are trying to put her to sleep. She swings at one of the men . . . She has no soul, they conclude, she does not know right from wrong. "Be still," they shout at her. "Be humble, trust us," they demand. "We have souls," they proclaim, "we know what is right," they approach her with their medicine, "for you." She does not understand this language. She devours them.[34]

In this passage from *Woman and Nature: The Roaring Inside Her*, Susan Griffin completes the exorcism of scientific culture, which, she argues, has bounded women for centuries. Griffin, writing a book about women's ways of thinking about nature and their links to nature, spends most of her text critiquing scientific traditions, detailing how positivistic models, particularly of animal life, have been used to limit women's freedom. She discusses the ways her culture has denigrated African Americans and American Indians by placing them closer to nature, but she goes on to posit that Euro-American women are caught in a trap as well. White women's enfoldment into culture springs from the sense that without taming they will revert to the same animalistic behaviors assigned to women of color. Griffin argues that Euro-American women have had their sexual natures perverted by their participation in intellectual traditions splitting nature from culture. She pushes Euro-American women to disassociate themselves from the taming done by scientific culture and return to more intuitive, "wilder" ways of knowing the natural world and their own nature. Only by coming into their own animal presence will Euro-American women see the connections between their oppression by the dominant, male culture and the destruction of the earth.[35]

Griffin knows that her audience, which is dominated by white, educated, middle- and upper-class women, will have at least a popular knowledge of the history of science. Since the early nineteenth century, this class of women has been expected to be aware of major trends in natural history. One sign of their "progress" (in contrast to that of African American and American Indian women) up the ladder of civilization has been their general participation in amateur science, particularly in botany and ornithology. Often such participation took the form of helping scientific husbands or educating youngsters—either one's own children or someone else's—through popular books and nature study curricula in the schools. Griffin's general grasp of the history of science itself reflects middle-class women's traditions in nature study. For all her radical utopian call to change, she also speaks as the most recent voice in the split between men and women over the meanings of nature and female nature that have developed over the last century.

Griffin is correct that, from its inception, Euro-American women's nature study has been conducted within the context of Western scientific traditions. Early women birders, for example, found a space for their work within the burgeoning scientific interest in field observation. But they did not always have the same interests in nature as men. They, and the men they worked with, agreed that women spoke from within the domestic sphere about issues appropriate to their sex. From Susan Fenimore Cooper to Florence Merriam, women brought the moral values of home into the naturalist's round and used their different vision of nature to critique excesses of science and industrial society. These commentaries were muted, however, by the women's apparent confidence that their concerns were taken seriously, that they and the men they worked with believed in the values of America domestica and together they would nourish and protect them. The real differences between men and women only surfaced in a wide, public forum, when Rachel Carson criticized "Neanderthal" science for threatening the future of the American environment. The male response to Carson exposed the dangerous marginalization of women's domestic sphere (and their concepts of nature) that their collaboration with the naturalist tradition had masked.

Although nineteenth-century female naturalists did not seem to grasp the ways that their culture "mocked" their separate sphere, at least one novelist did. Sarah Orne Jewett's late nineteenth-century stories crossed the boundary between the literary domestic novel and the nature essay, posing a more problematic relationship between the female naturalist and the public round than the naturalists were able to do themselves.[36] Jewett voiced her analysis from within the constraints of nineteenth-century sensibility. An early British traveler meeting any of Jewett's heros in *The Country of the Pointed Firs* or her other short stories would have celebrated the discovery of another American Eve. Jewett's stories are set in a dying New England whaling village. Secluded from the materialistic lures and threats of the city, her heros model a genteel but humble country life driven by virtue, modesty, and selfless devotion to the domestic round. They are appreciative of and knowledgeable about their native terrain.

Jewett supported late nineteenth-century women's efforts to protect nature. Her interest in the Audubon women's attempts to end the slaughter of birds is evidenced in "A White Heron," in which a young girl, Sylvie, refuses to reveal the location of a heron's nest to a visiting ornithologist who is hunting for just such a specimen. Almira Todd, the woman who rents the narrator of the stories a room in the village, is an accomplished herbalist. Esther Hight of "A Dunnet Shepherdess" and "William's Wedding" rejects life as a schoolteacher and moves back home to an isolated stretch of land where she tends her sheep with a devotion commensurate with that shown her ailing mother. Joanna, whose story appears in *The Country of the Pointed Firs*, was duped by a cad from the city. Retiring alone to an isolated island, she communes with the small animal life of the place.[37]

None of Jewett's protagonists are "natural" women in the contemporary meaning—in the meaning Griffin has in mind when she has her lion devour the scientists. All act within nineteenth-century, middle-class gender proscriptions about the role of cultured females. In this way, they remain surrounded by culture. Her life among the sheep refines Esther, the little shepherdess. Joanna's retirement to the hermitage supports rather than subverts gentility—she isolates herself out of shame for being tricked by a scoundrel. Implicit in such behavior is women's role as conservator of the values of home, family, and civilization in the face, not of wild nature, but of irresponsible men bred by the new urban wilderness. Sylvie first hears the whistle of the ornithologist as she remembers a "great red-faced boy" from the "noisy town" who used to frighten her (229). The narrator of *The Country of the Pointed Firs* retreats to Dunnet Landing seeking "the centre of civilization" (2). Such opposition of a civilized rural community to the impinging city has earned Jewett a reputation as a pastoralist.[38]

But something is awry in this pastoral image. Men from the public sphere come here only for plunder, not for refuge. They threaten nature and women when they appear. They make it difficult for women to achieve a full domestic life: in the end, Sylvie must choose between the heron and the ornithologist. She chooses the bird after seeing him at his nest watching over his family. In saving the bird, she saves as well the values of America domestica.[39] The problem is that to do so, she has to give up her own future as a wife and mother. When Jewett's narrator supposes that Sylvie might have chosen the ornithologist and loyally served him as a dog might, she pointedly critiques the subordination of women to men (239). Sylvie's choice represents the real sacrifices forced by the marginalization of women culture's in late nineteenth-century America.

The image of Sylvie as a dog might suggest that her choice is between taming (the domesticated animal giving its loyalty to its owner) and a wild life (the natural woman living freely in nature), but this is not the duality Jewett poses. For Sylvie's sacrifice to function as a heroic act, it has to forward the virtues of woman's sphere. Sylvie does not "value the heron for its heronness" but for its domesticity.[40] The green world validates women's critique of the dominant culture. Jewett's women, with the female naturalists of the day, see nature in what we might call sanitized terms. The vocabulary they use to describe their own virtue is the vocabulary they apply to nature. Men from the city threaten this gentility in both women and nature by bringing violence and sexuality into the country. Were Sylvie to marry the ornithologist, she would become his "dog" serving the goals of the hunt. If these men cannot be tamed by women's culture, then domesticity (and nature) must become a refuge from them—and the threats they pose.

To achieve this refuge in the natural world and in women's nature, Jewett renders her characters sexless in a most basic way. Her heros are either too young or too old to have children. For example, Esther, the shepherdess, waits until middle age to marry William, a local man. Jewett bestows upon her not a human child, but a lamb to complete her family.[41] Removed from any connection of their nature love with their own biology, the women are freed to nurture the herons, sheep, and plants of the world. Such a role is gained by alienation from their own links to animals in any but a romanticized way. We know, for example, that any shepherdess in tending her flock would learn about sex, birth, and death. Such knowledge is suppressed in Jewett's rendering of Esther to cast her as a nunlike being. These are not women who create life but who conserve life—they are nurturer's in a "higher" sense.

Viewed from this perspective, Sylvie's power as a spokesperson for nature is achieved by her alienation from her own natural cycles and potential. Nature becomes a purified, cleansed other, existing only in the context of the assigned gender roles of nineteenth-century middle-class culture. Jewett knew that women's appeal to these symbols of domesticity did not garner them as much influence in the public sphere as their advocates implied. She had only a hint, however, of images of nature and women's nature that might return potency to both. Almira Todd is more than a botanist who specializes in herbs. Her herb plot bespeaks ancient power: "There were some strange and pungent odors that roused a dim sense of remembrance of something in the forgotten past. Some of these might once have belonged to sacred and mystic rites, and have some occult knowledge handed down the centuries; but now they pertained only to humble compounds brewed at intervals with molasses or vinegar or spirits in a small caldron on Mrs. Todd's kitchen stove" (3–4). Like Florence Merriam's worry that female birds lost their true nature in scientific nomenclature, Jewett here hints that women of her rank may have denied their own strength and lost touch with nature in settling into genteel domesticity. These turn-of-the-century questions about the constraints implicit in women's subordination continued to build in the twentieth century as women struggled to find a new vocabulary for naming themselves and nature and as men strained to maintain control of both endeavors.[42]

By the mid-twentieth century both nature and women had changed in ways that challenged the pastoral view of the environment and Victorian codes of behavior. Rather than locating God in the green world, Americans had found the atom, in whose heart lay the potential destruction of the world. By the time Jean Stafford wrote *The Mountain Lion* in 1947, middle-class white women had proven themselves able, if not acceptably so, to work alongside men in the aggressive world of the city. Yet they were not expected to involve themselves in either the science or the policies governing that world. The development of the Atomic Age was almost exclusively the province of men, as was most of the science attendant upon it. Such history informed the responses of many male professionals to Rachel Carson's *Silent Spring*.

The early decades of the twentieth century also ushered in more open discussion of sex, including some legitimizing of female sexual desires. Matching their work patterns, however, women quickly found that their assumed sexual freedom only provided another justification for their relegation to the domestic round. Freudian psychology, specifically as it was applied to women's sexuality, played an important role in assigning them to the confines of home. Freud and his followers taught women to see their sexuality as passive, even masochistic; their primary goal in the sexual act was the pleasure that came from maternity. As their work was not to interfere with home life, so their orgasms were primarily for conception. Although middle-class women appeared to have more freedom than their Victorian sisters, in many ways their lives were as tightly bound by ideology.[43] In this inherently contradictory atmosphere, Stafford wrote a novel that critiques the shared repressions of the Victorian and Atomic ages but fails to overcome them.

*The Mountain Lion* is set in the American West in the early twentieth century. The action alternates between the civilized pleasures of life in a suburb of Covina, California, and the more rugged ranching life of the Colorado Rockies. Stafford chronicles the coming of age of a sister and brother (Molly and Ralph) as they reject pastoral suburbs for wild mountains, in the process growing from childhood (Molly is ten at the beginning and fourteen at the end) to maturity. Ranch life offers less romantic pictures of human-animal interactions than Jewett's pastoral village. Horses are stubborn, fractious animals; pigs and goats are butchered and skinned in graphic detail; coyotes are poisoned; cattle are valued only insofar as they produce and are never seen as the domestic pet Jewett envisioned in her sheep. Managing nature for a profit, the ranch represents the market domination of the green world that Jewett warned about fifty years earlier. Ranch life contrasts with the children's Victorian domesticity in Covina, where their widowed mother protects them from both the dangers of the city and the wilds, trying to create just the domestic refuge that Jewett's heros enjoyed. Yet by 1949 Stafford recognized the refuge for what it was, a constraining island of domesticity adrift on the waters of rapid social change.

The children's reactions to the ranch seem to be determined by the same gender codes that bounded the lives of Jewett's men and women. Ralph learns to ride, helps his uncle in ranching, including butchering and birthing, and hopes one day to live there permanently. Molly rides reluctantly and avoids all knowledge of the real life of the ranch, regarding the summers as a chance simply to stroll through the mountains, diary in hand. Very close until the first summer on the ranch, brother and sister grow apart when Molly refuses to share in Ralph's new knowledge of sex, amassed from his work with the stock. Unlike Jewett, Stafford could not conceive of a girl or woman participating in the running of a ranch who would not soon lose her innocence of the facts of reproduction. More clearly than Jewett, she also understood that culture defines those "facts" just as it defines all the meanings of nature, and that we then turn that understanding on ourselves. For Molly to accept her society's definition of nature would mean accepting a similar definition of herself as female—this she refuses to do. The result is a girl apparently alienated from nature (as nature is defined by her culture), but alienated to preserve her innocence and her freedom.[44]

Symbolizing her choice, Molly resists acknowledging her own physicality. Denying her body, even embarrassed by the word, "Molly thought of herself as a long wooden box with a mind inside" (177). Her rigid denial of sexuality, coupled with her disdain for the adolescent preening of her two older sisters, has led at least one critic to see her as representative of all the deformities of Victorian culture.[45] But Molly is much more complex than that. In her life and death she represents not culture but nature resisting the grip of culture. Molly denies knowledge not to grow into proper Victorian womanhood, but to escape from it. If we know that Sylvie is both a lady and a nature lover, we know that Molly will never be a lady and is much more directly connected with nature than as its lover, Molly is known for her antisocial behavior, her "ugly" appearance, her immersion into the unfeminine life of the mind. Stafford's hero equates growing up with becoming fat: Molly plans never to grow fat (181).[46]

She is as alien and disturbing to her family and society as the mountain lion whose pursuit establishes the title of the book. Only she respects the lioness's fearsome power. Sighting the creature in the mountains with her brother and uncle, she is terrified and remembers seeing a caged lioness in Balboa Park. Whereas her mother and sisters regarded the zoo animal as a close relative of the cat, Molly recognized its wildness. For months afterward she dreamed that the creature pursued her through the streets of San Diego (212).

Understanding that Molly is a wild beast surrounded by culture, caged by her society into a space that does not fit her, explains much of her behavior. The tightest cage is Covina, where her mother, sisters, and clergyman each work to socialize her. Rather than offering a secure refuge from the marketplace, middle-class domesticity is shown to be riddled with the false values that nineteenth-century women labored to keep at bay.[47] In this world Molly becomes self-destructive. Like an animal chewing its paw in a trap, she willfully burns her hand after being told that sisters do not marry their brothers. The connection between Molly and the cat becomes clear in her one moment of tenderness toward the animal. Looking at the scar left on her hand, she loses all fear of the lion and feels only sadness for the beast (212). Without her escape to the mountains, where people seem to leave her alone, Molly might well have killed herself. But the mountains offer no shelter from society either. The wilderness is being plundered to fill the needs of the city. Wild lions and wild girls are both at the mercy of that acquisitive drive. The ranch owner wants to exterminate the lion. At one point Molly hopes the animal will either leave the territory or be caught in a skunk trap before her brother or uncle can kill her (214). The cat does neither, and neither does Molly. In the end, both are sacrificed to culture as the uncle kills the cat and Ralph accidentally shoots Molly.

The conclusion of *The Mountain Lion* offers an alternative ending to "A White Heron," the ending Jewett rejected in favor of isolating Sylvie, forever nine years old and forever in an idealized garden that served as a refuge from the threats of male-dominated society. Ralph's interest in both Molly and the lion is a form of possession. Just as he cannot allow the lion to exist outside his influence, neither can he allow Molly. Once he is filled with knowledge, so must she be, though he knows that such knowledge will destroy her love for him. As the ornithologist had tried to implicate Sylvie in his form of nature study by making her participate in his hunt, so Ralph finally whispers stories of sex to Molly. When she resists, her reward is death.

Molly's only hope is to embrace the wildness and turn it back on culture; this is what Jewett sensed when she suggested that women had lost contact with the power in nature. But this route of escape is complicated by the line dividing white women from women of color. The only other human character in the book sharing the lion's wildness is the black woman, Magdalene, who cooks at the ranch. Stafford's portrait of this woman contains all the limiting stereotypes of African American women as sexually licentious, potentially violent animals. Cast as a woman lacking in any sensitivity, Magdalene "was not in the least kind; she was always smoldering with an inward rage or a vile amusement over something sexual or something unfortunate, and she spoke chiefly in obscene or blasphemous expletives" (98). Molly understands that Magdalene's connection with wilderness also includes a wisdom about the world that no one else on the ranch shares: "she was wonderfully wise. She knew when it was going to rain and when someone was going to get sick and when a cow was going to get through a fence" (98). Of the three representatives of wildness, Magdalene is located farthest outside culture. While her distance from the forces of civilization makes her appear the most powerful (she is never threatened with death), such a portrayal masks African American women's equal vulnerability to the forces attempting to control Molly and the lion, and it denies her any real threat as a force critiquing the dominant values.

Molly sees something of herself in Magdalene and for a time believes that the woman is her true mother. Magdalene remains one of the few people never relegated to the "fat" group in Molly's world. And it is Magdalene who breaks through to Ralph, allowing him to face what he has done, when she utters the last words of the novel: "Lord Jesus. The pore little old piece of white trash" (231). Stafford could not conceive of a white woman who could serve as the rightful chorus to Molly's death. Her understanding of how much middle-class society had alienated such women from nature and from their own natures made it impossible for her to envision such a person. The only alternative lay in a woman who contained wildness.

Linking Magdalene, Molly, and the mountain lion, Stafford hinted at the connections between cultural control of nature, male control of women, and white control of blacks. She was herself too mired in racist and sexist stereotypes to invest the black woman, the girl, or the lion with the power to devour patriarchal tradition. Her narrative, like Jewett's, suggests more freedom than it can deliver. This was a fact she vaguely sensed when she wrote a preface to the reprint of *The Mountain Lion* in 1971 acknowledging her remorse over killing off Molly (xvii). But the lion and Magdalene offer clues to how the next generation of Euro-American writers might finally unwind themselves from the burdens of Victorian culture and imagine a hero who not only recognizes the lion in her nature, but also turns on culture and devours it.

In the 1971 preface to *The Mountain Lion*, Stafford acknowledged a new influence on women and their writings when she noted the growing impact of "women's liberation" in her culture. The 1970s witnessed the emergence of women's critique of gender constraints, including questions about sexual mores and much debate about the importance of biology as a determinant of gender.[48] Margaret Atwood's 1972 novel, *Surfacing*, served as a touchstone for some of the discussion. An account of a contemporary Canadian woman who throws off technological society, symbolized by the "Americans," to return to the isolated island of her youth and conceive a new form of life, a wild child she will not teach to speak, Atwood's fiction received mixed reviews in the feminist community. On one hand, the book was problematic in its removal of women from the repressions of urban life and in its suggestion that motherhood offered ultimate fulfillment; on the other hand, it was praised for proposing that women's spirituality sprang from sources within their separate culture, a culture drawing strength from traditional connections with the green world.[49]

Lost in the discussion was the understanding that Atwood's fiction arose from a preceding history. That history included the suspicion in white, middle-class women's culture that in solving the problem of appearing both more civilized and more "natural" than men, women had become alienated from what they were trained to preserve and protect. Unlike African American and American Indian women, white women's bogeyman has been the specter of too much culture, too much genteel appreciation of nature. In *Surfacing*, Atwood lays open the contradictions in overcivilizing women because of their perceived biological closeness to nature and tries to create a white woman choosing to live outside the bounds of culture, within the terms of nature. In so doing, however, she finds herself sharing similar difficulties with women of color. She fronts the dangers of conjoining biology and gender in a way that suggests women are less human than men.

Like Griffin's female lioness trapped in a room, encircled by scientists ready to define her soul, Margaret Atwood offers a protagonist who sees herself as a captive animal encased in the artificial spaces of scientific/technological society. The primary metaphor for such enclosure is the glass specimen jar. The story revolves around the hero's return to the isolated island of her youth. Critics have interpreted the island as the green world existing in opposition to the plastic city.[50] In fact, the island serves as a pastoral preserve defined by urban-generated needs. The woman's father, a botanist working for the government in resource management, controls the island and defines its meaning. In the high-tech, lab-science-dominated world of the 1970s, he represents the nineteenth-century field naturalist and he defines nature in nineteenth-century ways as a rational, predictable, knowable system.[51]

The protagonist recognizes that their life on the island fulfilled some broad-based social need for a pastoral quotient in modern life, some nostalgic link to the genteel nature of Jewett's time. Her childhood on the island, within the context of new forms of scientific dominance and control of nature through biotechnology, functions like the preserved specimen of an extinct animal. She grows up within the glass jar but cannot return to it once she has lost her innocence in technological America: "[My parents] never knew . . . why I left. Their own innocence, the reason I couldn't tell them; perilous innocence, closing them in glass, their artificial garden, greenhouse. They didn't teach us about evil, they didn't understand about it, how could I describe it to them? They were from another age, prehistoric, when everyone got married and had a family, children growing in the yard like sunflowers; remote as Eskimos or mastodons" (169). This is the cleansed green world of Jewett's women, in which procreation takes place under a cabbage leaf and nature is pacific. The self-contained cabin calls to mind many of the home-based sanctuaries of nineteenth-century birders, in which birds discretely retired to the shadows to mate. Ironically, it offers the perfect display case in Hurston's "Museum of Unnatural History" for the middle-class white family.

Out of date though it is, life on the island is preferable to the new projections of culture upon nature the hero encounters in the American city. Beside the pastoral specimen jar is the new, plastic bucket into which everything not created by human artifice is dumped for disposal. The key is the child whom the protagonist aborted, which act alienated her from her parents and their nineteenth-century island. Scattered throughout are images of the fetus in a glass specimen jar, until the woman, finally facing the illegal abortion, remembers that the child did not receive even that much dignity: "They scraped it into a bucket and threw it wherever they throw them, it was traveling through the sewers by the time I woke" (168). She feels that in allowing the abortion she has given herself up to the forces of technology, reflected in her suspicion that while she was knocked out, the doctors pumped her veins full of red plastic.

The critical act that Atwood accomplishes centers on this image of woman as object, subjected to the manipulations of male-dominated culture. Nineteenth-century domestic codes had masked fears about white women's sexuality by elevating females to protectors of a tamed nature. Jewett recognized how this ideology functioned to marginalize women, but she offered no critique of the sexual repression at its heart. By mid-century Stafford was able to lay open the fears about the disruptive potential that had informed white women's relegation to a sexually cleansed, domesticated garden. By the late twentieth century, however, white women were openly taking control of definitions of sexuality and challenging attempts to confine their sex to the sheltered spaces of middle-class suburbs. As Molly discovered, in dropping the veil of gentility white, middle-class women faced a new risk: they discovered themselves vulnerable to the same animal symbolism that women of color had experienced for generations.

Atwood names the secrets that Molly's brother, Ralph, had whispered in her ear. One of the men on the island tells an off-color joke about how a "split beaver" would be the most appropriate symbol on Canada's flag. The man who tells this joke is outraged by the exploitation of the beaver population. At the same time, he makes a pun when he uses the term *beaver* to refer to sexual relations between trappers and Indian women (141). The protagonist initially misses the pun (like Molly, these are stories she would prefer not to hear), then recognizes in it the traditional lore of male/female and human/animal relations: "a part of the body, a dead animal" (141). Atwood's narrator states what Stafford, and perhaps Jewett, hinted: "anything we could do to the animals we could do to each other: we practiced on them first" (143). Bestiality again surfaces as a way of describing men's love of women.

Such imagery sets up the abortion, which the narrator has unwillingly at the behest of her married lover; he tells her that, after all, the fetus is not human, it is only an animal (170). We are reminded of how we use our ideas about animals to structure gender relationships. Atwood has said that the book is not meant as an antiabortion text.[52] Besides her critique of simplistic separations between nature and culture, Atwood charts the loss of women's power in the choice of whether and how to bear children. The story of the protagonist's child is actually presented in two forms. At first she tells us that she had a husband, became pregnant because he forced her to, that he monitored her body daily in protecting his fetus, and that he promptly took ownership of the child upon its birth. That this story of woman as breeding vessel to her husband is as credible as the story of woman as sexual object to her lover makes Atwood's point about the alienation of women from their own creative power.

The effect of the abortion is to separate her head from her body. As had Molly in *The Mountain Lion*, she shuts down the conduit from body to brain and imagines herself trapped in the specimen jar: "at some point my neck must have closed over, pond freezing over a wound, shutting me into my head; since then everything had been glancing off me, it was like being in a vase . . . Bottles distort for the observer too: frogs in the jam jar stretched wide, to them watching I must have appeared grotesque" (126). On one level Atwood has written a book very much within the terms established by Jewett and Stafford, for her hero never experiences the sensual connectedness to nature expressed in Silko's and Hurston's tales of Yellow Woman and the rose of the world. Such sensuality is too loaded with meanings of love, and love, she discovers, is a term of ownership, a term she repeatedly refuses. For example, her married friends, David and Anna, engage in destructive power struggles in which sexual pleasure is a trap. Anna, on the point of orgasm, makes a sound of "pure pain," "an animal's at the moment the trap closes" (99). Realizing that the twentieth-century rediscovery of white women's sexuality was not in itself a source of freedom, the protagonist appears as lacking in a way out as Stafford's Molly.

Reading Molly's resistance as merely prudishness misses the point of her connection with a mountain lion. Stafford sensed that Molly could find a freer self in connecting with her own wild nature, but she could not find a socially acceptable method of release. Atwood poses a more radical solution. What if the hero chooses to enter animal presence, to act as the fearful wild woman that domesticity is supposed to control? In the conclusion of the novel, Atwood shatters the glass jar that has controlled women's nature. Like Silko and Morrison, the natural world she calls forth is not pacific, but filled with blood and danger and the spirits of the dead. Splitting from Jewett, who, like most of her society, saw the green world as a tame space preserved by and for white women, Atwood plays out what happens when a woman throws off domesticity and nature becomes wild.

Freed from the constrictions of gentility, the sexual act neither reduces her to a "split beaver" nor binds her to husband in an artificial home located outside nature's household. For the vision to work, men must be pulled into the natural realm as well. The protagonist's lover becomes as wild as she and loses his control over her. She is released into communion with cycles of life and death, connected with the animal world physically and spiritually. The farther she goes into nature, the closer she comes to the spirits of the dead until she feels her aborted child surfacing anew in her body and learns that "nothing has died, everything is alive, everything is waiting to become alive"

(186). Further symbolizing her rejection of modern technological culture, she is guided into the spirit world by ancient tribal drawings on hidden rocks around the island.

When *Surfacing* appeared in the early 1970s Marge Piercy criticized it for lacking a political agenda, for failing to suggest what the protagonist would do when she returned to the real world of work, child care, sexism, and racism.[53] Piercy could not see that Atwood was attacking a problem at the core of sexist and racist ideology: the use of artificial, hierarchical divisions between nature and culture to assign women a status lower than men. *Surfacing* does have a political agenda. Springing from the environmentalist decades following *Silent Spring*, Atwood's novel carries the same message—though in a radically different context—as Carson's work. The only escape from the destructive cycles set in motion by the Atomic Age is renewal of our understanding of earth's processes and our dependence on those processes. Writing also at the height of the feminist movement, Atwood spoke directly to women—in particular, Euro-American women—encouraging them to find a route back into sacred animal presence. Rachel Carson found the strength to criticize the scientific establishment in part through her and other women's feelings of kinship with animals, but Carson did not herself bring to consciousness the deeply oppositional stance from which she and her colleagues critiqued dominant cultural ideas about the connections of women and nature. A decade later, Margaret Atwood could take that step and suggest that kinship with nonhuman animals potentially empowered both women and nature.

IV

Comparing the meanings of nature in African American, American Indian, and Euro-American literatures suggests points of contact and areas of contradiction. American Indian and African American writers have drawn on their understanding of precontact environmental beliefs to write an oppositional literature laying claim to the North American continent as home. Having experienced dispossession and alienation from the land in several hundred years of postcontact history, the nineteenth- and twentieth-century writers I discuss must first renew rights to read nature within the terms of their own history. Such renewal requires a critique of white assumptions about the ways people of color think about nature. Specifically, the writers grapple with white projections of their people as representatives of a lower order of human consciousness, more in touch with the intuitive animal than the rational human. Rather than debunking the story of their connectedness to nature, these writers reject white folks' self-image as rational outsiders to the exigencies of the environment. They privilege less dualistic readings of nature in their presentations of American Indian and African American tribal beliefs. This is a particularly useful oppositional strategy. It denies the right of Euro-Americans to establish the frame of reference—design the museum case—in which nature will be viewed. The appeal to the spirit informing all life also allows women of color to reject animalistic stereotypes without taking up the mantle of the middle-class white woman dwelling in her genteel garden.

North American inheritors of the Euro-American scientific tradition have had a rather different journey to make in their expressive literature of nature appreciation. Well entrenched by the late nineteenth century as at once assistants to male naturalists and voices for pastoral nature against an urban wilderness, they had lost touch with stories connecting them with nature through their nature as animals. I have argued that their relegation to a tamed green world separated "proper" white women from women of color and such "degenerates" as prostitutes. As stereotypes about white women's sexuality shifted in the post-Freudian period, and as nature was seen as less and less pacific, the suppressed connection of all women to degraded animals became visible, as did their role as subjects of scientific experiment. Like Silko and Morrison, Atwood responded with a radical revision of the relationship between nature and culture. Accepting Euro-American women's tradition as protectors of the creatures of earth's household, Atwood rejected their unnatural ranking above their animal kin in patriarchal stereotypes of genteel womanhood.

These stories help explain why Euro-American women have played the roles they have in American conservation and environmental history of the dominant culture. The narratives also reveal the reasons underpinning American Indian and African American women's invisibility as actors in such history. Natural history has often viewed women of color as subjects of study, useful in determining human/animal classification systems. Scientific findings describing the "nature" of African American and American Indian women have been used in Euro-American society to justify various forms of dominance. Nineteenth- and twentieth-century narratives by such women suggest that they have been aware of these issues and have sought to express their opposition to the stereotypes and proffer their own forms of nature lore and appreciation. Within the contemporary canon of prominent nature essayists, however, only Leslie Silko has achieved any standing. African American women's voices remain unrecorded. Although Alice Walker has written some fine essays in the naturalist tradition, her work does not appear in collections. What is needed is a contemporary Zora Neale Hurston to name what it is that white publishers of natural history collections at the end of the twentieth century will not print.[54]

Euro-American women have established themselves among the ranks of respected nature essayists and have contributed to conservation and environmental movements of the nineteenth and twentieth centuries. The conflicts raised by Rachel Carson's *Silent Spring*, however, unveiled the split between men's and women's environmental values that had been building since the nineteenth century. Always, women naturalists evidenced a sense of difference from men in their endeavors but only voiced a muted critique of their place in environmental history. A more pointed analysis of the problems with women's assigned role in nature study and appreciation was first raised in Jewett's stories of American Eves. Jewett suggested that rather than having an equal voice in defining America domestica, women were subordinated in a pastoral landscape among tamed creatures. This domestic space served as a female retreat from the pressures of city life, but it was at once vulnerable and marginal to the agencies of the marketplace. When Rachel Carson was characterized as a nun of nature, who had devoted her life to birds because she had no family of her own, she was reminded of that restricted image of women's space.

A particularly problematic aspect of Carson's challenge was her acknowledgment that the pain and suffering of other animals deserved compassion on a par with humans—revealing a deeper and more troubling bond with animals than domestic women were supposed to feel. Carson's contemporary, Jean Stafford, fronted these issues, laying open the connection between domination of animals and control of female sexuality, in her story of a girl's bond with a mountain lion. Susan Griffin and Margaret Atwood picked up the thread in the 1970s, proposing that women's freedom was connected with recognizing the sacred in wild animals. None of these women devoted their lives to observing wild animals, but their writings suggested that women who did might experience conflicts, both with their male colleagues and in their own sense of a woman's proper responsibility to another animal. Accounts of wildlife observers support the truth to Griffin's contention that women's attunement to the "roaring inside her" poses a threat as well as a fulfillment.

# 7

# Women and Wildlife

*The nearest female was old Effie, mother of six, whom I had known since 1967. She'd had a new baby in my absence, little Maggie . . . Effie glanced my way while chewing on a stalk of celery. She looked away, then did a double-take myopic scrutiny as if not believing her eyes. Then she tossed the celery aside and began walking rapidly toward me.*

*Meantime Tuck, another female I had known nearly as long, appeared out of the underbrush and started to pick up Maggie . . . then Tuck too did a second take. She dropped Maggie and walked right up in front of me, resting her weight on her arms so that her face was level with mine and only a couple of inches away. She stared intently into my eyes, and it was eye-to-eye contact for thirty or forty seconds. Not knowing quite what to do, for I had never had this reaction from gorillas before, I squished myself flat on the bed of vegetation. Whereupon she smelled my head and neck, then lay down beside me . . . and embraced me! . . . embraced me! . . . embraced me! GOD, she* did *remember!*

—From Dian Fossey's journal

FROM 1966 until her murder in 1985, Dian Fossey devoted her life to studying the mountain gorillas inhabiting the rain forests along the borders of Zaire and Rwanda. The first person to develop a technique for habituating the animals to intimate observation, she has been the object of much popular interest. Fossey is one of three women who have been famous for detailed studies of primates—the others are Jane Goodall and Biruté Galdikas. Her adventures in the African wilderness exemplified British and American fears about what might happen to women who ventured too far outside the bounds of domesticity. In her early work with gorillas Fossey, who was dubbed *Nyiramachabelli* (the old lady who lives in the forest without a man) by the Africans who worked at her research camp, seemed to mirror fictional characters like Sarah Orne Jewett's Sylvie. Shown in National Geographic films living alone (meaning without a white male companion) in an isolated camp, naming the gorillas whose comrade she appeared to be, she looked like a nun of nature whose presence signified a pacified green world. One of the most popular images of Fossey was a photograph of the first intimate touch between human and mountain gorilla when Peanuts, a young male, laid his hand in hers.

Fossey herself imagined her research camp to be a sanctuary for wild animals. However, funded by the scientific research community and located in a developing country, Fossey's project was subject to the intrusions posed by international economic development and the goals of modern scientific management. The peaceful idyll stereotyped in her "taming" of a mountain gorilla unraveled as she displayed her loyalty to the animals in violent defense of their preserve from both native Africans and international conservation management groups. When her behavior failed to match the image of the genteel domestic female, another story took its place. The Hollywood film, *Gorillas in the Mist*, implies that the arc of Fossey's life began its downward slide into violence and death when she rejected a marriage proposal from a National Geographic photographer. Renouncing traditional bonds of home and family, she placed herself in jeopardy. Like Jean Stafford's Molly, her allegiance to wild beasts made her a wild woman, leaving her vulnerable to the violence visited upon other animals. Fossey, popular culture suggests, was killed once she stepped outside the bounds of domestic space and into the landscape of wilderness.[1]

Fossey's fame also demonstrates the extent to which twentieth-century women have established a name for themselves in contemporary animal behavioral studies. Their most important work has revised traditional ideas about the lives of large, social mammals, particularly the primates. Some scholars believe that they were able to make this contribution because women's gender socialization prepared them to ask questions about animal behavior that were different from those of their male colleagues.[2] Women who stepped into sustained work with wild animals have often done so as assistants to men. Early narratives about how to study animals were developed by male naturalist-explorers. Women had to find a niche for their work that addressed the demands of the field while fulfilling gender stereotypes about female domesticity. In reducing Fossey's life to a simplistic choice between wild animals or domestic civilization, the Hollywood film about her death fails to suggest how women's gender socialization informed her passionate pleas for the mountain gorilla. Women have been taught that, as females, their strengths lie in empathy with and concern for other individuals. They have entered the habitat of wolves, gorillas, and elephants expecting to immerse themselves in a network of relationships requiring reciprocity and ethical responsibility. Contrary to the popular image of Dian Fossey as a woman lost to the bounds of civilization, her work was founded on the history of American women's struggles to create a niche within wildlife study and to have their findings change the way the dominant culture viewed other animals.

During the twentieth century, American ideas about wild animals, particularly game animals and predators, underwent extensive change. Near-extermination of the buffalo in the 1880s alerted many Americans to the dangers facing wildlife. By the turn of the century, sportsmen, scientists, and club women campaigned to protect native creatures. Increasing professionalism in zoology and wildlife management between the first and second world wars created a cadre of scientists whose findings revised negative perceptions of predators like the wolf, grizzly, cougar, and coyote. Their efforts complemented attempts to educate the public in the need for ecologically responsible preservation of habitats for various large mammals. As one of the last major sources of large game at the turn of the twentieth century, Africa drew a number of influential Americans who helped other colonial powers establish parks and game preserves following the American model. Ever-increasing numbers of field naturalists worked for and in such preserves in America and Africa, creating a new animal mythology. For example, Adolph Murie's *Wolves of Mt. McKinley* (1944) changed the stereotypical wolf from ferocious man-eater to complex social animal. American and African wild animals began turning up in natural history museums in lifelike dioramas representing not only the violent side of nature but also peaceful moments of familial affection.

Photographs and moving pictures increasingly portrayed wild creatures on their daily round, often with bits of humanizing play.[3]

By the late nineteenth century, women accompanied naturalist husbands on botanical and zoological collecting expeditions. Single women also began to work as explorers, plant collectors, and field ornithologists.[4] Large mammal studies represented a natural extension of these activities. American wives of naturalists collected big game and predators with their husbands, mounted animals for exhibit, photographed and filmed wildlife in America and Africa, and wrote popular accounts of their exploits. Such reports educated the American public about wildlife. They also provided American women with new ways to think about their connection with creatures previously presented as threatening to their safety (not to mention disturbing to their psyche).

Nevertheless, women's efforts were bounded by the dominant male narrative of contact with the wilderness. That narrative, for scientist-naturalists as well as hunters, had to do with the search for and capture of the trophy animal. Women who entered the domain of zoological collecting helped gun down specimens and complete family groups to take back for display in natural history museums. They became trophy photographers, assisting their husbands in making popular motion picture films of animals in their haunts. They helped collect live animals for sale or donation to American zoos. In zoos, they displayed the trophy with a bit of its native habitat. Participation in such activities did not mean that women dropped gender-coded ideas about white, middle-class females' appropriate responses to nature. In stepping into wilderness to fulfill a collecting agenda set by scientific naturalists, women experienced conflicts between their role as nurturer and the violence connected with field exploration. Sometimes they managed to negotiate a compromise, but often they openly acknowledged the gender-weighted guilt attached to their actions. The most honest faced the load of violence and death surrounding these kinds of trophy collecting.

As women went about the business of helping male naturalists, they developed a narrative about the best way for a Euro-American woman to involve herself with a wild creature. For many women who went on safaris to the American West or Africa, the lure was the opportunity to interact with animals in their habitat. They shared similar motivations with women who devised open-air gardens for watching native birds and insects and field ornithologists who left their suburban neighborhoods to discover how birds lived in their home territories. Perhaps the first expression of this wish to see into the lives of other creatures was Susan Fenimore Cooper's wistful comment in 1850 that she had never managed to see the Otsego otters at play in the snow.

Observing large mammals, however, required more determination and a stronger stomach for violent episodes of life in the wilds. Women interested in communicating with the beaver, coyote, wolf, elephant, chimpanzee, or gorilla wanted more than to sit patiently watching the nest. The trophy of such endeavors was the moment of mutual recognition between human and wild creature, the moment when, like Margaret Atwood's hero, their own connectedness to other animals surfaced. Dian Fossey's joy in the recognition and embrace of the gorilla, Tuck, represents such a trophy. Histories of such contact are contained in popular field narratives by women who spent years observing a species of large mammal. Building off their self-image as conservers and their long-standing interest in animals as social individuals, women field observers defended the right of specific animals to live out their lives appropriately. Acknowledging that their step into animal presence sometimes harmed the very animals they wanted to preserve, they tried to develop ethical rules for human-animal interaction. The clash between Dian Fossey and international scientific conservation organizations arose partly from her espousal of these gender-based ethics.


I

Martha Maxwell's career as a scientific trophy collector and taxidermist began innocently enough. Wisconsin's Baraboo Collegiate Institute, a small women's college that her sisters attended in 1862, had no zoological collection for the students. The professor asked for some young lady with "more skilful fingers than I, [to] assist me in putting up some birds."[5] Maxwell, who had developed an interest in taxidermy while living with her husband in Colorado, took up the challenge. Her birds not only served to educate young ladies in science, they also decorated her mother's parlor. When Maxwell returned to her husband's home on the outskirts of Boulder, Colorado, in 1868, she put her new skill to good use decorating the interior. Her sister, Mary Dartt, described the animal "tableau" in her parlor: "Birds looked down in listening attitudes into the music-book upon the organ; scolded each other from the corners of neighboring picture-frames . . . the smaller animals of the neighborhood were represented among the rocks [at the foot of a tree], and the whole formed a picture not less interesting than novel."[6] Maxwell's ornaments were popular with family and friends, usually drawing a crowd of admiring youngsters to view the latest addition to the scene. In proper Victorian fashion she was educating and entertaining, within the bounds of home, the next generation.

Maxwell took a somewhat more expansive view of her efforts, however. An ardent feminist, she saw her work in taxidermy as an effort to prove women's capabilities in both art and science. Living in the West during the period of widespread slaughter of the buffalo and other native animals, she was concerned that Colorado's wildlife was disappearing. She artificially preserved animals threatened with extinction to educate the public in the need for their actual preservation. As interest grew in the animals in her parlor, she conceived of a small natural history museum that would serve the same purpose as the large museums in the East. Her scientific approach led to a correspondence with Spencer Baird and Robert Ridgway at the Smithsonian Institution in 1869. Over the next decade she received much help from these scientists and returned the favor by sending the Smithsonian duplicates of the rarer species she collected. One of her proudest achievements was Ridgway's naming of a subspecies of screech owl after her.

Her taxidermy just preceded the explosion in animal preservation and display techniques that would begin in the 1880s. Perhaps growing out of her early vision of stuffed animals as parlor ornaments, she was a pioneer in placing specimens in naturalistic poses and in realistic habitats.[7] Maxwell was not shy about publicizing the gender of the artist-scientist in her displays. In her exhibit for the Colorado-Kansas display at the Philadelphia Centennial Exposition in 1876, she placed a sign at the front announcing that the diorama was "Woman's Work" (Figure 42).[8] In displays like Maxwell's, wildlife of the American West appeared simultaneously as museum specimens and parlor ornaments, drawing both the animals and their terrain into America domestica—nature conceived as Americans' proper home. As well as establishing a place for women in science and art, Maxwell's efforts demonstrated how women's work could support nineteenth-century expansion along the western frontier.

Yet certain aspects of Maxwell's achievement raised troubling questions about the propriety of her endeavors. Unlike women who conducted civic improvement campaigns, she was not beautifying the suburbs or designing parks in the cities. Unlike women who studied birds, she was neither creating sanctuary for small animals of the garden and neighborhood nor passively sitting at the nest admiring the parenting skills of hummingbirds in the Rockies.

FIGURE 42. *Martha Maxwell's (1831–81) exhibit at the Philadelphia Centennial Exposition. (Historical Society of Pennsylvania, Philadelphia, Pa.)*

And unlike scientific illustrators, she had to withstand physically taxing, often unpleasant labor. Martha Maxwell took up a gun, adventured into unknown terrain, shot large game and predators, then skinned and stuffed her trophies (Figure 43). To make up her family groupings, she killed not only the male animal sought after by sportsmen but also the mother and infants. Her sister's litany of the type of questions raised by viewers of the Philadelphia exhibit suggests that the public found her to be a most unusual woman. According to Mary Dartt, the audience was of the opinion that Maxwell must be a hardened pioneer woman living in a cave, possibly with some Indian background.[9] Dartt's response to this image was to write a biography of her sister suggesting that a Euro-American woman engaged in trophy hunting could still maintain the proper domestic role as long as she kept her educational goal firmly in sight.

Mary Dartt's account of her sister's life, *On the Plains and Among the Peaks; or, How Mrs. Maxwell Made Her Natural History Collection*, helps explain how Euro-American women of the late nineteenth century justified (some might say, rationalized) their work in terrain filled with masculine images of virile challenge, bloody initiation, and violent domination.[10] Dartt's narrative sets her sister's collecting activities within the context of responsible sportsmanship and scientific preservation. In creating her beautiful dioramas, Maxwell shared the same conservationist goals as the Audubon club women who wrote articles encouraging moral restraint among sporthunters.[11] Even her potentially disturbing efforts to collect whole families could be read as an act of domestic preservation. Such interpretation required a good deal of rhetorical slight of hand, such as that demonstrated in the description of how Maxwell assembled a hawk family.

Searching for infant hawks and eggs, because "science has at present more interest in the eggs and young of animals," Maxwell enlisted her husband's help in attempting to rob a nest. Unfortunately, the mother arrived on the scene, leading to Martha's judgment that she should be shot as "it would be cruel to leave her to grieve over the loss of her children." Having "quiet[ed] all apprehension of danger from her beak and talons," Maxwell removed one youngster and an egg. She then took "upon herself the maternal responsibility" until both chicks were of a "desirable size," when "a little chloroform induced them to stop growing." Such language soothes over the murderous image of a woman despoiling a mother's home for her own ends, suggests that the hawk was done a favor, and implies that the infants were not dead but merely captured in time. However dishonest such rhetoric may appear to

FIGURE 43. *Martha Maxwell in collecting attire. (Colorado Historical Society, Denver)*

the contemporary reader, Maxwell believed that she had engaged in an act of preservation. When asked how she could destroy such animals, she answered: "There isn't a day you don't tacitly consent to have some creature killed that you may eat it. I never take life for such carnivorous purposes! All must die sometime; I only shorten the period of consciousness that I may give their forms a perpetual memory; and I leave it to you, which is the more cruel? to kill to eat, or to kill to *immortalize*?" [12] Maxwell found a match between scientific interest in preserving perfect specimens in dioramas and women's goal of conserving life, including the wildlife of North America.

Martha Maxwell died in 1881, as taxidermy was becoming professionalized in natural history collections in the Field Museum in Chicago and the American Museum of Natural History in New York. With the notable exception of Delia Akeley, wife of Carl Akeley, one of the leaders in the development of new techniques for preserving and mounting wildlife, few women surfaced as practitioners of the craft during the late nineteenth and early twentieth centuries. Although Maxwell's methods were indeed remarkable, after 1880 taxidermy became a corporate enterprise. Her momentary rise to fame did not send multitudes of women into the field. Women's declining participation in various scientific careers as they were professionalized suggests one reason for the dearth of women.[13]

Yet neither Martha Maxwell nor her sister Mary Dartt was comfortable with the contortions required to subsume the trophy hunt into women's sphere. The hunt posed a major problem for women who wanted to work in the field. But if they did not follow Maxwell into taxidermy, women of the late nineteenth and early twentieth centuries did join the scientific hunt. Their narratives reveal a continuing struggle to match gender codes with the bloody results of the chase.[14]

The public parading past Maxwell's Colorado exhibit found the variety of wildlife astonishing. In part because she had collapsed the whole state into a very small space, the western landscape seemed to be teeming with animals, re-creating early nineteenth-century images of abundance. Although Maxwell never questioned American expansion into the West, she tried to explain how much wildlife was threatened with extinction due to irresponsible hunting and settlement patterns. One of her messages was the necessity of preserving habitats for these animals. By the 1880s many influential Americans were aware that western wildlife was fast disappearing. During this period hunting was prohibited in Yellowstone National Park, partly to protect the last remnants of buffalo. Simultaneously, affluent Europeans and Americans who had used the American West as a sporting ground turned their attention to the African continent. In Africa, elites found the opportunity to continue the hunt but in more "responsible, sportsmanlike" modes. Africa also offered scientists live specimens of large mammals that had been all but extinguished in America. Colonial European powers enlisted the aid of Americans in developing parks based on the Yellowstone model to preserve the wildlife valued by European and American elites. Giving little thought to the rights or needs of native Africans, scientists engaged in such preservation efforts while simultaneously collecting trophy animals for display in American museums alongside the dioramas of American buffalo, caribou, cougars, and wolves.[15]

Carl Akeley, one of the first Americans to work in Africa for the development of wildlife preserves, provided the excuse for several women to test their skills as trophy hunters in the early twentieth century. Pioneering in the establishment of large animal dioramas in natural history museums, Akeley led collecting expeditions financed by the Field Museum and the American Museum of Natural History. Akeley expected his wives, Delia and then Mary Jobe, to prove their prowess by shooting at least one revered African game animal—elephant, lion, buffalo, leopard, or rhino. He also led novelist Mary Hastings Bradley, her husband, and her five-year-old daughter, Alice, on a safari to collect, among other creatures, mountain gorillas for the American Museum (Figure 44). These women produced popular narratives of their adventures, stories that regaled readers with the thrills of the hunt while virtuously arguing for the need to preserve Africa's wildlife. Their mixed message has contributed to the contradictory image that Delia Akeley has earned in feminist history. On one hand she is portrayed as a hero who never killed animals for pleasure, whereas on the other she is pictured as a "joyous and unrepentant hunter."[16] These women's accounts reveal that they struggled with the contradictions in their roles and chose carefully how they would engage in the hunt.

In 1906 Delia Akeley accompanied her husband to Africa; it was her first safari. Their goal was to collect an elephant group for an ambitious diorama in the Field Museum. Although Delia's initial function was to collect birds, butterflies, and flowers, she quickly came to accept the tradition that, for food and safety, every white member of the expedition had be ready to kill larger animals. Both Carl and Delia had permits to kill elephants. According to Delia, Carl envisioned an elephant exhibit containing his and her first elephants. Game laws restricted the number of elephants any one individual could collect. When Carl killed his quota without having collected a perfect male specimen, he asked Delia to continue the hunt.[17] She collected two specimens on this trip, one their trophy animal—a bull elephant with huge, perfect tusks. Her elephant became the centerpiece in the massive display that Carl built in the Field Museum after their return in 1907. That exhibit played a role in Mary Bradley's decision to take little Alice and join her husband and Carl

FIGURE 44. *Mary Hastings Bradley and Alice Bradley on safari (1921–22). (Photograph by H. E. Bradley, Neg./Trans. no. 258778, Department of Library Services, American Museum of Natural History, New York City)*

Akeley on a collecting safari.[18] In published accounts of their journeys, Delia Akeley and Mary Bradley constructed a consistent story of women's responses to the scientific trophy hunt, including an elaborate rationale for the specific animals killed. Their narrative mirrors Mary Dartt's and Martha Maxwell's tale about women's responsibilities as scientific collectors in the American West.

Delia Akeley refused to shoot the first likely elephant sighted on the 1906 expedition. "Mr. Akeley" had collected his first elephant but found the specimen unsuitable because it had only one tusk. At last, the company came upon a candidate. Carl and R. J. Cunningham, the "white hunter" Carl hired to teach him how to track and kill elephants, told Delia to shoot it: "But I couldn't have raised my gun to save our lives. I wanted to look, just look, at that magnificent creature that had come down to us from the unknown past." The elephant charged off, leaving Delia with an acutely disappointed husband, whom she promised "not to make such a mistake again." In the ensuing several weeks Carl exhausted his permits, and Delia had to come up with the perfect trophy. She did not let him down.[19] Following her success, Cunningham "christened" her "Elephant Hunter." Her elephant became the symbolic trophy of the expedition—the perfect specimen preserved in the natural history museum. Were that all of Akeley's experience, we might see her as a joyous hunter, but in this tale of the 1906 expedition and in her account of a similar elephant hunt in 1909, Delia was careful to embed her victory in a larger chronicle rationalizing the deaths she had caused.

Her first elephant was not, in fact, perfect. On closer examination, she discovered "in his back . . . a great festering wound caused by a poisoned spear. The iron blade had worked its way into his flesh to his ribs and he must have suffered agonies."[20] In her own mind Delia Akeley—like Martha Maxwell before her—had removed this animal from a world of pain to the greater realm of the immortals. In her account of the 1909 expedition to collect a group for the American Museum, Akeley went to great lengths to justify collecting elephants at all as well as her own participation in the enterprise. She prefaced the actual hunt by a long discussion of elephant history—a history that, Delia assured the reader, was the real reason she and Carl had returned to Africa.[21] Delia contrasted their work as responsible scientists, following hunting regulations to the letter, with unscrupulous poachers (white and native Africans) who were threatening the future of Africa's wildlife. However much the press might have played upon the image of women like Delia Akeley as the female equivalent of the "great white hunter," her self-image was more akin to all the women who worked within the walls of natural history museums. These institutions were extensions of home; women's work within them was to educate the public about nature—in particular, about the domestic side of flora and fauna. Akeley and her husband were seeking the middle-class, twentieth-century version of a family. The elephant group they planned would include an old patriarch, a younger male, a female, and a calf.[22]

In addition to fulfilling her public role as an educated, middle-class wife, Delia also justified her collecting activities as an effort to preserve her own domestic life. Her husband was sick for most of the 1909 expedition. She went in search of elephants to "secure the desired specimen so Mr. Akeley could leave the country before it claimed him for its own." Carl's psychic health was none too good either. Dispirited after a mauling in an elephant attack, he felt that he had to prove his mettle by resuming the chase. His wife went with him to back up his recovery of virility. Delia's account of the hunt that restored Carl's morale also attempted to justify her use of a gun in socially acceptable terms. Stalking elephants in a dense fog around an apparently deserted hut, she stumbled on three small children in the path of a charging elephant: "As the wounded leviathan bore down on us with terrific speed, screaming like a siren, something touched my leg. Glancing quickly down I beheld, crouching in the doorway, a little girl with a tiny baby in her arms and over her shoulder peered the terrified face of another child. For a second I was petrified with horror, and then, with but one thought in my mind, I gripped my gun and pulled the trigger."[23] With one shot Delia supported her husband in his life-work, protected the young of another woman's home, and bagged a specimen to educate the children trooping through the American Museum of Natural History.

Mary Hastings Bradley located her efforts as a hunter in similar rhetoric. Throughout *On the Gorilla Trail*, Bradley carefully distanced herself from any bloodthirsty imagery while stalking elephants, lions, and crocodiles. Although she did kill lions and crocodiles (and wounded an elephant), she always proffered an elaborate rationale for their deaths. Further, she refused to turn her rifle on other animals. She would not kill a Thomas cob because he was so beautiful and never reports aiming her gun at a gorilla.[24] Neither she nor Carl Akeley's secretary, Martha Miller, hunted the mountain gorillas that were the primary goal of Akeley's 1921 safari with the Bradleys. Akeley's stated purpose for collecting a gorilla family for his American Museum dioramas was to encourage the removal of the animal from the game lists, slowing its (again "inevitable") extinction enough to allow for the study of gorilla social life. Popular images of the gorilla as a fierce, bloodthirsty animal had to be revised to reflect what Akeley thought was a more peaceful, shy creature not really fitting the classification of "big game." Donna Haraway has probed the ironies in Akeley's need to first conquer the animal in order to preserve it. She notes that Mary Bradley's account of Akeley's 1921 collecting expedition is the "white woman's" version of the narrative, but she does not suggest what that version might be.[25]

Carl Akeley and Jack Bradley had every intention of killing gorillas in Africa, but Mary Bradley did not. Describing her motivations for accompanying the group into gorilla terrain, Mary imagined that she "was going into his country. I was trying to penetrate his domain and spy upon affairs that were undoubtedly his own concern, but I was not going to thrust myself and what might be an uncongenial New World personality upon his attention." Although she shared the men's interest in sighting a trophy animal—the mature silverback male of legend—she described him as "Peter Pan": "Wary and elusive were his invariably given characteristics. Now I rather liked that in him. He could be as elusive as Peter Pan. I had no intention of frustrating any social barriers he wished erected. My New England blood could be as proudly reserved as his. He could rely upon me not to make undue advances." Just as Carl Akeley killed the first gorillas he encountered, so too Jack Bradley brought down the first perfect specimen he met. Mary at first notes her excitement at the sight of "a male gorilla in his savage haunts," but his death only buttresses her argument for the preservation of the animal and its removal from the game lists. The silverback fled his attackers and "looked back over his shaggy shoulder as the gun crashed again, as if trying to comprehend this sudden assault upon his solitudes. I shall never forget the humanness of that black, upturned face." Although she tasted gorilla meat, she ate only a little, finding it difficult to get "over the family feeling of sampling grandfather Africanus."[26]

Bradley's narrative concludes with observations of gorilla bands that supported Akeley's grounds for preserving the animals for scientific study. Mary found their family structure especially intriguing: "The question arises whether those bands consisted of two or more respectable monogamous couples and their marriageable daughters—maiden gorillas yet unculled by roving gallants—or whether it consisted of a couple of gorilla gentlemen and their respective harems or of unassorted and liberally inclined ladies and gentlemen."[27] The gorillas collected on this expedition ultimately raised the same question for the public viewing Akeley's diorama in the African Hall at the American Museum.

Bradley's published narrative thus served as a white woman's argument for the preservation of African wildlife, particularly the mountain gorilla. Carl Akeley took his wife and Mary Bradley along on this expedition to "reduce the potency of game" (specifically gorilla) for hunting by showing that "inexperienced women" could kill them.[28] Although that may have been his goal, Bradley actually rendered the gorilla less potent as a game animal by her sympathetic account of gorillas as social creatures, deserving of the same courtesy by visitors to their domain as any human neighbor. A successful romantic novelist, she had the rhetorical skills to rehabilitate the gorilla. From a fearsome monster charging through the jungle, he became Peter Pan—the perennial boy who refuses to grow up, residing forever (one hopes) in a green land that lucky little girls like five-year-old Alice Bradley occasionally get to visit.

Martha Maxwell, Delia Akeley, and Mary Hastings Bradley might have been depicted in popular accounts as unusual women because each took up a gun and hunted, not as frontierswomen might have for meat, but for intellectual pursuits with unsettling links to sporthunting. Their own narratives, however, suggest that the gun held rather a different meaning for them than for their male counterparts. Killing a large or threatening animal contained no connotations of dominance. They described the moment of death often with great ambivalence. The trophy did not signify a step into the charmed circle of adulthood. These women were already adults, going about the grown-up business of creating texts to educate the public about nature. Believing with their husbands and scientific mentors that certain species of wildlife faced imminent extinction, that some animals would continue to exist only in museums, and that preservation of what could be saved depended on the taking of scientific trophies, they found reasons in women's role and women's narratives to kill whole animal families. Although some of them refused to participate in every hunt, their presence implicated them in every death and their narratives labored to control the meaning of their involvement.

A click of the shutter preserved Martha Maxwell seated in front of her Colorado diorama and Mary Bradley on safari. In addition to preserving the exploits of scientific trophy hunters, the camera served as a valuable tool in immortalizing vanishing species. Further, as sporthunters recognized the threat of extinction facing game animals, they saw the virtue in substituting trophy hunting by camera for bagging every perfect specimen spotted.[29] Two of the first photographers to turn the camera on big game were Allen Grant and Mary Augusta Wallihan. In 1889 this husband-and-wife team set out to photograph the wildlife of Colorado and Wyoming. They published trophy images of deer, elk, antelope, buffalo, cougars, coyotes, foxes, and bears in *Hoofs, Claws, and Antlers of the Rocky Mountains* (1894) and *Camera Shots at Big Game* (1901). Teddy Roosevelt provided introductions to both books, emphasizing the need to preserve American wildlife and championing the challenges of camera hunting as a complement or even alternative to some forms of sporthunting with rifles.[30] In her biographical sketch for the earliest collection of photographs, Mrs. Wallihan stated their mutual goal: "Mr. Wallihan and myself still work together, happy in our effort of trying to preserve the game in photography for the world at large."[31]

Mary Wallihan's skill as a camerawoman did not release her from the rifle. Living on the western frontier, the couple depended on game for their meat. Revelatory of her helpmate status, Wallihan ruefully noted that she often had to take up the gun in preference to the camera: "in the fall of 1891 my husband told me I must get the winter's meat while he took photographs of the deer."[32] Mary was an adept shot. One plate in *Hoofs, Claws, and Antlers* documents two bucks that she killed with one shot; the last plate in the book captures her standing proudly beside "her 30th deer."[33] Mary Wallihan also managed to work in a good deal of photography, however. Looking on her camera as a new sort of gun, she used the two artifacts interchangeably. But the rifle was more troublesome than the camera: "I sit almost breathless, watching for them to come into the gulch and then down to the chosen spot. Suddenly they appear—the leader in full view, then another and another until all are in sight. On they come right up in front. I want that big buck. Click! goes the shutter, and I have them all. Now I will try another kind of gun, so I raise my rifle slowly and carefully, so they do not see any movement; but the camera is in the way. I drew a bead on the big fellow and fired, but somehow the fawn came in the way and got the bullet in the neck. So much for not holding my gun tight."[34] Reflecting developments in the hunting ethic, Wallihan's unfortunate killing of a fawn suggests the conflicts awaiting middle-class, urban women who looked to photography as a more gender-appropriate means of gaining entry to the parlors of wild animals. As she well knew, life among big game animals in the wild at the turn of the century required a gun. Women who wanted to try their hand at photography would also have to learn to use a rifle.

Teddy Roosevelt's concern about the future of wild animals extended to Africa. The interest among American and colonial elites in preserving classic big game animals made camera safaris to "darkest Africa" increasingly popular in the early twentieth century. While German and British photographers pioneered still and motion photography, Carl Akeley invented motion picture camera equipment that allowed him to take some of the first action shots of mountain gorillas on his 1921 expedition with the Bradleys.[35] Donna Haraway argues that Akeley was a transitional figure in the shift from guns to cameras. Seeing his camera as an extension of the gun, he held his finger off the trigger long enough to press the shutter.[36] Akeley "fathered" the American couple who first hoped to remove the gun altogether from trophy hunting. Martin and Osa Johnson had already established themselves as capable filmmakers in wild terrain when Akeley encouraged them to film the animals of East Africa. During the 1920s and 1930s they made many safaris, living for several years at an isolated lake in Kenya. Their films of elephants, gorillas, and lions were popular in the United States. They alternated between safaris and lecture tours until Martin's death in an airplane crash in 1937. Osa Johnson left comprehensive accounts of her feelings about the role of a female wildlife photographer in *I Married Adventure* and *Four Years in Paradise*.[37]

Neither Osa nor Martin had grown up in the hunting tradition that informed Roosevelt's conservation ethic, nor had either participated in scientific collecting. Middle-class, small-town midwesterners, they had no idea of how to go about filming action shots of wild animals, only that such a career would constitute the adventure of their lives. Putting together their first safari in Nairobi in 1921, the Johnsons consulted with Blaney Percival, the game warden in British East Africa. Percival told them that they would have to shoot fresh meat for their porters or hire a professional hunter to do so. Further, he warned, they might have to shoot the wildlife they were filming if they were threatened. Martin was dismayed. His father, who went along for the trip, reported that Martin had never killed anything in his life, being the kind of boy to bring them home alive.

Although Martin and Osa shared the photographic work, he had been a professional photographer when they married. Realizing that the need to kill animals might end the safari, and that she really only worked as his assistant, Osa took on the job of hunter: "Martin's going to have his hands full taking pictures—that's what we're here for. I guess I'm really going to have to learn to shoot." Reminiscent of Delia Akeley's justification of her collecting activities as the only way to get her husband safely out of the jungle and Mary Wallihan's rueful job of getting the winter's meat, Osa sacrificed her own reluctance to kill a living creature for their photographic career. After a few misses, she proved to be an excellent shot, seldom failing to provide meat for the table. Throughout her narratives, however, she never allowed the reader to assume that this was a role she enjoyed. Like Martin, she was there to film the animals. Even bringing home Christmas dinner was a hollow victory: "There lay the giant bustard. Thirty-five pounds of delicious African turkey. I held him up. He was a beauty. The feathers of his tail were spotted, his handsome chest a pearl grey. His long beak and the proud little white pompom crest on his head were splotched with red where the bullet had entered. As I looked at him, I realized as never before that there was more joy in shooting with a camera than a gun"[38] (Figure 45). Apparently, neither Osa nor Martin ever confused the camera with the gun. They had a clear understanding of the difference between collecting an animal's skin and collecting its image. But this did not release them from the violence attached to the trophy hunt.

Their goal, and the reason Carl Akeley was so supportive of their work, was to film what they imagined as authentic Africa. Rather than exaggerating the fearsome, violent aspects of wildlife, they hoped to show a community of creatures assuming many of the same nurturing roles seen in human fami-

FIGURE 45. *Osa Johnson (1894–1953) titled this image of her hunting prowess "Osa Brings Home the Dinner" when she published it in* Four Years in Paradise *(1941). (Martin and Osa Johnson Safari Museum, Chanute, Kans.)*

lies, to "show the animals, not hunted and afraid, but natural and unaware, untroubled by man."[39] The problem with this objective was that it made for boring motion picture footage. Often the Johnsons had to "stir up" the quarry. One filmed while the other engaged in some sort of maneuver to get the antelope or elephants or lions in motion. Audiences in America might take some interest in the variety of animals who came down to a lake to drink, or in the playful antics of a baby lion and its mother, but a rhino was most exciting when it charged. The Johnsons discovered that encouraging a charge sometimes required killing the animal to save their own necks.

As their expertise increased, they began to move in closer to the animals they filmed, and here too they put themselves and the wildlife at risk. Osa reportedly killed only one elephant in her life, and its death came from their desire to get a close-up shot. In standard heroic fashion, Osa and Martin had a pact to "keep grinding" the film no matter how terrifying the situation. On this occasion, an elephant charged Martin: "True to our pact I kept on grinding; I kept screaming too, and my gun-bearer stood ready at my side with my rifle. Terror then was added to terror as the rest of the herd tore after their leader. One part of my brain told me that this would be a magnificent picture, the other told me that unless I brought the lead elephant down, Martin would be trampled. I snatched my gun and fired."[40] Osa did not pause at the trigger of her rifle to take a photographic trophy of the animal she intended to kill; the pause was in the camera action. Dead, the creature had no value for her. In all of her accounts of such kills, she tried to justify her actions in the light of human safety.

Martin and Osa attempted to carve out a space for their wildlife observations within the scientific collecting establishment and the popular entertainment market. They might have encouraged a charging rhino, but they also resisted the temptation to capture every filmic trophy if it might endanger the animal's life. Stumbling on an opportunity to photograph a lioness and her cubs dining on oryx, they chose not to film: "Even if we didn't shoot any pictures, we didn't have to shoot any animals." While filming at Lake Paradise, they forbade scientific collectors from shooting even perfect specimens, although Osa helped collect impala for the American Museum in another part of the country. Discovering that hunters were using their photographic blinds, they tore down the blinds and moved on.[41] In such actions the Johnsons pulled away from nineteenth-century attitudes about wildlife and critiqued activities harming privileged animals.

However intrusive and unsettling the gun may have been during their safaris, life in the African jungle fulfilled Osa's own interest in observing wild-life. She was particularly fond of elephants and lions. In her narratives, wild animals take on individual characteristics and humanlike qualities that she attempted to capture on film. It was not the terrifying charge of a bull elephant that Osa worked hardest at filming, but the night in her sweet potato garden when a family of elephants went digging for vegetables. She felt that such images of elephants would encourage American school children to value the animal. Similarly, a lion good-naturedly fathering a family of frolicsome infants would promote the preservation of a creature misunderstood as simply violent and bloodthirsty.[42]

In keeping with her female interest in family life, Osa portrays an Africa that is most often tenanted by animals living domestic lives close to the model provided by mid-twentieth-century middle-class America. She felt a responsibility in both her photography and her writings to educate Americans in this new view of wildlife in order to protect the animals for future generations. She also saw herself as a nurturer of the particular animals whose acquaintance she made. Here she parted ways with Martin. In one of the rare instances of a reported disagreement between the pair, Osa killed an impala to feed a starving lioness and her cubs. Although Martin thought that she was being overly solicitous, the event triggered a section of her narrative detailing the harsh conditions faced by many of the animals and the constant threats to the domesticity Osa so valued.[43]

In the end, however, her legacy was the body of film shot in the wild. Inevitably, she read their films as the contribution she and her husband made to the artificial preservation of an endangered animal group: "We were attempting . . . to make an authentic film record of vanishing wildlife as it existed in its last and greatest stronghold. And if, in some over-civilized future, cities should crowd out the elephants and war should bomb the giraffes from the plains and the baboons from the treetops, our films would stand—a record for posterity."[44] Obviously, authenticity was measured by the extent to which the Johnsons' vision of African wildlife matched that being constructed by scientists like Carl Akeley. Since Akeley was after a more peaceful image of the jungle, that is what the Johnsons found.[45] Peace was earned in the belief that all the animals lived in patriarchal family units. It would be several decades before the public realized that lion prides and elephant groups are composed mainly of females and their young and therefore, by middle-class standards, serve as poor models for the American image of the nuclear family.[46] But for the moment, the photographic construction of a properly domestic jungle

FIGURE 46. *Delia Akeley (1875–1970) and J. T., Jr. (Photograph by Carl E. Akeley, Neg./Trans. no. 211788, Department of Library Services, American Museum of Natural History, New York City)*

held sway and informed the final sort of trophy hunt in which American women participated—the search for a live specimen to take back home.

Mary Bradley reported with some relief that Carl Akeley had no intention of bringing back a live gorilla specimen on their safari, "although for some moments he dallied with the idea and I held an agonized breath, seeing myself walking the floor with the wailing infant."[47] The image of a white woman holding an infant ape had struck a popular chord in the 1980s with the work of Dian Fossey and Jane Goodall, but British and American women have been cast as excellent foster mothers of such animals since the 1920s. Running through the narratives of both Delia Akeley and Osa Johnson was their feeling, often substantiated by their husbands, that they were "good with animals." Akeley adopted a vervet monkey and the Johnsons kept a gibbon and an orangutan as pets. Several wealthy women who followed their husbands on safari returned home with baby chimps and gorillas. The adventure usually ended in the banishment of the adult pet to a zoo or circus after it had become a menace to its human mother. Women of the period also developed a reputation as good zoo managers, largely due to the fame of Belle Benchley. Benchley was instrumental in building the San Diego Zoo collection and wrote a popular account about her friends the apes. Martin and Osa Johnson were so pleased with Benchley's accommodations that they sold the San Diego Zoo two mountain gorillas they had collected in 1930.[48]

There were many reasons why a woman would care for a young wild animal. Augusta Hoyt took on the gorilla baby, Toto, after her husband and his native African hunters had killed the infant's family trying to collect yet another gorilla for the American Museum's African Hall. The Johnsons adopted Kalowatt, their gibbon, when they found her starving on a native woman's boat in Borneo. Delia Akeley took on a "scientific study" of wild animals in their habitat while collecting specimens for the museum. She had her porters capture a vervet so she could prove that wild animals were cleaner in their ways than captives. Intending to release the animal, she became attached to her. Dubbed "J. T., Jr.," the vervet lived with the Akeleys for more than nine years (Figure 46). Belle Benchley adopted her first ape at the zoo. Working as an accountant at the newly opened San Diego Zoo in 1925, Benchley went out one day to get to know the animals she had experienced only as figures in a ledger. Taken by the grace and beauty of a female gibbon, she spent so much time at the cage that the animal she named "Gibby" became habituated to her. From then on, Benchley made it a point to become the familiar of every ape in the zoo. She was particularly enamored of infants and mothered them at every opportunity (Figure 47).[49]

Much as these animals were treated as children, they were exotic children, trophies of the women's ability to cross the species barrier and capture the heart of a wild animal. As living ornaments, the animals were given special attention. Often the ape or monkey had his or her own personal attendant, usually a hired native child, or as the animal grew larger, an adult keeper. Women who were mistresses of such creatures showed them in public. Osa Johnson once carried her orang, Bessie, to the steps of the New York Public Library as a benefit for the Animal Humane Association. Like camera images and stuffed specimens in museum cases, the animals served as a cross between entertainment and education.

Once Belle Benchley became director of the San Diego Zoo, she looked upon the capture of another exotic species much as Carl Akeley had valued the addition of another diorama to his African Hall. Zoo cages became the equivalent of museum cases. Describing a new home under construction for

FIGURE 47. *Belle Benchley with infant lowland gorillas Albert, Bouba, and Bata on their arrival at the San Diego Zoo in 1949. (Zoological Society of San Diego, San Diego, Calif. Photographer unknown.)*

the gibbons, Benchley touted the "little corner shelves [that] would permit them to arrange themselves like ornaments in an old-fashioned whatnot." The best trophy was a family group. Delia Akeley was sorry that J. T., Jr., never had the opportunity to have a baby of her own. When Martin and Osa Johnson captured the young mountain gorillas who ended up in the San Diego Zoo, Osa was sure they were a pair of "sweethearts" who "would be company for each other and . . . afford a valuable scientific study." The study would be a new understanding of gorilla family life. As it happened, both were male. Belle Benchley completed the story with a protracted search for mates, feeling that the gorilla display was incomplete without a family.[50]

As with the stuffed specimens in museums and flickering images in motion picture houses, there was an element of guilt attached to these living trophies. The sin involved in collecting living animals was magnified by the women's lengthy connections to their friends. After seeing an infant gorilla through bouts of pneumonia, or being the first recipient of an orang's kiss, or sharing the rare joy of a captive gibbon's first child, to be responsible for sending the pet to a cage in a zoo, or having it put to sleep, was devastating for the women involved.

Belle Benchley handled the problem much as had Martha Maxwell. San Diego was the first American zoo to breed gibbons in captivity. The death of the first mother and infant saddened Benchley and spurred her to call upon the expertise of scientists then studying the animals in the wild to help design an exhibit assuring the survival of family groups. Looking at her new gibbon collection, Benchley fantasized about their Edenic family life in their natural habitat but quickly pointed out the virtues of their life in the zoo. She felt no regret, declaring that "their life is full and happy and complete. They feel no need to glance behind to see if an enemy is near; they join no hurried rush for wild figs and plums lest other creatures steal their living from them. This is no place for slips and broken bones; each youngster is perfection so far as his physical appearance goes, as he spends his time swinging and singing as he who walks on the trees has done from time immemorial." Skimming over the fact that the first gibbon family had died partly as a result of mishandling at the zoo and that many of the animals became so ill they were put to sleep or succumbed to human diseases, Benchley envisioned the zoo as an immortal haven in which an endless chain of perfect commodities would be bred.[51]

Belle Benchley had not, however, spent much time with animals in their habitat. Delia Akeley had, and she recognized the harm that she caused in taking her vervet out of Africa. Her narrative of the animal's life, *J. T., Jr.: The Biography of an African Monkey*, is suffused with guilt about keeping the animal in captivity. When the vervet severely bit her mistress, Akeley elaborately justified her behavior, suggesting that the animal was at once an "unfortunate prisoner" and a hyperactive "child." Finally, she placed J. T. in a zoo. Describing her painful visits to the cage, she reminded her friends that she had "thoughtlessly robbed" the monkey of her freedom. The title of Akeley's account of her observations of the vervet suggests that she engaged in much more than a scientific study of an animal. Regarding J. T.'s life as worthy of a biography brought the animal within the human range of responsibility. In her book Akeley stated that after having caused the monkey such misery, J. T.'s death seemed a release for them both. The biography informed the public about the painful results of America's ostensibly innocent interest in keeping exotic animals—either at home or in zoos. Apprising her readers of the cruel methods used to capture circus and zoo animals, Akeley cast Americans as "barbaric" in their insensitivity to the suffering taking place in zoos across the country. For Akeley, new habitat cages like those being built in San Diego would not enhance the scientific study of these animals: "The real truth about the life and habits of apes and monkeys can be learned only through exhaustive study. Years must be spent by the student in the lonely and per- haps unhealthy forests where the animals dwell. No caged animal or museum specimen can tell us the fascinating life history of the wild, free creatures."[52]

## I I

Delia Akeley's narrative explains how white, middle-class women could immerse themselves in animal behavioral studies in the wild after generations of cultural sheltering from contact with undomesticated creatures other than birds and small animals of the suburban garden and neighborhood woods. Women had a long tradition of habituating birds to their presence. The large, social, intelligent species they encountered in the wild offered expanded op- portunities for much more sophisticated forms of interaction. Akeley found that "one of the greatest joys on my African journeys has been my ability to win the confidence of both birds and animals." In one instance, she inspired a flock of birds to light on her shoulders while she sat motionlessly observing a group of baboons. Her communication with the birds seemed to engage the interest of a male baboon: "I began to coquet with him, as I had seen them doing with one another; I moved my head from side to side; I scratched myself under the arm and yawned boldly; when I grunted and imitated their bark, he not only answered back but he jumped off the rock and walked toward me." She found the ensuing three-way communication between herself, the male, and the rest of the troop humorous, but she did not laugh because "monkeys are very quick to sense laughter at their expense."[53] Like the early female orni- thologists who found a way into the field when observations of the bird in its habitat became important, Akeley found that her apparent ability to read rules of social etiquette helped her succeed with animals in the jungle just as surely as at home in New York.

Not surprisingly, her subjects displayed appropriate gender roles. As had the Victorian ornithologists, Akeley read gender stereotypes of the early twen- tieth century into animal society. Her flirtation with the male baboon was modeled on behavior she had seen in female baboons. Although she felt that occasionally they behaved as wildly as "flappers," Akeley was confident of each female's interest in settling down with a mate. Most of her observations focus on family groups, often emphasizing "human-like" relations among parents and children. One courageous exemplar revealed herself to Akeley in just such a family group. When a leopard attacked her troop, Akeley reported seeing this female hand her infant to another and charge forward to hold off the predator while the others escaped: "ever since that time the baboon mother has had a leading place in my gallery of heroines. She could easily have made her escape with her baby, for she was much larger and stronger than her companions, but she voluntarily gave up her baby and faced the dreaded enemy while the others ran." The courageous mother was part of a garden-raiding troop that local tribesmen had asked Akeley to kill. Her view of the baboons as social beings with rights to life informed her refusal to assist the local people by shooting the intrusive baboons: "Knowing how amazingly human these animals are and feeling about them as I do, it would have been cold-blooded murder and I would have been haunted by the crime for the rest of my life." [54]

Of course, there were reasons to kill even a baboon—if, for example, it seemed he was about to attack Akeley herself. She dutifully reported on the fierce aspects of animal life that she witnessed. But she was reluctant to make any generalizations about the violence of animals, preferring to use even their more problematic traits as evidence of their closeness to humans: "the apes and monkeys vary in their dispositions as much as do human beings. One animal may be lazy, another energetic, one aggressive and ready to attack without provocation, while another may be a pacifist and run away to avoid trouble." [55]

Delia Akeley was isolated in the jungle, was often the only white woman in the group, and met wild animals whose fearsomeness was widely reputed. Popular imagery portrayed her as a courageous explorer stepping into wild terrain, but press accounts also emphasized that she lost none of her womanly demeanor in her exploits. Her ability to maintain both roles sprang from her success as a hunter and safari leader in her own right. After her divorce from Carl, Akeley led her own expeditions. But, according to the press, her approach to the animals and native peoples was one of dominance. She maintained her distance from this wilderness.[56] Such popular stereotypes only told half the story. In her mind, Akeley was immersed in a highly socialized network of animals whose living arrangements mirrored her own and with whom she could communicate. She felt little distance from or control over wildlife. The native human populations of Africa were another matter, however. Akeley couched her concern for African animals in such a way as to give deference to the animals and set herself off from native Africans. As wild animals were drawn into her net of humanity, African peoples were excluded.

Akeley argued for the hunting rights of African tribes, bemoaned the destruction of native cultures by white developers, and praised the "natural" freedoms of tribal women. Yet her portraits of Africans, both as a group and as individuals, placed them outside the circle of enchantment Akeley had drawn around herself and wildlife. Baboons might display variation in their character, but tribesmen were uniformly "lazy." Wild animals were clean in their ways, whereas pygmies lived in "filth." In Akeley's narrative, no African—woman or man—ever displays the sort of heroism she locates in a female baboon. Although two chapters in her *Jungle Portraits* ostensibly deal with her observations of African peoples, most of her narrative suggests that she never experienced in such work the intimacy she felt with wild animals. While on an elephant hunt with the pygmies, whom she presumably was studying, Akeley saved a chimp from their arrows. "Mother Africa" rewarded her with a present of wild animals: "Suddenly I became conscious of two bright eyes peering down at me from a limb. Presently I could see black faces fringed in white rising and lowering over the leaves, and I realized that the tree was full of inquisitive little monkeys. I forgot my misery and the Pygmies."[57]

Although Akeley used the term *animals* to describe both tribal peoples and monkeys, her frames of reference were quite different. Native Africans were "primitives"; Akeley read them through the nineteenth-century Victorian filter that placed blacks on a lower rung of the evolutionary ladder than whites. As Zora Neal Hurston well knew, racist images of her people as animalistic carried well into the twentieth century. Apes, on the other hand, were the beneficiaries of the developing impression that animals had a mental life. Nature writing was popular in America at the turn of the century. In much of this work, authors described heroic animals consciously laying down their lives for their families, much as Akeley had witnessed in her baboon matriarch.[58] Narratives like hers, where one set of values about Africans appears against another set of values about wildlife, reveal the shifts in ranking: as animals rose, Africans sank in the hierarchy. Thus, the leader of the pygmy group she lived with for several months was in her eyes an "unwashed, forest-dwelling savage, with habits lower than the wild beasts whose flesh he feeds upon."[59] In Delia Akeley's world, a society that ate chimpanzees ranked lower than other animals.[60]

Akeley's reading of the relationships of tribal peoples with animals justified her passion to come into intimate contact with animals. Although in the 1980s the most popular aspect of women's close observation of wild animals was their work with primates, in fact American women have been fascinated with a wide variety of species—in both North America and Africa. If some women's early participation in traditional forms of trophy gathering was often an excuse to live among wildlife, many other women have spent an extended period of time in isolated terrain to bring back a less tangible sort of trophy. These naturalists want more than a glimpse of gorillas in their parlor: they want to know the entire family over several generations, and they want the gorillas to know them.

Women who take up residence alongside wild animals extend the boundaries of home to include wolves' dens and elephants' gathering places. As their trophies of human family life include memories of a child's first smile or first words, so the trophies of wildlife observation appear in the moment of first contact—the first human try at a wolf howl returned by the real wolf, the first exchange of sympathy between grieving elephant and concerned human. Interested in knowing what another animal wants of its life, women—when they have an answer—turn their attention to the preservation of habitats that will support their new friends' way of living. These women have been instrumental in changing conceptions of wildlife among scientists and the public in the twentieth century. Each also has made her study of a specific species the occasion to call for wildlife conservation. While species preservation is a goal, these women also advocate the right of individual animals they have known to live out their lives in peace and freedom.

In the decades following Delia Akeley's exhortations to observe live animals in their habitat, American women gained some visibility engaging in just such study. During the 1930s, Wendell and Lucie Chapman published several photographic texts documenting their years in the Rockies watching elk, beaver, and coyote. The Chapmans were amateurs who took up cameras after Wendell's retirement from business. Their popular accounts of wildlife in the West emphasized their dislike of hunting. Their photographs show no perfect specimens collected in the interest of science, nor did they kill any animals in the pursuit of photographic trophies. Taking up the Akeleys' and Johnsons' theme of the wilderness as a peaceful space filled with animals pursuing typical domestic lives, the Chapmans proved it with images of themselves carrying on conversations with habituated beaver and in warm-hearted, insider accounts of a coyote and his family.[61]

The scientific side of such work is represented in the writings of Theodora and John Stanwell-Fletcher, both of whom had advanced training in zoology. They lived in an isolated region of north-central British Columbia from 1937 to 1941 studying the wildlife, particularly timber wolves. In addition to their scientific papers, Theodora wrote a journal of those years. Published in 1946,

*Driftwood Valley* was one of the first accounts suggesting that a white, middle-class woman could stalk and be stalked by wolves and find the experience enjoyable. Like the Johnsons, the Stanwell-Fletchers disliked the requirements of scientific collecting. Theodora collected only a few small birds—she was, in fact, proud of her status as "the only white woman in the world who, having been on an expedition into big game country, has returned without 'getting her bear.'" Although she and her husband sketched and photographed animals, her real trophy was her feeling that the timber wolves around their cabin had become habituated to them: "the wolves are well aware of our presence and habits, and like us! They even allow their young to be near us. With their remarkable gift of understanding, they have apparently come to realize that there is nothing to fear from us, that we like them, that we are interested in their welfare." Understanding that, as a group, wolves helped maintain the elk and other animals at levels the habitat could handle, the couple also witnessed individual wolves demonstrate so much family feeling and intelligence around the cabin that neither husband nor wife could collect these predators after making their acquaintance.[62] Theodora Stanwell-Fletcher advocated both species preservation and gentle dealing with individual animals.

In the early 1940s Sally Carrighar began publishing her accounts of animal communities. Similar to Rachel Carson's *Under the Sea Wind*, Carrighar's *One Day on Beetle Rock* dispenses with a human narrator. Carrighar reveals nature through imaginative rendering of animal consciousness. Following the animal adventure stories that helped kindle popular interest in wildlife at the turn of the century, Carrighar's book changed the viewpoint from the older focus on one heroic animal to a newer understanding of animal communities. Although the author was not a trained naturalist, she called on the scientific community to help her understand what she saw. Her first book included a foreword by Robert C. Miller, director of the California Academy of Sciences, validating that hers were stories "of actual animals in an actual place, as the author has observed them . . . This is real natural history."[63]

Based on her long-term study of wildlife in California's Sequoia National Park, *One Day on Beetle Rock* relates each animal's daily round, emphasizing the intricate web of relationships that make up the community. Individual animals have "characters" of their own (a spinster grouse, a furious weasel, a failing buck). Each also represents its species and serves as a link in an unbroken chain of dependencies. The chain is not hierarchical. Every animal, from the lizards warming themselves in the sun to the black bear guiding her young along the rock's shelf, has equal value in Carrighar's eyes. She carefully rehabilitates problematic creatures like the predators. A starving coyote, for example, is grounded in the earth's cycles as Carrighar imagines him finally succeeding in his hunt at the proper moment: "The Coyote slept—only briefly, but when he awoke nothing remained of the rain but a bright mist. The clouds above the trees were a fresher, softer gray; the air felt as if some wariness had been abandoned. This was hunters' weather. The earth itself seemed lazy, pleased, warm, overconfident. Some new arrangement of natural forces, of tensions and pressures, would make the pursuing kind of nerves and muscles more effective than the fleeing kind."[64] Carefully noting the coyote's high failure rate as a predator, Carrighar also cast his hunt as family business. He had a famished mate and cubs dependent on him to bring home food.

Carrighar found her lifework in *One Day on Beetle Rock*. She went on to become one of America's most prolific animal writers. Several other books followed the *Beetle Rock* format—detailing the interactions of a community over the course of a day or a season. In the 1960s she wrote a popular account of ethology, using her skills at imagining animal consciousness to explain new behavioral studies. Her last book, *The Twilight Seas: An Account of a Blue Whale's Journey*, appeared in 1975 in support of developing international efforts to protect marine mammals.[65] Her most interesting narrative, however, is her autobiography, *Home to the Wilderness* (1973). Carrighar first realized that she had a way with animals in the 1930s while working in Hollywood on a movie that included a trained lion. She weathered many false starts before realizing that her interest in animals could be used in a career as a nature writer. Although she attended Wellesley College for a time, she had little training in zoology. Without the funds to return to college, Carrighar introduced herself to scientists at the University of California and the California Academy of Sciences. Like many before her, she found a niche as an amateur dependent on the advice of male naturalists. Through these men, and others in the U.S. Forest Service, she gradually built a reputation as a serious, reliable narrator.

In the late 1930s Carrighar began a series of extended stays at Beetle Rock, living for months at a time in a Forest Service cabin. Her goal was to produce a new kind of ecological study: "to portray the pattern but devote most attention to individual creatures in it. I wanted to tell how these animals were related to one another but to show chiefly what was interesting to the creatures themselves. They did not see themselves as strands in a net. They were concerned with surviving, finding mates, rearing young, and getting through every day with as little stress and as much satisfaction as possible. How did they do it, each one with his numerous neighbors?"[66] Victimized by a perfectionist, rejecting mother, Carrighar had decided against having children of her own. Never married, she was involved in a long-term relationship when the Beetle Rock study began. She reported that once she realized she would "go on and on into a farther and farther wilderness," she broke off the relationship. Wilderness then became her home and wildlife her progeny. Recounting a day when many wild animals had come into her cabin at Beetle Rock to escape a raiding goshawk, she closed her autobiography with an Edenic scene: "I was looking around at [the wildlife] with satisfaction and out through the door to the wider green walls beyond, I thought, suddenly, This is the home I have come to. I know now what home means to most people, not only walls but a shelter-touch for the heart and mind. Here I have found it, home at last—and with all these delightful children."[67]

During the 1930s and 1940s, women established themselves in both popular and scientific circles as contributors to the emerging fields of animal ecology and ethology. As they published their accounts of extended animal observation, they not only helped change cultural prejudices against species like the wolf, they also suggested that women could find a space for themselves in the wilderness among wildlife—a space built from their domestic roles as wives and mothers but encouraging expansion of those roles as the meanings of both wilderness and wildlife altered. If ecology suggested that threatening predators such as the wolf were actually preserving habitats and ethology raised the status of the wolf to social animal—a loving family member and loyal friend—then there was little reason for women to be protected from such animals. In fact, women could imagine, as Theodora Stanwell-Fletcher once did, that male wolves sang to them as surely as they sang to their mates: "Like a breath of wind, rising slowly, softly, clearly to a high, lovely note of sadness and longing; dying down on two distinct notes so low that our human ears could scarcely catch them. It rose and died, again and again. A wolf singing the beauty of the night, singing it as no human voice had ever done, calling on a mate to share the beauty of it with him, to come to him, to love him. Over and over it sang, so tenderly and exquisitely that it seemed as if the voice were calling to me and I could hardly keep from crying."[68]

As ecologists and ethologists increasingly valued preservation of wildlife in the wilderness rather than in urban museums, older modes of trophy collecting declined. Women experienced somewhat less ambivalence about their activities. By the early 1950s, for example, field naturalists were more conservative in their specimen collecting and more interested in the triumphant sighting of an animal going about its business in its own habitat.[69] The new trophy was a badge of friendship with a wild animal on its own terms. Whereas earlier generations of live trophy collectors had tried to fit their animals into homes in the city, by the 1950s the goal was to strike up a long-term relationship with a wild creature on its home ground. Women's interest in such study gained more credibility within the field itself. Yet this new, apparently less violent form of collecting carried its own imperatives, leading to guilt matched only by that experienced by Delia Akeley as she watched her vervet slowly die in a zoo cage.

In 1958 Lois Crisler published her personal narrative of the joys and terrors awaiting those women for whom the wolf's call was so powerful that nothing else would do but to look deeply into its eyes on its home ground. Lois and her husband Herb lived for eighteen months in the Arctic wilds of the Brooks Range filming animals for a Disney movie featuring the caribou. Arriving at an isolated lake in the Range, Lois asked herself: "'What *do* I want?' My answer was instant. 'To be where "the people that walk on four legs" are. For the rest I can pick myself up, get off the couch of uncorseted slackness. Tauten my muscles and take the direction of the desire under the desires.'"[70] Her challenge was not survival in a harsh environment, but communication with other species, seen from the first as "people" with all the rights accorded human animals. Determined to film wolves on the tundra, Herb Crisler had asked their pilot to arrange for the capture of a litter of wolves. Two cubs were obtained from Eskimos at the beginning of their first summer camp on the Brooks Range. With these animals, Trigger and Lady, Lois fulfilled her "desire under the desires." Not only did she live among the wolves, wolverines, and caribou of the Arctic, but she also shared her tundra home with a pair of "four-leggeds."

Picking up on the Stanwell-Fletchers' observations that the wolf is a highly social animal, Lois wrote detailed descriptions of the wolves' interactions with each other and with the Crislers. Here was no momentary brush with a tantalizing baboon in the forest or a brief howl with hidden creatures, but an intimate, extended observation. Once camp was established, the wolves were allowed out of their pen and off the leash. To Lois's astonishment, rather than running to freedom, the young animals returned to the Crislers, leading her to think of herself as a "part of their pack." Lois's goal was to mold her life to their needs, to "try to live in a degree of freedom with animals not human-oriented." The couple's superficial job of filming the animals was grounded in the deeper desire to share a friendship with them while also acknowledging that "animals without wilderness are a closed book."[71] Living with a pair of wolves in their home range seemed the perfect way to learn about their habits and characters.

*Arctic Wild,* Lois's account of how she and Herb shared a cabin with wolves, offered Americans what A. Starker Leopold called in 1958 "the most meticulous and complete description of wolf mannerisms and behavior that has been written."[72] In addition to vivid images of wolves "smiling" and "talking," Lois included a particularly significant trophy of communication. Sharing eye contact with growling Trigger, Lois reassured him: "the wolf had read my eyes! The thing happens so fleetingly, the animal's wild inexorable intelligence seizes the knowledge so instantaneously that the wonder is I ever blundered into awareness of this deepest range of communication . . . your true feeling looks out of your eyes, the animal reads it. The wolf has a characteristic way of looking at your eyes. He does not stare, his eyes merely graze yours in passing. I learned at last to have my eyes ready for that unguarded instant when the wolf's eyes brushed mine." (Figure 48) She hoped the message her eyes sent to Trigger was that she respected him as a "free being, neither doglike nor humanlike, but wolf and wild." Her reward for breaking through "anthropomorphism" was a vision of the wolf's "selfness." Humans who gain such reward, she argued, are explorers on a par with "Cortez and may have the authentic delight of spying new worlds."[73]

Lois Crisler assumed that this venture was morally correct. By the 1950s both wild land and wild life were gaining a privileged status in America. To be out on the tundra working to preserve native animals was considered heroic, worthy of funding by no less popular a figure than Walt Disney. Marking the ethical boundaries set by the Crislers, Lois emphasized their reluctance to take along guns and their commitment to filming only "real" action, not set-up scenes.[74] The habituated wolves, Trigger and Lady, had many opportunities to leave them for a life with other wolves. On occasions when they were late returning from hunting forays, Lois and Herb worried that the wolves had left for good. Before the year and a half was over, Lady was killed by a female rival and Trigger left with a wolf pack. Yet, at some point in the venture, the initial objective became obscured, overshadowed by the other trophy— a marketable film. How better to display wolves' true social nature, their remarkable emotion and intelligence, than in images of family life? Given their limited time on the tundra, the Crislers could not rely on Trigger and Lady for such imagery. Lois reported that Herb initially hoped to film wild cubs

FIGURE 48. *Lois Crisler (1897–1971) and one of her Arctic wolves. (University of Washington Libraries, Seattle)*

raised in the den, but thwarted in his first try, he raided a den and brought home five babies for Trigger and Lady to adopt.

The stolen cubs forever altered Lois's innocent immersion into the lives of the four-leggeds. When Herb surprised her with the infants late one night, she "involuntarily . . . shrank." Although she took on a nurturing role with the cubs (a role she gladly shared with Lady), she was haunted by thoughts of the other mother crying for her children. When a strange female wolf hung around the camp, Lois wondered if she might be the mother, Trigger tried to lead the pups off into the tundra toward this female but was prevented by the Crislers. Finally, he went off to form his own family. The Crislers filled in, arranging a "good howl" with the pups and encouraging them to test out new territory.

The humans had only so long on the tundra, not long enough to raise young wolves to maturity. When the film was finished and the money consumed, they had to return home. Less than a year old, with no adult wolves to lead them, the five cubs were doomed to starvation if left behind and to captivity if taken along. Wrenched by a guilt first expressed years earlier by Delia Akeley, Lois laid bare their violation of those they considered their friends: "What was right to do in a situation unright from its beginning—the hour the pups were stolen from their den?"[75] Unwilling to kill the cubs, Lois and Herb shipped them back to their cabin in Colorado. There they constructed a pen covering several acres. The wolves escaped and all but one, Alatna, were killed by local people still obsessed—like much of the American West during that period—with exterminating the wolf. Lois dedicated the next seven years to seeing that Alatna had some semblance of a wolf's life in the wild. The wolf had a series of dog mates, producing several litters of puppies, many of whom had to be killed because they were "vicious" or to control the population in the pens. At last, Lois, forced to leave the cabin by her impending divorce from Herb, euthanized Alatna and all her family.

Lois Crisler relates the story of those seven years in *Captive Wild*. It is a remarkable tale of human-wolf friendship earned by Crisler's ceaseless efforts to protect the wolf from the crippling effects of captivity, to maintain Alatna's autonomy and sense of control in a situation denying both. The female wolf and the female human shared a private and exclusive bond. And, Lois asserted, both were affected: "I had not dreamed until now that I had something to give Alatna—and she had been able to receive it—besides my main effort and preoccupation, which had been, so passionately, to keep her as herself, to keep her heart confident and free. But I had given her something—I did not know what in a wolf's mind. I had given her of my humanness. She had given me of her wolfness. We were both different. She was still all wolf. I was, I thought, more human." Once on the road of a wrong decision, Lois Crisler lived up to her felt debt to the stolen cub and ended Alatna's life to honor their bond of friendship. In the end, her long relationship with the wolves was paid for in "involvement, concern, action." *Captive Wild* concludes at the moment that Crisler destroys Alatna while remembering the wolf "free with her fellow wolves on the tundra in the old big days of her youth" and her own inclusion in the "symphony [they] played among themselves."[76]

Crisler suggests that the intimate observation practiced in long-term animal behavioral studies compels the human participant to take responsibility for the knowledge gained. Knowing that wolves are social animals, she felt obligated to ensure that her wolf had an opportunity to fulfill that role, even if it meant sacrificing seven years of her own autonomy. Though it might appear that the binding action was the theft of the cubs from their parents' den, other women wildlife observers argue that any extended friendship with such animals requires action to secure four-legged individuals the rights to their own society. Since Crisler's books appeared in the 1950s and 1960s, other women have published similar studies of American wildlife. One of the most prolific is Hope Ryden, who has written observational/activist accounts of the beaver, bobcat, and coyote.[77] As earlier writers shifted their interest from the American West to Africa, the contemporary period has seen as much work with African wildlife as with North American animals. By the 1970s and 1980s women had become famous for their studies of chimps, gorillas, orangutans, lions, and elephants. In part due to Louis Leakey's gender-selective sponsorship of Jane Goodall, Dian Fossey, and Biruté Galdikas as primate watchers, a mystique surrounds women who work with apes.

What makes Lois Crisler's narratives somewhat old-fashioned is the sense that there are only two options for her wolf cubs—death or a life as captives. Goodall, Fossey, and Galdikas offer a third alternative—reintroduction of wildlife into their home terrain.[78] That effectively happened to Trigger during the Crislers' eighteen-month study in the Brooks Range. Crisler felt the rightness of such a solution and imaginatively sent Alatna back to the tundra at the moment of her death. Reintroduction assumes that the best place for a wild animal is home terrain. The new generation of animal friends feel bound to return stolen animals to life in the wild. Such return is connected with an equally important obligation to the wildlife they study: interfering with the daily lives of their intimates as little as possible. While the Crislers felt something of this duty, the expectations for contemporary animal observers are more rigid. There are scientific reasons for interfering as little as possible with the objects of study. Popular narratives by the most recent generation of female naturalists also locate a rationale in moral duties to the wild animal. Obligations spring not only from perceived correlations between animal and human society identified as a result of the study, but also from individual bonds of friendship that women feel with their animal informants.[79] Thus, moments of intimate contact between researcher and subject, on the subject's home ground, become trophies signifying women's success as well-behaved guests in the parlors of four-legged individuals.

Dian Fossey is the American woman most famed for her advocacy of the right of African wildlife to autonomy. As the first person to habituate mountain gorillas to close, extended human observation, Fossey perfected a technique allowing her access to their daily activities. Her approach depended on adapting herself to gorillas' perceptions of how animals should behave in the forest, and resisting the urge to push herself too much upon her subjects. Fossey imitated gorilla sounds and mannerisms, climbed trees to satisfy their curiosity about her, and never followed a troop when they decided to move away from the contact point. Realizing that habituation might orient some individuals too much to a human, she resisted her own inclination to turn the animals into pets.[80] Although her tactics matched widely accepted practice in animal behavioral studies, in her popular account of her study, *Gorillas in the Mist*, she gives her methods an ethical content as well. How Fossey studied the animals was implicitly connected with her perception of their rights as four-legged individuals.

Fossey's interest in African wildlife preceded her collaboration with Louis Leakey. She approached him about the gorillas after taking out a personal loan to go on a long-awaited safari. On her first, brief contact with the mountain gorillas in 1963, she had been impressed by the animals' individuality. After her return as a funded observer in 1967, she discovered a wide range of behavioral variations among the animals, confirming her sense that each was a unique individual. Watching these apparently autonomous creatures living together in family groups typically headed by a dominant male with several mates, Fossey described their individuality through their behavior among kin. Leakey was interested in primates for the light they might shed on early human society. Fossey's research received funding for the contribution it might make to unraveling this puzzle. This question informs her descriptions of the silverback Beethoven's group as a "family unit" offering a "behavioral example for human society."[81]

Gorillas mean more, however, than any generalization humans might make about their living arrangements. Group 5, Beethoven's family, consisted of unique personalities whom Fossey considered her friends. She had not observed them as an outsider, hidden behind a blind, never interacting with the subject. Fossey achieved the goal implicit in most women's narratives I have discussed: she developed an intimate relationship with the animals. Intimacy means mutual recognition, communication, an answer to the question—"what do you want?" Moments when Fossey feels recognized, accepted, even included in gorilla daily life become the trophies of her narrative and support her sense of personal responsibility for the protection not only of the species, but also of these animals, her friends.

Most attention has been paid to Fossey's relationship with the male, Digit, whose death was used to publicize the plight of the mountain gorillas. Nevertheless, her book, *Gorillas in the Mist*, is filled with many examples of the moment when gorilla and human gaze on or touch one another in trust. Once, assuming that a group had moved on, Fossey stood to look for signs of their direction: "Suddenly I heard a noise in the foliage by my side and looked directly into the beautifully trusting face of Macho, who stood gazing up at me. She had left her group to come to me. On perceiving the softness, tranquillity, and trust conveyed by Macho's eyes, I was overwhelmed by the extraordinary depth of our rapport. The poignancy of her gift will never diminish." Later, when Macho was killed defending her infant, Kweli, from capture, Fossey remembered this moment and Macho's tenderness with Kweli. Her point was not only that the deaths meant the loss of two more gorillas in an endangered population, but also that these were individuals whose lives Fossey had shared. When Fossey made her home in the mountains of Rwanda, she found her most supportive friends among the gorillas (Figure 49).[82]

Fossey broke with the dominant scientific and conservationist establishment over how to study and manage the mountain gorilla population in Parc de Volcans. One highly visible sign of the gorilla's status in her mind was the burial ground that she began in her research camp. Here Digit, Macho, Kweli, and others rested in individual graves with named markers. Once Fossey's work began to draw other researchers to the area, she often clashed with her students and colleagues over their responsibility to gorillas—dead or alive. After a male whom Fossey had studied for seven years died, one of the students appeared at her door with the skin in a bag: "'This is Rafiki's skin and I want to take it home with me.' The ghoulish statement hit me with shattering force. This gruesome violation of the majesty, strength, and dignity of Rafiki seemed an intolerable sacrilege. I promptly confiscated the trophy, revolted by the request." Fossey, who had come to the study of gorillas as an amateur drawn to the animals themselves, was often unsympathetic with graduate students' views of scientific inquiry. She found the students more concerned with "obtaining observational data for their doctoral degrees" than with the welfare of their informants. The difference between herself and many of her assistants, she argued, was that her work was "not about building one's reputation on data, but preserving life."[83]

These tensions with students over the rights of their subjects were symptomatic of the more basic split between Fossey and those scientists and conservation groups she relied on for funding. Her disagreements with the establishment developed partly around the privilege she granted gorillas over African people. Just as Delia Akeley's images of primates were influenced by her negative responses to tribal peoples, so Fossey's intimacy with gorillas contrasted

FIGURE 49. *Macho and Kweli. (Photograph by Dian Fossey. Reprinted by permission of Russell and Volkening, New York, N.Y., as agents for the author.)*

sharply with her insensitivity to native Rwandans. *Gorillas in the Mist* offers an impassioned plea for the protection of the mountain gorillas from agricultural and pastoral threats to their habitat. Reminiscent of Akeley's intervention to protect chimps from pygmies, Fossey waged a fierce battle to remove Rwandan people from the Parc de Volcans, the wildlife preserve that Carl Akeley had originally helped develop and in which she located her Karisoke Research Center. Fossey had little understanding of or respect for native Africans. The conclusion to *Gorillas* indicates that she sympathized with the complex economic pressures confronting the Rwandan government and citizenry given the imperatives of world market forces. Yet the introduction to her study presents these same people as nothing more than a set of eternally warring tribes, mired in ancient customs. Fossey was sometimes contemptuous of her Rwandan staff and visited a similar attitude on governmental representatives. Moreover, because Rwandans did not appear to Fossey to be endangered and mountain gorillas were, she gave deference to the gorillas.[84]

Although Fossey supported almost any conservation effort, she felt that building a tourist market and educating Rwandans in the ecological and economic benefits of the gorilla worked too slowly. These measures were developed by international consortia of wildlife management and conservation professionals and were proffered by these groups as sensitive to the property rights of African peoples. Dubbing these management schemes "theoretical conservation," Fossey contended that "gorillas . . . do not have time to wait." Her method, "active conservation," was to enforce laws against poaching and grazing within the park. Witnessing the violent deaths of animals who had become her friends, she gradually stepped up her own efforts to the point where she felt obligated to terrorize those Africans she held responsible. Her radical intervention in the park management structure led to much tension with scientific and conservation groups like the National Geographic Society, which ultimately withdrew its support from her project, declaring that her approach was not scientific enough and that she was too emotionally involved with the gorillas. When Fossey argued that the gorillas did not have time, she was speaking not only of the species but also of individuals she knew would die while the long-term schemes developed. Her radical split with scientists involved in modern conservation techniques was based on her equal concern for species and individual preservation.[85]

Fossey's trophy was not the skin, the image, or the book about gorilla behavior, but contact with the animal itself. Like Lois Crisler, she discovered that even this seemingly innocent need for intimacy across the species barrier carried a burden of pain and guilt. While the Karisoke Research Camp became a haven comparable to Sally Carrighar's Sierra cabin, with habituated wildlife mingling among humans, Karisoke was also an island resting uneasily in the mingled waters of African, European, and American conservation agendas.

Pressures on the camp's status as a wildlife sanctuary forced Fossey into actions for which she felt guilt and sorrow. Even more tragically, she discovered that her alien presence itself threatened the preserve. Driven by her passion to save the gorillas, she retaliated against native herders by killing their cows: "I hate myself for doing this. The poor cows just won't die, won't die. I can't stand seeing this." Familiar with the raising of infant gorillas, Fossey was asked to care for sickly infants captured for zoos. She felt like a "traitor" for complying but was blackmailed by threats to raid her study groups if she did not. The deaths of Macho, her mate Uncle Bert, and the infant Kweli were the result of such retaliation when a gorilla infant died while in Fossey's care. Because of her "active conservation" raids, by the time of Macho's death international conservation groups were pressing Fossey to leave Rwanda. Colleagues suggested that she had brought about the deaths of Macho, Uncle Bert, and Kweli and that she should leave before other animals died in what began to look like a vendetta against her. However, the greatest blow came with the realization that some of the gorillas were dying of human-induced diseases. Fossey had to face the fact that her successful habituation procedure, which had allowed researchers close contact with the animals, also caused their deaths: "The horrid thing is, it might not have been just the tourists. [Nunkie] could have been infected by one of my own students!"[86]

Donna Haraway has argued that Louis Leakey's entire group of women working with primates, including Fossey, symbolically serve as a mediating link between white men and the "dark continent" in a postcolonial age. Touching the hand of the gorilla on one side and the hand of man on the other, white women ameliorate the guilt of colonial history and suggest an ostensibly peaceful mode for the return of Western culture to Africa. This is the message of the famous image of Fossey's fingertip-to-fingertip contact with a young male gorilla, recorded by a (male) photographer for *National Geographic* and captured in the Hollywood film of her life, as a triangle made up of gorilla and woman as objects of a masculine photographic eye.[87] Fossey's descriptions of gorilla behavior and her habituation techniques appeared to pose no threat to the dominant culture. Leakey chose women to study the primates because he felt that their gender-coded sensitivity to interpersonal relations would encourage just the sort of interaction Fossey succeeded in establishing.

He failed to recognize, however, that gender roles included other, potentially more troubling, imperatives. Dian Fossey trained in occupational therapy in part because she had not been able to handle the scientific training necessary for a veterinary career.[88] Like some other women, she found the sciences alienating and chose a career more "in keeping" with women's perceived strengths. While the men funding her study may have seen her as an amateur helpmate playing a role similar to Martha Maxwell and Delia Akeley in creating the twentieth-century living museum—the tourist game preserve—Fossey had another vision. Acknowledging her gift of developing intimate relationships with wild animals, she also held herself accountable for the behavior incumbent on those who would enter the private domain of another household. Forced to choose between the growing science of wildlife study and management and the traditional duty of a woman to protect friends and family, she chose the latter. In making that decision, Fossey posed a threat to the controlling elites in both scientific and conservation circles. After proving herself a capable observer and an able fund-raiser for wildlife causes, she questioned the whole enterprise by openly criticizing the establishment's methods and goals. Like Susan Griffin's lioness, ringed by the scientific establishment, Fossey refused to be put in her place.[89]

Her biographer, Farley Mowat, has suggested that, for all Fossey's attraction to men, most of her real confidants and friends were women. Mostly among them could she find colleagues who understood and supported her desire to secure the safety of the gorillas. Fossey seemed to be conscious of the gendered reading that might be given to her feelings for the gorillas. Removed as head of the Karisoke Research Center, denied funds that had been raised to support her aggressive conservation program, and ostracized from most conservation groups, she saw herself as an "abandoned mother of fifty-seven, the number of gorillas now in the study area. To care for them I have to get work or sell something. I could try selling my body, but there wouldn't be many takers for Fossil Fossey, so I must try something else."[90] One group concerned with wildlife did not fail her. The American Humane Society awarded her the Joseph Wood Krutch Medal after the publication of *Gorillas in the Mist* and made her a grant of five thousand dollars in honor of her work "in the cause of animal protection."[91] From its inception in the nineteenth century, women were deeply involved in the animal rights movement. One strand in early protection efforts arose from the belief that wild animals left to suffer the bullets of incompetent hunters or denied adequate habitats to thrive were as much victims of human mistreatment as cruelly treated domestic animals. The Humane Society understood that Fossey was battling for the right of individual animals to a "normal" life as much as she was fighting for the survival of an endangered species.

This account of women's involvement in wildlife study, as seen through trophy-gathering behavior, should not be read as purely progressive. Every

FIGURE 50. *Peggy Bauer. (Courtesy of Erwin and Peggy Bauer)*

sort of trophy still exists, although some are less favored and have evolved into more socially accepted practices. American women are a distinct minority among sporthunters, but sporthunting in general has decreased with the development of more benign uses of wildlife. Although specimen collecting persists in zoology and ecology, and more women have entered these fields, scientists tred more lightly in the ecosystem than they did at the turn of the century. Nor is live specimen collecting in much favor except in drastic efforts to save threatened species, particularly since the 1973 enactment of the Convention on International Trade in Endangered Species of Wild Fauna and Flora. The early gathering of animal trophies on safaris has been replaced by attempts to develop human-animal communication with captive subjects and to breed endangered species in zoos. Women have gained some recognition and have worked on an equal footing with men in these endeavors, the most famous being Penny Patterson's efforts to teach her gorilla Koko to communicate through sign language. Like her earlier ancestors, Koko is a cross between a scientific project and an entertaining diversion—both laboratory experiment and trained circus act. Reflecting the guilt attached to such treatment, Patterson has recently tried to set up Koko with a family of her own.[92]

Rather than heading out on safari to collect an exotic creature for the

FIGURE 51. *A gray wolf* (Canis lupus), *Denali, North Park, Alaska (1987). (Photograph by Peggy Bauer, courtesy of Erwin and Peggy Bauer)*

local natural history museum or zoo, professional and amateur naturalists in the late twentieth century collect trophy photographs and sketches. Women are developing reputations as professional wildlife photographers and artists. Capping the long-standing tradition of husband-and-wife photographic teams are Erwin and Peggy Bauer. The Bauers became known for photographing native American wildlife, but they also document endangered species worldwide. Taught the art by her husband, Peggy Bauer is now a wildlife photographer in her own right (Figures 50, 51, 52). The Bauers have written several guides for amateur wildlife photographers, continuing Teddy Roosevelt's admonition to trophy hunters to realize that a good photograph of a white-tailed deer can be as much a testament to tracking skill as a pair of antlers in the den. Women are also establishing themselves in this field on their own. In addition to pursuing a successful career as a wildlife photographer, Irene Hinke Sacilotto leads photography workshops for amateurs and professionals.[93]

Women have gradually begun to work their way into wildlife painting as

FIGURE 52. *A grizzly (*Ursus arctos horribilis*), McNeil River, Alaska. (Photograph by Peggy Bauer, courtesy of Erwin and Peggy Bauer)*

well. Long a male-dominated genre, with a market made up mostly of men interested in artistic depictions of game animals, wildlife painting first included women bird artists. The most prestigious bird art show in the country, the Leigh Yawkey Woodson Art Museum's annual exhibition, includes some of the most accomplished women in the field. Recently Leigh Yawkey has begun a wildlife art exhibition. Marking the continued gender divisions in the field, women are a distinct minority of those represented in the shows.[94] One of the finest contemporary artists is Lindsay Scott, whose pencil drawings

FIGURE 53. Dust Storm *(Pied crows and zebras), by Lindsay B. Scott. (Courtesy of the artist)*

of African animals often emphasize interdependent communities of wildlife: *Dust Storm* depicts the interplay between zebras and pied crows (Figure 53). Although some of the women are themselves hunters, many pursue their art out of a desire for simple contact with nature. All share a deep commitment to conservationist ethics. Scott has said of *Dust Storm*: "soon the whole zebra herd will have disappeared into the dust—a symbolic representation of the deplorable extinction of so many species." Janet Heaton, another contemporary artist working in Africa, evokes a similar feeling in a pastel of elephants entitled *Surviving in Shadows*, drawn to remind her audience of the dangers facing these creatures (Figure 54).[95]

Within the scientific establishment, field naturalists rely increasingly on the camera to document the habitat and behavior of animals. Whereas earlier in the century women often played second fiddle to husbands engaged in camera documentation, the new generation of female ecologists and ethologists makes many of its own pictures. Although the most popular image of Dian Fossey is as an object of the photographic eye, posed with the gorillas, she also took many of her own photographs (see Figure 49). These prints held both private and scientific meaning. Fossey displayed them as public documents, but she also read them as representations of personal family history.[96]

Throughout her fourteen-year study of African elephants, Cynthia Moss has used the camera to help her identify individuals and delineate the complex net of social bonds existing within and between matriarchal groupings. Moss

FIGURE 54. Surviving in Shadows *(African elephants), by Janet N. Heaton. (Courtesy of the artist)*

has discovered that photographs—rather than serving as static artifacts, taken to freeze a vanishing species into a timeless model—help construct elephantine versions of history (Figure 55). She compared images of Teresia, one of her oldest subjects, taken in the 1960s by Norman Myers, with her own recent images of the animal and her group. The comparison helped her construct the elephant's biography. Teresia's life story supported Moss's contention that elephants have "their knowledge, their traditions, and their memories," a social history that must be respected in management schemes.[97]

Finally, increasing numbers of women are contributing to the most recent form of trophy collecting—intimate interaction with animals on their home ground. Cynthia Moss's narrative of her work with elephants demonstrates that women are not restricted to primate studies. Moss, an authority on elephant behavior, has encouraged several other women to enter the field. In addition to presenting fine studies of elephant groups, Moss's *Elephant Memories* shows the impact women are making on field studies and the support they provide each other as colleagues and friends. Her account of her research group of five or six women and several men gathered around the

FIGURE 55. *Cynthia Moss captioned this photograph "Agatha of the AAs Stops and Feels and Gently Moves Her Mother Annabelle's Skull" in* Elephant Memories *(1988). (Photograph by Cynthia Moss, courtesy of the artist)*

campfire at night "gossiping" about their elephant friends subverts the stereo-type of a self-denying nun isolated from human contact by her devotion to wild animals. *Elephant Memories* also offers sensitive portrayals of the Maasai tribe's traditional interaction with elephants and argues for Kenya's right to self-determination on the issue of wildlife preservation. Moss does not pull wildlife into the bounds of home while excluding tribal peoples as the "other." Two of her research assistants are Maasai women, who add the perceptions and voices of native women to behavioral studies of life among the animals.[98]

For all women's visibility in field studies of live animals, in some ways they often remain outsiders to the methods and goals of modern scientific con-servation. Like Dian Fossey, Cynthia Moss has battled for credibility within the establishment. The funds to cover her first two years with the elephants in Kenya's Amboseli National Park came from money she had saved from other jobs. Learning most of her observational techniques as a research assis-tant for Iain Douglas-Hamilton, who pioneered photographic techniques for identifying individual elephants, Moss has not earned formal professional cre-dentials. The respect she has achieved comes from her long-term dedication to studying the elephants.[99]

Narratives like *Elephant Memories* depict nature as much less genteel and pacific than those written by nineteenth-century female naturalists. Reflect-ing the late twentieth-century's openness to the discussion of sexual behavior, Moss presents graphic descriptions of mating patterns. But signifying a con-tinued concern with the gender of field observers, she notes that she has been called a "female chauvinist" for concentrating on female elephants. Counter-ing such charges, she describes the discoveries she and a female colleague have made about the sexual behavior of bulls. She also argues that the females are important to any understanding of elephant social life and thus justify her specific interest in their behavior. Such comments serve as well to defend Moss's credibility as a reliable, objective observer of the animals. What she has seen, however, often puts her objectivity to the test. Witnessing the suffering and death, either from natural causes or the hand of man, of individual ani-mals with whom she has a feeling of kinship, Moss has been torn between a personal sense of obligation to help the individual and her family and her scientific goal of nonintrusive study of the patterns of elephant life.[100]

As something of an outsider, she, like Fossey before her, feels free to criti-cize any tendency to see elephants as objects subject to efficient management. Echoing Fossey's view that "gorillas are their own owners," Moss believes that "an elephant is its own being." Appalled by culling programs that kill whole family groups to prevent elephants from overgrazing trees, Moss argues for a more cautious approach. She suggests that we do not really know enough about how elephants and plants interact to develop a workable model for management by culling and should introduce intrusive techniques with extreme care. The real issue is not preserving elephants for ivory harvests and as tourist commodities, but assuring their "way of life," the opportunity to play out their matriarchal, multigenerational family and community history:

> Killing the elephants seems the simplest and most direct solution, but only to people who have not watched individuals over 14 years; have not seen the elephants greet one another with trumpets of joy; seen elephants, adults and calves alike, running and playing across an open pan in the moonlight; seen elephants trying to lift and hold up a stricken companion; seen a female stand by her dead baby for four days; or seen a seven-year-old calf gently fondle and stroke and feel the jaw of his dead mother. Elephants are not so many rodents to be exterminated; they deserve something better than that and I am not afraid to say that ethics and morality should be essential considerations in our decisions for their future.[101]

Ethics and morality have figured heavily in women's attempts not only to study but to communicate with, befriend, and protect wild animals. In the nineteenth and early twentieth centuries, women interested in large game animals, predators, and exotic wildlife had few options except to follow the traditions established by men. Many had to enter the hunt, which often conflicted with their sense of woman's responsibility to conserve life. As the methods and goals of wildlife science and management changed in the twentieth century, more space developed for women's studies of animal behavior. In turn, women's interest in animal individuality led them to ask different questions and pose new possibilities. Their findings encouraged men in the field to revise traditional ideas about animal society.

As their knowledge of other animals has increased, women have broadened their own sense of proper interactions with them. In the nineteenth and early twentieth centuries, female observers acted out fairly simple maternal roles with wildlife. They adopted infants and brought wild creatures into human culture as pets and zoo specimens. Long-term field studies resulted in more respect for the animal's right to its own habitat and society. Women are central voices in efforts to reintroduce social animals to the wild and to preserve sufficient habitats for animals to maintain their social structure.

Throughout, however, their appeals have been based on more than simply a concern for the preservation of species. Women's belief in the *rights* of individual animals, played out in their long-term involvement in animal humane movements, is reflected in their contemporary battles to save the lives and habitats of specific animals they have studied. These attachments sometimes violate the rules of modern scientific management. Clashes over the nature of human responsibility to wildlife, like that evidenced in Fossey's life, lay open the continued importance of gender codes in defining men's and women's approaches to the wild.

Late twentieth-century feminism has influenced some of the women conducting animal behavioral studies. Women trained within the scientific establishment have raised much the same critique of stereotypes about women and animals that Susan Griffin provided in *Woman and Nature*. Suggesting that previous animal studies have been influenced by male assumptions based on patriarchal models, these researchers have focused their work on female roles in animal society.[102] Two issues are at stake: women's place in human society and human responsibility to nature. Recently, another group of women has begun to develop an environmental philosophy grounded in ecology and feminism. Ecological feminists believe that changes in power relations between men and women could improve our dealings with the environment. Inheriting over 150 years of female tradition, ecofeminism represents American women's most recent collective attempt to bring the values of home to bear on public environmental decision-making processes.

# 8

## "She Unnames Them" *The Utopian Vision of Ecological Feminism*

*When you realize the value of all life, you dwell less on what is past and concentrate more on the preservation of the future.*
—The final entry in Dian Fossey's journal

AMERICAN WOMEN'S most significant contributions to nature study, conservation, and the environmental movement have occurred during the same period as critical developments in feminist activism. In the nineteenth and twentieth centuries American women have waged political campaigns for such rights as suffrage, equal education, employment and pay, and reproductive choice. Although a few naturalists and environmentalists over the past 150 years have been involved in the women's rights battles of their time, feminist activism has rarely combined with environmental politics.[1] The 1960s and 1970s witnessed the latest period in which fears about the pollution of the earth coincided with anger at the oppression of women. In contrast to earlier periods, during these decades a cohesive group of American women merged these concerns.

Ecological feminists, or ecofeminists, identify disturbing connections between the domination of women and the domination of nature, and they argue that these associations explain the violent attitudes toward both nature and women pervading Western culture. Arising in part out of feminist spirituality, women's peace initiatives, and a growing genre of women's speculative fiction, ecological feminism works to cross boundaries by injecting ecological goals into the women's movement and by including the feminist critique of patriarchy in the environmental movement. Ecofeminists hope to change society: their concern is for the future; their goal is a new mode of interaction between humans and nature.[2]

Ecofeminists have developed various strategies for translating their utopian visions into practice. For example, in the early 1980s founding member Ynestra King and others instigated a series of antimilitarist demonstrations, dubbed the Women's Pentagon Action. King has also helped organize conferences combining theoretical discussions of women's relationship with nature and activist workshops on the politics of environmental protection. As well as providing forums for the discussion of national agendas, these meetings have supported local women's efforts to remedy environmental pollution in their communities. In collections of essays such as *Reclaim the Earth: Women Speak Out for Life on Earth* (1983), *Healing the Wounds: The Promise of Ecofeminism* (1989), and *Reweaving the World: The Emergence of Ecofeminism* (1990), academic and lay women have come together to describe both their public battles and their personal struggles to live within utopian ideals.[3]

One of the initiating texts for ecofeminism was Rosemary Radford Ruether's *New Woman/New Earth: Sexist Ideologies and Human Liberation* (1975).[4] Plumbing classical philosophy, Christian theology, Freudian psychology, and classism, racism, and sexism in the age of science and industry, Ruether argues that Western culture has come to identify women with nature, while nature has become merely a field for the exercise of male power and control. She concludes her study with a call for revolution: "How do we change the self-concept of a society from the drives toward possession, conquest, and accumulation to the values of reciprocity and acceptance of mutual limitation?" Ruether poses the answer in a new synthesis of feminism and ecology. Her utopian projection calls for communalized family and work arrangements, equal distribution of decision making between men and women and among all levels of society, and an "ecological technology" focused on the development of nonpolluting and renewable energy sources.[5]

Following Ruether's lead, a number of writers including Susan Griffin, Elizabeth Dodson Gray, Carolyn Merchant, and Andrée Collard have expanded on the ideological roots of the link between women and nature.[6] They argue that Judeo-Christian assertions of a duality between God and creation and a hierarchy placing humans next to God in dominion over nature have been intimately connected with women's repression because, in Western patriarchal culture, human dominion has meant *male* domination. As the chain of being was secularized and rationalized during the scientific revolution, the dominated "other" came to include not only women, but also "primitive" peoples and the poor, as well as nonhuman animals, plants, and the physical landscape. Although some scholars have raised questions about specific aspects of the historical lineage of sexism, racism, and classism outlined by Ruether, Gray, Merchant, and Collard, the broad narrative of these writers has been influential. Collectively, this group has provided a useful model for explaining a set of symbolic connections that are widely current in contemporary culture.[7]

A good deal of the material laying out the ecofeminist agenda is expressed theoretically. American women's science fiction and fantasy literature of the late twentieth century give specificity to ecofeminism's cultural critique and alternative vision. I find Ursula K. Le Guin's tales helpful for grounding the main issues in ecofeminism. Le Guin's early science fiction, particularly *The Left Hand of Darkness* (1969) and *The Dispossessed* (1974), has become a part of the feminist literary canon.[8] Her work is particularly useful in considering what the ecofeminist agenda might mean for the way we actually live because she fleshes out the details of the natural world her characters inhabit. A representative selection of Le Guin's work on this theme appears in *Buffalo Gals and Other Animal Presences* (1987), a collection of short stories and poems describing human relations with rocks, trees, acorn woodpeckers, cats, coyotes, and "alien life forms" inhabiting present and future worlds.

In the introduction to *Buffalo Gals*, Le Guin argues that stories and myths in which animals talk serve to mock and subvert the "phallological" notion that only "Civilized Man" has a voice worthy of attention: "So long as 'man' 'rules,' animals will make rude remarks about him. Women and unruly men will tell their daughters and sons what the fox said to the ox, what Raven told South Wind."[9] Each piece in the collection centers on communication between nonhuman animals (and in a couple of stories, plants) and humans, most often women. Le Guin keeps the blurred boundary between women and nature very much in view—from the novella "Buffalo Gals, Won't You Come Out Tonight," in which a female coyote points out the sexism in a hunter's comparison of the animal to his wife ("Hell, will you look at that damn coyote in broad daylight big as my wife's ass," 47), to tales such as "The Wife's Story," in which it is unclear whether the heros are human or nonhuman animals.

"The Wife's Story" offers a particularly effective reversal of accepted symbols. A female voice tells of the gradual change in her mate from a "good father" into someone the children fear. Initially, they seem to be a close-knit family and community. Yet there is something a bit different about their lives.

For example, the family keeps a nocturnal schedule. In fact, the first clue to the husband's change is his wakefulness during the day. When he returns to the family at night, he smells different and his children begin to fear him. Finally, the wife witnesses his mutation into a monster: "And he turned his face. It was changing while I looked. It got flatter and flatter, the mouth flat and wide, and the teeth grinning flat and dull, and the nose just a knob of flesh with nostril holes, and the ears gone, and the eyes gone blue . . . He stood up then on two legs. I saw him, I had to see him, my own dear love turned into the hateful one" (70). The man attacks his family but is driven off and killed by the "pack" that we now recognize as a community of wolves. Looking at his corpse, his wife hopes he will return to his wolf shape, but he remains human even in death.

"The Wife's Story" reverses the typical werewolf yarn in which the horror lies in the moment the human turns into a wolf. Here wolf society constitutes the norm while the terror is located in the shift to a human shape. Le Guin's tale also upends the classic story of the alluring "half-breed" woman who is always on the verge of wildness, like Pauline Johnson's hero in *The Moccasin Maker*. In "The Wife's Story," the "other"—the woman who is also animal— serves as the voice of reason explaining the man's descent into humanity. As he mutates into a man, her husband is alienated from his wife and children, changing from father into a domineering creature wreaking violence on his family and thus on nature.

Le Guin offers a vision of the moment when men separated themselves from nature and grounded women in nature. She locates the problem not in women's connection with the green world, but in men's false separation from it. The pack's attack on the husband symbolizes the sort of revolution called for by ecofeminists—a revolution that returns all humans to their place within the community of plants and animals.

One of the major problems in bringing an ecological perspective to feminist theory is evidenced by the ease with which the reader accepts Le Guin's woman/wolf. Women tread in dangerous waters when they call on their connection with other animals to argue their view of human relationships with nature. Unlike the communal pack Le Guin imagines, actual women speak within a male-dominated culture that continues to marginalize females by appealing to their closeness to nature. In her call for a new synthesis of ecology and feminism, Rosemary Ruether warns that ecofeminists must be careful how they argue the question of women's connection with nature. Writing about the late twentieth century, she shares the same fears expressed by the nineteenth-century novelist, Sarah Orne Jewett. Ruether cautions: "The concern with ecology could repeat the mistakes of nineteenth century romanticism with its renewed emphasis on the opposite, 'complementary natures' of men and women. Women will again be asked to be the 'natural' wood-nymph and earth mother and to create places of escape from the destructive patterns of the dominant culture."[10] There is a good deal of disagreement within the feminist movement over how to interpret and express what it means to be a woman, how to balance the relative importance of biological, sexual differences against socially constructed gender roles, how even to delineate the line between the two. Thus, one difficulty in incorporating an ecological perspective into feminism centers around tensions within the feminist movement regarding the definition of women's "true nature."

Carolyn Merchant argues that different feminist schools of thought offer varying potentialities for synthesis with an environmental agenda. Dividing the feminist movement into liberal, radical, socialist, and Marxist camps, she finds that radical feminism has, to date, had the most influence on ecofeminism, but that socialist feminism may offer a better model for an "ecological revolution." According to Merchant, radical feminists (and their ecofeminist adherents) contend that "human nature is grounded in human biology. Humans are biologically sexed and socially gendered. Sex/gender relations give men and women different power bases."[11] Ecofeminists identified with radical feminism focus on women's "physical" connection with the earth as a result of their menstrual cycle, pregnancy, and childbirth. For Elizabeth Dodson Gray, Andrée Collard, and Ariel Kay Salleh, the problem is not women's alignment with nature, but the patriarchal culture's alienation from women's physical experience in the push to dominate the earth. The solution to the violent relationships of patriarchy, they contend, lies in emphasizing values arising from women's connection with nature. Some radical ecofeminist literature has looked for models of such values in women's spirituality, particularly as expressed in ancient goddess mythologies.[12]

Ecofeminists with a more socialist bent find such biologically linked essentialism troubling. Merchant, Rosemary Ruether, and Ynestra King locate the dualities between male-and-female/mind-and-nature/reason-and-emotion in the specific history of Western culture. While not denying the part played by sexual difference in defining these divisions, socialist feminists emphasize gender-coded interpretations of biology as the source for women's connections with nature. They maintain that gender socialization has been used in capitalist, patriarchal culture to further women's oppression. Thus, the apparently "natural" connection of women with nature is a myth serving to subjugate both; to argue that such symbolism reflects organic truth is to risk continuing forms of domination in Western culture that have unbalanced the relations of humans with each other and the rest of nature.[13]

Yet these groups are not as clearly divided as they appear. Elizabeth Dodson Gray, for example, maintains that women's bodily processes may sensitize them to environmental cycles, but she also warns against casting human-based images of female and male onto the earth:

> Some women today are still projecting female attributes upon nature. In some feminist circles "The Great Mother" and "The Goddess" are the preferred images used to describe the planet earth . . . Now I must tell you that this gives me great cause for concern because it is the old game of projection *upon* nature *from* the human *for* human needs . . . such projecting always prevents us . . . from discovering the true identity of the other. In this case the truth is that nature *is* itself. It is neither male human *nor* female human . . . The ground we walk upon is not "Mother Earth"; it is living soil with a chemistry and a biology of its own which we must come to understand and respect.[14]

Gray asserts that for women to take on this responsibility means that they must deal honestly with their own tendencies to reduce nature to fit human needs—even when those needs come out of feminist agendas. Her goal is an understanding of nature emphasizing interaction: "environmental cycles *manage* themselves. They are self-organizing. They are not dependent upon us. Rather, we are dependent upon them. It is the reverse of the Judeo-Christian dream of man's dominion over nature."[15] Carolyn Merchant argues that socialist feminism "incorporates many of the insights of radical feminism, but views both nature and human nature as historically and socially constructed." Socialist feminists agree with radical feminists that gender analysis is critical to understanding power relations within society, but they tend to view nature as material rather than spiritual. Yet a socialist feminist like Merchant frames her image of self-acting nature in terms mirroring Gray's: "Nonhuman nature is dynamic and alive. As a historical actor, nature interacts with human beings through mutual ecological relations." For all their differences, Merchant sees radical feminism and socialist feminism sharing much commonality in such environmental visions.[16]

Since 1975, when Rosemary Ruether cautioned women to be aware of the dangers in embracing socially constructed links between women and nature, ecofeminists have struggled to chart a course denying romantic images of woman as passive earth mother while affirming women's particular contribution to improving human relations with nonhuman nature. Their literary sisters have mined the same tensions in more concrete terms. In her novella, "Buffalo Gals, Won't You Come Out Tonight," Le Guin explores why women identify with nonhuman animals, how women might express their connection with nature without unduly projecting Western ideas about gender on the earth, and whether women must choose between loyalty to nature or to culture.

"Buffalo Gals" is the tale of a young girl, Myra, who survives an airplane crash in the desert aided by a female coyote and her compatriots. In keeping with her interest in giving "voice" to nonhuman animals, Le Guin's coyote talks, as do all the other animals in her "village." Abandoned by her human mother and in pain from an eye lost in the accident, the girl bonds with the animal, who licks her aching wound. The healing eye affects the girl's vision. Sometimes Coyote looks human; sometimes she is a scruffy gray beast. Coyote renames Myra "Buffalo Gal," or "Gal" for short. Coyote takes Gal back to her home, where she lives in a community of animals. Gal knows that these are nonhuman animals and cannot understand why they all look like people to her. Coyote explains that we are all "people" but "resemblance is in the eye." That the girl's first recognition of these interconnections comes with the healing touch of a she-coyote symbolically links woman to nature through traditional images of the female as care giver.

Locating the connection between women and nature in the physical form of a coyote, however, Le Guin goes on to deny much of the romanticism accompanying concepts of women's identification with "mother earth." Coyote behaves like the mocking trickster of American Indian legend, leaving Gal to note that "a lot of things were hard to take about Coyote as a mother" (32).[17] Knowing how readily her audience accepts identification of women with animals, Le Guin makes a point of highlighting this animal's "otherness." When Gal recognizes the truth to Coyote's contention that "this is my country . . . I made it. Every goddam sage brush" (22), she has come to an ecological understanding of the webs of life that make even "varmints" critical to a healthy habitat, and she has gained a feminist recognition of the potential diversity to being female.

Finally, Le Guin speculates on how we might rethink the nature-culture duality so that woman's identification with nature does not deny her access to culture. Echoing the classic Euro-American tale of the girl child's choice between nature or culture, told and retold in women's fiction from Sarah Orne Jewett to Margaret Atwood, Gal tells Coyote that she does not want to grow up, for in maturity she will lose her sense of connection with the plants and animals. But Gal cannot refuse to grow up, any more than she can become Coyote's child. Such a resolution would affirm the duality that humans have created and land women in a separate garden while men went about the destruction of the earth. Gal must acknowledge her species as her own: "they're your folks . . . All yours. Your kith and kin and cousins and kind. Bang! Pow! There's Coyote! Bang! There's my wife's ass! Pow! There's anything— BOOOOOM! Blow it away, man! BOOOOOOM!" (47). Gal returns to the world of men bearing an ecofeminist understanding of the dual oppression of nonhuman nature and women and the gift of integrated sight. The animals replace her wounded eye with one made of pine pitch. When she goes home, she will see with both eyes, joining culture and nature into one vision.

Carolyn Merchant's *The Death of Nature* documents the patriarchal domination of women and nature engendered in part by the founders of the scientific revolution, but it locates in the newer science of ecology the potential for overcoming Western models of duality and hierarchy. Envisioning the earth as a home/household, ecology implicitly legitimates woman's role in human caretaking of the natural resources on which all life depends.[18] Ecofeminists find inspiration in the literature of ecology, particularly those texts calling for a new social order in keeping with an interdependent ecosystem.

For some, however, it has proved as difficult to bring feminism to bear on ecology as to bring ecological understanding into feminism. Some argue that men in the ecological movement share a continuing fascination with masculinist-scientific solutions to environmental degradation. Andrée Collard suggests that respected figures like René Dubos and Barry Commoner continue to locate the solution to the environmental crisis in a technological fix and rely on troubling metaphors of the earth as a female to be seduced. Marti Kheel finds in Aldo Leopold's support of hunting a "reduction of the animal to object status," belying his reputation as a "pioneer of deep ecology and ecophilosophy."[19]

Ecofeminists, in fact, have found much to criticize in a number of radical environmental groups. Deep ecology—the philosophical movement relying on ecology to argue for an extension of moral consideration to the whole biotic community—shares many values with ecofeminism. Deep ecologists assert that contemporary threats to the earth stem from the Western anthropocentric tradition. Melding philosophy and ecology, deep ecologists want to place humans properly within nature, no more or less privileged than all other forms of life.[20] Yet ecofeminists have criticized deep ecologists for centering their analysis on human mastery of the earth rather than on a recognition of male domination of women and nature. They find the pronouncements of deep ecologists filled with the language of positivism, dualism, and hierarchy.[21]

Similarly, ecofeminists have been leery of supporting the arguments other environmental philosophers have used to extend human rights to nonhuman beings. They say that animal rights theoreticians engage in universal rule making informed by the hierarchical ranking of some forms of life over others. They see this aspect of environmental philosophy closely aligned with the natural rights doctrine traditionally used in Western culture to justify treating nature as an object for human manipulation.[22] For example, Marti Kheel finds the approach Peter Singer takes to extend natural rights to nonhumans problematic. Singer, she contends, shifts the animal liberation movement from its roots in concrete, emotional identification with animals to a philosophy "proudly ground[ing] itself in rationality." Believing that contemporary animal rights theorists have generated rules granting moral standing only to those "beings who are thought to resemble" humans, Kheel and others have maintained that such hierarchies do not fit well with female ways of knowing nonhuman life. Ecofeminists assert that women's gender-role socialization leads them to see "ethics and ethical meaning *emerging out of* particular situations . . . rather than being *imposed on* those situations." On the whole, Kheel observes, women respect animals' difference from as well as their similarity to us and value other species even when they are not drawn into human culture by abstract rules.[23]

In contrast to their differences with animal rights philosophy, ecofeminists often support animal rights activism. Important texts in the movement, like Gray's *Green Paradise Lost* and Collard's *Rape of the Wild*, are highly critical of the manipulation of animals in the interests of science and agriculture. Major collections of ecofeminist writings include animal rights essays.[24] Those working to change the treatment of animals find little to inspire them in the rationalist debate about which animals should have legal standing. Rather, they are moved by their feeling for animals as a class of "other" often subject to the same forms of domination visited upon women.

The men with whom ecofeminism has formed the closest ties are the popular interpreters of quantum physics. Many ecofeminists find a sympathetic text in Fritjof Capra's *The Tao of Physics*.[25] Taken with Capra's assertion that "quantum theory forces us to see the universe not as a collection of physical objects, but rather as a complicated web of relations between the various parts of a unified whole," ecofeminists use the shifting boundaries between matter and energy to argue with any sort of duality, particularly the assertion that nature is merely the passive subject of objective scrutiny.[26] Kheel holds that the subatomic world offers a model of human-nature relations as a constantly changing field of possibilities: "Just as quantum physics cannot predict atomic events with certainty at exact times and specific places, so too we cannot postulate that one species or one individual is of greater or lesser value than another. The attempt to formulate universal, rational rules of conduct ignores the constantly changing nature of reality. It also neglects the emotional-instinctive or spontaneous component in each particular situation, for in the end, emotion cannot be contained by boundaries and rules; in a single leap it can cross the boundaries of space, time, and species."[27] Thus, Kheel suggests, quantum physics offers us a view of nature that blurs the boundaries between humans and animals, self and other, and reason and emotion.

Ecofeminism's reliance on metaphysical interpretations of quantum physics to support its theoretical and political stance demonstrates the movement's interest in broadening the basis for its cultural critique. Concerned that the dominant culture will simplify ecofeminism into a women's back-to-nature movement, sharing affinities primarily with feminist spirituality, many ecofeminists emphasize their links with selected male domains—physics is a particularly useful foil in this effort. Like ecology, quantum physics, as described by an interpreter like Capra, questions the positivist, hierarchical image of the world from within male culture and incidentally validates from outside female culture the resistance of ecofeminism to mechanistic world-views.[28]

In "Schrödinger's Cat" Ursula Le Guin gives literary form to Kheel's notion that quantum physics offers a good model for understanding human-nature interactions. Le Guin bases her story on the physicist Erwin Schrödinger's "parable cat, a figment-cat, the amusing embodiment of a daring hypothesis." Schrödinger described an imaginary cat-in-the-box experiment as one way to explain the apparently odd behavior of the subatomic world. The experiment involves placing a cat in a completely sealed box with a device that can kill the cat. A random event (decay of a radioactive atom) determines whether or not the device is triggered. The only way to know if the cat is dead or alive is to look in the box. According to classical physics, moments after the experiment has begun the cat is either dead or alive. According to quantum theory, the cat is potentially in either state until the moment the experimenter opens the box and sees the cat.[29] Le Guin creates an "actual, biographico-historical cat" who leaps into the middle of a story she is writing, changing its conclusion.

Initially, the cat is the only reliable presence in an unpredictable world, a parable universe in which the common matter and energy of our everyday lives behave like subatomic particles. As though the earth were a particle under investigation, everything heats up and speeds up. Stove burners go on for no predictable reason; hot water flows from cold water taps; animals crack "the sound barrier. You knew of swallows only by the small, curved sonic booms that looped about the eaves of old houses in the evening" (161). Amid all of this the cat remains "a real cool cat" (161). A man appears at the door (to the author he resembles a dog), recognizes the cat as "Schrödinger's Cat," and proceeds to unpack a box and gun for performing the experiment. The man/dog, dubbed Rover, explains how the experiment illustrates the unavoidable element of unpredictability in science and asserts: "it is beautifully demonstrated that if you desire certainty, any certainty, you must create it yourself" by lifting the lid of the box (164). Spontaneity and uncertainty consume the rest of the story. The narrator refuses to sacrifice the cat by placing him in the box. The cat (behaving in true feline fashion) then jumps in on its own. When they open the box to see if the cat is alive or dead, he has disappeared. As she suggests to Rover that "we really could use larger boxes," the roof of the house lifts off "just like the lid of a box, letting in the unconscionable, inordinate light of the stars" (166).

Imagining Schrödinger's cat as a real animal also leads Le Guin to ponder the meanings of animals as subjects of scientific study. In the story, the woman sees the cat as "her" cat, having established a caring relationship with him, whereas Rover sees the cat as an experimental object. Mirroring eco-feminism's defense of animal rights, Le Guin argues: "an animal perceived by the experimenting scientist not as an object, nor as a subject in the sense of the word 'subject of an experiment,' . . . but as subject in the philosophical/grammatical sense of a sentient presence of the same order as the scientist's existence . . . would profoundly change the nature, and probably the results, of the experiments" (157). Animal experiments assume that it is possible to control the other—to study objectively a subject in a predictable trial. Rover's experiment depends on the cat behaving as an object, but the cat follows his own, unpredictable path. In suggesting that the narrator of the story better understands this "subjectivity" of the cat through her caring relationship with him, Le Guin exemplifies the distinction between animal rights seen as a body of universal rules applied to objectified life-forms and animal rights seen as the extension of friendship to familiars.

Carrying her point into a critique of the tendency of some linguists to "deny the capacity of apes to talk" (just as their "intellectual forebears denied the capacity of women to think"), Le Guin constructs a series of speculations on the communicative modes of animals, plants, and even rocks. The plant communication story shares ecofeminism's ecological ground. Le Guin questions the ranking of life based on human-derived norms of sentience, and even the valuing of biological over physical nature. Nature's artifacts are equally filled with meaning, she suggests, if we just listen with the right attitude. In the "Editorial by the President of the Therolinguistics Association," the author criticizes scientists for assuming that plants do not communicate. What if a "non-communicative, vegetative art exists?" (174). Such an art might be "not a communication, but a reception." Ending on a utopian note, Le Guin's imaginary editor predicts a day when humans will not only read the language of plants but "the first geolinguist, . . . ignoring the delicate, transient lyrics of the lichen, will read beneath it the still less communicative, still more passive, wholly atemporal, cold, volcanic poetry of the rocks: each one a word spoken, how long ago, by the earth itself, in the immense solitude, the immenser community, of space" (175). Stories like this acknowledge the integrity of the other, recognize diversity over duality, and celebrate nature as a household whose individual parts are of equal importance to the whole.

Speculative fiction like Le Guin's provides a good illustration of many of the points of ecofeminism, in part because the movement is so future-oriented. Ecofeminists want to reform human interactions with nonhuman nature and recast human society along pluralistic lines. Ynestra King asserts that "ecofeminism supports utopian visions of harmonious, diverse, decentralized communities, urging only those technologies based on ecological principles, as the only practical solution for the continuation of life on earth."[30] Leaders of the movement stress that they are not advocating a return to "primitive" society or a rejection of intellect and knowledge in favor of stereotypical "feminine" emotion. Ecofeminists oppose the environmental degradation and materialism resulting from industrial technology, the threat to all life posed by a militarized economy, and arrogant disregard of human rights to self-determination in advances in biotechnology. They locate the problem not solely in science and technology itself, but in the ethics applied to decision making about technology.[31]

Out of their commitment to feminist goals of pluralism, and their belief that ecology teaches there are no hierarchies "among persons, between persons and the rest of the world," ecofeminist leaders have stressed the need for the movement to include concerns outside the white middle class. Much remains to be done to make ecofeminism truly representative of a broad social base, but some African American women are beginning to see in the movement a forum for addressing environmental threats to the rural and inner city poor, while American Indian women are finding support for concerns about radioactive wastes on their homelands. These women have taken ecofeminism to task for being mired in theory and reminded members of the environmental activism at the heart of the movement. Describing the efforts of lower-class black women to keep their neighborhoods from becoming dumps for surrounding affluent areas, Cynthia Hamilton has shown how fighting a thirteen-acre solid waste incinerator in south-central Los Angeles empowered and radicalized the women. Hamilton's study of the Los Angeles venture suggests that the divisions of class and race typical of environmentalism are beginning to break down in such community activism. Demonstrating how these new social movements cut across such boundaries, Hamilton documents how white and black women, both poor and middle-class, formed a citizens' coalition that pushed the city council to reconsider the decision to locate the incinerator in their district. Building on these trends within the United States, ecofeminism hopes to develop an international base including not only European and American women, but also women working on environmental and women's rights issues around the world.[32]

Such diversity is not without conflict. Some white ecofeminists celebrate the commonality of women's culture and attempt to merge their newfound goddess traditions with indigenous beliefs of women of color. Many women of color have criticized such ahistorical theorizing. They resist the appropriation of their culture and argue that such attempts at synthesis fail to recognize white women's part in imperialism. Yet a few women are finding a match between their history on the land and the values of ecofeminism. Laguna Pueblo writer Paula Gunn Allen mingles traditional stories and new-age concepts to heal human society's relationship with "grandmother" earth. African

American activist Rachel Bagby calls on her mother's work with an inner city urban gardening group as a mirror of the egalitarian organizational approaches advocated in ecofeminist conferences.[33]

Whatever the fate of the pluralist agenda potentially in ecofeminism's future, one image—that of a web—aptly synthesizes the movement's most fundamental vision. In the 1980s ecofeminists in Great Britain and America engaged in a variety of nonviolent protests at military installations and nuclear power plants. The most powerful image of women's opposition to nuclear culture, and a symbol of the threats to nature posed by atomic weapons and nuclear energy, has been a web woven around and through the metal gates "securing" the installation.[34] The web carries both feminist and ecological meaning. Women's creative art as weavers is conjoined with a symbol of nature's interconnectedness. The web, handmade and asymmetrical, is set in stark contrast to the hard-edged, isolated, guarded symbols of patriarchal culture. In such nonviolent protest, women announce their consciousness of the difference between male and female culture and their intention to start anew, creating a future in which humans live within terms set by the earth.

In the last story in *Buffalo Gals and Other Animal Presences*, Le Guin also weaves a different future onto the artifacts of patriarchal culture. "She Unnames Them" imagines Eve reversing Adam's task of naming the beasts, rejecting not only the private names given household pets, but also "all the Linnaean qualifiers that had trailed along behind them for two hundred years like tin cans tied to a tail" (195). Unnaming the animals brings her closer to them. Without the hierarchy of names, they come to know each other in sensuous, physical contact, recognizing the fear and the attraction in their interaction. Refusing to make an "exception" for herself, she casts off the name Adam gave her: "You and your father lent me this—gave it to me, actually. It's been really useful, but it doesn't seem to fit very well lately." Adam, busy "fitting parts together," doesn't hear her comment "I hope the garden key turns up" as she leaves to live with the others (196). Like the orbital patterns of yarn strung against linear fences of the military-industrial landscape, unnaming the animals (including the female human) is a gendered statement of affiliation with the earth and a rejection of the alienation and separation embedded in language as well as technology.

Making it clear that the idealized garden is itself a part of that alienating mind-set—her hero needs no fabricated key to a mythical garden—Le Guin refuses a future located in some millennial return to Eden. Spurning a fantasized paradise, she denies the dangerous possibility that women will be placed there, keepers of a pastoral landscape useful only as a retreat from the real affairs of men. As Elizabeth Dodson Gray suggests, perhaps the "Fall was not down into sin and our worst self but more ironically a Fall *up*—a Fall *up* in which we fail to accept or 'claim' our full humanness, and the finitude of our bodies, and our mortality"; if this is so, then "this finite planet and the here-and-now *is* our Eden." [35]

Informed by the twentieth-century sciences of ecology and quantum physics and engendered out of contemporary feminist thought, ecofeminism seems to owe slight debt to the female naturalists, gardeners, artists, and writers of the nineteenth century. Indeed, there would appear to be little connection between Susan Fenimore Cooper, whose work was shepherded by her father and whose politics were antifemale suffrage, and the young women of the 1980s blockading nuclear power plants. Ecofeminists have paid limited attention to the history of Euro-American women's contributions to nature study and environmental values. Focused on understanding the roots of patriarchal culture's attitude toward women and nature, most historical analysis has emphasized Neoplatonic thought, early Christianity, and the scientific revolution. Carolyn Merchant, the most rigorous historian considering the sources for contemporary connections between the call for women's rights and for the rights of nature, has paid some attention to nineteenth- and early twentieth-century history. She has yet to establish the extent to which early female naturalists or Progressive Era women's clubs might have played a part in articulating and popularizing the values informing ecofeminism. Marti Kheel suspects that earlier women's gender socialization set them at odds with dominant environmental values. She offers no history, however, to flesh out the assertion or to provide links between women of the nineteenth and twentieth centuries. Rachel Carson is most often mentioned as a touchstone, but only Merchant has really probed her importance to the movement. In fact, ecofeminist images of Carson as the leading light in a select group of female progenitors serve to isolate her in much the same way as do canonical histories of American conservation that pose her as the singular woman in a field of men. Uncomfortable with Victorian, Euro-American women's history, some ecofeminists have concluded that the major sources for their values are located in prehistory, in early forms of goddess worship.[36]

Carolyn Merchant and Ynestra King have suggested that ecofeminism could benefit from more historical analysis. They argue that the case for the alternative values arising out of women's concern with home verges on essentialism and lacks a firm grounding in social and economic history. Merchant and King agree with women of color that the lack of a historical perspective also unfairly universalizes experiences and values that are in fact tied to racial and class differences. And they contend that such generalizations sometimes mean that key voices in ecofeminism have dodged the issue of Euro-American women's participation in the domination of both nature and other peoples.[37] Where, then, does ecofeminism fit into the history of American women's nature values? In what respects has this movement split with women's traditional work in natural history and the environmental movement? Is ecofeminism in debt to women's middle-class, domestic role as well as to modern ecology, quantum physics, and radical feminism? Has the movement oversimplified women's history in an effort to pose an essential dualism between men and women, between culture and nature?

Ecofeminist writings sometimes give the impression that this is the first generation of women to grasp the importance of gender socialization in defining women's vision of nature. Yet conscious appeals to gender roles have long informed Euro-American women's appreciation of nature. Nineteenth-century women (and men) were well aware of gender as an issue in defining the work that women might do. Susan Fenimore Cooper, Mary Treat, Lucy Say, Helen Lawson, and Graceanna Lewis first showed how American women might join aspects of the naturalist's round with their domestic lives. Strolling the family grounds, creating habitats for familiar birds, drawing artifacts collected by naturalists, or developing educational materials for children, these women drew clear connections between the conservation of home and family and the preservation of nature. Throughout the nineteenth and twentieth centuries women, who were encouraged by men who agreed, told themselves that it was their duty to nurture the American landscape in trust for succeeding generations. They preserved nature in historic gardens, herbaria, natural history displays, and zoo collections. With words, paintbrush, and camera, they documented vanishing flora and fauna. Such work enhanced the image of women as uniquely sensitive to the meanings of plants and animals—as having a way with and a responsibility for the natural world.

Women's modes of participation in natural history provide the model for a good many of the values espoused by ecofeminists celebrating women's connections to nature. Popular belief supports the rightness of women's work "re-weaving the web" because for over one hundred years middle-class Euro-American women have engaged in such work and have seen it particularly tied to their gender. Ecofeminists, more concerned with the question of how these connections between women and nature allowed men to dominate both, find this model troubling. They focus on the constraints implied in women's relegation to the domestic sphere. Some have cast women, along with nature, as an oppressed class that did not participate in the masculine agenda of domination. There are two problems with this reading. First, it assumes that women have played little public role in American knowledge about and development of nature's resources. Second, and more important, it implies that women's relegation to the domestic round excluded them from participation in the surge to dominate nature.[38]

During the nineteenth and twentieth centuries, women have been significant voices among the influential elites in defining the value of nature. Susan Cooper, Mary Treat, Beatrix Farrand, Mary Hunter Austin, Osa Johnson, and Rachel Carson played major roles in developing and popularizing for a national audience trends in such areas as landscape design, scientific ecology, wildlife management, and environmental protection. Some of these women aligned themselves with "unruly men"—men who challenged widespread attempts to develop the natural resources of the country. Women joined in such efforts because they believed that the particular environmental agendas supported values deriving from domestic culture. They also found that they sometimes shared these values with like-minded men. Certainly, men controlled and defined the progress of natural history and resource development, and women entered male terrain in their work. The landscapes of home and its attendant garden were not, however, excluded from this terrain. For example, influential men and women agreed that one meaningful way to describe America's flora and fauna was in terms of a native household. As keepers of the home, women gained some standing in the attempt to domesticate the continent.

More critically, while ecofeminists point out the constraints on women's lives in a domestic garden, they nevertheless situate the critique offered by women's culture in the home-based values deriving from those lives. In this scenario, the oppressed—more closely identified with nature—speak more eloquently for nature. Not much attention has been paid to the fact that much of women's domestic history is grounded in the experiences of middle-class Euro-Americans. Female naturalists who carried the values of the domestic round into the public arena often did so from a base of privilege.

Women had a public voice because the values of middle-class family life were conflated with the domestication of the landscape to justify expansionist goals in the nineteenth and early twentieth centuries. By the 1850s American elites were defining the country's distinctiveness in part by its native plants and animals. As New World flora and fauna were incorporated into America domestica—America imagined as home to a new society defined as nature's nation—the national self-image and women's roles meshed. The domestication of the biophysical landscape blurred divisions between public and private space. Press reports of the exploits of women like Martha Maxwell, Mary Agnes Chase, and Delia Akeley linked appropriate female activity with burgeoning nationalism. In emerging images of the United States as at once consumer and caretaker of natural resources worldwide, the mesh between women's domesticity and America domestica often conjoined traditional middle-class white women's values with expansionist agendas. This is a rather more complex form of oppression than ecofeminism has identified, and it offers a social and economic context for explaining the sort of power white women wielded in the nineteenth century and for analyzing how their values served as instruments of dominion.

Even though the dominant culture may have enfolded domesticity into the expansionist agenda in the nineteenth and early twentieth centuries, women also attempted to set themselves off from marketplace materialism and scientific manipulation of natural resources. Like the ecofeminists of the late twentieth century, many women naturalists and conservationists argued that their differences with the dominant culture arose from the special context of female life. Susan Cooper's resistance to scientific nomenclature, Celia Thaxter's appreciation of the common plants in her mother's garden, Olive Thorne Miller's delight in the birds flying freely in and out of her aviary, and Sally Carrighar's wildlife sanctuary on Beetle Rock reflected values that the women located within the bounds of home and domesticity. Ecofeminists, emphasizing the virtue of humility, skeptical about the adequacy of scientific nomenclature to capture nature, and believing that women's culture offers an alternative to male modes of interacting with nature, carry on a tradition begun by these earlier middle-class white women as much as they create a new movement out of contemporary ecology, quantum physics, or premodern goddess worship.[39]

The shared history of gendered difference in male/female ways of looking at nature, however, does not necessarily link earlier female conservationists to the political goals of contemporary ecofeminism. Carolyn Merchant has shown how the Progressive Era women's sense of the separate sphere, of their roles as conservers of home and family, effectively excluded them from the rising professional class of natural resource managers who came to control environmental policy in the twentieth century. Some ecofeminists have argued that difference based on complementarity sets up a "tacit consent" to male dominance of nature. Earlier women are not given much credit for offering more than a "grumble" about the state of affairs. Ecofeminists see their own critique calling first and foremost for the "abolition of male privilege" in determining the course of human-nature interactions. They resist attempts to subsume feminism under a broad environmental agenda, carefully state their differences with the ecological movement, and selectively embrace only those scientists sympathetic to feminist readings of culture.[40] Although nineteenth- and early twentieth-century women often did find themselves supporting male agendas, their history also includes a frequently overlooked strain of more active opposition to patriarchal prerogatives. Well before the advent of ecofeminism, influential American women began to question their subordination to male naturalists, to criticize the environmental decisions made by patriarchy, and to articulate their values as distinct from those of the dominant culture.

Sometimes women's nature study strained against definitions of women's "nature." During the nineteenth century, women like Lucy Say and Martha Maxwell noticed the constrictions. Mary Hunter Austin invested southwestern American deserts with qualities modeled on the liberated New Woman of the early twentieth century—a woman (and a landscape) who followed her own desires. In raising questions about male dominance, these women articulated the ecofeminist position that patriarchal prerogatives have unfairly limited women's contributions to nature study and conservation. Austin went further, making the connection between patriarchal oppression of women and nature and arguing that liberating women would also free nature.

Since the late nineteenth century, the willingness of influential women to do more than sit on the sidelines has led to increasingly pointed critiques of mainstream environmental decisions made by professional males. Skepticism about scientific nomenclature suggested more broad-based questions about scientific methods. One hundred years after Susan Fenimore Cooper worried that taxonomy disenfranchised ordinary citizens from a confident understanding of nature, Rachel Carson encouraged her readers not to be intimidated by the intricacies of scientific jargon. Nineteenth-century women's love of the native plants of their yards and neighborhoods blossomed in the twentieth century into women's political efforts to control housing and transportation development, regulate herbicides, and cultivate native plants in public spaces. From Lucy Furman's leadership of the Anti-Steel Trap League, to Rosalie

Edge's attacks on the Audubon power elite, to Rachel Carson's involvement in the Animal Welfare Institute's animal rights work, women have set themselves against the male establishment, arguing from a concern for the pain and suffering of individual animals.

Both sides in these battles were well aware of the gender divisions informing much of the difference of opinion. As the history of the male response to Lady Bird Johnson, Rachel Carson, and Dian Fossey shows, the issue has not been only that men and women looked at nature differently, but also what right women have had to inject their values into the public sphere. In the decades between the Progressive Era and the mid-twentieth century, connections between women's domesticity and the nation's image as America domestica eroded. America was defined by its scientific and technical prowess; rhetorical reliance on the image of "nature's nation" seemed old-fashioned and parochial. During these decades, the split between suburban green space as a place of refuge and cities as the location of commerce and industry emerged as a national standard. Though women continued to work as naturalists and to participate in conservationist politics, their role in the domestic round was not as central to the country's self-definition as it had been earlier in the nineteenth century.

The woman in the garden began to look marginal, frivolous, decorative, disconnected from national agendas. She certainly was not perceived to be in any position to launch a public critique of the scientific and industrial establishment. When Rachel Carson did just that, the response was to remind her that women's place was in the suburban garden, not the congressional hearing room. Carson looks singularly important to ecofeminism because of this history. Her highly publicized conflict with the male establishment demonstrates, for the most recent generation of feminists, how the patriarchy has tried to use the gendered connection of women with nature to contain their voices of opposition. Yet, perhaps more visibly than any woman before or since, Carson forced influential men to respond to concerns arising directly out of women's culture. This history of gender-based conflict with the dominant culture and assertion of women's traditional values informs much of the ecofeminist movement.[41]

Ecofeminists also see Carson as a foremother because she helped popularize an ecological view that, along with the feminist critique, grounds the movement. Carson understood that the values of home encompassed a good deal more of the universe than the limited 1950s' version of the suburban bungalow, flower garden, and bird bath. In *Silent Spring*, she educated the public in the ecological meanings of home, encouraging her readers to make connections between the suburb and the city, their own home and the habitats of wild animals, the health of the ecosystem and their children's health. Carson also reminded her readers that home and the woman in charge of it were not tame and secure but participated in the interactive struggles of all life. For Carson, the best way to experience that supposedly tame middle-class yard was at night: "Most of us walk unseeing through the world, unaware alike of its beauties, its wonders, and the strange and sometimes terrible intensity of the lives that are being lived about us . . . But we see with an understanding eye only if we have walked in the garden at night and here and there with a flashlight have glimpsed the mantis stealthily creeping upon her prey. Then we sense something of the drama of the hunter and the hunted. Then we begin to feel something of that relentlessly pressing force by which nature controls her own." [42]

Ecofeminists cite the 1978 publication of Susan Griffin's *Woman and Nature: The Roaring Inside Her* for shining a new light on patriarchal assumptions about women's domestication and bringing to consciousness the meanings of wildness in women's lives and in the natural world. [43] Griffin names few women who rejected exaggerated domesticity and responded to wilderness, instead casting a generic female in the role of the predatory lioness who, in devouring her captors, returns women to their true power. This sense that American women's history offers little critique of the positivist view of the world dominating recent American culture suggests that ecofeminists have failed to follow Carson's advice. A little flashlight exploration of their foremothers' gardens turns up a variety of women in mid-twentieth-century America who probed how the image of the tamed garden had ceased to serve as an adequate model either of the natural world or of women's nature.

Fictional accounts like Jean Stafford's *The Mountain Lion* apprised 1950s' women of the dangers posed by the attenuation of their domestic space into the isolated yards of repetitive middle-class neighborhoods and encouraged them to look more closely at their own wild potential and its oppression in modern culture. Also by mid-century, Zora Neale Hurston had exposed how fears about wild women were projected onto women of color to keep them out of the very garden that white middle-class women were trying to expand. In *Their Eyes Were Watching God*, Hurston laid open how black women's identification with beasts of burden constrained their lives. Rejecting stereotypes of blacks as a people insensitive to nature, she created a hero who was deeply moved by the beauties and wonders of the green world and well aware of its power.

Women like Belle Benchley, Delia Akeley, and Lois Crisler, who worked with live animals during this period, moved the bounds of the middle-class woman's garden far outside the suburbs and established women's right to speak for wildlife in the public sphere. Their narratives illuminate how the urge to read nature as a domestic garden oppressed the lives of nonhuman animals. Their anguished confessions of the violence and death involved in trophy collecting served as real-life emblems of the murder of Molly and her mountain lion. When Crisler closes her narrative with the confession that, at last, she had to kill Alatna because there was no safe space for her in settled northern Colorado, she makes the same critique of her culture's domination of nature that Stafford does in the mountain lion's death. She also offers a model of the white, middle-class woman that is different from that posed by 1950s' stereotypes.

Ecofeminism owes many of its assumptions about women's connection with wild terrain and wild animals to women of the middle decades of the twentieth century who struggled to come into deeper contact with the plants and animals of the garden and who voiced, directly and indirectly, their disaffection from the dominant modes of controlling nature. Ecofeminists have extended their white, middle-class predecessors' critique by making much more explicit the connections between the oppression of nature and women's oppression, and by counseling all women to embrace the wildness in their nature and turn that wildness back upon culture. Griffin's *Woman and Nature* has been singularly influential because the book envisions the girl and the lion triumphing over social forces that would study, domesticate, and kill them both.[44] There is, however, a utopian strain to this immersion in nature that fails to address fully what Carson was talking about when she sent women into the night garden.

Griffin and her followers assume that women's interaction with the earth has caused and will cause no harm. Such is the meaning in the image of women stepping into nature as healers, reweaving a broken web. Women are assumed to be at one with earth's processes; they understand and accept naturally occurring pain and suffering as they understand and accept the pain of giving birth. The quarrel is with Western, capitalist, patriarchal culture and the unnatural violence and destruction visited upon nature by that culture. But the accounts of women like Akeley, Crisler, and more recently Jane Goodall, Dian

Fossey, and Cynthia Moss, suggest that women who truly enter the wild face a constant struggle. On one hand, gender socialization encourages them to protect individual animals with whom they interact and identify. On the other hand, the goals of objective, scientific study conjoined with ecological respect for the inherent correctness of nature's cycles counsel them not to interfere with other beings' lives. They sometimes doubt the "rightness" of nature's way when they see, and are tempted to redress, violence and death visited upon an animal by her own kind. Further, while these women often locate the source of pain and death to animal familiars in the dominant culture's drive to control nature, they also question how their own gender's long-standing desire to come into close contact with wild animals has threatened the very beings they have loved. Ecofeminism has not yet considered what it has meant or will mean when women grapple with the moral conflicts raised by field studies, or how women should deal with the responsibility when their own efforts—even when motivated by the best intentions—go awry.[45]

White ecofeminists take much more interest in the nature values of women of color than did their predecessors. They often quote American Indian and African American women writers, whose different cultures counter male, Western beliefs and whose critique, ecofeminists argue, parallels their own disagreements with patriarchy. These African American and American Indian women find spiritual value in nature and argue for respectful dealings with mother earth. Like Zora Neale Hurston's Janie, they locate power in their own people's connection with the common plants of mother's and grandmother's gardens. African American and American Indian women's musings on the meanings of plants in their lives have, in turn, served as a source of inspiration for Euro-American ecofeminists like Carol Christ.[46]

Ecofeminist leaders argue that the presence of such voices in the movement bespeaks its sensitivity to diversity, yet the message that they have developed is singular and sometimes troubling in its coherence. A writer like Susan Griffin is well aware that women of color have borne an extra burden of oppression. *Woman and Nature* aptly notes the history that supposed "in the *female* Hottentot one can see the monkey more clearly." She also recognizes that the domestic garden was restricted to white women, whose domination was expressed in their alienation from nature. Ultimately, however, she universalizes women's experience, locating freedom and power in the return to wildness, expressed as reclaiming one's animal nature. Griffin does not probe why women of color might find the call of the wild somewhat more troublesome than their white sisters, why they might suggest that white women's release from the garden fails to address their rather different forms of oppression. Ecofeminists have not grappled with the reasons why white women are more willing to situate freedom in the lion's roar and why their American Indian and African American sisters locate it in a flower displaying "the color purple." Until the movement begins to draw upon the work of writers like Toni Morrison and Leslie Silko, both of whom explore the diverse symbolism in women's animality, ecofeminism will not begin to come to grips with the different experiences and traditions among women trying to forge the environmental future.[47]

Ecofeminism enjoys a much richer women's history than its leaders have yet discovered. Much of the movement's critique of the dominant culture's environmental values is not new but continues American women's narrative of their own unique role in the study and preservation of nature. The women who pushed the Audubon bird preservation efforts, organized Progressive Era conservation and urban beautification campaigns, supported Rachel Carson in women's clubs and gardening groups, and founded the contemporary animal rights movement demonstrate that women's work in nature is not limited to isolated females serving as assistants to husbands and fathers. Ecofeminism's particular contribution has been to extend the meanings of women's traditional oppositional role by insisting on the connections between the oppression of women and the oppression of nature in Western culture. Their critique illuminates the gendered struggles at the heart of the visible splits over environmental issues that have developed between men and women during the twentieth century. But ecofeminists also believe that women's culture provides a valuable clue to how humans should live on the earth in the future. Such an assumption raises the question of the ways that American women actually have chosen to center themselves in nature. Only by cultivating its own history, giving voice to women's collective work nurturing, preserving, and depicting the plants and animals of our home, will ecofeminism shape the answer to how women's culture can offer a better future. Then ecofeminists may fulfill Susan Fenimore Cooper's call to American women to take themselves and the natural world seriously, to speak for the fate of the earth.

# Notes

PREFACE

1. Schmitt, *Back to Nature*, xiii. Illustrating Schmitt's point, the only women whose work appears in Lyon's *This Incomperable Lande*, a new anthology of American nature writing, are Rachel Carson and Annie Dillard.
2. Harding and O'Barr, *Sex and Scientific Inquiry*; Keller, *Feeling for the Organism*; Rossiter, *Women Scientists*.
3. Merchant, *Ecological Revolutions*, 81, 92, 112, 166–72, 250–54.
4. For a good discussion of the urban, middle-class bias informing early nature appreciation, see Schmitt, *Back to Nature*.

CHAPTER ONE

1. Kohlstedt, "In from the Periphery"; Rossiter, *Women Scientists*, 1–26; Rudolph, "How It Developed That Botany" and "Women in Nineteenth Century American Botany"; Scott, *Making the Invisible Woman Visible*, 64–107. The standard biography on Phelps is Balzau, *Almira Hart Lincoln Phelps*.
2. Phelps, *Familiar Lectures on Botany*, 219.
3. Merchant, *Ecological Revolutions*, 233–46, 251.
4. Fox-Genovese, *Within the Plantation Household*, 116–18, 192–241; Kolodny, *Land Before Her*, 53–54, 146–48. For a good study of the continuing connections of poor, white, southern women to the land they work, see Hagood, *Mothers of the South*.
5. Scott, *Making the Invisible Woman Visible*, 64–107; Rudolph, "Women in Nineteenth-Century American Botany"; Smallwood and Smallwood, *Natural History*, 104–5; Pease and Pease, *Ladies, Women, and Wenches*, 74–75. Baym argues that Willard had less impact on the production of teachers than did Mary Lyon and Catharine Beecher ("Women and the Republic," 21). Willard did train some teachers, and the fact remains that most of the early female educators were trained in the Northeast.
6. Burstyn, "Early Women in Education." Kohlstedt ("In from the Periphery") also discusses women's reluctance to take a visibly public role in such endeavors. For an extensive study of the men's self-image, see Bush, *Dream of Reason*.

7. D. E. Allen, *Naturalist in Britain*, 48–49, 74–75, 127–31; Barber, *Heyday of Natural History*, 125–39; Merchant, *Death of Nature*, 253–75.

8. Americans were well aware of this literature. For an example of the dialogue from the American side, see Steele, *Summer Journey*, 210.

9. Trollope, *Domestic Manners*, 103; Martineau, *Society in America*, 1:197.

10. Bremer, *Homes of the New World*, 1:19.

11. Ibid., 2:84 (quotation). For examples of Martineau's commentary on American women's restricted roles in public life, see Yates, *Harriet Martineau*, 51–85, 134–39. Travel narratives offer a litany of criticism on American women's secluded lives; for more examples, see Trollope, *Domestic Manners*, 103; Bremer, *Homes of the New World*, 1:19, 2:85, 141, 519; Houstoun, *Texas*, 82, 191; Murray, *Letters*, 35.

12. Bremer, *Homes of the New World*, 2:85; Bird, *Englishwoman in America*, 365; Trollope, *Domestic Manners*, 114.

13. Bremer, *Homes of the New World*, 1:515; Murray, *Letters*, 144.

14. For self-conscious references to class in their characterizations of American women, see Trollope, *Domestic Manners*, 82; Houstoun, *Texas*, 129.

15. Trollope, *Domestic Manners*, 28; Bird, *Lady's Life*, 50.

16. Martineau, *Society in America*, 1:226; Bremer, *Homes of the New World*, 2:51. Bremer's primary sources for information on American Indians were Henry Rowe Schoolcraft and Margaret Fuller, whose writings she called upon when she arrived in the Midwest. Her descriptions of American Indian life in the region mirror these texts (2:26–55). Although Yates has rightly lauded Martineau's intellectual stance against slavery (*Harriet Martineau*, 40–41), she does not address the actual images of black women that Martineau provided while in America.

17. Forten, *Journal*, 46–47. Documentation of an exchange of letters with Martineau occurs on 89, 95. For examples of Forten's attitudes toward nature, see 48, 58 (Mammoth Cave), 137, 150, 152, 201. For a good study of her attempts to deal with the tensions between her racial identification and her gender-role as a middle-class woman, see Braxton, "Poet's Retreat."

18. Trollope, *Domestic Manners*, 279–80; Martineau, *Society in America*, 1:192; Cumming, *Granite Crags*, 242–43.

19. Bremer, *Homes of the New World*, 1:360–61. Bremer's narrative contains a wealth of natural description. For examples of a female nature, see 1:75, 359, 515.

20. Ibid., 2:587 (quotation). Amelia Murray also visited the Holbrooks (*Letters*, 16, 198–99). Charleston had a reputation as a cultural center for nature study, and by the 1840s many women were participating in the enjoyable "botanizing" hobby. For further information on Charleston and Mrs. Holbrook, see Smallwood and Smallwood, *Natural History*, 102–30.

21. Bremer, *Homes of the New World*, 1:271–72.

22. Trollope, *Domestic Manners*, 191; Martineau, *Society in America*, 1:196; Murray, *Letters*, 34–35.

23. Cumming, *Granite Crags*, 28, 240, 261, 333.

24. Rudolph's examination of the increasing participation of women in the study of botany verifies this building tradition. He finds some botanists before the Civil

War, but significant numbers appear in the 1870s–1890s ("Women in Nineteenth-Century American Botany," 1348).

25. Bremer, *Homes of the New World*, 1:207. In a letter remembering her time with Downing, Bremer mentions his appreciation of Susan Cooper's work, "Letter to His Friends" (Downing, *Rural Essays*, lxix). American women writers themselves felt some ambiguity about their roles. For a study of literary women's struggles to balance the private life of the domestic sphere with public authorship, see Kelley, *Private Woman*.

26. Houstoun, *Texas*, 173.

27. Rossiter, *Women Scientists*, 4.

28. Women's interest in botany mirrors other trends in nineteenth-century women's history that saw appeals to the morals deriving from the domestic sphere used to open public space for women's voice (Kelley, *Private Woman*, 248; Smith-Rosenberg, *Disorderly Conduct*, 86; Cott, *Bonds of Womanhood*, 199–201).

29. For shifts in taste here, see D. E. Allen, *Naturalist in Britain*, 75. Seaton provides a survey of these books in "The Flower Language Books of the Nineteenth Century."

30. Grandville, *Flowers Personified*. For a history of the production of the plates and the book, see Wick, Introduction and Notes for *Court of Flora*.

31. Grandville, *Flowers Personified*, iii, 15, 12, 16–17.

32. Wick argues that Grandville and company were themselves concerned that the scientific study of plants was draining the natural world of meaning and made their book in an effort to "humanize the pursuit of science, dwelling at length upon the simple yet fulfilling pleasures afforded by nature" (Introduction and Notes for *Court of Flora*).

33. Grandville, *Flowers Personified*, 25 (quotation). On the debates in America between the value of Linnaeus or Jussieu, see Rudolph, "Introduction of the Natural System."

34. Hale, *Flora's Interpreter*, iv, 21.

35. Hooper, *Lady's Book of Flowers*, 203–4.

36. Ibid., 192.

37. Grandville, *Flowers Personified*, 14.

38. For more background on Marcet's influence in America, see Rossiter, *Women Scientists*, 3–4.

39. Marcet, *Conversations on Vegetable Physiology*, 13–14.

40. Ibid., 195.

41. Ibid., 199.

42. On the developing ecological understanding of nature in the eighteenth and nineteenth centuries, see Worster, *Nature's Economy*.

43. Rudolph, "Introduction of the Natural System," for example, lists all the women who supported Linnaeus and does not mention Marcet as an influence in America.

44. On Eaton's influence, see Rudolph, "Women in Nineteenth-Century American Botany," 1347.

45. Phelps is the single woman whose name routinely appears in general histories of

botany in America. See, for example, Ewan, *Short History of Botany*, 39–40.

46. Phelps, *Familiar Lectures on Botany*, 9; Scott, *Making the Invisible Woman Visible*, 286–87.

47. On women's role in scientific education, see Scott, *Making the Invisible Woman Visible*, Kohlstedt, "In from the Periphery"; Burstyn, "Early Women in Education."

48. Phelps, *Familiar Lectures on Botany*, 128, 130; Rudolph, "How It Developed That Botany," 463.

49. Rossiter, *Women Scientists*, 7; Kohlstedt, "In from the Periphery," 87; Scott, *Making the Invisible Woman Visible*, 89–107.

50. Phelps, *Familiar Lectures on Botany*, 14–15.

51. Ibid., Preface, 14, 226.

52. Rossiter, *Women Scientists*, 7.

53. Phelps, *Familiar Lectures on Botany*, 200. Phelps's mention of "civil history" is apt here because her sister, Emma Willard, was as committed to women's education in human history as Almira was to their education in natural history (Baym, "Women and the Republic," 1–23).

54. Burstyn, "Early Women in Education," 62–63.

55. D. E. Allen, *Naturalist in Britain*, 125–40.

56. Agassiz, *First Lesson in Natural History*, 62–63.

57. Ibid., 46–47.


CHAPTER TWO

1. On the early history of the nature essay, see Hanley, *Natural History in America*, 16–31, 103–19, 176–92, 224–38; Huth, *Nature*, 14–54, 87–105; Welker, *Birds and Men*, 91–149.

2. Margaret Fuller's account of her own travels through the West, *Summer on the Lakes*, contained much nature description, but nature study was secondary to Fuller's narrative of human society on the frontier.

3. On the cult of domesticity, see Cott, *Bonds of Womanhood*; Welter, *Dimity Convictions*.

4. On James's attitudes toward women as evidenced in his fiction, see Bradsher, "Women in the Works of James Fenimore Cooper." The standard biography of Susan is Cunningham, "Susan Fenimore Cooper." On the strong influence of her father on her life and work, see Maddox, "Susan Fenimore Cooper."

5. The primary source for information on Susan's family history is her "Small Family Memories," in J. F. Cooper, *Correspondence*, 1:9–72. William Cooper's *Guide in the Wilderness*, although not a natural history, contains much information on the lay of the land around Cooperstown. On the landscape aesthetic of Downing, see Leighton, *American Gardens*, 163–72. Susan thanks "Dr. De Kay and Mr. Downing . . . for their kindness in directing her course on several occasions" (*Rural Hours*, 406). All further references to *Rural Hours* are cited parenthetically in the text.

6. Kelley, *Private Woman*, xi, 248.

7. Her father's role in the publication of *Rural Hours*, and Bryant's and Irving's responses to the book, are documented in two published sets of correspondence: J. F. Cooper, *Letters and Journals*, 6:131, 216–17, 232, 234, and *Correspondence*, 3:640–41, 671–72, 681, 685–86, 690–92. Thoreau's interest in the book is reported by David Jones in his introduction to the 1968 reprint of *Rural Hours* (Syracuse: Syracuse University Press), xxxvii. On Downing's suggestion to Bremer, see the first chapter of this book.

8. Huth, *Nature*, 34, 48, 51, 89. For a focused study on the meanings of this sort of middle-landscape life during the century, see Stilgoe, *Borderland*. Stilgoe is one of the first commentators to emphasize Susan Fenimore Cooper's contribution to the celebration of country life (24).

9. Knapp, *Country Rambles*, 11. For an excellent discussion of Gilbert White's work and influence in mid-nineteenth-century America, see Worster, *Nature's Economy*, 3–25.

10. On the development of a middle-class ideal of domestic retirement and its connections to maternal associations, see Cott, *Bonds of Womanhood*, 149–59. In 1870 Cooper published an antisuffrage article, "Female Suffrage: A Letter to the Christian Women of America." On her later charitable work, see Cunningham, "Susan Fenimore Cooper." Here Cooper parted company with many of the most popular literary domestics, who, Kelley argues, felt "mocked" by their culture, found women "betrayed" in the home, and supported the call to women's rights (*Private Woman*, 309, 335).

11. Kurth notes that in the 1887 edition of *Rural Hours*, Cooper deleted a good deal of this moralizing, religious material in deference to different reader preferences of the day ("Susan Fenimore Cooper," 137–38).

12. Knapp, *Country Rambles*, 18.

13. On the influence of Thomson on Cooper's text, see Kurth, "Susan Fenimore Cooper," 144.

14. Her role here fits into a similar sort of "noblesse oblige" that Kelley identifies among the literary domestics who shared Cooper's station in life (*Private Woman*, 295).

15. Of course, the Euro-Americans had not been the first to domesticate the region, although they presented themselves as doing so. For accounts of the American Indians' impact on land in the Northeast, see Cronon, *Changes in the Land*; Merchant, *Ecological Revolutions*.

16. Stilgoe, *Borderland*, 115.

17. Huth pinpoints the rise of the conservationist impulse in America in the publication, in 1864, of George Perkins Marsh's *Man and Nature*, noting that prior to this date conservationist voices were isolated and few (*Nature*, 167–69).

18. J. F. Cooper, *Letters and Journals*, 6:149.

19. On the rise of Arbor Day in America in the early 1870s, see Huth, *Nature*, 171. On the development of the bird essay, see Welker, *Birds and Men*, 177–99; Brooks, *Speaking for Nature*, 133–81.

20. S. F. Cooper, *Elinor Wyllys*, 7–8.

21. On the search for privacy and seclusion from the city in the suburbs, and the restricted size of the grounds in the less expensive subdivisions, see G. Wright, *Building the Dream*, 98–113; Stilgoe, *Borderland*, 152–53. Wright comments on the urge in the last half of the century to bring nature indoors and open the house to the out-of-doors with added windows and living rooms decorated with dried leaves, but women engaged in such an endeavor were still restricted to the space inside or directly contiguous to their home. The suburbs of the majority did not contain within their round the varied natural landscape just outside Susan Cooper's door.

22. Susan shared this landscape aesthetic with her father. For a description of his views on the subject, see Nevius, *Cooper's Landscapes*.

23. The sentiment expressed here both reflects and extends the distinctions Victorian middle-class women made between "conspicuous housekeeping" and "homekeeping." Gillian Brown argues that such women converted market commodities purchased for the home into personal possessions through family use, building up emotional attachments to objects over time (*Domestic Individualism*, 47). Cooper suggests that the best such possessions are those that draw us closer to nature by modeling organic forms. She here contrasts frivolous consumerism to responsible domesticity. Her lack of interest in her home's interior amenities also forms a subtle critique of women who would spend more time arranging the parlor furniture than admiring nature's artifacts out in the fresh air.

24. For Wilson's influence on bird lore, see Huth, *Nature*, 25. Cooper had read Wilson and mentions him in *Rural Hours*, 347.

25. On the upholsterer bee, see Knapp, *Country Rambles*, 53, 284–85. On hedgehogs, see ibid., 97–98, 296–97. In support of her description of the bee, Cooper quoted from "Acheta Domestica," the name Miss L. M. Budgen used in publishing her *Episodes of Insect Life*, 3:86–88. Budgen explained that the purpose of her book was to build sympathy for insects by associating "them as much as possible with our domestic habits,—the summer's stroll,—the winter's walk" (vii). Her text includes charming illustrations of insects behaving as humans, offered in part to teach moral lessons through close observation. She often presents herself—the male "Acheta Domestica"—as a well-dressed grasshopper or cricket studying the habits of insects.

26. Maddox, "Susan Fenimore Cooper," 145.

27. Worster, *Nature's Economy*, 11–20.

28. Knapp, *Country Rambles*, 97–98.

29. Cooper no doubt garnered the general values expressed here from John Ruskin and his American followers; but, as with most every other idea she had about nature, she then looked for the application to woman's sphere. On Ruskin's influence on the popularization of wildflowers, see Blunt, *Art of Botanical Illustration*, 231; Foshay, *Reflections of Nature*, 37.

30. Gillian Brown argues that a number of nineteenth-century women shared Cooper's suspicion of much such consumerist display (*Domestic Individualism*, 46–47).

31. Rossiter demonstrates how important the years 1870 to 1890 were for women's

participation in natural history (*Women Scientists*, 86). For biographies of Treat, see Harshberger, *Botanists of Philadelphia*, 298–302; Weiss, "Mrs. Mary Treat," 258–73. Treat groups spiders and wasps together under the general heading "insects" in *Home Studies*.

32. Like many scientists of the time, including Darwin in his later years, Treat was convinced that evolution could be triggered by geography. See her comments on the potential for development of a new species of cow as a result of the consumption of a certain plant in *Home Studies*, 220. For a good history of the development of evolutionary ideas, see Eiseley, *Darwin's Century*. All further references to *Home Studies* are cited parenthetically in the text.

33. I am not suggesting that Treat was somehow ahead of her time. As Donald Worster has demonstrated, Darwin's evolutionary theory could be read two ways—one that sanctioned violence and dominance and one that saw in natural selection an image of human immersion into the web of nature. Worster argues that Darwin himself came around to this second view in his later years. My point is that, having a choice, Mary Treat, for reasons partially connected to women's culture, was in the biocentric camp at a time when many of her compatriots were not. See Worster, *Nature's Economy*, 178–87.

34. See Welker, *Birds and Men*, 178–208; Brooks, *Speaking for Nature*, 105; Dunlap, *Saving America's Wildlife*, 13–16. Ainley argues, in addition, that ornithology has been less professionalized than other branches of science, leaving an opening for women amateurs not available in other fields ("Field Work and Family," 60). For a general history of women's work in clubs during this period, including conservation activities, see Blair, *Clubwoman as Feminist*, 119.

35. Schmitt discusses the general tendency of this literature, men's and women's, to engage in "Christian ornithology"—the application of moral lessons to bird behavior—but he does not discuss the women's application of such morals to lessons about gender (*Back to Nature*, 36–38).

36. O. T. Miller, *In Nesting Time*, 152. All further references are cited parenthetically in the text.

37. On the relationships between the New Woman, the True Woman, and the cult of domesticity, see Smith-Rosenberg, *Disorderly Conduct*, 173–76; Blair, *Clubwoman as Feminist*, 99–100. Merriam married late and pursued her own research throughout her life. The most complete biography is Kofalk, *No Woman Tenderfoot*. Most of the women ornithologists, Miller included, drew a line between songbirds and such predators as hawks and owls. They, along with male Audubon members, advocated eradicating such destroyers of family life. In this, they were as likely to take up a gun as their male colleagues (Dunlap, *Saving America's Wildlife*, 15).

38. In addition to Kofalk's biography of Merriam, see Brooks, *Speaking for Nature*, 171–75.

39. Merriam, *A-Birding on a Bronco*, 218. All further references are cited parenthetically in the text.

40. Quoted in Kofalk, who also reports that Merriam published under her maiden name after her marriage (*No Woman Tenderfoot*, 51).

41. Smith-Rosenberg notes that those in the first wave of New Women—Merriam's generation—remained tied to Victorian romantic vocabularies in describing their own sexuality, even while the next generation was openly flaunting their sexual behavior (*Disorderly Conduct*, 284). Some of this reticence clearly informed what the nature writers had to say about bird behavior.

42. Welker, *Birds and Men*, 190. Paul Brooks is to be credited for first recognizing the women's achievements as both insightful and inspirational in *Speaking for Nature*, 163–81.

43. See Huth, *Nature*, 95–104; Welker, *Birds and Men*, 176–84.

44. For a history of the "nature fakers" argument between Burroughs and Earnest Thompson Seton in which Mabel Osgood Wright's observations play a key role, see Brooks, *Speaking for Nature*, 213. For full treatments of the nature fakers battles, see Dunlap, *Saving America's Wildlife*, 27–31; Schmitt, *Back to Nature*, 45–56.

45. Douglas, *Feminization of American Culture*, 397. Douglas argues that the sentimental novelists were pawns of industrial society, espousing "passivity" as a virtue that ultimately denied them real power (and literary greatness). In her study she does not consider literary naturalists or discuss how their work might have been painted with the large brush of masculine dismissal that occurred near the end of the century. Gillian Brown has recently countered Douglas's image of these writers as passive consumers (of things and ideas), posing some domestic novelists as engaged in a sophisticated critique of patriarchy, including the corrupting effects of the marketplace on domestic values (*Domestic Individualism*, 17–18).

46. Rossiter, *Women Scientists*, 79; Welker, *Birds and Men*, 206.

47. Nash chronicles the rise of the "cult of wilderness" in America (*Wilderness*, 141–60). He includes Burroughs and Thoreau as precursors to this masculinized cult. My reading of their contribution suggests that, at different points in their careers (and to fit different needs in cultural history), they have been claimed by both camps.

48. McCulloch-Williams, *Next to the Ground*, 139–40; Kumin, *In Deep*, 75.

49. Rich, *We Took to the Woods*, 319–20; Hubbell, *Country Year*, 120–21.

50. Kumin, *In Deep*, 178.

51. Merchant, "Women of the Progressive Conservation Movement." The standard biography of Austin is Stineman, *Mary Austin*. On her reputation as a nature essayist and her work as a conservationist, see Brooks, *Speaking for Nature*, 183–92; Blend, "Mary Austin." Austin admired Muir. In *Land of Little Rain* (152), she contrasted his approach to nature with that of scientific professionals who fail to see the moral precepts in their developing understanding of the biophysical environment.

52. Nash, *Wilderness*, 200–271.

53. Hoover, *Gift of the Deer*, 114; Zwinger, *Beyond the Aspen Grove*, 68, 80; J. Johnson, *Inland Island*, 53.

54. The quotation is from Austin's stories of women's lives in the Mojave (*Lost Borders*, 10–11). On her contradictory attitudes toward feminism, see Stineman, *Mary Austin*, 129–30. On her support for the younger generation's struggle for a female

sexual vocabulary, see Smith-Rosenberg, *Disorderly Conduct*, 284–85. On her differences with other Progressive Era women (including naturalists) on the meanings of home and domesticity, see Blend, "Mary Austin," 14, 31–32. For a full discussion of female imagery in her work, see Norwood, "The Photographer and the Naturalist."

55. Kumin, *In Deep*, 87.
56. J. Johnson, *Inland Island*, 90.
57. Austin, *Land of Little Rain*, 88.
58. J. Johnson, *Inland Island*, 9.
59. Zwinger, "Thoreau on Women," 3 (Thoreau's quotation).
60. See Zwinger and Teale's account of their journey in *A Conscious Stillness*.
61. Women (and men) who write about nature refer primarily to male authorities, both for scientific proof and for sensitive evocations of flora and fauna. That I chose not to include Annie Dillard in my discussion of contemporary female nature essayists shows how effectively such silencing sometimes works. Dillard's *Pilgrim at Tinker Creek* has earned more recognition than any of the books discussed in this chapter. Dillard is a skilled nature writer, but no more so than Josephine Johnson. That Dillard is female enters rarely into her account of the seasonal round of her cabin. Nor does the cabin itself bear the emotional meanings of home. Dillard has stated that she wrote *Tinker Creek* off 1,103 note cards in a library carrel. Rachel Carson receives a brief mention, in a chapter including references to Joseph Wood Krutch, Rutherford Platt, Edwin Way Teale, and Arthur Stanley Eddington (162–84). Describing the books she reads as including men and women, Dillard names only the men: "Knud Rasmussen, Sir John Franklin, Peter Freuchen, Scott, Peary, and Bird; Jedediah Smith, Peter Skene Ogden, and Milton Sublette; or Daniel Boone" (43). Based as it is in Dillard's education, *Tinker Creek* reflects our contemporary inheritance of that late nineteenth-century effort to remasculinize science and nature writing. *Tinker Creek*'s fame rests in part on its appeal to that tradition. On her writing method, see Major, "Pilgrim of the Absolute," 363.
62. Zwinger, "Thoreau on Women," 3.

CHAPTER THREE

1. For Cowing's Death Valley illustrations, see Coville, "Botany of the Death Valley Expedition," plates 1–12, 14–15, 19–21.
2. The description of Colden's accomplishments is found in Rickett, "Jane Colden as Botanist," 24.
3. On the importance of landscape painting, see Novak, *Nature and Culture*; on still lifes and popular magazines and prints, see Gerdts, Brindle, and Secrist, *American Cornucopia*; on the artists and the government surveys, see Goetzmann, *Exploration and Empire*, 333–55; on Wilson and Audubon, see Welker, *Birds and Men*, 18–91, and Hanley, *Natural History in America*, 47–85.
4. Gerdts, Brindle, and Secrist comment on women's traditions in flower painting and prints in *American Cornucopia*, 4–12, and Gerdts documents women's strong

participation in the outdoor art schools of the period in "Teaching of Painting Out-of-Doors," 25–40. Foshay mentions Dewing, Robbins, and Bridges as flower painters (*Reflections of Nature*, 59–62, 109, 126). On Martin, see Coffin, "Audubon's Friend." On Bridges's work on birds, see Sharf, "Fidelia Bridges." Robbins wrote an informative autobiography on the motivations and trials of women landscape painters of the period, in which she remembered learning flower lore and love from her mother ("Reminiscences of a Flower Painter").

5. Goetzmann's *Exploration and Empire* is the standard text on the expeditionary artists. For the impact of the surveys on landscape art, and for the best example of the importance of landscape painting to cultural history, see Novak, *Nature and Culture*. Neither of these histories mentions women. On women's lives on the frontier and in the West, see Kolodny, *Land Before Her*; Schlissel, *Women's Diaries*.

6. The primary biographical material on Colden is in James, *Notable American Women*, 357–58, and Hall, "Jane Colden," 17–21.

7. James, *Notable American Women*, 357 (first quotation); Rickett, "Jane Colden as Botanist," 22 (second quotation).

8. On life-styles of women of Colden's class, see Ryan, *Womanhood*, 69–94.

9. Rickett, "Jane Colden as Botanist," 25.

10. Moriarty, as the title indicates, attempted to touch all the bases in this little book—noting that it was intended for amateur gardeners, painters, and the schoolroom (v–viii). The period between 1820 and 1860 witnessed an explosion in popular interest in drawing generally; women's flower work was part of this wave (Marzio, "American Drawing Books").

11. Brindle and White, *Flora Portrayed*, 11.

12. Rossiter, *Women Scientists*, 3.

13. Gerdts, Brindle, and Secrist, *American Cornucopia*, 8. For a study of the Peale family tradition of still-life painting, see Born, "Female Peales," 12–14.

14. For a good study of this process in bird etching, see C. E. Jackson, *Bird Etchings*.

15. Terminology in this field is not standard. The original term for the study of shells was *conchology*, later replaced by *malacology* as more inclusive of the animals and their shells. For a discussion, see Dance, *Shell Collecting*, 270–74.

16. On the founding of the Academy of Natural Sciences of Philadelphia, see Smallwood and Smallwood, *Natural History*, 155–65; on the history of American books on shells, see Dance, *Shell Collecting*, 184–87; for biographies of the malacologists, see R. T. Abbott, *American Malacologists*.

17. On shell collecting in England, see D. E. Allen, *Naturalist in Britain*, 125–28.

18. R. T. Abbott, *American Malacologists*, 1. Shell collecting was only one of a number of seaside collecting activities in which American women engaged. They were also significant participants in algology, the study of algae, filling many an album with beautiful specimens (D. Warner, *Graceanna Lewis*, 102).

19. *Conchologists' Exchange* 1 (March–April 1887): 56.

20. Frierson, "How Uniones Emigrate," 139. For a biography of Frierson, see R. T. Abbott, *American Malacologists*, 102.

21. Planton Collection, Academy of Natural Sciences of Philadelphia (hereafter cited

as ANSP). The sketchbook was donated to the academy by the Planton heirs in 1920. The only suggestion as to its dating is a handwritten poem by Anna Bache, tipped into the journal and dated 1833.

22. R. T. Abbott, *American Malacologists*, 2–27.

23. Dance, *Shell Collecting*, 36.

24. Quoted in Weiss and Ziegler, *Thomas Say*, 192.

25. Information on Lucy Way Sistare's relatives appears in a brief family chronology she wrote, located in the Lucy Say Collection, ANSP. Her connection to Madam Fretageot is mentioned in Weiss and Ziegler, *Thomas Say*, 213, and W. E. Wilson, *The Angel and the Serpent*, 105, 139. Maclure's school in Philadelphia was undoubtedly run along the same lines as the New Harmony schools he later organized—that is, teaching natural history by objects (Wilson, 185).

26. For information on the production of *American Conchology*, see Weiss and Ziegler, *Thomas Say*, 192–93; W. E. Wilson, *The Angel and the Serpent*, 183–84.

27. Lucy Say (in New York) to Dr. William Price (of Cincinnati), January 29, 1835, Lucy Say Collection, ANSP. On Lucy's dislike of the domestic round and her preference for the East, see Weiss and Ziegler, *Thomas Say*, 142–43.

28. Quotation reprinted in Weiss and Ziegler, *Thomas Say*, 215.

29. Ibid., 217.

30. Rossiter, *Women Scientists*, 75.

31. Smallwood and Smallwood, *Natural History*, 187.

32. Dance (*Shell Collecting*) documents the explosion in identification—in 1758 Linnaeus had described 700 mollusks; 2,244 were known by 1817, 17,321 by mid-century, and 44,482 by 1891 (189–91). Throughout the late nineteenth century, wealthy women were major collectors (218–20).

33. On Philadelphia's prominence in producing illustrated scientific books, see Wood, "Prints and Scientific Illustration," 179–80.

34. "Biography of A. Lawson, prepared for the Academy of Natural Sciences of Philadelphia by his daughter Malvina," Alexander Lawson Collection, ANSP, p. v.

35. Although Binney's text began appearing after Lawson's death, the major work was done earlier. Helen Lawson's death was reported in "Minutes of the Board of Lady Managers," School of Design for Women, February 1, 1853, Philadelphia, Archives of the Historical Society of Pennsylvania.

36. Smallwood and Smallwood, *Natural History*, 188.

37. Lawson usually earns mention in standard references on early American artists like David H. Wallace's *New-York Historical Society's Dictionary of Artists in America, 1564–1860*. Her works were exhibited in shows of the Pennsylvania Academy of the Arts in the 1830s and 1840s (Rutledge, *Cumulative Record of Exhibition Catalogues*, 124).

38. For biographical information on Pilsbry, see R. T. Abbott, *American Malacologists*, 143–44; on Pilsbry's and Tyron's work on the *Manual*, see Dance, *Shell Collecting*, 186–87.

39. Pilsbry's comment was recorded in the ANSP copy of Binney by Maurice Phillips, a scientific editor at the academy in the 1940s and 1950s.

40. For the Congo materials, see Pilsbry, "Land Mollusks"; Pilsbry and Bequet, "Aquatic Mollusks." Information on Winchester's tutelage of Pilsbry in the art of scientific illustration is contained in Phillips and Phillips, *Guide to the Manuscript Collections*, 269. The "New York Land and Fresh-water Mollusks" monograph was never published (Phillips and Phillips, 269).

41. Pilsbry, *Land Mollusca*.

42. Rossiter, *Women Scientists*, 73–160.

43. On women at the academy, see Schmitz, "Women in Science."

44. The publication history of photographs of Henry Pilsbry and his female assistants illustrates the pattern. The Academy of Natural Sciences of Philadelphia holds many photographic portraits of Pilsbry. In one he is seated with two female assistants standing behind, one of whom was probably Helen Winchester. Several similar portraits were made at the time. Yet, in published images of Pilsbry, the women have been blacked out, enshrining Pilsbry in solitary fame and masking the collaboration his publications required.

45. For example, Virginia Orr Maes worked at the academy as a scientific assistant from 1955 until her marriage in 1963, at which point she gave up her salary and became a research associate (Robertson, "Virginia Orr Maes").

46. An example of the impact of Pilsbry's and Winchester's illustrated works, and of women's involvement in regional study, is provided in the letters collected in honor of Pilsbry's eighty-fifth birthday in 1947. Many letters were from husband/wife teams who, like Joshua and Ruth Bailey of the San Diego Natural History Museum, worked together in the field. Others were signed by women working on local mollusks in universities, museums, and clubs in regional cities like Topeka and Buffalo. See "Letters to Dr. Pilsbry on the Occasion of his 85th," Pilsbry Collection, ANSP.

47. James, *Notable American Women*, 686–87.

48. Furbish, "Evening in the Maine Woods," 5–6, unpublished manuscript, Furbish Collection, Bowdoin College Library, Brunswick, Maine. Furbish published portions of this lecture in two articles, entitled "A Botanist's Trip to the Aroostook," in *American Naturalist*.

49. Miss E. L. Turner, "Bird Photography for Women," 180; Pearson, "Which Would You Choose?," 250. The poem asks which woman a young man would choose for a companion, "the maid who can shoot or the camera girl?"

50. Miss E. L. Turner, "Bird Photography for Women," 190.

51. Stanwood, "Hermit Thrush." For one of her most famous articles and series of photographs of baby chickadees, see "Tenants of Birdsacre."

52. Quoted in Bonta, "Cordelia Stanwood," 45.

53. Brooks, *Speaking for Nature*, 177–80.

54. Porter, *Moths of the Limberlost*, 117–18.

55. Ibid., 111, 134.

56. Biddle and Lowrie, *Notable Women of Pennsylvania*, 161–62; Harshberger, *Botanists of Philadelphia*, 233–36. Lewis's description of her career appears in Havaford, *Daughters of America*, 260–62. The most extensive biography of Lewis is

D. Warner's *Graceanna Lewis*. On Quaker women's participation in nature study, see Bacon, *Mothers of Feminism*, 163–64.

57. A. B. Comstock, *Comstocks of Cornell*, 53–105, 130, 143–44, 150, 168, 179, 190, 229, 234; Mallis, *American Entomologists*, 126–38; Rossiter, *Women Scientists*, 64. For her most extensive set of illustrations in her husband's work, see J. H. Comstock, *Introduction to Entomology*. On the Nature Study movement, see Schmitt, *Back to Nature*, 77–95.

58. In her autobiography, Comstock noted that she could have earned more than she did from her illustrating, but she and her husband felt that the *Introduction to Entomology* was more important (*Comstocks of Cornell*, 166–67). Apparently the couple was not rich but well off enough to make such decisions. Comstock was able to finish her degree because Cornell waived her tuition (ibid., 144). Much to their mutual disappointment, the Comstocks never had children.

59. Ryan, *Womanhood*, 198–216. Ryan notes that the cohort of women born between 1865 and 1874 "married less and less frequently than any group before or since" (206). See also Chafe, *American Woman*, 48–65.

60. Rossiter, *Women Scientists*, 218–47. For a general survey of women's tasks in Agriculture, see Baker, "Women in the U.S. Department of Agriculture."

61. Chase to Mildred Gilman, n.d., Chase Collection, Hunt Institute for Botanical Documentation, Pittsburgh (hereafter cited as Hunt Institute).

62. Biographical information on Agnes Chase is taken from Fosberg and Swallen, "Agnes Chase," and Mildred Gilman, "Agnes Chase: My Most Unforgettable Character," unpublished manuscript, Chase Collection, Hunt Institute.

63. Mildred Gilman, "Agnes Chase," 3; Rossiter, *Women Scientists*, 116. Chase, more than her contemporary Florence Merriam, thus fit the model for the first generation of "New Women" described by Smith-Rosenberg (*Disorderly Conduct*, 176–77).

64. Reported in Mildred Gilman, "Agnes Chase," 5–6, and "Mrs. Agnes Chase, Botanist, Is Dead."

65. Hitchcock credited Chase with all the spikelet illustrations for the *Manual of the Grasses*, 15. See Chase's comments on the importance of spikelets in her *First Book of Grasses*, 13.

66. Between 1913 and 1940 Chase made collecting trips to Brazil, Puerto Rico, and Venezuela (Fosberg and Swallen, "Agnes Chase," 146). In a newspaper report on her seventy-ninth birthday, she described herself as a "plain old woman . . . there isn't anything interesting about me" (Schultz, "Mrs. Agnes Chase"). Describing the results of one of her expeditions to Brazil in 1925, the *Official Record* of the U.S. Department of Agriculture reported that "the Grass Herbarium of the department is the largest and most valuable grass herbarium in the world" ("Brazil Explored For New Grasses").

67. Chase, *First Book of Grasses*, v.

68. Hitchcock, *Manual of the Grasses*, 15.

69. Chase, "Toodles," 1, unpublished manuscript, Chase Collection, Hunt Institute.

70. White and Neumann, "Collection of Pomological Watercolors," 103. The authors

list the artists and their contributions as well as providing some biographical information.

71. Ibid., 106–7. Passmore's watercolor folio is in the National Agricultural Library, Beltsville, Md.; included with the folio are two brief biographies of Passmore, who died in 1911.

72. Books encouraging the study and preservation of local wildflowers were popular throughout the nineteenth and twentieth centuries. Many were written and/or illustrated by women; two of note are Dana, *How to Know the Wildflowers*, and Embury, *American Wildflowers*.

73. White and Schallert ("Illustrations") list the artists and the volumes in which their work appears.

74. The Forest Service Collection is housed at the Hunt Institute. For examples of Hughey's work in print, see Little, *Southwestern Trees, Yearbook of Agriculture: Trees* (1949), and *Yearbook of Agriculture: Grass* (1948).

75. For example, most of the yearbooks included an editorial preface stressing the importance of knowledge about America's plants and animals in preserving the country's way of life, although the definitions for such preservation were linked to the historical moment. Thus, in his 1948 preface to the *Grass* issue, Clinton Anderson noted how important grasses were in the effort to make America secure and increase the beauty of the landscape, which beauty brought "serenity . . . a quality we and the troubled world need" (v–vi). For a history of the development of the Department of Agriculture and its basis in the practical application of scientific knowledge, see Dupree, *Science in the Federal Government*, 149–84.

76. Vita, Elaine Hodges File, Hunt Institute.

77. Exhibition catalog, "GNSI Natural Science Illustration Exhibit."

78. The "Directory of Members" of the Guild for 1988 lists members by specialty.

79. Ibid., 17–18.

80. Buell, "Grace Albee."

81. Dowden also takes an ecological approach in much of her work, particularly the relationships of insects and plants. For other fine examples of her work, see *From Flower To Fruit* and *The Clover and the Bee*.

82. Dowden, "Something About the Author," 83.

83. Chase to Margaret Gilman, n.d., Chase Collection, Hunt Institute.


CHAPTER FOUR

1. For a biography of Lawrence, see Lacy's Introduction to Lawrence's *Gardening for Love*. *Gardening for Love* includes many of the letters Lawrence exchanged with southern gardeners. All further references to this work are cited parenthetically in the text.

2. The standard history on early American horticulture is Hedrick's *History of Horticulture*, which discusses Grant (64–65), Pinckney (127–28), and Logan (89–135). See also Prior, "Letters of Martha Logan," 38–47; J. H. Wilson, "Dancing Dogs"; Hollingsworth, *Her Garden*. On reading Grant's description of the work of the

Dutch women, Grace Tabor, a turn-of-the-century historian of American gardens, was moved to marvel: "So the women were the gardeners; and they spun and wove and knit, also—and found time to take tea with a neighbor or to entertain one at home! How did they ever do it?" (*Old-Fashioned Gardening*, 74). Garden spaces have a long tradition as woman's domain, a tradition well expressed by J. B. Jackson in *Necessity for Ruins*, 26–27.

3. Downing, *Rural Essays*, 44–55; Loudon, *Gardening for Ladies*, 16–17. On these and other efforts to encourage women as gardeners, see Leighton, *American Gardens*, 91–97. In preparing Loudon's book for the American audience, Downing deleted her chapters on kitchen gardens, thus reinforcing the image of the leisured American woman in an ornamental floral landscape (Tice, *Gardening*, 58).

4. Beecher and Stowe, *American Woman's Home*, 384–88. Earlier editions of this text, published as *A Treatise on Domestic Economy*, included similar advice but not the illustration. See, for example, the 1851 edition authored by Beecher (New York: Harper and Brothers, 1851). On Beecher's influence on home design, see K. T. Jackson, *Crabgrass Frontier*, 61–63.

5. For a fulsome reading of the domestic scene depicted in the *Harper's* illustration, see Tice, *Gardening*, 12.

6. Kolodny, *Land Before Her*, 93–158. For a good example of the specifically domestic limits to frontier women's gardening role, see Kolodny's comments on Caroline Kirkland's *A New Home*, 146–48.

7. A. Warner, *Gardening By Myself*, 42.

8. Although garden historians like Leighton seem to agree with Downing and company about Victorian women's aversion to gardens, their histories are packed with references to women's gardens and their gardening activities throughout the nineteenth century. See the inconsistencies in Leighton (*American Gardens*, 99, 109–10, 213, 216–18), in which women of the 1820s to 1860s are variously seen fainting away at the thought of gardening, taking part in horticultural society meetings and shows, and joining with their husbands in the making of gardens. Some of the confusion about what women actually did in the garden seems to arise from reading too much into their exclusion from men's associations, such as the Massachusetts Horticultural Society (MHS). Thus, Thornton ("Moral Dimensions of Horticulture," 9) asserts that, because horticultural societies were composed of men, messages appearing in *Godey's Lady's Book* (1840) concerning the moral power of work with plants were aimed at men. Women did not have to be official members of the society to work with plants, as Leighton reveals: in 1845 a member of the MHS complimented the work of women's flower exhibits by noting that "the plants of the garden are cultivated with us by hands as delicate as their own tendrils" (110). Doell's study of New York State Gardens, *Gardens of the Gilded Age*, suggests that throughout this period women engaged in gardening, and that some commentators recognized their efforts (118).

9. Garden club women are well aware of this stereotype. The seventy-fifth anniversary chronicle of the Garden Club of America includes several cartoons depicting such a lady—including one showing the "Compleat G.C.A. Member" in her tweed suit

with a name tag pinned on with a diamond pin (Olcott, *Winds of Change*, 49, 75, 221).

10. Treat, *Injurious Insects*; M. O. Wright, *Garden of a Commuter's Wife* and *The Garden, You, and I*; Chase, "Toodles," Mrs. Gerrie Davis, interview with Michael Steiber, September 6, 1977, and Chase to Prof. Walter V. Brown, November 18, 1949—all in Chase Collection, Hunt Institute. Wright's garden is pictured in McCauley, *Joy of Gardens*, 116. For a survey of American and British garden "autobiographies," see Seaton, "Garden Autobiography."

11. C. Thaxter, *Island Garden*, v. All further references are cited parenthetically in the text. For a good description of the biophysical landscape of the Isles of Shoals, see K. L. Jacobs, "Celia Thaxter."

12. For biographical details on Thaxter, see James, *Notable American Women*, 441–43; Fields and Lamb, Introduction to Celia Thaxter, *Letters*; R. Thaxter, *Sandpiper*.

13. C. Thaxter, *Among the Isles of Shoals*, 129–30.

14. C. Thaxter, *Letters*, 17.

15. On the history of garden paintings, see Gerdts, "Artist's Garden" and *Down Garden Paths*. This image of women as passive consumers of the garden persists in current scholarship. For example, John Stilgoe, in *Borderland*, a study of the meanings of the suburb in American culture, spends a great deal of time describing middle-class women as observers of and commentators on a landscape created for them by borderland husbands. With the exception of their work in village improvement societies, women have gardens made for them to relax in (202), visit in (209), and use as a base for consumption of goods (except plants) (210).

16. In another painting done of Thaxter's garden, Hassam seems to have replaced her with a white poppy, familiarly called "The Bride" (*Island Garden*, 74, 95). The white color itself forms part of the code. On the pictorial interest in the naturalistic garden, see Gerdts, *Down Garden Paths*, 111.

17. Here I have collapsed an involved history of landscape design that began in part with American appreciation of eighteenth-century British walking gardens and was further influenced by the nineteenth-century English garden architect, John Loudon. Loudon's distinctions between the "picturesque" and the "gardenesque" were important to Downing as he adapted English innovations to American terrain and social circumstances. Olmsted, too, was influenced by English landscape aesthetics. Within the broad values I have outlined, a good deal of change, and some heated debates, took place over the course of the nineteenth century. The specific emphasis in Hassam's painting on perennial flowers reflects, for example, the influence of the English popularizer of cottage gardens, Gertrude Jekyll. For a summary of some of this history, see Leighton, *American Gardens*, 144–206; Morrow, *Dictionary of Landscape Architecture*, 351–52. On the landscape painting tradition, see Novak, *Nature and Culture*, 101–34, 226–73.

18. R. Thaxter, *Sandpiper*, 115, 176. Her work in the garden on Star Island is described in Robbins, "Reminiscences of a Flower Painter," 540–41.

19. C. Thaxter, *Letters*, ix–x.

20. Celia Thaxter did note, however, that she was not profligate in picking wildflow-

ers, cognizant as she was of the "wholesale destruction" going on at the time (ibid., 93).

21. A description of this style is found in Thomas Mawson's *The Art and Craft of Garden Making* (1900), in which he dubs the approach the "naturalesque." Mawson is quoted in Balmori, McGuire, and McPeck, *Farrand's American Landscapes*, 74. On Downing's love of this sort of landscape, see also Leighton, *American Gardens*, 179–84.

22. For a description of the bedding-out craze of the Victorian period, creating intricately patterned designs and ribbon borders, see Leighton, *American Gardens*, 241–48; Hollingsworth, *Her Garden*, 139–42. Nevins ("Triumph of Flora," 906) notes that Thaxter's rejection of the geometric formality of this phase of garden history "distinguishes" the Appledore garden, but Doell's study of New York State gardens indicates that the "grandmother's" or "old-fashioned" garden was one of many styles used in flower beds of the period (*Gardens of the Gilded Age*, 86). Thaxter was not alone in understanding the best sort of garden for the middle-class woman who would do the work herself. In 1872 Anna Warner, while citing the authority of Peter Henderson, the American popularizer of the bedding-out craze, encouraged her middle-class readers to pursue the "fair, rich profusion" of the "old-fashioned" garden over these new styles (*Gardening By Myself*, 61–65). Although middle-class women had old-fashioned gardens in part because they had to, the turning point for wealthier women seems to have come early in the twentieth century with the publication of Helena Rutherford Ely's *A Woman's Hardy Garden* (1903). Ely was of the class that could afford the staff necessary for the more intricate beds but preferred the naturalized style. On Ely, see Hollingsworth, *Her Garden*, 139–42.

23. C. Thaxter, *Letters*, 91; R. Thaxter, *Sandpiper*, 43. On Thaxter's urge to share her plants with the locals, see *Island Garden*, 55; Robbins, "Reminiscences of a Flower Painter," 541.

24. On the fashion for wearing dead birds, see her article, "A Woman's Heartlessness." On her dislike of her husband's hunting endeavors, see C. Thaxter, *Letters*, 29, 39, 181.

25. Downing, *Rural Essays*, 53.

26. C. Thaxter, *Letters*, 54.

27. On developments in professional landscape design, see Leighton, *American Gardens*, 144–95; Newton, *Design on the Land*, 246–352.

28. Charles Sargent was also associated with one of the major journals for horticultural enthusiasts, *Garden and Forest*, first offered in 1888. Mary Treat provided columns for *Garden and Forest*, as did many other women. Women were avid correspondents in the pages of the journal, offering travel narratives, notes from their gardens, and encouragement for civic planting efforts. An editorial in the issue of October 12, 1892, encouraged women to look at landscape architecture as a particularly suitable career (vol. 5, no. 242, p. 482).

29. For biographical information on Farrand, see Balmori, McGuire, and McPeck, *Farrand's American Landscapes*. On the interest in gardens built on the Italian

model, see Newton, *Design on the Land*, 372–73; Doell, *Gardens of the Gilded Age*, 12. On the Sargents' suburban garden, see Schmitt, *Back to Nature*, 63–67.

30. Balmori, McGuire, and McPeck, *Farrand's American Landscapes*, 16.

31. Shelton, *Beautiful Gardens*, xvii. The four consultants were Mrs. Francis King, Mrs. Banyer Clarkson, Mrs. Edward Harding, and Mrs. Percy Kennaday. On the country place movement, see Newton, *Design on the Land*, 427–46; Schmitt, *Back to Nature*, 28–29.

32. Hill, *Forty Years of Gardening*, 274–75; Barrington, "A Fielde of Delite," 198–91, 241; Shelton, *Beautiful Gardens*, color plate 6, plates 100–103. For an overview of women's work as garden amateurs and landscape architects, see Nevins, "Triumph of Flora," 904–22.

33. Newton, *Design on the Land*, 273; Nevins, "Triumph of Flora," 913. On the emphasis on women as designers of plant material, see D. M. Anderson, *Women, Design*, xvi, 15, 21, 41. In the late 1860s, members of the New England Woman's Club had founded, with the assistance of the Massachusetts Horticultural Society, a short-lived school to prepare young women for work as horticulturists. The school closed after three years, when the Bussey College for Horticulture began admitting women. Although such schools were aimed at a different class of student than the landscape design institutions, they further document the prevalence of the belief that work with plants was a suitable occupation for turn-of-the-century women (Blair, *Clubwoman as Feminist*, 34–35).

34. Hartt, "Women and the Art of Landscape Gardening," 697 and 699 (quotations). On the emphasis on "domestic" design, see Brown and Maddox, "Women and the Land"; D. M. Anderson, *Women, Design*.

35. On the room theme in Dumbarton Oaks and the plan of the Abby Aldrich Rockefeller garden, see Balmori, McGuire, and McPeck, *Farrand's American Landscapes*, 58–66, 74–76. On the use of the Green Garden for entertainment, see Balmori, "Beatrix Farrand at Dumbarton Oaks," 85. On the search for privacy in the flight from the city, see K. T. Jackson, *Crabgrass Frontier*, 58; Stilgoe, *Borderland*, 55–196.

36. On the general resurgence of interest in historical furniture and gardens, see Stilgoe, *Borderland*, 219, 290.

37. Balmori, McGuire, McPeck, *Farrand's American Landscapes*, 16; [Farrand], "The Garden as a Picture," 2 (quotation).

38. Nevins ("Triumph of Flora," 913) provides a detailed list of the women landscape architects of the period and information on their publications. Farrand inspired Marian Cruger Coffin, who designed many gardens in elite suburbs of New York City (Teutonico, "Marian Cruger Coffin").

39. Johnston, "What a Woman Can Do with a Camera," 6. For biographical material on Johnston, see Daniel and Smock, *Talent for Detail*; on Hewitt, about whom little biographical material exists, see Close, *Portrait of an Era*.

40. Nevins ("Triumph of Flora," 913) cites Sipprell and Perrett. Beals photographed a number of scenes appearing in Shelton's *Beautiful Gardens*.

41. Schmitt, *Back to Nature*, 29, 63–65. Stilgoe documents the incredible surge in plant consumption that occurred after 1910 as more and more families came to locate

one source of recreation in the design and maintenance of their lots (*Borderland*, 199). *Gardens of the Gilded Age*, Doell's study of New York State gardens, discusses the spread of garden design fashions into middle-class landscapes.

42. For background on the values expressed here, see Dean, *Livable House*; Hutcheson, *Spirit of the Garden*; Van Rensselaer, *Art Out-Of-Doors*. Close provides a good summary of what technically are termed *style gardens* of the period, many of which aimed to re-create a European landscape in an American setting. Close also discusses the tendency of the photographers to emphasize "symmetry and enclosure" in their highly selective images of the gardens (*Portrait of an Era*, n.p.).

43. Stilgoe, *Borderland*, 186–206.

44. For the history of exotic plant introductions into American gardens, and how specific styles, plants, and garden furniture carried marks of status, see Tice, *Gardening*.

45. Quoted in Daniel and Smock, *Talent for Detail*, 32.

46. For a good history of one aspect of club women's urban cleanup efforts, see Hoy, "Municipal Housekeeping."

47. For graphic descriptions of the limitations posed by the rectangular design of small lots in less affluent residential suburbs, see Stilgoe, *Borderland*, 159–61; K. T. Jackson, *Crabgrass Frontier*, 136.

48. Tice (*Gardening*, 70–71) documents the demand for less expensive designs and plant material.

49. McCauley, *Joy of Gardens*, 20. All further references are cited parenthetically in the text.

50. L. Y. King, *Little Garden*, 25. All further references are cited parenthetically in the text. For biographical information on King, see Hollingsworth, *Her Garden*, 143–54. In part, King was reacting to the trend toward openness in suburban spaces first articulated by Frank J. Scott in *The Art of Beautifying Suburban Home Grounds of Small Extent* (1870); Scott found fences, high walls, and shrub screens "unchristian and unneighborly" (Leighton, *American Gardens*, 255). The designs in Scott's book lack the sort of private spaces that could function as outdoor rooms. Scott, however, assumed that the lots would be at least one-half acre. Stilgoe charts the changing values in the early 1900s (and changing lot sizes) that encouraged the creation of "nooks," particularly as spaces of private retreat for women (*Borderland*, 198–202).

51. In his study of the early suburbs of the mid-nineteenth century, Archer argues that residents were not denying the city; rather, they were attempting to carry city amenities out to the country ("Country and City," 139–56). The garden literature indicates that by the turn of the century, the focus had shifted to protecting some vestige of the country setting within the increasingly congested environments of suburbs.

52. Clark documents the tendency of pattern book authors and suburban developers to depict the suburban house as isolated and private, belying the close quarters of many of the actual developments (*American Family Home*, 99).

53. Louise Beebe Wilder, for example, made a garden in such circumstances, using

many native wildflowers from the surrounding woods in her painstakingly designed rock gardens (*Adventures in My Garden*). Louisa King encouraged those
suburbanites with automobiles to drive them out into the woods to collect wildflowers for home gardens (*Little Garden*, vii).

54. L. Y. King, *Pages from a Garden Notebook*, 199.

55. The most extensive biography of Sessions is MacPhail's *Kate Sessions: Pioneer Horticulturist*. For information on her influence on residential landscapes in San Diego,
see ibid., 47, 53, 109; Cockerell, "Kate Olivia Sessions," 176. On her interest in
native and drought-hardy plants, see Padilla, *Southern California Gardens*, 170, 269.

56. MacPhail, *Kate Sessions*, 73. Just as early women bird photographers had to cope
with proper attire in unique circumstances, gardening women received advice on
clothing. In particular, they were encouraged to be wary of "a mannish costume,
with manners and customs to correspond" (Varley, "Gardening Clothes," 165).
Sessions apparently was unmoved by such counsel.

57. MacPhail, *Kate Sessions*, 45. On California women's work with plants, see Lothrop,
"Women Pioneers"; Padilla, *Southern California Gardens*, 212–20.

58. For evidence of the rise of garden clubs, see Hollingsworth, *Her Garden*, 147;
Crosby, *Fifty Years of Service*, 10; Olcott, *Winds of Change*. The membership of
the Garden Club of America included some of the wealthiest and most influential
women of the late nineteenth and early twentieth centuries. These women were
largely responsible for determining elite tastes in garden styles. For a comprehensive study of their gardens across the country, see Griswold and Weller, *Golden Age
of American Gardens*.

59. Davis, *History of Nevada*, 2:773. On the varied membership of one such club, see
L. Y. King, *Pages from a Garden Notebook*, 240–41.

60. On the rise of village improvement societies, garden clubs, and the city beautification movement, see Huth, *Nature*, 183–85; Schmitt, *Back to Nature*, 70–71;
Stilgoe, *Borderland*, 213–15; W. H. Wilson, "J. Horace McFarland." On Progressive Era women and these movements, see W. H. Wilson, "More Almost Than the
Men"; Vance, *May Mann Jennings*, 80–100. Wortman argues that women's clubs
were key to the shift from passive "true" woman to activist ("Domesticating the
Nineteenth-Century American City," 547).

61. Cranz, *Politics of Park Design*, 61–101, and "Women in Urban Parks," S85–S90.

62. Duncan, *Joyous Art of Gardening*, 4.

63. For a good example of the upsurge in interest in such gardens, see Tabor, *Old-
Fashioned Gardening*. Stilgoe discusses the general trend early in the century to
return to American history for house and yard design, as well as the popularity
of do-it-yourself projects for the family, seeing these as primary expressions of an
antiurban sentiment (*Borderland*, 290). Duncan may have disliked the cramped life
of the city, but she did not ignore its requirements; rather she, along with many of
the "municipal housekeepers," took an active part in redesigning the city to offer
a more healthful, restful space.

64. Wortman, "Domesticating the Nineteenth-Century American City," 555–56.

65. In his descriptions of these communities, Clarence S. Stein emphasized the im-

portance of enclosed green spaces, stressing the residents' use of them for flower beds and vegetable gardens (*Toward New Towns for America*, 28). Newton praises Cautley's "sensitive handling of plant materials [which] brought to completion a surprising atmosphere of almost suburban charm in the city blocks of Sunnyside Gardens" (*Design on the Land*, 489). For a good critique of the Garden City movement, see J. Jacobs, *Death and Life*, 19–21.

66. Cautley, "Planting at Radburn," 26. All further references are cited parenthetically in the text.

67. Cautley, *Garden Design*, 121.

68. For an excellent survey of these catalogs and their use by a middle-class woman, see K. S. White, *Onward and Upward in the Garden*.

69. Lawrence, Dormon and her sister-in-law Ruth, and the fiction writer Eudora Welty formed another network of middle-class women gardeners who corresponded with each other and with the farm women regarding regional plants. Dormon was an illustrator and writer who encouraged the use and preservation of native Louisiana plants in books like *Natives Preferred*. Lawrence often cited this network in her garden columns in the *Charlotte Observer*. These columns have been collected in Lawrence's *Through the Garden Gate*.

70. Lawrence, *A Southern Garden*, xxvi. Lawrence was apparently a member of a female line of gardeners. *Little Bulbs* mentions her consultation of her mother's garden book (12–21) and memories of plants growing in her grandmother's garden and preserved in her own (130).

71. Westmacott, "Pattern and Practice in Traditional Black Gardens in Rural Georgia," unpublished manuscript, 65. Westmacott notes that several of the gardens in his study were managed entirely by women (Westmacott, University of Georgia, letter to the author, June 14, 1989).

72. Cranz (*Politics of Park Design*) provides a comprehensive study of the goals of park designers; Hester ("Process CAN Be Style") documents the historical lack of a participatory process in landscape design.

73. S. B. Warner, *To Dwell Is To Garden*, 13–23; Francis, Cashdan, and Paxson, *Community Open Spaces*, 17–30.

74. S. B. Warner, *To Dwell Is To Garden*, 69, 91, 93.

75. Ibid., 99–122; Hester, "Process CAN Be Style," 52.

76. S. B. Warner, *To Dwell Is To Garden*, xv.

77. Francis, Cashdan, and Paxson, *Community Open Spaces*, 195.

78. L. J. Gould cites her commitment to environmental improvement that springs from within the community (*Lady Bird Johnson*, 103).

79. For example, S. B. Warner cites the leadership of Augusta Bailey, who had been involved in "an old-fashioned beautification program," in the Boston community gardening movement (*To Dwell Is To Garden*, 27). Of course, as Ryan documents, urban African American women have held strong political leadership roles in their communities; their work in community gardens is but one aspect of their activism (*Womanhood in America*, 303–4).

80. For recent popular gardening books, see Perényi, *Green Thoughts*; S. B. Stein, *My*

*Weeds*. The continued vitality of local garden clubs and the national network of gardening women is demonstrated in the activities and publications of the National Council of State Garden Clubs, which in 1978 had a membership of 364,131 among 12,965 local clubs in all fifty states (Crosby, *Fifty Years of Service*, 17).

81. On the difficulties faced by professional women in the 1940s and 1950s, see Chafe, *American Woman*, 174–225; Ryan, *Womanhood*, 278–90. On the decline of women landscape architects, see Brown and Maddox, "Women and the Land," 69. On the predominance of women in small-scale residential design, see Newton, *Design on the Land*, 444–45. No women professionals appear in Kassler's catalog of influential modernists, *Modern Gardens and the Landscape*. Women architects share a similar history. Although some women worked in large firms in the modern period, they were few and not well known. Women's most visible impact during this period was as "architectural critics." Catherina Bauer, Jane Jacobs, Sibyl Moholy-Nagy, and Ada Louise Huxtable each criticized modern architecture's excesses, often raising questions about human needs and human scale. (See Torre, *Women in American Architecture*, 88–143.) For an overview of the tendency of modern architects and planners to ignore women's needs in designing the environment and to exclude women as professionals, see Wekerle, Peterson, and Morley, *New Space for Women*.

82. Hester, "Process CAN Be Style," 50 (first quotation); Tunnard, *Gardens in the Modern Landscape*, 108–10 (second quotation). For a general summary of the modern period, see Morrow, *Dictionary of Landscape Architecture*, 354–56. Clark reports on the changing fashion in residential architecture during these decades, noting that *House and Garden* ranch house models would be landscaped with a "highly stylized version of nature" (*American Family Home*, 212).

83. Lawrence, *Gardening for Love*, 18. Lawrence was also unhappy with the traditional female stereotype of being better with plant material than design.

84. Brown and Maddox, "Women and the Land," 69.

85. Spirn practices what she preaches. She has worked with the Boston Urban Gardeners on the design and development of their projects (S. B. Warner, *To Dwell Is To Garden*, 33).

86. Spirn, *Granite Garden*, 5.

87. Whyte, *Last Landscape*, 327.


CHAPTER FIVE

1. A. G. Hill, *Forty Years of Gardening*, 127.

2. Merchant, "Women of the Progressive Conservation Movement."

3. Ibid., 70; Doughty, *Feather Fashions*, 43–50. Bird protection campaigns joined the interests of those engaged in benign uses of wildlife with sporthunting elites upset over the decimation of game populations (see Dunlap, *Saving America's Wildlife*, 3–17).

4. Dunlap, *Saving America's Wildlife*, 92–97; Hays, *Beauty, Health, and Permanence*, 112; Mighetto, "Wildlife Protection"; J. Turner, *Reckoning with the Beast*, 92–93.

5. Merchant, "Women of the Progressive Conservation Movement," 77–79; Fox, *John Muir*, 344.
6. Ryan, *Womanhood*, 261.
7. Chafe, *American Woman*, 237; Ryan, *Womanhood*, 281.
8. Hays documents the divisions between hunting and antihunting agendas (*Beauty, Health, and Permanence*, 111–12). On women's place in such conflicts, see Fox, *John Muir*, 334–36. Dunlap agrees that political involvement in conservation organizations generally stabilized for a time after World War II but argues that the stage was set for the upswings of the 1960s by a proliferation of popular books and films depicting wild animals (*Saving America's Wildlife*, 103).
9. L. L. Gould, *Lady Bird Johnson*, 60 (quotation).
10. Hays charts the overlap in the 1960s of earlier concerns for the protection of natural environments and new fears about threats posed by industrial pollution of air and water. Although he argues that the post–World War II agenda shifted from conservation issues to environmental concerns, he notes that the term *conservation* continued to be used by the new generation of environmentalists (*Beauty, Health, and Permanence*, 54–56). L. L. Gould's comprehensive study of Lady Bird Johnson's environmental agenda convincingly demonstrates her wide-ranging commitment to quality-of-life issues facing urban America. Quoting from her diaries and speeches, he shows the first lady's concern about air and water pollution and urban blight, as well as interest in wilderness preservation and city beautification (*Lady Bird Johnson*, 36, 38, 42, 44, 62, 202).
11. L. L. Gould, *Lady Bird Johnson*, 51–61 (quotations, 60–61). Gould cites instances where the president clearly evidenced an "implicit masculine uneasiness with natural beauty as a cultural value" (224).
12. Ibid., 146, 150–51.
13. L. L. Gould argues that Lady Bird Johnson deserves a place beside Rachel Carson as one of the founders of the contemporary environmental movement (ibid., 245). While Gould convincingly demonstrates Johnson's contributions (particularly in the preservation of native wildflowers), Carson's scientific training and literary skill in *Silent Spring* made her voice more influential to a broad public.
14. Hays, *Beauty, Health, and Permanence*, 53–55.
15. For evaluations of Carson's centrality to a public shift in environmental attitudes, see Fox, *John Muir*, 292; Dunlap, *DDT*, 98–125, and *Saving America's Wildlife*, 105; Perkins, *Insects, Experts*, 33.
16. Perkins (*Insects, Experts*) has done the most on Carson's critique of entomology; Brooks (*House of Life*) chronicles her network of correspondence with other scientists as she built the arguments in *Silent Spring*; and Graham (*Since Silent Spring*) provides a good history of the scientific and governmental responses to *Silent Spring*.
17. Fox (*John Muir*) provides some research suggestions for the study of women's contributions to conservation and environmentalism. L. L. Gould (*Lady Bird Johnson*) suggests a continuing tradition in women's activism from the 1920s to the 1960s. Dunlap (*Saving America's Wildlife*) provides some history of female contri-

butions to wildlife preservation efforts. No one has demonstrated how women's agendas drew them together in effective coalitions for public change during these years. Hynes (*Recurring Silent Spring*) argues that Carson's "work is a watershed for women" in the environmentalist movement (50) but does not make any direct links between Carson and the other women conservationists of her time.

18. The best biography of Carson is Brooks, *House of Life*, from which my summary of her early years is drawn.

19. Ibid., 34.

20. Ibid., 127–31, 319.

21. "The Real World Around Us," speech given to Theta Sigma Phi, April 21, 1954, Columbus, Ohio, pp. 2–3, 16–17, Rachel Carson Collection, Beinecke Library, Yale University (hereafter cited as Carson Collection, BL/YU). These comments are reprinted in Brooks, *House of Life*, 132.

22. Announcement of the selection of *The Edge of the Sea* as the "outstanding book of the year" by the Letters Committee, National Council of Women, November 27, 1956, Carson Collection, BL/YU. On the limitation of women's scientific careers in the 1930s and 1940s and the rise of "women's prizes," see Rossiter, *Women Scientists*, 315.

23. On the home/household imagery of ecology, see Worster, *Nature's Economy*, 37; Merchant, "Earthcare," 6–111. For a more complete discussion of Carson's use of these metaphors in her published works, see Norwood, "The Nature of Knowing."

24. Carson, *Edge of the Sea*, 55.

25. Worster quotes from Ernest Haeckel (who coined the term *ecology* in the nineteenth century): "The living organisms of the earth constitute a single economic unit resembling a household or family dwelling intimately together in conflict as well as in mutual aid" (*Nature's Economy*, 192).

26. Carson, *Edge of the Sea*, 3.

27. Ibid., 100. For comments on scientific nomenclature versus true understanding, see *Edge of the Sea*, vii–viii.

28. "The Real World Around Us," 15, Carson Collection, BL/YU, quoted by permission of Frances Collin, Trustee of the Carson Collection. On Carson's reluctance to join clubs, see Brooks, *House of Life*, 320.

29. "The Real World Around Us," 15–16. Sections of this speech appear in Carson's last text, *The Sense of Wonder*, and in Brooks, *House of Life*, 324–26.

30. "The Real World Around Us," 17, quoted in Brooks, *House of Life*, 326. Carson first evinced concern about the dangers of DDT in 1945 (Brooks, *House of Life*, 228).

31. "For the Attention of League Members Most Interested in Food Safety," leaflet published by the Swarthmore, Pa., League of Women Voters, 1962; Carson to Jane Brown Gemmill, Co-Chairman, Food Safety Committee, League of Women Voters, Swarthmore, Pa., January 22, February 9, 1962. Leaflet and letters in Carson Collection, BL/YU.

32. Citing Talcott Parsons as evidence, Ryan presents a strong case for the confining impact of the "feminine mystique" on middle-class women of the 1950s, arguing

that women's ideological (if not actual) relegation to the home made them less willing than previous generations to carry the concerns of domestic life into the public sphere (*Womanhood*, 260–61). In this judgment, she neglects the efforts of such public-spirited groups as the League of Women Voters. Hays discusses the league's contribution to air and water pollution agendas in the 1960s (*Beauty, Health, and Permanence*, 460).

33. Brooks, *House of Life*, 257.

34. *Silent Spring* campaign file (for proofs' mailing list); Pauline Tomkins, General Director, AAUW, Washington, D.C., to Anne Ford, Houghton Mifflin, June 4, 1962; Edith H. Sherrard, Staff Associate, Social and Economic Issues, AAUW, to Carson, November 8, 1962. File and letters in Carson Collection, BL/YU. See also Sterling, *Sea and Earth*, 176.

35. On industry's response to *Silent Spring*, see Brooks, *House of Life*, 296–98; Graham, *Since Silent Spring*, 48–68. The woman garden expert was Cynthia Westcott, the "plant doctor," who initially wrote a very critical review of *Silent Spring*. Using both her own experience and materials prepared by the Entomological Society of America, she asserted that chemicals had actually done little harm and asked, "would you sit by and let the flies destroy the citrus crop or would you approve an eradication program that may inconvenience tourists, injure paint on automobiles, possibly kill some fish but ensure the continuance of Vitamin C for our nation's health?" ("The Question Has Two Sides"). The argument that chemicals protect the country and the world from famine and food shortages is debunked in Perkins, "Insects, Food, and Hunger."

36. Correspondence between Mrs. J. Lewis (Ruth) Scott and Carson, June 16, September 18, 28, October 6, December 15, 1961, January 29, February 2, 1962, February 5, 8, September 8, 1963, Carson Collection, BL/YU.

37. Speech to Garden Club of America's annual meeting, Philadelphia, January 8, 1963, p. 5, Carson Collection, BL/YU.

38. Carson, *Silent Spring*, 24.

39. For discussions of these hazards, see *Silent Spring*, 24, 38, 97–98, 153, 158–59.

40. For example, in 1963 the Federation of Homemakers circulated among its members a document entitled "Additional Ammunition." It was a copy of Carson's June 4, 1963, statement on "Environmental Hazards, Control of Pesticides, and Other Chemical Poisons" before a subcommittee of the Committee on Government Operations, Carson Collection, BL/YU.

41. Carson, *Silent Spring*, 170, 186.

42. Acceptance speech for Woman of Conscience award, National Council of Women, Washington, D.C., June 19, 1963, Carson Collection, BL/YU, quoted by permission of Frances Collin, Trustee of the Carson Collection.

43. On Carson's connection to such circles, see Fox, *John Muir*, 292–93; Brooks, *House of Life*, 79, 99.

44. Mrs. J. Lewis (Ruth) Scott, "Conservation Report, June 1961, Roadside Vegetation Management Project, Number 1," Audubon Society of Western Pennsylvania, Carson Collection, BL/YU.

45. For examples of Carson's enjoyment of bird-watching, see Carson to Shirley Briggs, July 14, 1942, and Carson to Ada Govan, March 22, 1946, Carson Collection, BL/YU.
46. A good example of the "Conservation in Action" series is "Mattamuskeet: A National Wildlife Refuge."
47. Dunlap, *Saving America's Wildlife*, 94–96; Fox, *John Muir*, 174–82, 338–35. Taylor ("Oh, Hawk of Mercy!") provides a history of Edge's work and an interview. The tone of Taylor's article reflects the period's dislike of Edge's intensity about the issues.
48. Dunlap, *Saving America's Wildlife*, 93–94. Dunlap notes that in most organizations of the time, "men did the managing, women the protesting" (93).
49. Quoted in Brooks, *House of Life*, 8–9.
50. Carson, *Under the Sea Wind*, 74, and *Silent Spring*, 54 (quotation), 83.
51. Quoted in Brooks, *House of Life*, 232.
52. Brooks (ibid., 233) quotes Carson's crediting of Huckins's personal letter for the genesis of *Silent Spring*. On the Huckins-Carson friendship, see Sterling, *Sea and Earth*, 147.
53. Carson, *Silent Spring*, 72–73. For other citations of women's letters, see pp. 97–98, 106–7.
54. Ibid., 73.
55. Quoted in Brooks, *House of Life*, 232.
56. On the importance of birding activities to the rise of animal rights movements and wildlife protection, and women's involvement in both, see Doughty, *Feather Fashions*, 43–50; Mighetto, "Wildlife Protection," 38–42; J. Turner, *Reckoning with the Beast*, 125–37.
57. On women's dominance of the humane education movement, see J. Turner, *Reckoning with the Beast*, 76. On the ties between animal rights organizations and the Audubon societies and women's participation in both groups, see Doughty, *Feather Fashions*, 43–44.
58. J. Turner, *Reckoning with the Beast*, 135–36. Thomas argues that seventeenth-century theology, which taught that "the continuation of every species was surely a part of the divine plan," helped set the stage for widespread acceptance of ecology in the nineteenth and twentieth centuries (*Man and the Natural World*, 278).
59. Quoted in Brooks, *House of Life*, 272.
60. *Silent Spring*, 95. For other comments on wildlife kills, see 51, 65, 67. Nash (*Rights of Nature*, 79–80) states that Carson did not extend rights to animal victims in *Silent Spring* because she was arguing that cruelty to animals "diminished" human beings. I contend that both in her private life and in her public pronouncements, Carson deliberately placed herself in league with the new initiatives of the humane movement.
61. Brooks, *House of Life*, 253 (Carson's letter to the *Washington Post*); J. Turner, *Reckoning with the Beast*, 117–21; Rowan, *Of Mice, Models, and Men*, 49–60. The Animal Welfare Institute continues to work for animal rights (see Leavitt, *Animals and Their Legal Rights*).

62. Correspondence between Carson and Christine Stevens, April 21, 23, 1959, July 26, 1962, January 7, 1964, Carson Collection, BL/YU. Carson recommended that Stevens read Lois Crisler's *Arctic Wild* and correspond with Crisler about predator control efforts in Alaska. Carson and Crisler were incensed at Fish and Wildlife predator poisoning campaigns (Carson to Crisler, May 7, 1959, Carson Collection, BL/YU). Carson encouraged Marjorie Spock to acquaint herself with Stevens's work (Carson to Spock, January 29, 1960, Carson Collection, BL/YU). Carson also wrote a preface to an Animal Welfare Institute publication, *Humane Biology Projects*, which was reprinted in the *Atlantic Naturalist* 15 (October–December 1960): 249. In this statement, Carson argued that biology should be taught first through observation of live animals in the field, not by "placing unnatural restraints upon living creatures or . . . subjecting them to unnatural conditions or to changes in their bodily structure." Finally, in joining the Defenders of Wildlife, Carson aligned herself with the radical wing of wildlife conservation groups: Defenders was founded on the coals of the Anti-Steel Trap League and was unafraid to take on hunting interests (Dunlap, *Saving America's Wildlife*, 132–34).

63. Quoted in Brooks, *House of Life*, 315. Carson's work in the animal rights arena was summarized by Ann Cottrell Free in a *Defenders of Wildlife Bulletin* in 1963–64 (quoted in Brooks, *House of Life*, 316–17).

64. In letters to Marjorie Spock on March 26, 1958, and January 29, 1960 (Carson Collection, BL/YU), Carson mentions her submission to the *Atlantic Naturalist* of an article by Dr. C. J. Briejer, a Dutch scientist whose work Spock had translated, and of other material on court cases involving spraying campaigns for Briggs to place in the *Atlantic Naturalist*. Brooks documents Carson's role in the publication of Dr. Briejer's article (*House of Life*, 240). World War II opened up journalistic work for women, some of whom were war correspondents, while others held jobs from which they had previously been excluded—on the copy desk, for example. By January 1945 there were 135 women in the House and Senate galleries. Prior to the war, women had made a name for themselves as columnists, and between 1930 and 1970 some of the most famous "alternative," dissenting journalists were women. To illustrate, Dorothy Day gained prominence in the peace movement through the *Catholic Worker* and Ada Louise Huxtable was a founding member of the Urban Writer's Society, a group working on city problems and the environment. On women's contributions to journalism, see Emery and Emery, *The Press and America*, 439, 574, 577; Mott, *American Journalism*.

65. Correspondence between Carson and Ann Free, December 1, 7, 1959, January 5, 1960, August 9, 1961, March 25, 1962, Carson Collection, BL/YU. See also Free, "A Humane Question."

66. Quoted in Brooks, *House of Life*, 253.

67. Correspondence between Carson and Agnes (Mrs. Eugene) Meyer, June 18, 24, November 26, 1962, Carson Collection, BL/YU. Permission to quote Agnes Meyer received from Katharine Graham and Frances Collin, Trustee of the Carson Collection.

68. Schwartz, "Great Underwater Adventure."

69. Women first took up underwater diving in numbers in the 1950s—as scuba divers. By 1976 women's participation had grown considerably, to include approximately 40,000 "certified female sport divers, instructors, researchers, and professional commercial divers" (Eugenie Clark, quoted in LaBastille, *Women and Wilderness*, 168). On Clare Booth Luce, see "A Versatile Lady's New Adventure," 68; on Simone Cousteau, see Dugan and Dugan, "She Lives with Adventure," 41. Tillman ("Recreation Goes Underwater," 62–63) describes the joys of family scuba diving.

70. Dugan and Dugan, "She Lives with Adventure," 112.

71. On the history of women's exclusion from direction of Woods Hole and their early work in marine biology, see Rossiter, *Women Scientists*, 86–88.

72. LaBastille includes an interview with Clark in which she recounts this experience (*Women and Wilderness*, 167).

73. Quotation from Carson's 1954 speech to Theta Sigma Phi, reprinted in Brooks, *House of Life*, 115. On her only expedition in diving equipment, see ibid., 113–14.

74. Not that there were that many women in Fish and Wildlife in the 1930s and 1940s. Carson was among the first two professional women hired by the service. She, Shirley Briggs, and Kay Howe, an illustrator for the agency, made trips in teams to do research for Fish and Wildlife publications like the Conservation in Action series. For a narrative of her adventures with Howe while doing such work, see Carson to Briggs, September 28, 1946, Carson Collection, BL/YU. For her account of a trip with Briggs to the Florida Everglades, see Brooks, *House of Life*, 81–83.

75. Her most extensive correspondence of this sort was carried on with Marjorie Spock, who had instituted a widely publicized suit in May 1957 to stop DDT spraying on Long Island. The connection to Spock is discussed in Brooks, *House of Life*, 234, 258.

76. "Appeal Could Halt Dieldrin"; Swarts, "Papa Is Wrong"; "Controversy over Insecticide Divides a City."

77. Editorial, *Cambridge Banner*, October 13, 1962; R. D. Symons to Carson, May 12, 1962, Carson Collection, BL/YU; Leonard, "Review of *Silent Spring*" and "The Public and *Silent Spring*"; Bean, "The Noise of *Silent Spring*." For other examples of gender-based attacks on Carson, see Graham, *Since Silent Spring*, 50, 56, 88. On the links between Carson and Kelsey, see Dunlap, *DDT*, 104–5. It is important to stress that Carson had close, supportive friendships with men as well as women; her correspondence is filled with warm letters to both. Hynes probably exaggerates when she argues that Carson "kept [men] at a distance" (*Recurring Silent Spring*, 65). My contention is rather that among certain men Carson elicited antagonism based in part on her sex.

78. Ryan points out a similar bounding of women's freedom among men whose wives worked—women should not be so successful as to challenge their husband's position as primary breadwinner in the family (*Womanhood*, 286).

79. Quoted in Brooks, *House of Life*, 241.

80. Perkins states that "biological control in the U.S. nearly died as a recognizable field

of research from the 1940s to the 1960s" (*Insects, Experts*, 68).

81. For an overview of this issue, see Harding and O'Barr, *Sex and Scientific Inquiry*.

82. Kuhn, *Structure of Scientific Revolutions*, 5–8.

83. Carson, *Silent Spring*, 261.

84. Perkins (*Insects, Experts*) argues that the book did not work the paradigm change among entomologists that Carson sought—rather, insect resistance to pesticides proved most important in changing scientific entomology. He also notes, however, that the public furor about pesticides generated by the book led to increased funding for research into biological control (33, 90).

85. Kuhn states that "one of the strongest . . . rules of scientific life is the prohibition of appeals to heads of state or to the populace at large in matters scientific" (*Structure of Scientific Revolutions*, 168). Perkins (*Insects, Experts*, 32–33) and Dunlap (*DDT*, 122–23) argue that some of the scientific community's negative response to the book sprang from their sense that science was a closed community, not to be intruded upon by "outsiders" of any kind. Ironically, Kuhn has shown that the initial push for a revolutionary paradigm in science often comes from an outsider to the field (133, 144).

86. "Tomorrow's Spring," address given at the "All-Women Conference," sponsored by the National Council of Women of the United States, New York City, October, 11, 1962, pp. 1–11, Carson Collection, BL/YU, quoted by permission of Frances Collin, Trustee of the Carson Collection.


CHAPTER SIX

1. On the origins of ideas connecting women to a disruptive nature, see Merchant, *Death of Nature* and *Ecological Revolutions*. On the ways that biological models of "women's nature" have constricted their social freedom, see Bleier, *Science and Gender*; Russett, *Sexual Science*.

2. I have chosen to focus this chapter on fiction and memoir. As Denise Levertov's "Come Into Animal Presence" suggests, poets, too, offer a rich source of insight into women's struggle to reconnect with the animal kingdom.

3. Both Fox (*John Muir*, 355–56) and Hays (*Beauty, Health, and Permanence*, 305–7) discuss recent attempts by environmentalist groups to broaden their ethnic base.

4. Hurston, "What White Publishers Won't Print."

5. For more complete histories of the application of such notions to African Americans and American Indians, see Berkhofer, *White Man's Indian*; W. R. Comstock, "On Seeing with the Eye of the Native European"; Dudley and Novak, *Wild Man Within*; Fredrickson, *Black Image*; S. J. Gould, *The Mismeasure of Man*.

6. Gilman, "Black Bodies, White Bodies." On the alleged "wild" passions of American Indian and African American women, see Dearborn, *Pocahontas's Daughters*, 113–20. Collins further explores the use of these connections between black women and white prostitutes in the antebellum South, arguing that "Black 'whores' make white 'virgins' possible" (*Black Feminist Thought*, 175–76).

7. Carby, *Reconstructing Womanhood*, 20.

8. Linderman, *Pretty-shield*, 151. All further references are cited parenthetically in the text.

9. Hultkrantz, "North American Indian Religions," 89. Merchant, for example, argues that worldviews of the northern New England tribes located "no nature-culture demarcation" between humans and other animals, and that "Myth and ritual together constituted an environmental ethic that operated to hinder over-exploitation of animals" (*Ecological Revolutions*, 44–47). For a good review of the current debate on American Indian environmentalism, see R. White, "Native Americans and the Environment." For a suggestive study on the interactive processes through which Euro-Americans and American Indians may have constructed the figure of Mother Earth as a key symbol in contemporary tribal belief systems, see Gill, *Mother Earth*. On these values as expressed specifically by conservationists, see Fox, *John Muir*, 349–51. Martin ("American Indian as Miscast Ecologist") points out some of the fallacies in the image of American Indians as more responsible in their dealings with the land.

10. Pretty-shield's stories were about life before the mid-nineteenth-century contact with Euro-Americans but after the introduction of the horse by the Spaniards. At least one scholar has suggested that the coming of the horse meant much less power for plains women (Liberty, "Hell Came With Horses"), while another asserts that, for the Pawnees, horses led to dissension between men and women (R. White, "Cultural Landscape," 36).

11. Quoted in Van Steen, *Pauline Johnson*, 3.

12. Parker, Introduction to *The Moccasin Maker*, 6. All further references to *The Moccasin Maker* are cited parenthetically in the text.

13. Smith and Allen, "Earthy Relations," 178. All further references to Silko's collection, *Storyteller*, are cited parenthetically in the text.

14. A fine example of American Indian environmental specificity was evidenced recently in a collection of essays meant to showcase the best contemporary nature writers. The sole woman of color included was Leslie Silko, who produced an essay on the spiritual meanings of the desert home of the Hopi, "Landscape, History, and the Pueblo Imagination."

15. Marshall, *Praisesong for the Widow*, 37–39.

16. Walker, *Our Mothers' Gardens*, 143. All further references are cited parenthetically in the text.

17. For an extended analysis of the landscapes of Walker's fiction, see Dixon, *Ride Out the Wilderness*, 94–108. Barbara Christian has explored the nature imagery in Morrison's previous novels in *Black Feminist Criticism*, 47–80. See also Dixon's study of Morrison's landscapes, pp. 141–69.

18. Morrison, *Beloved*, 6. All further references are cited parenthetically in the text.

19. Yellin ("Texts and Contexts") argues convincingly for Jacobs's authorship of the narrative. For an analysis of Jacobs's struggle to write through the expected conventions of true womanhood in order to revise the cult of domesticity to fit her own circumstances, see Carby, *Reconstructing Womanhood*, 45–61. On the historical sources for *Beloved*, see Christian, "'Somebody Forgot,'" 331, 336.

20. Jacobs, *Incidents in the Life*, 19. All further references are cited parenthetically in the text. Carby documents other instances of slave women's understanding of their links to animals (*Reconstructing Womanhood*, 37–38).

21. Willis, "Crushed Geraniums," 211. Fox-Genovese's survey of slave and slaveholder narratives indicates that it was common for white women of the higher classes to use slaves to tend their ornamental gardens (*Within the Plantation Household*, 117).

22. Carby, *Reconstructing Womanhood*, 27.

23. Dixon, *Ride Out the Wilderness*, 23. On the meanings of graveyards in African American communities, see Vlach, *Afro-American Tradition*, 146–47.

24. Fox-Genovese's study of the power relations between female slaves and male masters in the antebellum South emphasizes the extent to which women "lived always on the edge of an abyss, always confronted a dangerous world" (*Within the Plantation Household*, 396).

25. Carby notes that the North was not much better, that much of Jacobs's narrative exposes the racism and collusion northerners practiced. At one point, Jacobs cast northerners as "bloodhounds" in service to slavery (Carby, *Reconstructing Womanhood*, 55–56).

26. Fox-Genovese, *Within the Plantation Household*, 301; Christian, "'Somebody Forgot,'" 330–31. J. Jones argues that African women, as participants in subsistence agriculture at home, brought with them much plant knowledge and skill, but that given the variety in gender divisions among African tribes and the disruptive effects of plantation field labor, it is difficult to generalize about slave women's agricultural expertise (*Labor of Love*, 39).

27. Levine, *Black Culture*, 73. For an extensive discussion of the intertwining of African slaves' beliefs and their experiences in the South, see ibid., 3–81.

28. On Hurston's work collecting tales and beliefs with links to African traditions, see M. B. Brown, "Zora Neale Hurston."

29. Hurston, *Their Eyes Were Watching God*, 35. All further references are cited in the text.

30. My reading here is based on Walker's analysis of the relationship between Janie and Tea Cake as defined in his display of ownership (*Our Mothers' Gardens*, 305–6); see also Collins, *Black Feminist Thought*, 188–89. Willis notes that in leaving Killicks and taking up with Starks, Janie experiences a shift in role from beast of burden to "domestic pet." Willis ignores the tensions between Janie and Tea Cake in her interpretation of their lives on the muck as utopian (*Specifying*, 48–50). On Hurston's understanding of the connections between being a pet and being victimized and her understanding of this form of domination, see Collins, *Black Feminist Thought*, 174–75.

31. Christian argues that this inclusion of African worldviews in a historical novel about a slave is part of Morrison's attempt to retrieve a portion of African American history that was suppressed in narratives and novels produced by blacks in the nineteenth century. This is part of the historic revision that she sees contemporary novelists performing ("'Somebody Forgot,'" 330, 340).

32. Parrinder, *African Traditional Religion*, 53.

33. Much of Walker's writing locates female creativity and connection to nature in African American women's garden activities, including memories of her mother's garden and the discovery that Hurston herself had a flower garden (*Our Mothers' Gardens*, 114, 241).

34. S. Griffin, *Woman and Nature*, 187.

35. Ibid., 31, 103–6. Ortner ("Is Female to Male as Nature Is to Culture?") early posited these dualities as cultural universals. Later scholars have disagreed, finding that the opposition of nature to culture and male to female is not predominant across cultures. All do agree, however, on the importance of the duality between nature and culture for British and American Victorians. For revisions of Ortner, see MacCormack and Strathern, *Nature, Culture, and Gender*; Rosaldo, "Use and Abuse of Anthropology"; Collier and Yanagisako, *Gender and Kinship*.

36. Kelley argues that literary domestics felt that dominant culture "mocked" the serious values originating in home and raised a defense of their sphere in their novels (*Private Woman*, 309). Jewett was one of the "local color" or "regional" New England writers who concentrated on evoking the sense of place in her fiction. In describing the whaling villages of the region, she emphasized the biophysical landscape and located her characters in a natural setting much as Susan Cooper had centered herself in Otsego.

37. "A White Heron" and several other stories appear in a collection of Jewett's works that includes the novel, *The Country of the Pointed Firs*. The novel itself is composed of short vignettes on various characters. All further references are to this collection and are cited parenthetically in the text.

38. Stouck, "*Country of the Pointed Firs*"; Magowan, "Pastoral and the Art of Landscape."

39. Cary (*Appreciation of Sarah Orne Jewett*) and Pratt ("Women and Nature") see "A White Heron" as a prefeminist attempt to break free of scientific/technical control of the world and enter some other relationship with nature. While this is true, I argue that the story is very much grounded in the historical moment, that the other relationship with nature was one women naturalists of her time had a hand in defining. That Sylvie's space is invaded by a scientist rather than a man collecting birds for use in fashion suggests that Jewett was aware that women were trying at this time to find a way into bird study in keeping with their own values. Jewett echoed Olive Thorne Miller's warning that they could not enter by way of the gun. Miller, however, more sanguine than Jewett that scientific culture offered them a niche, suggested that ornithology was changing. Jewett cautioned that the women should be wary of such science and remain true to their own "nature." Thus, Jewett envisions Sylvie, who is a wonderfully expert watcher at the nest, as an instinctive naturalist in no need of training or advice from the ornithologist. In this way, Jewett preserves America domestica from intrusion by the scientist, whom she depicts as a representative of the threatening values of the city. It does not help his cause that he tries to pay Sylvie, who lives in modest poverty, to lead him to the bird. In this, he represents the intrusion of the false values of the market economy just as surely as if he were hunting the bird for its use in women's hats.

40. Pratt argues that Sylvie is not "plumbing" nature for "usable aesthetic images" but accepting it on its own terms ("Women and Nature," 479). I argue, rather, that she is plumbing nature for usable domestic images.

41. There are men in the village, and they become subsumed in the gentility women create. Like William, however, these men have been factored out of the public stage and are not involved in the aggressive expansionism of the day. There are also very few of them.

42. Smith-Rosenberg argues that it was at the turn of the twentieth century that women began to seek a vocabulary that would describe, rather than mask, their sexuality. She also documents the struggles between men and women to control language describing this sexuality (*Disorderly Conduct*, 245–96).

43. Ryan, *Womanhood*, 262–67; May, *Homeward Bound*, 92–161.

44. Shutting her ears to Ralph's stories of the differences between male and female horses, she asserts that they are simply different species. At various points in her life she considers marriage to the neighbor's dog, a horse at the ranch, and her brother (Stafford, *The Mountain Lion*, 125). All further references to *The Mountain Lion* are cited parenthetically in the text.

45. See Pilkington's Introduction to *The Mountain Lion*, xiii.

46. Roberts argues that *The Mountain Lion* was based on Stafford's childhood and suggests that she may have suffered from anorexia (*Jean Stafford*, 259–65, 322). If Stafford is here suggesting that Molly is anoretic, it is not because she imagines Molly to be enmeshed in the same marketing of slenderness that some have argued drives such urges in contemporary young women. Rather, her anorexia fits with the nineteenth-century rejection of marketplace invasion of private domesticity (the anoretic refuses consumption and garners an ultimate form of self-control) that Gillian Brown outlines in *Domestic Individualism*, 189–93.

47. Reflecting, perhaps, the 1950s' emphasis on the middle-class home as the seat of consumer society and the emergence of that role in the nineteenth century, Stafford casts Molly's mother and sisters as shallow, artificial materialists, much like the hothouse flowers Susan Cooper warned against.

48. These debates did not wane in the 1980s. For examples of the discussion that spanned the decade, see Spelman, "Woman as Body"; Hite, "Writing—and Reading—the Body."

49. Christ, "Margaret Atwood"; Piercy, "Margaret Atwood."

50. Pratt, *Archetypal Patterns*, 158.

51. Atwood, *Surfacing*, 44. All further references are cited parenthetically in the text.

52. Quoted in Christ, "Margaret Atwood," 328.

53. Piercy, "Margaret Atwood," 44.

54. Silko's essay, "Landscape, History, and the Pueblo Imagination," was the only piece by a woman of color in the recent *Antaeus* collection of contemporary nature writers. Although it provides a sensitive rendition of Pueblo beliefs about nature, Silko's essay does not tackle the problems inherent in Euro-Americans' interpretation of American Indian environmentalism. Both Alice Walker's *Our Mother's Gardens* and *Living by the Word* include essays considering her feelings for nature.

Such essays also delve into the race and class issues dividing African American and Euro-American environmental values. Their political tone does not quite fit the approach taken in most of the nature essays appearing in collections. For another representative sampling of contemporary nature writers similarly limited to Euro-American perspectives, see Trimble, *Words from the Land*.

CHAPTER SEVEN

1. In his biography of Fossey, *Woman in the Mists*, Mowat provides a sympathetic overview of her life; Hayes offers a more critical view in *The Dark Romance of Dian Fossey*. For an alternative interpretation of popular stereotypes about Fossey and other women who work with primates, see Haraway, *Primate Visions*, 146–85.

2. A good survey of these issues is Fedigan and Fedigan's "Gender and the Study of Primates."

3. The best history of wildlife perception and policy is Dunlap's *Saving America's Wildlife*. For other commentary on these developments, see Nash, *Wilderness*; Haraway, *Primate Visions*.

4. One of the most famous wives to go on an early collecting expedition was Elizabeth Agassiz, wife of Louis; see her account, *A Journey in Brazil* (1868). In the American West, J. G. Lemmon and his wife Sara Allen Plummer collected plants during the 1880s in California, Nevada, and Arizona. Like Florence Merriam Bailey and her husband Vernon, the Lemmons shared a passion for nature study; see his account of their honeymoon trip collecting in the Santa Catalina Mountains of Arizona, "A Botanical Wedding Trip" (1881), and Crosswhite, "'J. G. Lemmon and Wife.'" California, particularly San Francisco, drew naturalists in the late nineteenth and early twentieth centuries, many of them women. Kate Sessions, the San Diego landscaper, was good friends with one of the most famous—Alice Eastwood. Never married, Eastwood devoted her life to plant collecting, much of it in isolated areas of Colorado and California. On the California naturalists, see Ewan, "San Francisco as a Mecca." On Eastwood, see C. G. Wilson, *Alice Eastwood's Wonderland*. Other solitary women combined even more exotic travel with nature study. One of the most famous was Ynes Mexia, whose reports on plants and animals in Mexico, Brazil, and Ecuador combined wilderness adventure with scientific observations. (See Tinling, *Women into the Unknown*, 181–88; Mexia, "Botanical Trails in Old Mexico" and "Birds of Brazil.")

5. Benson, *Martha Maxwell*, 68. This is the only complete biography of Maxwell, and I rely on it heavily for factual information. Much of Benson's history, including this quotation, is based on the account of her life by Maxwell's sister, Mary Dartt, entitled *On the Plains and Among the Peaks*, 17.

6. Dartt, *On the Plains*, 34.

7. Benson, *Martha Maxwell*, 79, 85, 97, 104, 170–71. On the aesthetics of natural history museum displays, see ibid., 140–41; Parr, "The Habitat Group"; Haraway, *Primate Visions*, 36–38.

8. Benson, *Martha Maxwell*, 133.

9. Dartt, *On the Plains*, 5–9.

10. Haraway provides a good reading of the masculine imagery in scientific collecting and taxidermy during the late nineteenth and early twentieth century (*Primate Visions*, 38–42).

11. Dartt, *On the Plains*, 25–26, 33–34, 124–30. Dartt's narrative constructs a reformed Eve who first takes up the gun to save her sister from a snake, then shoots her specimens as part of her effort to make more realistic displays, and never, never violates the "rights" of her prey to a quick and painless death.

12. Maxwell quoted in ibid., 69–73, 119.

13. On the extent to which Progressive Era women were excluded from professional environmental activities and scientific careers, see Merchant, "Women of the Progressive Conservation Movement"; Rossiter, *Women Scientists*. Haraway argues that scientific collecting and taxidermy were so neurotically masculine that no stories of women's work in these areas were allowed to surface in the establishment; such women threatened the integrity of the narrative of initiation into manhood through bloody dominance of wild animals (*Primate Visions*, 40, 52). One wonders, then, what to make of Elliott Coues's public celebration of Martha Maxwell's achievements as a collector and taxidermist (Dartt, *On the Plains*, 217). Rather than posing a threat to the story of virility that male scientists were constructing in the late nineteenth century, Maxwell's mode of collecting—as conveyed by herself and her sister—seems to have been accepted as a complement to the men's story in its focus on women's maintenance of *their* role through such activity. Coues does not mention the conflicts Maxwell and her sister had to settle to make her work mesh with the goals of masculine science.

14. Little attention has been paid to women's work as zoological collectors for scientific institutions, perhaps because scholars have tended to believe the popular image that women did not hunt. While they are a minority, women certainly have engaged in various hunting activities, of which scientific collecting is one. This was true not only of Martha Maxwell but also of Annie Montague Alexander, patron of the Museum of Vertebrate Zoology at the University of California, Berkeley. During the early twentieth century, Montague collected paleontological specimens and recent mammals for the museum (Zullo, "Annie Montague Alexander").

15. On American involvement in these efforts, see Dunlap, *Saving America's Wildlife*, 7; Nash, *Wilderness*, 350–59. For an excellent collection of essays on the history and problems of the importation of colonial conservation methods and goals into Africa, see Anderson and Grove, *Conservation in Africa*.

16. Tinling (*Women into the Unknown*, 11) and Olds (*Women of the Four Winds*, 84) envision Delia as a somewhat reluctant hunter, whereas Haraway (*Primate Visions*, 49) stresses her enjoyment of the hunt.

17. D. Akeley, "My First Elephant," 16–26; Olds, *Women of the Four Winds*, 82–91.

18. Bradley, *On the Gorilla Trail*, 2–3.

19. D. Akeley, "My First Elephant," 29 (quotation, 20–21).

20. Ibid., 29.

21. D. Akeley, *Jungle Portraits*, 82.

22. Seeing what they expected to see in elephant groups, early collectors had not realized that elephants lived in matriarchies. On elephant social organization, see Moss, *Elephant Memories*.

23. D. Akeley, *Jungle Portraits*, 84–94 (quotations, 84, 94).

24. Bradley, *On the Gorilla Trail*, 65–67, 168, 177.

25. Haraway, *Primate Visions*, 31–35, 386.

26. Bradley, *On the Gorilla Trail*, 5, 115–16.

27. Ibid., 133.

28. C. E. Akeley, *In Brightest Africa*, 226; Haraway, *Primate Visions*, 34 (quotation).

29. For a history of wildlife photography, see Guggisberg, *Early Wildlife Photographers*.

30. Roosevelt in Wallihan and Wallihan, *Hoofs, Claws, and Antlers* (unpaged) and *Camera Shots*, 11–12. Roosevelt was not, of course, arguing for an end to hunting, but for a sort of release valve that would lead to a decline in professional hunting in particular.

31. Wallihan and Wallihan, *Hoofs, Claws, and Antlers*.

32. Ibid.

33. Ibid., "Deer Plate #28, Doubles at One Shot" and "Deer Plate #43, Mrs. Wallihan's 30th Deer."

34. Wallihan and Wallihan, *Camera Shots*, 75.

35. Guggisberg, *Early Wildlife Photographers*, 95–103.

36. Haraway, *Primate Visions*, 43.

37. Osa Johnson's *I Married Adventure* contains the story of both of their lives up to Martin's death.

38. Ibid., 204–5, 218–19, 233; O. Johnson, *Four Years in Paradise*, 109 (bustard quotation).

39. O. Johnson, *Four Years in Paradise*, 72. Haraway (*Primate Visions*, 45) quotes from their prospectus seeking funding from the American Museum for a film depicting various species of animal babies and maternal care.

40. O. Johnson, *I Married Adventure*, 288.

41. O. Johnson, *Four Years in Paradise*, 41 (quotation), and *I Married Adventure*, 254, 296–98.

42. O. Johnson, *Four Years in Paradise*, 74, and *I Married Adventure*, 308–9. Schaller found that pride groups actually spend little time at play (*The Serengeti Lion*, 55). Although the Johnsons did contribute to the understanding that lions have another life besides the kill, lions (and lionesses) can pose more of a threat to cubs than the Johnsons depicted. For a study of pride behavior, see Rudnai, *Social Life of the Lion*.

43. O. Johnson, *Four Years in Paradise*, 148–52.

44. O. Johnson, *I Married Adventure*, 9.

45. Haraway, *Primate Visions*, 44.

46. For a popular overview of changing ideas about such wildlife, see Rensberger, *Cult of the Wild*. For more rigorous studies, see Rudnai, *Social Life of the Lion*; Moss, *Elephant Memories*.

47. Bradley, *On the Gorilla Trail*, 4.

48. Haraway (*Primate Visions*, 43, 151) argues that the image of the woman nurturer developed with the contemporary group of women Louis Leakey sent into the African jungle, but the narratives of the 1920s and 1930s indicate that both men and women assumed that women would play a key role in nurturing the first specimens brought back to America. For a journalistic, and heavily biased, history of these women, see Emily Hahn's *Eve and the Apes*. Hahn is herself a collector of apes as pets. On Delia Akeley's and Osa Johnson's "way" with animals, see D. Akeley, *Jungle Portraits*, 65, and O. Johnson, *Four Years in Paradise*, 139.

49. Hahn, *Eve and the Apes*, 42 (on Hoyt); O. Johnson, *I Married Adventure*, 174; D. Akeley, *J. T., Jr.*, 1–4; Benchley, *My Friends*, 4–11, 117.

50. Hahn, *Eve and the Apes*, 42, 60; O. Johnson, *I Married Adventure*, 191–92, 342; D. Akeley, *J. T., Jr.*, 233, 242; Benchley, *My Friends*, 17 (quotation), 188, 192.

51. Benchley, *My Friends*, 62 (quotation). I am not suggesting that Benchley was not upset by the death of animals; she was devastated when one of her special friends died. But one method for handling her grief was to rationalize that they lived happier lives in the zoo than they might have in the wild. Osa Johnson was prone to similar thinking. Upset about the way that Martin captured the two gorillas for the zoo, she reminded herself that they went on to live with "joyous gusto" in the San Diego Zoo (*I Married Adventure*, 342).

52. Akeley, *J. T., Jr.*, 11, 237–38, 245, xxiv (quotation). Familiar with the story of J. T., Mary Bradley refused to allow Alice to bring home a monkey for a pet and made the occasion an opportunity in her own narrative to chastise zoos in general (*On the Gorilla Trail*, 219).

53. D. Akeley, *Jungle Portraits*, 65–67.

54. Ibid., 54, 58.

55. Ibid., 69–70, 159, 27–28 (quotation).

56. Olds, *Women of the Four Winds*, 114–15.

57. Ibid., 189–90, 203, 208, 212–15, 219, 221–22, 224 (quotation).

58. On changing ideas about wild animals, see Dunlap, *Saving America's Wildlife*, 13–17, 19–33; Mighetto, "Science, Sentiment, and Anxiety." On nineteenth- and twentieth-century British and American images of native Africans as "primitives" and more expendable than African wildlife, see Anderson and Grove, *Conservation in Africa*; Torgovnick, *Gone Primitive*.

59. D. Akeley, *Jungle Portraits*, 203.

60. This viewpoint conflicts with Nash's argument that the extension of rights to animals followed a neatly linear progression after the extension of rights to slaves and women. Nash (*Rights of Nature*, 7) depends on legal history for the construction of his model of the gradual expansion of rights to other species, but I contend that social history reveals a somewhat less progressive narrative. Nor was Akeley's solution the only approach taken on this issue. Other women of her generation believed that Euro-Americans could turn away from their "civilization" and find a truer, more meaningful life in tribal cultures. Another important figure in women's shift into wildlife observation was Mary Hunter Austin. Whereas Akeley envisioned Africans as a people with little feeling for the plants and animals of their

native land, Austin offered portraits of American Indians whose history on the North American continent lent credulity to their beliefs about animals. Making a virtue of necessity, Austin argued, Indian tribes living in America's deserts had the best sense of how to live among other animals. An early twentieth-century feminist, Austin invested American Indian women with strength and nobility bred from their perceived closeness to nature. The hero of her nature classic, *The Land of Little Rain*, is Seyavi, a basket maker whose life is completely integrated with the landscape. Unfortunately, in her enthusiasm to connect Seyavi to other animals, Austin compares her to a "stray" dog, "slinking savage and afraid." Austin chose one of the most racist stereotypes that her own culture held about American Indian women to describe a "new" way of interacting with nature. As Leslie Silko shows in *Storyteller*, dominant culture has used such images of American Indian women as a means of suppression. Regardless of Austin's goodhearted motives, she stereotyped Paiutes as much as Delia Akeley did pygmies (*Land of Little Rain*, 105–6).

61. Chapman and Chapman, *Beaver Pioneers*, *Little Wolf*, and *Wilderness Wanderers*.
62. Stanwell-Fletcher, *Driftwood Valley*, 139, 354–55.
63. R. C. Miller, Introductory Note in Carrighar, *Beetle Rock*, 1. On Carrighar's contribution to the new, ecological trend in nature writing, see Dunlap, *Saving America's Wildlife*, 88.
64. Carrighar, *Beetle Rock*, 125.
65. See Carrighar, *Teton Marsh*, *Icebound Summer*, *Wild Heritage*, and *Twilight Seas*. On the Marine Mammal Protection Act of 1972, see Dunlap, *Saving America's Wildlife*, 142. Joan McIntyre, founder of Project Jonah, an activist group working to save the whales, has also written about cetaceans. Her 1974 publication, *Mind in the Waters*, is a popular collection of essays on whales and dolphins.
66. Carrighar, *Home to the Wilderness*, 278.
67. Ibid., 301, 330.
68. Stanwell-Fletcher, *Driftwood Valley*, 134.
69. An excellent history of changing attitudes in specimen collecting is embedded in Margaret Murie's *Two in the Far North*, her journal of her life as the wife of naturalist Olaus Murie. Covering the period in American wildlife study from the 1920s to the 1960s, Murie's narrative signified many changes when in her 1956 entry she stressed that scientists collected very few specimens, focusing their studies on living animals in their habitat (273). Making a similar point, Dunlap (*Saving America's Wildlife*, 74–76) contrasts the field methods of Olaus and his younger brother Adolph.
70. Crisler, *Arctic Wild*, 11.
71. Ibid., 91–92.
72. Leopold, Foreword to *Arctic Wild*, xvii.
73. Crisler, *Arctic Wild*, 157–58.
74. Ibid., 77, 32–34; Dunlap, *Saving America's Wildlife*, 101–2.
75. *Arctic Wild*, 223, 248, 267–68, 294.
76. *Captive Wild*, 234–38. For all the emotional honesty of *Captive Wild*, Lois did

not directly acknowledge the part Herb had played in stealing the young wolves. *Captive Wild* slides over the taking of the cubs with the comment that they were "acquired . . . taken as puppies from a wild ravaged den" (4). Unless one has read *Arctic Wild*, it is unclear who violated the den.

77. Ryden, *God's Dog*, *Bobcat Year*, and *Lily Pond*.

78. Haraway, *Primate Visions*, 129–32, 398–99.

79. Grier (*Biology of Animal Behavior*) provides a textbook description of the distancing scientific approach when he cautions that "this currently is a complex world of ethics, rules, regulations, and laws pertaining to live animals, both wild and captive . . . For the welfare and protection of all concerned—instructors, students, property owners, neighbors, and the animals themselves—both instructors and students must be alert to and familiar with the possible legal, ethical, and safety ramifications of *whatever* is being done with the animals" (657). On the relationships Goodall, Fossey, and Galdikas shared with their study animals, see Montgomery, *Walking with the Great Apes*.

80. Fossey, *Gorillas*, 12–14, 61, 199. See also Mowat, *Woman in the Mists*, 340.

81. Fossey, *Gorillas*, 70, 86, 104–5. Zoologists, ethologists, and cultural and biological anthropologists continue to argue the validity of interpreting animal social life using models developed from observation of human groups, and vice versa. Sperling analyzes the trends in anthropology from the 1960s to the 1980s, arguing that data on social animals like the great apes has been read to anthropomorphize the animals or animalize humans—depending on the researcher's goals. Having "re-habilitated" tribal peoples to the extent that their societies are no longer read by western intellectual elites as examples of the primitive, the great apes, in this scenario, then became next in line as models of early human society. Not only is another species observed through the lens of human society, but also, like the tribal peoples studied at the turn of the century, animals are denied individualism. Fedigan and Fedigan add another dimension to such analysis in arguing that the entry of influential women into primate studies has led to increased interest in individual variation. This was certainly true of Fossey's work. See Sperling, *Animal Liberators*, 157–93, and "Baboons with Briefcases"; Haraway, *Primate Visions*, 146–48; Fedigan and Fedigan, "Gender and the Study of Primates," 52. For ethology's perspective on the related question of how to speak about the intelligence, social life, and symbolic behavior of animals, see Grier, *Biology of Animal Behavior*, 585; J. L. Gould, *Ethology*, 278–93; D. R. Griffin, *Animal Thinking*, 155–210.

Although Fossey's work was supported by those, like Leakey, whose agenda was a better understanding of human behavior, and her popularity arose in part from wide-ranging developments in human-animal communication and in sociobiology, her interest lay in wildlife conservation, not social theory. That her work has been used in various debates concerning the links between human and animal society is another story.

82. Fossey, *Gorillas*, 18, 201 (quotation), 212–14.

83. Ibid., 150 (first quotation), 162; Mowat, *Woman in the Mists*, 281 (second quotation).

84. Fossey, *Gorillas*, 20–21, 238–42. On her attitudes toward Africans and Rwandan resentment of her treatment, see Shoumatoff, *African Madness*, 5–42. For commentary on the threats development poses to the lives and cultures of indigenous peoples in Africa, see Burger, *Report from the Frontier*.

85. Fossey, *Gorillas*, 58. On the tensions between Fossey and funding sources such as the National Geographic Society, see Mowat, *Woman in the Mists*, 237–38. Historians of postcolonial conservation initiatives in Africa would see little difference between the approaches at issue here. Most conservation projects have served to perpetuate colonial models in which a government program designed by a metropolitan elite controls and displaces rural people in order to preserve wild animals, thus displaying little real concern for the property rights of locals or respect for their traditions. See McCormick, *Reclaiming Paradise*, 43–46; Lindsay, "Integrating Parks and Pastoralists," 149–67. I argue that a basic difference between Fossey's efforts and these newer "ecodevelopment" approaches lies in Fossey's impassioned concern for individual animals with whom she had formed intimate ties.

86. Fossey, *Gorillas*, 122, 131; Mowat, *Woman in the Mists*, 108, 188, 196–98, 339.

87. Haraway, *Primate Visions*, 148–50.

88. Mowat, *Woman in the Mists*, 2.

89. The popular image of Fossey was as a scientist working on animal behavior, but her techniques were more related to old-fashioned natural history studies. She did not benefit from the new, more rigorous methods of observation, many of which were being developed by better-trained women working in animal behavior studies. Fossey's contributions to the science of animal behavior were the rich data collected on individual animals and longtime fieldwork in difficult terrain. But much of the power of her critique of international conservation approaches came from the perception that she spoke as a scientist. On women's contributions to new field study methods, see Fedigan and Fedigan, "Gender and the Study of Primates," 44.

90. Mowat, *Woman in the Mists*, 191, 238, 310 (Fossey quotation). Fedigan and Fedigan correctly caution against assuming that women have concentrated in primate studies out of a gendered interest in mothering "cute, furry, little animals . . . Adult primates in nature seldom strike the researcher as sweet or simply entertaining." But they go on to argue that women primatologists, as well as other women scientists, have been more conscious of their emotional connectedness to their research subjects, and that gender socialization helps explain these tendencies ("Gender and the Study of Primates," 51–52). In her ironic image of herself as abandoned mother to fifty-seven adult gorillas, Fossey both acknowledged that the scientific men with whom she worked trivialized her concerns by playing on such stereotypes and supported her own sense that important gender divisions played a role in her differences with the scientific conservation community.

91. Mowat, *Woman in the Mists*, 321.

92. Scheffer, "Benign Uses of Wildlife"; Kellert and Berry, *Knowledge, Affection, and*

Basic Attitudes, 59; Dunlap, Saving America's Wildlife, 152; Haraway, Primate Visions, 143–46.

93. Bauer and Bauer, Photographing Wild Texas, 10; Sacilotto, "Osprey Photo Workshops."

94. Cotton, "Wildlife Art"; Peterson, "Bird Art." The Leigh Yawkey Woodson Art Museum's 1989 "Birds in Art" catalog includes ninety-eight artists, of which fifteen are female and two are husband/wife teams. The 1987 "Wildlife in Art" catalog includes sixty-eight artists, of whom three are female, and the 1990 "Wildlife: The Artist's View" catalog includes eighty-nine artists, of whom nineteen are female. On the hunting tradition in wildlife painting, see Hammond, Twentieth-Century Wildlife Artists. Hammond's collection of the best artists of the century includes only one woman.

95. Birds in Art, Exhibition catalog, 104 (quotation). A number of the women artists combine hunting with wildlife painting—see Vivi K. Crandall's biography in Wildlife in Art, Exhibition catalog, 33. Nancy Glazier, on the other hand, loves to simply mingle with buffalo, elk, and moose (Wechsler, "N. Glazier," 38). On Janet Heaton's "Survival in the Shadows," see Wildlife: The Artist's View, Exhibition catalog, 46.

96. Fossey was disturbed about the use of one of her photographs of Digit in support of Rwandan tourist efforts, feeling that it was an invasion of "privacy" (Gorillas, 183).

97. Moss, Elephant Memories, 248, 316 (quotation). Teresia was born in 1922, the year Delia Akeley called for an extended study of elephant family life. Moss was privileged to know her during her last years as matriarch of a family group and leader in the wider social networks of the Amboseli elephants.

98. Moss, Elephant Memories, 197, 225, 297–304, 312. Haraway argues that Moss, in earlier work, contributed to "decentering" primates from the woman-animal discussion and added to feminist readings of primate group behavior. She also mentions Moss's work with tribal women (Primate Visions, 403, 416).

99. Moss, Elephant Memories, 30; Bartlett, "First She Fell in Love." Lister groups Moss with two other women, Jane Goodall and Fiona Guiness, who have provided long-term studies of animals that are "simply irreplaceable by shorter-term studies" ("A Wild Social Life," 480).

100. Moss, Elephant Memories, 89–118 (on mating behavior), 101 (the "female chauvinist" quotation). For examples of her attempts to balance objectivity and her sense of the elephants as intimates whose individual survival she cares about, see pp. 58, 155–56. Moss's study has been lauded for offering sensitive depictions of elephant social life, which raise questions about the extent to which elephants should be excluded from human feelings for "kin and community" (Eisenberg, "Family Portraits," 84).

101. Moss, Elephant Memories, 29–30, 305 (quotations, 37, 317); Mowat, Woman in the Mists, 319 (Fossey quotation).

102. Fedigan and Fedigan, "Gender and the Study of Primates," 44–45.

CHAPTER EIGHT

1. Of the women discussed in earlier chapters, Almira Lincoln Phelps, Agnes Chase, and Mary Austin demonstrated some commitment to the women's rights agendas of their time. Susan Fenimore Cooper, on the other hand, lobbied against the suffrage movement. Merchant notes that, whereas Progressive Era women involved in conservation activities disagreed on the suffrage question, the opposing camps drew on conservation rhetoric to argue for their positions ("Women of the Progressive Conservation Movement," 75–76).

2. On the history and objectives of ecofeminism, see Merchant, "Earthcare" and "Ecofeminism"; Y. King, "Healing the Wounds."

3. Y. King, "Ecology of Feminism," 25; Plant, *Healing the Wounds*; Caldecott and Leland, *Reclaim the Earth*; Diamond and Orenstein, *Reweaving the World*.

4. Merchant locates the genesis of the term itself in a 1974 essay by the French writer Françoise d'Eaubonne ("Ecofeminism," 100).

5. Ruether, *New Woman/New Earth*, 186–211 (quotation, 205). On Ruether's significance, see Plumwood, "Ecofeminism," 121–23. On the early roots of ecofeminism, see Y. King, "What Is Ecofeminism?," 702.

6. See S. Griffin, *Woman and Nature*; Gray, *Green Paradise Lost*; Merchant, *Death of Nature*; Collard, *Rape of the Wild*.

7. This literature has itself engendered a good bit of commentary, particularly among environmental philosophers. My brief summary of their work synthesizes the findings. Environmental philosophers have been interested in the different emphases among some of these women and have raised critical questions about the historical validity of parts of their narratives. Plumwood has posed the most extended critique; see also Warren, "Feminism and Ecology" and "The Power and the Promise"; Zimmerman, "Feminism, Deep Ecology."

8. See Copper, "Voice of Women's Spirituality"; Sargent, "A New Anarchism," 30–32; Brewer, "Surviving Fictions"; Barr, *Future Females*; Rosinsky, *Feminist Futures*. Of course, not all feminist science fiction falls into the ecofeminist camp. For a review of some contemporary authors who celebrate technology more than many ecofeminists might, see Haraway, "Manifesto for Cyborgs," 98–99.

9. Le Guin, *Buffalo Gals*, 10–12 (quotation, 12). All further references are cited parenthetically in the text.

10. Ruether, *New Woman/New Earth*, 204.

11. Merchant, "Ecofeminism," 100–101. Merchant bases her analysis of the schools within the feminist movement on Jaggar, *Feminist Politics*.

12. Gray, *Green Paradise Lost*, 112–16; Collard, *Rape of the Wild*, 114–15, 137–38; Salleh, "Deeper Than Deep Ecology," 340.

13. Merchant, "Ecofeminism," 102–3; Ruether, "Toward an Ecological-Feminist Theory," 148; Y. King, "What Is Ecofeminism?," 702. See also Warren, "Feminism and Ecology"; Merchant, *Ecological Revolutions*, 269–70.

14. Gray, "Nature as an Act of Imagination," 20.

15. Ibid., 20.

16. Merchant, "Ecofeminism," 103–5.

17. For an ecofeminist commentary on male writers' use of a male coyote as the "Spirit of the Earth" and "Mama Coyote's" response, see Doubiago, "Mama Coyote Talks to the Boys."

18. Merchant, *Death of Nature*, 290–95, and "Earthcare." For ecology based on the image of the earth as "household," see Worster, *Nature's Economy*, 192.

19. Collard, *Rape of the Wild*, 142–49; Kheel, "Ecofeminism," 133–34.

20. For a summary and history of the movement, see Sessions, "The Deep Ecology Movement."

21. Salleh, "Deeper Than Deep Ecology," 340; Cheney, "Eco-feminism," 118. Zimmerman ("Feminism, Deep Ecology") analyzes the two movements.

22. Zimmerman characterizes natural rights theory as a "masculinist moral system" and argues that ecofeminism critiques it as androcentric, hierarchical, dualistic, atomistic, and abstract ("Feminism, Deep Ecology," 28–29).

23. Kheel, "Liberation of Nature," 142, and "Ecofeminism," 133–35; Warren, "The Power and the Promise," 136–37. Deep ecologists share similar concerns about theoretical animal rights models but do not see the issues as bound up in the dichotomy between abstraction and concrete experience or between reason and emotion (Sessions, "The Deep Ecology Movement," 116–18).

24. See Gray, *Green Paradise Lost*, 140–43; Collard, *Rape of the Wild*, 57–104. Kheel's "From Healing Herbs" speaks in favor of the animal liberation movement in Plant, *Healing the Wounds*, 108; Benney, "All of One Flesh," is included in Caldecott and Leland, *Reclaim the Earth*; S. Abbott, "The Origins of God," appears in Diamond and Orenstein, *Reweaving the World*. The special issue of *Woman of Power* on nature includes Newkirk, "Animal Rights and the Feminist Connection," and Walker, "Why Did the Balinese Chicken Cross the Road?."

25. In this interest in the new physics, ecofeminists and some deep ecologists share a common ground. Sessions includes Capra as a key figure in the wing of deep ecology interested in developing a new ethics from the changed worldview apparently offered by the new physics ("The Deep Ecology Movement," 119). Capra has made a greater impact with these groups than other, perhaps more rigorous, popularizers like Stephen Hawking (*Brief History of Time*) because he pushes the metaphysical meanings of physics.

26. Capra, *The Tao of Physics*, as quoted in Kheel, "Liberation of Nature," 136. For other appeals to quantum physics in ecofeminist literature, see Gray, *Green Paradise Lost*, 61–68; S. Griffin, "Split Culture," 11; Spretnak, "Toward An Ecofeminist Spirituality," 129; Ruether, "Toward an Ecological-Feminist Theory," 145. Ecofeminists are drawn particularly to Capra because of his suggestion that the problem is an overemphasis on masculine forms of thinking about the world (Sessions, "The Deep Ecology Movement," 117). Robin Morgan uses quantum physics as a model of what to expect of a new feminist revolution (*Anatomy of Freedom*, 281–316).

27. Kheel, "Liberation of Nature," 141.

28. For a heated exchange on just this issue, see Sale, "Ecofeminism"; Y. King, "What Is Ecofeminism?."

29. Hawking (*Brief History of Time*, 53–63) provides a good outline of quantum physics. Carol Hill, in her fantasy novel, *The Eleven Million Mile High Dancer*, offers a nice retelling of the cat-in-the-box experiment, noting that there is little agreement among physicists about the validity of extending the weird behavior of subatomic particles to our more commonly experienced world (446–47).

30. Y. King, "Ecology of Feminism," 25.

31. Ibid., 23; Henderson, "The Warp and the Weft," 212–13; Ruether, *New Woman/New Earth*, 204–11.

32. Hamilton, "Women, Home, and Community"; Y. King, "Ecology of Feminism," 24; Merchant, "Earthcare," 13; Bagby, "A Power of Numbers" and "Building the Green Movement"; W. Brown, "Roots"; Jones and Maathai, "Greening the Desert"; Anand, "Saving Trees"; Shiva, "Indian Women."

33. Y. King, "Healing the Wounds," 112–13; P. G. Allen, "The Woman I Love"; Bagby, "A Power of Numbers."

34. For a collection of such images, see Cook and Kirk, *Greenham Women Everywhere*.

35. Gray, *Green Paradise Lost*, 158.

36. Merchant concluded *The Death of Nature* with the hint that there might be some connection between nineteenth-century women's feminism and environmental activism and the resurgence of both issues among late twentieth-century women (294). In "Women of the Progressive Conservation Movement" and *Ecological Revolutions*, however, she does not return to the question. Her "Earthcare" offers a sensitive reading of Carson's use of the concept of earth as our home. Focused on women's place in developments in scientific ecology, Merchant locates the history preceding Carson in only one woman, the nineteenth-century home economist Ellen Swallow. This is a lineage Hynes repeats in "Ellen Swallow, Lois Gibbs, and Rachel Carson." In this context, it is no wonder that ecofeminism sees itself as something new under the sun. Spretnak, for example, locates the sources of eco-feminism in "nature-based religion, usually that of the Goddess," "our own experiential explorations" into Marxist feminism, and cultural trends in environmentalism. Citing an essay by Celia Thaxter on her difficulties in converting some women to the Audubon bird campaigns, Spretnak globally dismisses earlier women as "team players, defenders of patriarchal, anthropocentric values, which is exactly what we were raised to be, too—until we figured out that the game was dreadfully wrong." Carson receives a slight nod from Spretnak as a "beacon" (along with Thoreau and Muir) whom ecofeminists have come to "appreciate" ("Toward an Ecofeminist Spirituality," 5). In an essay on the meaning of the hunt in Aldo Leopold's ecophilosophy, Kheel alludes to the "female-imaged natural world" but offers no counterexamples to Leopold to support her contention that women's relationship to animals differs from men's ("Ecofeminism," 135).

37. Merchant, "Ecofeminism," 103–5; Y. King, "Healing the Wounds," 111–13.

38. For an example of such reading, see Dinnerstein ("Survival on Earth," 197), who

argues that women, shut out of the public realm, have been able to offer only "a subordinate's critique, sealed off from the flow of formal historic event." Merchant gives a more sophisticated reading of the place of women in "capitalist culture," suggesting that definitions of their role as reproducers deeply implicated them in the flow of history. By the mid-nineteenth century, nature split into a utilitarian and a romantic or moral sphere. Women were primarily voices in the romantic sphere. Their role was to reproduce, in part through nature study, a "refuge from the stress of competition." Thus, she argues, women played a complementary role in economic progress (*Ecological Revolutions*, 247). As I see the uses of the concept of America domestica, the clear duality between the private and public spheres Merchant identifies became, after 1850, somewhat blurred.

39. For example, Kheel ("From Healing Herbs") continues the interest in women's traditional connections to plants, particularly herbal healing traditions, and Plant (*Healing the Wounds*, 1–3) views local timber trucked past her home to sawmills as "sisters and brothers . . . literally a part of us that is dying." Like their predecessors, such women locate within women's culture a different sort of botanical knowledge that is sometimes at odds with science and defined by plants common to the home and locale. Kheel ("Ecofeminism," 135–37) and Ingrid Newkirk ("Animal Rights and the Feminist Connection"), one of the founders of People for the Ethical Treatment of Animals, also appeal to women's identification with other animals. Each sets herself (and women's culture) in opposition to the dominant scientific and agricultural modes of manipulating nonhumans by according nonhumans the right to live out their domestic lives with a measure of freedom similar to that granted humans.

40. The most visible split with male environmentalists has been in the ecofeminist critique of deep ecology; see, for example, Kheel, "Ecofeminism." On the constraints of the separate spheres model, see Merchant, "Women of the Progressive Conservation Movement," 77. The grumbling imagery is from Dinnerstein, who asserts that women have served as "court jesters" who engaged only in a "complicitous grumble (maternal, but cowed; unimpressed, but self-deprecating; worried, but sheepishly proud of our big boys; amused by their silly bravado, but protective of their tender egos; afraid *for* them, but afraid *of* them; angry and contemptuous, but deferent; doubtful, but dazzled)" ("Survival on Earth," 199).

41. One of the most recent ecofeminist collections is dedicated to Carson. In Diamond and Orenstein's *Reweaving the World*, Grace Paley lauds Carson as proof of women's "ecological and feminist . . . other way of understanding" nature (iii).

42. Carson, *Silent Spring*, 220.

43. Orenstein, "Artists As Healers," 281. Merchant suggests a richer group of writers but notes that Griffin was one of the most popular ("Earthcare," 8).

44. In *Woman and Nature*, Griffin continually links the physical invasion of women's bodies with the destruction of nature. Thus, a woman's death following a bungled abortion is set within the context of the slaughter of an elephant matriarch, and both are presented as the text for women's active resistance to patriarchy (214–18). Griffin has been particularly inspirational to Carol Christ, whose writings on

feminist spirituality routinely appear in ecofeminist collections. Christ suggests that it is through this connection to the wild, and the attitude of humility and awe it conveys, that women return to goddess worship ("Rethinking Theology and Nature," 58).

45. Griffin rarely mentions the many narratives of women who dedicated their lives to wild animals. At one point she draws on a quote from Jane Goodall to offer her own version of what it must mean to be a woman studying a wild animal. There is no sense of the moral dilemmas Goodall faced as she discovered that chimp society was not based on some middle-class version of domesticity and civility (*Woman and Nature*, 196–97). For a more considered discussion of the responsibilities humans feel when they "extend sympathy" to other animals, based in part on Goodall's work with the chimps, see Midgley, *Animals and Why They Matter*, 119–21. In *Adam's Task*, animal trainer Vicki Hearne also probes the responsibilities humans take on when they seek any sort of interaction with other animals. In much ecofeminist literature, nature often seems to serve more as an oppositional category than as a physical space filled with plants and animals. At least one ecofeminist has acknowledged her own ignorance of the green world and described her attempts to get back to nature (Spretnak, "Toward an Ecofeminist Spirituality," 7). The two major anthologies of ecofeminist writings appearing to date— Plant's *Healing the Wounds* and Diamond and Orenstein's *Reweaving the World*— play on women's roles as healers.

46. Christ, "Rethinking Theology and Nature," 64–65. On Hurston's influence, see Walker, *Our Mother's Gardens*, 93–116; on the importance of Walker's own mother's garden to her creativity, see pp. 231–43. Both major collections of ecofeminist writings include a number of essays by women of color; each writer locates her differences with the dominant culture in a concern specifically for the green world and in her traditional valuing of that world. For examples, see P. G. Allen, "The Woman I Love"; Bagby, "Daughters of Growing Things"; Gwaganad, "Speaking for the Earth." Although Marie Wilson provides a more holistic description of her people's environmental beliefs than most, she too locates her most powerful connections in the green world: "What do we cherish most in the corner of our gardens? The compost. Where do we put it? Around the tender new life to give it a good start in the new created life it will become. If I had any way of describing myself that would be the way I would like to be described" (Wilson and Plant, "Wings of the Eagle," 212).

47. S. Griffin, *Woman and Nature*, 31; on the dangers of being trapped in the garden, see pp. 103–6. Christ cites Walker's *The Color Purple* as a key text in locating an "alternative theological vision" in the main character's recognition of God in flowers in the field. Walker has written a number of pointed and racially sensitive essays on animal rights, but these have yet to receive much attention in ecofeminist theory (*Living by the Word*, 3–8, 139–52). One of the most revealing attempts to universalize difference is Elizabeth Dodson Gray's image of the rainbow: "The rainbow is like a banner or flag, waving as a symbol of diversity over the movements of ethnicity and difference, celebrating the dissolution of the norm and

of monochromatic uniformity. Let's hear it for the chocolate brown of the good earth and dark skins! Hurrah for roseate tones of sunsets and Indian skins. Cheers for the yellows of sunlight and oriental skins. Here's to the blue-purple of skies and butterflies. Let's celebrate the green of trees and all of nature's 'niggers,' and let's storm the law courts till we acknowledge the intrinsic value of *all* in the creation's rainbow" (*Green Paradise Lost*, 149–50). Though the goals of the passage may be laudable, Gray achieves a holistic earth by grounding all people of color in nature. Where in this scenario are the white skins? As women of color have often noted about feminism, whites again serve as the background, the space containing the rainbow, controlling its shape.

# Bibliography

Abbott, R. Tucker, ed. *American Malacologists: A National Register of Professional and Amateur Malacologists and Private Shell Collectors and Biographies of Early American Mollusk Workers Born between 1618 and 1900.* Falls Church, Va.: American Malacologists, 1973–74.

Abbott, Sally. "The Origins of God in the Blood of the Lamb." In *Reweaving the World*, edited by Irene Diamond and Gloria Feman Orenstein, 35–40.

Abir-Am, Pnina G., and Dorinda Outram, eds. *Uneasy Careers and Intimate Lives: Women in Science, 1789–1979.* New Brunswick, N.J.: Rutgers University Press, 1987.

Agassiz, Elizabeth Cabot. *First Lesson in Natural History.* Boston: Little, Brown and Co., 1859.

———. *A Journey in Brazil.* Boston: Ticknor and Fields, 1868.

Ainley, Marianne Goszwingertonyi. "Field Work and Family: North American Women Ornithologists, 1900–1950." In *Uneasy Careers and Intimate Lives*, edited by Pnina G. Abir-Am and Dorinda Outram, 60–77.

Akeley, Carl E. *In Brightest Africa.* Garden City, N.Y.: Doubleday, Page and Co., 1924.

Akeley, Delia. *J. T., Jr.: The Biography of an African Monkey.* New York: Macmillan, 1928.

———. *Jungle Portraits.* New York: Macmillan, 1930.

———. "My First Elephant." In *All True!: The Record of Actual Adventures That Have Happened to Ten Women of Today.* New York: Brewer, Warren and Putnam, 1931.

Allen, David Elliston. *The Naturalist in Britain: A Social History.* London: Allen Lane, 1976.

Allen, Paula Gunn. "The Woman I Love Is a Planet; The Planet I Love Is a Tree." In *Reweaving the World*, edited by Irene Diamond and Gloria Feman Orenstein, 52–57.

"America in Bloom: The Work of the Country Garden Clubs, East and West." *Craftsman* 29 (November 1915): 144–51.

Anand, Anita. "Saving Trees, Saving Lives: Third World Women." In *Reclaim the Earth*, edited by Leonie Caldecott and Stephanie Leland, 182–87.

Anderson, Clinton. Foreword to *The Yearbook of the United States Department of Agriculture: Grass*. Washington, D.C.: U.S. Department of Agriculture, 1948.

Anderson, David, and Richard Grove, eds. *Conservation in Africa: Peoples, Policies, and Practice*. Cambridge: Cambridge University Press, 1987.

Anderson, Dorothy May. *Women, Design, and the Cambridge School*. West Lafayette, Ind.: PDA Publishers Corp., 1980.

"Appeal Could Halt Dieldrin." *Virginia Pilot*, January 12, 1963.

Archer, John. "Country and City in the American Romantic Suburb." *Journal of the Society of Architectural Historians* 42 (May 1983): 139–56.

Atwood, Margaret. *Surfacing*. New York: Warner Books, 1972.

Austin, Mary. *The Flock*. Boston: Houghton Mifflin, 1906.

———. *The Land of Journey's Ending*. New York: Century Co., 1924.

———. *The Land of Little Rain*. 1903. Reprint. Albuquerque: University of New Mexico Press, 1974.

———. *Lost Borders*. New York: Harper and Brothers, 1909.

Bacon, Margaret Hope. *Mothers of Feminism: The Story of Quaker Women in America*. San Francisco: Harper and Row, 1986.

Bagby, Rachel. "Building the Green Movement." *Woman of Power* 9 (Spring 1988): 11–18.

———. "Daughters of Growing Things." In *Reweaving the World*, edited by Irene Diamond and Gloria Feman Orenstein, 231–48.

———. "A Power of Numbers." In *Healing the Wounds*, edited by Judith Plant, 91–95.

Baker, Gladys. "Women in the U.S. Department of Agriculture." *Agricultural History* 50 (January 1976): 190–201.

Ballinger, Franchot. "The Responsible Center: Man and Nature in Pueblo and Navaho Ritual Songs and Prayers." *American Quarterly* 30 (Spring 1978): 90–107.

Balmori, Diana. "Beatrix Farrand at Dumbarton Oaks." *Heresies* 3 (1981): 83–86.

Balmori, Diana, Diane Kostial McGuire, and Eleanor M. McPeck. *Beatrix Farrand's American Landscapes: Her Gardens and Campuses*. Sagaponack, N.Y.: Sagapress, 1985.

Balzau, Emman Lydia. *Almira Hart Lincoln Phelps: Her Life and Work*. Philadelphia: Science Press Printing Co., 1936.

Barber, Lynn. *The Heyday of Natural History, 1820–1870*. London: J. Cape, 1980.

Barr, Marlene S., ed. *Future Females: A Critical Anthology*. Bowling Green, Ohio: Bowling Green State University Popular Press, 1981.

Barrington, Amy L. "A Fielde of Delite: The Country Home of Two Well-Known Artists—Mr. and Mrs. Albert Herter." *House Beautiful* (April 1919): 189–91, 241.

Bartlett, Kay. "First She Fell in Love with Africa, Then Elephants." *Albuquerque Journal*, May 30, 1988.

Basso, Keith. "'Stalking with Stories': Names, Places, and Moral Narratives among the Western Apaches." *Antaeus* 57 (Autumn 1986): 95–116.

Bauer, Erwin, and Peggy Bauer. *Photographing Wild Texas*. Austin: University of Texas Press, 1985.

Baym, Nina. "Women and the Republic: Emma Willard's Rhetoric of History." *American Quarterly* 43 (March 1991): 1–23.

Bean, William B., M.D. "The Noise of *Silent Spring*." *Archives of Internal Medicine* 112 (September 1963): 311.

Beecher, Catharine E., and Harriet Beecher Stowe. *The American Woman's Home; or, Principles of Domestic Science*. New York: J. B. Ford and Co., 1869.

Benchley, Belle J. *My Friends, the Apes*. Boston: Little, Brown and Co., 1944.

Benney, Norma. "All of One Flesh: The Rights of Animals." In *Reclaim the Earth*, edited by Leonie Caldecott and Stephanie Leland, 141–51.

Benson, Maxine. *Martha Maxwell: Rocky Mountain Naturalist*. Lincoln: University of Nebraska Press, 1986.

Berkhofer, Robert F., Jr. *The White Man's Indian: Images of the American Indian from Columbus to the Present*. New York: Alfred A. Knopf, 1978.

Biddle, Gertrude, and Sarah Lowrie. *Notable Women of Pennsylvania*. Philadelphia: University of Pennsylvania Press, 1942.

Binney, Amos. *The Terrestrial Air-Breathing Mollusks of the United States*. . . . 5 vols. Boston: Little and Brown, 1851–78.

Bird, Isabella L. [pub. under Isabella L. Bishop]. *The Englishwoman in America*. 1856. Reprint. Madison: University of Wisconsin Press, 1966.

————. *A Lady's Life in the Rocky Mountains*. 1879. Reprint. Norman: University of Oklahoma Press, 1960.

*Birds in Art*. Exhibition catalog. Wausau, Wis.: Leigh Yawkey Woodson Art Museum, 1989.

Blair, Karen J. *The Clubwoman as Feminist: True Womanhood Redefined, 1868–1914*. New York: Holmes and Meier, 1980.

Bleier, Ruth, ed. *Feminist Approaches to Science*. New York: Pergamon Press, 1986.

————. *Science and Gender: A Critique of Biology and Its Theories on Women*. New York: Pergamon Press, 1984.

Blend, Benay. "Mary Austin and the Western Conservation Movement: 1900–1927." *Journal of the Southwest* 30 (Spring 1988): 12–34.

Blunt, Wilfrid. *The Art of Botanical Illustration*. New York: Charles Scribner's Sons, 1951.

Bonta, Marcia. "Cordelia Stanwood: Pioneer Student of Nesting Behavior." *Bird-watcher's Digest* (May–June 1983): 40–47.

Born, Wolfgang. "The Female Peales: Their Art and Tradition." *American Collector* 15 (August 1946): 12–14.

Bradley, Mary Hastings. *On the Gorilla Trail*. New York: D. Appleton and Co., 1922.

Bradsher, Frieda Katherine. "Women in the Works of James Fenimore Cooper." Ph.D. dissertation, University of Arizona, 1979.

Braxton, Joanne M. "A Poet's Retreat: The Diaries of Charlotte Forten Grimké (1837–1914)." In *Wild Women in the Whirlwind*, edited by Joanne M. Braxton and Andrée Nicola McLaughlin, 70–88.

Braxton, Joanne M., and Andrée Nicola McLaughlin. *Wild Women in the Whirl-wind: Afra-American Culture and the Contemporary Literary Renaissance.* New Brunswick, N.J.: Rutgers University Press, 1990.

"Brazil Explored for New Grasses." U.S. Department of Agriculture, *Official Record* 4 (August 12, 1925): 1, 5.

Bremer, Fredrika. *The Homes of the New World: Impressions of America.* 2 vols. Translated by Mary Howitt. New York: Harper and Brothers, 1853.

Brewer, Maria Minich. "Surviving Fictions: Gender and Difference in Postmodern and Postnuclear Narrative." *Discourse: Berkeley Journal for Theoretical Studies in Media and Culture* 9 (Spring–Summer 1987): 37–52.

Brindle, John V., and James J. White. *Flora Portrayed: Classics of Botanical Art from the Hunt Institute Collection.* Pittsburgh: Hunt Institute for Botanical Documentation, 1985.

Brooks, Paul. *The House of Life: Rachel Carson At Work.* Boston: Houghton Mifflin, 1972.

—————. *Speaking for Nature: How Literary Naturalists from Henry Thoreau to Rachel Carson Have Shaped America.* Boston: Houghton Mifflin, 1980.

Brown, Catherine, and Celia Newton Maddox. "Women and the Land: A Suitable Profession." *Landscape Architecture* (May 1982): 65–69.

Brown, Gillian. *Domestic Individualism: Imagining Self in Nineteenth-Century America.* Berkeley and Los Angeles: University of California Press, 1990.

Brown, Mary Beth. "Zora Neale Hurston in the Caribbean: Women in Religion and Society." In *A Rainbow Round Her Shoulder: The Zora Neale Hurston Symposium Papers,* edited by Ruthe T. Sheffey, 104–18. Baltimore: Morgan State University Press, 1982.

Brown, Wilmette. "Roots: Black Ghetto Ecology." In *Reclaim the Earth,* edited by Leonie Caldecott and Stephanie Leland, 73–85.

Budgen, Miss L. M. *Episodes of Insect Life.* 3 vols. New York: J. S. Redfield, Clinton Hall; Boston: B. B. Mussey and Co., 1851–52.

Buell, Glenda. "Grace Albee, 91, An Engraver Still in Vogue." *Providence Journal,* October 22, 1981.

Burger, Julian. *Report from the Frontier: The State of the World's Indigenous Peoples.* London and Atlantic Highlands, N.J.: Zed Books, 1987.

Burstyn, Joan N. "Early Women in Education: The Role of the Anderson School of Natural History." *Boston University Journal of Education* 159 (August 1977): 50–64.

Bush, Clive. *The Dream of Reason: American Consciousness and Cultural Achievement from Independence to the Civil War.* New York: St. Martin's Press, 1978.

Caldecott, Leonie, and Stephanie Leland, eds. *Reclaim the Earth: Women Speak Out for Life on Earth.* London: The Women's Press, 1983.

Capps, Walter Holden, ed. *Seeing with a Native Eye: Essays on Native American Religion.* New York: Harper and Row, 1976.

Capra, Fritjof. *The Tao of Physics.* 1975. Reprint. New York: Bantam Books, 1983.

Carby, Hazel V. *Reconstructing Womanhood: The Emergence of the Afro-American Woman Novelist*. New York: Oxford University Press, 1987.

Carrighar, Sally. *Home to the Wilderness*. Boston: Houghton Mifflin, 1973.

———. *Icebound Summer*. New York: Alfred A. Knopf, 1953.

———. *One Day on Beetle Rock*. New York: Alfred A. Knopf, 1944.

———. *One Day at Teton Marsh*. New York: Alfred A. Knopf, 1947.

———. *The Twilight Seas: A Blue Whale's Journey*. 1975. Reprint. New York: E. P. Dutton, 1989.

———. *Wild Heritage*. Boston: Houghton Mifflin, 1965.

Carson, Rachel. *The Edge of the Sea*. Boston: Houghton Mifflin, 1955.

———. "Mattamuskeet: A National Wildlife Refuge." Conservation in Action Series, no. 4. Washington, D.C.: U.S. Fish and Wildlife Service, 1947.

———. *The Sea Around Us*. New York: Oxford University Press, 1951.

———. *The Sense of Wonder*. New York: Harper and Row, 1956.

———. *Silent Spring*. 1962. Reprint. New York: Fawcett, 1964.

———. *Under the Sea Wind: A Naturalist's Picture of Ocean Life*. 1941. Reprint. New York: Oxford University Press, 1952.

Cary, Richard, ed. *Appreciation of Sarah Orne Jewett: Twenty-nine Interpretive Essays*. Waterville, Maine: Colby College Press, 1973.

Cautley, Marjorie Sewell. *Garden Design: The Principles of Abstract Design as Applied to Landscape Composition*. New York: Dodd, Mead and Co., 1935.

———. "Planting at Radburn." *Landscape Architecture* 21 (October 1930): 23–29.

Chafe, William H. *The American Woman: Her Changing Social, Economic, and Political Role, 1920–1970*. New York: Oxford University Press, 1972.

Chapman, Wendell, and Lucie Chapman. *Beaver Pioneers*. New York: Charles Scribner's Sons, 1937.

———. *The Little Wolf: A Story of the Coyote of Our Rocky Mountains*. New York: Charles Scribner's Sons, 1936.

———. *Wilderness Wanderers: Adventures among Wild Animals in Rocky Mountain Solitudes*. New York: Charles Scribner's Sons, 1937.

Chase, Agnes. *The First Book of Grasses: The Structure of Grasses Explained for Beginners*. New York: Macmillan, 1922.

Cheney, Jim. "Eco-feminism and Deep Ecology." *Environmental Ethics* 9 (Summer 1987): 115–45.

Christ, Carol P. "Margaret Atwood: The Surfacing of Women's Spiritual Quest and Vision." *Signs: Journal of Women in Culture and Society* 2 (Winter 1976): 316–30.

———. "Rethinking Theology and Nature." In *Reweaving the World*, edited by Irene Diamond and Gloria Feman Orenstein, 58–69.

Christian, Barbara. *Black Feminist Criticism: Perspectives on Black Women Writers*. New York: Pergamon Press, 1985.

———. "'Somebody Forgot to Tell Somebody Something': African-American Women's Historical Novels." In *Wild Women in the Whirlwind*, edited by Joanne M. Braxton and Andrée Nicola McLaughlin, 326–41.

Clark, Clifford Edward, Jr. *The American Family Home: 1800–1960*. Chapel Hill: University of North Carolina Press, 1986.

Close, Leslie Rose. *Portrait of an Era in Landscape Architecture: The Photographs of Mattie Edwards Hewitt*. Exhibition catalog. Bronx, N.Y.: Wave Hill, 1983.

Cockerell, T. D. A. "Kate Olivia Sessions and California Floriculture." *Bios* (December 1943): 167–79.

Coffin, Annie Roulhac. "Audubon's Friend—Maria Martin." *New York Historical Society Quarterly* 49 (January 1965): 29–51.

Colden, Jane. *The Botanic Manuscript of Jane Colden*. Edited by H. W. Rickett and Elizabeth C. Hall. New York: Garden Club of Orange and Duchess Counties, 1963.

Collard, Andrée, with Joyce Contrucci. *Rape of the Wild: Man's Violence against Animals and the Earth*. Bloomington: Indiana University Press, 1989.

Collier, Jane, and Sylvia J. Yanagisako. *Gender and Kinship: Essays Toward a Unified Analysis*. Stanford, Calif.: Stanford University Press, 1987.

Collins, Patricia Hill. *Black Feminist Thought: Knowledge, Consciousness, and the Politics of Empowerment*. Boston: Unwin Hyman, 1990.

Comstock, Anna Botsford. *The Comstocks of Cornell: John Henry Comstock and Anna Botsford Comstock*. Edited by Glenn W. Herrick and Ruby Green Smith. Ithaca, N.Y.: Comstock Publishing Associates, a division of Cornell University Press, 1953.

————. *Handbook of Nature Study*. 1911. Reprint. Ithaca, N.Y.: Comstock Publishing Co., 1939.

Comstock, John H. *An Introduction to Entomology*. Ithaca, N.Y.: Comstock Publishing Co., 1920.

Comstock, W. Richard. "On Seeing with the Eye of the Native European." In *Seeing with a Native Eye*, edited by Walter Holden Capps, 58–78.

"Controversy over Insecticide Divides a City." *National Observer*, February 25, 1963.

Cook, Alice, and Gwyn Kirk. *Greenham Women Everywhere: Dreams, Ideas, and Actions from the Women's Peace Movement*. London: Pluto Press, 1983.

Cooper, James Fenimore. *Correspondence of James Fenimore Cooper*. Edited by his grandson, James Fenimore Cooper. 2 vols. New Haven: Yale University Press, 1922.

————. *The Letters and Journals of James Fenimore Cooper*. Edited by James Franklin Beard. 6 vols. Cambridge: Harvard University Press, 1968.

Cooper, Susan Fenimore [pseud. Amabel Penfeather]. *Elinor Wyllys; or, The Young Folk of Longbridge*. Anon. 2 vols. Philadelphia: Carey and Hart, 1846.

————. "Female Suffrage: A Letter to the Christian Women of America." *Harper's New Monthly Magazine* 41 (August, September 1870): 438–46, 594–600.

————. *Rural Hours*. By a Lady. New York: George P. Putnam, 1850.

————. "Small Family Memories." In *Correspondence of James Fenimore Cooper*, edited by James Fenimore Cooper, 1:9–72.

Cooper, William. *A Guide in the Wilderness*. New York: Gilbert and Hodges, 1810.

Copper, Baba. "The Voice of Women's Spirituality in Futurism." In *The Politics of Women's Spirituality: Essays on the Rise of Spiritual Power within the Feminist Movement*, edited by Charlene Spretnak, 497–510. Garden City, N.Y.: Anchor Press/Doubleday, 1982.

Cott, Nancy F. *The Bonds of Womanhood: Woman's Sphere in New England, 1780–1835*. New Haven: Yale University Press, 1977.

Cotton, Barbara. "Wildlife Art: The Female Perspective." *Sports Afield* 196 (November 1986): 71–75.

Coville, Frederick Vernon. "Botany of the Death Valley Expedition." *Contributions from the U.S. National Herbarium* 4 (November 1893).

Cranz, Galen. *The Politics of Park Design: A History of Urban Parks in America*. Cambridge: MIT Press, 1982.

———. "Women in Urban Parks." *Signs: Journal of Women in Culture and Society* 5 (Supp. Spring 1980): S79–S95.

Crisler, Lois. *Arctic Wild*. 1958. Reprint. New York: Harper and Row, 1973.

———. *Captive Wild*. New York: Harper and Row, 1968.

Cronon, William. *Changes in the Land: Indians, Colonists, and the Ecology of New England*. New York: Hill and Wang, 1983.

Crosby, Mrs. Robert R. *Fifty Years of Service: National Council of State Garden Clubs, 1929–1979*. St. Louis, Mo.: National Council of State Garden Clubs, 1979.

Crosswhite, Frank S. "'J. G. Lemmon and Wife': Plant Explorers in Arizona, California, and Nevada." *Desert Plants* 1 (August 1979): 12–21.

Cumming, C[onstance] F. Gordon. *Granite Crags*. Edinburgh: William Blackwood and Sons, 1884.

Cunningham, Anna K. "Susan Fenimore Cooper—Child of Genius." *New York History* 25 (July 1944): 339–50.

Dana, Mrs. William Starr [Frances Theodora]. *How to Know the Wildflowers: A Guide to the Names, Haunts, and Habits of Our Common Wildflowers*. New York: Charles Scribner's Sons, 1893.

Dance, S. Peter. *Shell Collecting: An Illustrated History*. Berkeley and Los Angeles: University of California Press, 1966.

Daniel, Pete, and Raymond Smock. *A Talent for Detail: The Photographs of Miss Frances Benjamin Johnston, 1889–1910*. New York: Harmony Books, 1974.

Dartt, Mary. *On the Plains and Among the Peaks; or, How Mrs. Maxwell Made Her Natural History Collection*. Philadelphia: Claxton, Remsen and Haffelfinger, 1879.

Davis, Charles T., and Henry Louis Gates, Jr., eds. *The Slave's Narrative*. New York: Oxford University Press, 1985.

Davis, Sam P. *The History of Nevada*. Vol. 2. Reno: Elms Publishing Co., 1913.

Dean, Ruth. *The Livable House: Its Garden*. New York: Moffat, Yard and Co., 1917.

Dearborn, Mary V. *Pocahontas's Daughters: Gender and Ethnicity in American Culture*. New York: Oxford University Press, 1986.

Diamond, Irene, and Gloria Feman Orenstein, eds. *Reweaving the World: The Emergence of Ecofeminism*. San Francisco: Sierra Club Books, 1990.

Dillard, Annie. *Pilgrim at Tinker Creek*. New York: Bantam Books, 1975.

Dinnerstein, Dorothy. "Survival on Earth: The Meaning of Ecofeminism." In *Healing the Wounds*, edited by Judith Plant, 192–200.

Dixon, Melvin. *Ride Out the Wilderness: Geography and Identity in Afro-American Literature*. Urbana: University of Illinois Press, 1987.

Doell, M. Christine Klim. *Gardens of the Gilded Age: Nineteenth-Century Gardens and Home Grounds of New York State*. Syracuse, N.Y.: Syracuse University Press, 1986.

Dormon, Caroline. *Natives Preferred*. Baton Rouge, La.: Claitor's Book Store, 1965.

Doubiago, Sharon. "Mama Coyote Talks to the Boys." In *Healing the Wounds*, edited by Judith Plant, 40–45.

Doughty, Robin W. *Feather Fashions and Bird Preservation: A Study in Nature Protection*. Berkeley and Los Angeles: University of California Press, 1975.

Douglas, Ann. *The Feminization of American Culture*. New York: Alfred A. Knopf, 1977.

Dowden, Anne Ophelia. *The Clover and the Bee: A Book of Pollination*. New York: Thomas Y. Crowell, 1984.

———. *From Flower to Fruit*. New York: Thomas Y. Crowell, 1990.

———. "Something About the Author." Autobiography Series 10, 75–86. Detroit: Gale Research, Inc., [1990].

———. *Wild Green Things in the City: A Book of Weeds*. New York: Thomas Y. Crowell, 1972.

"Dowden, Anne Ophelia." *Third Annual Exhibition, Hunt Botanical Institution*. Exhibition catalog. Pittsburgh: Hunt Botanical Institute, 1972.

Downing, Andrew Jackson. *Rural Essays: Horticulture—Landscape Gardening—Rural Architecture—Trees—Agriculture—Fruit, Etc.* New York: Worthington Co., 1890.

Dudley, Edward, and Maximillian E. Novak. *The Wild Man Within: An Image in Western Thought from the Renaissance to Romanticism*. Pittsburgh: University of Pittsburgh Press, 1972.

Dugan, James, and Ruth Dugan. "She Lives with Adventure." *McCall's* 83 (January 1956): 41, 112.

Duncan, Frances. *The Joyous Art of Gardening*. New York: Charles Scribner's Sons, 1917.

Dunlap, Thomas R. " 'The Coyote Itself'—Ecologists and the Value of Predators." *Environmental Review* 7 (Spring 1983): 54–70.

———. *DDT: Scientists, Citizens, and Public Policy*. Princeton, N.J.: Princeton University Press, 1981.

———. *Saving America's Wildlife*. Princeton, N.J.: Princeton University Press, 1988.

Dupree, A. Hunter. *Science in the Federal Government: A History of Policies and Activities to 1940*. Cambridge: Harvard University Press, 1957.

Eiseley, Loren. *Darwin's Century: Evolution and the Men Who Discovered It*. Garden City, N.Y.: Doubleday, 1958.

Eisenberg, John F. "Family Portraits." *Natural History* 97 (March 1988): 80, 82, 84.

Ely, Helen Rutherford. *A Woman's Hardy Garden*. New York: Macmillan, 1903.

Embury, Emma C. *American Wildflowers in Their Native Haunts*. New York: D. Appleton and Co., 1844.

Emery, Edwin, and Michael Emery. *The Press and America: An Interpretive History of the Mass Media*. 5th ed. Englewood Cliffs, N.J.: Prentice Hall, 1984.

Ewan, Joseph. "San Francisco as a Mecca for Nineteenth-Century Naturalists." In *A Century of Progress in the Natural Sciences, 1853–1953*, edited by Ernest B. Babcock, J. Wyatt Durham, and George S. Myers, 1–65. San Francisco: California Academy of Sciences, 1955.

———, ed. *A Short History of Botany in the United States*. New York: Hafner Publishing Co., 1969.

[Farrand], Beatrix Jones. "The Garden as a Picture." *Scribners* 62 (July 1907): 2–11.

Fedigan, Linda Marie, and Laurence Fedigan. "Gender and the Study of Primates." In *Gender and Anthropology: Critical Reviews for Research and Teaching*, edited by Sandra Morgen, 41–64. Washington, D.C.: American Anthropological Association, 1989.

Forten, Charlotte L. [Grimké]. *The Journal of Charlotte L. Forten: A Free Negro in the Slave Era*. Edited by Ray Allen Billington. 1953. Reprint. New York: Collier Books, 1961.

Fosberg, F. R., and J. R. Swallen. "Agnes Chase." *Taxon* 8 (June 1959): 145–51.

Foshay, Ella M. *Reflections of Nature: Flowers in American Art*. New York: Alfred A. Knopf in association with the Whitney Museum of American Art, 1984.

Fossey, Dian. *Gorillas in the Mist*. Boston: Houghton Mifflin, 1983.

Fox, Stephen. *John Muir and His Legacy: The American Conservation Movement*. Boston: Little, Brown and Co., 1981.

Fox-Genovese, Elizabeth. *Within the Plantation Household: Black and White Women of the Old South*. Chapel Hill: University of North Carolina Press, 1988.

Francis, Mark, Lisa Cashdan, and Lynn Paxson. *Community Open Spaces: Greening Neighborhoods through Community Action and Land Conservation*. Washington, D.C.: Island Press, 1984.

Frederickson, George M. *The Black Image in the White Mind: The Debate on Afro-American Character and Destiny, 1817–1914*. New York: Harper and Row, 1971.

Free, Ann Cottrell. "A Humane Question: Proper Care for Science's Animals." *Sunday Star* (Washington, D.C.), November 15, 1959.

Freibert, Lucy M. "World Views in Utopian Novels by Women." In *Women and Utopia: Critical Interpretations*, edited by Marleen Barr and Nicholas D. Smith, 67–84. Lanham, Md.: University Press of America, 1983.

Frierson, Lorraine. "How Unioneo Emigrate." *The Nautilus* 12 (May 1898–April 1899): 139–40.

Fuller, Margaret. *Summer on the Lakes, in 1843*. Boston: Little and Brown, 1844.

Furbish, Kate. "A Botanist's Trip to the 'Aroostook.'" *American Naturalist* 15, 16 (May–June 1881, May–June 1882): 397–99, 469–70.

Gerdts, William H. "The Artist's Garden: American Floral Painting, 1850–1915." *Portfolio* 4 (July–August 1982): 44–51.

———. *Down Garden Paths: The Floral Environment in American Art*. Rutherford,

N.J.: Fairleigh Dickinson University Press, 1983.

——— . "The Teaching of Painting Out-of-Doors in America in the Late Nineteenth Century." In *In Nature's Ways: American Landscape Painting of the Late Nineteenth Century*, edited by William H. Gerdts and Bruce Weber, 25–40. Exhibition catalog. Norton Gallery of Art: West Palm Beach, Fla., 1987.

Gerdts, William H., John V. Brindle, and Sally Secrist. *American Cornucopia: Nineteenth-Century Still Lifes and Studies*. Catalog of a bicentennial exhibition. Pittsburgh: Hunt Institute for Botanical Documentation, 1976.

Gill, Sam D. *Mother Earth: An American Story*. Chicago: University of Chicago Press, 1987.

Gilman, Sander L. "Black Bodies, White Bodies: Toward an Iconography of Female Sexuality in Late Nineteenth-Century Art, Medicine, and Literature." *Critical Inquiry* 12 (Autumn 1985): 204–42.

Goetzmann, William H. *Exploration and Empire: The Explorer and the Scientist in the Winning of the American West*. New York: Alfred A. Knopf, 1966.

Gould, James L. *Ethology: The Mechanisms and Evolution of Behavior*. New York: W. W. Norton and Co., 1982.

Gould, Lewis L. *Lady Bird Johnson and the Environment*. Lawrence: University Press of Kansas, 1988.

Gould, Stephen Jay. *The Mismeasure of Man*. New York: W. W. Norton and Co., 1981.

Govan, Ada. *Wings At My Window*. New York: Macmillan, 1940.

Grace, George, and David H. Wallace, eds. *New-York Historical Society's Dictionary of Artists in America, 1564–1860*. New Haven: Yale University Press, 1957.

Graham, Frank, Jr. *Since Silent Spring*. Boston: Houghton Mifflin, 1970.

Grandville, J. J. *The Flowers Personified*. Translated by N. Cleveland. New York: R. Martin, 1847. Reprinted as *The Court of Flora (Les Fleurs Animées)*, with an introduction and notes by Peter A. Wick. New York: George Braziller, 1981.

Gray, Elizabeth Dodson. *Green Paradise Lost*. Wellesley, Mass.: Roundtable Press, 1981. (First published in 1979 as *Why the Green Nigger?* by the same press.)

——— . "Nature as an Act of Imagination." *Woman of Power* 9 (Spring 1988): 18–21.

Grier, James W. *Biology of Animal Behavior*. New York: Times/Mirror, 1984.

Griffin, Donald R. *Animal Thinking*. Cambridge: Harvard University Press, 1984.

Griffin, Susan. "Split Culture." In *Healing the Wounds*, edited by Judith Plant, 7–17.

——— . *Woman and Nature: The Roaring Inside Her*. New York: Harper and Row, 1978.

Griswold, Mac, and Eleanor Weller. *The Golden Age of American Gardens: Proud Owners, Private Estates, 1890–1940*. New York: Henry N. Abrams in association with the Garden Club of America, 1991.

Guggisberg, C. A. W. *Early Wildlife Photographers*. New York: Taplinger Publishing Co., 1977.

*Guild of Natural Science Illustrators' Natural Science Illustration Exhibit*. Exhibition catalog. Washington, D.C.: National Museum of Natural History, 1986.

Gwaganad. "Speaking for the Earth: The Haida Way." In *Healing the Wounds*, edited by Judith Plant, 76–79.

Hagood, Margaret Jarman. *Mothers of the South: Portraiture of the White Tenant Farm Woman*. 1939. Reprint. New York: W. W. Norton and Co., 1977.

Hahn, Emily. *Eve and the Apes*. New York: Winfeld and Nicolson, 1988.

Haldeman, S. S. *A Monograph of the Freshwater Univalve Mollusca of the United States*. . . . Philadelphia: Academy of Natural Sciences, 1842, 1845.

Hale, Sarah Josepha. *Flora's Interpreter: or, The American Book of Flowers and Sentiments*. Boston: Marsh, Capen and Lyon, 1832.

Hall, Elizabeth C. "The Gentlewoman, Jane Colden, and Her Manuscript on New York Native Plants." Introduction to *Botanic Manuscript*, by Jane Colden, 17–21.

Hamilton, Cynthia. "Women, Home, and Community: The Struggle in an Urban Environment." In *Reweaving the World*, edited by Irene Diamond and Gloria Feman Orenstein, 215–22.

Hammond, Nicholas. *Twentieth-Century Wildlife Artists*. Woodstock, N.Y.: Overlook Press, 1986.

Hanley, Wayne. *Natural History in America: From Mark Catesby to Rachel Carson*. New York: Quadrangle/New York Times Book Co., 1977.

Haraway, Donna. "A Manifesto for Cyborgs: Science, Technology, and Socialist Feminism in the 1980s." *Socialist Review* 80 (March–April 1985): 65–107.

———. *Primate Visions: Gender, Race, and Nature in the World of Modern Science*. New York: Routledge, 1989.

Harding, Sandra, and Jean F. O'Barr. *Sex and Scientific Inquiry*. Chicago: University of Chicago Press, 1987.

Harshberger, John W. *The Botanists of Philadelphia and Their Work*. Philadelphia: T. C. Davis and Son, 1899.

Hartt, Mary Bronson. "Women and the Art of Landscape Gardening." *The Outlook* 88 (March 28, 1908): 694–704.

Havaford, Phebe. *Daughters of America; or, Women of the Century*. Augusta, Maine: True and Co., 1882.

Hawking, Stephen W. *A Brief History of Time: From the Big Bang to Black Holes*. New York: Bantam Press, 1988.

Hayes, Harold T. P. *The Dark Romance of Dian Fossey*. New York: Simon and Schuster, 1990.

Hays, Samuel P. *Beauty, Health, and Permanence: Environmental Politics in the United States, 1955–1985*. Cambridge: Cambridge University Press, 1987.

Hearne, Vicki. *Adam's Task: Calling Animals By Name*. New York: Alfred A. Knopf, 1987.

Hedrick, U. P. *A History of Horticulture in America to 1860*. New York: Oxford University Press, 1950.

Henderson, Hazel. "The Warp and the Weft: The Coming Synthesis of Eco-Philosophy and Eco-Feminism." In *Reclaim the Earth*, edited by Leonie Caldecott and Stephanie Leland, 203–14.

Hester, Randolph T., Jr. "Process CAN Be Style: Participation and Conservation in Landscape Architecture." *Landscape Architecture* 73 (May 1983): 49–55.

Hill, Anna Gilman. *Forty Years of Gardening*. New York: Frederick A. Stokes Co., 1938.

Hill, Carol. *The Eleven Million Mile High Dancer*. New York: Penguin Books, 1986.

Hitchcock, A. S. *Manual of the Grasses of the United States.* Washington, D.C.: U.S. Government Printing Office, 1935.

Hite, Molly. "Writing—and Reading—the Body: Female Sexuality and Recent Feminist Fiction." *Feminist Studies* 14 (Spring 1988): 121–42.

Hollingsworth, Buckner. *Her Garden Was Her Delight*. New York: Macmillan, 1962.

Hooper, Lucy, ed. *The Lady's Book of Flowers and Poetry, to which Are Added a Botanical Introduction, a Complete Floral Dictionary, and a Chapter on Plants in Rooms*. New York: J. C. Riker, 1848.

Hoover, Helen. *The Gift of the Deer*. 1965. Reprint. Boston: Houghton Mifflin, 1981.

Houstoun, Matilda Charlotte. *Texas and the Gulf of Mexico: or, Yachting in the New World*. Philadelphia: G. B. Zieber and Co., 1845.

Hoy, Suellen. "'Municipal Housekeeping': The Role of Women in Improving Urban Sanitation Practices, 1880–1917." In *Pollution and Reform in American Cities, 1870–1930*, edited by Martin V. Melosi, 173–98. Austin: University of Texas Press, 1980.

Hubbell, Sue. *A Country Year: Living the Questions*. New York: Random House, 1986.

Hultkrantz, Ake. "The Contribution of the Study of North American Indian Religions to the History of Religions." In *Seeing with a Native Eye*, edited by Walter Holden Capps, 86–106.

Hurston, Zora Neale. *Their Eyes Were Watching God*. 1937. Reprint. Urbana: University of Illinois Press, 1978.

———. "What White Publishers Won't Print." In *I Love Myself When I Am Laughing. . . .*, edited by Alice Walker, 169–73. Old Westbury, N.Y.: Feminist Press, 1979.

Hutcheson, Martha Brookes. *The Spirit of the Garden*. Boston: Atlantic Monthly Press, 1923.

Huth, Hans. *Nature and the American Mind: Three Centuries of Changing Attitudes*. Berkeley and Los Angeles: University of California Press, 1957.

Hynes, H. Patricia. "Ellen Swallow, Lois Gibbs, and Rachel Carson: Catalysts of the American Environmental Movement." *Woman of Power* 9 (Spring 1988): 37–41, 78–80.

———. *The Recurring Silent Spring*. New York: Pergamon Press, 1989.

Jackson, Christine E. *Bird Etchings: The Illustrators and Their Books*. Ithaca: Cornell University Press, 1985.

Jackson, J. B. *The Necessity for Ruins and Other Topics*. Amherst: University of Massachusetts Press, 1980.

Jackson, Kenneth T. *Crabgrass Frontier: The Suburbanization of the United States*. New York: Oxford University Press, 1985.

Jacobs, Harriet. *Incidents in the Life of a Slave Girl*. Edited by Lydia Maria Child. 1861. Reprinted with an introduction and notes by Walter Teller. San Diego: Harcourt Brace Jovanovich, 1973.

Jacobs, Jane. *The Death and Life of Great American Cities*. New York: Random House, 1961.

Jacobs, Katherine L. "Celia Thaxter and Her Island Garden." *Landscape* 24 (1980): 12–17.

Jaggar, Alison. *Feminist Politics and Human Nature*. Totowa, N.J.: Rowman and Allanheld, 1983.

James, Edward T., ed. *Notable American Women, 1607–1950*. Cambridge: Harvard University Press, 1971.

Jewett, Sarah Orne. *The Country of the Pointed Firs and Other Stories*. Selected and introduced by Mary Helen Chase. Introduction to the Norton edition by Marjorie Pryse. New York: W. W. Norton and Co., 1981.

Johnson, E[mily] Pauline. *The Moccasin Maker*. Toronto: William Briggs, 1913.

Johnson, Josephine. *The Inland Island*. Columbus: Ohio State University Press, 1969.

Johnson, Osa. *Four Years in Paradise*. London, New York, and Melbourne: Hutchinson and Co., 1941.

———. *I Married Adventure: The Lives and Adventures of Martin and Osa Johnson*. Garden City, N.Y.: Garden City Publishing Co., 1940.

Johnston, Frances Benjamin. "What a Woman Can Do with a Camera." *Ladies' Home Journal* (September 1897): 6–7.

Jones, Jacqueline. *Labor of Love, Labor of Sorrow: Black Women, Work, and the Family from Slavery to the Present*. New York: Vintage Books, 1986.

Jones, Maggie, and Wangari Maathai. "Greening the Desert: Women of Kenya Reclaim Land." In *Reclaim the Earth*, edited by Leonie Caldecott and Stephanie Leland, 112–14.

Kassler, Elizabeth B. *Modern Gardens and the Landscape*. New York: Museum of Modern Art, 1964.

Keller, Evelyn Fox. *A Feeling for the Organism: The Life and Work of Barbara McClintock*. San Francisco: W. H. Freeman, 1983.

Kellert, Stephen R., and Joyce K. Berry. *Knowledge, Affection, and Basic Attitudes toward Animals in American Society*. American Attitudes, Knowledge, and Behaviors toward Wildlife and Natural Habitats, Phase III. Washington, D.C.: U.S. Fish and Wildlife Service, 1980.

Kelley, Mary. *Private Woman, Public Stage: Literary Domesticity in Nineteenth-Century America*. New York: Oxford University Press, 1984.

Kheel, Marti. "Ecofeminism and Deep Ecology: Reflections on Identity and Difference." In *Reweaving the World*, edited by Irene Diamond and Gloria Feman Orenstein, 128–37.

———. "From Healing Herbs to Deadly Drugs: Western Medicine's War against the Natural World." In *Healing the Wounds: The Promise of Ecofeminism*, edited Judith Plant, 96–111.

———. "The Liberation of Nature: A Circular Affair." *Environmental Ethics* 7 (Summer 1985): 135–49.

King, Louisa Yeomans [Mrs. Francis]. *The Little Garden*. Boston: Atlantic Monthly Press, 1921.

———. *Pages from a Garden Notebook*. New York: Charles Scribner's Sons, 1921.

King, Ynestra. "The Ecology of Feminism and the Feminism of Ecology." In *Healing the Wounds*, ed. Judith Plant, 18–29.

———. "Healing the Wounds: Feminism, Ecology, and the Nature/Culture Dualism." In *Reweaving the World*, edited by Irene Diamond and Gloria Feman Orenstein, 106–21.

———. "What Is Ecofeminism?" *Nation* (December 12, 1987): 702, 730–32.

Knapp, John Leonard. *Country Rambles in England; or, Journal of a Naturalist, with notes and additions by the author of "Rural Hours."* 1829. Reprint. Edited and annotated by Susan Fenimore Cooper. Buffalo, N.Y.: Phinney and Co., 1853.

Kofalk, Harriet. *No Woman Tenderfoot: Florence Merriam Bailey, Pioneer Naturalist*. College Station: Texas A&M University Press, 1989.

Kohlstedt, Sally Gregory. "In from the Periphery: American Women in Science, 1830–1880." *Signs: Journal of Women in Culture and Society* 4 (Autumn 1978): 81–96.

Kolodny, Annette. *The Land Before Her: Fantasy and Experience of the American Frontiers, 1630–1860*. Chapel Hill: University of North Carolina Press, 1984.

———. *The Lay of the Land: Metaphor as Experience and History in American Life and Letters*. Chapel Hill: University of North Carolina Press, 1975.

Kuhn, Thomas S. *The Structure of Scientific Revolutions*. 2d ed. Chicago: University of Chicago Press, 1970.

Kumin, Maxine. *In Deep: Country Essays*. Boston: Beacon Press, 1987.

Kurth, Rosaly Torna. "Susan Fenimore Cooper: A Study of Her Life and Works." Ph.D. dissertation, Fordham University, 1974.

LaBastille, Anne. *Women and Wilderness: Professions and Lifestyles*. San Francisco: Sierra Club Books, 1980.

Lacy, Allen. Introduction to *Gardening for Love*, by Elizabeth Lawrence, 1–22.

La Tour, Mme. Charlotte de [pseud. of Mme. Louise Contambert]. *Le Langage des Fleurs*. Paris: Audot, 1819.

Lawrence, Elizabeth. *Gardening for Love: The Market Bulletins*. Edited by Allen Lacy. Durham: Duke University Press, 1987.

———. *The Little Bulbs: A Tale of Two Gardens*. 1957. Reprint. Durham: Duke University Press, 1986.

———. *A Southern Garden: A Handbook for the Middle South*. 1942. Reprint. Chapel Hill: University of North Carolina Press, 1984.

———. *Through the Garden Gate*. Edited by Bill Neal. Chapel Hill: University of North Carolina Press, 1990.

Leavitt, Emily Stewart. *Animals and Their Legal Rights: A Survey of American Laws from 1641–1978*. Washington, D.C.: Animal Welfare Institute, 1978.

Le Guin, Ursula K. *Buffalo Gals and Other Animal Presences*. New York: New American Library, 1987.

———. "A Very Warm Mountain." *Parabola* 5 (1980): 46–52.

Leighton, Ann. *American Gardens of the Nineteenth Century: "For Comfort and Affluence."* Amherst: University of Massachusetts Press, 1987.

Lemmon, John Gill. "A Botanical Wedding Trip." *The Californian: A Western Monthly Magazine* 4 (July–December 1881): 517–25.

Leonard, John. "The Public and *Silent Spring*." *NAC News and Pesticide Review* (October 1964): 5.

———. "Review of *Silent Spring*." *Time*, September 28, 1962.

Leopold, A. Starker. Foreword to *Arctic Wild*, by Lois Crisler.

Levine, Lawrence W. *Black Culture and Black Consciousness: Afro-American Folk Thought from Slavery to Freedom*. New York: Oxford University Press, 1977.

Liberty, Margot. "Hell Came With Horses: Plains Indian Women in the Equestrian Era." *Montana Magazine of Western History* (Summer 1982): 10–19.

Linderman, Frank. *Pretty-shield: Medicine Woman of the Crows*. Lincoln: University of Nebraska Press, 1972. (First published in 1932 as *Red Mother* [New York: John Day Co.]).

Lindsay, W. K. "Integrating Parks and Pastoralists: Some Lessons from Amboseli." In *Conservation in Africa*, edited by David Anderson and Richard Grove, 149–68.

Lister, Adrian. "A Wild Social Life." *Nature* 334 (August 11, 1988): 480.

Little, Elbert L., Jr. *Southwestern Trees: A Guide to the Native Species of New Mexico and Arizona*. Washington, D.C.: U.S. Department of Agriculture, 1950.

Lothrop, Gloria Ricci. "Women Pioneers and the California Landscape." *The Californians* (May–June 1986): 16–23.

Loudon, Mrs. Jane. *Gardening for Ladies and Companion to the Flower Garden*. Edited by A. J. Downing. New York: Wiley and Halstead, 1849.

Lyon, Thomas J. *This Incomperable Lande: A Book of American Nature Writing*. Boston: Houghton Mifflin, 1989.

McCauley, Lena May. *The Joy of Gardens*. Chicago: Rand McNally and Co., 1911.

MacCormack, Carol P., and Marilyn Strathern, eds. *Nature, Culture, and Gender*. Cambridge: Cambridge University Press, 1980.

McCormick, John. *Reclaiming Paradise: The Global Environmental Movement*. Bloomington: Indiana University Press, 1989.

McCulloch-Williams, Martha. *Next to the Ground: Chronicles of a Countryside*. New York: McClure, Phillips and Co., 1902.

McIntyre, Joan, comp. *Mind in the Waters: A Book to Celebrate the Consciousness of Whales and Dolphins*. New York: Charles Scribner's Sons, and Sierra Club Books, San Francisco, 1974.

MacPhail Elizabeth C. *Kate Sessions: Pioneer Horticulturist*. San Diego: San Diego Historical Society, 1976.

Maddox, Lucy B. "Susan Fenimore Cooper and the Plain Daughters of America." *American Quarterly* 40 (June 1988): 131–47.

Magowan, Robin. "Pastoral and the Art of Landscape in *The Country of the Pointed Firs*." In *Appreciation of Sarah Orne Jewett*, edited by Richard Cary, 187–95.

Major, Mike. "Pilgrim of the Absolute." *America* 138 (May 6, 1978): 363–64.

Mallis, Arnold. *American Entomologists*. New Brunswick, N.J.: Rutgers University Press, 1971.

Marcet, Mrs. Jane. *Conversations on Vegetable Physiology; Comprehending the Elements of*

*Botany, with Their Application to Agriculture*. New York: Sleight and Robinson, 1830.

Marshall, Paule. *Praisesong for the Widow*. New York: E. P. Dutton, 1984.

Martin, Calvin. "The American Indian as Miscast Ecologist." *History Teacher* 14 (February 1981): 243–52.

Martineau, Harriet. *Society in America*. 3 vols. London: Saunders and Otley, 1837.

Marzio, Peter C. "American Drawing Books." In *Philadelphia Printmaking: American Prints Before 1860*, edited by Robert F. Looney, 9–42. West Chester, Pa.: Tinicum Press, 1977.

Mawson, Thomas. *The Art and Craft of Garden Making*. London: B. T. Batsford, 1900.

May, Elaine Tyler. *Homeward Bound: American Families in the Cold War Era*. New York: Basic Books, 1988.

Merchant, Carolyn. *The Death of Nature: Women, Ecology, and the Scientific Revolution*. San Francisco: Harper and Row, 1980.

———. "Earthcare: Women and the Environment." *Environment* 23 (June 1981): 6–13, 38–40.

———. "Ecofeminism and Feminist Theory." In *Reweaving the World*, edited by Irene Diamond and Gloria Feman Orenstein, 100–105.

———. *Ecological Revolutions: Nature, Gender, and Science in New England*. Chapel Hill: University of North Carolina Press, 1989.

———. "Women of the Progressive Conservation Movement, 1900–1916." *Environmental Review* 8 (Spring 1984): 57–86.

Merriam, Florence A. *A-Birding on a Bronco*. Boston: Houghton Mifflin, 1896.

——— [published under Florence Merriam Bailey]. *Birds of New Mexico*. New Mexico: New Mexico Department of Game and Fish, 1928.

Mexia, Ynez. "Birds of Brazil." *The Gull* 12 (July–August 1930): unpaged.

———. "Botanical Trails in Old Mexico: The Lure of the Unknown." *Madroño: Journal of the California Botanical Society* 1 (September 1929): 227–38.

Middleton, Dorothy. *Victorian Lady Travellers*. London: Routledge and Kegan Paul, 1965.

Midgley, Mary. *Animals and Why They Matter*. Athens: University of Georgia Press, 1983.

Mighetto, Lisa. "Science, Sentiment, and Anxiety: American Nature Writing at the Turn of the Century." *Pacific Historical Review* 54 (February 1985): 33–50.

———. "Wildlife Protection and the New Humanitarianism." *Environmental Review* 12 (Spring 1988): 37–49.

Miller, Olive Thorne. *In Nesting Time*. Boston: Houghton Mifflin, 1888.

Miller, Robert C. Introductory Note. In *One Day on Beetle Rock*, by Salla Carrighar, 1.

Montgomery, Sy. *Walking with the Great Apes: Jane Goodall, Dian Fossey, Biruté Galdikas*. Boston: Houghton Mifflin, 1991.

Morgan, Robin. *The Anatomy of Freedom: Feminism, Physics, and Global Politics*. Garden City, N.Y.: Anchor Press/Doubleday, 1984.

Moriarty, Henrietta Maria. *Fifty Plates of Green-House Plants, Drawn and Coloured From Nature. . . .* London: T. Bensley, 1807.

Morrison, Toni. *Beloved.* New York: Alfred A Knopf, 1987.

Morrow, Baker H. *A Dictionary of Landscape Architecture.* Albuquerque: University of New Mexico Press, 1987.

Moss, Cynthia. *Elephant Memories: Thirteen Years in the Life of an Elephant Family.* New York: William Morrow and Co., 1988.

Mott, Frank Luther. *American Journalism: A History, 1690–1960.* 3d ed. New York: Macmillan, 1962.

Mowat, Farley. *Woman in the Mists: The Story of Dian Fossey and the Mountain Gorillas of Africa.* New York: Warner Books, 1987.

"Mrs. Agnes Chase, Botanist, Is Dead." *New York Times,* September 26, 1963.

Mulvey, Christopher. *Anglo-American Landscapes: A Study of Nineteenth-Century Anglo-American Travel Literature.* Cambridge: Cambridge University Press, 1983.

Murie, Margaret E. *Two in the Far North.* 1962. Reprint. Anchorage: Alaska Northwest Publishing Co., 1978.

Murray, Amelia. *Letters from the United States, Cuba, and Canada.* New York: G. P. Putnam, 1856.

Nash, Roderick. *The Rights of Nature: A History of Environmental Ethics.* Madison: University of Wisconsin Press, 1989.

———. *Wilderness and the American Mind.* New Haven: Yale University Press, 1967 (3d ed., 1982).

Nevins, Deborah. "The Triumph of Flora: Women and the American Landscape, 1890–1935." *Antiques* 127 (April 1985): 904–22.

Nevius, Blake. *Cooper's Landscapes: An Essay on the Picturesque Vision.* Berkeley and Los Angeles: University of California Press, 1976.

Newkirk, Ingrid. "Animal Rights and the Feminist Connection." *Woman of Power* 9 (Spring 1988): 67–69.

Newton, Norman T. *Design on the Land: The Development of Landscape Architecture.* Cambridge: Harvard University Press, 1971.

Norwood, Vera. "Heroines of Nature: Four Women Respond to the American Landscape." *Environmental Review* 8 (Spring 1984): 34–57.

———. "The Nature of Knowing: Rachel Carson and the American Environment." *Signs: Journal of Women in Culture and Society* 12 (Summer 1987): 740–60.

———. "The Photographer and the Naturalist: Laura Gilpin and Mary Austin in the Southwest." *Journal of American Culture* 5 (Summer 1982): 1–29.

Novak, Barbara. *Nature and Culture: American Landscape Painting, 1825–1875.* New York: Oxford University Press, 1980.

Olcott, Diana Morgan. *Winds of Change, 1963–1988: Seventy-fifth Anniversary Chronicle of the Garden Club of America.* Trenton, N.J.: Parker Printing Co., 1988.

Olds, Elizabeth Fagg. *Women of the Four Winds: The Adventures of Four of America's First Women Explorers.* Boston: Houghton Mifflin, 1985.

Orenstein, Gloria Feman. "Artists As Healers: Envisioning Life-Giving Culture." In

*Reweaving the World*, edited by Irene Diamond and Gloria Feman Orenstein, 279–87.

Ortner, Sherry. "Is Female to Male as Nature Is to Culture?" In *Woman, Culture, and Society*, edited by Michele Zimbalist Rosaldo and Louise Lamphere, 66–87. Stanford, Calif.: Stanford University Press, 1974.

Padilla, Victoria. *Southern California Gardens*. Berkeley and Los Angeles: University of California Press, 1961.

Parker, Sir Gilbert. Introduction to *The Moccasin Maker*, by E. Pauline Johnson, 5–8.

Parr, A. E. "The Habitat Group." *Curator* 2 (1959): 107–28.

Parrinder, Geoffrey. *African Traditional Religion*. London: Sheldon Press, 1974.

Pearson, T. Gilbert. "Which Would You Choose?" *Bird-Lore* 17 (May–June 1915): 250.

Pease, Jane H., and William H. Pease. *Ladies, Women, and Wenches: Choice and Constraint in Antebellum Charleston and Boston*. Chapel Hill: University of North Carolina Press, 1990.

Perényi, Eleanor. *Green Thoughts: A Writer in the Garden*. New York: Random House, 1983.

Perkins, John H. *Insects, Experts, and the Insecticide Crisis*. New York: Plenum Press, 1982.

———. "Insects, Food, and Hunger: The Paradox of Plenty for U.S. Entomology, 1920–1970." *Environmental Review* 7 (Spring 1983): 71–96.

Peterson, Roger Tory. "Bird Art." *Natural History* (September 1983): 66–74.

Petulla, Joseph M. *American Environmental History*. 1977. Reprint. Columbus, Ohio: Merrill Publishing Co., 1988.

Phelps, Almira Hart Lincoln. *Familiar Lectures on Botany, Practical, Elementary, and Physiological*. 1829. Reprint. New York: Huntington and Savage, 1846.

Phillips, Venia T., and Maurice E. Phillips. *Guide to the Manuscript Collections in the Academy of Natural Sciences of Philadelphia*. Special publication no. 5. Philadelphia: Academy of Natural Sciences of Philadelphia, 1963.

Piercy, Marge. "Margaret Atwood: Beyond Victimhood." *American Poetry Review* 2 (November–December 1973): 41–44.

Pilkington, William T. Introduction to *The Mountain Lion*, by Jean Stafford, vii–xv.

Pilsbry, Henry. *Land Mollusca of North America*. Academy of Natural Sciences of Philadelphia Monographs, no. 3, vol. 2, pt. 1. Philadelphia: Academy of Natural Sciences of Philadelphia, 1946.

———. "The Land Mollusks of the Belgian Congo." In *Bulletin of the American Museum of Natural History*, vol. 40. New York: American Museum of Natural History, 1919.

Pilsbry, Henry, and J. Bequet. "The Aquatic Mollusks of the Belgian Congo." *Bulletin of the American Museum of Natural History*, vol. 53. New York: American Museum of Natural History, 1927.

Plant, Judith, ed. *Healing the Wounds: The Promise of Ecofeminism*. Philadelphia: New Society Publishers, 1989.

Plumwood, Val. "Ecofeminism: An Overview and Discussion of Positions and Arguments." *Australasian Journal of Philosophy* supp. 64 (June 1986): 120–38.

Porter, Gene Stratton. *Homing with the Birds*. Garden City, N.Y.: Doubleday, Page and Co., 1919.

——. *Moths of the Limberlost*. Garden City, N.Y.: Doubleday, Page and Co., 1912.

Pratt, Annis. *Archetypal Patterns in Women's Fiction*. Bloomington: Indiana University Press, 1981.

——. "Women and Nature in Modern Fiction." *Contemporary Literature* 13 (Autumn 1972): 476–90.

Prior, Mary Barbot. "Letters of Martha Logan to John Bartram, 1760–1763." *South Carolina Historical Magazine* 59 (1958): 38–46.

Rensberger, Boyce. *The Cult of the Wild*. Garden City, N.Y.: Anchor Press/Doubleday, 1977.

Rich, Louise Dickinson. *We Took to the Woods*. Philadelphia: J. B. Lippincott Co., 1942.

Rickett, H. W. "Jane Colden as Botanist in Contemporary Opinion." In *Botanic Manuscript*, by Jane Colden, 22–25.

Robbins, Ellen. "Reminiscences of a Flower Painter." *New England Magazine* 14 (June–July 1886): 440–51, 532–45.

Roberts, David. *Jean Stafford: A Biography*. Boston: Little, Brown and Co., 1988.

Robertson, Robert. "Virginia Orr Maes (1920–1986): Biography and Malacological Bibliography." *Proceedings of the Academy of Natural Sciences of Philadelphia* 138 (1987): 527–32.

Rosaldo, Michele Zimbalist. "The Use and Abuse of Anthropology: Reflections on Feminism and Cross-Cultural Understanding." *Signs: Journal of Women in Culture and Society* 5 (Spring 1980): 389–417.

Rosinsky, Natalie M. *Feminist Futures: Contemporary Women's Speculative Fiction*. Ann Arbor, Mich.: UMI Research Press, 1984.

Rossiter, Margaret W. *Women Scientists in America: Struggles and Strategies to 1940*. Baltimore: Johns Hopkins University Press, 1982.

Rowan, Andrew N. *Of Mice, Models, and Men: A Critical Evaluation of Animal Research*. Albany: State University of New York Press, 1984.

Rudnai, Judith A. *The Social Life of the Lion: A Study of the Behaviour of Wild Lions in the Nairobi National Park, Kenya*. Wallingford, Pa.: Washington Square East, Publishers, 1973.

Rudolph, Emanuel D. "How It Developed That Botany Was the Science Thought Most Suitable for Victorian Young Ladies." *Children's Literature* 2 (1973): 92–97.

——. "The Introduction of the Natural System of Classification of Plants to Nineteenth-Century American Students." *Archives of Natural History* 10 (April 1982): 461–68.

——. "Women In Nineteenth-Century American Botany: A Generally Unrecognized Constituency." *American Journal of Botany* 69 (1982): 1346–55.

Ruether, Rosemary Radford. *New Woman/New Earth: Sexist Ideologies and Human Liberation*. New York: Seabury Press, 1975.

———. "Toward an Ecological-Feminist Theory of Nature." In *Healing the Wounds*, edited by Judith Plant, 145–51.

Russett, Cynthia Eagle. *Sexual Science: The Victorian Construction of Womanhood*. Cambridge: Harvard University Press, 1989.

Rutledge, Anna Wells, ed. *Cumulative Record of Exhibition Catalogues, Pennsylvania Academy of the Fine Arts, 1807–1870, the Society of Artists, 1800–1814, [and] the Artist's Fund Society, 1835–1845*. Philadelphia: American Philosophical Society, 1955.

Ryan, Mary P. *The Empire of the Mother: American Writing about Domesticity, 1830–1860*. New York: Haworth Press, 1982.

———. *Womanhood in America: From Colonial Times to the Present*. New York: Franklin Watts, 1983.

Ryden, Hope. *Bobcat Year*. New York: Viking Press, 1981.

———. *God's Dog: A Celebration of the North American Coyote*. New York: Lyons and Burford, 1979.

———. *Lily Pond: Four Years with a Family of Beavers*. New York: William Morrow and Co., 1989.

Sacilotto, Irene Hinke. "Osprey Photo Workshops and Tours." Baltimore: Osprey Photo Workshops and Tours, 1990.

Sale, Kirkpatrick. "Ecofeminism—A New Perspective." *Nation* (September 26, 1987): 302–4.

Salleh, Ariel Kay. "Deeper Than Deep Ecology: The Eco-Feminist Connection." *Environmental Ethics* 6 (Winter 1984): 339–46.

Sargent, Lyman Tower. "A New Anarchism: Social and Political Ideas in Some Recent Feminist Eutopias." In *Women and Utopia: Critical Interpretations*, edited by Marleen Barr and Nicholas D. Smith, 3–33. Lanham, Md.: University Press of America, 1983.

Say, Thomas. *American Conchology*. Illustrated by Lucy Say. New Harmony, Ind.: Printed at the School Press, 1830–34. (Originally issued in seven parts.)

Schaller, George B. *The Serengeti Lion: A Study of Predator-Prey Relations*. Chicago: University of Chicago Press, 1972.

Scheffer, Victor B. "Benign Uses of Wildlife." *International Journal for the Study of Animal Problems* 1 (1980): 19–32.

Schlissel, Lillian. *Women's Diaries of the Westward Journey*. New York: Schocken Books, 1982.

Schmitt, Peter J. *Back to Nature: The Arcadian Myth in Urban America*. 1969. Reprint. Baltimore: Johns Hopkins University Press, 1990.

Schmitz, Jan. "Women in Science." *Academy News* 7 (Autumn 1984): 5–7.

Schultz, Esther. "Mrs. Agnes Chase, World Scientist." *Saint Louis Star Times*, March 10, 1949.

Schwartz, Robert L. "The Great Underwater Adventure." *Life* 45 (November 24, 1958): 135–36.

Scott, Anne Firor. *Making the Invisible Woman Visible*. Urbana: University of Illinois Press, 1984.

Scott, Frank J. *The Art of Beautifying Suburban Home Grounds of Small Extent.* . . . New York: D. Appleton, 1870.

Seaton, Beverly. "The Flower Language Books of the Nineteenth Century." *Morton Arboretum Quarterly* 16 (1980): 1–11.

———. "The Garden Autobiography." *Garden History: The Journal of the Garden History Society* 7 (Spring 1979): 101–20.

Sessions, George. "The Deep Ecology Movement: A Review." *Environmental Review* 11 (Summer 1987): 105–25.

Sharf, Frederic A. "Fidelia Bridges, 1834–1923: Painter of Birds and Flowers." *Essex Institute Historical Collections* 104 (July 1968): 217–37.

Shelton, Louise. *Beautiful Gardens in America*. New York: Charles Scribner's Sons, 1928.

Shiva, Vandana. "Indian Women and the Chipko Movement." *Woman of Power* 9 (Spring 1988): 26–31.

Shoumatoff, Alex. *African Madness*. New York: Vintage Books, 1990.

Shteir, Ann. "Women and Plants: A Fruitful Topic." *Atlantis* 6 (Spring 1981): 114–23.

Silko, Leslie Marmon. "Landscape, History, and the Pueblo Imagination." *Antaeus* 57 (Autumn 1986): 83–94.

———. *Storyteller*. New York: Seaver Books, 1981.

Singer, Peter. *Animal Liberation: A New Ethics for Our Treatment of Animals*. New York: Random House, 1975.

Smallwood, William Martin, and Mabel Sarah Coon Smallwood. *Natural History and the American Mind*. New York: Columbia University Press, 1941.

Smith, Patricia Clark, and Paula Gunn Allen. "Earthy Relations, Carnal Knowledge: Southwestern American Indian Women Writers and the Landscape." In *The Desert Is No Lady: Southwestern Landscapes in Women's Writing and Art*, edited by Vera Norwood and Janice Monk, 174–96. New Haven: Yale University Press, 1987.

Smith-Rosenberg, Carroll. *Disorderly Conduct: Visions of Gender in Victorian America*. New York: Alfred A. Knopf, 1985.

Spelman, Elizabeth. "Woman as Body: Ancient and Contemporary Views." *Feminist Studies* 8 (Spring 1982): 108–31.

Sperling, Susan. *Animal Liberators: Research and Morality*. Berkeley and Los Angeles: University of California Press, 1988.

———. "Baboons with Briefcases: Feminism, Functionalism, and Sociobiology in the Evolution of Primate Gender." *Signs: Journal of Women in Culture and Society* 17 (Autumn 1991): 1–27.

Spirn, Anne Whiston. *The Granite Garden: Urban Nature and Human Design*. New York: Basic Books, 1984.

Spretnak, Charlene. "Toward an Ecofeminist Spirituality." In *Healing the Wounds*, edited by Judith Plant, 127–32.

Stafford, Jean. *The Mountain Lion*. 1947. Reprinted with an introduction by William Pilkington. Albuquerque: University of New Mexico Press, 1972.

Stanwell-Fletcher, Theodora C. *Driftwood Valley*. Boston: Little, Brown and Co., 1946.

Stanwood, Cordelia J. "The Hermit Thrush: The Voice of the Northern Woods." *Bird-Lore* 12 (May–June 1910): 100–103.

———. "Tenants of Birdsacre." *House Beautiful* 48 (October 1920): 280–81, 314.

Steele, Mrs. [Eliza R.] *A Summer Journey in the West*. New York: J. S. Taylor, 1841.

Stein, Clarence S. *Toward New Towns for America*. Cambridge: MIT Press, 1966.

Stein, Sara B. *My Weeds: A Gardener's Botany*. New York: Harper and Row, 1988.

Sterling, Philip. *Sea and Earth: The Life of Rachel Carson*. New York: Thomas Y. Crowell, 1970.

Stilgoe, John R. *Borderland: Origins of the American Suburb, 1820–1939*. New Haven: Yale University Press, 1988.

Stineman, Esther Lanigan. *Mary Austin: Song of a Maverick*. New Haven: Yale University Press, 1989.

Stouck, David. "*The Country of the Pointed Firs*: A Pastoral of Innocence." In *Appreciation of Sarah Orne Jewett*, edited by Richard Cary, 249–54.

Swarts, Mrs. Ida H. "Papa Is Wrong." *Virginia Pilot*, January 16, 1963.

Tabor, Grace. *Old-Fashioned Gardening: A History and Reconstruction*. New York: McBride, Nast and Co., 1913.

Taylor, Robert Lewis. "Oh, Hawk of Mercy!" *New Yorker* 24 (April 17, 1948): 31–45.

Teutonico, Jeanne Marie. "Marian Cruger Coffin: The Long Island Estates." M.S. thesis, Columbia University, 1983.

Thaxter, Celia. *Among the Isles of Shoals*. Boston: J. R. Osgood and Co., 1873.

———. *An Island Garden*. Boston: Houghton Mifflin, 1894.

———. "A Woman's Heartlessness." [1886]. (Reprinted in pamphlet form by the Audubon Society of the State of New Jersey, 1899, 7 pp.)

———. *Letters of Celia Thaxter*. Edited by Annie Fields and Rose Lamb. Boston: Houghton Mifflin, 1895.

Thaxter, Rosamond. *Sandpiper: The Life of Celia Thaxter*. Sanbornville, N.H.: Wake-Brook House, 1962.

Thomas, Keith. *Man and the Natural World: A History of Modern Sensibility*. New York: Pantheon, 1983.

Thornton, Tamara Plakins. "The Moral Dimensions of Horticulture in Antebellum America." *New England Quarterly* 57 (March 1984): 3–24.

Tice, Patricia M. *Gardening in America: 1830–1910*. Rochester, N.Y.: The Strong Museum, 1984.

Tillman, Al. "Recreation Goes Underwater." *Recreation* 48 (February 1955): 62–63.

Tinling, Marion. *Women into the Unknown: A Sourcebook on Women Explorers and Travelers*. New York: Greenwood Press, 1989.

Torgovnick, Marianna. *Gone Primitive: Savage Intellects, Modern Lives*. Chicago: University of Chicago Press, 1990.

Torre, Susana. *Women in American Architecture: A Historic and Contemporary Perspective*. New York: Whitney Library of Design, 1977.

Treat, Mary. *Home Studies in Nature*. New York: Harper and Brothers, 1885.

———. *Injurious Insects of the Farm and Garden*. New York: Orange Judd Co., 1882.

Trimble, Stephen, ed. *Words from the Land: Encounters with Natural History Writing*. Salt Lake City, Utah: Peregrine Smith Books, 1989.

Trollope, Mrs. *Domestic Manners of the Americans*. London: Whittaker, Treacher, and Co., 1832.

Tunnard, Christopher. *Gardens in the Modern Landscape*. New York: Charles Scribner's Sons, 1938. Rev. 1948.

Turner, Miss E[mma] L. "Bird Photography for Women." *Bird-Lore* 17 (May–June 1915): 175–90.

Turner, James. *Reckoning with the Beast: Animals, Pain, and Humanity in the Victorian Mind*. Baltimore: Johns Hopkins University Press, 1980.

Vance, Linda D. *May Mann Jennings: Florida's Genteel Activist*. Gainesville: University Presses of Florida, 1985.

Van Rensselaer, Mariana Griswold [Mrs. Schuyler]. *Art Out-Of-Doors: Hints on Good Taste in Gardening*. New York: Charles Scribner's Sons, 1893.

Van Steen, Marcus. *Pauline Johnson: Her Life and Work*. Toronto: Musson Book Co., 1965.

Varley, Elsie D. "Gardening Clothes for the Woman with the Hoe." *Countryside Magazine and Suburban Life* 12 (March 1911): 165.

Vecsey, Christopher T., and Robert W. Venables. *American Indian Environments: Ecological Issues in Native American History*. Syracuse, N.Y.: Syracuse University Press, 1980.

"A Versatile Lady's New Adventure." *Life* 43 (August 5, 1957): 68.

Vlach, John Michael. *The Afro-American Tradition in Decorative Arts*. Cleveland: Cleveland Museum of Art, 1978.

Walker, Alice. *In Search of Our Mothers' Gardens: Humanist Prose*. San Diego: Harcourt Brace Jovanovich, 1983.

———. *Living by the Word: Selected Essays, 1973–1987*. San Diego: Harcourt Brace Jovanovich, 1989.

———. "Why Did the Balinese Chicken Cross the Road?" *Woman of Power* 9 (Spring 1988): 50. Reprinted in *Living by the Word*, by Alice Walker, 170–73.

Wallace, David H. *New-York Historical Society's Dictionary of Artists in America, 1564–1860*. New Haven: Yale University Press, 1957.

Wallihan, Allen Grant, and Mrs. Wallihan [Mary Augusta]. *Camera Shots at Big Game*. New York: Doubleday, Page and Co., 1901.

———. *Hoofs, Claws, and Antlers of the Rocky Mountains*. Denver: Frank S. Thayer, 1894.

Warner, Anna. *Gardening By Myself*. New York: Anson D. F. Randolph and Co., 1872.

Warner, Deborah. *Graceanna Lewis: Scientist and Humanitarian*. Washington, D.C.: Smithsonian Institution Press, 1979.

Warner, Sam Bass. *To Dwell Is To Garden: A History of Boston's Community Gardens.* Boston: Northeastern University Press, 1987.

Warren, Karen J. "Feminism and Ecology: Making Connections." *Environmental Ethics* 9 (Spring 1987): 3–20.

———. "The Power and the Promise of Ecological Feminism." *Environmental Ethics* 12 (Summer 1990): 125–46.

Wechsler, Chuck. "N. Glazier: A Passion for Painting." *Wildlife Art News* 4 (May–June 1985): 36–40.

Weiss, Harry. "Mrs. Mary Treat, 1830–1923, Early New Jersey Naturalist." *Proceedings of the New Jersey Historical Society* 73 (1955): 258–73.

Weiss, Harry, and Grace M. Ziegler. *Thomas Say: Early American Naturalist.* Springfield, Ill.: Charles C. Thomas, 1931.

Wekerle, Gerda R., Rebecca Peterson, and David Morley, eds. *New Space for Women.* Boulder, Colo.: Westview Press, 1980.

Welker, Robert Henry. *Birds and Men: American Birds in Science, Art, Literature, and Conservation, 1800–1900.* Cambridge: Harvard University Press, 1955.

Welter, Barbara. *Dimity Convictions: The American Woman in the Nineteenth Century.* Athens: Ohio University Press, 1976.

Westcott, Cynthia. "The Question Has Two Sides." *National Gardener* 33 (1962): 30.

Wharton, Edith. *Italian Villas and Their Gardens.* New York: Century Co., 1910.

White, Gilbert. *The Natural History of Selborne.* 1789. Reprint. London: Chatto and Windus, 1890.

White, James J., and Erik A. Neumann. "The Collection of Pomological Watercolors at the U.S. National Arboretum." *Huntia* 4 (1982): 103–17.

White, James J., and Ruth F. Schallert. "Illustrations in the *Contributions from the U.S. National Herbarium,* 1890–1974." *Huntia* 6 (1986): 147–63.

White, Katharine S. *Onward and Upward in the Garden.* Edited by E. B. White. New York: Farrar, Straus, Giroux, 1979.

White, Richard. "The Cultural Landscape of the Pawnees." *Great Plains Quarterly* 2 (1982): 31–40.

———. "Native Americans and the Environment." In *Scholars and the Indian Experience: Critical Reviews of Recent Writing in the Social Sciences,* edited by W. R. Swagerty, 179–204. Bloomington: Indiana University Press, 1984.

Whyte, William. *The Last Landscape.* Garden City, N.Y.: Doubleday, 1968.

Wick, Peter. Introduction and Notes for *The Court of Flora,* by J. J. Grandville, unpaged.

Wilder, Louise Beebe. *Adventures in My Garden and Rock Garden.* Garden City, N.Y.: Doubleday, Doran and Co., 1928.

*Wildlife: The Artist's View.* Exhibition catalog. Wausau, Wis.: Leigh Yawkey Woodson Art Museum, 1990.

*Wildlife in Art.* Exhibition catalog. Wausau, Wis.: Leigh Yawkey Woodson Art Museum, 1987.

Willis, Susan. "Crushed Geraniums: Juan Francisco Manzano and the Language of

Slavery." In *The Slave's Narrative*, edited by Charles T. Davis and Henry Louis Gates, Jr., 199–224.

———. *Specifying: Black Women Writing the American Experience*. Madison: University of Wisconsin Press, 1987.

Wilson, Carol Green. *Alice Eastwood's Wonderland: The Adventures of a Botanist*. San Francisco: California Academy of Sciences, 1955.

Wilson, Joan Hoff. "Dancing Dogs of the Colonial Period: Women Scientists." *Early American Literature* 7 (Winter 1973): 225–35.

Wilson, Marie, and Judith Plant. "Wings of the Eagle: A Conversation with Marie Wilson." In *Healing the Wounds*, edited by Judith Plant, 212–18.

Wilson, William E. *The Angel and the Serpent*. Bloomington: Indiana University Press, 1964.

Wilson, William H. "J. Horace McFarland and the City Beautiful Movement." *Journal of Urban History* 7 (May 1981): 315–34.

———. "'More Almost Than the Men': Mira Lloyd Dock and the Beautification of Harrisburg." *Pennsylvania Magazine of History and Biography* 99 (October 1975): 490–99.

Wood, Charles B. "Prints and Scientific Illustration in America." In *Prints in and of America to 1850*, edited by John D. Morse, 161–91. Charlottesville: University Press of Virginia, 1970.

Worster, Donald. *Nature's Economy: A History of Ecological Ideas*. Cambridge: Cambridge University Press, 1977.

Wortman, Marlene Stein. "Domesticating the Nineteenth-Century American City." *Prospects* 3 (1977): 531–72.

Wright, Gwendolyn. *Building the Dream: A Social History of Housing in America*. New York: Pantheon Books, 1981.

Wright, Mabel Osgood. *The Garden of a Commuter's Wife*. New York: Grosset and Dunlap, 1901.

———. *The Garden, You, and I*. New York: Macmillan, 1906.

Yates, Gale Graham, ed. *Harriet Martineau on Women*. New Brunswick, N.J.: Rutgers University Press, 1985.

*The Yearbook of the United States Department of Agriculture: Grass*. Washington, D.C.: U.S. Department of Agriculture, 1948.

*The Yearbook of the United States Department of Agriculture: Trees*. Washington, D.C.: U.S. Department of Agriculture, 1949.

Yellin, Jean Fagan. "Texts and Contexts of Harriet Jacobs' Incidents in the Life of a Slave Girl: Written by Herself." In *The Slave's Narrative*, edited by Charles T. Davis and Henry Louis Gates, Jr., 262–82.

Young, M. Jane. *Signs from the Ancestors: Zuni Cultural Symbolism and Perceptions of Rock Art*. Albuquerque: University of New Mexico Press, 1988.

Zimmerman, Michael E. "Deep Ecology and Feminism: The Emerging Dialogue." In *Reweaving the World*, edited by Irene Diamond and Gloria Feman Orenstein, 138–54.

———. "Feminism, Deep Ecology, and Environmental Ethics." *Environmental Ethics* 9 (Spring 1987): 21–44.

Zullo, Janet Lewis. "Annie Montague Alexander: Her Work in Paleontology." *Journal of the West* 8 (April 1969): 183–99.

Zwinger, Ann. *Beyond the Aspen Grove*. New York: Random House, 1970.

———. "Thoreau on Women." *Thoreau Society Bulletin*, no. 164 (Summer 1983): 3–7.

Zwinger, Ann, and Edwin Way Teale. *A Conscious Stillness: Two Naturalists on Thoreau's Rivers*. Amherst: University of Massachusetts Press, 1984.

# Index

211, 212–13, 224, 229, 250–51, 324
(n. 90); male dominance in, 211–12;
women's ethics in, 242, 244–45, 246,
251, 259; influence of feminism, 260.
*See also* Nature study
Animal Welfare Institute, 162
Anti-Steel Trap League, 158
Antivivisection, xiv, 162
Arbor Day, 35, 127, 129
Art, xviii, 12, 24; depicting native plants
and animals, 56; male vs. female participation in, 56, 58; nature as popular subject, 56, 94; garden painting,
103–5. *See also* Birds: photography
of, as female pursuit; Botanical illustration; Flower painting; Garden
photography; Scientific illustration;
Shell illustration; Wildlife: art; Wild-
life: photography
Atwood, Margaret, 207, 213, 268—
*Surfacing*, 202–6; women associated
with animals, 202, 204–6; on spirit in
nature, 205–6
Audubon, John James, 56; *Birds of
America*, 61
Audubon clubs, 43, 147, 154, 157, 216
Austin, Mary, 49, 53, 277, 279; *The Flock*,
49; *The Land of Journey's Ending*, 49;
*The Land of Little Rain*, 49, 51–52; as
New Woman, 50; on American Indian
women, 321–22 (n. 60)

Bagby, Rachel, 274
Bailey, Vernon, 43, 53
Baird, Spencer, 214
Bartram, William, 59; *Travels*, 25
Bauer, Erwin, 253
Bauer, Peggy, 253
Beautification, city, xiv, 138, 139, 142,
145–46; and garden clubs, 121, 129–
31
Beecher, Catharine: *The American
Woman's Home*, 99–100

Benchley, Belle, 282; relationships with
zoo animals, 231; rationalizes animal
captivity, 233
Binney, Amos, 61; *The Terrestrial Air-
Breathing Mollusks*, 66
Bird, Isabella, 5, 6, 11
Birds: protection of, xiv, 42–43, 46, 109,
155, 195; photography of, as female
pursuit, 72, 74
Bliss, Mildred, 115
Botanical illustration, 71, 87, 94
Botany: in women's education, 2–3, 13,
17–21, 59; popular texts for women,
11–13, 17–20; women's participation
in, 47
Bradley, Jack, 222–23
Bradley, Mary Hastings, 219–20, 224;
*On the Gorilla Trail*, 222; observes
gorilla social life, 223
Bremer, Fredrika, 6, 8–9, 11, 16, 27,
40; on American women as hothouse
plants, 4–5
Bridges, Fidelia, 56
Briggs, Shirley, 157, 163
Bryant, William Cullen, 26, 27
Burroughs, John, 26, 47; *Wake-Robin*, 46

Capra, Fritjof: *The Tao of Physics*, 269–70
Carby, Hazel, 175
Carrighar, Sally, xiv, xx, 249, 278; *One
Day on Beetle Rock*, 238; *Home to the
Wilderness*, 239; *The Twilight Seas*, 239;
biography of, 239–40
Carson, Rachel, xiv, xix, 275, 277, 279,
280; *The Sea Around Us*, 147, 150, 153,
164–65, 166; and women's networks,
147–48; interest in animal homes, 148;
biography of, 148, 150; *The Edge of
the Sea*, 150, 151; *Under the Sea Wind*,
150, 238; male vs. female responses to,
150–52, 165–70, 312 (n. 77); ecosystem as home, 151–52, 156; field study
method, 152; on women's role, 152–

242–44; *Captive Wild*, 244; destroys
Alatna, 244
Cumming, Constance Gordon, 7, 9, 10

Dartt, Mary, 213, 218; *On the Plains and
Among the Peaks*, 216
Darwin, Charles, 41, 53, 109
Dean, Ruth: *The Livable House*, 117
De Candolle, Augustin Pyramus, 17
Deep ecology: criticized by ecological
feminists, 268–69
Defenders of Wildlife, 162
Domesticity: and nature study, xvii, 1–5,
7–11, 17, 20–22, 26–31, 78, 164–66,
194–95, 251, 276, 278; and nature,
35–40, 43–46, 148, 196, 317 (n. 40);
and animal study, 41–46, 211–12, 240;
and sexuality, 46, 50–51; and women's
nature art, 97; and gardening, 106–7,
109–10, 123, 142; marginalized, 144–
46, 168, 171, 196–97, 198–99, 203,
208, 280; and environmental threats,
169–71; and women's trophy hunts,
214, 216–18, 221–22, 319 (n. 13)
Dormon, Caroline, 136
Dowden, Anne Ophelia: *Wild Green
Things in the City*, 94
Downing, Andrew Jackson, 4, 11, 26, 27,
36, 99, 101, 105, 109, 114, 141
Dubos, René, 268
Dumbarton Oaks, 115
Duncan, Frances: *The Joyous Art of Gardening*, 130

Eastwood, Alice, 127
Eaton, Amos, 19; *Manual of Botany*, 22
Ecofeminism. *See* Ecological feminism
Ecological feminism, 260; and women
of color, xx, 273–74, 283–84; defined, 261–62; utopianism, 262, 272,
282; activism, 262, 273; critique of
Western patriarchy, 262–63, 274; on
biological sex vs. socially constructed
gender, 264–66; and feminist spiri-

tuality, 265, 270; and ecology, 266,
268–69; and animal rights, 269; and
quantum physics, 269–70; critique
of positivism, 270–72; critique of
technological science, 272–73, 274;
analysis of, 275, 277–79, 281–84; and
Rachel Carson, 275, 280–81; place
in women's history, 275–82, 284, 328
(n. 36)
Edge, Rosalie, 158, 279–80
Elephants, 219–22, 225, 229, 245, 255–
59
Environmental movement: urban pollution, 145, 146; women's contributions
to, 147–48, 153–56, 169–71, 262; and
women of color, 173, 273
Ethology. *See* Animal study
Euro-American women, xvii, 206; identification with flowers, 12–13, 17;
bounded by culture, 174–75, 176,
185, 194, 201; as nature's defenders,
195; associated with animals, 196–97,
199–200, 202; alienated from nature,
197, 199, 202, 204–5; locate sacred in
nature, 197, 206; response to animal
stereotypes, 204–6; and domination
of nature, 276, 277–78; and wild
nature, 281–83, 330 (n. 45)
European travelers, 195; as naturalists, 4;
image of American women, 4–11, 99;
on African American and American
Indian women, 5–7

Farrand, Beatrix, xix, 120, 164, 277;
biography of, 110–11; as landscape designer, 114–17; use of familiar plants,
115; designs middle-class garden,
121, 124
Flower painting, 56, 60
Forten, Charlotte [Grimké], 6–7, 173
Fossey, Dian, xix, xx, 209, 213, 230, 255,
258, 261, 280, 282; popular images
of, 210–11; field method, 245–47;
on rights of gorillas, 246, 247, 249,

251; *Gorillas in the Mist* (book), 246, 248–49, 251; breaks with scientific establishment, 247, 250–51; animals vs. Africans, 247–49; active conservation, 249; implicated in gorilla deaths, 249–50

Fox-Genovese, Elizabeth, 3, 186

Free, Ann Cottrell, 163

Freeman, Dorothy, 161

Frierson, Lorraine, 62

Furbish, Kate, 71, 72, 74

Furman, Lucy, 158, 279

Galdikas, Biruté, 210, 245

Garden Club of America, 147, 155

Garden clubs, 113, 121; national movement, 127, 129; work on city beautification, 129–31; support of conservation, 143, 145, 157; concern about chemical pesticides, 154–55

Gardening: by rural women, 98–99, 133–34, 136–37; women's shared traditions, 98–99, 133–34, 136–38, 305 (n. 69); as appropriate female endeavor, 99–101, 106–7, 109–10, 112, 114–15, 122–23, 130, 299 (n. 8); old-fashioned gardens, 108–9, 122–23, 130–31, 133, 301 (n. 22); symbolic of moral character, 110, 119–20, 121, 123, 130; popularity of nurseries and seed merchants, 124–25; by African American women, 136–38, 305 (n. 79). *See also* Landscape design

Garden literature, xix, 106; women predominant in, 101, 112–14, 117, 121; aimed at middle-class suburbanites, 121–24; aimed at urban, working classes, 130–32; reflects upper-class values, 133. *See also* Thaxter, Celia

Garden of Eden, 1–2, 4, 6, 7, 11, 20, 33, 110, 123, 141, 186, 240, 274–75

Garden photography, 111, 112; women's employment in, 118; influence on garden styles, 118–19, 303 (n. 42)

Garden styles. *See* Landscape design

Gill, Mary Wright, 87; friendship with Agnes Chase, 86

Gilman, Sander, 175

Goodall, Jane, 210, 230, 245, 282

Gorillas. *See* Primates

*Gorillas in the Mist* (Hollywood film), 210–11, 250

Gould, Lewis, 145

Grandville, J. J.: *The Flowers Personified*, 12–13

Gray, Asa, 11, 41, 72

Gray, Elizabeth Dodson, 262, 265, 266; *Green Paradise Lost*, 269

Griffin, Susan, 251, 262; *Woman and Nature*, xxiii, 194, 260, 281, 282, 283

Guild of Natural Science Illustrators, 91

Haar, Charles, 145

Haldeman, S. S., 61; *Monograph of the Freshwater Univalve Mollusca*, 66

Hale, Sarah Josepha: *Flora's Interpreter*, 16, 17

Halliday, Nancy, 92

Hamilton, Cynthia, 273

Haraway, Donna, 222, 225, 250

Harrison, Ruth: *Animal Machines*, 162

Hassam, Frederick Childe, 137, 141; *Celia Thaxter in Her Garden*, 103–5, 110

Hays, Samuel P., 146

Heaton, Janet: *Surviving in Shadows*, 255

Heiges, Bertha, 87

Herter, Adele, 113

Hewitt, Mattie Edwards, 118

Heyerdahl, Thor: *Kon Tiki*, 150, 166

Hicks, Rosa Viola, 136

Hill, Anna: and Gray Gardens, 113; *Forty Years of Gardening*, 113, 143

Hitchcock, A. S.: *Manual of the Grasses*, 83, 86

Hodges, Elaine, 91

Holbrook, Mrs. John Edwards, 8, 9

Do wicked men always prosper ~~wh~~

Subject of work: proble ~~~~

Work concludes evil is nothing, all manner of
fortune good, adversity makes
virtue possible, God knows what
He is doing, & all is for the best.

Bk two: Fortune is always changeable - that is
her nature
In what does happiness consist?
even pleasure is not happiness, since it
enslaves the mind & turns man's
attention away from what could
make him happy.

Bk 3    Only Sovereign God is true happiness
substance of God is goodness

Book 4 - nothing more powerful than God, & if
God is goodness, then evil cannot be
absolute & evil men cannot triumph,
evil are punished by doing evil - they
deprive themselves of good that might
be theirs - wickedness turns men into
beasts. Evil hath no place in God's
providence; Therefore all manner of
fortune is good- if wicked prosper & virtuous
suffer. It is because

Bk 5 - B. ~~is assured him his free will even~~
though everything is a manifestation
of God's providence. God's foreknowledge does not prevent free exercise of man's knowledge & will. Man's
spirit imposes on itself the necessity
of doing well, since God sees all.

*manner of malice*
*Value of adversity*
*which challenges his*
*spirit, makes him*
*virtuous,*

# BOETHIUS

# THE LOEB CLASSICAL LIBRARY

## VOLUMES ALREADY PUBLISHED

### LATIN AUTHORS

AMMIANUS MARCELLINUS. J. C. Rolfe. 3 Vols.

APULEIUS : THE GOLDEN ASS (METAMORPHOSES). W. Adlington (1566). Revised by S. Gaselee.

ST. AUGUSTINE : CITY OF GOD. 7 Vols. Vol. I. G. E. McCracken. Vol. II. W. M. Green. Vol. III. D. Wiesen. Vol. IV. P. Levine. Vol. V. E. M. Sanford and W. M. Green. Vol. VI. W. C. Greene. Vol. VII. W. M. Green.

ST. AUGUSTINE, CONFESSIONS OF. W. Watts (1631). 2 Vols.

ST. AUGUSTINE : SELECT LETTERS. J. H. Baxter.

AUSONIUS. H. G. Evelyn White. 2 Vols.

BEDE. J. E. King. 2 Vols.

BOETHIUS : TRACTS AND DE CONSOLATIONE PHILOSOPHIAE. Rev. H. F. Stewart and E. K. Rand. Revised by S. J. Tester.

CAESAR : ALEXANDRIAN, AFRICAN AND SPANISH WARS. A. G. Way.

CAESAR : CIVIL WARS. A. G. Peskett.

CAESAR : GALLIC WAR. H. J. Edwards.

CATO AND VARRO : DE RE RUSTICA. H. B. Ash and W. D. Hooper.

CATULLUS. F. W. Cornish ; TIBULLUS. J. B. Postgate ; and PERVIGILIUM VENERIS. J. W. Mackail.

CELSUS : DE MEDICINA. W. G. Spencer. 3 Vols.

CICERO : BRUTUS AND ORATOR. G. L. Hendrickson and H. M. Hubbell.

CICERO : DE FINIBUS. H. Rackham.

CICERO : DE INVENTIONE, etc. H. M. Hubbell.

CICERO : DE NATURA DEORUM AND ACADEMICA. H. Rackham.

CICERO : DE OFFICIIS. Walter Miller.

CICERO : DE ORATORE, etc. 2 Vols. Vol. I : DE ORATORE, Books I and II. E. W. Sutton and H. Rackham. Vol. II : DE ORATORE, Book III ; DE FATO ; PARADOXA STOICORUM ; DE PARTITIONE ORATORIA. H. Rackham.

CICERO : DE REPUBLICA, DE LEGIBUS. Clinton W. Keyes.

1

# THE LOEB CLASSICAL LIBRARY

CICERO: DE SENECTUTE, DE AMICITIA, DE DIVINATIONE. W. A. Falconer.

CICERO: IN CATILINAM, PRO MURENA, PRO SULLA, PRO FLACCO. New version by C. Macdonald.

CICERO: LETTERS TO ATTICUS. E. O. Winstedt. 3 Vols.

CICERO: LETTERS TO HIS FRIENDS. W. Glynn Williams, M. Cary, M. Henderson. 4 Vols.

CICERO: PHILIPPICS. W. C. A. Ker.

CICERO: PRO ARCHIA, POST REDITUM, DE DOMO, DE HARUSPICUM RESPONSIS, PRO PLANCIO. N. H. Watts.

CICERO: PRO CAECINA, PRO LEGE MANILIA, PRO CLUENTIO, PRO RABIRIO. H. Grose Hodge.

CICERO: PRO CAELIO, DE PROVINCIIS CONSULARIBUS, PRO BALBO. R. Gardner.

CICERO: PRO MILONE, IN PISONEM, PRO SCAURO, PRO FONTEIO, PRO RABIRIO POSTUMO, PRO MARCELLO, PRO LIGARIO, PRO REGE DEIOTARO. N. H. Watts.

CICERO: PRO QUINCTIO, PRO ROSCIO AMERINO, PRO ROSCIO COMOEDO, CONTRA RULLUM. J. H. Freese.

CICERO: PRO SESTIO, IN VATINIUM. R. Gardner.

[CICERO]: RHETORICA AD HERENNIUM. H. Caplan.

CICERO: TUSCULAN DISPUTATIONS. J. E. King.

CICERO: VERRINE ORATIONS. L. H. G. Greenwood. 2 Vols.

CLAUDIAN. M. Platnauer. 2 Vols.

COLUMELLA: DE RE RUSTICA, DE ARBORIBUS. H. B. Ash, E. S. Forster, E. Heffner. 3 Vols.

CURTIUS, Q.: HISTORY OF ALEXANDER. J. C. Rolfe. 2 Vols.

FLORUS. E. S. Forster; and CORNELIUS NEPOS. J. C. Rolfe.

FRONTINUS: STRATAGEMS AND AQUEDUCTS. C. E. Bennett and M. B. McElwain.

FRONTO: CORRESPONDENCE. C. R. Haines. 2 Vols.

GELLIUS. J. C. Rolfe. 3 Vols.

HORACE: ODES AND EPODES. C. E. Bennett.

HORACE: SATIRES, EPISTLES, ARS POETICA. H. R. Fairclough.

JEROME: SELECT LETTERS. F. A. Wright.

JUVENAL AND PERSIUS. G. G. Ramsay.

LIVY. B. O. Foster, F. G. Moore, Evan T. Sage, A. C. Schlesinger and R. M. Geer (General Index). 14 Vols.

LUCAN. J. D. Duff.

LUCRETIUS. W. H. D. Rouse. Revised by M. F. Smith.

MANILIUS. G. P. Goold.

MARTIAL. W. C. A. Ker. 2 Vols. Revised by E. H. Warmington.

MINOR LATIN POETS: from PUBLILIUS SYRUS to RUTILIUS NAMATIANUS, including GRATTIUS, CALPURNIUS SICULUS,

# THE LOEB CLASSICAL LIBRARY

NEMESIANUS, AVIANUS, with " Aetna," " Phoenix " and other poems. J. Wight Duff and Arnold M. Duff.

OVID : THE ART OF LOVE AND OTHER POEMS. J. H. Mozley.

OVID : FASTI. Sir James G. Frazer.

OVID : HEROIDES AND AMORES. Grant Showerman. Revised by G. P. Goold.

OVID : METAMORPHOSES. F. J. Miller. 2 Vols. Vol. I. Revised by G. P. Goold.

OVID : TRISTIA AND EX PONTO. A. L. Wheeler.

PETRONIUS. M. Heseltine ; SENECA : APOCOLOCYNTOSIS. W. H. D. Rouse. Revised by E. H. Warmington.

PHAEDRUS AND BABRIUS (Greek). B. E. Perry.

PLAUTUS. Paul Nixon. 5 Vols.

PLINY : LETTERS, PANEGYRICUS. B. Radice. 2 Vols.

PLINY : NATURAL HISTORY. 10 Vols. Vols. I-V. H. Rackham. Vols. VI-VIII. W. H. S. Jones. Vol. IX. H. Rackham. Vol. X. D. E. Eichholz.

PROPERTIUS. H. E. Butler.

PRUDENTIUS. H. J. Thomson. 2 Vols.

QUINTILIAN. H. E. Butler. 4 Vols.

REMAINS OF OLD LATIN. E. H. Warmington. 4 Vols. Vol. I (Ennius and Caecilius). Vol. II (Livius, Naevius, Pacuvius, Accius). Vol. III (Lucilius, Laws of the XII Tables). Vol. IV (Archaic Inscriptions).

SALLUST. J. C. Rolfe.

SCRIPTORES HISTORIAE AUGUSTAE. D. Magie. 3 Vols.

SENECA : APOCOLOCYNTOSIS. Cf. PETRONIUS.

SENECA : EPISTULAE MORALES. R. M. Gummere. 3 Vols.

SENECA : MORAL ESSAYS. J. W. Basore. 3 Vols.

SENECA : NATURALES QUAESTIONES. T. H. Corcoran. 2 Vols.

SENECA : TRAGEDIES. F. J. Miller. 2 Vols.

SENECA THE ELDER. M. Winterbottom. 2 Vols.

SIDONIUS : POEMS AND LETTERS. W. B. Anderson. 2 Vols.

SILIUS ITALICUS. J. D. Duff. 2 Vols.

STATIUS. J. H. Mozley. 2 Vols.

SUETONIUS. J. C. Rolfe. 2 Vols.

TACITUS : AGRICOLA AND GERMANIA. M. Hutton ; DIALOGUS. Sir Wm. Peterson. Revised by R. M. Ogilvie, E. H. Warmington, M. Winterbottom.

TACITUS : HISTORIES AND ANNALS. C. H. Moore and J. Jackson. 4 Vols.

TERENCE. John Sargeaunt. 2 Vols.

TERTULLIAN : APOLOGIA AND DE SPECTACULIS. T. R. Glover ; MINUCIUS FELIX. G. H. Rendall.

VALERIUS FLACCUS. J. H. Mozley.

# THE LOEB CLASSICAL LIBRARY

Varro : De Lingua Latina. R. G. Kent. 2 Vols.
Velleius Paterculus and Res Gestae Divi Augusti.
F. W. Shipley.
Virgil. H. R. Fairclough. 2 Vols.
Vitruvius : De Architectura. F. Granger. 2 Vols.

## GREEK AUTHORS

Achilles Tatius. S. Gaselee.
Aelian : On the Nature of Animals. A. F. Scholfield.
3 Vols.
Aeneas Tacticus, Asclepiodotus and Onasander. The
Illinois Greek Club.
Aeschines. C. D. Adams.
Aeschylus. H. Weir Smyth. 2 Vols.
Alciphron, Aelian and Philostratus : Letters. A. R.
Benner and F. H. Fobes.
Apollodorus. Sir James G. Frazer. 2 Vols.
Apollonius Rhodius. R. C. Seaton.
The Apostolic Fathers. Kirsopp Lake. 2 Vols.
Appian : Roman History. Horace White. 4 Vols.
Aratus. Cf. Callimachus : Hymns and Epigrams.
Aristides. C. A. Behr. 4 Vols. Vol. I.
Aristophanes. Benjamin Bickley Rogers. 3 Vols. Verse
trans.
Aristotle : Art of Rhetoric. J. H. Freese.
Aristotle : Athenian Constitution, Eudemian Ethics.
Virtues and Vices. H. Rackham.
Aristotle : The Categories. On Interpretation. H. P.
Cooke ; Prior Analytics. H. Tredennick.
Aristotle : Generation of Animals. A. L. Peck.
Aristotle : Historia Animalium. A. L. Peck. 3 Vols.
Vols. I and II.
Aristotle : Metaphysics. H. Tredennick. 2 Vols.
Aristotle : Meteorologica. H. D. P. Lee.
Aristotle : Minor Works. W. S. Hett. " On Colours,"
" On Things Heard," " Physiognomics," " On Plants,"
" On Marvellous Things Heard," " Mechanical Prob-
lems," " On Invisible Lines," " Situations and Names of
Winds," " On Melissus, Xenophanes, and Gorgias."
Aristotle : Nicomachean Ethics. H. Rackham.
Aristotle : Oeconomica and Magna Moralia. G. C.
Armstrong. (With Metaphysics, Vol. II.)
Aristotle : On the Heavens. W. K. C. Guthrie.

4

# THE LOEB CLASSICAL LIBRARY

ARISTOTLE : ON THE SOUL, PARVA NATURALIA, ON BREATH.
W. S. Hett.

ARISTOTLE : PARTS OF ANIMALS. A. L. Peck : MOVEMENT
AND PROGRESSION OF ANIMALS. E. S. Forster.

ARISTOTLE : PHYSICS. Rev. P. Wicksteed and F. M. Corn-
ford. 2 Vols.

ARISTOTLE : POETICS ; LONGINUS ON THE SUBLIME. W. Hamilton Fyfe ; DEMETRIUS ON STYLE. W. Rhys Roberts.

ARISTOTLE : POLITICS. H. Rackham.

ARISTOTLE : POSTERIOR ANALYTICS. H. Tredennick ; TOPICS.
E. S. Forster.

ARISTOTLE : PROBLEMS. W. S. Hett. 2 Vols.

ARISTOTLE : RHETORICA AD ALEXANDRUM. H. Rackham.
(With PROBLEMS, Vol. II.)

ARISTOTLE : SOPHISTICAL REFUTATIONS. COMING-TO-BE AND
PASSING-AWAY. E. S. Forster ; ON THE COSMOS. D. J.
Furley.

ARRIAN : HISTORY OF ALEXANDER AND INDICA. 2 Vols.
Vol. I. P. Brunt. Vol. II. Rev. E. Iliffe Robson.

ATHENAEUS : DEIPNOSOPHISTAE. C. B. Gulick. 7 Vols.

BABRIUS AND PHAEDRUS (Latin). B. E. Perry.

ST. BASIL : LETTERS. R. J. Deferrari. 4 Vols.

CALLIMACHUS : FRAGMENTS. C. A. Trypanis ; MUSAEUS :
HERO AND LEANDER. T. Gelzer and C. Whitman.

CALLIMACHUS : HYMNS AND EPIGRAMS, AND LYCOPHRON.
A. W. Mair ; ARATUS. G. R. Mair.

CLEMENT OF ALEXANDRIA. Rev. G. W. Butterworth.

COLLUTHUS. Cf. OPPIAN.

DAPHNIS AND CHLOE. Cf. LONGUS.

DEMOSTHENES I : OLYNTHIACS, PHILIPPICS AND MINOR
ORATIONS : I-XVII AND XX. J. H. Vince.

DEMOSTHENES II : DE CORONA AND DE FALSA LEGATIONE.
C. A. and J. H. Vince.

DEMOSTHENES III : MEIDIAS, ANDROTION, ARISTOCRATES,
TIMOCRATES, ARISTOGEITON. J. H. Vince.

DEMOSTHENES IV-VI : PRIVATE ORATIONS AND IN NEAERAM.
A. T. Murray.

DEMOSTHENES VII ; FUNERAL SPEECH, EROTIC ESSAY, EX-
ORDIA AND LETTERS. N. W. and N. J. DeWitt.

DIO CASSIUS : ROMAN HISTORY. E. Cary. 9 Vols.

DIO CHRYSOSTOM. 5 Vols. Vols. I and II. J. W. Cohoon.
Vol. III. J. W. Cohoon and H. Lamar Crosby. Vols. IV
and V. H. Lamar Crosby.

DIODORUS SICULUS. 12 Vols. Vols. I-VI. C. H. Oldfather.
Vol. VII. C. L. Sherman. Vol. VIII. C. B. Welles. Vols.

IX and X. Russel M. Geer. Vols. XI and XII. F. R. Walton. General Index. Russel M. Geer.

DIOGENES LAERTIUS. R. D. Hicks. 2 Vols. New Introduction by H. S. Long.

DIONYSIUS OF HALICARNASSUS : CRITICAL ESSAYS. S. Usher. 2 Vols.

DIONYSIUS OF HALICARNASSUS : ROMAN ANTIQUITIES. Spelman's translation revised by E. Cary. 7 Vols.

EPICTETUS. W. A. Oldfather. 2 Vols.

EURIPIDES. A. S. Way. 4 Vols. Verse trans.

EUSEBIUS : ECCLESIASTICAL HISTORY. Kirsopp Lake and J. E. L. Oulton. 2 Vols.

GALEN : ON THE NATURAL FACULTIES. A. J. Brock.

THE GREEK ANTHOLOGY. W. R. Paton. 5 Vols.

THE GREEK BUCOLIC POETS (THEOCRITUS, BION, MOSCHUS). J. M. Edmonds.

GREEK ELEGY AND IAMBUS WITH THE ANACREONTEA. J. M. Edmonds. 2 Vols.

GREEK MATHEMATICAL WORKS. Ivor Thomas. 2 Vols.

HERODES. Cf. THEOPHRASTUS : CHARACTERS.

HERODIAN. C. R. Whittaker. 2 Vols.

HERODOTUS. A. D. Godley. 4 Vols.

HESIOD AND THE HOMERIC HYMNS. H. G. Evelyn White.

HIPPOCRATES AND THE FRAGMENTS OF HERACLEITUS. W. H. S. Jones and E. T. Withington. 4 Vols.

HOMER : ILIAD. A. T. Murray. 2 Vols.

HOMER : ODYSSEY. A. T. Murray. 2 Vols.

ISAEUS. E. S. Forster.

ISOCRATES. George Norlin and LaRue Van Hook. 3 Vols.

[ST. JOHN DAMASCENE]: BARLAAM AND IOASAPH. Rev. G. R. Woodward, Harold Mattingly and D. M. Lang.

JOSEPHUS. 9 Vols. Vols. I-IV. H. St. J. Thackeray. Vol. V. H. St. J. Thackeray and Ralph Marcus. Vols. VI and VII. Ralph Marcus. Vol. VIII. Ralph Marcus and Allen Wikgren. Vol. IX. L. H. Feldman.

JULIAN. Wilmer Cave Wright. 3 Vols.

LIBANIUS : SELECTED WORKS. A. F. Norman. 3 Vols. Vols. I and II.

LONGUS : DAPHNIS AND CHLOE. Thornley's translation revised by J. M. Edmonds ; and PARTHENIUS. S. Gaselee.

LUCIAN. 8 Vols. Vols. I-V. A. M. Harmon. Vol. VI. K. Kilburn. Vols. VII and VIII. M. D. Macleod.

LYCOPHRON. Cf. CALLIMACHUS : HYMNS AND EPIGRAMS.

LYRA GRAECA. J. M. Edmonds. 3 Vols.

LYSIAS. W. R. M. Lamb.

# THE LOEB CLASSICAL LIBRARY

Manetho. W. G. Waddell; Ptolemy: Tetrabiblos. F. E. Robbins.

Marcus Aurelius. C. R. Haines.

Menander. F. G. Allinson.

Minor Attic Orators. 2 Vols. K. J. Maidment and J. O. Burtt.

Musaeus: Hero and Leander. *Cf.* Callimachus: Fragments.

Nonnos: Dionysiaca. W. H. D. Rouse. 3 Vols.

Oppian, Colluthus, Tryphiodorus. A. W. Mair.

Papyri. Non-Literary Selections. A. S. Hunt and C. C. Edgar. 2 Vols. Literary Selections (Poetry). D. L. Page.

Parthenius. *Cf.* Longus.

Pausanias: Description of Greece. W. H. S. Jones. 4 Vols. and Companion Vol. arranged by R. E. Wycherley.

Philo. 10 Vols. Vols. I-V. F. H. Colson and Rev. G. H. Whitaker. Vols. VI-X. F. H. Colson. General Index. Rev. J. W. Earp.
Two Supplementary Vols. Translation only from an Armenian Text. Ralph Marcus.

Philostratus: The Life of Apollonius of Tyana. F. C. Conybeare. 2 Vols.

Philostratus: Imagines; Callistratus: Descriptions. A. Fairbanks.

Philostratus and Eunapius: Lives of the Sophists. Wilmer Cave Wright.

Pindar. Sir J. E. Sandys.

Plato: Charmides, Alcibiades, Hipparchus, The Lovers, Theages, Minos and Epinomis. W. R. M. Lamb.

Plato: Cratylus, Parmenides, Greater Hippias, Lesser Hippias. H. N. Fowler.

Plato: Euthyphro, Apology, Crito, Phaedo, Phaedrus. H. N. Fowler.

Plato: Laches, Protagoras, Meno, Euthydemus. W. R. M. Lamb.

Plato: Laws. Rev. R. G. Bury. 2 Vols.

Plato: Lysis, Symposium, Gorgias. W. R. M. Lamb.

Plato: Republic. Paul Shorey. 2 Vols.

Plato: Statesman, Philebus. H. N. Fowler; Ion. W. R. M. Lamb.

Plato: Theaetetus and Sophist. H. N. Fowler.

Plato: Timaeus, Critias, Clitopho, Menexenus, Epistulae. Rev. R. G. Bury.

Plotinus. A. H. Armstrong. 6 Vols. Vols. I-III.

# THE LOEB CLASSICAL LIBRARY

PLUTARCH : MORALIA. 16 Vols. Vols. I-V. F. C. Babbitt.
Vol. VI. W. C. Helmbold. Vol. VII. P. H. De Lacy and
B. Einarson. Vol. VIII. P. A. Clement, H. B. Hoffleit.
Vol. IX. E. L. Minar, Jr., F. H. Sandbach, W. C.
Helmbold. Vol. X. H. N. Fowler. Vol. XI. L. Pearson,
F. H. Sandbach. Vol. XII. H. Cherniss, W. C. Helmbold.
Vol. XIII, Parts 1 and 2. H. Cherniss. Vol. XIV. P. H.
De Lacy and B. Einarson. Vol. XV. F. H. Sandbach.

PLUTARCH : THE PARALLEL LIVES. B. Perrin. 11 Vols.

POLYBIUS. W. R. Paton. 6 Vols.

PROCOPIUS : HISTORY OF THE WARS. H. B. Dewing. 7 Vols.

PTOLEMY : TETRABIBLOS. *Cf.* MANETHO.

QUINTUS SMYRNAEUS. A. S. Way. Verse trans.

SEXTUS EMPIRICUS. Rev. R. G. Bury. 4 Vols.

SOPHOCLES. F. Storr. 2 Vols. Verse trans.

STRABO : GEOGRAPHY. Horace L. Jones. 8 Vols.

THEOPHRASTUS : CHARACTERS. J. M. Edmonds ; HERODES,
etc. A. D. Knox.

THEOPHRASTUS : DE CAUSIS PLANTARUM. G. K. K. Link and
B. Einarson. 3 Vols. Vol. I.

THEOPHRASTUS : ENQUIRY INTO PLANTS. Sir Arthur Hort.
2 Vols.

THUCYDIDES. C. F. Smith. 4 Vols.

TRYPHIODORUS. *Cf.* OPPIAN.

XENOPHON : ANABASIS. C. L. Brownson.

XENOPHON : CYROPAEDIA. Walter Miller. 2 Vols.

XENOPHON : HELLENICA. C. L. Brownson.

XENOPHON : MEMORABILIA AND OECONOMICUS. E. C. Marchant ; SYMPOSIUM AND APOLOGY. O. J. Todd.

XENOPHON : SCRIPTA MINORA. E. C. Marchant and G. W.
Bowersock.

CAMBRIDGE, MASS.          LONDON
HARVARD UNIV. PRESS    WILLIAM HEINEMANN LTD.

# CONTENTS

# INTRODUCTION

In this re-issue in 1973 of Boethius' *Theological Tractates* and *Consolation of Philosophy* the Loeb Classical Library has taken advantage of much revision and re-translation by S. J. Tester, of the Department of Classics, University of Bristol. The original rendering of the *Tractates* for the Library by Dr. H. F. Stewart and Professor E. K. Rand, besides inaccuracies, contained omissions, obscurities, paraphrases, and some needless archaisms ; and the translation of the *Consolatio* by " I. T." (1609), despite its virtues and the revision by Dr. Stewart, was too far removed from the purposes of the Loeb series, and has been relinquished. In this reprint therefore much of the translation of the *Tractates* and the whole of the translation of the *Consolatio*, with the notes also, are the work of Tester, whose aim was, in addition to correction, to produce throughout the volume a homogeneous rendering, reasonably literal, which would make philosophical sense. The following note on the text, written by Rand in 1918, still applies : " The text of the *Opuscula Sacra* is based on my own collations of all the important manuscripts of these works. In preparing the text of the *Consolatio* I have used the apparatus in Peiper's edition (Teubner, 1871), since his reports, as I know in the case of the

# INTRODUCTION

Tegernseensis, are generally accurate and complete ; I have depended also on my own collations or excerpts from various of the important manuscripts, nearly all of which I have at least examined, and I have also followed, not always but usually, the opinions of Engelbrecht in his admirable article, *Die Consolatio Philosophiae des Boethius* in the *Sitzungsberichte* of the Vienna Academy, CXLIV, (1902), 1-60. The present text, then, has been constructed from only part of the material with which an editor should reckon, though the reader may at least assume that every reading in the text has, unless otherwise stated, the authority of some manuscript of the ninth or tenth century ; in certain orthographical details, evidence from the text of the *Opuscula Sacra* has been used without special mention of this fact."

Of the specially renowned *Consolatio* there appeared in the Middle Ages (during which it was among the most popular of philosophical manuals) many translations including King Alfred's into Anglo-Saxon late in the ninth century, Chaucer's into English before 1382, and various renderings into French, German, Italian, Spanish, and Greek, before the end of the fifteenth century ; commentaries such as that of Asser (Alfred's instructor) and Robert Grosseteste, Bishop of Lincoln ; and imitations. Later came the " Englishings " of Queen Elizabeth I. Modern editions and translations are numerous. Until the present century the best editions were those of T. Obbarius (Jena, 1843) containing the *Consolatio* only but including much information about Boethius himself, the manuscripts, and earlier editions ; and of R. Peiper (Leipzig, 1871) containing the *Consolatio* and the *Tractates*. Stewart and Rand's translation of

# INTRODUCTION

the *Tractates* for the Loeb Series in 1918, in which they derived much help from the medieval commentary by John the Scot and the one by Gilbert de la Porrée, was the first English rendering. Since then, some important work has appeared of which note especially the following : editions of the *Consolatio* by A. Fortescue and G. D. Smith, London, 1925 ; G. Weinberger in *Corpus Scriptorum Ecclesiasticorum Latinorum* LXVII, Vienna, 1934 ; L. Bieler in *Corpus Christianorum*, Ser. Lat., XCIV, Turnhout, 1957 ; E. Rapisarda (with translation), Catania, 1961 ; and the 2nd edition, with translation, of the *Tractates* by the same author, *Opuscoli teologici*, Catania, 1960 ; also F. Klingner, de Boethii consolatione Philosophiae, in *Philol. Untersuch.* XXVII, Berlin, 1921 ; M. Schanz, in *Geschichte d. Röm. Literatur*, Teil IV, *Boethius*, Berlin, 1921 ; H. R. Patch, *The tradition of Boethius*, Oxford, 1935 (with a good bibliography) ; and P. Courcelle's *La Consolation de Philosophie dans la tradition littéraire ; antécédents et postérité de Boèce*, Paris, 1967, with bibliography on pp. 383-402.

We reprint here the Life of Boethius by Stewart and Rand from our original issue.

E. H. W.

# BOETHIUS

## THE
## THEOLOGICAL TRACTATES
### WITH AN ENGLISH TRANSLATION BY
### H. F. STEWART, D.D.
#### FELLOW OF TRINITY COLLEGE, CAMBRIDGE

AND

### E. K. RAND, Ph.D.
#### PROFESSOR OF LATIN IN HARVARD UNIVERSITY

AND

### S. J. TESTER
#### DEPARTMENT OF CLASSICS, UNIVERSITY OF BRISTOL

## THE CONSOLATION OF
## PHILOSOPHY
### WITH AN ENGLISH TRANSLATION BY
### S. J. TESTER

CAMBRIDGE, MASSACHUSETTS
HARVARD UNIVERSITY PRESS
LONDON
WILLIAM HEINEMANN LTD
MCMLXXVIII

*American*
ISBN 0-674-99083-8

*British*
ISBN 0 434 99074 4


*First printed* 1918
*Reprinted* 1926, 1936, 1938, 1946, 1953, 1962, 1968
*New edition* 1973
*Reprinted* 1978

*Printed in Great Britain*

# LIFE OF BOETHIUS

Anicius Manlius Severinus Boethius, of the famous Praenestine family of the Anicii, was born about 480 A.D. in Rome. His father was an ex-consul; he himself was consul under Theodoric the Ostrogoth in 510, and his two sons, children of a great granddaughter[a] of the renowned Q. Aurelius Symmachus, were joint consuls in 522. His public career was splendid and honourable, as befitted a man of his race, attainments, and character. But he fell under the displeasure of Theodoric, and was charged with conspiring to deliver Rome from his rule, and with corresponding treasonably to this end with Justin, Emperor of the East. He was thrown into prison at Pavia, where he wrote the *Consolation of Philosophy*, and he was brutally put to death in 524. His brief and busy life was marked by great literary achievement. His learning was vast, his industry untiring, his object unattainable—nothing less than the transmission to his countrymen of all the works of Plato and Aristotle, and the reconciliation of their apparently divergent views. To form the idea was a silent judgement on the learning of his day ; to realize it was more than one man could accomplish ; but Boethius accomplished much. He translated the Εἰσαγωγή of Porphyry, and the whole of Aristotle's Ὄργανον. He wrote a double commentary on the Εἰσ

---

[a] Rusticiana, daughter of Q. Aurelius Memmius Symmachus. Boethius's sons were Anicius Manlius Severinus Boethius, and Q. Aurelius Memmius Symmachus.

αγωγή, and commentaries on the *Categories* and the *De Interpretatione* of Aristotle, and on the *Topica* of Cicero. He also composed original treatises on the categorical and hypothetical syllogism, on Division and on Topical Differences. He adapted the arithmetic of Nicomachus, and his textbook on music, founded on various Greek authorities, was in use at Oxford and Cambridge until modern times. His five theological *Tractates* are here, together with the *Consolation of Philosophy*, to speak for themselves.

Boethius was the last of the Roman philosophers, and the first of the scholastic theologians. The present volume serves to prove the truth of both these assertions.

The *Consolation of Philosophy* is indeed, as Gibbon called it, " a golden volume, not unworthy of the leisure of Plato or of Tully." To belittle its originality and sincerity, as is sometimes done, with a view to saving the Christianity of the writer, is to misunderstand his mind and his method. The *Consolatio* is not, as has been maintained, a mere patchwork of translations from Aristotle and the Neoplatonists. Rather it is the supreme essay of one who throughout his life had found his highest solace in the dry light of reason. His chief source of refreshment, in the dungeon to which his beloved library had not accompanied him, was a memory well stocked with the poetry and thought of former days. The development of the argument is anything but Neoplatonic ; it is all his own.

And if the *Consolation of Philosophy* admits Boethius to the company of Cicero or even of Plato, the theological *Tractates* mark him as the forerunner of St. Thomas. It was the habit of a former generation

to regard Boethius as an eclectic, the transmitter of
a distorted Aristotelianism, a pagan, or at best a
luke-warm Christian, who at the end cast off the
faith which he had worn in times of peace, and
wrapped himself in the philosophic cloak which
properly belonged to him. The authenticity of
the *Tractates* was freely denied. We know better
now. The discovery by Alfred Holder, and the
illuminating discussion by Hermann Usener,[a] of a
fragment of Cassiodorus are sufficient confirmation of
the manuscript tradition, apart from the work
of scholars who have sought to justify that tradition from internal evidence. In that fragment
Cassiodorus definitely ascribes to his friend Boethius
" a book on the Trinity, some dogmatic chapters, and
a book against Nestorius."[b] Boethius was without
doubt a Christian, a Doctor and perhaps a martyr. Nor
is it necessary to think that, when in prison, he put
away his faith. If it is asked why the *Consolation
of Philosophy* contains no conscious or direct reference
to the doctrines which are traced in the *Tractates*
with so sure a hand, and is, at most, not out of
harmony with Christianity, the answer is simple.
In the *Consolation* he is writing philosophy ; in the
*Tractates* he is writing theology. He observes what
Pascal calls the orders of things. Philosophy
belongs to one order, theology to another. They
have different objects. The object of philosophy
is to understand and explain the nature of the world
around us ; the object of theology is to understand

---

[a] *Anecdoton Holderi*, Leipzig, 1877.
[b] *Scripsit librum de sancta trinitate et capita quaedam
dogmatica et librum contra Nestorium.* On the question of
the genuineness of Tr. iv *De fide catholica* see note p. 52.

and explain doctrines delivered by divine revelation. The scholastics recognized the distinction,[a] and the corresponding difference in the function of Faith and Reason. Their final aim was to co-ordinate the two, but this was not possible before the thirteenth century. Meanwhile Boethius helps to prepare the way. In the *Consolation* he gives Reason her range, and suffers her, unaided, to vindicate the ways of Providence. In the *Tractates* Reason is called in to give to the claims of Faith the support which it does not really lack.[b] Reason, however, has still a right to be heard. The distinction between *fides* and *ratio* is proclaimed in the first two *Tractates*. In the second especially it is drawn with a clearness worthy of St. Thomas himself ; and there is, of course, the implication that the higher authority resides with *fides*. But the treatment is philosophical and extremely bold. Boethius comes back to the question of the substantiality of the divine Persons which he has discussed in Tr. I. from a fresh point of view. Once more he decides that the Persons are predicated relatively ; even Trinity, he concludes, is not predicated substantially of deity. Does this square with catholic doctrine ? It is possible to hear a note of challenge in his words to John the Deacon, *fidem si poterit rationemque coniunge.* Philosophy states the problem in unequivocal terms. Theology is required to say whether they commend themselves.

One object of the scholastics, anterior to the final co-ordination of the two sciences, was to harmonize and codify all the answers to all the questions

[a] Cp. H. de Wulf, *Histoire de la philosophie médiévale* (Louvain and Paris, 1915), p. 332.
[b] See below, *De Trin.* vi *ad fin.*, p. 31.

that philosophy raises. The ambition of Boethius was not so soaring, but it was sufficiently bold. He set out, first to translate, and then to reconcile, Plato and Aristotle ; to go behind all the other systems, even the latest and the most in vogue, back to the two great masters, and to show that they have the truth, and are in substantial accord. So St. Thomas himself, if he cannot reconcile the teaching of Plato and Aristotle, at least desires to correct the one by the other, to discover what truth is common to both, and to show its correspondence with Christian doctrine. It is reasonable to conjecture that Boethius, if he had lived, might have attempted something of the kind. Were he alive to-day, he might feel more in tune with the best of the pagans than with most contemporary philosophic thought.

In yet one more respect Boethius belongs to the company of the schoolmen. He not only put into circulation many precious philosophical notions, served as channel through which various works of Aristotle passed into the schools, and handed down to them a definite Aristotelian method for approaching the problem of faith ; he also supplied material for that classification of the various sciences which is an essential accompaniment of every philosophical movement, and of which the Middle Ages felt the value. The uniform distribution into natural sciences, mathematics and theology which he recommends may be traced in the work of various teachers up to the thirteenth century, when it is finally accepted and defended by St. Thomas in his commentary on the *De Trinitate.*

H. F. S.<br>E. K. R. 1918

# BOETHIUS
# THE THEOLOGICAL TRACTATES
# THE CONSOLATION
# OF PHILOSOPHY

# ANICII MANLII SEVERINI BOETHII

V.C. ET INL. EXCONS. ORD. PATRICII

## INCIPIT LIBER QUOMODO

# TRINITAS UNUS DEUS
# AC NON TRES DII

AD Q. AURELIUM MEMMIUM SYMMACHUM

V.C. ET INL. EXCONS. ORD. ATQUE PATRICIUM SOCERUM

Investigatam diutissime quaestionem, quantum
nostrae mentis igniculum lux divina dignata est,
formatam rationibus litterisque mandatam offerendam
vobis communicandamque curavi tam vestri cupidus
5 iudicii quam nostri studiosus inventi. Qua in re quid
mihi sit animi quotiens stilo cogitata commendo, tum
ex ipsa materiae difficultate tum ex eo quod raris id
est vobis tantum conloquor, intelligi potest. Neque
enim famae iactatione et inanibus vulgi clamoribus
10 excitamur ; sed si quis est fructus exterior, hic non

2

# THE TRINITY IS ONE GOD NOT THREE GODS

## A TREATISE BY
## ANICIUS MANLIUS SEVERINUS BOETIIIUS

MOST HONOURABLE, OF THE ILLUSTRIOUS ORDER OF
EX-CONSULS, PATRICIAN

### TO HIS FATHER-IN-LAW, QUINTUS AURELIUS MEMMIUS SYMMACHUS

MOST HONOURABLE, OF THE ILLUSTRIOUS ORDER OF
EX-CONSULS, PATRICIAN

I HAVE very long pondered this question, so far as the divine light has deemed it fitting for the spark of my intelligence to do so. Now, having set it forth in logical order and cast it into literary form, I have caused it to be presented and communicated to you, being as much desirous of your judgement as zealous for my own discovery. You can readily understand what I feel in this matter whenever I try to write down what I think both from the actual difficulty of the topic and from the fact that I discuss it only with the few—I may say with no one but yourself. It is indeed no vain striving after fame or empty popular applause that prompts me ; but if there be any exter-

potest aliam nisi materiae similem sperare sententiam.
Quocumque igitur a vobis deieci oculos, partim ignava
segnities partim callidus livor occurrit, ut contume-
liam videatur divinis tractatibus inrogare qui talibus
15 hominum monstris non agnoscenda haec potius quam
proculcanda proiecerit. Idcirco stilum brevitate con-
traho et ex intimis sumpta philosophiae disciplinis
novorum verborum significationibus velo, ut haec
mihi tantum vobisque, si quando ad ea convertitis
20 oculos, conloquantur; ceteros vero ita submovimus, ut
qui capere intellectu nequiverint ad ea etiam legenda
videantur indigni. Sane[1] tantum a nobis quaeri
oportet quantum humanae rationis intuitus ad divinitatis valet celsa conscendere. Nam ceteris quoque
25 artibus idem quasi quidam finis est constitutus, quo-
usque potest via rationis accedere. Neque enim medicina aegris semper affert salutem ; sed nulla erit culpa
medentis, si nihil eorum quae fieri oportebat omiserit.
Idemque in ceteris. At quantum haec difficilior
30 quaestio est, tam facilior esse debet ad veniam.
Vobis tamen etiam illud inspiciendum est, an ex
beati Augustini scriptis semina rationum aliquos in
nos venientia fructus extulerint. Ac de proposita
quaestione hinc sumamus initium.

# I

Christianae religionis reverentiam plures usurpant,
sed ea fides pollet maxime ac solitarie quae cum
propter universalium praecepta regularum, quibus

[1] sed ne *the best MSS.*

---

[a] *Cf.* the discussion of human *ratio* and divine *intelligentia*
in *Cons.* v, pr. 4 and 5.
[b] *e.g.* Aug. *De Trin.*

nal reward, we may not look for more warmth in the
verdict than the subject itself arouses. So, apart
from yourself, wherever I turn my eyes, they fall on
either the apathy of the dullard or the jealousy of the
shrewd, and a man who should cast his thoughts
before such unnatural creatures of men, I will not say
to consider but rather to trample under foot, would
seem to bring discredit on the study of divinity. So
I purposely use brevity and wrap up the ideas I draw
from the deep questionings of philosophy in new and
unaccustomed words such as speak only to you and
to myself, that is, if you ever look at them. The rest
of the world I simply disregard since those who cannot
understand seem unworthy even to read them. We
should of course press our inquiry only so far as the
insight of man's reason is allowed to climb the height
of heavenly knowledge.[a] For in other arts the same
point is set as a sort of limit, as far as which the way
of reason can reach. Medicine, for instance, does not
always bring health to the sick, though the doctor will
not be to blame if he has left nothing undone which
should have been done. So with the other arts. In
the present case the very difficulty of the quest claims
a lenient judgement. You must however examine
whether the seeds of argument sown in my mind by
St. Augustine's writings[b] have borne fruit. And now
let us make a beginning on the question proposed.

# I

There are many who claim as theirs the dignity
of the Christian religion ; but that form of faith is
most valid and only valid which, both on account of
the universal character of the rules and doctrines

eiusdem religionis intellegatur auctoritas, tum prop-
5 terea, quod eius cultus per omnes paene mundi terminos emanavit, catholica vel universalis vocatur.
Cuius haec de trinitatis unitate sententia est: "Pater,"
inquiunt, "deus filius deus spiritus sanctus deus."
Igitur pater filius spiritus sanctus unus non tres dii.
10 Cuius coniunctionis ratio est indifferentia. Eos enim
differentia comitatur qui vel augent vel minuunt, ut
Arriani qui gradibus meritorum trinitatem variantes
distrahunt atque in pluralitatem diducunt. Principium
enim pluralitatis alteritas est ; praeter alteritatem
15 enim nec pluralitas quid sit intellegi potest. Trium
namque rerum vel quotlibet tum genere tum specie
tum numero diversitas constat ; quotiens enim idem
dicitur, totiens diversum etiam praedicatur. Idem
vero dicitur tribus modis : aut genere ut idem homo
20 quod equus, quia his idem genus ut animal ; vel
specie ut idem Cato quod Cicero, quia eadem species
ut homo ; vel numero ut Tullius et Cicero, quia unus
est numero. Quare diversum etiam vel genere vel
specie vel numero dicitur. Sed numero differentiam
25 accidentium varietas facit. Nam tres homines neque
genere neque specie sed suis accidentibus distant ;
nam vel si animo cuncta ab his accidentia separemus,
tamen locus cunctis diversus est quem unum fingere
nullo modo possumus ; duo enim corpora unum locum

---

a From the Athanasian Creed.
b The terms *differentia*, *numerus*, *species*, are used expertly,
as would be expected of the author of the *In Isag. Porph.
Commenta.* See S. Brandt's edition of that work (in the
Vienna *Corpus*, 1906), s.v. *differentia*, etc.

through which the authority of that same religion is perceived, and because its form of worship has spread throughout almost all the world, is called catholic or universal. The belief of this faith concerning the Unity of the Trinity is as follows : " the Father " they say " is God, the Son is God, the Holy Spirit is God."[a] Therefore Father, Son, and Holy Spirit are one God, not three Gods. The cause of this union is absence of difference[b] : difference cannot be avoided by those who add to or take from the Unity, as for instance the Arians, who, by graduating the Trinity according to merit, break it up and convert it to Plurality. For the principle of plurality is otherness ; for apart from otherness plurality is unintelligible. In fact, the diversity of three or more things lies in genus or species or number ; for as often as " same " is said, so often is " diverse " also predicated. Now sameness is predicated in three ways. By genus ; e.g. a man is the same as a horse, because they have the same genus, animal. By species ; e.g. Cato is the same as Cicero, because they have the same species, man. By number ; e.g. Tully and Cicero, because he is one in number. Similarly diversity is expressed by genus, species, and number. Now numerical difference is caused by variety of accidents ; for three men differ neither by genus nor species but by their accidents, for even if we mentally remove from them all other accidents,[c] still the places for each are diverse, which we cannot by any means make into one place, since two bodies will not occupy one place, and place

---

[c] This method of mental abstraction is employed more elaborately in *Tr.* iii (*vide infra*, p. 44) and in *Cons.* v, pr. 4, where the notion of divine foreknowledge is abstracted in imagination.

30 non obtinebunt, qui est accidens. Atque ideo sunt
numero plures, quoniam accidentibus plures fiunt.

## II

Age igitur ingrediamur et unumquodque ut intellegi atque capi potest dispiciamus ; nam, sicut optime
dictum videtur, eruditi est hominis unumquodque ut
ipsum est ita de eo fidem capere temptare.

5    Nam cum tres sint speculativae partes, *naturalis*,
in motu inabstracta ἀνυπεξαίρετος (considerat enim
corporum formas cum materia, quae a corporibus
actu separari non possunt, quae corpora in motu
sunt ut cum terra deorsum ignis sursum fertur,
10 habetque motum forma materiae coniuncta), *mathematica*, sine motu inabstracta (haec enim formas
corporum speculatur sine materia ac per hoc sine
motu, quae formae cum in materia sint, ab his
separari non possunt), *theologica*, sine motu abstracta
15 atque separabilis (nam dei substantia et materia et
motu caret), in naturalibus igitur rationabiliter, in
mathematicis disciplinaliter, in divinis intellectualiter
versari oportebit neque diduci ad imaginationes, sed
potius ipsam inspicere formam quae vere forma
20 neque imago est et quae esse ipsum est et ex qua

---

*a* By Cicero (*Tusc.* v. 7. 19).
*b* *Cf.* the similar division of philosophy in *Isag. Porph.*
ed. Brandt, pp. 7 ff.
*c* *Sc.* though they may be separated in thought.

is an accident. Wherefore it is because men are made plural by their accidents that they are plural in number.

## II

Come, then, let us begin and consider each several point, as far as it can be grasped and understood ; for as has been wisely said,[a] in my opinion, it is a scholar's duty to try to formulate his belief about each thing according as it actually is.

Speculative Science may be divided into three kinds[b] : Physics, Mathematics, and Theology. Physics deals with motion and is not abstract or separable (*i.e.* ἀνυπ∊ξαίρ∊τος) ; for it is concerned with the forms of bodies together with their constituent matter, which forms cannot be separated in reality from their bodies.[c] These bodies are in motion, the earth, for instance, tending downwards, and fire tending upwards, and the form which is joined with the matter takes on its motion. Mathematics does not deal with motion and is not abstract, for it investigates forms of bodies apart from matter, and therefore apart from motion, which forms, however, being connected with matter cannot be really separated from bodies. Theology does not deal with motion and is abstract and separable, for the Divine Substance is without either matter or motion.

In Physics, then, we shall be bound to use scientific, in Mathematics, systematical, in Theology, intellectual concepts ; and in Theology we should not be diverted to play with imaginations, but rather apprehend that form which is pure form and no image, which is very being and the source of being. For all

esse est. Omne namque esse ex forma est. Statua
enim non secundum aes quod est materia, sed
secundum formam qua in eo insignita est effigies
animalis dicitur, ipsumque aes non secundum terram
25 quod est eius materia, sed dicitur secundum aeris figuram. Terra quoque ipsa non secundum ἄποιον ὕλην
dicitur, sed secundum siccitatem gravitatemque quae
sunt formae. Nihil igitur secundum materiam esse
dicitur sed secundum propriam formam. Sed divina
30 substantia sine materia forma est atque ideo unum et
est id quod est. Reliqua enim non sunt id quod sunt.
Unum quodque enim habet esse suum ex his ex quibus
est, id est ex partibus suis, et est hoc atque hoc, id est
partes suae coniunctae, sed non hoc vel hoc singulari-
35 ter, ut cum homo terrenus constet ex anima corpore-
que, corpus et anima est, non vel corpus vel anima in
partem ; igitur non est id quod est. Quod vero non
est ex hoc atque hoc, sed tantum est hoc, illud vere
est id quod est ; et est pulcherrimum fortissimumque
40 quia nullo nititur. Quocirca hoc vere unum in quo
nullus numerus, nullum in eo aliud praeterquam id
quod est. Neque enim subiectum fieri potest ; forma
enim est, formae vero subiectae esse non possunt.
Nam quod ceterae formae subiectae accidentibus

---

[a] ῎Αποιος ὕλη=τὸ ἄμορφον, τὸ ἀειδές of Aristotle. *Cf.* οὔτε
γὰρ ὕλη τὸ εἶδος (ἡ μὲν ἄποιος, τὸ δὲ ποιότης τις) οὔτε ἐξ ὕλης
(Alexander Aphrod. *De Anima*, 17. 17) ; εἰ δὲ τοῦτο, ἄποιος
δὲ ἡ ὕλη, ἄποιον ἂν εἴη σῶμα (id. *De anima libri mantissa*,
124. 7).
[b] This is Realism. *Cf.* " Sed si rerum veritatem atque

being is dependent on form.   For a statue is not called
a likeness of a living thing on account of the bronze
which is its matter, but on account of the form
whereby that likeness is impressed upon it : and the
bronze itself is not called bronze because of the earth
which is its matter, but because of the form of bronze.
Likewise earth itself is not called earth by reason of
unqualified matter,[a] but by reason of dryness and
weight, which are forms.   So nothing is said to be because of its matter, but because of its distinctive
form.   But the Divine Substance is form without
matter, and is therefore one, and is its own essence.
But other things are not their own essences, for each
thing has its being from the things of which it is
composed, that is, from its parts.   It is This *and* That,
*i.e.* it is its parts in conjunction ; it is not This *or* That
taken apart.   Earthly man, for instance, since he
consists of soul and body, is body *and* soul, not body
*or* soul, separately ; therefore he is not his own
essence.   That on the other hand which does not
consist of This and That, but is only This, is really its
own essence, and is altogether beautiful and stable
because it does not depend upon anything.   Wherefore that is truly one in which is no number, in which
nothing is present except its own essence.   Nor can it
become the substrate of anything, for it is form, and
forms cannot be substrates.[b]   For if humanity, like

integritatem perpendas, non est dubium quin vere sint.
Nam cum res omnes quae vere sunt sine his quinque
(*i.e.* genus species differentia propria accidentia) esse non
possint, has ipsas quinque res vere intellectas esse non
dubites, " *Isag. in Porph. ed. pr.* i (Migne, *P.L.* lxiv, col. 19,
Brandt, pp. 26 ff.).   The passages show that Boethius is
definitely committed to the Realistic position, although in
his *Comment. in Porphyr. a se translatum* he holds the scales

11

45 sunt ut humanitas, non ita accidentia suscipit eo quod
ipsa est, sed eo quod materia ei subiecta est ; dum
enim materia subiecta humanitati suscipit quodlibet
accidens, ipsa hoc suscipere videtur humanitas. Forma
vero quae est sine materia non poterit esse subiectum
50 nec vero inesse materiae, neque enim esset forma sed
imago. Ex his enim formis quae praeter materiam
sunt, istae formae venerunt quae sunt in materia et
corpus efficiunt. Nam ceteras quae in corporibus
sunt abutimur formas vocantes, dum imagines sint.
55 Adsimulantur enim formis his quae non sunt in
materia constitutae. Nulla igitur in eo diversitas,
nulla ex diversitate pluralitas, nulla ex accidentibus
multitudo atque idcirco nec numerus.

### III

Deus vero a deo nullo differt, ne vel accidentibus
vel substantialibus differentiis in subiecto positis dis-
tent. Ubi vero nulla est differentia, nulla est omnino
pluralitas, quare nec numerus ; igitur unitas tantum.
5 Nam quod tertio repetitur deus, cum pater ac filius
et spiritus sanctus nuncupatur, tres unitates non
faciunt pluralitatem numeri in eo quod ipsae sunt, si
advertamus ad res numerabiles ac non ad ipsum
numerum. Illic enim unitatum repetitio numerum
10 facit. In eo autem numero qui in rebus numerabilibus
constat, repetitio unitatum atque pluralitas minime
facit numerabilium rerum numerosam diversitatem.

---

between Plato and Aristotle, " quorum diiudicare sententias
aptum esse non duxi " (cp. Hauréau, *Hist. de la philosophie
scolastique*, i. 120). As a fact in the *Comment. in Porph.*
he merely postpones the question, which in the *De Trin.* he
settles.

other forms, is a substrate for accidents, it does not receive accidents through the fact that it exists, but through the fact that matter is subjected to it. For when the matter which is subject to humanity receives any accident, humanity itself seems to receive it. But form which is without matter will not be able to be a substrate, nor indeed to be in matter, else it would not be form but an image. For from these forms which are outside matter have come those forms which are in matter and produce a body. We misname the entities that reside in bodies when we call them forms, since they are mere images ; for they only resemble those forms which are not incorporate in matter. In God, then, is no difference, no plurality arising out of difference, no multiplicity arising out of accidents, and accordingly no number either.

### III

Now God differs from God in no respect, for there cannot be divine essences distinguished either by accidents or by substantial differences belonging to a substrate. But where there is no difference, there is no sort of plurality and accordingly no number ; here, therefore, is unity alone. For whereas we say God thrice when we name the Father, Son, and Holy Spirit, these three unities do not produce a plurality of number in their own essences, if we think of numerable things and not of number itself. For in that case the repetition of ones does make a number ; but in that number which consists in numerable things, the repetition of ones and their plurality do not by any means produce numerical difference in the objects counted. For there are two

13

Numerus enim duplex est, unus quidem quo numeramus, alter vero qui in rebus numerabilibus constat.
15 Etenim unum res est ; unitas, quo unum dicimus.
Duo rursus in rebus sunt ut homines vel lapides ;
dualitas nihil, sed tantum dualitas qua duo homines
vel duo lapides fiunt. Et in ceteris eodem modo.
Ergo in numero quo numeramus repetitio unitatum
20 facit pluralitatem ; in rerum vero numero non facit
pluralitatem unitatum repetitio, vel si de eodem
dicam " gladius unus mucro unus ensis unus."
Potest enim unus tot vocabulis gladius agnosci ;
haec enim unitatum iteratio potius est non nume-
25 ratio, velut si ita dicamus " ensis mucro gladius,"
repetitio quaedam est eiusdem non numeratio diver-
sorum, velut si dicam " sol sol sol," non tres soles
effecerim, sed de uno totiens praedicaverim.

Non igitur si de patre ac filio et spiritu sancto
30 tertio praedicatur deus, idcirco trina praedicatio
numerum facit. Hoc enim illis ut dictum est im-
minet qui inter eos distantiam faciunt meritorum.
Catholicis vero nihil in differentia constituentibus
ipsamque formam ut est esse ponentibus neque aliud
35 esse quam est ipsum quod est opinantibus recte
repetitio de eodem quam enumeratio diversi videtur
esse cum dicitur "deus pater deus filius deus spiritus
sanctus atque haec trinitas unus deus," velut "ensis
atque mucro unus gladius," velut " sol sol sol
40 unus sol."

---

[a] The same words are used to illustrate the same matter
in the *Comment. in Arist.* περὶ ἑρμηνείας, 2nd ed. (Meiser),
56. 12.

14

kinds of number : one with which we count and the other which consists in numerable things. For indeed, " one " is a thing ; " unity " is that by which we call a thing one. Again " two " belongs to the class of things, as men or stones ; but not so duality ; duality is merely that whereby two men or two stones are denoted ; and similarly for the rest. Therefore in the case of that number by which we number, the repetition of ones makes plurality ; but in the number consisting in things the repetition of ones does not make plurality, as, for example, if I say of one and the same thing, " one sword, one brand, one blade."[a] For one sword can be recognized in so many words ; for this is rather the iteration of ones, not their numeration, just as if we were to say " sword, brand, blade," this is a sort of repetition of the same thing not a numeration of different things, just as if I were to say " sun sun sun " I should not have produced three suns, but I should have spoken that many times of one thing.

So then if God be predicated thrice, of Father, Son, and Holy Spirit, the threefold predication does not result in plural number. The risk of that, as has been said, attends only on those who distinguish them according to merit. But Catholic Christians, allowing no difference of merit in God, and positing that form to be as it really is, nor thinking his essence to be other than it is, rightly regard the statement " the Father is God, the Son is God, the Holy Spirit is God, and this Trinity is one God," not as an enumeration of different things but as a reiteration of one and the same thing, like the statement, " blade and brand are one sword " or " sun, sun, and sun are one sun."

Sed hoc interim ad eam dictum sit significationem
demonstrationemque qua ostenditur non omnem unitatum repetitionem numerum pluralitatemque perficere. Non vero ita dicitur " pater ac filius et spiritus
45 sanctus " quasi multivocum quiddam ; nam mucro et
ensis et ipse est et idem, pater vero ac filius et spiritus
sanctus idem equidem est, non vero ipse. In qua re
paulisper considerandum est. Requirentibus enim :
" Ipse est pater qui filius ? " " Minime," inquiunt.
50 Rursus : " Idem alter qui alter ? " Negatur. Non
est igitur inter eos in re omni indifferentia ; quare
subintrat numerus quem ex subiectorum diversitate
confici superius explanatum est. De qua re breviter
considerabimus, si prius illud, quem ad modum de
55 deo unum quodque praedicatur, praemiserimus.

## IV

Decem omnino praedicamenta traduntur quae de
rebus omnibus universaliter praedicantur, id est substantia, qualitas, quantitas, ad aliquid, ubi, quando,
habere, situm esse, facere, pati. Haec igitur talia
5 sunt qualia subiecta permiserint ; nam pars eorum in
reliquarum rerum praedicatione substantia est, pars
in accidentium numero est. At haec cum quis in
divinam verterit praedicationem, cuncta mutantur
quae praedicari possunt. Ad aliquid vero omnino
10 non potest praedicari, nam substantia in illo non est
vere substantia sed ultra substantiam ; item qualitas
et cetera quae venire queunt. Quorum ut amplior
fiat intellectus exempla subdenda sunt.

Nam cum dicimus " deus," substantiam quidem

16

Let this be enough for the present to establish my meaning and to show that not every repetition of units produces number and plurality. Still in saying " Father, Son, and Holy Spirit," we are not using synonymous terms. For " brand and blade " are the same and identical, but " Father, Son, and Holy Spirit," though the same, are not identical. This point deserves a moment's consideration. For to those who ask, " Is the Father the same as the Son ? " Catholics answer " Not at all." Again : " Is the one the same as the other ? " The answer is no. There is not, therefore, complete indifference between them ; and so number does come in—number which we explained was the result of diversity of substrates. We will briefly debate this point when we have done examining how particular predicates can be applied to God.

<h2 style="text-align:center">IV</h2>

There are in all ten categories which can be universally predicated of all things, namely, Substance, Quality, Quantity, Relation, Place, Time, Condition, Situation, Activity, Passivity. Now these are such as their subjects allow ; for some of them denote real substantive attributes of other things, others belong to the class of accidental attributes. But when anyone turns these to predication of God, all the things that can be predicated are changed. Relation, for instance, cannot be predicated at all of God ; for substance in Him is not really substantial but super-substantial. So with quality and the other possible attributes, of which we must add examples for the sake of better understanding.

For when we say God, we seem indeed to denote a

15 significare videmur, sed eam quae sit ultra substantiam ; cum vero " iustus," qualitatem quidem
sed non accidentem, sed eam quae sit substantia sed
ultra substantiam. Neque enim aliud est quod est,
aliud est quod iustus est, sed idem est esse deo quod
20 iusto. Item cum dicitur " magnus vel maximus,"
quantitatem quidem significare videmur, sed eam
quae sit ipsa substantia, talis qualem esse diximus
ultra substantiam ; idem est enim esse deo quod
magno. De forma enim eius superius monstratum
25 est quoniam is sit forma et unum vere nec ulla
pluralitas. Sed haec praedicamenta talia sunt, ut in
quo sint ipsum esse faciant quod dicitur, divise quidem
in ceteris, in deo vero coniuncte atque copulate hoc
modo : nam cum dicimus " substantia " (ut homo vel
30 deus), ita dicitur quasi illud de quo praedicatur ipsum
sit substantia, ut substantia homo vel deus. Sed
distat, quoniam homo non integre ipsum homo est ac
per hoc nec substantia ; quod enim est, aliis debet
quae non sunt homo. Deus vero hoc ipsum deus est ;
35 nihil enim aliud est nisi quod est, ac per hoc ipsum
deus est. Rursus " iustus," quod est qualitas, ita
dicitur quasi ipse hoc sit de quo praedicatur, id est
si dicamus " homo iustus vel deus iustus," ipsum
hominem vel deum iustos esse proponimus ; sed
40 differt, quod homo alter alter iustus, deus vero idem
ipsum est quod est iustum. " Magnus " etiam homo

---

ᵃ Gilbert de la Porrée in his commentary on the *De Trin.*
makes Boethius's meaning clear. " Quod igitur in illo
substantiam nominamus, non est subiectionis ratione quod
dicitur, sed ultra omnem quae accidentibus est subiecta
substantiam est essentia, absque omnibus quae possunt
accidere solitaria omnino " (Migne, *P.L.* lxiv. 1283). *Cf.*
Aug. *De Trin.* vii. 10.

substance ; but it is such as is supersubstantial. When
we say of him, " He is just," we do indeed mention
a quality, but not an accidental quality—rather such
as is substantial and, in fact, supersubstantial.[a] For
God is not one thing because he is, and another thing
because he is just ; with him to be just and to be God
are one and the same. So when we say, " He is great
or the greatest," we seem indeed to predicate quantity, but it is such as to be the same as this substance
which we have declared to be supersubstantial ; for
with him to be great and to be God are all one.
Again, concerning his form, we have already shown
that he is form, and truly one without any plurality.
Now the categories we have mentioned are such that
they give to the thing to which they are applied the
character which they express, in a divided manner in
other things, but in God in a conjoined and united
manner, in the following way. When we name a
substance, as man or God, it is named as though that
of which the predication is made were itself substance,
as if man or God were substance. But there is a
difference : since man is not simply and entirely man,
and therefore is not substance after all. For what
he is he owes to other things which are not man. But
God is simply and entirely God, for he is nothing else
than what he is, and therefore is simply God. Again
just, which is a quality, is said as though it were that
of which it is predicated ; that is, if we were to say
" a just man or just God," we are asserting that man
or God is just. But there is a difference, for man is
one thing, and a just man another. But God himself is
identical with the just. So a man or God is said to be
great, and it would appear that man himself is great

19

vel deus dicitur atque ita quasi ipse sit homo magnus
vel deus magnus ; sed homo tantum magnus, deus
vero ipsum magnus exsistit.  Reliqua vero neque de
45 deo neque de ceteris praedicantur.  Nam ubi vel de
homine vel de deo praedicari potest, de homine ut
in foro, de deo ut ubique, sed ita ut non quasi ipsa
sit res id quod praedicatur de qua dicitur.  Non
enim ita homo dicitur esse in foro quem ad modum
50 esse albus vel longus nec quasi circumfusus et deter-
minatus proprietate aliqua qua designari secundum
se possit, sed tantum quo sit illud aliis informatum
rebus per hanc praedicationem ostenditur.

De deo vero non ita, nam quod ubique est ita dici
55 videtur non quod in omni sit loco (omnino enim in
loco esse non potest) sed quod omnis ei locus adsit
ad eum capiendum, cum ipse non suscipiatur in loco ;
atque ideo nusquam in loco esse dicitur, quoniam
ubique est sed non in loco.  " Quando " vero eodem
60 praedicatur modo, ut de homine heri venit, de
deo semper est.  Hic quoque non quasi esse aliquid
dicitur illud ipsum de quo hesternus dicitur adventus,
sed quid ei secundum tempus accesserit praedicatur.
Quod vero de deo dicitur " semper est," unum
65 quidem significat, quasi omni praeterito fuerit, omni
quoquo modo sit praesenti est, omni futuro erit.
Quod de caelo et de ceteris inmortalibus corporibus
secundum philosophos dici potest, at de deo non ita.
Semper enim est, quoniam " semper " praesentis est
70 in eo temporis tantumque inter nostrarum rerum

---

[a] *i.e.* according to their substance.

or that God is great. But man is merely great ; God himself *is* essentially great.

The remaining categories are not predicated of God nor yet of other things.[a] For place can be predicated of man or of God—of man as " in the market-place " ; of God as " everywhere "—but in neither case is the predicate identical with that of which it is predicated. For " in the market-place " is not said of a man in the same way as " white " or " tall " nor so to speak, is he encompassed and determined by some property which enables him to be described in terms of his substance ; this predicate of place simply declares how far his substance is given a particular setting amid other things.

It is otherwise, of course, with God. " He is everywhere " seems to mean not that he is in every place, for he cannot be in any place at all—but that every place is present to him for him to occupy, although he himself is not received by any place, and therefore he is said to be nowhere in place, since he is everywhere but not in any place. Now time is predicated in the same way, as, of a man, " He came yesterday," of God, " He ever is." Here again it is not as if " he of whom yesterday's coming is predicated " is said actually to be something, but what is added to him in terms of time is predicated. But what is said of God, " ever is," signifies only one thing, that he was, as it were, in all the past, is in all the present—however that term be used—and will be in all the future. According to the philosophers this may be said of the heavens and of other immortal bodies, but of God it is said in a different way. He is ever, because " ever " is with him a term of present time, and there is this great difference

praesens, quod est nunc, interest ac divinarum, quod
nostrum " nunc " quasi currens tempus facit et sempi-
ternitatem, divinum vero " nunc " permanens neque
movens sese atque consistens aeternitatem facit ; cui
75 nomini si adicias " semper," facies eius quod est nunc
iugem indefessumque ac per hoc perpetuum cursum
quod est sempiternitas.

Rursus habere vel facere eodem modo ; dicimus
enim " vestitus currit " de homine, de deo " cuncta
80 possidens regit." Rursus de eo nihil quod est esse
de utrisque dictum est, sed haec omnis praedicatio
exterioribus datur omniaque haec quodam modo
referuntur ad aliud. Cuius praedicationis differentiam sic facilius internoscimus : qui homo est vel
85 deus refertur ad substantiam qua est aliquid, id est
homo vel deus ; qui iustus est refertur ad qualitatem
qua scilicet est aliquid, id est iustus, qui magnus ad
quantitatem qua est aliquid, id est magnus. Nam in
ceteris praedicationibus nihil tale est. Qui enim
90 dicit esse aliquem in foro vel ubique, refert quidem
ad praedicamentum quod est ubi, sed non quo aliquid
est velut iustitia iustus. Item cum dico " currit " vel
" regit " vel " nunc est " vel " semper est," refertur
quidem vel ad facere vel ad tempus—si tamen
95 interim divinum illud semper tempus dici potest—
sed non quo aliquo aliquid est velut magnitudine

---

*a* The doctrine is Augustine's, *cf. De Civ. Dei*, xi. 6,
xii. 16 ; but Boethius's use of *sempiternitas*, like his
word-building, seems to be peculiar to himself. Claudianus
Mamertus, speaking of applying the categories to God,
uses *sempiternitas* as Boethius uses *aeternitas*. *Cf. De Statu
Animae*, i. 19. Apuleius seems to use both terms interchangeably, *e.g. Asclep.* 29-31. On Boethius's distinction
between time and eternity see *Cons.* v, pr. 6, and Rand, *Der*

between the present of our affairs, which is now, and the divine present : our " now " connotes changing time and sempiternity ; but God's " now," abiding, unmoved, and immovable, connotes eternity. If you add *semper* to *eternity*, you will get the flowing, incessant and thereby perpetual course of our present time, that is to say, sempiternity.[a]

It is just the same with the categories of condition and activity. For example, we say of a man, " He runs, clothed," of God, " He rules, possessing all things." Here again nothing substantial is asserted of either subject ; in fact all this kind of predication arises from what lies outside substance, and all of these predicates refer, so to speak, to something other than substance. And we easily distinguish the difference of this sort of predication in this way : the terms "man " and " God " refer to the substance in virtue of which the subject is—man or God. The term " just " refers to the quality in virtue of which the subject is something, viz. just ; the term " great " to the quantity in virtue of which he is something, viz. great. Now in other kinds of predication there is nothing like this. For he who says that someone is in the market or everywhere, is surely referring to the category of place, but not to anything by reason of which he is something, as he is just in virtue of justice. So when I say, " he runs, he rules, he is now, he is ever," reference is surely made to activity or time—if indeed God's " over " can be described as time—but not to anything in virtue of which he is something, as he is great in virtue of greatness.

*dem B. zugeschr. Trakt. de fide*, pp. 425 ff., and Brandt in *Theol. Littzg.*, 1902, p. 147.

magnum. Nam situm passionemque requiri in deo
non oportet, neque enim sunt.

Iamne patet quae sit differentia praedicationum ?
100 Quod aliae quidem quasi rem monstrant aliae vero
quasi circumstantias rei; quodque illa quae ita praedicantur, ut esse aliquid rem ostendant, illa vero ut
non esse, sed potius extrinsecus aliquid quodam modo
affigant. Illa igitur, quae aliquid esse designant,
105 secundum rem praedicationes vocentur. Quae cum
de rebus subiectis dicuntur, vocantur accidentia secundum rem ; cum vero de deo qui subiectus non est,
secundum substantiam rei praedicatio nuncupatur.

V

Age nunc de relativis speculemur pro quibus
omne quod dictum est sumpsimus ad disputationem ;
maxime enim haec non videntur secundum se facere
praedicationem quae perspicue ex alieno adventu
5 constare perspiciuntur. Age enim, quoniam dominus
ac servus relativa sunt, videamus utrumne ita sit ut
secundum se sit praedicatio an minime. Atqui si
auferas servum, abstuleris et dominum ; at non etiam
si auferas albedinem, abstuleris quoque album, sed
10 interest, quod albedo accidit albo, qua sublata perit
nimirum album. At in domino, si servum auferas,

---

<sup>a</sup> *Dominus* and *servus* are similarly used as illustration,
*In Cat.* (Migne, *P.L.* lxiv. 217).

Finally, we must not look for the categories of situation and passivity in God, for they simply are not to be found in him.

Have I now made clear the difference between the kinds of predication ? Because one set points, as it were, to the thing, the other set to the circumstances of the thing ; and because those things which are predicated in the first way point to a thing as being something, but the others do not point to it as being something, but rather in some way attach something external to it. Those which describe a thing as being something may be called objective predications ; when they are said of things as subjects they are called objective accidents. But when they are said of God, who is not a subject at all, it is called predication according to the substance.

## V

Let us now consider relationships to which all the foregoing remarks have been preliminary ; for these especially, which are clearly seen to exist because of something else coming in, do not seem to produce predication by themselves. For instance, since master and slave [a] are relative terms, let us see whether either of them is such that it is a predication by itself or not. But if you suppressed the term slave, you would simultaneously suppress the term master. On the other hand, though you suppressed the term whiteness, you would not suppress some white thing, though the fact is important that whiteness belongs as an accident to a white thing, and when it is removed, obviously the white thing ceases to be a white thing. But in the case of master, if you sup-

perit vocabulum quo dominus vocabatur ; sed non accidit servus domino ut albedo albo, sed potestas quaedam qua servus coercetur. Quae quoniam sublato
15 deperit servo, constat non eam per se domino accidere sed per servorum quodam modo extrinsecus accessum.

Non igitur dici potest praedicationem relativam quidquam rei de qua dicitur secundum se vel addere vel minuere vel mutare. Quae tota non in eo quod
20 est esse consistit, sed in eo quod est in comparatione aliquo modo se habere, nec semper ad aliud sed aliquotiens ad idem. Age enim stet quisquam. Ei igitur si accedam dexter, erit ille sinister ad me comparatus, non quod ille ipse sinister sit, sed quod
25 ego dexter accesserim. Rursus ego sinister accedo, item ille fit dexter, non quod ita sit per se dexter velut albus ac longus, sed quod me accedente fit dexter atque id quod est a me et ex me est, minime vero ex sese.

30 Quare quae secundum rei alicuius in eo quod ipsa est proprietatem non faciunt praedicationem, nihil alternare vel mutare queunt nullamque omnino variare essentiam. Quocirca si pater ac filius ad aliquid dicuntur nihilque aliud ut dictum est diffe-
35 runt nisi sola relatione, relatio vero non praedicatur ad id de quo praedicatur quasi ipsa sit et secundum rem de qua dicitur, non faciet alteritatem rerum de qua dicitur, sed, si dici potest, quo quidem modo id quod vix intelligi potuit interpretatum est, persona-

press the term slave, the term by which he was called master disappears. But slave is not an accidental quality of master, as whiteness is of a white thing ; that accidental quality is a certain power by which the slave is coerced. Now since that power goes when the slave is removed, it is plain that it does not belong as an accident to the master by itself, but because of the accession of slaves, which is as it were external.

It cannot therefore be affirmed that predication of relationship by itself adds or takes away or changes anything in the thing of which it is said. It wholly consists not in that which is simply being, but in that which is being in some way in comparison, not always with another thing but sometimes with itself. For suppose a man standing. If I go up to him on the right and stand beside him, he will be left, in comparison with me, not because he is left in himself, but because I have come up to him on the right. Again, if I come up to him on the left, he becomes right, not because he is right in himself, as he may be white or tall, but because he becomes right in virtue of my approach, and what he is depends entirely on me, and not in the least on himself.

Accordingly those things which do not produce predication according to the essential property of a thing cannot alter, change, or disturb any essence in any way. Wherefore if father and son are predicates of relation, and, as we have said, have no other difference but that of relation, but relation is not predicated with reference to that of which it is predicated as if it were the thing itself and objectively predicated of it, it will not imply an otherness of the things of which it is said, but, in a phrase which aims at interpreting what we could hardly understand, an

27

40 rum. Omnino enim magna regulae est veritas in
rebus incorporalibus distantias effici differentiis non
locis. Neque accessisse dici potest aliquid deo, ut
pater fieret ; non enim coepit esse umquam pater
eo quod substantialis quidem ei est productio filii,
45 relativa vero praedicatio patris. Ac si meminimus
omnium in prioribus de deo sententiarum, ita cogi-
temus processisse quidem ex deo patre filium deum
et ex utrisque spiritum sanctum ; hos, quoniam in-
corporales sint, minime locis distare. Quoniam vero
50 pater deus et filius deus et spiritus sanctus deus, deus
vero nullas habet differentias quibus differat ab deo,
a nullo eorum differt. Differentiae vero ubi absunt,
abest pluralitas ; ubi abest pluralitas, adest unitas.
Nihil autem aliud gigni potuit ex deo nisi deus ; et
55 in rebus numerabilibus repetitio unitatum non facit
modis omnibus pluralitatem. Trium igitur idonee
constituta est unitas.

VI

Sed quoniam nulla relatio ad se ipsum referri
potest, idcirco quod ea secundum se ipsum est praedicatio quae relatione caret, facta quidem est trinitatis numerositas in eo quod est praedicatio relationis,
5 servata vero unitas in eo quod est indifferentia vel
substantiae vel operationis vel omnino eius quae secundum se dicitur praedicationis. Ita igitur substantia continet unitatem, relatio multiplicat trini-
28

otherness of persons. For there is indeed great truth
in the rule that distinctions in incorporeal things are
established by differences and not by spatial separation. It cannot be said that any accident was added
to God, that he might become the Father ; for he
never began to be Father, since the begetting of the
Son belongs to his very substance ; however, the
predication of father, as such, is relative. And if we
bear in mind all the propositions made concerning
God in the previous discussion, let us consider that
God the Son proceeded from God the Father, and
the Holy Ghost from both, and that they cannot
possibly be spatially different, since they are incorporeal. But since the Father is God, the Son is God,
and the Holy Spirit is God, but God has no differences
distinguishing him from God, he differs from none
of the others. But where there are no differences
there is no plurality ; where there is no plurality there
is unity. Again, nothing but God could be begotten
of God, and lastly, in concrete enumerations the
repetition of units does not in any way produce
plurality. Thus the Unity of the Three is suitably
established.

## VI

But since no relation can be related to itself,
inasmuch as one which makes a predicate by itself
is a predication which lacks relation, the manifoldness
of the Trinity is produced in the fact that it is predication of a relation, and the unity is preserved
through the fact that there is no difference of substance, or operation, or generally of that kind of
predication which is made on its own. So then, the
substance preserves the unity, the relation makes

tatem ; atque ideo sola singillatim proferuntur atque
10 separatim quae relationis sunt. Nam idem pater qui
filius non est nec idem uterque qui spiritus sanctus.
Idem tamen deus est pater et filius et spiritus sanctus,
idem iustus idem bonus idem magnus idem omnia
quae secundum se poterunt praedicari. Sane scien-
15 dum est non semper talem esse relativam praedicationem, ut semper ad differens praedicetur, ut est
servus ad dominum ; differunt enim. Nam omne
aequale aequali aequale est et simile simili simile
est et idem ei quod est idem idem est ; et similis
20 est relatio in trinitate patris ad filium et utriusque
ad spiritum sanctum ut eius quod est idem ad id
quod est idem. Quod si id in cunctis aliis rebus
non potest inveniri, facit hoc cognata caducis rebus
alteritas. Nos vero nulla imaginatione diduci sed
25 simplici intellectu erigi et ut quidque intellegi potest
ita aggredi etiam intellectu oportet.

Sed de proposita quaestione satis dictum est.
Nunc vestri normam iudicii exspectat subtilitas quaestionis ; quae utrum recte decursa sit an minime,
30 vestrae statuet pronuntiationis auctoritas. Quod si
sententiae fidei fundamentis sponte firmissimae opitu-
lante gratia divina idonea argumentorum adiumenta
praestitimus, illuc perfecti operis laetitia remeabit
unde venit effectus. Quod si ultra se humanitas
35 nequivit ascendere, quantum inbecillitas subtrahit
vota supplebunt.

---

[a] *Cf. Cons.* v, pr. 4 and 5, especially in pr. 5 the passage
" quare in illius summae intellegentiae acumen si possumus
erigamur " (page 418).

up the Trinity. Hence only terms belonging to relation may be applied singly and separately. For the Father is not the same as the Son, nor is either of them the same as the Holy Spirit. Yet Father, Son, and Holy Spirit are the same God, the same in justice, in goodness, in greatness, and in everything that can be predicated by itself. One must not forget that relative predication is not always such that it is always predicated with reference to something different, as slave is with reference to master ; for they are different. For equals are equal, likes are like, identicals are identical, each with other ; and the relation in the Trinity of Father to Son, and of both to Holy Spirit is like a relation of identicals. But if a relation of this kind cannot be found in all other things, this is because of the otherness natural to all perishable, transitory objects. But we ought not to be led astray by any imagination, but raised up by pure understanding and, so far as anything can be understood, thus far also we should approach it with our understanding.[a]

But enough has now been said of the question which was proposed. The subtle reasoning of the argument awaits the standard of your judgement ; the authority of your verdict will decide whether it has been run through on a straight course or not. If, the grace of God helping me, I have furnished some fitting support in argument to an article which stands quite firmly by itself on the foundation of Faith, the joy felt for the finished work will flow back to the source whence its effecting came. But if human nature has failed to reach beyond its limits, whatever my weakness takes away, my prayers will make up.

# ANICII MANLII SEVERINI BOETHII

V.C. ET INL. EXCONS. ORD. PATRICII

## AD IOHANNEM DIACONUM

## UTRUM PATER ET FILIUS ET SPIRITUS SANCTUS DE DIVINITATE SUBSTANTIALITER PRAEDICENTUR

Quaero an pater et filius ac spiritus sanctus de divinitate substantialiter praedicentur an alio quolibet modo ; viamque indaginis hinc arbitror esse sumendam, unde rerum omnium manifestum constat exor-
5 dium, id est ab ipsis catholicae fidei fundamentis. Si igitur interrogem, an qui dicitur pater substantia sit, respondetur esse substantia. Quod si quaeram, an filius substantia sit, idem dicitur. Spiritum quoque sanctum substantiam esse nemo dubitaverit. Sed cum
10 rursus colligo patrem filium spiritum sanctum, non plures sed una occurrit esse substantia. Una igitur substantia trium nec separari ullo modo aut disiungi potest nec velut partibus in unum coniuncta est, sed est una simpliciter. Quaecumque igitur de divina
15 substantia praedicantur, ea tribus oportet esse communia ; idque signi erit quae sint quae de divinitatis

32

# ANICIUS MANLIUS SEVERINUS BOETHIUS

MOST HONOURABLE, OF THE ILLUSTRIOUS ORDER OF
EX-CONSULS, PATRICIAN

## to JOHN THE DEACON

## WHETHER FATHER, SON, AND HOLY SPIRIT ARE SUBSTANTIALLY PREDICATED OF THE DIVINITY

I ASK whether Father, Son, and Holy Spirit are predicated of the divinity substantially or in any other way. And I think that the method of our inquiry must be borrowed from what is admittedly the surest source of all truth, namely, the fundamental doctrines of the catholic faith. If, then, I ask whether he who is called the Father is a substance, the answer is that he is a substance. And if I ask whether the Son is a substance, the reply is the same. So, too, no one would doubt that the Holy Spirit is also a substance. But when, on the other hand, I take together Father, Son, and Holy Spirit, the result is not several substances but one substance. The one substance of the Three, then, cannot be separated in any way or divided, nor is it combined into one as if from parts : it is simply one. Everything, therefore, that is predicated of the divine substance must be common to the Three, and this will be a sign of what sort of thing

substantia praedicentur, quod quaecumque hoc modo
dicuntur, de singulis in unum collectis tribus singulariter praedicabuntur. Hoc modo si dicimus :
20 " Pater deus est, filius deus est, spiritus sanctus deus
est," pater filius ac spiritus sanctus unus deus. Si igitur
eorum una deitas una substantia est, licet dei nomen
de divinitate substantialiter praedicari.

Ita pater veritas est, filius veritas est, spiritus
25 sanctus veritas est ; pater filius et spiritus sanctus
non tres veritates sed una veritas est. Si igitur una
in his substantia una est veritas, necesse est veritatem
substantialiter praedicari. De bonitate de incommutabilitate de iustitia de omnipotentia ac de ceteris
30 omnibus quae tam de singulis quam de omnibus
singulariter praedicamus manifestum est substantialiter dici. Unde apparet ea quae cum in singulis
separatim dici convenit nec tamen in omnibus dici
queunt, non substantialiter praedicari sed alio modo ;
35 qui vero iste sit, posterius quaeram. Nam qui pater
est, hoc vocabulum non transmittit ad filium neque
ad spiritum sanctum. Quo fit ut non sit substantiale
nomen hoc inditum ; nam si substantiale esset, ut
deus ut veritas ut iustitia ut ipsa quoque substantia,
40 de ceteris diceretur.

Item filius solus hoc recipit nomen neque cum
aliis iungit sicut in deo, sicut in veritate, sicut in
ceteris quae superius dixi. Spiritus quoque non est
idem qui pater ac filius. Ex his igitur intellegimus
45 patrem ac filium ac spiritum sanctum non de ipsa
divinitate substantialiter dici sed alio quodam modo ;

---

<sup>a</sup> *i.e. personaliter* (Ioh. Scottus *ad loc.*).

is predicated of the substance of the divinity, that all those things which are said of it in this way will also be predicated severally of each of the Three combined into one. For instance if we say " the Father is God, the Son is God, and the Holy Spirit is God," then Father, Son, and Holy Spirit are one God. If then their one godhead is one substance, the name of God may with right be predicated substantially of the divinity.

Similarly the Father is truth, the Son is truth, and the Holy Spirit is truth ; Father, Son, and Holy Spirit are not three truths, but one truth. If, then, the one substance in them is one truth, truth must of necessity be predicated substantially. So goodness, immutability, justice, omnipotence and all the other things which we predicate of the Persons singly and collectively are plainly said of them substantially. Hence it appears that what may be predicated of each single one but cannot be said of all is not predicated substantially, but in some other way ; in what way I shall enquire presently. For he who is Father does not transmit this name to the Son nor to the Holy Spirit. Hence it follows that this name is not attached to him as something substantial ; for if it were substantial, as God, truth, justice, or substance itself, it would be affirmed of the other Persons.

Similarly the Son alone receives this name ; nor does he associate it with the other Persons, as in the case of the titles God, truth, and the other predicates which I have already mentioned. The Spirit too is not the same as the Father and the Son. From these things, then, we understand that Father, Son, and Holy Spirit are not predicated of the divinity in a substantial manner, but in some other way.[a] For if

si enim substantialiter praedicaretur, et de singulis
et de omnibus singulariter diceretur. Haec vero ad
aliquid dici manifestum est ; nam et pater alicuius
50 pater est et filius alicuius filius est, spiritus alicuius
spiritus. Quo fit, ut ne trinitas quidem substantialiter de deo praedicetur ; non enim pater trinitas
(qui enim pater est, filius ac spiritus sanctus non
est) nec trinitas filius nec trinitas spiritus sanctus
55 secundum eundem modum, sed trinitas quidem in
personarum pluralitate consistit, unitas vero in
substantiae simplicitate.

Quod si personae divisae sunt, substantia vero
indivisa sit, necesse est quod vocabulum ex personis
60 originem capit id ad substantiam non pertinere ; at
trinitatem personarum diversitas fecit, trinitas igitur
non pertinet ad substantiam. Quo fit ut neque
pater neque filius neque spiritus sanctus neque trinitas
de deo substantialiter praedicetur, sed ut dictum est
65 ad aliquid. Deus vero 'veritas iustitia bonitas omnipotentia substantia inmutabilitas virtus sapientia et
quicquid huiusmodi excogitari potest substantialiter
de divinitate dicuntur. Haec si se recte et ex fide
habent, ut me instruas peto ; aut si aliqua re forte
70 diversus es, diligentius intuere quae dicta sunt et
fidem si poterit rationemque coniunge.

---

[a] *i.e. sed personaliter* (Ioh. Scottus *ad loc.*).
[b] *Vide supra*, Introduction, p. xiv.

each term were predicated substantially it would be affirmed of the three Persons both separately and collectively. It is evident that these terms are relative, for the Father is some one's Father, the Son is some one's Son, the Spirit is some one's Spirit. Hence not even Trinity is predicated substantially[a] of God ; for the Father is not Trinity—since he who is Father is not Son and Holy Spirit—nor yet, by parity of reasoning, is the Son Trinity nor the Holy Spirit Trinity, but the Trinity consists in plurality of Persons, the unity in simplicity of substance.

Now if the Persons are separate, while the substance is undivided, it must needs be that that term which is derived from Persons does not belong to Substance. But the diversity of Persons makes the Trinity, wherefore Trinity does not belong to substance. Hence neither Father, nor Son, nor Holy Spirit, nor Trinity is predicated substantially of God, but only relatively, as we have said. But God, truth, justice, goodness, omnipotence, substance, immutability, virtue, wisdom and all other conceivable predicates of the kind are said of the divinity substantially.

If these things are right and in accordance with the Faith, I pray you confirm me ; or if you are in any point of another opinion, examine carefully what has been said, and if possible, reconcile faith and reason.[b]

## ITEM EIUSDEM

### AD EUNDEM

## QUOMODO SUBSTANTIAE IN EO QUOD SINT BONAE SINT CUM NON SINT SUBSTANTIALIA BONA

Postulas, ut ex Hebdomadibus nostris eius quaestionis obscuritatem quae continet modum quo substantiae in eo quod sint bonae sint, cum non sint
substantialia bona, digeram et paulo evidentius mon-
5 strem ; idque eo dicis esse faciendum, quod non sit
omnibus notum iter huiusmodi scriptionum.  Tuus
vero testis ipse sum quam haec vivaciter fueris ante
complexus.  Hebdomadas vero ego mihi ipse commen-
tor potiusque ad memoriam meam speculata conservo
10 quam cuiquam participo quorum lascivia ac petulantia
nihil a ioco risuque patitur esse seiunctum.[1]  Prohinc
tu ne sis obscuritatibus brevitatis adversus, quae cum
sint arcani fida custodia tum id habent commodi, quod
cum his solis qui digni sunt conloquuntur.  Ut igitur

[1] seiunct. *Rand* ; coniunct. *the best* MSS. : disiunct. *vulg.*,
*Vallinus.*

---

[a] " Groups of Seven."  Similarly Porphyry divided the
works of Plotinus into six *Enneades* or groups of nine.

# FROM THE SAME
## TO THE SAME

## HOW SUBSTANCES ARE GOOD IN VIR-
## TUE OF THEIR EXISTENCE WITH-
## OUT BEING SUBSTANTIAL GOODS

You ask me to state and explain somewhat more
clearly that obscure question in my *Hebdomads* [a] concerning the manner in which substances are good in
virtue of existence without being substantial goods.[b]
You urge that this demonstration is necessary because the method of this kind of treatise is not clear
to all. I can bear witness with what eagerness you
have already attacked the subject. But I think over
my *Hebdomads* with myself, and I keep my speculations in my own memory rather than share them with
any of those pert and frivolous persons who will not
tolerate an argument unless it is made amusing.
Wherefore do not you take objection to obscurities
consequent on brevity, which are the sure treasure-
house of secret doctrine and have the advantage that
they speak only with those who are worthy. I have

---

[b] *Cf.* discussion on the nature of good in *Cons.* iii, m. 10
and pr. 11 (*infra*, pp. 284 ff.).

15 in mathematica fieri solet ceterisque etiam disciplinis,
praeposui terminos regulasque quibus cuncta quae
sequuntur efficiam.

I. Communis animi conceptio est enuntiatio quam
quisque probat auditam. Harum duplex modus est.
20 Nam una ita communis est, ut omnium sit hominum,
veluti si hanc proponas : " Si duobus aequalibus
aequalia auferas, quae relinquantur aequalia esse,"
nullus id intellegens neget. Alia vero est doctorum
tantum, quae tamen ex talibus communibus animi
25 conceptionibus venit, ut est : " Quae incorporalia
sunt, in loco non esse," et cetera ; quae non vulgus
sed docti comprobant.

II. Diversum est esse et id quod est ; ipsum enim
esse nondum est, at vero quod est accepta essendi
30 forma est atque consistit.

III. Quod est participare aliquo potest, sed ipsum
esse nullo modo aliquo participat. Fit enim partici-
patio cum aliquid iam est ; est autem aliquid, cum
esse susceperit.

35 IV. Id quod est habere aliquid praeterquam quod
ipsum est potest ; ipsum vero esse nihil aliud praeter
se habet admixtum.

V. Diversum est tantum esse aliquid et esse
aliquid in eo quod est ; illic enim accidens hic
40 substantia significatur.

---

<sup>a</sup> On this mathematical method of exposition *cf. Cons.*
iii, pr. 10 (*infra*, p. 281).
  <sup>b</sup> *Esse*=Aristotle's τὸ εἶναι ; *id quod est*=τὸ τί.
  <sup>c</sup> *Consistere*=ὑποστῆναι.

therefore followed the example of the mathematical [a] and cognate sciences and laid down bounds and rules according to which I shall develop all that follows.

I. A common conception of the mind is a statement which anyone accepts as soon as he hears it. Of these there are two kinds. For one is common in that all men possess it ; as, for instance, if you say, " If you take equals from two equals, the remainders are equal." Nobody who grasps that would deny it. But the other kind is intelligible only to the learned, though it is derived from the same class of common conceptions ; as " Things which are incorporeal are not in space," and the like ; these conceptions are approved as obvious to the learned but not to the common herd.

II. Being and the thing that is [b] are different. For simple being awaits manifestation, but the thing that is is and exists as soon as it has received the form which gives it being. [c]

III. What is, can participate in something, but simple being does not participate in any way in anything. For participation is effected when something already is ; but something is, when it has acquired being.

IV. That which is can possess something besides what it is itself. But simple being has no admixture of aught besides itself.

V. Merely to be something and to be something in virtue of existence are different ; the former signifies an accident, the latter a substance.

VI. Omne quod est[1] participat eo quod est esse ut sit ; alio vero participat ut aliquid sit. Ac per hoc id quod est participat eo quod est esse ut sit ; est vero ut participet alio quolibet.

45 VII. Omne simplex esse suum et id quod est unum habet.

VIII. Omni composito aliud est esse, aliud ipsum est.

IX. Omnis diversitas discors, similitudo vero
50 appetenda est ; et quod appetit aliud, tale ipsum esse naturaliter ostenditur quale est illud hoc ipsum quod appetit.

Sufficiunt igitur quae praemisimus ; a prudente vero rationis interprete suis unumquodque aptabitur
55 argumentis.

Quaestio vero huiusmodi est. Ea quae sunt bona sunt ; tenet enim communis sententia doctorum omne quod est ad bonum tendere, omne autem tendit ad simile. Quae igitur ad bonum tendunt
60 bona ipsa sunt. Sed quemadmodum bona sint, in-quirendum est, utrumne participatione an substantia ? Si participatione, per se ipsa nullo modo bona sunt ; nam quod participatione album est, per se in eo quod ipsum est album non est. Et de ceteris qualitatibus
65 eodem modo. Si igitur participatione sunt bona, ipsa per se nullo modo bona sunt : non igitur ad bonum tendunt. Sed concessum est. Non igitur participatione sunt bona sed substantia. Quorum vero substantia bona est, id quod sunt bona sunt ;

----

[1] est *omitted by the best* MSS.

[a] *Id quod est esse*=τὸ εἶναι.

# QUOMODO SUBSTANTIAE

VI. Everything that is participates in absolute being [a] in order to exist; but it participates in something else in order to be something. Hence that which is participates in absolute being in order to exist, but it exists in order to participate in something else.

VII. Every simple thing possesses as a unity its existence and its particular being.

VIII. In every composite thing existence is one thing, its particular being is another.

IX. All diversity repels, likeness must be attracted. That which seeks something else is demonstrably of the same nature as that which it seeks.

These preliminaries are enough then for our purpose. The intelligent interpreter of the discussion will supply the arguments appropriate to each point.

Now the problem is this. Things which are, are good. For the common opinion of the learned holds that everything that is tends to good and everything tends to its like. Therefore things which tend to good are themselves good. We must, however, inquire how they are good—by participation or by substance. If by participation, they are in no wise good in themselves; for a thing which is white by participation is not white in itself by virtue of its own being. So with all other qualities. If then they are good by participation, they are in no way good in themselves; therefore they do not tend to good. But we have agreed that they do. Therefore they are good not by participation but by substance. But of those things whose substance is good the particular

70 id quod sunt autem habent ex eo quod est esse.
Esse igitur ipsorum bonum est ; omnium igitur rerum
ipsum esse bonum est. Sed si esse bonum est, ea
quae sunt in eo quod sunt bona sunt idemque illis
est esse quod boni esse ; substantialia igitur bona
75 sunt, quoniam non participant bonitatem. Quod si
ipsum esse in eis bonum est, non est dubium quin
substantialia cum sint bona, primo sint bono similia
ac per hoc hoc ipsum bonum erunt ; nihil enim illi
praeter se ipsum simile est. Ex quo fit ut omnia
80 quae sunt deus sint, quod dictu nefas est. Non
sunt igitur substantialia bona ac per hoc non in his
est esse bonum ; non sunt igitur in eo quod sunt
bona. Sed nec participant bonitatem ; nullo enim
modo ad bonum tenderent. Nullo modo igitur sunt
85 bona.

Huic quaestioni talis poterit adhiberi solutio.
Multa sunt quae cum separari actu non possunt,
animo tamen et cogitatione separantur ; ut cum
triangulum vel cetera a subiecta materia nullus actu
90 separat, mente tamen segregans ipsum triangulum
proprietatemque eius praeter materiam speculatur.
Amoveamus igitur primi boni praesentiam paulisper
ex animo, quod esse quidem constat idque ex omnium
doctorum indoctorumque sententia barbararumque
95 gentium religionibus cognosci potest. Hoc igitur
paulisper amoto ponamus omnia esse quae sunt bona
atque ea consideremus quemadmodum bona esse
possent, si a primo bono minime defluxissent. Hinc

---

[a] *Cf.* the similar *reductio ad absurdum* in *Tr.* 5 (*infra*, p. 100).
[b] *Vide supra*, p. 7, n. *c*.

being is good. But they owe their particular being
to absolute being. Their existence therefore is good ;
therefore mere existence of all things is good. But if
their existence is good, things which exist are good
in virtue of their existence, and their existence is the
same as the existence of the good. Therefore they
are substantial goods, since they do not participate
in goodness. But if the particular being in them is
good, there is no doubt but that since they are
substantial goods, they are like the first good, and
thereby they will be that good itself ; for nothing is
like it save itself. Hence all things that are, are God
—an impious assertion. Wherefore they are not
substantial goods, and so there is not in them good
existence ; therefore they are not good in virtue of
their existence. But neither do they participate in
goodness ; for they would in no wise tend to good.
Therefore they are in no wise good.[a]

This problem will admit of the following solution.[b]
There are many things which are separated by a
mental process, though they cannot be separated in
fact. No one, for instance, actually separates a
triangle or other mathematical figure from the underlying matter ; but separating it mentally one considers the triangle itself and its properties apart from
matter. Let us therefore remove from the mind for
a moment the presence of the first good, which it is
certainly agreed exists, as can be known from the
opinion of all men, learned and unlearned, and from
the religious beliefs of savage races. This having
been thus for a moment removed, let us postulate
that all things that are good exist, and let us consider how they could possibly be good if they did not
derive from the first good. This leads me to perceive

intueor aliud in eis esse quod bona sunt, aliud quod
100 sunt. Ponatur enim una eademque substantia bona
esse alba, gravis, rotunda. Tunc aliud esset ipsa illa
substantia, aliud eius rotunditas, aliud color, aliud
bonitas ; nam si haec singula idem essent quod ipsa
substantia, idem esset gravitas quod color, ⟨color⟩[1]
105 quod bonum et bonum quod gravitas—quod fieri
natura non sinit. Aliud igitur tunc in eis esset esse,
aliud aliquid esse, ac tunc bona quidem essent, esse
tamen ipsum minime haberent bonum. Igitur si ullo
modo essent, non a bono ac bona essent ac non idem
110 essent quod bona, sed eis aliud esset esse aliud bonis
esse. Quod si nihil omnino aliud essent nisi bona
neque gravia neque colorata neque spatii dimensione
distenta nec ulla in eis qualitas esset, nisi tantum
bona essent, tunc non res sed rerum viderentur esse
115 principium nec potius viderentur, sed videretur ;
unum enim solumque est huiusmodi, quod tantum
bonum aliudque nihil sit. Quae quoniam non sunt
simplicia, nec esse omnino poterant, nisi ea id quod
solum bonum est esse voluisset. Idcirco quoniam
120 esse eorum a boni voluntate defluxit, bona esse
dicuntur. Primum enim bonum, quoniam est, in eo
quod est bonum est ; secundum vero bonum, quoniam
ex eo fluxit cuius ipsum esse bonum est, ipsum quoque bonum est. Sed ipsum esse omnium rerum ex eo
125 fluxit quod est primum bonum et quod bonum tale est
46

that their goodness and their existence are two different things. For let us suppose that one and the same good substance is white, heavy and round. Then its particular substance, its roundness, colour and goodness would all be different things. For if each of these qualities were the same as its particular substance, weight would be the same thing as colour, colour as goodness, and goodness as weight—which is contrary to nature. Then in that case existence in them would be one thing, their particular being another, and then they would be good, but they would not have their particular being good. Therefore if they existed in any way, they would not be from the good and so good, and they would not be the same because good, but for them existence would be one thing, being good another. But if they were nothing else at all except good, and were neither heavy nor coloured[1] nor extended in a spatial dimension, and there were in them no quality save only that they were good, then they (or rather it) would seem to be not things but the principle of things ; for there is one thing alone of this kind, that is only good and nothing else. But since they are not simple, they could not even exist at all unless that which is the one sole good had willed them to exist. They are called good simply because their existence has derived from the will of the good. For the first good, since it exists, is good in virtue of its existence ; but the secondary good, since it has derived from that whose existence is itself good, is itself also good. But the particular being of all things has derived from that which is the first good and which is such a

---

[1] ⟨color⟩ *supplied by Tester.*

ut recte dicatur in eo quod est esse bonum. Ipsum
igitur eorum esse bonum est ; tunc enim in eo.

Qua in re soluta quaestio est. Idcirco enim licet
in eo quod sint bona sint, non sunt tamen similia
130 primo bono, quoniam non quoquo modo sint res
ipsum esse earum bonum est, sed quoniam non
potest esse ipsum esse rerum, nisi a primo esse
defluxerit, id est bono ; idcirco ipsum esse bonum est
nec est simile ei a quo est. Illud enim quoquo modo
135 sit bonum est in eo quod est ; non enim aliud est
praeterquam bonum. Hoc autem nisi ab illo esset,
bonum fortasse esse posset, sed bonum in eo quod
est esse non posset. Tunc enim participaret forsitan
bono ; ipsum vero esse quod non haberent a bono,
140 bonum habere non possent. Igitur sublato ab his
bono primo mente et cogitatione, ista licet essent
bona, tamen in eo quod essent bona esse non possent,
et quoniam actu non potuere exsistere, nisi illud ea
quod vere bonum est produxisset, idcirco et esse
145 eorum bonum est et non est simile substantiali bono
id quod ab eo fluxit ; et nisi ab eo fluxissent, licet
essent bona, tamen in eo quod sunt bona esse non
possent, quoniam et praeter bonum et non ex bono
essent, cum illud ipsum bonum primum [est]¹ et ipsum
150 esse sit et ipsum bonum et ipsum esse bonum. At
non etiam alba in eo quod sunt alba esse oportebit
ea quae alba sunt, quoniam ex voluntate dei fluxerunt

¹ [est] *deleted by Tester.*

48

good that it is rightly said to be good in virtue of its existence. Therefore their particular being is good ; for then it is in the first good.

Thereby the problem is solved. For though they are good in virtue of their existence, they are not therefore like the first good, since their particular being is not good under all circumstances, but because the particular being of things cannot exist unless it has derived from the first being, that is, the good ; therefore their particular being is good, but it is not like that from which it derives. For that is good in any conditions in virtue of its existence ; for it is nothing else than good. But if the former were not derived from that good, it could perhaps be good, but it could not be good in virtue of its existence. For in that case it might perhaps participate in the good ; but their particular being, which such things would not have from the good, they could not have as good. Therefore, the first good being removed from these things by a mental process, these things, though they might be good, yet could not be good in virtue of their existence, and since they could not actually have existed unless that which is truly good had produced them, therefore their existence is good and yet that which has derived from the substantial good is not like its source ; and unless they had derived from it, though they were good yet they could not be good in virtue of their existence, since they would be both apart from the good and not derived from it, while that very first good is existence itself and good itself and good existence itself. But will not those things which are white also have to be white in virtue of their being white, since they have derived from the will of God that they should be

ut essent alba? Minime. Aliud est enim esse, aliud
albis esse ; hoc ideo, quoniam qui ea ut essent effecit
155 bonus quidem est, minime vero albus. Voluntatem
igitur boni comitatum est ut essent bona in eo quod
sunt ; voluntatem vero non albi non est comitata
talis eius quod est proprietas ut esset album in eo
quod est ; neque enim ex albi voluntate defluxerunt.
160 Itaque quia voluit esse ea alba qui erat non albus,
sunt alba tantum ; quia vero voluit ea esse bona qui
erat bonus, sunt bona in eo quod sunt. Secundum
hanc igitur rationem cuncta oportet esse iusta,
quoniam ipse iustus est qui ea esse voluit ? Ne hoc
165 quidem. Nam bonum esse essentiam, iustum vero
esse actum respicit. Idem autem est in eo esse
quod agere ; idem igitur bonum esse quod iustum.
Nobis vero non est idem esse quod agere ; non enim
simplices sumus. Non est igitur nobis idem bonis
170 esse quod iustis, sed idem nobis est esse omnibus in
eo quod sumus. Bona igitur omnia sunt, non etiam
iusta. Amplius bonum quidem generale est, iustum
vero speciale nec species descendit in omnia. Idcirco
alia quidem iusta alia aliud omnia bona.

white ? By no means. For existence is one thing,
their being white is another ; and that because he who
produced them so that they existed is indeed good,
but certainly not white. It is therefore in accordance
with the will of the good that they should be good in
virtue of their existence ; but that which is a property
of a thing like whiteness is not in accordance with the
will of him who is not white, that it should be white
in virtue of its existence ; for such things have not
derived from the will of one who is white. And so
they are white simply because one who was not white
willed them to be white ; but because he willed them
to be good who was good, they are good in virtue of
their existence. Ought, then, according to this
reasoning, all things to be just, since he himself is
just who willed them to exist ? That is not so either.
For being good refers to essence, being just, to
action. But in him being and acting are the same ;
and therefore being good is the same as being just.
But for us being is not the same as acting ; for we are
not simple. Therefore being good is not the same
for us as being just, but being is the same for all of
us in virtue of our existence. Therefore all things are
good, but not also just. Moreover, good is a genus,
but just is a species, and this species does not apply
to all. Therefore some things are just, others are
something else, but all things are good.

# DE FIDE CATHOLICA

Christianam fidem novi ac veteris testamenti
pandit auctoritas ; et quamvis nomen ipsum Christi
vetus intra semet continuerit instrumentum eumque
semper signaverit affuturum quem credimus per par-
5 tum virginis iam venisse, tamen in orbem terrarum
ab ipsius nostri salvatoris mirabili manasse probatur
adventu.

Haec autem religio nostra, quae vocatur christiana
atque catholica, his fundamentis principaliter nititur
10 asserens : ex aeterno, id est ante mundi constitutionem, ante omne videlicet quod temporis potest
retinere vocabulum, divinam patris et filii ac spiritus
sancti exstitisse substantiam, ita ut deum dicat
patrem, deum filium, deum spiritum sanctum, nec
15 tamen tres deos sed unum : patrem itaque habere
filium ex sua substantia genitum et sibi nota ratione
coaeternum, quem filium eatenus confitetur, ut non
sit idem qui pater est : neque patrem aliquando
fuisse filium, ne rursus in infinitum humanus animus
20 divinam progeniem cogitaret, neque filium in eadem

---

*a* The conclusions adverse to the genuineness of this
tractate, reached in the dissertation *Der dem Boethius
zugeschriebene Traktat de Fide Catholica* (*Jahrbücher für kl.
Phil.* xxvi (1901), Supplementband) by one of the editors, now
seem to both unsound. This fourth tractate, though lacking,
in the best mss., either an ascription to Boethius or a title,
is firmly imbedded in two distinct recensions of Boethius's
theological works. There is no reason to disturb it. Indeed

# ON THE CATHOLIC FAITH[a]

THE Christian Faith is proclaimed by the authority of
the New Testament and of the Old ; but although the
Old scripture [b] contains within its pages the name of
Christ and constantly gives token that he will come
who we believe has already come by his birth of the
Virgin, yet the diffusion of that faith throughout the
world dates from the actual miraculous coming of our
Saviour.

Now this our religion which is called Christian and
Catholic is supported chiefly on these foundations
which it asserts : From eternity, that is, before the
establishment of the world, before all, that is, that
can be given the name of time, there has existed the
divine substance of Father, Son, and Holy Spirit in
such wise that our religion calls the Father God, the
Son God, and the Holy Spirit God, and yet not three
Gods but one. Thus the Father has the Son, begotten of his substance and coeternal with himself
after a manner that he alone knows. Him we confess to be Son in the sense that he is not the same as
the Father. Nor has the Father ever been Son, so
the human mind must not imagine a divine lineage

the *capita dogmatica* mentioned by Cassiodorus can hardly
refer to any of the tractates except the fourth.

   [b] For *instrumentum*=Holy Scripture *cf.* Tertull. *Apol.*
18, 19, *Adv. Hermog.* 19, etc. ; for *instrumentum*=any historical writing *cf.* Tert. *De Spect.* 5.

53

natura qua patri coaeternus est aliquando fieri
patrem, ne rursus in infinitum divina progenies
tenderetur : sanctum vero spiritum neque patrem
esse neque filium atque ideo in illa natura nec
25 genitum nec generantem sed a patre quoque pro-
cedentem vel filio ; qui sit tamen processionis istius
modus ita non possumus evidenter dicere, quemadmodum generationem filii ex paterna substantia non
potest humanus animus aestimare. Haec autem ut
30 credantur vetus ac nova informat instructio. De
qua velut arce religionis nostrae multi diversa et
humaniter atque ut ita dicam carnaliter sentientes
adversa locuti sunt, ut Arrius qui licet deum dicat
filium, minorem tamen patre multipliciter et extra
35 patris substantiam confitetur. Sabelliani quoque
non tres exsistentes personas sed unam ausi sunt
affirmare, eundem dicentes patrem esse qui filius est
eundemque filium qui pater est atque spiritum
sanctum eundem esse qui pater et filius est ; ac per
40 hoc unam dicunt esse personam sub vocabulorum
diversitate signatam.

　　Manichaei quoque qui duo principia sibi coaeterna
et adversa profitentur, unigenitum dei esse non
credunt. Indignum enim iudicant, si deus habere
45 filium videatur, nihil aliud cogitantes nisi carnaliter,
ut quia haec generatio duorum corporum commixtione procedit, illic quoque indignum esse intellectum
huiusmodi applicare ; quae res eos nec vetus facit

---

　　*a* Boethius is no heretic. By the sixth century *vel* had
often no separative force. Cp. " Noe cum sua vel trium
natorum coniugibus," Greg. Tur. *H.F.* i. 20. Other examples
in Bonnet, *La Latinité de Grég. de Tours*, p. 313, and in
Brandt's edition of the *Isag.* Index, s.v. *vel*.
　　*b* *Vide Cons.* i, pr. 3 (*infra*, p. 142), and *cf.* Dante, *De Mon.*
iii. 16. 117.

stretching back into infinity ; nor does the Son, being of the same nature in virtue of which he is coeternal with the Father, ever become Father, so that the divine lineage might not stretch again into infinity. But the Holy Spirit is neither Father nor Son, and therefore, albeit of the same nature, neither begotten, nor begetting, but proceeding as well from the Father as the Son.[a]   Yet what the manner of that procession is we are not able to state clearly just as the human mind is unable to understand the generation of the Son from the substance of the Father.   But these articles are laid down for our belief by the teaching of the Old and New Testaments.   Concerning which citadel,[b] as it were, of our religion many men have spoken in a hostile way, having different opinions based on human and, so to speak, carnal feelings. Arius, for instance, who, while calling the Son God, declares him to be in various ways inferior to the Father and of another substance.   The Sabellians also have dared to affirm that there are not three separate Persons but only one, saying that the Father is the same as the Son and the Son the same as the Father and the Holy Spirit the same as the Father and the Son ; and so they declare that there is but one Person signified under the diversity of names.

The Manichaeans, too, who profess two coeternal and contrary principles, do not believe in the only-begotten Son of God.   For they consider it unworthy of God that he should be thought to have a Son, their thinking being only on a carnal level, as that since human generation arises from the mingling of two bodies, in the case of God also it is unworthy to apply a notion of this sort ; whereas their view finds

BOETHIUS

recipere testamentum neque in integro novum.
50 Nam sicut illud omnino error eorum non recipit ita
ex virgine generationem filii non vult admittere, ne
humano corpore polluta videatur dei fuisse natura.
Sed de his hactenus ; suo enim loco ponentur sicut
ordo necessarius postularit.

55 Ergo divina ex aeterno natura et in aeternum
sine aliqua mutabilitate perdurans sibi tantum conscia
voluntate sponte mundum voluit fabricare eumque
cum omnino non esset fecit ut esset, nec ex sua
substantia protulit, ne divinus natura crederetur,
60 neque aliunde molitus est, ne iam exsititisse aliquid
quod eius voluntatem existentia propriae naturae
iuvaret atque esset quod neque ab ipso factum esset
et tamen esset ; sed verbo produxit caelos, terram
creavit, ita ut caelesti habitatione dignas caelo
65 naturas efficeret ac terrae terrena componeret. De
caelestibus autem naturis, quae universaliter vocatur
angelica, quamvis illic distinctis ordinibus pulchra
sint omnia, pars tamen quaedam plus appetens quam
ei natura atque ipsius auctor naturae tribuerat de
70 caelesti sede proiecta est ; et quoniam angelorum
numerum, id est supernae illius civitatis cuius cives
angeli sunt, imminutum noluit conditor permanere,
formavit ex terra hominem atque spiritu vitae ani-
mavit, ratione composuit, arbitrii libertate decoravit

---

[a] *In integro=prorsus* ;  *cf.* Brandt, *op. cit.* Index, s.v.
*integer.*
[b] The doctrine is orthodox, but note that Boethius does
not say *ex nihilo creavit.*
[c] *Vide infra, Cons.* iv, pr. 6, p. 360 l. 54.

no authority in the Old Testament and absolutely [a] none in the New. Yea, their error which altogether refuses this notion will also not admit the generation of the Son from a virgin, lest the nature of God seem to have been polluted by the human body. But enough of this for the present ; the points will be presented in the proper place as the proper arrangement demands.

The divine nature then, abiding from eternity and unto eternity without any change, by the exercise of a will known only to himself, determined of himself to fashion the world, and brought it into being when it was absolutely naught, nor did he produce it from his own substance, lest it should be thought divine by nature, nor did he set about it after any model, lest it should be thought that anything had already come into being which might help his will by the existence of an independent nature, and that there existed something that had not been made by him and yet existed ; but by his word he brought forth the heavens, and created the earth [b] that so he might make natures worthy of a heavenly place for the heavens, and also fit earthly things to earth. But although in heaven all things are beautiful and arranged in due order, yet one part of the heavenly creation which is universally termed angelic, [c] seeking more than their nature and the author of that nature had granted them, was cast forth from its heavenly seat ; and because the Creator did not wish the number of the angels, that is of that heavenly city whose citizens the angels are, to remain diminished, he formed man out of the earth and breathed into him the breath of life ; he endowed him with reason, he adorned him with freedom of choice and estab-

75 eumque praefixa lege paradisi deliciis constituit, ut,
si sine peccato manere vellet, tam ipsum quam eius
progeniem angelicis coetibus sociaret, ut quia superior
natura per superbiae malum ima petierat, inferior
substantia per humilitatis bonum ad superna con-
80 scenderet. Sed ille auctor invidiae non ferens
hominem illuc ascendere ubi ipse non meruit permanere, temptatione adhibita fecit etiam ipsum
eiusque comparem, quam de eius latere generandi
causa formator produxerat, inoboedientiae suppliciis
85 subiacere, ei quoque divinitatem affuturam pro-
mittens, quam sibi dum arroganter usurpat elisus
est. Haec autem revelante deo Moysi famulo suo
comperta sunt, cui etiam humani generis conditionem
atque originem voluit innotescere, sicut ab eo libri
90 prolati testantur. Omnis enim divina auctoritas his
modis constare videtur, ut aut historialis modus sit,
qui nihil aliud nisi res gestas enuntiet, aut allegoricus,
ut non illic possit historiae ordo consistere, aut certe
ex utrisque compositus, ut et secundum historiam et
95 secundum allegoriam manere videatur. Haec autem
pie intelligentibus et veraci corde tenentibus satis
abundeque relucent. Sed ad ordinem redeamus.

Primus itaque homo ante peccatum cum sua con-
iuge incola paradisi fuit. At ubi aurem praebuit
100 suasori et conditoris praeceptum neglexit attendere,
exul effectus, terram iussus excolere atque a paradisi
sinu seclusus in ignotis partibus sui generis posteri-
tatem transposuit atque poenam quam ipse primus
homo praevaricationis reus exceperat generando
105 transmisit in posteros. Hinc factum est ut et cor-

lished him in the joys of Paradise, establishing the law beforehand that if he would remain without sin he would add him and his offspring to the angelic hosts ; so that as the higher nature had fallen low through the evil of pride, the lower substance might ascend on high through the good of humility. But the father of envy, loath that man should climb to the place where he himself did not deserve to remain, put temptation before him and his consort, whom the Creator had brought forth out of his side for the continuance of the race, and laid them open to punishment for disobedience, promising man also the gift of Godhead, the arrogant attempt to seize which had caused his expulsion. All this was revealed by God to his servant Moses, whom he vouchsafed to teach the creation and origin of mankind, as the books written by him declare. For the divine authority seems always to be conveyed in these ways—the historical, which simply announces facts ; the allegorical, which is such that historical order cannot be preserved in it ; or else the two combined, such that it seems to be established both according to history and according to allegory. All this is abundantly clear to pious hearers and steadfast believers.

But let us return to the order of our discourse ; the first man, before sin came, dwelt with his consort in Paradise. But when he gave ear to the persuader and failed to keep the commandment of his Creator, he was banished, bidden to till the ground, and being shut out from the shelter of Paradise he carried abroad in unknown regions the children of his race ; in begetting whom he transmitted to those that came after, the punishment which he, the first man, had incurred by being guilty of his transgression. Hence

porum atque animarum corruptio et mortis proveniret
interitus primusque mortem in Abel filio suo meruit
experiri, ut quanta esset poena quam ipse exceperit
probaret in subole. Quod si ipse primus moreretur,
110 nesciret quodam modo ac, si dici fas est, nec sentiret
poenam suam, sed ideo expertus in altero est, ut
quid sibi iure deberetur contemptor agnosceret et
dum poenam mortis sustinet, ipsa exspectatione
fortius torqueretur. Hoc autem praevaricationis
115 malum, quod in posteros naturaliter primus homo
transfuderat, quidam Pelagius non admittens proprii
nominis haeresim dedicavit, quam catholica fides a
consortio sui mox reppulisse probatur. Ab ipso
itaque primo homine procedens humanum genus ac
120 multiplici numerositate succrescens erupit in lites,
commovit bella, occupavit terrenam miseriam quia[1]
felicitatem paradisi in primo patre perdiderat. Nec
tamen ex his defuerunt quos sibi conditor gratiae
sequestraret eiusque placitis inservirent ; quos licet
125 meritum naturae damnaret, futuri tamen sacramenti
et longe postmodum proferendi faciendo participes
perditam voluit reparare naturam. Impletus est
ergo mundus humano genere atque ingressus est
homo vias suas qui malitia propriae contumaciae
130 despexerat conditorem. Hinc volens deus per
iustum potius hominem reparare genus humanum
quam manere protervum, poenalem multitudinem
effusa diluvii inundatione excepto Noe iusto homine

[1] qui *or* quod *MSS.*

it came to pass that corruption both of their bodies and souls ensued, and the destruction which is death ; and he was the first to deserve to experience death in his own son Abel, in order that he might learn through his child the greatness of the punishment that he himself was to receive. For if he had died first he would in some sense not have known, and if one may so say not have felt, his punishment ; but he tasted it in another in order that he might perceive the due reward of his contempt, and doomed to death himself, might be the more powerfully tormented by the apprehension of it. But this evil of transgression which the first man had by natural propagation transmitted to posterity, was denied by one Pelagius who so set up the heresy which goes by his name and which the Catholic faith, as is known, at once banished from its bosom. So the human race that sprang from the first man and mightily increased and multiplied, broke into strife, stirred up wars, and became the heir of earthly misery, because it had lost the blessedness of Paradise in its first parent. Yet among them there were not lacking those whom the Author of Grace set apart for himself and who were obedient to his precepts ; and though the fault of their nature condemned them, yet God by making them partakers in the mystery to come, long afterwards to be revealed, vouchsafed to restore their fallen nature. So the world was filled by the human race and man who in the wickedness of his own arrogant disobedience had despised his Creator began to walk in his own ways. Hence God willing rather to restore mankind through one just man than that it should remain contumacious, suffered all the guilty multitude to perish by the wide waters of a flood, save only Noah, the just man, with his children

cum suis liberis atque his quae secum in arcam intro-
135 duxerat interire permisit. Cur autem per arcae
lignum voluerit iustos eripere, notum est divinarum
scripturarum mentibus eruditis. Et quasi prima
quaedam mundi aetas diluvio ultore transacta est.

Reparatur itaque humanum genus atque propriae
140 naturae vitium, quod praevaricationis primus auctor
infuderat, amplecti non destitit. Crevitque con-
tumacia quam dudum diluvii unda puniverat et qui
numerosam annorum seriem permissus fuerat vivere,
in brevitate annorum humana aetas addicta est.
145 Maluitque deus non iam diluvio punire genus
humanum, sed eodem permanente eligere víros per
quorum seriem aliqua generatio commearet, ex qua
nobis filium proprium vestitum humano corpore
mundi in fine concederet. Quorum primus est
150 Abraham, qui cum esset aetate confectus eiusque
uxor decrepita, in senectute sua repromissionis
largitione habere filium meruerunt. Hic vocatus
est Isaac atque ipse genuit Iacob. Idem quoque
duodecim patriarchas non reputante deo in eorum
155 numero quos more suo natura produxerat. Hic ergo
Iacob cum filiis ac domo sua transigendi causa
Aegyptum voluit habitare atque illic per annorum
seriem multitudo concrescens coeperunt suspicioni
esse[1] Aegyptiacis imperiis eosque Pharao magna
160 ponderum mole premi decreverat et gravibus oneri-
bus affligebat. Tandem deus Aegyptii regis domina-
tionem despiciens diviso mari rubro, quod numquam

---

[1] suspiciones *or* suspicione *or* suspicio *or* subici *the better* MSS.

[a] *e.g.* Ishmael also κατὰ σάρκα γεγέννηται, Gal. iv. 23.
[b] *Cf.* " populus dei mirabiliter crescens . . . quia . . . erant
suspecta . . . laboribus premebatur," Aug. *De Civ. Dei*, xviii. 7.
For other coincidences see Rand, *op. cit.* pp. 423 ff.

and all that he had brought with him into the ark. The reason why he wished to save the just by the wood of the ark is known to all minds learned in the Holy Scriptures. Thus what we may call the first age of the world was ended by the avenging flood.

Thus the human race is restored, and yet it does not cease to embrace the vice of its own nature with which the first author of transgression had infected it. And the arrogance increased which had once been punished by the waters of the flood, and man who had been suffered to live for a long series of years was reduced to the brief span of ordinary human life. Yet would not God again punish mankind by a flood, but rather, letting it continue, he chose from it men of whose line a generation should arise out of which he might in the last age of the world grant us his own Son, clothed in a human body. Of these men Abraham is the first, and although he was stricken in years and his wife very old, they had in their old age the reward of a son in fulfilment of a promise. This son was named Isaac and he begat Jacob, who in his turn begat the Twelve Patriarchs, God not reckoning in their number those whom nature in its ordinary course produced.[a] This Jacob, then, together with his sons and his household determined to dwell in Egypt for the purpose of trafficking ; and the multitude of them increasing there in the course of many years began to be a cause of suspicion to the Egyptian rulers, and Pharaoh ordered them to be oppressed by exceeding heavy tasks [b] and afflicted them with grievous burdens. At length God, minded to set at naught the tyranny of the king of Egypt, divided the Red Sea—a marvel such as nature had never known before—and led across his host under

63

antea natura ulla cognoverat, suum transduxit exer-
citum auctore Moyse et Aaron.  Postea igitur pro
165 eorum egressione altis Aegyptus plagis vastata est,
cum nollet dimittere populum.  Transmisso itaque
ut dictum est mari rubro venit per deserta eremi
ad montem qui vocatur Sinai, ibique universorum
conditor deus volens sacramenti futuri gratia populos
170 erudire per Moysen data lege constituit, quemadmodum et sacrificiorum ritus et populorum mores
instruerentur.  Et cum multis annis multas quoque
gentes per viam debellassent, venerunt tandem ad
fluvium qui vocatur Iordanis duce iam Iesu Nave
175 filio atque ad eorum transitum quemadmodum aquae
maris rubri ita quoque Iordanis fluenta siccata sunt ;
perventumque est ad eam civitatem quae nunc
Hierosolyma vocatur.  Atque dum ibi dei populus
moraretur, post iudices et prophetas reges instituti
180 leguntur, quorum post Saulem primatum David de
tribu Iuda legitur adeptus fuisse.  Descendit itaque
ab eo per singulas successiones regium stemma
perductumque est usque ad Herodis tempora, qui
primus ex gentilibus memoratis populis legitur
185 imperasse.  Sub quo exstitit beata virgo Maria quae
de Davidica stirpe provenerat, quae humani generis
genuit conditorem.  Hoc autem ideo quia multis
infectus criminibus mundus iacebat in morte, electa
est una gens in qua dei mandata clarescerent, ibique
190 missi prophetae sunt et alii sancti viri per quorum
admonitionem ipse certe populus a tumore pervicaciae
revocaretur.  Illi vero eosdem occidentes in suae
nequitiae perversitate manere voluerunt.

the authority of Moses and Aaron. Thereafter to achieve their departure Egypt was laid waste with sore plagues, because they would not let the people go. So, after crossing the Red Sea, as I have told, they came through the desert of the wilderness to the mount which is called Sinai, where God the Creator of all, wishing to prepare the nations for the sake of the mystery to come, laid down by a law given through Moses how both the rites of sacrifices and the national customs should be ordered. And after fighting down many tribes in many years amidst their journeyings they came at last to the river called Jordan, with Joshua the son of Nun now as their captain, and, for their crossing, the streams of Jordan were dried up as the waters of the Red Sea had been ; so they finished their course to that city which is now called Jerusalem. And while the people of God abode there we read that there were set up first judges and prophets and then kings, of whom we read that after Saul the first king, David of the tribe of Judah ascended the throne. So from him the royal race descended from father to son and lasted till the days of Herod who, we read, was the first taken out of the peoples called Gentile to bear sway. In whose days rose up the blessed Virgin Mary, sprung from the stock of David, she who bore the Maker of the human race. But it was just because the world lay in death, stained with its many sins, that one race was chosen in which the commands of God might shine clear ; to it prophets and other holy men were sent, to the end that by their warnings that people at least might be called back from their swollen obstinacy. But they slew these holy men and chose rather to abide in the perversity of their own wickedness.

Atque iam in ultimis temporibus non prophetas
195 neque alios sibi placitos sed ipsum unigenitum suum
deus per virginem nasci constituit, ut humana salus
quae per primi hominis inoboedientiam deperierat
per hominem deum rursus repararetur et quia
exstiterat mulier quae causam mortis prima viro
200 suaserat, esset haec secunda mulier quae vitae
causam humanis visceribus apportaret. Nec vile
videatur quod dei filius ex virgine natus est, quoniam
praeter naturae modum conceptus et editus est.
Virgo itaque de spiritu sancto incarnatum dei filium
205 concepit, virgo peperit, post eius editionem virgo
permansit ; atque hominis factus est idemque dei
filius, ita ut in eo et divinae naturae radiaret splendor
et humanae fragilitatis appareret assumptio. Sed
huic tam sanae atque veracissimae fidei exstiterant
210 multi qui diversa garrirent et praeter alios Nestorius
et Eutyches repertores haereseos exstiterunt, quorum
unus hominem solum, alter deum solum putavit
asserere nec humanum corpus quod Christus induerat
de humanae substantiae participatione venisse. Sed
215 haec hactenus.

Crevit itaque secundum carnem Christus, baptizatus
est, ut qui baptizandi formam erat ceteris tributurus,
ipse primus quod docebat exciperet. Post baptismum
vero elegit duodecim discipulos, quorum unus traditor
220 eius fuit. Et quia sanam doctrinam Iudaeorum
populus non ferebat, eum inlata manu crucis sup-
66

And now at the last days of time, in place of prophets and other men well-pleasing to him, God decreed that his only-begotten Son himself should be born of a virgin that so the salvation of mankind which had been lost through the disobedience of the first man might be restored again by the God-man, and that inasmuch as it was a woman who had first persuaded a man to that which brought death there should be this second woman who should carry in a human womb him who brings life. Nor let it be deemed a thing unworthy that the Son of God was born of a virgin, for it was out of the course of nature that he was conceived and brought to birth. Virgin then she conceived, by the Holy Spirit, the incarnate Son of God, virgin she bore him, virgin she continued after his birth ; and he became the Son of Man and likewise the Son of God that in him the glory of the divine nature might shine forth and at the same time his assumption of human weakness be made clear. Yet against this article of faith so wholesome and altogether true there rose up many who babbled other doctrine, and especially Nestorius and Eutyches, inventors of heresy, arose, of whom the one thought fit to say that he was man alone, the other that he was God alone and that the human body which Christ put on had not come by participation in human substance. But enough on this point.

So Christ grew after the flesh, and was baptized in order that he who was to give the form of baptism to others should first himself receive what he taught. But after his baptism he chose twelve disciples, one of whom was his betrayer. And because the people of the Jews would not bear sound doctrine they laid hands upon him and destroyed him with the torment

plicio peremerunt. Occiditur ergo Christus, iacet
tribus diebus ac noctibus in sepulcro, resurgit a
mortuis, sicut ante constitutionem mundi ipse cum
225 patre decreverat, ascendit in caelos ubi, in eo quod
dei filius est, numquam defuisse cognoscitur, ut
assumptum hominem, quem diabolus non permiserat
ad superna conscendere, secum dei filius caelesti
habitationi sustolleret. Dat ergo formam discipulis
230 suis baptizandi, docendi salutaria, efficientiam quoque
miraculorum atque in universum mundum ad vitam
praecipit introire, ut praedicatio salutaris non iam in
una tantum gente sed orbi terrarum praedicaretur.
Et quoniam humanum genus naturae merito, quam
235 ex primo praevaricatore contraxerat, aeternae poenae
iaculis fuerat vulneratum nec salutis suae erat
idoneum, quod eam in parente perdiderat, medici-
nalia quaedam tribuit sacramenta, ut agnosceret
aliud sibi deberi per naturae meritum, aliud per
240 gratiae donum, ut natura nihil aliud nisi poenae
summitteret, gratia vero, quae nullis meritis attributa
est, quia nec gratia diceretur si meritis tribueretur,
totum quod est salutis afferret.

Diffunditur ergo per mundum caelestis illa
245 doctrina, adunantur populi, instituuntur ecclesiae,
fit unum corpus quod mundi latitudinem occuparet,
cuius caput Christus ascendit in caelos, ut necessario
caput suum membra sequerentur. Haec itaque
doctrina et praesentem vitam bonis informat operibus
68

of the cross. Christ, then, is slain ; he lies three days and three nights in the tomb ; he rises again from the dead as he had predetermined with his Father before the foundation of the world ; he ascends into heaven whence we know that he was never absent, because he is Son of God, in order that as Son of God he might raise together with him to the heavenly habitation man whose flesh he had assumed, whom the devil had hindered from ascending to the places on high. Therefore he bestowed on his disciples the form of baptizing, and of teaching saving truth, and the power to work miracles, and bade them go throughout the whole world to give it life, in order that the message of salvation might be preached no longer in one nation only but to the whole world. And because the human race was wounded by the darts of eternal punishment by the fault of the nature which it had inherited from the first transgressor and was not fitted for its salvation because it had lost it in its first parent, he instituted certain health-giving sacraments that mankind might recognize that one thing was due to it through the fault of nature, but another thing through the gift of grace, nature simply subjecting to punishment, but grace, which is not won by any merits, since it would not be called grace if it were due to merits, conferring all that belongs to salvation.

Therefore is that heavenly instruction spread throughout the world, the peoples are knit together, churches are founded, and, filling the broad earth, one body formed, whose head, even Christ, ascended into heaven in order that the members might of necessity follow their head. Thus this teaching both instructs this present life in good works, and pro-

250 et post consummationem saeculi resurrectura corpora
nostra praeter corruptionem ad regna caelestia
pollicetur, ita ut qui hic bene ipso donante vixerit,
esset in illa resurrectione beatissimus, qui vero male,
miser post munus resurrectionis adesset. Et hoc est
255 principale religionis nostrae, ut credat non solum
animas non perire, sed ipsa quoque corpora, quae
mortis adventus resolverat, in statum pristinum
futura de beatitudine reparari. Haec ergo ecclesia
catholica per orbem diffusa tribus modis probatur
260 exsistere : quidquid in ea tenetur, aut auctoritas est
scripturarum aut traditio universalis aut certe propria et particularis instructio. Sed auctoritate tota
constringitur, universali traditione maiorum nihilo-
minus tota, privatis vero constitutionibus et propriis
265 informationibus unaquaeque vel pro locorum varietate
vel prout cuique bene visum est subsistit et regitur.
Sola ergo nunc est fidelium exspectatio qua credimus
affuturum finem mundi, omnia corruptibilia trans-
itura, resurrecturos homines ad examen futuri iudicii,
270 recepturos pro meritis singulos et in perpetuum atque
in aeternum debitis finibus permansuros ; solumque
esse praemium beatitudinis contemplationem conditoris—tanta dumtaxat, quanta a creatura ad crea-
torem fieri potest,—ut ex eis reparato angelico
numero superna illa civitas impleatur, ubi rex est
275 virginis filius eritque gaudium sempiternum, delec-
tatio, cibus, opus, laus perpetua creatoris.

70

mises that after the end of the world our bodies shall rise incorruptible to the kingdom of heaven, to the end that he who has lived well on earth by God's gift should be altogether blessed in that resurrection, but he who has lived amiss should, with the gift of resurrection, enter upon misery. And this is a firm principle of our religion, to believe not only that men's souls do not perish, but that their very bodies, which the coming of death had destroyed, are restored to their first state through the blessedness that is to be. This Catholic church, then, spread throughout the world, is known to exist by three marks : whatever is believed in it has the authority of the Scriptures, or of universal tradition, or at least of its own and proper teaching. And the whole church is bound by that authority, as is the whole church no less by the universal tradition of the Fathers, while each separate church exists and is governed by its private constitution and its proper rites according to difference of locality and the approval of each. There is therefore now but one expectation of the faithful by which we believe that the end of the word will come, that all corruptible things shall pass away, that men shall rise for the test of the judgement to come, that each shall receive reward according to his deserts and abide in the lot assigned to him perpetually and eternally ; and that the sole reward of blessedness is the contemplation of the Creator, so far, that is, as the creature may look on the Creator, to the end that the number of the angels may be restored from these and that heavenly city filled where the Virgin's Son is King and where will be everlasting joy, delight, food, labour, and unending praise of the Creator.

# ANICII MANLII SEVERINI BOETHII

v.c. et inl. excons. ord. patricii

## INCIPIT LIBER

# CONTRA EUTYCHEN ET NESTORIUM

domino sancto ac venerabili patri IOHANNI
DIACONO BOETHIUS filius

Anxie te quidem diuque sustinui, ut de ea quae
in conventu mota est quaestione loqueremur. Sed
quoniam et tu quominus venires occupatione distractus es et ego in crastinum constitutis negotiis
5 implicabor, mando litteris quae coram loquenda
servaveram. Meministi enim, cum in concilio
legeretur epistola, recitatum Eutychianos ex duabus
naturis Christum consistere confiteri, in duabus
negare : catholicos vero utrique dicto fidem prae-
10 bere, nam et ex duabus eum naturis consistere
et in duabus apud verae fidei sectatores aequaliter
credi. Cuius dicti novitate percussus harum coniunc-

---

<sup>a</sup> Evidently the letter addressed to Pope Symmachus
by the Oriental bishops (*vide* Mansi, *Concil.* viii. 221 ff.), in
which they inquire concerning the safe middle way between
the heresies of Eutyches and Nestorius. The date of the

72

# A TREATISE AGAINST
# EUTYCHES AND NESTORIUS

BY

## ANICIUS MANLIUS SEVERINUS
## BOETHIUS

MOST HONOURABLE, OF THE ILLUSTRIOUS ORDER OF
EX-CONSULS, PATRICIAN

TO HIS SAINTLY MASTER AND REVEREND FATHER
## JOHN THE DEACON HIS SON BOETHIUS

I HAVE been long and anxiously waiting for you that
we might discuss the problem which was raised at the
meeting. But since *your* duties have prevented your
coming and *I* shall be for some time involved in my
business engagements, I am setting down in writing
what I had been keeping to say by word of mouth.

Now you remember how, when the letter *a* was
read in the assembly, it was read out that the
Eutychians confess that Christ is formed from two
natures but does not consist of them, but that
Catholics give credence to both propositions, for
among followers of the true Faith he is equally believed to be of two natures and in two natures. Struck

bishops' letter, and consequently, in all probability, of
Boethius's tractate was 512.

tionum quae ex duabus naturis vel in duabus consis-
terent differentias inquirebam, multum scilicet referre
15 ratus nec inerti neglegentia praetereundum, quod
episcopus scriptor epistolae tamquam valde necessarium praeterire noluisset. Hic omnes apertam
esse differentiam nec quicquam in eo esse caliginis
inconditum confusumque strepere nec ullus in tanto
20 tumultu qui leviter attingeret quaestionem, nedum
qui expediret inventus est.

Adsederam ego ab eo quem maxime intueri cupie-
bam longius atque adeo, si situm sedentium recorderis,
aversus pluribusque oppositis, ne si aegerrime quidem
25 cuperem, vultum nutumque eius aspicere poteram ex
quo mihi aliqua eius darentur signa iudicii. Atqui
ego quidem nihil ceteris amplius afferebam, immo
vero aliquid etiam minus. Nam de re proposita aeque
nihil ceteris sentiebam ; minus vero quam ceteri ipse
30 afferebam, falsae scilicet scientiae praesumptionem.
Tuli aegerrime, fateor, compressusque indoctorum
grege conticui metuens ne iure viderer insanus, si
sanus inter furiosos haberi contenderem. Meditabar
igitur dehinc omnes animo quaestiones nec deglutie-
35 bam quod acceperam, sed frequentis consilii iteratione
ruminabam. Tandem igitur patuere pulsanti animo
fores ęt veritas inventa quaerenti omnes nebulas
Eutychiani reclusit erroris. Unde mihi maxime
subiit admirari, quaenam haec indoctorum hominum

---

    *a* Obviously his father-in-law Symmachus. *Vide* p. 76,
*eius cuius soleo iudicio*, etc.
    *b* *Cf.* Hor. *Serm.* i. 3. 82 ; ii. 3. 40.

by the novelty of this assertion I began to inquire
into the differences between unions formed from two
natures and unions which consist in two natures, for
the point which the bishop who wrote the letter
refused to pass over because of its gravity, seemed to
me of importance and not one to be idly and carelessly
slurred over. On that occasion all loudly protested
that the difference was evident, that there was in this
matter no obscurity, confusion or perplexity, and in
the general storm and tumult there was found no one
who really touched the edge of the problem, much
less anyone who solved it.

I was sitting a long way from the man whom I
especially wished to watch,[a] and if you recall the
arrangement of the seats, I was turned away from
him, with so many between us, that however much I
desired it I could not see his face and expression and
glean therefrom any sign of his opinion. Personally,
indeed, I had nothing more to contribute than the
rest, in fact rather somewhat less. For, about the
question at issue my feelings in no way coincided with
the others'; but my own contribution was less than
theirs in that it did not imply a false assumption of
knowledge. I was, I admit, much put out, and being
overwhelmed by the mob of ignorant speakers, I held
my peace, fearing lest I should be rightly set down as
insane if I held out for being sane among those mad-
men.[b] So I continued to ponder all the questions in
my mind, not swallowing what I had heard, but rather
chewing the cud of constant meditation. At last the
door opened to my mind's knocking, and the truth
which I found in my inquiry disclosed all the fogs of
the Eutychian error. And with this discovery a great
wonder came upon me at the vast temerity of

40 esset audacia qui inscientiae vitium praesumptionis
atque inpudentiae nube conentur obducere, cum non
modo saepe id quod proponatur ignorent, verum in
huiusmodi contentionibus ne id quidem quod ipsi
loquantur intellegant, quasi non deterior fiat in-
45 scientiae causa, dum tegitur.

Sed ab illis ad te transeo, cui hoc quantulumcumque
est examinandum prius perpendendumque transmitto.
Quod si recte se habere pronuntiaveris, peto ut mei
nominis hoc quoque inseras chartis ; sin vero vel
50 minuendum aliquid vel addendum vel aliqua mutatione variandum est, id quoque postulo remitti, meis
exemplaribus ita ut a te revertitur transcribendum.
Quae ubi ad calcem ducta constiterint, tum demum
eius cuius soleo iudicio censenda transmittam. Sed
55 quoniam semel res a conlocutione transfertur ad stilum,
prius extremi sibique contrarii Nestorii atque Eutychis
summoveantur errores ; post vero adiuvante deo,
Christianae medietatem fidei temperabo. Quoniam
vero in tota quaestione contrariarum sibimet αἱρέσεων
60 de personis dubitatur atque naturis, haec primitus
definienda sunt et propriis differentiis segreganda.

I

Natura igitur aut de solis corporibus dici potest
aut de solis substantiis, id est corporeis atque incorporeis, aut de omnibus rebus quae quocumque modo
esse dicuntur. Cum igitur tribus modis natura dici

---

*a Cf. infra, de Cons.* i, pr. 4 (p. 144) : *oportet vulnus de-*
*tegas.*

76

unlearned men who seek with a cloud of impudent presumption to cover up the vice of ignorance, for not only do they often fail to grasp the point at issue, but in debates of this kind they do not even understand their own statements, as if the cause of ignorance is not made worse when it is covered up.[a]

I turn from them to you, and to you I submit this little essay for your first consideration and judgement. If you pronounce it to be sound I beg you to place it among the other writings of mine ; but if there is anything to be struck out or added or changed in any way, I would ask you to let me have your suggestions, in order that I may enter them in my copies just as they come back from you. When this revision has been duly accomplished, then I will send the work on to be judged by the man to whom I always submit everything.[b] But since the pen is now to take the place of the living voice, let there first be cleared away the extreme and self-contradictory errors of Nestorius and Eutyches ; after that, by God's help, I will set out in order the middle way of the Christian Faith. But since in this whole question of self-contradictory heresies the matter of debate is persons and natures, these terms must first be defined and distinguished by their proper differences.

## I

Nature, then, may be predicated either of bodies alone or of substances alone, that is, of corporeals and incorporeals, or of all things which are said to exist in any way at all. Since, then, nature can be predicated in three ways, it must obviously be defined in

[b] *Vide supra*, p. 75, and *De Trin.* p. 3.

5 possit, tribus modis sine dubio definienda est. Nam
si de omnibus rebus naturam dici placet, talis definitio
dabitur quae res omnes quae sunt possit includere.
Erit ergo huiusmodi : " natura est earum rerum
quae, cum sint, quoquo modo intellectu capi pos-
10 sunt." In hac igitur definitione et accidentia et
substantiae definiuntur ; haec enim omnia intellectu
capi possunt. Additum vero est " quoquo modo,"
quoniam deus et materia integro perfectoque intellectu intelligi non possunt, sed aliquo tamen
15 modo ceterarum rerum privatione capiuntur. Idcirco
vero adiunximus " quae cum sint," quoniam etiam
ipsum nihil significat aliquid sed non naturam.
Neque enim quod sit aliquid sed potius non esse
significat ; omnis vero natura est. Et si de omnibus
20 quidem rebus naturam dici placet, haec sit naturae
definitio quam superius proposuimus. Sin vero de
solis substantiis natura dicitur, quoniam substantiae
omnes aut corporeae sunt aut incorporeae, dabimus,
definitionem naturae substantias significanti huius-
25 modi : " natura est vel quod facere vel quod pati
possit." " Pati " quidem ac " facere, " ut omnia
corporea atque corporeorum anima ; haec enim in
corpore et a corpore et facit et patitur. " Facere "
vero tantum ut deus ceteraque divina. Habes igitur
30 definitionem eius quoque significationis naturae quae
tantum substantiis applicatur. Qua in re substantiae
quoque est reddita definitio. Nam si nomen naturae
substantiam monstrat, cum naturam descripsimus
78

three ways. For if you choose to predicate nature of
all things, a definition will be given of such a kind as
to be able to include all things that are. It will
accordingly be something of this kind : " Nature
belongs to those things which, since they exist, can
in some way be apprehended by the intellect." This
definition, then, includes the definition of both accidents and substances, for they all can be apprehended
by the intellect. But I add " in some way " because
God and matter cannot be apprehended by the intellect, be it never so whole and perfect, but still they
are apprehended in some way through the removal
of other things. The reason we add the words, " since
they exist," is that even the word " nothing " itself
signifies something, though not nature. For it signifies, indeed, not that something is, but rather
non-existence ; but every nature exists. And if we
choose to predicate nature of all things, the definition
will be as we have given it above.

But if nature is predicated of substances alone,
we shall, since all substances are either corporeal or
incorporeal, give to nature signifying substances a definition of the following kind : " Nature is either that
which can act or that which can be acted upon."
On the one hand, be acted upon and act, as all
corporeals and the soul of corporeals ; for the soul
acts and is acted upon in the body and by means of
the body. On the other hand, only act, as God and
other divine substances.

Here, then, you have the definition of that signification of nature which is only applied to substances.
This definition comprises also the definition of substance. For if the word nature indicates substance,
when we have described nature we have also given a

79

substantiae quoque est assignata descriptio. Quod si
35 naturae nomen relictis incorporeis substantiis ad corporales usque contrahitur, ut corporeae tantum substantiae naturam habere videantur, sicut Aristoteles
ceterique et eiusmodi et multimodae philosophiae
sectatores putant, definiemus eam, ut hi etiam qui
40 naturam non nisi in corporibus esse posuerunt. Est
autem eius definitio hoc modo : " natura est motus
principium per se non per accidens." Quod " motus
principium " dixi hoc est, quoniam corpus omne habet
proprium motum, ut ignis sursum, terra deorsum.
45 Item quod " per se principium motus " naturam esse
proposui et non " per accidens," tale est, quoniam
lectum quoque ligneum deorsum ferri necesse est, sed
non deorsum per accidens fertur. Idcirco enim quia
lignum est, quod est terra, pondere et gravitate
50 deducitur. Non enim quia lectus est, deorsum cadit,
sed quia terra est, id est quia terrae contigit, ut
lectus esset ; unde fit ut lignum naturaliter esse
dicamus, lectum vero artificialiter. Est etiam alia
significatio naturae per quam dicimus diversam esse
55 naturam auri atque argenti in hoc proprietatem
rerum monstrare cupientes, quae significatio naturae
definietur hoc modo : " natura est unam quamque
rem informans specifica differentia." Cum igitur tot
modis vel dicatur vel definiatur natura, tam catholici
60 quam Nestorius secundum ultimam definitionem
duas in Christo naturas esse constituent ; neque
enim easdem in deum atque hominem differentias
convenire.

description of substance. But if we neglect incorporeal substances and confine the name nature to corporeal substances so that they alone appear to possess the nature of substance—which is the view of Aristotle and the adherents both of his and various other schools—we shall define nature as those do who have posited nature as not existing except in bodies. Now, its definition is as follows : " Nature is the principle of movement, *per se* and not accidental." I said " principle of movement " because every body has its proper movement, as fire upwards, earth downwards. Again, that I propose that nature is " the principle of movement *per se* and not accidental " is so expressed because a wooden bed is necessarily borne downward and is not carried downward by accident. For it is drawn downward by weight and heaviness because it is of wood, *i.e.* an earthly material. For it falls downwards not because it is a bed, but because it is earth, that is, because it has happened of earth that it should be a bed ; hence we call it wood in virtue of its nature, but bed in virtue of the art that shaped it.

Nature has, further, another signification according to which we speak of the different nature of gold and silver, wishing thereby to indicate the special property of things ; this signification of nature will be defined as follows : " Nature is the specific difference that gives form to anything." Thus, although nature is predicated or defined in so many ways, both Catholics and Nestorius hold that there are in Christ two natures according to our last definition, but the same differences cannot apply to God and man.

# BOETHIUS

## II

Sed de persona maxime dubitari potest, quaenam
ei definitio possit aptari. Si enim omnis habet natura
personam, indissolubilis nodus est, quaenam inter
naturam personamque possit esse discretio ; aut si
5 non aequatur persona naturae, sed infra terminum
spatiumque naturae persona subsistit, difficile dictu
est ad quas usque naturas persona perveniat, id est
quas naturas conveniat habere personam, quas a
personae vocabulo segregari. Nam illud quidem
10 manifestum est personae subiectam esse naturam nec
praeter naturam personam posse praedicari. Vestiganda sunt igitur haec inquirentibus hoc modo.

Quoniam praeter naturam non potest esse persona
quoniamque naturae aliae sunt substantiae, aliae
15 accidentes et videmus personam in accidentibus non
posse constitui (quis enim dicat ullam albedinis vel ni-
gredinis vel magnitudinis esse personam ?), relinquitur
ergo ut personam in substantiis dici conveniat. Sed
substantiarum aliae sunt corporeae, aliae incorporeae.
20 Corporearum vero aliae sunt viventes, aliae minime ;
viventium aliae sunt sensibiles, aliae minime ; sen-
sibilium aliae rationales, aliae inrationales. Item in-
corporearum aliae sunt rationales, aliae minime, ut
pecudum vitae ; rationalium vero alia est inmutabilis
25 atque inpassibilis per naturam ut deus, alia per
creationem mutabilis atque passibilis, nisi inpassibilis
gratia substantiae ad inpassibilitatis firmitudinem
permutetur ut angelorum atque animae. Ex quibus

---

<sup>a</sup> For a similar example of the method of *divisio cf.* Cic.
*De Off.* ii. 3. 11. *Cf.* also *Isag. Porph. edit. prima*, i. 10
(ed. Brandt, p. 29).

## II

But the proper definition of person is a matter of very great perplexity. For if every nature has person, the difference between nature and person is a hard knot to unravel ; or if person is not taken as the equivalent of nature but is a term of less scope and range, it is difficult to say to what natures it may be extended, that is, to what natures the term person may be applied and what natures are dissociate from it. For one thing is clear, namely that nature is a substrate of person, and that person cannot be predicated apart from nature.

We must, therefore, conduct our inquiry into these points as follows.

Since person cannot exist apart from nature and since natures are either substances or accidents and we see that person cannot consist in accidents (for who can say there is any person of whiteness or blackness or size ?), it therefore remains that person is properly predicated of substances. But of substances, some are corporeal and others incorporeal. And of corporeals, some are living and others not ; of living substances, some are sensitive and others not ; of sensitive substances, some are rational and others irrational.[a] Similarly of incorporeal substances, some are rational, others not (for instance the animating spirits of beasts) ; but of rational substances one is immutable and impassible by nature, as God, another which in virtue of its creation is mutable and passible unless by the grace of the impassible substance it be transformed to the unshaken impassibility which belongs to angels and to the soul.

omnibus neque in non viventibus corporibus personam
30 posse dici manifestum est (nullus enim lapidis ullam
dicit esse personam), neque rursus eorum viventium
quae sensu carent (neque enim ulla persona est
arboris), nec vero eius quae intellectu ac ratione
deseritur (nulla est enim persona equi vel bovis
35 ceterorumque animalium quae muta ac sine ratione
vitam solis sensibus degunt), at hominis dicimus esse
personam, dicimus dei, dicimus angeli. Rursus substantiarum aliae sunt universales, aliae particulares.
Universales sunt quae de singulis praedicantur ut
40 homo, animal, lapis, lignum ceteraque huiusmodi
quae vel genera vel species sunt ; nam et homo de
singulis hominibus et animal de singulis animalibus
lapisque ac lignum de singulis lapidibus ac lignis
dicuntur. Particularia vero sunt quae de aliis minime
45 praedicantur ut Cicero, Plato, lapis hic unde haec
Achillis statua facta est, lignum hoc unde haec mensa
composita est. Sed in his omnibus nusquam in
universalibus persona dici potest, sed in singularibus
tantum atque in individuis ; animalis enim vel gene-
50 ralis hominis nulla persona est, sed vel Ciceronis
vel Platonis vel singulorum individuorum personae
singulae nuncupantur.

### III

Quocirca si persona in solis substantiis est atque
in his rationabilibus substantiaque omnis natura est
nec in universalibus sed in individuis constat,
reperta personae est definitio : " naturae rationabilis
5 individua substantia." Sed nos hac definitione
eam quam Graeci ὑπόστασιν dicunt terminavimus.

---

[a] Boethius's definition of *persona* was adopted by St.

Now from all this it is clear that person cannot be predicated of bodies which have no life (for no one ever says that a stone has a person), nor yet of living things which lack sense (for neither is there any person of a tree), nor finally of that which is bereft of mind and reason (for there is no person of a horse or ox or any other of the animals which dumb and without reason live a life of sense alone), but we say there is a person of a man, of God, of an angel. Again, some substances are universal, others are particular. Universals are those which are predicated of individuals, as man, animal, stone, plank and other things of this kind which are either genera or species ; for man is predicated of individual men just as animal is of individual animals, and stone and plank of individual stones and planks. But particulars are those which are never predicated of other things, as Cicero, Plato, this stone from which this statue of Achilles was hewn, this plank out of which this table was made. But in all these things person cannot anywhere be predicated of universals, but only of particulars and individuals ; for there is no person of man as animal or a genus ; only of Cicero, Plato, or other single individuals are single persons named.

### III

Wherefore if person belongs to substances alone, and these rational, and if every substance is a nature, and exists not in universals but in individuals, we have found the definition of person : " The individual substance of a rational nature." [a] Now by this definition we Latins have described what the Greeks call Thomas (*S. Th.* I[a] II[ae] 29. 1), and was regarded as classical by the Schoolmen.

85

# BOETHIUS

Nomen enim personae videtur aliunde traductum, ex his scilicet personis quae in comoediis tragoediisque eos quorum interest homines repraesentabant. Per-
10 sona vero dicta est a personando, circumflexa paenultima. Quod si acuatur antepaenultima, apertissime a sono dicta videbitur ; idcirco autem a sono, quia concavitate ipsa maior necesse est volvatur sonus. Graeci quoque has personas πρόσωπα vocant ab eo
15 quod ponantur in facie atque ante oculos obtegant vultum : παρὰ τοῦ πρὸς τοὺς ὦπας τίθεσθαι. Sed quoniam personis inductis histriones individuos homines quorum intererat in tragoedia vel in comoedia ut dictum est repraesentabant, id est Hecubam vel
20 Medeam vel Simonem vel Chremetem, idcirco ceteros quoque homines, quorum certa pro sui forma esset agnitio, et Latini personam et Graeci πρόσωπα nuncupaverunt. Longe vero illi signatius naturae rationabilis individuam subsistentiam ὑποστάσεως no-
25 mine vocaverunt, nos vero per inopiam significantium vocum translaticiam retinuimus nuncupationem, eam quam illi ὑπόστασιν dicunt personam vocantes ; sed peritior Graecia sermonum ὑπόστασιν vocat individuam subsistentiam. Atque, uti Graeca utar oratione in
30 rebus quae a Graecis agitata Latina interpretatione translata sunt : αἱ οὐσίαι ἐν μὲν τοῖς καθόλου εἶναι δύνανται· ἐν δὲ τοῖς ἀτόμοις καὶ κατὰ μέρος μόνοις ὑφίστανται, id est : essentiae in universalibus quidem esse possunt, in solis vero individuis et particularibus
35 substant. Intellectus enim universalium rerum ex

---

ᵃ Implying a short penultimate.

ὑπόστασις. For the word " person " seems to be
borrowed from a different source, namely from the
masks (*personae*) which in comedies and tragedies
used to represent the people concerned. Now *persona*
with a circumflex on the penultimate is derived from
*personare*. But if the accent is put on the ante-
penultimate [a] the word will clearly be seen to come
from *sonus* " sound," and it is from *sonus* for this
reason, that the sound that is produced is necessarily
greater from the very hollowness of the mask. The
Greeks, too, call these masks πρόσωπα from the fact
that they are placed over the face and conceal the
countenance in front of the eyes : παρὰ τοῦ πρὸς τοὺς
ὦπας τίθεσθαι (from being put up against the face).
But since, as we have said, it was by the masks they
put on that actors represented the individual
people concerned in a tragedy or comedy—Hecuba
or Medea or Simo or Chremes,— so also of all other
men who could be clearly recognized by their appearance the Latins used the name *persona*, the Greeks
πρόσωπα. But the Greeks far more clearly called
the individual subsistence of a rational nature by the
name ὑπόστασις, while we through want of appropriate words have kept the name handed down to us,
calling that *persona* which they call ὑπόστασις ; but
Greece with its richer vocabulary gives the name
ὑπόστασις to the individual subsistence. And, if I
may use Greek in dealing with matters which were
dealt with by Greeks before they came to be interpreted in Latin : αἱ οὐσίαι ἐν μὲν τοῖς καθόλου εἶναι
δύνανται· ἐν δὲ τοῖς ἀτόμοις καὶ κατὰ μέρος μόνοις
ὑφίστανται, that is : essences can indeed exist in
universals, but they subsist in individuals and particulars alone. For the understanding of universals is

87

particularibus sumptus est. Quocirca cum ipsae subsistentiae in universalibus quidem sint, in particularibus vero capiant substantiam, iure subsistentias parti-
culariter substantes ὑποστάσεις appellaverunt. Neque
40 enim pensius subtiliusque intuenti idem videbitur
esse subsistentia quod substantia.

Nam quod Graeci οὐσίωσιν vel οὐσιῶσθαι dicunt, id
nos subsistentiam vel subsistere appellamus ; quod
vero illi ὑπόστασιν vel ὑφίστασθαι, id nos substantiam
45 vel substare interpretamur. Subsistit enim quod ipsum
accidentibus, ut possit esse, non indiget. Substat
autem id quod aliis accidentibus subiectum quoddam,
ut esse valeant, subministrat ; sub illis enim stat, dum
subiectum est accidentibus. Itaque genera vel species
50 subsistunt tantum ; neque enim accidentia generibus
speciebusve contingunt. Individua vero non modo
subsistunt verum etiam substant, nam neque ipsa
indigent accidentibus ut sint ; informata enim sunt
iam propriis et specificis differentiis et accidentibus
55 ut esse possint ministrant, dum sunt scilicet subiecta.
Quocirca εἶναι atque οὐσιῶσθαι esse atque subsistere,
ὑφίστασθαι vero substare intellegitur. Neque enim
verborum inops Graecia est, ut Marcus Tullius alludit,
sed essentiam, subsistentiam, substantiam, personam
60 totidem nominibus reddit, essentiam quidem οὐσίαν,
subsistentiam vero οὐσίωσιν, substantiam ὑπόστασιν,
personam πρόσωπον appellans. Ideo autem ὑποστάσεις
Graeci individuas substantias vocaverunt, quoniam
ceteris subsunt et quibusdam quasi accidentibus sub-
65 positae subiectaeque sunt ; atque idcirco nos quoque
eas substantias nuncupamus quasi subpositas, quas illi[1]

[1] quas illi *Vallinus* : quasi *or* quas *the better* MSS.

<hr>

[a] *Tusc.* ii. 15. 35.

taken from particulars. Wherefore since subsistences themselves are present in universals but acquire substance in particulars they rightly gave the name ὑπόστασις to subsistences which acquired substance through the medium of particulars. For to no one looking at it with any care or penetration will subsistence and substance appear identical.

For our equivalents of the Greek terms οὐσίωσις οὐσιῶσθαι are respectively *subsistentia* and *subsistere*, while their ὑπόστασις ὑφίστασθαι are represented by our *substantia* and *substare*. For a thing has subsistence when it does not require accidents in order to be, but that thing has substance which supplies to other things, accidents to wit, a substrate enabling them to be ; for it " stands under " (*sub-stat*) those things while it is " put under " (*sub-iectum*) the accidents. Thus genera and species have only subsistence, for accidents do not attach to genera and species. But individuals have not only subsistence but also substance, for neither do they depend on accidents for their being ; for they are already provided with their proper and specific differences and they enable accidents to be by being, that is, their subjects. Wherefore *esse* and *subsistere* represent εἶναι and οὐσιῶσθαι, while *substare* represents ὑφίστασθαι. For Greece, as Marcus Tullius [a] playfully says, is not short of words, but provides as many equivalents for *essentia, subsistentia, substantia* and *persona*—οὐσία for *essentia*, οὐσίωσις for *subsistentia*, ὑπόστασις for *substantia*, πρόσωπον for *persona*. But the Greeks called individual substances ὑποστάσεις because they underlie the rest and are put under and subject to certain things such as accidents ; and therefore we also call them substances as being

ὑποστάσεις, cumque etiam πρόσωπα nuncupent easdem
substantias, possumus nos quoque nuncupare personas.
Idem est igitur οὐσίαν esse quod essentiam, idem
70 οὐσίωσιν quod subsistentiam, idem ὑπόστασιν quod
substantiam, idem πρόσωπον quod personam. Quare
autem de inrationabilibus animalibus Graecus ὑπόστασιν non dicat, sicut nos de eisdem nomen substantiae praedicamus, haec ratio est, quoniam nomen
75 hoc melioribus applicatum est, ut aliqua id quod est
excellentius, tametsi non descriptione naturae secundum id quod ὑφίστασθαι atque substare est, at certe
ὑποστάσεως vel substantiae vocabulis discerneretur.

Est igitur et hominis quidem essentia, id est οὐσία,
80 et subsistentia, id est οὐσίωσις, et ὑπόστασις, id
est substantia, et πρόσωπον, id est persona ; οὐσία
quidem atque essentia quoniam est, οὐσίωσις vero
atque subsistentia quoniam in nullo subiecto est,
ὑπόστασις vero atque substantia, quoniam subest
85 ceteris quae subsistentiae non sunt, id est οὐσιώσεις ;
est πρόσωπον atque persona, quoniam est rationabile
individuum. Deus quoque et οὐσία est et essentia,
est enim et maxime ipse est a quo omnium esse pro-
ficiscitur. Est οὐσίωσις, id est subsistentia (subsistit
90 enim nullo indigens) ; et ὑφίστασθαι : substat enim.
Unde etiam dicimus unam esse οὐσίαν vel οὐσίωσιν,
id est essentiam vel subsistentiam deitatis, sed tres
ὑποστάσεις, id est tres substantias. Et quidem secundum hunc modum dixere unam trinitatis essentiam,
95 tres substantias tresque personas. Nisi enim tres in
deo substantias ecclesiasticus loquendi usus exclu-
deret, videretur idcirco de deo dici substantia, non
90

" put under "—ὑποστάσεις, and since they also term the same substances πρόσωπα, we too can call them persons. So οὐσία is identical with essence, οὐσίωσις with subsistence, ὑπόστασις with substance, πρόσωπον with person. But the reason why the Greek does not use ὑπόστασις of irrational animals while we predicate the term substance of them is this : this term has been applied to things of higher value, in order that in some way what is more excellent might be distinguished, if not by a description of nature answering to the literal meaning of ὑφίστασθαι = substare, at any rate by the words ὑπόστασις and substantia.

To begin with, then, man has essence, i.e. οὐσία, subsistence, i.e. οὐσίωσις, ὑπόστασις, i.e. substance, and πρόσωπον, i.e. person : οὐσία or essentia because he exists, οὐσίωσις or subsistence because he is not in any subject, ὑπόστασις or substance because he is subject to the other things which are not subsistences or οὐσιώσεις, while he is πρόσωπον or person because he is a rational individual. Next, God is οὐσία or essence, for he is and is especially that from which proceeds the being of all things. He is οὐσίωσις, i.e. subsistence, for he subsists in absolute independence ; and ὑφίστασθαι, for he is substance. Whence we go on to say that there is one οὐσία or οὐσίωσις, i.e. one essence or subsistence of the Godhead, but three ὑποστάσεις, that is three substances. And indeed, following this use, men have spoken of One essence of the Trinity, three substances and three persons. For did not the language of the Church forbid us to say that there are three substances in God,[a] substance might seem for this reason to be predicated of God,

---

[a] For a similar submission of his own opinion to the usage of the Church cf. the end of Tr. i and of Tr. ii.

quod ipse ceteris rebus quasi subiectum supponeretur,
sed quod idem omnibus uti praeesset ita etiam quasi
100 principium subesset rebus, dum eis omnibus οὐσιῶσθαι
vel subsistere subministrat.

## IV

Sed haec omnia idcirco sint dicta, ut differentiam
naturae atque personae id est οὐσίας atque ὑποστάσεως
monstraremus.   Quo vero nomine unumquodque
oporteat appellari, ecclesiasticae sit locutionis arbi-
5 trium.   Hoc interim constet quod inter naturam
personamque differre praediximus, quoniam natura
est cuiuslibet substantiae specificata proprietas,
persona vero rationabilis naturae individua substantia.   Hanc in Christo Nestorius duplicem esse
10 constituit eo scilicet traductus errore, quod putaverit
in omnibus naturis dici posse personam.   Hoc enim
praesumpto, quoniam in Christo duplicem naturam
esse censebat, duplicem quoque personam esse confessus est.   Qua in re eum falsum esse cum definitio
15 superius dicta convincat, tum haec argumentatio
evidenter eius declarabit errorem.   Si enim non est
Christi una persona duasque naturas esse manifestum
est, hominis scilicet atque dei (nec tam erit insipiens
quisquam, utqui utramque earum a ratione seiungat),
20 sequitur ut duae videantur esse personae ;  est enim
persona ut dictum est naturae rationabilis individua
substantia.

Quae est igitur facta hominis deique coniunctio ?
Num ita quasi cum duo corpora sibimet apponuntur,
25 ut tantum locis iuncta sint et nihil in alterum ex

92

not because he is set under other things like a substrate, but because, just as he is before all things,
so he is as it were the principle beneath all things,
supplying them all with οὐσιῶσθαι or subsistence.

## IV

You must consider that all I have said so far has
been for the purpose of marking the difference
between nature and person, that is, οὐσία and
ὑπόστασις. The exact name by which each should
be called must be left to the decision of ecclesiastical usage. For the time being let that distinction
between nature and person hold which I have
affirmed, viz. that nature is the specific property of
any substance, and person the individual substance
of a rational nature. Nestorius affirmed that in Christ
person was twofold, being led astray by thinking that
person can be predicated of every nature. For on
this assumption, understanding that there was in
Christ a twofold nature, he declared that there was
likewise a twofold person. And although the definition which we have already given is enough to prove
Nestorius wrong in this, his error shall be clearly declared by the following argument. If the person of
Christ is not single, and if it is clear that there are in
him two natures, to wit, of man and of God (and no
one will be so foolish as to fail to include either in the
definition), it follows that there must apparently be
two persons ; for person, as has been said, is the individual substance of a rational nature.

What kind of union, then, between God and man
has been effected ? Is it as when two bodies are laid
the one against the other, so that they are only joined

alterius qualitate perveniat ? Quem coniunctionis
Graeci modum κατὰ παράθεσιν vocant. Sed si ita
humanitas divinitati coniuncta est, nihil horum ex
utrisque confectum est ac per hoc nihil est Christus.
30 Nomen quippe ipsum unum quiddam significat
singularitate vocabuli. At si duabus personis manentibus ea coniunctio qualem superius diximus facta
est naturarum, unum ex duobus effici nihil potuit ;
omnino enim ex duabus personis nihil umquam fieri
35 potest. Nihil igitur unum secundum Nestorium
Christus est ac per hoc omnino nihil. Quod enim
non est unum, nec esse omnino potest ; esse enim
atque unum convertitur et quodcumque unum
est est. Etiam ea quae ex pluribus coniunguntur
40 ut acervus, chorus, unum tamen sunt. Sed esse
Christum manifeste ac veraciter confitemur ; unum
igitur esse dicimus Christum. Quod si ita est,
unam quoque Christi sine dubitatione personam esse
necesse est. Nam si duae personae essent, unus
45 esse non posset ; duos vero esse dicere Christos nihil
est aliud nisi praecipitatae mentis insania. Cur enim
omnino duos audeat Christos vocare, unum hominem
alium deum ? Vel cur eum qui deus est Christum
vocat, si eum quoque qui homo est Christum est
50 appellaturus, cum nihil simile, nihil habeant ex
copulatione coniunctum ? Cur simili nomine diver-
sissimis abutatur naturis, cum, si Christum definire
cogitur, utrisque ut ipse dicit Christis non possit
unam definitionis adhibere substantiam ? Si enim
55 dei atque hominis diversa substantia est unumque in
utrisque Christi nomen nec diversarum coniunctio

94

locally, and nothing of the quality of the one reaches the other—the kind of union which the Greeks term κατὰ παράθεσιν " by juxtaposition " ? But if humanity has been united to divinity in this way no one thing has been formed out of the two, and hence Christ is nothing. The very name of Christ, indeed, denotes by its singular number a unity. But if the two persons continued and such a union of natures as we have above described took place, no unity could have been formed from the two things, for nothing can ever possibly be formed out of two persons. Therefore Christ is, according to Nestorius, in no respect one, and therefore he is absolutely nothing. For what is not one cannot exist at all either ; because being and unity are convertible terms, and whatever is one is. Even things which are made up of many items, such as a heap or chorus, are nevertheless one. Now we openly and truly confess that Christ is ; therefore we say that Christ is one. And if this is so, then without doubt the person of Christ must be one also. For if there were two persons he could not be one ; but to say that there are two Christs is nothing else than the madness of a distraught mind. For why should he ever dare to name two Christs, one man, the other God ? Or why does he call him Christ who is God, if he is also going to call him Christ who is man, when the two have no common factor, no coherence from being joined ? Why should he wrongly use the same name for two utterly different natures, when, if he is compelled to define Christ, he cannot, as he himself admits, apply the one substance of his definition to both Christs ? For if the substance of God is different from that of man, and the one name of Christ applies to both, and the combination

95

substantiarum unam creditur fecisse personam, aequivocum nomen est Christi et nulla potest definitione
concludi. Quibus autem umquam scripturis nomen
60 Christi geminatur ? Quid vero novi per adventum
salvatoris effectum est ? Nam catholicis et fidei
veritas et raritas miraculi constat. Quam enim
magnum est quamque novum, quam quod semel
nec ullo alio saeculo possit evenire, ut eius qui solus
65 est deus natura cum humana quae ab eo erat diver-
sissima conveniret atque ita ex distantibus naturis
una fieret copulatione persona ! Secundum Nestorii
vero sententiam quid contingit novi ? " Servant,"
inquit, " proprias humanitas divinitasque personas."
70 Quando enim non fuit divinitatis propria humanitatisque persona ? Quando vero non erit ? Vel quid
amplius in Iesu generatione contingit quam in cuiuslibet alterius, si discretis utrisque personis discretae
etiam fuere naturae ? Ita enim personis manentibus
75 illic nulla naturarum potuit esse coniunctio, ut in
quolibet homine, cuius cum propria persona subsistat,
nulla est ei excellentissimae substantiae coniuncta
divinitas. Sed fortasse Iesum, id est personam
hominis, idcirco Christum vocet, quoniam per eam
80 mira quaedam sit operata divinitas. Esto. Deum
vero ipsum Christi appellatione cur vocet ? Cur vero
non elementa quoque ipsa simili audeat appellare
vocabulo per quae deus mira quaedam cotidianis
motibus operatur ? An quia inrationabiles sub-
85 stantiae non possunt habere personam qua[1] Christi
vocabulum excipere possint ?[2] Nonne in sanctis

[1] quae *MSS.*    [2] possit *Vallinus.*

---

[a] *Cf.* the discussion of *aequivoca*=ὁμώνυμος in *Isag. Porph.*
*Vide* Brandt's Index.

of different substances is not believed to have formed
one person, the name of Christ is equivocal [a] and
cannot be comprised in any definition. But in what
Scriptures is the name of Christ ever made double ?
Or what new thing has been wrought by the coming
of the Saviour ? For the truth of the faith and
the unwontedness of the miracle alike remain, for
Catholics, unshaken. For how great and unprece-
dented a thing it is—unique and incapable of repetition in any other age—that the nature of him who is
God alone should come together with human nature
which was entirely different from God and thus form
from different natures by conjunction a single person !
But according to the opinion of Nestorius, what happens that is new ? " Humanity and divinity," quoth
he, " keep their proper persons." Well, when had
not divinity and humanity each its proper person ?
And when will this not be so ? Or wherein is the
birth of Jesus more significant than that of any other
child, if, the two persons remaining distinct, the
natures also were distinct ? For while the persons
remained so there could be no union of natures in
Christ, as in the case of any man at all, so long as his
proper person subsists, there is no conjunction of
divinity with his substance, however excellent it be.
But perhaps he would call Jesus, *i.e.* the human person, Christ, because through that person divinity
wrought certain wonders. Agreed. But why should
he call God himself by the name of Christ ? Why
should he not make bold to call the very elements by
that name, through which in their daily movements
God works certain wonders ? Is it because irrational
substances cannot possess a person enabling them to
receive the name of Christ ? Is not the action of

hominibus ac pietate conspicuis apertus divinitatis
actus agnoscitur ? Nihil enim intererit, cur non
sanctos quoque viros eadem appellatione dignetur,
90 si in adsumptione humanitatis non est una ex con-
iunctione persona. Sed dicat forsitan, " Illos quoque
Christos vocari fateor, sed ad imaginem veri Christi."
Quod si nulla ex homine atque deo una persona
coniuncta est, omnes ita veros Christos arbitrabimur
95 ut hunc qui ex virgine genitus creditur. Nulla
quippe in hoc adunata persona est ex dei atque
hominis copulatione sicut nec in eis, qui dei spiritu
de venturo Christo praedicebant, propter quod etiam
ipsi quoque appellati sunt Christi. Iam vero sequitur,
100 ut personis manentibus nullo modo a divinitate
humanitas credatur adsumpta. Omnino enim disiuncta sunt quae aeque personis naturisque separantur, prorsus inquam disiuncta sunt nec magis inter
se homines bovesque disiuncti quam divinitas in
105 Christo humanitasque discreta est, si mansere personae. Homines quippe ac boves una animalis com-
munitate iunguntur ; est enim illis secundum genus
communis substantia eademque in universalitatis
collectione natura. Deo vero atque homini quid
110 non erit diversa ratione disiunctum, si sub diversitate
naturae personarum quoque credatur mansisse discretio ? Non est igitur salvatum genus humanum,
nulla in nos salus Christi generatione processit, tot
prophetarum scripturae populum inlusere credentem,
115 omnis veteris testamenti spernatur auctoritas per
quam salus mundo Christi generatione promittitur.

---

<sup>a</sup> Universalitas=τὸ καθόλου.

divinity seen plainly in men of holy life and notable piety ? For there will be no reason for him not to call holy men also by that same name, if in the assumption of humanity there is not one person out of the conjunction. But perhaps he will say, " I allow that such men are called Christs, but it is because they are in the image of the true Christ." But if no one person has been formed of the union of God and man, we shall consider all of them just as true Christs as him who, we believe, was born of a virgin. For no person has been made one by the joining of God and man either in him or in them who by the Spirit of God foretold the Christ to come, for which cause they too were called Christs. So now it follows that so long as the persons remain, we cannot in any wise believe that humanity has been assumed by divinity. For things which differ alike in persons and natures are altogether separate ; they are, I say, utterly separate, and men and oxen are not more separate than are divinity and humanity apart in Christ, if the persons have remained. Men indeed and oxen are joined in the single common category, animal, for according to their genus they have a common substance and the same nature in the collection which forms the universal.[a] But God and man will be at all points fundamentally different if we are to believe that distinction of persons continued under difference of nature. Then the human race has not been saved, Christ's begetting has brought us no salvation, the writings of so many prophets have but beguiled the people that believed in them, contempt is poured upon the authority of the whole Old Testament which promised to the world salvation by the birth of Christ. It is plain that salvation has not

99

# BOETHIUS

Non autem provenisse manifestum est, si eadem in persona est quae in natura diversitas. Eundem quippe salvum fecit quem creditur adsumpsisse; 120 nulla vero intellegi adsumptio potest, si manet aeque naturae personaeque discretio. Igitur qui adsumi manente persona non potuit, iure non videbitur per Christi generationem potuisse salvari. Non est igitur per generationem Christi hominum salvata 125 natura—quod credi nefas est.

Sed quamquam permulta sint quae hunc sensum inpugnare valeant atque perfringere, de argumentorum copia tamen haec interim libasse sufficiat.

## V

Transeundum quippe est ad Eutychen qui cum a veterum orbitis esset evagatus, in contrarium cucurrit errorem asserens tantum abesse, ut in Christo gemina persona credatur, ut ne naturam 5 quidem in eo duplicem oporteat confiteri; ita quippe esse adsumptum hominem, ut ea sit adunatio facta cum deo, ut natura humana non manserit. Huius error ex eodem quo Nestorii fonte prolabitur. Nam sicut Nestorius arbitratur non posse esse naturam 10 duplicem quin persona fieret duplex, atque ideo, cum in Christo naturam duplicem confiteretur, duplicem credidit esse personam, ita quoque Eutyches non putavit naturam duplicem esse sine duplicatione personae et cum non confiteretur duplicem esse per-

---

ᵃ For a similar *reductio ad absurdum* ending in *quod nefas est* see *Tr.* iii (*supra*, p. 44). *Generatio* is properly begetting by a male.

ᵇ The ecclesiastical *via media*, with the relegation of opposing theories to the extremes, which meet in a common

100

been brought us, if there is the same difference in person that there is in nature. No doubt he saved that humanity which we believe he assumed ; but no assumption can be conceived, if the distinction abides alike of nature and of person. Hence man who could not be assumed as long as the person continued, will rightly appear incapable of salvation by Christ's begetting. Wherefore man's nature has not been saved by Christ's begetting—an impious conclusion.[a]

But although there are many arguments strong enough to assail and demolish the Nestorian view, let us for the moment be content with this small selection from the store available.

## V

I must now pass to Eutyches who, wandering from the path of primitive doctrine, has rushed into the opposite error [b] and asserts that so far from our having to believe in a twofold person in Christ, we must not even confess a double nature ; man, he maintains, was so assumed that such a union was made with God that the human nature did not remain. His error springs from the same source as that of Nestorius. For just as Nestorius thinks there could not be a double nature unless the person were doubled, and therefore, confessing the double nature in Christ, has perforce believed the person to be double, so also Eutyches deemed that the nature was not double without the doubling of the person, and since he did not confess a double person, he

fount of falsity, owes something to Aristotle and to our author. *Vide infra*, p. 120.

15 sonam, arbitratus est consequens, ut una videretur
esse natura. Itaque Nestorius recte tenens duplicem
in Christo esse naturam sacrilege confitetur duas
esse personas ; Eutyches vero recte credens unam
esse personam impie credit unam quoque esse
20 naturam. Qui convictus evidentia rerum, quando-
quidem manifestum est aliam naturam esse hominis
aliam dei, ait duas se confiteri in Christo naturas
ante adunationem, unam vero post adunationem.
Quae sententia non aperte quod vult eloquitur. Ut
25 tamen eius dementiam perscrutemur, adunatio haec
aut tempore generationis facta est aut tempore
resurrectionis. Sed si tempore generationis facta
est, videtur putare et ante generationem fuisse
humanam carnem non a Maria sumptam sed aliquo
30 modo alio praeparatam, Mariam vero virginem
appositam ex qua caro nasceretur quae ab ea sumpta
non esset, illam vero carnem quae antea fuerit esse
et divisam atque a divinitatis substantia separatam ;
cum ex virgine natus est, adunatum esse deo, ut una
35 videretur facta esse natura. Vel si haec eius
sententia non est, illa esse poterit dicentis duas ante
adunationem, unam post adunationem, si adunatio
generatione perfecta est, ut corpus quidem a Maria
sumpserit, sed, antequam sumeret, diversam deitatis
40 humanitatisque fuisse naturam ; sumptam vero unam
factam atque in divinitatis cessisse substantiam.
Quod si hanc adunationem non putat generatione
sed resurrectione factam, rursus id duobus fieri arbi-
trabitur modis ; aut enim genito Christo et non
45 adsumente de Maria corpus aut adsumente ab eadem
102

thought it followed that the nature should be regarded as single. Thus Nestorius, rightly holding
nature to be double Christ, sacrilegiously professes
the persons to be two ; whereas Eutyches, rightly
believing the person to be single, impiously believes
that the nature also is single. And being confuted
by the plain evidence of facts, since it is clear that
the nature of man is one thing, that of God another,
he declares his belief to be : two natures in Christ
before the union and only one after the union. Now
this statement does not express clearly what he
means. However, let us scrutinize his folly. It is
plain that this union took place either at the moment
of begetting or that of resurrection. But if it happened at the moment of begetting, Eutyches seems
to think that even before that He was human flesh,
not taken from Mary but prepared in some other
way, while the Virgin Mary was brought in to give
birth to flesh that had not been taken from her ; that
this flesh, which already existed, was apart and
separate from the substance of divinity, but that
when he was born of the Virgin he was united to God,
so that it seemed that one nature was made. Or if
that is not his opinion, it could be this, if he says that
there were two natures before the union and one
after, supposing the union to be effected by begetting
so that the body indeed he took from Mary but
before he took it the natures of Godhead and
humanity were different : but the nature assumed
became one with that of Godhead into the substance
of which it passed. But if he thinks that this union
was effected not by begetting but resurrection, again
he will believe this to happen in two ways ; either
Christ was born but did *not* assume a body from Mary

103

carnem, usque dum resurgeret quidem, duas fuisse
naturas, post resurrectionem unam factam. De
quibus illud disiunctum nascitur, quod interro-
gabimus hoc modo : natus ex Maria Christus aut
50 ab ea carnem humanam traxit aut minime. Si non
confitetur ex ea traxisse, dicat quo homine indutus
advenerit, utrumne eo qui deciderat praevaricatione
peccati an alio ? Si eo de cuius semine ductus est
homo, quem vestita divinitas est ? Nam si ex
55 semine Abrahae atque David et postremo Mariae
non fuit caro illa qua natus est, ostendat ex cuius
hominis sit carne derivatus, quoniam post primum
hominem caro omnis humana ex humana carne
deducitur. Sed si quem dixerit hominem a quo
60 generatio sumpta sit salvatoris praeter Mariam
virginem, et ipse errore confundetur et adscribere
mendacii notam summae divinitati inlusus ipse videbitur, quando quod Abrahae atque David promittitur
in sanctis divinationibus, ut ex eorum semine toti
65 mundo salus oriatur, aliis distribuit, cum praesertim,
si humana caro sumpta est, non ab alio sumi potuerit
nisi unde etiam procreabatur. Si igitur a Maria non
est sumptum corpus humanum sed a quolibet alio,
per Mariam tamen est procreatum quod fuerat prae-
70 varicatione corruptum, superius dicto repellitur
argumento. Quod si non eo homine Christus indutus est qui pro peccati poena sustinuerat mortem,
illud eveniet ex nullius hominis semine talem potuisse
nasci qui fuerit sine originalis poena peccati. Ex

---

[a] The use of this kind of argument by Boethius allays
any suspicion as to the genuineness of *Tr.* iv which might
be caused by the use of allegorical interpretation therein.
Note also that in the *Consolatio* the framework is allegory,
which is also freely applied in the details.

or he *did* assume flesh from her, and there were, until indeed he rose, two natures which became one after the Resurrection. From these alternatives a disjunction arises which we will examine as follows : Christ who was born of Mary either did or did not take human flesh from her. If Eutyches does not admit that he took it from her, then let him say dressed in what manhood he came—that which had fallen through the transgression of sin or another ? If it was the manhood of that man from whose seed all men descend, what manhood did divinity invest ? For if that flesh in which he was born came not of the seed of Abraham and of David and finally of Mary, let Eutyches show from what man's flesh he descended, since, after the first man, all human flesh is derived from human flesh. But if he shall name any human besides Mary the Virgin from whom the Saviour's begetting came, he will both be himself confounded by error, and, himself a dupe, will seem to stamp with falsehood the very Godhead for thus transferring to others the promise of the sacred oracles made to Abraham and David *a* that of their seed salvation should arise for all the world, especially since if human flesh was taken it could not be taken from any other but him of whom it was begotten. If, therefore, his human body was not taken from Mary but from any other, yet that was engendered through Mary which had been corrupted by transgression, Eutyches is confuted by the argument already stated. But if Christ did not put on that manhood which had endured death in punishment for sin, it will result that of no man's seed could ever one have been born who should be without punishment for original sin. Therefore flesh like this

75 nullo igitur talis sumpta est caro ; unde fit ut noviter
videatur esse formata. Sed haec aut ita hominum
visa est oculis, ut humanum putaretur corpus quod
revera non esset humanum, quippe quod nulli
originali subiaceret poenae, aut nova quaedam vera
80 nec poenae peccati subiacens originalis ad tempus
hominis natura formata est ? Si verum hominis
corpus non fuit, aperte arguitur mentita divinitas,
quae ostenderet hominibus corpus, quod cum verum
non esset, tum fallerentur ii[1] qui verum esse arbitra-
85 rentur. At si nova veraque non ex homine sumpta
caro formata est, quo tanta tragoedia generationis ?
Ubi ambitus passionis ? Ego quippe ne in homine
quidem non stulte fieri puto quod inutiliter factum
est. Ad quam vero utilitatem facta probabitur tanta
90 humilitas divinitatis, si homo qui periit generatione
ac passione Christi salvatus non est, quoniam negatur
adsumptus ? Rursus igitur sicut ab eodem Nestorii
fonte Eutychis error principium sumpsit, ita ad
eundem finem relabitur, ut secundum Eutychen
95 quoque non sit salvatum genus humanum, quoniam
non is qui aeger esset et salvatione curaque egeret,
adsumptus est. Traxisse autem hanc sententiam
videtur, si tamen huius erroris fuit ut crederet non
fuisse corpus Christi vere ex homine sed extra atque
100 adeo in caelo formatum, quoniam cum eo in caelum
creditur ascendisse. Quod exemplum continet tale :
" non ascendit in caelum, nisi qui de caelo descendit."

[1] hii *or* hi MSS.

---

*a* Another *reductio ad absurdum* or *ad impietatem, cf.
supra*, p. 100, note *a*.

was taken from no man; whence it would appear to
have been new-formed. But did this flesh then
either so appear to human eyes that the body was
deemed human which was not really human, because
it was not subject to any primal penalty, or was
some new true nature of man formed for the time,
not subject to the penalty for original sin ? If it was
not a truly human body, the Godhead is plainly
convicted of falsehood for displaying to men a body
which since it was not real thus deceived those who
thought it real. But if flesh had been formed new
and real and not taken from man, to what purpose
was the tremendous drama of the begetting ? Where
the scene of his Passion ? I cannot but consider
foolish even a human action that is useless. And to
to what useful end shall we say this great humiliation
of Divinity was wrought if ruined man has not been
saved by the begetting and Passion of Christ—for
they denied that he was taken into Godhead ? Once
more then, just as the error of Eutyches took its rise
from the same source as that of Nestorius, so it sinks
into the same end inasmuch as according to Eutyches
also the human race has not been saved,[a] since man
who was sick and needed health and salvation was not
taken into Godhead. Yet this is the conclusion he
seems to have drawn, if he erred so deeply as to
believe that Christ's body was not formed really from
man but from a source outside him and indeed in
heaven, since it is believed to have ascended into
heaven with him. Which is the meaning of the text :
" none hath ascended into heaven save him who
came down from heaven."

# BOETHIUS

## VI

Sed satis de ea parte dictum videtur, si corpus quod
Christus excepit ex Maria non credatur adsumptum.
Si vero adsumptum est ex Maria neque permansit perfecta humana divinaque natura, id tribus effici potuit
5 modis : aut enim divinitas in humanitatem translata
est aut humanitas in divinitatem aut utraeque in se
ita temperatae sunt atque commixtae, ut neutra substantia propriam formam teneret. Sed si divinitas
in humanitatem translata est, factum est, quod credi
10 nefas est, ut humanitate inmutabili substantia permanente divinitas verteretur et quod passibile atque
mutabile naturaliter exsisteret, id inmutabile per-
maneret, quod vero inmutabile atque inpassibile
naturaliter creditur, id in rem mutabilem verteretur.
15 Hoc igitur fieri nulla ratione contingit. Sed humana
forsitan natura in deitatem videatur esse conversa.
Hoc vero qui fieri potest, si divinitas in generatione
Christi et humanum animam suscepit et corpus ? Non
enim omnis res in rem omnem verti ac transmutari
20 potest. Nam cum substantiarum aliae sint corporeae,
aliae incorporeae, neque corporea in incorpoream
neque incorporea in eam quae corpus est mutari
potest, nec vero incorporea in se invicem formas
proprias mutant ; sola enim mutari transformarique
25 in se possunt quae habent unius materiae commune
subiectum, nec haec omnia, sed ea quae in se et facere
et pati possunt. Id vero probatur hoc modo : neque

# CONTRA EUTYCHEN

## VI

I think enough has been said on that aspect of the case, that is if it were not believed that the body which Christ received was taken from Mary. But if it was taken from Mary and the human and divine natures did not continue, each in its perfection, this could have happened in three ways. Either divinity was translated into humanity, or humanity into divinity, or both were so modified and mingled that neither substance kept its proper form. But if divinity was translated into humanity, that has happened which piety forbids us to believe, viz. while the humanity continued in unchangeable substance divinity was changed, and that which was by nature passible and mutable remained immutable, while that which we believe to be by nature immutable and impassible was changed into a mutable thing. But it accords with no reasoning that this should happen. But perchance the human nature may seem to have been changed into Godhead. Yet how can this be if divinity in Christ's begetting received both human soul and body ? Things cannot be promiscuously changed and interchanged. For since some substances are corporeal and others incorporeal, neither can a corporeal substance be changed into an incorporeal, nor can an incorporeal be changed into that substance which is body, nor yet incorporeals interchange their proper forms ; for only those things can be interchanged and transformed which possess the common substrate of the same matter, nor can all of these so behave, but only those which can act upon and be acted on by each other. Now this is proved as follows : bronze cannot be converted into

109

enim potest aes in lapidem permutari nec vero idem
aes in herbam nec quodlibet aliud corpus in quodlibet
30 aliud transfigurari potest, nisi et eadem sit materia
rerum in se transeuntium et a se et facere et pati
possint, ut, cum vinum atque aqua miscentur, utraque
sunt talia quae actum sibi passionemque communicent.
Potest enim aquae qualitas a vini qualitate aliquid
35 pati ; potest item vini ab aquae qualitate aliquid pati.
Atque idcirco si multum quidem fuerit aquae, vini vero
paululum, non dicuntur inmixta, sed alterum alterius
qualitate corrumpitur. Si quis enim vinum fundat
in mare, non mixtum est mari vinum sed in mare
40 corruptum, idcirco quoniam qualitas aquae multitudine sui corporis nihil passa est a qualitate vini,
sed potius in se ipsam vini qualitatem propria multitudine commutavit. Si vero sint mediocres sibique
aequales vel paulo inaequales naturae quae a se
45 facere et pati possunt, illae miscentur et mediocribus
inter se qualitatibus temperantur. Atque haec quidem in corporibus neque his omnibus, sed tantum
quae a se, ut dictum est, et facere et pati possunt
communi atque eadem materia subiecta. Omne enim
50 corpus quod in generatione et corruptione subsistit
communem videtur habere materiam, sed non omne
ab omni vel in omni vel facere aliquid vel pati potest.
Corpora vero in incorporea nulla ratione poterunt
permutari, quoniam nulla communi materia subiecta
55 participant quae susceptis qualitatibus in alterutram
110

stone nor indeed can the same bronze be changed
into grass, and generally no body can be transformed
into any other body unless the things which pass into
each other have a common matter and can act upon
and be acted on by each other, as when wine and
water are mingled both are of such a nature as to
allow reciprocal action and influence. For the quality
of water can be influenced in some degree by that of
wine, similarly the quality of wine can be influenced
by that of water. And therefore if there be a great
deal of water but very little wine, they are not said
to be mingled, but the one is brought to nothing by
the quality of the other. For if anyone pours wine
into the sea the wine is not mingled with the sea
but is brought to nothing in the sea, simply because
the quality of the water owing to its bulk has been
in no way effected by the quality of the wine, but
rather by its own bulk has changed the quality of the
wine into water. But if the natures which are capable of reciprocal action and influence are in moderate
proportion and equal or only slightly unequal, they
are really mingled and form a mixture with the
qualities which are in moderate relation to each other.
This indeed takes place in bodies but not in all bodies,
but only in those, as has been said, which are capable
of reciprocal action and influence, having the same
common material substrate. For every body which
subsists in conditions of birth and decay seems to
possess a common matter, but every body is not
capable of reciprocal action and influence on and by
every other. But bodies will not be able in any way
to be changed into incorporeals because they do not
share in any common material substrate which might
be changed into this or that thing by taking on its

permutetur. Omnis enim natura incorporeae substantiae nullo materiae nititur fundamento ; nullum
vero corpus est cui non sit materia subiecta. Quod
cum ita sit cumque ne ea quidem quae communem
60 materiam naturaliter habent in se transeant, nisi illis
adsit potestas in se et a se faciendi ac patiendi, multo
magis in se non permutabuntur quibus non modo
communis materia non est, sed cum alia res materiae
fundamento nititur ut corpus, alia omnino materiae
65 subiecto non egeat ut incorporeum.

Non igitur fieri potest, ut corpus in incorporalem
speciem permutetur, nec vero fieri potest, ut incorporalia in sese commixtione aliqua permutentur.
Quorum enim communis nulla materia est, nec in
70 se verti ac permutari queunt. Nulla autem est
incorporalibus materia rebus ; non poterunt igitur in
se invicem permutari. Sed anima et deus incorporeae
substantiae recte creduntur ; non est igitur humana
anima in divinitatem a qua adsumpta est permutata.
75 Quod si neque corpus neque anima in divinitatem
potuit verti, nullo modo fieri potuit, ut humanitas
converteretur in deum. Multo minus vero credi
potest, ut utraque in sese confunderentur, quoniam
neque incorporalitas transire ad corpus potest neque
80 rursus e converso corpus ad incorporalitatem, quando
quidem nulla his materia subiecta communis est quae
alterutris substantiarum qualitatibus permutetur.

At hi ita aiunt ex duabus quidem naturis Christum
consistere, in duabus vero minime, hoc scilicet in-
112

qualities. For the nature of no incorporeal substance rests upon a material basis ; but there is no body that has not matter as a substrate. Since this is so, and since not even those things which naturally have a common matter pass over into each other, unless they have the power of acting on each other and being acted upon by each other, far more will those things not suffer interchange which not only have no common matter but are different in substance, since one of them, being body, rests on a basis of matter, while the other, being incorporeal, cannot possibly stand in need of a material substrate.

It is therefore impossible for a body to be changed into an incorporeal species, nor is it ever possible for incorporeals to be changed into each other by some process of mingling. For things which have no common matter cannot be changed and converted one into another. But incorporeal things have no matter ; they will never, therefore, be able to be changed about among themselves. But the soul and God are rightly believed to be incorporeal substances ; therefore the human soul has not been changed into the divinity by which is was assumed. But if neither body nor soul could be turned into divinity, it could not possibly happen that humanity should be transformed into God. But it is much less credible that the two should be confounded together since neither can incorporality pass over to body, nor again, contrariwise, can body pass over into incorporality, when these have no common material substrate to be converted by the qualities of one or other of the two substances.

But the Eutychians say that Christ consists indeed of two natures, but not in two natures, meaning, no

85 tendentes, quoniam quod ex duabus consistit ita
unum fieri potest, ut illa ex quibus dicitur constare
non maneant ; veluti cum mel aquae confunditur
neutrum manet, sed alterum alterius copulatione corruptum quiddam tertium fecit, ita illud quidem quod
90 ex melle atque aqua tertium fit constare ex utrisque
dicitur, in utrisque vero negatur. Non enim poterit
in utrisque constare, quando utrorumque natura non
permanet. Ex utrisque enim constare potest, licet
ea ex quibus coniungitur alterutra qualitate corrupta
95 sint ; in utrisque vero huiusmodi constare non poterit,
quoniam ea quae in se transfusa sunt non manent
ac non sunt utraque in quibus constare videatur,
cum ex utrisque constet in se invicem qualitatum
mutatione transfusis.

100     Catholici vero utrumque rationabiliter confitentur,
nam et ex utrisque naturis Christum et in utrisque
consistere. Sed id qua ratione dicatur, paulo posterius
explicabo. Nunc illud est manifestum convictam
esse Eutychis sententiam eo nomine, quod cum tribus
105 modis fieri possit, ut ex duabus naturis una subsistat,
ut aut divinitas in humanitatem translata sit aut
humanitas in divinitatem aut utraque permixta sint,
nullum horum modum fieri potuisse superius dicta
argumentatione declaratur.

## VII

    Restat ut, quemadmodum catholica fides dicat, et

114

doubt, thereby, that a thing which consists of two natures can become one in such a way that the elements of which it is said to be made up disappear ; just as, for example, when honey is mixed with water neither remains, but each being brought to nothing by conjunction with the other produces a certain third thing, so that third thing which is produced by the combination of honey and water is said to consist of both, but not in both. For it will not be able to consist in both so long as the nature of both does not continue. For it can consist of both even though each element of which it is compounded has been brought to nothing by the quality of the other ; but it will not be able to consist in both natures of this kind since the elements which have been transmuted into each other do not continue, and both the elements in which it seems to consist cease to be, since it consists of two things translated into each other by change of qualities.

But Catholics in accordance with reason confess both, for they say that Christ consists both of and in two natures. How this can be affirmed I will explain a little later. One thing is now clear ; the opinion of Eutyches has been confuted on the ground that, although there are three ways by which of two natures one may subsist, viz. either divinity has been translated into humanity or humanity into divinity or both have been mixed together, the foregoing train of reasoning shows that no one of these ways could have been effected.

# VII

It remains for us to show how in accordance with

in utrisque naturis Christum et ex utrisque consistere
doceamus.

Ex utrisque naturis aliquid consistere duo signi-
5 ficat : unum quidem, cum ita dicimus aliquid ex
duabus naturis iungi sicut ex melle atque aqua, id
autem est ut ex quolibet modo confusis, vel si una
vertatur in alteram vel si utraeque in se invicem
misceantur, nullo modo tamen utraeque permaneant ;
10 secundum hunc modum Eutyches ait ex utrisque
naturis Christum consistere.

Alter vero modus est ex utrisque consistendi
quod ita ex duabus iunctum est, ut illa tamen ex
quibus iunctum esse dicitur maneant nec in alterutra
15 vertantur, ut cum dicimus coronam ex auro gemmisque
compositam. Hic neque aurum in gemmas translatum
est neque in aurum gemma conversa, sed utraque
permanent nec formam propriam derelinquunt. Talia
ergo ex aliquibus constantia et in his constare dicimus
20 ex quibus consistere praedicantur. Tunc enim possumus dicere coronam gemmis auroque consistere ;
sunt enim gemmae atque aurum in quibus corona
consistat. Nam in priore modo non est mel atque
qua in quibus illud quod ex utrisque iungitur constet.
25 Cum igitur utrasque manere naturas in Christo fides
catholica confiteatur perfectasque easdem persistere
nec alteram in alteram transmutari, iure dicit et in
utrisque naturis Christum et ex utrisque consistere :
in utrisque quidem, quia manent utraeque, ex utris-
30 que vero, quia utrarumque adunatione manentium
una persona fit Christi. Non autem secundum eam
116

the affirmation of Catholic belief Christ consists at once in and of both natures.

The statement that a thing consists of two natures bears two meanings ; one, when we say that anything is a union of two natures, as *e.g.* honey and water, where the union is such that in the combination, however the elements be confounded, whether by one nature changing into the other, or by both mingling with each other, the two entirely disappear. This is the way in which according to Eutyches Christ consists of two natures.

The other way in which a thing can consist of two natures is when it is so combined of two that the elements of which it is said to be combined continue without changing into each other, as when we say that a crown is composed of gold and gems. Here neither is the gold converted into gems nor is the gem turned into gold, but both continue without surrendering their proper form.

Things then like this, composed of various elements, we say consist also in the elements of which they are said to consist. For in this case we can say that a crown consists of gems and gold, for gems and gold are that in which the crown consists. For in the former mode of composition honey and water is not that in which the resulting union of both consists.

Since then the Catholic Faith confesses that both natures continue in Christ and that they both remain perfect, neither being transformed into the other, it says with right that Christ consists both in and of tho two natures ; *in* the two because both continue, *of* the two because the one person of Christ is formed by the union of the two continuing natures.

But the Catholic Faith does not hold the union

significationem ex utrisque naturis Christum iunctum
esse fides catholica tenet, secundum quam Eutyches
pronuntiat.   Nam ille talem significationem coniunc-
35 tionis ex utraque natura sumit, ut non confiteatur in
utrisque consistere, neque enim utrasque manere ;
catholicus vero eam significationem ex utrisque consistendi sumit quae illi sit proxima eamque conservet
quae in utrisque consistere confitetur.

40   Aequivocum igitur est " ex utrisque consistere " ac
potius amphibolum et gemina significatione diversa
designans : una quidem significatione non manere
substantias ex quibus illud quod copulatum est dicatur
esse coniunctum, alio modo significans ita ex utrisque
45 coniunctum, ut utraque permaneant.

Hoc igitur expedito aequivocationis atque ambigui-
tatis nodo nihil est ultra quod possit opponi, quin id
sit quod firma veraque fides catholica continet ; eundem Christum hominem esse perfectum, eundem deum
50 eundemque qui homo sit perfectus atque deus unum
esse deum ac dei filium, nec quaternitatem trinitati
adstrui, dum homo additur supra perfectum deum,
sed unam eandemque personam numerum trinitatis
explere, ut cum humanitas passa sit, deus tamen
55 passus esse dicatur, non quo ipsa deitas humanitas
facta sit, sed quod a deitate fuerit adsumpta.   Item
qui homo est, dei filius appellatur non substantia
divinitatis sed humanitatis, quae tamen divinitati
naturali unitate coniuncta est.   Et cum haec ita
60 intelligentia discernantur permisceanturque, tamen
unus idemque et homo sit perfectus et deus : deus
118

of Christ out of two natures according to that meaning which Eutyches puts upon it. For the meaning of the conjunction out of two natures which he adopts forbids him to confess that it consists in the two or that the two continue ; but the Catholic adopts such a meaning of its consisting of two as comes near to that of Eutyches, yet keeps the meaning which confesses that it consists in two.

" To consist of two natures " is therefore an equivocal or rather an ambiguous term of double meaning denoting different things ; according to one meaning the substances out of which the union is said to have been composed do not continue, according to another the union effected of the two is such that both natures continue.

When once this knot of equivocity and ambiguity has been untied, nothing further can be advanced to shake the true and solid content of the Catholic Faith, which is that the same Christ is perfect man, the same is God, and the same who is perfect man and God is one as God and Son of God ; that, however, quaternity is not added to the Trinity by the addition of man to perfect God, but that one and the same person completes the number of the Trinity, so that, although it was the humanity which suffered, yet God may be said to have suffered, not because manhood became Godhead itself but because it was assumed by Godhead. Further, he who is man is called Son of God not in virtue of divine but of human substance, which latter none the less was conjoined to divinity in a unity of natures. And although these things are distinguished and mixed together by the understanding, yet one and the same is perfect man and God : God because he was

119

quidem, quod ipse sit ex patris substantia genitus,
homo vero, quod ex Maria sit virgine procreatus.
Itemque qui homo, deus eo quod a deo fuerit ad-
65 sumptus, et qui deus, homo, quoniam vestitus homine
sit. Cumque in eadem persona aliud sit divinitas
quae suscepit, aliud quam suscepit humanitas, idem
tamen deus atque homo est. Nam si hominem intellegas, idem homo est atque deus, quoniam homo
70 ex natura, deus adsumptione. Si vero deum intellegas, idem deus est atque homo, quoniam natura deus
est, homo adsumptione. Fitque in eo gemina natura
geminaque substantia, quoniam homo-deus unaque
persona, quoniam idem homo atque deus. Mediaque
75 est haec inter duas haereses via sicut virtutes quoque
medium tenent. Omnis enim virtus in medio rerum
decore locata consistit. Siquid enim vel ultra vel infra
quam oportuerit fiat, a virtute disceditur. Medietatem igitur virtus tenet.
80　Quocirca, si quattuor haec neque ultra neque infra
esse possunt ut in Christo aut duae naturae sint
duaeque personae ut Nestorius ait, aut una persona
unaque natura ut Eutyches ait, aut duae naturae sed
una persona ut catholica fides credit, aut una natura
85 duaeque personae,[1] cumque duas quidem naturas
duasque personas in ea quae contra Nestorium dicta
est responsione convicerimus (unam vero personam
unamque naturam esse non posse Eutyche proponente
monstravimus neque tamen tam amens quisquam huc
90 usque exstitit, ut unam in eo naturam crederet sed
geminas esse personas), restat ut ea sit vera quam fide
catholica pronuntiat geminam substantiam sed unam

[1] quod nullus haereticus adhuc attigit *added by some MSS.*

---

[a] *Vide supra,* p. 100, note *b.*

begotten of the substance of the Father, but man because he was engendered of the Virgin Mary. And further he who is man is God in that man was assumed by God, and he who is God is man in that God was clothed with man. And although in the same person the divinity which took manhood is different from the humanity which it took, yet the same is God and man. For if you think of him as man, the same is man and God, being man by nature, God by assumption. But if you think of him as God, the same is God and man, being God by nature, man by assumption. And in him nature becomes double and substance double because he is God-man, and one person since the same is man and God. This is the middle way between two heresies, just as virtues also hold a middle place.[a] For every virtue has a place of honour midway between extremes. If anything happens, then, to a higher or lower degree than it should, it parts company with virtue. And so virtue holds a middle place.

Wherefore if these are the only four possibilities, no more and no less, viz. that in Christ are either two natures and two persons as Nestorius says, or one person and one nature as Eutyches says, or two natures but one person as the Catholic Faith believes, or one nature and two persons, and inasmuch as we have refuted the doctrine of two natures and two persons in our argument against Nestorius and incidentally have shown that the one person and one nature suggested by Eutyches is impossible, nor indeed has there ever been anyone so mad as to believe that there was in him one nature but two persons ; it remains that that must be true which the Catholic Faith affirms, viz. that the substance is

121

esse personam. Quia vero paulo ante diximus
Eutychen confiteri duas quidem in Christo ante
95 adunationem naturas, unam vero post adunationem,
cumque hunc errorem duplicem interpretaremur celare
sententiam, ut haec adunatio aut generatione fieret,
cum ex Maria corpus hominis minime sumeretur aut
ad sumptum[1] quidem ex Maria per resurrectionem
100 fieret adunatio, de utrisque quidem partibus idonee
ut arbitror disputatum est. Nunc quaerendum est
quomodo fieri potuerit ut duae naturae in unam
substantiam miscerentur.

## VIII

Verumtamen est etiam nunc et alia quaestio quae
ab his inferri potest qui corpus humanum ex Maria
sumptum esse non credunt, sed alias fuisse seque-
stratum praeparatumque quod in adunatione ex
5 Mariae utero gigni ac proferri videretur. Aiunt
enim : si ex homine sumptum est corpus, homo vero
omnis ex prima praevaricatione non solum peccato
et morte tenebatur, verum etiam affectibus pecca-
torum erat implicitus, eaque illi fuit poena peccati,
10 ut, cum morte teneretur obstrictus, tamen esset reus
etiam voluntate peccandi, cur in Christo neque
peccatum fuit neque voluntas ulla peccandi ? Et
omnino habet animadvertendam dubitationem talis
quaestio. Si enim ex carne humana Christi corpus
15 adsumptum est, dubitari potest, quaenam caro haec
quae adsumpta sit esse videatur. Eum quippe

---

[1] sumptum *MSS.* : adsumptum *printer's error* : ad sumptum
*Stewart or Rand.*

double, but the person one.  But as I have just now remarked that Eutyches confesses two natures in Christ before the union, but only one after the union, and since I explained that this error concealed two opinions, that the union was brought about either by begetting though the human body was certainly not taken from Mary ;  or, that the union was effected with what was taken indeed from Mary by means of the Resurrection, I have, it seems to me, argued the twofold aspect of the case as completely as it deserves.  What we have now to inquire is how it could come to pass that two natures were combined into one substance.

## VIII

Nevertheless there remains yet another question which can be advanced by those who do not believe that the human body was taken from Mary, but that the body was at some other time set apart and prepared, which in the moment of union appeared to be begotten and brought forth from Mary's womb.  For they say : if the body was taken from man, while every man was, from the time of the first transgression, not only bound by sin and death but also involved in sinful desires, and if his punishment for sin was that, although he was held bound by death, yet at the same time he should be guilty because of the will to sin, why was there in Christ neither sin nor any will to sin ?  And certainly such a question is attended by a difficulty which deserves attention. For if the body of Christ was assumed from human flesh, it is open to doubt of what kind we must consider that flesh to be which was assumed.

salvavit quem etiam adsumpsit; sin vero talem
hominem adsumpsit qualis Adam fuit ante peccatum,
integram quidem videtur humanam adsumpsisse
20 naturam, sed tamen quae medicina penitus non
egebat. Quomodo autem fieri potest, ut talem
adsumpserit hominem qualis Adam fuit, cum in
Adam potuerit esse peccandi voluntas atque affectio,
unde factum est ut etiam praetergressis divinis prae-
25 ceptis inobedientiae delictis teneretur adstrictus?
In Christo vero ne voluntas quidem ulla creditur
fuisse peccandi, cum praesertim si tale corpus
hominis adsumpsit quale Adae ante peccatum fuit,
non debuerit esse mortalis, quoniam Adam, si non
30 peccasset, mortem nulla ratione sensisset. Cum
igitur Christus non peccaverit, quaerendum est cur
senserit mortem, si Adae corpus ante quam peccaret
adsumpsit. Quod si talem statum suscepit hominis
qualis Adae post peccatum fuit, videtur etiam Christo
35 non defuisse necessitas, ut et delictis subiceretur et
passionibus confunderetur obductisque iudicii regulis
bonum a malo non sincera integritate discerneret,
quoniam has omnes poenas Adam delicti praevaricatione suscepit.

40 Contra quos respondendum est tres intellegi
hominum posse status: unum quidem Adae ante
delictum in quo, tametsi ab eo mors aberat nec
adhuc ullo se delicto polluerat, poterat tamen in eo
voluntas esse peccandi: alter in quo mutari potuisset,
45 si firmiter in dei praeceptis manere voluisset, tunc
enim id addendum foret ut non modo non peccaret
aut peccare vellet sed ne posset quidem aut peccare
aut velle delinquere. Tertius status est post delictum

124

In truth, the manhood which he assumed he likewise saved ; but if he assumed such manhood as Adam had before sin, he appears to have assumed a human nature complete indeed, but one which was in no need of healing. But how can it be that he assumed such manhood as Adam had when there could be in Adam both the will and the desire to sin, whence it came to pass that even after the divine commands had been broken, he was still held captive to sins of disobedience ? But we believe that in Christ there was never even any will to sin, though especially if he assumed such a human body as Adam had before his sin, he ought not to have been mortal, since Adam, had he not sinned, would in no wise have experienced death. Since, then, Christ never sinned, it must be asked why he suffered death if he assumed the body of Adam before he sinned. But if he took on such condition of man as was Adam's after sin, it seems that even on Christ lay the necessity of being both subject to sin and perplexed by passions, and, since the canons of judgement were obscured, of distinguishing good from evil without perfect soundness, since Adam by his sinful transgression incurred all these penalties.

Against whom we must reply that there are three conditions of men to envisage : one, that of Adam before his sin, in which, though death was not with him and he had not yet defiled himself with any sin yet there could be within him the will to sin ; the second, that in which he could have suffered change had he chosen to abide steadfastly in the commands of God, for then it might have been further granted him not only not to sin or wish to sin, but to be incapable of sinning or of wanting to transgress. The

in quo mors illum necessario subsecuta est et peccatum
50 ipsum voluntasque peccati.  Quorum summitatum
atque contrariorum haec loca sunt : is status qui
praemium esset, si in praeceptis dei Adam manere
voluisset et is qui poenae fuit, quoniam manere
noluit ; in illo enim nec mors esset nec peccatum
55 nec voluntas ulla peccati, in hoc vero et mors et
peccatum et delinquendi omnis affectio omniaque in
perniciem prona nec quicquam in se opis habentia,
ut post lapsum posset adsurgere.  Ille vero medius
status in quo praesentia quidem mortis vel peccati
60 aberat, potestas vero utriusque constabat, inter
utrumque statum est conlocatus.  Ex his igitur
tribus statibus Christus corporeae naturae singulas
quodam modo indidit causas ;  nam quod mortale
corpus adsumpsit ut mortem a genere humano
65 fugaret, in eo statu ponendum est quod post Adae
praevaricationem poenaliter inflictum est.  Quod
vero non fuit in eo voluntas ulla peccati, ex eo
sumptum est statu qui esse potuisset, nisi voluntatem
insidiantis fraudibus applicasset.  Restat igitur tertius
70 status id est medius, ille scilicet qui eo tempore fuit,
cum nec mors aderat et adesse poterat delinquendi
voluntas.  In hoc igitur Adam talis fuit ut mandu-
caret ac biberet, ut accepta digereret, ut laberetur
in somnum et alia quae ei non defuerunt humana
75 quidem sed concessa et quae nullam poenam mortis
inferrent.

Quae omnia habuisse Christum dubium non est ;

third condition is that after sin, in which man needs must be pursued by death and sin and the sinful will. Now the points of extreme divergence between these conditions are the following : that condition which would have been a reward if Adam had chosen to abide in God's laws ; and that which was his punishment because he would not abide in them ; for in the former there would have been no death nor sin nor any will to sin, in the latter there was death and sin and every desire to transgress, and a general tendency to ruin and a condition helpless to render possible a rise after the Fall. But that middle condition from which actual death or sin was absent, but the power for both remained, is situate between the other two.

Each one, then, of these three conditions somehow supplied to Christ a cause for his corporeal nature ; thus his assumption of a mortal body in order to drive death far from the human race belongs properly to that condition which was laid on man by way of punishment after Adam's transgression, whereas the fact that there was in Christ no will to sin is borrowed from that condition which might have been if Adam had not surrendered his will to the frauds of the tempter. There remains, then, the third or middle condition, to wit, that which existed at that time when death had not come and while the will to sin could yet be present. In this condition, therefore, Adam was such that he ate and drank, digested the food he took, fell asleep, and performed all the other functions which always belonged to him as man, though they were allowed and brought with them no penalty of death.

There is no doubt that Christ was in all points

nam et manducavit et bibit et humani corporis officio
functus est. Neque enim tanta indigentia in Adam
80 fuisse credenda est ut nisi manducasset vivere
non potuisset, sed, si ex omni quidem ligno escam
sumeret, semper vivere potuisset hisque non mori ;
idcirco paradisi fructibus indigentiam explebat.
Quam indigentiam fuisse in Christo nullus ignorat,
85 sed potestate non necessitate ; et ipsa indigentia ante
resurrectionem in eo fuit, post resurrectionem vero
talis exstitit ut ita illud corpus inmutaretur humanum,
sicut Adae praeter praevaricationis vinculum mutari
potuisset. Quodque nos ipse dominus Iesus Christus
90 votis docuit optare, ut fiat voluntas eius sicut in caelo
et in terra et ut adveniat eius regnum et nos liberet
a malo. Haec enim omnia illa beatissima humani
generis fideliter credentium inmutatio deprecatur.

Haec sunt quae ad te de fidei meae credulitate
95 scripsi. Qua in re si quid perperam dictum est, non
ita sum amator mei, ut ea quae semel effuderim
meliori sententiae anteferre contendam. Si enim
nihil est ex nobis boni, nihil est quod in nostris
sententiis amare debeamus. Quod si ex illo cuncta
100 sunt bona qui solus est bonus, illud potius bonum
esse credendum est quod illa incommutabilis bonitas
atque omnium bonorum causa perscribit.

---

[a] Adam did not need to eat in order to live, but if he had
not eaten he would have suffered hunger, etc.

thus conditioned ; for he ate and drank and discharged the function of the human body. For we must not think that there was such great need in Adam that unless he had eaten he could not have lived, but, if he had taken food from *every* tree, he would have been able to live for ever and by their fruits not die ; and so by the fruits of Paradise he satisfied a need.[a] And all know that in Christ the same need dwelt, but lying in his own power and not laid upon him. And this need was in him before the Resurrection, but after the Resurrection he was such that his human body was changed as Adam's could have been changed but for the bond of his transgression. Which, moreover, our Lord Jesus Christ himself taught us to desire in our prayers, asking that his will be done as in heaven so on earth, and that his Kingdom come, and that he may deliver us from evil. For that most blessed change of those of mankind who faithfully believe wards off all these things.

So much have I written to you concerning the acceptability of my belief. In which matter if I have said aught amiss, I am not so well pleased with myself as to try to press what I have once blurted out in the face of wiser judgement. For if nothing good comes from us there is nothing we should fancy in our opinions. But if all things are good that come from him who alone is good, that rather must be thought good which that unchangeable good and cause of all things indites.

# ANICII MANLII SEVERINI BOETHII

V.C. ET INL. EXCONS. ORD. EX MAG. OFF. PATRICII

# PHILOSOPHIAE CONSOLA-TIONIS

## LIBER I

### I

Carmina qui quondam studio florente peregi,
    Flebilis heu maestos cogor inire modos.
Ecce mihi lacerae dictant scribenda camenae
    Et veris elegi fletibus ora rigant.
5    Has saltem nullus potuit pervincere terror,
    Ne nostrum comites prosequerentur iter.
Gloria felicis olim viridisque iuventae
    Solantur maesti nunc mea fata senis.
Venit enim properata malis inopina senectus
10    Et dolor aetatem iussit inesse suam.
Intempestivi funduntur vertice cani
    Et tremit effeto corpore laxa cutis.
Mors hominum felix quae se nec dulcibus annis
    Inserit et maestis saepe vocata venit.
15    Eheu quam surda miseros avertitur aure
    Et flentes oculos claudere saeva negat.

BOETHIUS

# THE CONSOLATION OF PHILOSOPHY

## BOOK I

### I

Verses I made once glowing with content ;
Tearful, alas, sad songs must I begin.
See how the Muses grieftorn bid me write,
And with unfeigned tears these elegies drench my face.
But them at least my fear that friends might tread
    my path
Companions still
Could not keep silent : they were once
My green youth's glory ; now in my sad old age
They comfort me.
For age has come unlooked for, hastened by ills,
And anguish sternly adds its years to mine ;
My head is white before its time, my skin hangs loose
About my tremulous frame : I am worn out.
Death, if he come
Not in the years of sweetness
But often called to those who want to end their
    misery
Is welcome.   My cries he does not hear ;
Cruel he will not close my weeping eyes.

131

# BOETHIUS

Dum levibus male fida bonis fortuna faveret,
    Paene caput tristis merserat hora meum.
Nunc quia fallacem mutavit nubila vultum,
20    Protrahit ingratas impia vita moras.
Quid me felicem totiens iactastis amici ?
    Qui cecidit, stabili non erat ille gradu.

## I

Haec dum mecum tacitus ipse reputarem queri-
moniamque lacrimabilem stili officio signarem, ad-
stitisse mihi supra verticem visa est mulier reverendi admodum vultus, oculis ardentibus et ultra
5 communem hominum valentiam perspicacibus colore
vivido atque inexhausti vigoris, quamvis ita aevi
plena foret ut nullo modo nostrae crederetur aetatis,
statura discretionis ambiguae. Nam nunc quidem
ad communem sese hominum mensuram cohibebat,
10 nunc vero pulsare caelum summi verticis cacumine
videbatur ; quae cum altius caput extulisset, ipsum
etiam caelum penetrabat respicientiumque hominum
frustrabatur intuitum. Vestes erant tenuissimis filis
subtili artificio, indissolubili materia perfectae quas,
15 uti post eadem prodente cognovi, suis manibus ipsa
texuerat. Quarum speciem, veluti fumosas imagines
solet, caligo quaedam neglectae vetustatis obduxerat.
Harum in extrema margine ·$\Pi$· Graecum, in supremo
vero ·$\Theta$·, legebatur intextum. Atque inter utrasque
20 litteras in scalarum modum gradus quidam insigniti
videbantur quibus ab inferiore ad superius elementum

---

[a] For the twofold division of Philosophy, into Practical
and Theoretical.

# CONSOLATION I

While fortune favoured me—
How wrong to count on swiftly-fading joys—
Such an hour of bitterness might have bowed my
    head.
Now that her clouded, cheating face is changed
My cursed life drags on its long, unwanted days.
Ah why, my friends,
Why did you boast so often of my happiness ?
How faltering even then the step
Of one now fallen.

## I

While I was thinking these thoughts to myself in
silence, and set my pen to record this tearful complaint, there seemed to stand above my head a
woman. Her look filled me with awe ; her burning
eyes penetrated more deeply than those of ordinary
men ; her complexion was fresh with an ever-lively
bloom, yet she seemed so ancient that none would
think her of our time. It was difficult to say how tall
she might be, for at one time she seemed to confine
herself to the ordinary measure of man, and at
another the crown of her head touched the heavens ;
and when she lifted her head higher yet, she penetrated the heavens themselves, and was lost to the
sight of men. Her dress was made of very fine,
imperishable thread, of delicate workmanship : she
herself wove it, as I learned later, for she told me.
Its form was shrouded by a kind of darkness of forgotten years, like a smoke-blackened family statue
in the atrium. On its lower border was woven the
Greek letter $\Pi$ (P), and on the upper, $\Theta$ (Th),[a] and
between the two letters steps were marked like a
ladder, by which one might climb from the lower

*[handwritten margin note:]* like aThena

133

esset ascensus. Eandem tamen vestem violentorum
quorundam sciderant manus et particulas quas
quisque potuit abstulerant. Et dextera quidem eius
25 libellos, sceptrum vero sinistra gestabat.

Quae ubi poeticas Musas vidit nostro adsistentes
toro fletibusque meis verba dictantes, commota
paulisper ac torvis inflammata luminibus : " Quis,"
inquit, " has scenicas meretriculas ad hunc aegrum
30 permisit accedere quae dolores eius non modo nullis
remediis foverent, verum dulcibus insuper alerent
venenis ? Hae sunt enim quae infructuosis affectuum
spinis uberem fructibus rationis segetem necant homi-
numque mentes assuefaciunt morbo, non liberant.
35 At si quem profanum, uti vulgo solitum vobis, blan-
ditiae vestrae detraherent, minus moleste ferendum
putarem ; nihil quippe in eo nostrae operae laederen-
tur. Hunc vero Eleaticis atque Academicis studiis
innutritum ? Sed abite potius Sirenes usque in
40 exitium dulces meisque eum Musis curandum sanan-
dumque relinquite."

His ille chorus increpitus deiecit humi maestior
vultum confessusque rubore verecundiam limen tristis
excessit. At ego cuius acies lacrimis mersa caligaret
45 nec dinoscere possem, quaenam haec esset mulier
tam imperiosae auctoritatis, obstipui visuque in terram
defixo quidnam deinceps esset actura, exspectare
tacitus coepi. Tum illa propius accedens in extrema

---

ᵃ The Eleatics and the Academics were two ancient schools
of philosophy. That of Elea was founded by Xenophanes in
the mid-sixth century B.C. ; its best known representatives
are the great monist Parmenides and Zeno, the author of the
134

letter to the higher. But violent hands had ripped this dress and torn away what bits they could. In her right hand she carried a book, and in her left, a sceptre.

Now when she saw the Muses of poetry standing by my bed, helping me to find words for my grief, she was disturbed for a moment, and then cried out with fiercely blazing eyes : " Who let these theatrical tarts in with this sick man ? Not only have they no cures for his pain, but with their sweet poison they make it worse. These are they who choke the rich harvest of the fruits of reason with the barren thorns of passion. They accustom a man's mind to his ills, not rid him of them. If your enticements were distracting merely an unlettered man, as they usually do, I should not take it so seriously—after all, it would do no harm to us in our task—but to distract this man, reared on a diet of Eleatic and Academic thought ! [a] Get out, you Sirens, beguiling men straight to their destruction ! Leave him to *my* Muses to care for and restore to health." Thus upbraided, that company of the Muses dejectedly hung their heads, confessing their shame by their blushes, and dismally left my room. I myself, since my sight was so dimmed with tears that I could not clearly see who this woman was of such commanding authority, was struck dumb, my eyes cast down ; and I went on waiting in silence to see what she would do next. Then she came closer and sat on the end of

famous paradoxes concerned with motion. The Academics were the later (3rd and 2nd centuries B.C.) successors of Plato in the Academy in Athens ; theirs was a sceptical philosophy, in some respects not unlike contemporary analytical thought.

lectuli mei parte consedit meumque intuens vultum
50 luctu gravem atque in humum maerore deiectum
his versibus de nostrae mentis perturbatione con-
questa est.

## II

Heu quam praecipiti mersa profundo
Mens hebet et propria luce relicta
Tendit in externas ire tenebras,
Terrenis quotiens flatibus aucta
5 Crescit in inmensum noxia cura.
Hic quondam caelo liber aperto
Suetus in aetherios ire meatus
Cernebat rosei lumina solis,
Visebat gelidae sidera lunae
10 Et quaecumque vagos stella recursus
Exercet varios flexa per orbes,
Comprensam numeris victor habebat.
Quin etiam causas unde sonora
Flamina sollicitent aequora ponti,
15 Quis volvat stabilem spiritus orbem
Vel cur hesperias sidus in undas
Casurum rutilo surgat ab ortu,
Quid veris placidas temperet horas,
Ut terram roseis floribus ornet,
20 Quis dedit ut pleno fertilis anno
Autumnus gravidis influat uvis
Rimari solitus atque latentis
Naturae varias reddere causas,

---

*a* *Numeris* here refers to mathematical astronomy : from
Plato's pupil Eudoxus onwards, Greek astronomers were
concerned to make mathematical " models " (in the modern
philosophical sense) of the movements of the sun, moon and

# CONSOLATION I

my bed, and seeing my face worn with weeping and
cast down with sorrow, she bewailed my mind's
confusion bitterly in these verses :

## II

Ah ! How steep the seas that drown him !
His mind, all dulled, its own light fled,
Moves into outer dark, while noxious care
Swollen by earthbound winds
Grows beyond measure.
             This man
Used once to wander free under open skies
The paths of the heavens ; used to gaze
On rosy sunlight, and on the constellations
Of the cold new moon,
And on each star that on its wandering ways
Turns through its changing circles—all such things
He mastered and bound by number and law.[a]
Causes, moreover, he sought and knew :
Why the winds howl and stir up the waves of the sea,
What breath turns the fixed stars' sphere,
Why the sun rises in the red east
And sinks beneath the Western waves,
What warms the spring's calm hours
So that the earth is lovely with flowers of roses,
And who makes fruitful autumn heavy, as the year
    fills,
With the full grapes.  He sought and told
All Nature's secret causes.

planets—the " wandering stars "— which would enable their
positions and motions to be accurately computed.  Boethius
studied astronomy, and wrote a Latin textbook of the subject,
based on Ptolemy, which has not survived.

137

# BOETHIUS

Nunc iacet effeto lumine mentis
25      Et pressus gravibus colla catenis
Declivemque gerens pondere vultum
Cogitur, heu, stolidam cernere terram.

## II

Sed medicinae," inquit, " tempus est quam querelae." Tum vero totis in me intenta luminibus :
" Tune ille es," ait, " qui nostro quondam lacte
nutritus nostris educatus alimentis in virilis animi
5 robur evaseras ? Atqui talia contuleramus arma
quae nisi prior abiecisses, invicta te firmitate tuerentur. Agnoscisne me ? Quid taces ? Pudore an
stupore siluisti ? Mallem pudore, sed te, ut video,
stupor oppressit." Cumque me non modo tacitum
10 sed elinguem prorsus mutumque vidisset, admovit
pectori meo leniter manum et : " Nihil," inquit,
" pericli est ; lethargum patitur communem inlu-
sarum mentium morbum. Sui paulisper oblitus est ;
recordabitur facile, si quidem nos ante cognoverit.
15 Quod ut possit, paulisper lumina eius mortalium
rerum nube caligantia tergamus." Haec dixit ocu-
losque meos fletibus undantes contracta in rugam
veste siccavit.

## III

Tunc me discussa liquerunt nocte tenebrae
Luminibusque prior rediit vigor,

# CONSOLATION I

But now he lies
His mind's light languishing,
Bowed with these heavy chains about his neck,
His eyes cast down beneath the weight of care,
Seeing nothing
But the dull, solid earth.

## II

" But," she said, " now is the time for cure rather
than complaint." Then, gazing keenly and directly
on me, she said : " Are you the same man who was
once nourished with my milk, once fed on my diet,
till you reached your full manhood ? And did I not
furnish you with such weapons as would now keep
you steadfast and safe if you had not thrown them
away ? Do you recognize me ? Why do you say
nothing ? Were you silent because you were
ashamed or stupefied ? I should like to think that
you were ashamed, but I can see that you are quite
stupefied." Seeing that I was not merely silent, but
altogether speechless and dumb, she gently laid her
hand on my breast and said : " He is in no real
danger, but suffers only from lethargy, a sickness
common to deluded minds. He has for a little forgotten his real self. He will soon recover—he did,
after all, know me before—and to make this possible
for him, let me for a little clear his eyes of the mist
of mortal affairs that clouds them." And so saying
she gathered her dress into a fold and dried my eyes,
flowing as they were with tears.

## III

Then was the night dispersed, and darkness left me;
My eyes grew strong again.

139

Ut, cum praecipiti glomerantur sidera Coro
Nimbosisque polus stetit imbribus,
5    Sol latet ac nondum caelo venientibus astris,
Desuper in terram nox funditur ;
Hanc si Threicio Boreas emissus ab antro
Verberet et clausam reseret diem,
Emicat ac subito vibratus lumine Phoebus
10    Mirantes oculos radiis ferit.

## III

Haud aliter tristitiae nebulis dissolutis hausi
caelum et ad cognoscendam medicantis faciem
mentem recepi. Itaque ubi in eam deduxi oculos
intuitumque defixi, respicio nutricem meam cuius
5 ab adulescentia laribus obversatus fueram Philo-
sophiam. " Et quid," inquam, " tu in has exilii
nostri solitudines o omnium magistra virtutum supero
cardine delapsa venisti ? An ut tu quoque mecum
rea falsis criminationibus agiteris ?
10 " An," inquit illa, " te alumne desererem nec
sarcinam quam mei nominis invidia sustulisti, com-
municato tecum labore partirer ? Atqui Philosophiae
fas non erat incomitatum relinquere iter innocentis ;
meam scilicet criminationem vererer et quasi novum
15 aliquid acciderit, perhorrescerem ? Nunc enim
primum censes apud inprobos mores lacessitam periculis esse sapientiam ? Nonne apud veteres quoque
ante nostri Platonis aetatem magnum saepe certamen
cum stultitiae temeritate certavimus eodemque

---

<sup>a</sup> The cave of Aeolus, the lord of the winds ; " Thracian "
is a poetic adjective for " northern " (as seen from Greece).

140

# CONSOLATION I

Just as when north-west winds pile up the weather
And rain-clouds fill the sky and the sun is hidden,
And before the stars come out
Night comes flooding down upon the world ;
And then the north wind from the Thracian cavern [a]
Sweeps away night and lets the daylight out
So that the sparkling sunlight
Suddenly flashes on our wondering eyes.

## III

Just so the clouds of misery were dispelled, and I
drank in the clear light, recovering enough to recognize my healer's face. So, when I looked on her
clearly and steadily, I saw the nurse who brought
me up, whose house I had from my youth frequented,
the lady Philosophy. And I said : " Why have you
come, Queen of all the virtues, why have you come
down from your high seat in heaven to these wastes
where I am banished ? So that you too stand in the
dock with me, falsely accused ? " " Should I desert
you, my pupil ? " she replied ; " Should I not share
your labour and help to bear your burden, which you
bear because my name is hated ? It could not be
right that Philosophy should leave an innocent man
companionless on the road. Surely I should then be
afraid that I should be charged myself ; I should
shudder with horror at such an unheard-of thing !
Do you think that this is the first time that Wisdom
has been attacked and endangered by a wicked
society ? Did I not often of old also, before my
Plato's time, have to battle in mighty struggle with
arrogant stupidity ? And in his day, was I not beside

141

20 superstite praeceptor eius Socrates iniustae victoriam
mortis me adstante promeruit ? Cuius hereditatem
cum deinceps Epicureum vulgus ac Stoicum ceterique
pro sua quisque parte raptum ire molirentur meque
reclamantem renitentemque velut in partem praedae
25 traherent, vestem quam meis texueram manibus,
disciderunt abreptisque ab ea panniculis totam me
sibi cessisse credentes abiere. In quibus quoniam
quaedam nostri habitus vestigia videbantur, meos
esse familiares inprudentia rata nonnullus eorum
30 profanae multitudinis errore pervertit.

Quod si nec Anaxagorae fugam nec Socratis vene-
num nec Zenonis tormenta quoniam sunt peregrina
novisti, at Canios, at Senecas, at Soranos quorum nec
pervetusta nec incelebris memoria est, scire potuisti.
35 Quos nihil aliud in cladem detraxit nisi quod nostris
moribus instituti studiis improborum dissimillimi
videbantur. Itaque nihil est quod admirere, si in
hoc vitae salo circumflantibus agitemur procellis,
quibus hoc maxime propositum est pessimis displicere.
40 Quorum quidem tametsi est numerosus exercitus,
spernendus tamen est, quoniam nullo duce regitur,
sed errore tantum temere ac passim lymphante
raptatur. Qui si quando contra nos aciem struens
valentior incubuerit, nostra quidem dux copias suas in
45 arcem contrahit, illi vero circa diripiendas inutiles
sarcinulas occupantur. At nos desuper inridemus

---

[a] Anaxagoras of Clazomenae, the Pre-Socratic philosopher,
fled from Athens for fear of persecution in 450 b.c. ; Zeno
of Elea is said to have died helping to rid his native city of a
tyrant in the second half of the fifth century b.c. ; Socrates
was condemned to death in Athens in 399 b.c. ; Canius, or
better, Canus, Seneca and Soranus are quoted as types of the

his teacher Socrates when he won the prize of a martyr's death ? And after him the crowd of Epicureans and Stoics and the rest strove as far as they could to seize his legacy, carrying me off protesting and struggling, as if I were part of the booty, tearing my dress, which I wove with my own hands, and then went off with their torn-off shreds, thinking they possessed all of me. And because they seemed to be wearing certain bits of my dress, some were ignorantly accepted as my servants, and were abused by the delusions of the uneducated mob. But even if you knew nothing of Anaxagoras' flight from Athens, or Socrates' draught of hemlock, or Zeno's sufferings, all these being foreign events, surely you could have thought of Canius and Seneca and Soranus [a] whose stories are neither ancient nor obscure ? The only cause of their deaths was that they were brought up in my ways, so that their behaviour and pursuits were seen to be utterly different from those of wicked men. So it is no wonder if we are buffeted by storms blustering round us on the sea of this life, since we are especially bound to anger the wicked. Though their forces are large, yet we should hold them in contempt, for they are leaderless and are simply carried hither and thither at random in their crazed ignorance. If ever they range against us and press about us too strongly, Wisdom our captain withdraws her forces into her citadel, while our enemies busy themselves ransacking useless baggage. But we are safe from all their mad tumult and from our heights we can laugh at

" Stoic opposition " to the emperors : Canus died under Caligula in about A.D. 40, Seneca and Soranus under Nero in 65 and 66.

vilissima rerum quaeque rapientes securi totius furiosi
tumultus eoque vallo muniti quo grassanti stultitiae
adspirare fas non sit.

## IV

    Quisquis composito serenus aevo
    Fatum sub pedibus egit[1] superbum
    Fortunamque tuens utramque rectus
    Invictum potuit tenere vultum,
5    Non illum rabies minaeque ponti
    Versum funditus exagitantis aestum
    Nec ruptis quotiens vagus caminis
    Torquet fumificos Vesaevus ignes
    Aut celsas soliti ferire turres
10    Ardentis via fulminis movebit.
    Quid tantum miseri saevos tyrannos
    Mirantur sine viribus furentes ?
    Nec speres aliquid nec extimescas,
    Exarmaveris impotentis iram.
15    At quis quis trepidus pavet vel optat,
    Quod non sit stabilis suique iuris,
    Abiecit clipeum locoque motus
    Nectit qua valeat trahi catenam.

## IV

    Sentisne," inquit, " haec atque animo inlabuntur
tuo, an ὄνος λύρας ?   Quid fles, quid lacrimis manas ?

          ʼΕξαύδα, μὴ κεῦθε νόῳ.

5 Si operam medicantis exspectas, oportet vulnus de-
tegas."

---

[1] *Perhaps* iecit ;  *cf. Virg.* Georg. *ii. 491 sq.*

[a] *Iliad*, i. 363.

them as they carry off all those worthless things ;
we are protected by such a wall as may not be scaled
by raging stupidity.

### IV

He who has ground proud fate beneath his heel
Calm in his own well-ordered life
And has looked in the face good and ill fortune
Still able to keep erect his unconquered head,
He shall not be troubled by the rage or threats of the
  sea
Driving the turning tide up from the deep,
Nor by Vesuvius
However often it break from its deep forges
Flinging its smoking fires abroad,
Nor by the blazing thunderbolt
That strikes down lofty towers.
Why are wretched men so stupefied
By cruel tyrants raging with no real power ? *ref. to Theod.²*
Leave hope and fear aside
And anger is impotent, weaponless ;
But he who trembles with fear or desire,
Fickle at heart, nor master of himself, *talking about himself*
Has thrown away his shield, and left his post,
And links the chain by which he can be led.

### IV

 " Now," she said, " have you understood what I
have been saying ?  Has it penetrated your stricken
mind ?  Or are you like an ass hearing the sound of *different tone from former beginning*
a lyre ?  Why do you go on weeping, dissolving in
tears ?  As Homer says, ' Speak out, don't hide it in
your heart.'[a]  If you are looking for a healer's cure,

Tum ego collecto in vires animo : "Anne
adhuc eget admonitione nec per se satis eminet
fortunae in nos saevientis asperitas ? Nihilne te
10 ipsa loci facies movet ? Haecine est bibliotheca,
quam certissimam tibi sedem nostris in laribus ipsa
delegeras ? In qua mecum saepe residens de humanarum divinarumque rerum scientia disserebas ?
Talis habitus talisque vultus erat, cum tecum naturae
15 secreta rimarer, cum mihi siderum vias radio de-
scriberes, cum mores nostros totiusque vitae rationem
ad caelestis ordinis exempla formares ? Haecine
praemia referimus tibi obsequentes ? Atqui tu hanc
sententiam Platonis ore sanxisti : beatas fore res
20 publicas, si eas vel studiosi sapientiae regerent vel
earum rectores studere sapientiae contigisset. Tu
eiusdem viri ore hanc sapientibus capessendae rei
publicae necessariam causam esse monuisti, ne improbis flagitiosisque civibus urbium relicta guber-
25 nacula pestem bonis ac perniciem ferrent.

Hanc igitur auctoritatem secutus quod a te inter
secreta otia didiceram transferre in actum publicae ad-
ministrationis optavi. Tu mihi et qui te sapientium
mentibus inseruit deus conscii nullum me ad magis-
30 tratum nisi commune bonorum omnium studium
detulisse. Inde cum inprobis graves inexorabilesque
discordiae et quod conscientiae libertas habet, pro
tuendo iure spreta potentiorum semper offensio.

---

[a] *Republic*, 473 D.

you must lay bare the wound." So I gathered my strength of mind and said : " Do you really still need to ask ? Is my harsh treatment at fortune's hands not obvious enough ? Are you not affected by the very appearance of this room ? Do you not recognize the library, which you once chose for yourself as a secure dwelling-place in my house—the very room in which you used often to sit with me discoursing on the knowledge of all things human and divine ? Was this how I looked, was this my expression, when I used to seek out with you the secrets of Nature ? When with your rod you drew for me the paths of the stars ? When you shaped my character and the whole manner of my life according to celestial models ? Are these our rewards for obedient service to you ? It was you who established through the words of Plato the principle that those states would be happy where philosophers were kings or their governors were philosophers.[a] You, through that same Plato, told us that this was why philosophers must involve themselves in political affairs, lest the rule of nations be left to the base and wicked, bringing ruin and destruction on the good. It was in accordance with that teaching that I chose to apply in the practice of public administration what I learned from you In the seclusion of my private leisure. You, and God, who has set you in the minds of philosophers, know me well, and that I undertook office with no other motives than the common purposes of all good men. That is why there arose serious and irreconcilable disagreements with wicked men, and, as a consequence of keeping my conscience free, I have always maintained what is right and lawful in spite of the fact that I offended those more powerful than myself.

Quotiens ego Conigastum in inbecilli cuiusque
35 fortunas impetum facientem obvius excepi, quotiens
Trigguillam regiae praepositum domus ab incepta,
perpetrata iam prorsus iniuria deieci, quotiens
miseros quos infinitis calumniis inpunita barbarorum
semper avaritia vexabat, obiecta periculis auctoritate
40 protexi ! Numquam me ab iure ad iniuriam quisquam
detraxit. Provincialium fortunas tum privatis rapinis
tum publicis vectigalibus pessumdari non aliter
quam qui patiebantur indolui.

Cum acerbae famis tempore gravis atque inexplica-
45 bilis indicta coemptio profligatura inopia Campaniam
provinciam videretur, certamen adversum praefectum
praetorii communis commodi ratione suscepi, rege
cognoscente contendi et ne coemptio exigeretur,
evici. Paulinum consularem virum cuius opes Pala-
50 tinae canes iam spe atque ambitione devorassent, ab
ipsis hiantium faucibus traxi. Ne Albinum consularem
virum praeiudicatae accusationis poena corriperet,
odiis me Cypriani delatoris opposui. Satisne in me
magnas videor exacervasse discordias ? Sed esse apud
55 ceteros tutior debui qui mihi amore iustitiae nihil

---

*a* Nothing more is known of Trigguilla or of Conigastus,
who was the addressee of a letter from Cassiodorus, Boethius's successor as Master of the Offices to Theodoric,
the Ostrogothic king of Italy, 493–526 ( *Var.* viii. 28).

*b* *Coemptio* was a means by which supplies for troops, over
and above those provided for out of normal taxation, might
be obtained by compulsory purchase ; under later emperors
it was strictly limited by law except in the province of Thrace,
where taxation yielded insufficient revenue. It was clearly
open to abuse in the hands of unscrupulous administrators,

## CONSOLATION I

*as he goes on, he becomes more & more human*

How often did I stand in the way of Conigastus when he was trying to rob some weaker man of his wealth! How often did I frustrate Trigguilla, the Provost of the Royal Household, in committing some injustice—or even when he had actually committed it![a] How often did I protect poor wretches harassed with countless malicious charges by the constant and unchecked avarice of barbarians, though the exercise of my authority involved me in great dangers. No-one has ever turned me aside from the right, to commit injustice. That the fortunes of provincial families were ruined both by robbery by individuals and by taxation by the state grieved me no less than it did those who suffered so. When in a time of grievous famine it seemed there was to be by order a terrible and quite indefensible compulsory purchase of supplies which would have reduced the province of Campania to destitution, I took up the fight with the Praetorian Prefect for the sake of the common good, I fought against the enforcement of the purchase before the king, and I won.[b] The wealth of Paulinus, a man of consular rank, which had already in their ambitious hope been all but devoured by those dogs of the court, I snatched even from their gaping jaws. To prevent Albinus, another man of consular rank, being punished for a crime of *B. as a man* which he was found guilty before being tried, I made an enemy of his accuser Cyprian. Ought I not to have been satisfied with the amount of strong feeling I stirred up against myself? But surely I ought to have been that much the more safe with the others, since in my regard for justice I kept no favours

and the object here was to buy food cheaply and sell it back at an inflated price.

149

apud aulicos quo magis essem tutior reservavi.
Quibus autem deferentibus perculsi sumus ? Quorum
Basilius olim regio ministerio depulsus in delationem
nostri nominis alieni aeris necessitate compulsus est.
60 Opilionem vero atque Gaudentium cum ob innumeras
multiplicesque fraudes ire in exilium regia censura
decrevisset cumque illi parere nolentes sacrarum sese
aedium defensione tuerentur compertumque id regi
foret, edixit : uti ni intra praescriptum diem Ravenna
65 urbe decederent, notas insigniti frontibus pellerentur.
Quid huic severitati posse astrui videtur ? Atqui in
eo die deferentibus eisdem nominis nostri delatio
suscepta est. Quid igitur ? Nostraene artes ita meruerunt ? An illos accusatores iustos fecit praemissa
70 damnatio ? Itane nihil fortunam puduit si minus
accusatae innocentiae, at accusantium vilitatis ?[1] At
cuius criminis arguimur summam quaeris ? Senatum
dicimur salvum esse voluisse. Modum desideras ?
Delatorem ne documenta deferret quibus senatum
75 maiestatis reum faceret impedisse criminamur.

Quid igitur o magistra censes ? Infitiabimur
crimen, ne tibi pudor simus ? At volui nec umquam
velle desistam. Fatebimur ? Sed impediendi delatoris opera cessavit. An optasse illius ordinis salutem
80 nefas vocabo ? Ille quidem suis de me decretis, uti
hoc nefas esset, effecerat. Sed sibi semper mentiens
inprudentia rerum merita non potest inmutare nec

[1] vilitatis *Glareanus* ; vilitas MSS.

---

[a] He was no doubt offered a remission of his debts as a
bribe.

among the courtiers to ensure my own safety. Who are the accusers, then, by whom I have been brought down ? One of them, Basil, once in the king's service but dismissed, was forced to denounce me because of his burden of debts.[a] Two others were Opilio and Gaudentius : on account of their many different frauds they were condemned to exile by the king's judgement, but they refused to obey and took sanctuary in a temple. When the king learned of this he ordered that unless they left Ravenna by a certain date they should be branded on the forehead and driven out. Could they possibly have been more severely treated ? And yet on that very date the accusation against me was lodged, with their names on it ! I ask you ! Was that the reward my exercise of office had earned ? Did their previous conviction make them just accusers ? Was fortune not the least bit ashamed, if not that innocence was thus accused, at least that the accusers were so base ?

Do you want to know what, in a word, was the charge against me ? That I wanted to preserve the Senate. And how did I do that ? I am charged with preventing those accusers from bringing forward proofs whereby the Senate might have been convicted of treason. What then do you think, Lady ? Shall I deny the charge, so as not to cause you to be ashamed of me ? But I did want the Senate to be preserved, nor shall I ever cease to want it so. Shall I then confess to the charge ? But the chance of hindering their accuser has now passed. Shall I call it wrong to have wanted the preservation of the Senatorial order ? That order had itself made it wrong, by its decrees against me. But self-deceiving ignorance cannot change the true worth of anything,

151

mihi Socratico decreto fas esse arbitror vel occuluisse
veritatem vel concessisse mendacium. Verum id
85 quoquo modo sit, tuo sapientiumque iudicio aestimandum relinquo. Cuius rei seriem atque veritatem,
ne latere posteros queat, stilo etiam memoriaeque
mandavi.

Nam de compositis falso litteris quibus libertatem
90 arguor sperasse Romanam quid attinet dicere ?
Quarum fraus aperta patuisset, si nobis ipsorum con-
fessione delatorum, quod in omnibus negotiis maximas
vires habet, uti licuisset. Nam quae sperari reliqua
libertas potest ? Atque utinam posset ulla ! Re-
95 spondissem Canii verbo, qui cum a Gaio Caesare
Germanici filio conscius contra se factae coniurationis
fuisse diceretur : ' Si ego,' inquit, ' scissem, tu ne-
scisses.' Qua in re non ita sensus nostros maeror
hebetavit ut impios scelerata contra virtutem querar
100 molitos, sed quae speraverint effecisse vehementer
admiror. Nam deteriora velle nostri fuerit fortasse
defectus, posse contra innocentiam, quae sceleratus
quisque conceperit inspectante deo, monstri simile
est. Unde haud iniuria tuorum quidam familiarum
105 quaesivit : ' Si quidem deus,' inquit, ' est, unde
mala ? Bona vero unde, si non est ? ' Sed fas fuerit

---

[a] *Cf.* Plato, *Republic*, 485 and *Theaetetus*, 151 D.
[b] The authorship of this dilemma is unknown. Editors
have generally referred to Epicurus fr. 374, *ex* Lactantius,

nor do I think it would have been right for me, following Socrates' counsel,[a] to conceal the truth or admit to falsehood. But what the truth of the matter is, I leave to your judgement and to that of philosophers ; though so that the true details of this affair cannot lie concealed from later generations, I have written it down to be remembered. For what is the point of talking about those forgeries in which I am accused of having striven for Roman liberty ? Their falsity would have been evident for all to see, had I been allowed to use the confessions of my accusers themselves, for this always has most influence in all such matters as these. What freedom can now be hoped for ? Would there were any ! Then I should have replied with the words of Canius : when he was said by Caligula to have been aware of a conspiracy against his person, he replied : ' Had I known of it, you would not.' In this affair, grief has not so far blunted my sense that I complain that wicked men have tried to do evil to virtue, but rather I am amazed that they have succeeded in their hopes. For although it is perhaps a normal human failing to have evil desires, it is surely a monstrous thing in the sight of God that whatever an evil man conceives can actually be done to the innocent. So it was not without reason that one of your disciples asked : ' If there is a God, whence comes evil ? But whence good, if there is not ? '[b] It would be natural that

*De ira dei*, 13, 21 ; but that is a different problem (either God can prevent evil, and will not, or will, but cannot), and this one is surely not Epicurean. Its origins can be found in Plato (*cf*. *Republic*, 379, and *Schol. in Remp*. 379a : τύπος θεολογικὸς ὅτι πάντων ἀγαθῶν ὁ θεὸς αἴτιος, τῶν κακῶν δ' οὐδενός). It is probably from some Neo-platonist commentator, possibly Ammonius.

nefarios homines qui bonorum omnium totiusque
senatus sanguinem petunt, nos etiam quos propugnare
bonis senatuique viderant, perditum ire voluisse.
110 Sed num idem de patribus quoque merebamur?
Meministi, ut opinor, quoniam me dicturum quid
facturumve praesens semper ipsa dirigebas, meministi
inquam, Veronae cum rex avidus exitii communis
maiestatis crimen in Albinum delatae ad cunctum
115 senatus ordinem transferre moliretur, universi innocentiam senatus quanta mei periculi securitate de-
fenderim. Scis me haec et vera proferre et in nulla
umquam mei laude iactasse. Minuit enim quodam
modo se probantis conscientiae secretum, quotiens
120 ostentando quid factum recipit famae pretium. Sed
innocentiam nostram quis exceperit eventus vides;
pro verae virtutis praemiis falsi sceleris poenas
subimus. Et cuius umquam facinoris manifesta
confessio ita iudices habuit in severitate concordes ut
125 non aliquos vel ipse ingenii error humani vel fortunae
condicio cunctis mortalibus incerta submitteret? Si
inflammare sacras aedes voluisse, si sacerdotes impio
iugulare gladio, si bonis omnibus necem struxisse
diceremur, praesentem tamen sententia, confessum
130 tamen convictumve punisset. Nunc quingentis fere
passuum milibus procul muti atque indefensi ob
studium propensius in senatum morti proscriptionique
damnamur. O meritos de simili crimine neminem
posse convinci!

---

[a] Theodoric the Ostrogoth; see p. 148.

# CONSOLATION I

wicked men who wanted the blood of all good men
and of the whole Senate should want to destroy me
also, whom they saw fighting for good men and the
Senate. But surely I deserved differently from the
Senators themselves ? You remember, I expect,
since you yourself were with me directing all my
words and actions, how when the king<sup>a</sup> at Verona
tried to shift on to the whole Senatorial order the
charge of treason laid against Albinus, since he was
eager to do away with them all, I defended the innocence of the whole Senate with complete disregard
for my own peril. You know that I mention this
simply as the truth, not because I ever wished to sing
my own praises ; for the secret, mental satisfaction
of self approval is in some way lessened if a man by
revealing the deed reaps the reward of its being
talked about by others. But you see what the result
of my innocence has been : instead of being rewarded
for the good I did, I am punished for the evil I did
not do. Was there even any crime the clear admis-
sion of which made the judges so unanimously severe
that none was moved to moderation either by the
fallibility of man's mind or by that uncertainty of
fortune common to all mortals ? If I were accused
of trying to burn down a temple or of sacrilegiously
murdering priests, or of contriving the deaths of all
good men, I should be punished, and rightly—but
only having been present and tried, and either having
confessed or been found guilty. But now I am condemned to death, my goods confiscate, for too zeal-
ously supporting the Senate, although I am nearly
five hundred miles away and unable to speak in my
own defence. Ah me ! Surely I deserved that no one
could possibly be convicted on a charge like this !

155

135　Cuius dignitatem reatus ipsi etiam qui detulere
viderunt, quam uti alicuius sceleris admixtione
fuscarent, ob ambitum dignitatis sacrilegio me conscientiam polluisse mentiti sunt. Atqui et tu insita
nobis omnem rerum mortalium cupidinem de nostri
140　animi sede pellebas et sub tuis oculis sacrilegio locum
esse fas non erat. Instillabas enim auribus cogita-
tionibusque cotidie meis Pythagoricum illud ἕπου
θεῷ.[1] Nec conveniebat vilissimorum me spirituum
praesidia captare quem tu in hanc excellentiam com-
145　ponebas ut consimilem deo faceres. Praeterea
penetral innocens domus, honestissimorum coctus
amicorum, socer etiam sanctus et aeque ac tu ipsa[2]
reverendus ab omni nos huius criminis suspitione de-
fendunt. Sed, o nefas, illi vero de te tanti criminis
150　fidem capiunt atque hoc ipso videbimur affines fuisse
maleficio, quod tuis inbuti disciplinis, tuis instituti
moribus sumus. Ita non est satis nihil mihi tuam
profuisse reverentiam, nisi ultro tu mea potius offen-
sione lacereris. At vero hic etiam nostris malis
155　cumulus accedit, quod existimatio plurimorum non
rerum merita sed fortunae spectat eventum eaque
tantum iudicat esse provisa quae felicitas com-
mendaverit. Quo fit ut existimatio bona prima
omnium deserat infelices. Qui nunc populi rumores,
160　quam dissonae multiplicesque sententiae, piget
reminisci. Hoc tantum dixerim ultimam esse ad-
versae fortunae sarcinam, quod dum miseris aliquod

---

[1] θεόν MSS.
[2] ipsa Sitzmannus : ipso MSS.

---

[a] Not strictly a Pythagorean saying, but one of the
" ancient precepts " (vetera praecepta) of the Greeks, like
" Know thyself," taken in by many philosophical schools ;
cf. Cicero, De finibus, iii. 73.

# CONSOLATION I

Those who laid the charge know well its true worth. In order to smirch it with the stain of some foul deed, they lyingly alleged that I sullied my conscience in committing sacrilege in canvassing for high office. But you, Lady, dwelling in me, drove from my soul's depths all desire for mortal things, and to have made any room for sacrilege under your very eyes would have been wicked indeed, for daily you instilled into my ears and my mind the Pythagorean saying, ' Follow God ' [b] Now would it have been fitting for me to grasp for the support of baser spirits, since you were preparing me for such excellence, that you might make me like to God. Besides, the fact that my house hides no guilty secrets deep within, my friendship with good men, and the uprightness of my father-in-law— for he is as much to be revered as you yourself—all these protect me against any suspicion of this crime. But *they* are so wickedly impious that it is actually from you that they derive their proof of this great charge : I shall appear to have been a close party to such a misdeed precisely because I am steeped in your learning and trained in your ways. So it is not enough that reverence for you shall have done me no good : you too must be abused because I have offended. And now, to add to all my troubles, I know that common opinion looks not at the true deserts of any case but regards only the outcome of fortune, and judges only such things well foreseen as success commends. The result is that their good reputation is the first thing the unfortunate lose. I hate to think what tales are going round among the people, how many different opinions, about my case. This only I would say, that the final burden imposed by adverse fortune is that while any poor wretch is

157

crimen affingitur, quae perferunt meruisse creduntur.
Et ego quidem bonis omnibus pulsus, dignitatibus
165 exutus, existimatione foedatus ob beneficium supplicium tuli.

Videre autem videor nefarias sceleratorum officinas
gaudio laetitiaque fluitantes, perditissimum quemque
novis delationum fraudibus imminentem, iacere bonos
170 nostri discriminis terrore prostratos, flagitiosum quemque ad audendum quidem facinus impunitate, ad
efficiendum vero praemiis incitari, insontes autem
non modo securitate, verum ipsa etiam defensione
privatos. Itaque libet exclamare :

## V

O stelliferi cònditor orbis
Qui perpetuo nixus solio
Rapido caelum turbine versas
Legemque pati sidera cogis,
5 Ut nunc pleno lucida cornu
Totis fratris obvia flammis
Condat stellas luna minores,
Nunc obscuro pallida cornu
Phoebo propior lumina perdat,
10 Et qui primae tempore noctis
Agit algentes Hesperos ortus,
Solitas iterum mutet habenas
Phoebi pallens Lucifer ortu.
Tu frondifluae frigore brumae
15 Stringis lucem breviore mora :
Tu, cum fervida venerit aestas,
Agiles nocti dividis horas.
Tua vis varium temperat annum
Ut quas Boreae spiritus aufert

charged with some crime, he is thought to deserve all that he suffers. So I now, deprived of all my goods, stripped of my honours, and the object of evil gossip, am punished for my good service. And I seem to see the wicked in their factories of crime wallowing in their evil delight, all the corrupt now plotting new false accusations, while good men cower in fear, terrified by what has happened to me. The base and wicked are encouraged to greater boldness by their impunity, to greater crimes by their rewards ; and the innocent are deprived not only of safety but even of the chance to defend themselves. So I am moved to exclaim :

## V

O Maker of the circle of the stars,
Seated on your eternal throne,
Spinner of the whirling heavens,
Binding the constellations by your law—
As at one time the shining moon with crescent full,
Reflecting all the sun her brother's fire.
Hides all the lesser stars,
And at another closer to Phoebus pales
And loses all her light, her crescent dark ;
Or when, at fall of night,
Venus, as evening star, arises cold,
And then, as morning star, paling at sunrise,
Changes again her long-accustomed role ;—
You with the winter's cold when leaves pour down
Draw in the short day's light ;
You when the summer comes aflame
Hasten the passing of the night's swift hours.
The changing year is ordered by your power,
So that the leaves the north wind strips away

159

20      Revehat mites Zephyrus frondes
        Quaeque Arcturus semina vidit
        Sirius altas urat segetes.
        Nihil antiqua lege solutum
        Linquit propriae stationis opus.
25      Omnia certo fine gubernans
        Hominum solos respuis actus
        Merito rector cohibere modo.
        Nam cur tantas lubrica versat
        Fortuna vices ?   Premit insontes
30      Debita sceleri noxia poena,
        At perversi resident celso
        Mores solio sanctaque calcant
        Iniusta vice colla nocentes.
        Latet obscuris condita virtus
35      Clara tenebris iustusque tulit
        Crimen iniqui.
        Nil periuria, nil nocet ipsis
        Fraus mendaci compta colore.
        Sed cum libuit viribus uti,
40      Quos innumeri metuunt populi
        Summos gaudent subdere reges.
        O iam miseras respice terras
        Quisquis rerum foedera nectis.
        Operis tanti pars non vilis
45      Homines quatimur fortunae salo.
        Rapidos rector comprime fluctus
        Et quo caelum regis immensum
        Firma stabiles foedere terras."

## V

    Haec ubi continuato dolore delatravi, illa vultu placido nihilque meis questibus mota :   " Cum te,"

# CONSOLATION I

The west wind brings again in gentleness,
And what Arcturus saw as sleeping seed
As tall crops under Sirius burn dry.
Nothing escapes your ancient ordering
Or fails its proper office to fulfil.
With a sure purpose ruling and guiding all,
Man's acts alone
You will not, though you rightly could, constrain.
Why else does slippery fortune change so much?
The innocent endure the pains
That are the proper penalties of crime,
And evil ways sit in the thrones of kings,
And wicked men in unjust recompense
Trample beneath their heels the necks of the good.
Virtue's clear brightness lies obscured
In darkness hidden, and the just man bears
The unjust's calumnies.
Their perjuries hurt them not, nor their deceit,
Decked in false colours ;
And when they please to use their power,
Then they delight to overcome great kings
Whom countless peoples fear.
Look on this wretched earth,
Whoever you are who bind the world with law !
Of that great work far from the meanest part
We men are buffeted by fortune's seas.
Ruler, restrain their rushing waves and make the earth
Steady with that stability of law
By which you rule the vastness of the heavens.

## V

When I had done thus baying my unabated grief,
she said, with a calm expression, unaffected by my

inquit, "maestum lacrimantemque vidissem, ilico
miserum exsulemque cognovi. Sed quam id longin-
5 quum esset exilium, nisi tua prodidisset oratio, nescie-
bam. Sed tu quam procul a patria non quidem
pulsus es sed aberrasti ; ac si te pulsum existimari
mavis, te potius ipse pepulisti. Nam id quidem de
te numquam cuiquam fas fuisset. Si enim cuius
10 oriundus sis patriae reminiscare, non uti Atheniensium
quondam multitudinis imperio regitur, sed

εἷς κοίρανός ἐστιν, εἷς βασιλεύς

qui frequentia civium non depulsione laetetur ; cuius
agi frenis atque obtemperare iustitiae summa libertas
15 est. An ignoras illam tuae civitatis antiquissimam
legem, qua sanctum est ei ius exulare non esse quisquis in ea sedem fundare maluerit ? Nam qui vallo
eius ac munimine continetur, nullus metus est ne
exul esse mereatur. At quisquis eam inhabitare velle
20 desierit, pariter desinit etiam mereri. Itaque non
tam me loci huius quam tua facies movet nec biblio-
thecae potius comptos ebore ac vitro parietes quam
tuae mentis sedem requiro, in qua non libros sed id
quod libris pretium facit, librorum quondam meorum
25 sententias, collocavi. Et tu quidém de tuis in commune bonum meritis vera quidem, sed pro multitudine
gestorum tibi pauca dixisti. De obiectorum tibi vel
honestate vel falsitate cunctis nota memorasti. De
sceleribus fraudibusque delatorum recte tu quidem
30 strictim attingendum putasti, quod ea melius uberius-

---

complainings : " When I saw you weeping in your grief I knew at once that you were wretchedly banished ; but how remote was that banishment I should not have known if your speech had not told me. But how far from your homeland have you strayed ! Strayed, not been driven, I say ; or if you prefer to be thought of as driven, then how far have you driven yourself ! For in your case it could never have rightly been possible for anyone else to do this. You must remember what your native country is : not one like that of the old Athenians, governed by the rule of the many, but " there is one ruler, one king," [a] who delights in associating with his subjects, not in driving them out ; to be guided by his hand and obey his justice is true freedom. Surely you know the ancient and fundamental law of your city, by which it is ordained that it is not right to exile one who has chosen to dwell there ? No one who is settled within her walls and fortifications need ever fear the punishment of banishment : but whoever ceases to desire to live there has thereby ceased to deserve to do so. So I am moved more by the sight of you than of this place. I seek not so much a library with its walls ornamented with ivory and glass, as the storeroom of your mind, in which I have laid up not books, but what makes them of any value, the opinions set down in my books in times past. Now what *you* have said about your services to the common good is true, though you have mentioned but few of the great number of things you have done. The state of honesty, or rather the well-known dishonesty of the accusations against you, you have spoken of. You were of course right to think that you only needed to touch briefly on your accusers' crimes and deceits,

que recognoscentis omnia vulgi ore celebrentur.
Increpuisti etiam vehementer iniusti factum senatus.
De nostra etiam criminatione doluisti, laesae quoque
opinionis damna flevisti. Postremus adversum fortu-
35 nam dolor incanduit conquestusque non aequa meritis
praemia pensari, in extremo Musae saevientis, uti
quae caelum terras quoque pax regeret, vota posuisti.
Sed quoniam plurimus tibi affectuum tumultus incubuit diversumque te dolor, ira, maeror distrahunt,
40 uti nunc mentis es, nondum te validiora remedia contingunt. Itaque lenioribus paulisper utemur, ut
quae in tumorem perturbationibus influentibus in-
duruerunt, ad acrioris vim medicaminis recipiendum
tactu blandiore mollescant.

## VI

Cum Phoebi radiis grave
Cancri sidus inaestuat,
Tum qui larga negantibus
Sulcis semina credidit,
5      Elusus Cereris fide
Quernas pergat ad arbores.
Numquam purpureum nemus
Lecturus violas petas
Cum saevis aquilonibus
10      Stridens campus inhorruit,
Nec quaeras avida manu
Vernos stringere palmites,
Uvis si libeat frui ;

164

since they are all common topics of gossip among
ordinary people who recall them better and in fuller
detail. You have been more forceful in complaining
of the unjust actions of the Senate. And you have
bewailed the fact that I too am included under the
charge, you have wept for the harm done to my
reputation. In the end your grief flared against your
ill fortune, and complaining that your rewards were
not equal to your deserts you prayed at the end of
your outpourings in verse that that peace which
governs heaven might also govern earth. But since
you are buffeted by a tumult of different emotions,
and grief and anger and sorrow pull you in different
directions, for that is the state you are in, you are not
yet ready for strong medicines, so we shall for a little
use milder ones, so that by our gentler touch what
has swollen hard under the influence of all these
passions and worries may soften and become fit to be
treated with a sharper, stronger physic.

## VI

When heavy Cancer burns
Under the rays of the sun,
He who then sows his seed
In unreceiving furrows
Must, cheated of grain, go look
For acorns under oak trees.
Never would you seek in reddening woods
To gather violets,
When grasses shake their rustling spears
Under the fierce north winds.
Nor if you want full grapes would you greedily seek
To prune the vine in spring :

Autumno potius sua
15       Bacchus munera contulit.
Signat tempora propriis
Aptans officiis deus
Nec quas ipse coercuit
Misceri patitur vices.
20       Sic quod praecipiti via
Certum deserit ordinem
Laetos non habet exitus.

## VI

Primum igitur paterisne me pauculis rogatio-
nibus statum tuae mentis attingere atque temptare,
ut qui modus sit tuae curationis intellegam ? ”  “ Tu
vero arbitratu,” inquam, “ tuo quae voles ut respon-
5 surum rogato.”  Tum illa :  “ Huncine,” inquit,
“ mundum temerariis agi fortuitisque casibus putas,
an ullum credis ei regimen inesse rationis ? ”  “ Atqui,” inquam, “ nullo existimaverim modo ut fortuita
temeritate tam certa moveantur, verum operi suo
10 conditorem praesidere deum scio nec umquam fuerit
dies qui me ab hac sententiae veritate depellat.”

“ Ita est,” inquit.  “ Nam id etiam paulo ante ceci-
nisti, hominesque tantum divinae exsortes curae esse
deplorasti.  Nam de ceteris quin ratione regerentur,
15 nihil movebare.  Papae autem !  Vehementer admiror
cur in tam salubri sententia locatus aegrotes.  Verum
altius perscrutemur;  nescio quid abesse coniecto.

Sed dic mihi, quoniam ⟨a⟩ deo mundum regi non
**166**

## CONSOLATION I

Bacchus confers his gifts
In autumn rather.
God marks out the seasons
Each for its proper duty ;
Nor does he suffer the order he has fixed
To be disturbed.
So, whatever deserts that order
Rushing headlong
Comes to no happy ending.

## VI

" Now first of all, will you let me ask a few simple
questions, to probe and test the state of your mind,
so as to learn what kind of cure is best for your condition ? " " Ask what you will, as you think right,"
I replied, " and I will answer." " Do you think,
then," she said, " that this world is run by random
and chance events, or do you believe that it is
rationally directed ? " " Well, I could never imagine," I replied, " that anything so regular was
moved at random or by chance ; I know that God the
creator watches over and directs his work, nor could
there ever be such a time as would deprive me of the
certainty of that truth." " Good," she said. " That
is just what you spoke of a little time ago in your
verse, when you complained that man alone fell
outside the sphere of God's watchful care, for you
were sure enough that all the rest was governed by
reason. But I am really astonished that you should
sicken, holding as you do such a healthy opinion !
But, let us look into this more deeply ; something is
missing, I think. Now tell me, since you are not in
any doubt that the world is guided by God, do you

167

ambigis, quibus etiam gubernaculis regatur advertis ?
20 " Vix," inquam, " rogationis tuae sententiam nosco,
nedum ad inquisita respondere queam." " Num
me," inquit, " fefellit abesse aliquid, per quod, velut
hiante valli robore, in animum tuum perturbationum
morbus inrepserit ?  Sed dic mihi, meministine, quis
25 sit rerum finis, quove totius naturae tendat intentio? "
" Audieram," inquam, " sed memoriam maeror hebetavit."  " Atqui scis unde cuncta processerint ? "
" Novi," inquam, deumque esse respondi.  " Et qui
fieri potest, ut principio cognito quis sit rerum finis
30 ignores ?  Verum hi perturbationum mores, ea valentia est, ut movere quidem loco hominem possint, con-
vellere autem sibique totum exstirpare non possint.

Sed hoc quoque respondeas velim, hominemne te
esse meministi? " " Quidni," inquam, " meminerim ? "
35 " Quid igitur homo sit, poterisne proferre ? " " Hocine
interrogas an esse me sciam rationale animal atque
mortale ?  Scio et id me esse confiteor."  Et illa :
" Nihilne aliud te esse novisti ? "  " Nihil."

" Iam scio," inquit, " morbi tui aliam vel maximam
40 causam ; quid ipse sis, nosse desisti. Quare plenissime
vel aegritudinis tuae rationem vel aditum reconci-
liandae sospitatis inveni.  Nam quoniam tui oblivione
confunderis, et exsulem te et exspoliatum propriis
bonis esse doluisti.  Quoniam vero quis sit rerum finis
168

perceive what kind of governance it is guided by ? "
" I can scarcely understand your meaning," I said,
" much less answer the question." " I was not mistaken, was I, when I said that something was missing,
leaving as it were a crack in a strong wall, through
which the sickness of your troubles stole into your
mind ? But tell me, do you remember what is the
end of all things, towards what purpose does the
whole universe aim and move ? "

" I heard it once," I said, " but pain and grief have
weakened my memory."

" But at least you know where all things have
come from ? "

" Yes ; " and I said they came from God.

" Then since you know their origin, how can you
not know their end ? The nature and strength of
these troubles is such that they can dislodge a man,
but they cannot tear him out and completely uproot
him. Now I should like you to answer this : you
are aware that you are a man ? "

" How could I not be ? "

" Then can you say, what is a man ? "

" Are you asking me if I know that I am a mortal,
rational animal ? I do know that, and admit to being
such."

" And you do not know that you are anything
more ? "

" I am nothing more."

" Now I know," she said, " that other, more serious
cause of your sickness : you have forgotten what you
are. So I really understand why you are ill and how
to cure you. For because you are wandering, forgetful of your real self, you grieve that you are an exile
and stripped of your goods ; since indeed you do not

45 ignoras, nequam homines atque nefarios potentes
felicesque arbitraris. Quoniam vero quibus gubernaculis mundus regatur oblitus es, has fortunarum vices
aestimas sine rectore fluitare—magnae non ad morbum
modo verum ad interitum quoque causae. Sed sospi-
50 tatis auctori grates, quod te nondum totum natura
destituit. Habemus maximum tuae fomitem salutis
veram de mundi gubernatione sententiam, quod eam
non casuum temeritati sed divinae rationi subditam
credis. Nihil igitur pertimescas ; iam tibi ex hac
55 minima scintillula vitalis calor inluxerit. Sed quoniam
firmioribus remediis nondum tempus est et eam mentium constat esse naturam, ut quotiens abiecerint
veras falsis opinionibus induantur ex quibus orta perturbationum caligo verum illum confundit intuitum,
60 hanc paulisper lenibus mediocribusque fomentis at-
tenuare temptabo, ut dimotis fallacium affectionum
tenebris splendorem verae lucis possis agnoscere.

## VII

Nubibus atris
Condita nullum
Fundere possunt
Sidera lumen.
5 Si mare volvens
Turbidus Auster
Misceat aestum,
Vitrea dudum
Parque serenis
10 Unda diebus
Mox resoluto
Sordida caeno
Visibus obstat.

know the goal and end of all things, you think that
evil and wicked men are fortunate and powerful;
since indeed you have forgotten what sort of governance the world is guided by, you think these
fluctuations of fortune uncontrolled. All these are
quite enough to cause not merely sickness but even
death. But I thank the author of all health that you
have not yet wholly lost your true nature. The best
kindler of your health we have is your true opinion
of the governance of the world, that you believe it to
be subject not to the randomness of chance events
but to divine reason; do not be afraid, then, for
presently out of this tiny spark your vital warmth
will glow again. But it is not yet time for strong
medicines. Men's minds are obviously such that
when they lose true opinions they have to take up
false ones, and then a fog arises from these false
ideas, which obscures that true vision. So I shall try
for a while with gentle and moderate applications to
lessen that fog, so that when the darkness of those
deceptive ideas is removed, you may be able to
recognize the glory of the light of truth.

### VII

*abmt storm*

Stars in the dark clouds hid
Can give no light.
When the south wind's storm
Stirs up the rolling breakers of the sea,
The wave once glass-clear, calm
As settled days,
Now muddied with the stirred-up bottom
    sand
Obscures our sight.

Quique vagatur
15    Montibus altis
Defluus amnis,
Saepe resistit
Rupe soluti
Obice saxi.
20    Tu quoque si vis
Lumine claro
Cernere verum,
Tramite recto
Carpere callem,
25    Gaudia pelle,
Pelle timorem
Spemque fugato
Nec dolor adsit.
Nubila mens est
30    Vinctaque frenis,
Haec ubi regnant.''

# CONSOLATION I

A river wandering down the hills

Can be dammed and stopped by fallen rock

From the high crags.

You too, if you want

Clearly to see the truth

And to walk the right road straight,

Cast out joy,

Cast out fear,

Rid yourself of hope and grief.

The mind is clouded, checked,

Where these hold sway.

# ANICII MANLII SEVERINI BOETHII

## V.C. ET INL. EXCONS. ORD. PATRICII

# PHILOSOPHIAE CONSOLA-
# TIONIS

## LIBER PRIMUS EXPLICIT

## INCIPIT LIBER II

### I

Post haec paulisper obticuit atque ubi attentionem
meam modesta taciturnitate collegit, sic exorsa est :
" Si penitus aegritudinis tuae causas habitumque
cognovi, fortunae prioris affectu desiderioque tabescis.
5 Ea tantum animi tui sicuti tu tibi fingis mutata pervertit.   Intellego multiformes illius prodigii fucos et
eo usque cum his quos eludere nititur blandissimam
familiaritatem, dum intolerabili dolore confundat quos
insperata reliquerit.   Cuius si naturam mores ac
10 meritum reminiscare, nec habuisse te in ea pulchrum
aliquid nec amisisse cognosces, sed ut arbitror haud
multum tibi haec in memoriam revocare laboraverim.
Solebas enim praesentem quoque blandientemque
virilibus incessere verbis eamque de nostro adyto
15 prolatis insectabare sententiis.   Verum omnis subita
174

# BOETHIUS

# THE CONSOLATION OF PHILOSOPHY

## BOOK II

### I

THEN she was silent for a little, and having gained
my attention by her quiet modesty, she began thus :
" If I have properly understood the causes and the
nature of your sickness, you are faint with desire and
longing for your previous good fortune. It is simply
the change in your fortune, you imagine, which has
so much cast down your spirit. I know the many kinds
of tricks of that monster, fortune, and especially her
charming and friendly manner with those she is trying
to cheat, when she crushes with unbearable grief
those whom she leaves when they least expect it.
If you will just recall what she is and how she behaves,
and her true worth, you will recognize that you never
had anything worth having at her hands nor have you
lost anything. I do not think I should have to work
very hard to make you remember this. After all,
when she was with you, smiling on you, you used to
attack her with firm language and chase her with
arguments produced from our very sanctuary. But

175

mutatio rerum non sine quodam quasi fluctu contingit
animorum ; sic factum est ut tu quoque paulisper
a tua tranquillitate descisceres. Sed tempus est
haurire te aliquid ac degustare molle atque iucundum
20 quod ad interiora transmissum validioribus haustibus
viam fecerit. Adsit igitur Rhetoricae suadela dulcedinis quae tum tantum recto calle procedit, cum
nostra instituta non deserit cumque hac Musica laris
nostri vernacula nunc leviores nunc graviores modos
25 succinat.

Quid est igitur o homo quod te in maestitiam
luctumque deiecit ? Novum, credo, aliquid inusita-
tumque vidisti. Tu fortunam putas erga te esse
mutatam ; erras. Hi semper eius mores sunt ista
30 natura. Servavit circa te propriam potius in ipsa
sui mutabilitate constantiam. Talis erat cum
blandiebatur, cum tibi falsae inlecebris felicitatis
alluderet. Deprehendisti caeci numinis ambiguos
vultus. Quae sese adhuc velat aliis, tota tibi prorsus
35 innotuit. Si probas, utere moribus ; ne queraris. Si
perfidiam perhorrescis, sperne atque abice perniciosa
ludentem. Nam quae nunc tibi est tanti causa
maeroris, haec eadem tranquillitatis esse debuisset.
Reliquit enim te quam non relicturam nemo umquam
40 poterit esse securus. An vero tu pretiosam aestimas
abituram felicitatem ? Et cara tibi est fortuna
praesens nec manendi fida et cum discesserit adlatura
maerorem ? Quod si nec ex arbitrio retineri potest

176

such a sudden and complete change in a man's affairs does not happen without some sort of disturbance of the mind, and so even you have fallen for a little while from your proper serenity. But now it is time for you to take some gentle and pleasant physic, which taken and absorbed will prepare you to take stronger medicines. So let us use the sweet persuasiveness of rhetoric, which can only be kept on the right path if it does not swerve from our precepts, and if it harmonizes, now in a lighter, now in a graver mood, with the music native to our halls.

What then is it, man, that has cast you down so that you weep and wail so much? You have had an unusual shock, I think. You imagine that fortune's attitude to you has changed; you are wrong. Such was always her way, such is her nature. Instead, all she has done in your case is remain constant to her own inconstancy; she was just the same when she was smiling, when she deluded you with the allurements of her false happiness. You have merely discovered the changing face of that blind power: she who still conceals herself from others has completely revealed herself to you. If you like her, follow her ways without complaint. If you abhor her treachery, spurn and reject her, that sports so to a man's destruction. She, you think, is the cause of your great sorrow. Yet that same fortune should have set your heart at rest. For she has left you; and no-one will ever be able to feel sure that she is not going to leave him. Or do you think that happiness, which you are bound to lose? Is fortune so dear to you, while she is with you, although she cannot be trusted to stay with you, and will bring you sorrow when she leaves you? But if she cannot be held fast by your

177

et calamitosos fugiens facit, quid est aliud fugax
45 quam futurae quoddam calamitatis indicium ? Neque
enim quod ante oculos situm est, suffecerit intueri ;
rerum exitus prudentia metitur eademque in alterutro
mutabilitas nec formidandas fortunae minas nec
exoptandas facit esse blanditias. Postremo aequo
50 animo toleres oportet quidquid intra fortunae aream
geritur, cum semel iugo eius colla submiseris. Quod
si manendi abeundique scribere legem velis ei quam
tu tibi dominam sponte legisti, nonne iniurius fueris
et inpatientia sortem exacerbes quam permutare non
55 possis ? Si ventis vela committeres, non quo voluntas
peteret sed quo flatus impellerent, promoveres ; si
arvis semina crederes, feraces inter se annos ste-
rilesque pensares. Fortunae te regendum dedisti ;
dominae moribus oportet obtemperes. Tu vero
60 volventis rotae impetum retinere conaris ? At,
omnium mortalium stolidissime, si manere incipit,
fors esse desistit.

I

Haec cum superba verterit vices dextra
Et aestuantis more fertur Euripi,
Dudum tremendos saeva proterit reges
Humilemque victi sublevat fallax vultum
5 Non illa miseros audit aut curat fletus

---

<sup>a</sup> *Euripus* : the narrow strait which separates Euboea
from Boeotia, or any strait in which the tidal currents flow
strongly and variably.

willing it, and makes those she flees from miserable,
what is this fleeting goddess but a sure sign of misery
to come ? It is never enough for a man to contemplate what is before his eyes : prudence must measure
up how things will work out in future, and the very
changeableness and ambiguity of the future render
impotent the threats of fortune to inspire fear and
her flattery to awaken desire for it. Lastly, once you
have submitted your neck to her yoke, you must
calmly bear whatever happens to you on fortune's
own ground. And if you wanted to lay down rules
for her whom you have freely chosen as your mistress,
how long to stay and when to go, would you not be
wrong and would you not make your own lot, which
you could not change, much worse because of your
impatience ? If you spread your sails for the wind,
you must go where the wind takes you, not where
you wish to go ; when you cast your seed on the
ground, you must weigh the barren years against the
good. You have given yourself over to fortune's rule :
you must accommodate yourself to your mistress's
ways. Will you really try to stop the whirl of her
turning wheel ? Why, you are the biggest fool alive
—if it once stop, it ceases to be the wheel of fortune.

## I

So with imperious hand she turns the wheel of change
This way and that like the ebb and flow of the tide,[a]
And pitiless tramples down those once dread kings,
Raising the lowly face of the conquered—
Only to mock him in his turn ;
Careless she neither hears nor heeds the cries
Of miserable men : she laughs

*close to classical view of fortune in Greek art*

Ultroque gemitus dura quos fecit ridet.
Sic illa ludit, sic suas probat vires
Magnumque suis demonstrat[1] ostentum, si quis
Visatur una stratus ac felix hora.

## II

Vellem autem pauca tecum fortunae ipsius verbis
agitare.  Tu igitur an ius postulet, animadverte.
' Quid tu homo ream me cotidianis agis querelis ?
Quam tibi fecimus iniuriam ?  Quae tua tibi detraxi-
5 mus bona ?  Quovis iudice de opum dignitatumque
mecum possessione contende.  Et si cuiusquam
mortalium proprium quid horum esse monstraveris,
ego iam tua fuisse quae repetis, sponte concedam.

Cum te matris utero natura produxit, nudum rebus
10 omnibus inopemque suscepi, meis opibus fovi et
quod te nunc inpatientem nostri facit, favore prona
indulgentius educavi, omnium quae mei iuris sunt
affluentia et splendore circumdedi.  Nunc mihi
retrahere manum libet.  Habes gratiam velut usus
15 alienis, non habes ius querelae tamquam prorsus tua
perdideris.  Quid igitur ingemiscis ?  Nulla tibi a
nobis est allata violentia.  Opes honores ceteraque
talium mei sunt iuris.  Dominam famulae cognoscunt;
mecum veniunt, me abeunte discedunt.  Audacter
20 adfirmem, si tua forent quae amissa conquereris nullo

---

[1] monstrat *MSS.*

180

At the groans that she herself has mercilessly caused.
So she sports, so she proves her power,
Showing a mighty marvel to her subjects, when
The self-same hour
Sees a man first successful, then cast down.

*no providence as yet*

## II

But I should like to deal with you for a moment in fortune's own words ; and do you think whether she is not right. " Why, man, do you daily complain against me," she says, " what hurt have I done you ? What goods of yours have I taken from you ?  Contest with me the possession of wealth and office before any judge, and if you can show that any such thing is the property of any mortal, I shall immediately and perfectly readily grant that those things you want back were indeed yours.  When nature brought you out of your mother's womb, I accepted you, naked and poor in all respects ; I supported you, and, ready to be kind to you, even pampered you with my wealth, and over-indulgently spoiled you— which is precisely why you are now so angry with me. I surrounded you with every kind of affluence and splendour within my power.  Now I am pleased to draw back my hand.  You should thank me, as having enjoyed the use of what was not yours, not complain as if you had lost something of your own.  Now why lament ?  I have done no violence to you.  Wealth and honours and other such are under my control, they are my handmaids ; knowing their mistress, they come, and they go, with me.  I may say quite firmly that if those things the loss of which you complain of were really yours, you would never have lost

181

modo perdidisses. An ego sola meum ius exercere
prohibebor ? Licet caelo proferre lucidos dies eosdem-
que tenebrosis noctibus condere. Licet anno terrae
vultum nunc floribus frugibusque redimire, nunc
25 nimbis frigoribusque confundere. Ius est mari nunc
strato aequore blandiri, nunc procellis ac fluctibus
inhorrescere. Nos ad constantiam nostris moribus
alienam inexpleta hominum cupiditas alligabit ? Haec
nostra vis est, hunc continuum ludum ludimus ; rotam
30 volubili orbe versamus, infima summis summa infimis
mutare gaudemus. Ascende si placet, sed ea lege
ne utique[1] cum ludicri mei ratio poscet, descendere
iniuriam putes. An tu mores ignorabas meos ?
Nesciebas Croesum regem Lydorum Cyro paulo ante
35 formidabilem mox deinde miserandum rogi flammis
traditum misso caelitus imbre defensum ? Num te
praeterit Paulum Persi regis a se capti calamitatibus
pias inpendisse lacrimas ? Quid tragoediarum clamor
aliud deflet nisi indiscreto ictu fortunam felicia regna
40 vertentem ? Nonne adulescentulus δοιοὺς πίθους τὸν
μὲν ἕνα κακῶν τὸν δ' ἕτερον ἐάων in Iovis limine
iacere didicisti ? Quid si uberius de bonorum parte
sumpsisti ? Quid si a te non tota discessi ? Quid si
haec ipsa mei mutabilitas iusta tibi causa est sperandi
45 meliora ? Tamen ne animo contabescas et intra
commune omnibus regnum locatus proprio vivere
iure desideres.

---

[1] utique *Klussmann* ; uti MSS.

---

[a] *Cf.* Bacchylides iii. 23-62 ; Herodotus i. 86-87.
[b] *Cf.* Livy xlv. 7 ; but the story is probably from
Pacuvius's *fabula praetexta* (Roman play) *Paulus*, based on
the victory of L. Aemilius Paulus over the king of Macedon,
Perseus, in 168 B.C.
[c] Homer, *Iliad*, xxiv. 527.

them. Or will I alone be not allowed to exercise my
rights ? The sky may bring forth clear days, and
then hide them in the darkness of night ; the year
may weave a crown of flowers and fruits for the face
of the earth, and then confuse and obscure her
features with rain and frost ; the sea has a right to
smile with a smooth stillness, and then shudder and
rise with storms and great waves. But I, shall I be
bound by the insatiable desire of men to a constancy
quite foreign to my nature ? For this is my nature,
this is my continual game : turning my wheel swiftly
I delight to bring low what is on high, to raise high
what is down. Go up, if you will, but on this condition, that you do not really think it a wrong to have
to go down again whenever the course of my sport
demands. You were hardly unaware in my ways !
Did you not know the story of Croesus, the king of
the Lydians ; how he, not long before such a terror
to Cyrus, was soon wretchedly given over to be burnt,
but saved by a shower from heaven ? [a] Have you
forgotten how Aemilius Paulus, good man that he
was, shed tears over the fate of King Perses, whom
he had captured ? [b] What else is the cry of tragedy
but a lament that happy states are overthrown by the
indiscriminate blows of fortune ? Did you not learn as
a youth that on Jupiter's threshold there stand " two
jars, the evils in one, the blessings in the other " ? [c]
Suppose you have had more than your share of the
goods ; suppose I have not altogether deserted you ;
and suppose that this very changeableness of mine
is a fair cause for you to hope for better things to
come : still you must neither pine away, nor, set
as you are in a kingdom which embraces all men,
desire to live under a law peculiar to yourself.

## II

Si quantas rapidis flatibus incitus
    Pontus versat harenas
Aut quot stelliferis edita noctibus
    Caelo sidera fulgent
5  Tantas fundat opes nec retrahat manum
    Pleno copia cornu,
Humanum miseras haud ideo genus
    Cesset flere querellas.
Quamvis vota libens excipiat deus
10    Multi prodigus auri
Et claris avidos ornet honoribus,
    Nil iam parta videntur,
Sed quaesita vorans saeva rapacitas
    Alios[1] pandit hiatus.
15  Quae iam praecipitem frena cupidinem
    Certo fine retentent,
Largis cum potius muneribus fluens
    Sitis ardescit habendi ?
Numquam dives agit qui trepidus gemens
20    Sese credit egentem.'

## III

    His igitur si pro se tecum fortuna loqueretur,
quid profecto contra hisceres non haberes, aut si quid
est quo querelam tuam iure tuearis, proferas oportet.
Dabimus dicendi locum." Tum ego : " Speciosa
5 quidem ista sunt," inquam, " oblitaque Rhetoricae ac
Musicae melle dulcedinis ; tum tantum, cum audiun-
tur, oblectant. Sed miseris malorum altior sensus
est. Itaque cum haec auribus insonare desierint,

---

[1] altos *vulg.* ; alios *the best MSS.*

## CONSOLATION II

### II

Should Plenty pour from cornucopia full
As much in riches as the sand
Stirred up by wind-whipped seas, or as the countless
    stars
That shine in a clear night sky,
And never stay her hand,
Still would mankind not cease
Complaining of their wretchedness.
Even were God with much gold prodigal,
Answering men's prayers,
And heaped bright honours on those wanting them,
Their gains would seem to them
Nothing : ever their cruel gain-devouring greed
Opens new maws.  What curbs
Could check within firm bounds this headlong lust,
When even in those whose wealth is overflowing
The thirst for gain still burns ?
He is never rich
Who trembles and sighs, thinking himself in need."

_about human greed - no matter how much one has, always wants more_

### III

    Now if fortune spoke to you in this way in her own
defence, you would not know what to reply, would
you ?  If indeed you do have anything to say that
would justify your complaints, you must utter it— you
shall have your chance to speak now."
    " Such arguments," I said, " have a specious sweet-
ness, honeyed as they are with rhetoric and music.
While a man listens to them, they please him,
wretched though he is, but his sense of his wrongs
lies deeper, so that once they cease to sound in his

insitus animum maeror praegravat." Et illa : " Ita
10 est," inquit. " Haec enim nondum morbi tui remedia
sed adhuc contumacis adversum curationem doloris
fomenta quaedam sunt. Nam quae in profundum
sese penetrent, cum tempestivum fuerit admovebo.
Verumtamen ne te existimari miserum velis, an
15 numerum modumque tuae felicitatis oblitus es ?

Taceo quod desolatum parente summorum te
virorum cura suscepit delectusque in affinitatem prin-
cipum civitatis, quod pretiosissimum propinquitatis
genus est, prius carus quam proximus esse coepisti.
20 Quis non te felicissimum cum tanto splendore soce-
rorum, cum coniugis pudore, cum masculae quoque
prolis opportunitate praedicavit ? Praetereo, libet
enim praeterire communia, sumptas in adulescentia
negatas senibus dignitates ; ad singularem felicitatis
25 tuae cumulum venire delectat. Si quis rerum mortalium fructus ullum beatitudinis pondus habet, poteritne
illius memoria lucis quantalibet ingruentium malorum
mole deleri, cum duos pariter consules liberos tuos
domo provehi sub frequentia patrum, sub plebis
30 alacritate vidisti, cum eisdem in curia curules in-
sidentibus tu regiae laudis orator ingenii gloriam
facundiaeque meruisti, cum in circo duorum medius
consulum circumfusae multitudinis expectationem
186

ears he is oppressed again by the grief deep in his heart."

"That is so," she replied; "for they are not yet intended to be a cure for your ills, but just a sort of poultice for your hurt, which stubbornly resists curing. I shall apply more deeply penetrating remedies when the right time comes. Yet there is no reason why you should want to be pitied. Have you forgotten the number and the extent of your blessings? I shall not mention the fact that when you lost your own father you were cared for by men of the highest rank, and being chosen to become kin to the first men in the state, which is the most valuable kind of kinship, you became dear to them even before you were actually related by marriage. Who did not call you most happy, in having married into such a splendidly famous family, with such a chaste wife, and with the blessing of sons to follow you? I pass over also—for it is better to pass over what is common knowledge —the honours granted you in your youth, though denied to older men. I want to come to the very summit of your success, which was specially yours. If genuine happiness ever comes from the affairs of mortals, could the weight of any crowding ills, however great, obliterate the memory of that glory you experienced when you saw your two sons borne from your house together as consuls, in the crowd of Senators and the throng of the rejoicing populace; when you delivered the panegyric in praise of the king with them sitting in the curule chairs in the Senate House, and well deserved the praise you received for your splendid oratory; when between the two of them as consuls in the assembly you satisfied, with the largesse proper to a triumphal occasion, the

187

triumphali largitione satiasti ? Dedisti ut opinor
35 verba fortunae, dum te illa demulcet, dum te ut
delicias suas fovet. Munus quod nulli umquam
privato commodaverat abstulisti. Visne igitur cum
fortuna calculum ponere ? Nunc te primum liventi
oculo praestrinxit. Si numerum modumque laetorum
40 tristiumve consideres, adhuc te felicem negare non
possis. Quod si idcirco te fortunatum esse non
aestimas, quoniam quae tunc laeta videbantur abie-
runt, non est quod te miserum putes, quoniam quae
nunc creduntur maesta praetereunt. An tu in hanc
45 vitae scaenam nunc primum subitus hospesque venisti ? Ullamne humanis rebus inesse constantiam
reris, cum ipsum saepe hominem velox hora dissolvat ?
Nam etsi rara est fortuitis manendi fides, ultimus
tamen vitae dies mors quaedam fortunae est etiam
50 manentis. Quid igitur referre putas, tune illam
moriendo deseras an te illa fugiendo ?

### III

Cum polo Phoebus roseis quadrigis
Lucem spargere coeperit,
Pallet albentes hebetata vultus
Flammis stella prementibus.
5 Cum nemus flatu zephyri tepentis
Vernis inrubuit rosis,
Spiret insanum nebulosus auster :
Iam spinis abeat decus.

188

hopes and expectations of the mob crowding round you? I suppose you made fine phrases for fortune then, when she caressed and cuddled you as her darling! You received such a gift as she had never before bestowed on a private citizen. Do you want to reckon up your account with her? Now is the first time she has glanced grudgingly on you. If you weighed up the number and the kinds of joyful and sad things that have happened to you, you could not deny that up to now you have been fortunate. And if you now think yourself unfortunate, because the things that then seemed joyful to you are passed away, that is really no reason why you should think yourself wretched, for those things that you now think so miserable also pass away. Do you now enter on the stage of this life for the first time, a newcomer and a stranger? Do you think there is some constancy in human affairs, when man himself is so swiftly removed from the scene by flying time? Even if a man can, very rarely, rely on the gifts of fortune remaining with him, yet the last day of his life is a death also for what fortune does remain. Do you think it matters, then, whether you leave fortune behind by dying, or she leaves you?

### III

When Phoebus from his roseate car
Begins to spread his light across the sky,
His overwhelming fires
Dim the white faces of the paling stars.
Warmed by the west wind's gentle breath
The groves blush pink with roses in the spring;
Let but the stormy south wind madly blow
And the thorns are stripped of their loveliness.

*how fortune changes in weather*

189

Saepe tranquillo radiat sereno
10        Immotis mare fluctibus,
Saepe ferventes aquilo procellas
      Verso concitat aequore.
Rara si constat sua forma mundo,
      Si tantas variat vices,
15    Crede fortunis hominum caducis,
      Bonis crede fugacibus.
Constat aeterna positumque lege est
      Ut constet genitum nihil."

## IV

Tum ego : " Vera," inquam, " commemoras, o
virtutum omnium nutrix, nec infitiari possum pro-
speritatis meae velocissimum cursum. Sed hoc est
quod recolentem vehementius coquit. Nam in
5 omni adversitate fortunae infelicissimum est genus
infortunii fuisse felicem." " Sed quod tu," inquit,
" falsae opinionis supplicium luas, id rebus iure
imputare non possis. Nam si te hoc inane nomen
fortuitae felicitatis movet, quam pluribus maximisque
10 abundes mecum reputes licet. Igitur si quod in
omni fortunae tuae censu pretiosissimum possidebas,
id tibi divinitus inlaesum adhuc inviolatumque
servatur, poterisne meliora quaeque retinens de
infortunio iure causari ?
15 Atqui viget incolumis illud pretiosissimum generis
humani decus Symmachus socer et quod vitae pretio
non segnis emeres, vir totus ex sapientia virtutibusque
factus suarum securus tuis ingemiscit iniuriis. Vivit
uxor ingenio modesta, pudicitia pudore praecellens
190

# CONSOLATION II

Sometimes the sea gleams calm, serene,
Unruffled ;
Sometimes the north wind whips up raging storms
And overturns the sea.
Earth's beauty seldom stays, but ever changes.
Go on, then : trust in the passing fortunes,
The flecting pleasures of men !
It is decreed by firm, eternal law
Nothing that comes to be can firm remain."

## IV

" Lady," I answered, " you who nurture all the
virtues, what you say is true ; nor can I deny that I
did enjoy, however briefly, great prosperity. But it
is just that which most torments me, for in all the
adversities of fortune, the most unhappy kind of
misfortune is to have known happiness."
" But you cannot rightly blame anything else for
the fact that you are punished for your own wrong
ideas. For if you really take this empty notion of
fortuitous happiness seriously, you should consider
with me how much great good is still yours. So if
by God's will that one of your possessions which in
the whole reckoning of your fortune was most precious is still preserved unharmed and inviolate, can
you, keeping all that is best, rightly talk of your misfortune ? First, your father-in-law, Symmachus, that
most precious ornament of mankind, lives safely, and
being a man wholly formed in wisdom and virtue (a
state you would not be slow to purchase even at the
cost of your life) and therefore without concern for
his own troubles, he laments over yours. Then again,
your wife lives, a good woman excelling in modesty

20 et, ut omnes eius dotes breviter includam, patri
similis. Vivit inquam tibique tantum vitae huius
exosa spiritum servat quoque uno felicitatem minui
tuam vel ipsa concesserim, tui desiderio lacrimis ac
dolore tabescit.

25     Quid dicam liberos consulares quorum iam, ut in
id aetatis pueris, vel paterni vel aviti specimen elucet
ingenii? Cum igitur praecipua sit mortalibus vitae
cura retinendae, o te si tua bona cognoscas felicem,
cui suppetunt etiam nunc quae vita nemo dubitat

30 esse cariora ! Quare sicca iam lacrimas. Nondum est
ad unum omnes exosa fortuna nec tibi nimium valida
tempestas incubuit, quando tenaces haerent ancorae
quae nec praesentis solamen nec futuri spem temporis
abesse patiantur.''

35     '' Et haereant,'' inquam, '' precor ; illis namque
manentibus, utcumque se res habeant, enatabimus.
Sed quantum ornamentis nostris decesserit, vides.''
Et illa : '' Promovimus,'' inquit, '' aliquantum, si te
nondum totius tuae sortis piget. Sed delicias tuas

40 ferre non possum qui abesse aliquid tuae beatitu-
dini tam luctuosus atque anxius conqueraris. Quis
est enim tam conpositae felicitatis ut non aliqua ex
parte cum status sui qualitate rixetur ? Anxia enim
res est humanorum condicio bonorum et quae vel

45 numquam tota proveniat vel numquam perpetua
subsistat. Huic census exuberat, sed est pudori
degener sanguis ; hunc nobilitas notum facit, sed
angustia rei familiaris inclusus esse mallet ignotus.

192

and propriety and—to sum up all her gifts in one phrase—a woman like her father ; she lives, I say, and goes on living though she detests this life, only for you—and I must admit that in this alone is your happiness lessened, that she is wasting away in tears in her grievous longing for you. Need I speak of your sons, both consuls, who already show, for children of their age, a likeness to their father's or grandfather's nature ? Now although it is men's special concern to preserve their own lives, are you not happy, if you recognize your blessings, you who still possess those things which no one doubts are dearer than life ? So now dry your tears. Fortune does not yet hate every single one of your family, nor has too violent a storm overwhelmed you, when those anchors still hold firm which ensure that neither present consolation nor future hope shall be wanting."

" I pray they may continue to hold firm," said I. " For so long as they are there, I shall not drown, whatever happens. But you can see how many of my former distinctions have disappeared."

" Come, we have taken a small step forward," she said, " if you are no longer grieved by the whole of your present state. But I cannot tolerate your luxuriating in your grief to such an extent, peevishly complaining that something is lacking in your happiness. For who is so completely happy that he does not find something to quarrel with in his own condition ? For the condition of human good fortune is never free from worry ; a man never wholly possesses it, nor does it last for ever. One man has a good deal of property, but is ashamed of his low birth ; another is known for his high birth, but prefers to remain ignored, shut in by his personal poverty. Another

Ille utroque circumfluus vitam caelibem deflet ; ille
50 nuptiis felix orbus liberis alieno censum nutrit heredi.
Alius prole laetatus filii filiaeve delictis maestus
inlacrimat. Idcirco nemo facile cum fortunae suae
condicione concordat ; inest enim singulis quod
inexpertus ignoret, expertus exhorreat. Adde quod
55 felicissimi cuiusque delicatissimus sensus est et nisi ad
nutum cuncta suppetant, omnis adversitatis insolens
minimis quibusque prosternitur ; adeo perexigua sunt
quae fortunatissimis beatitudinis summam detrahunt.
Quam multos esse coniectas qui sese caelo proximos
60 arbitrentur, si de fortunae tuae reliquiis pars eis
minima contingat ? Hic ipse locus quem tu exilium
vocas, incolentibus patria est ; adeo nihil est miserum
nisi cum putes contraque beata sors omnis est aequa-
nimitate tolerantis. Quis est ille tam felix qui cum
65 dederit inpatientiae manus, statum suum mutare non
optet ? Quam multis amaritudinibus humanae felicitatis dulcedo respersa est ! Quae si etiam fruenti
iucunda esse videatur, tamen quo minus cum velit
abeat retineri non possit. Liquet igitur quam sit mor-
70 talium rerum misera beatitudo quae nec apud aequa-
nimos perpetua perdurat nec anxios tota delectat.

Quid igitur o mortales extra petitis intra vos po-
sitam felicitatem ? Error vos inscitiaque confundit.
Ostendam breviter tibi summae cardinem felicitatis.
194

is rich in both birth and property, but bewails his single state, while another is happily married but being childless preserves and increases his wealth for someone else's children to inherit ; and he who is blessed with children sadly weeps for his son's or daughter's faults. So, scarcely a man is easily happy with the state of his own fortunes ; in every case there are aspects unknown to those not experiencing them but dreadful to those who are. Consider also that he who is most happy is also the most delicately sensitive, so that unless everything is exactly as he wants it to be, he is so unused to any adversity that he is put out by even the least upset. Even the very tiniest thing can topple the most fortunate from the summit of their happiness. Think how many there are who would think themselves close to paradise if they possessed even the least part of what remains of your fortunes ! This place itself, which you call a place of exile, is home to those who live here. So nothing is miserable unless you think so, and on the other hand a man who bears all with contentment, finds every state a happy one. Who is so happy that once he gives in to discontent he would not choose to change his condition ? How many bitter troubles spoil with their spattering the sweetness of a man's happiness ! A happiness which even if it seem plea sant to a man when he enjoys it, yet cannot be prevented from passing when it will. So it is very clear how wretched is the happiness of mortal affairs, since it neither endures for the contented nor alto-gether satisfies the uneasy.

Why then do you mortals look outside for happiness when it is really to be found within yourselves ? Error and ignorance confuse you. Let me briefly show you

75 Estne aliquid tibi te ipso pretiosius ? Nihil inquies.
Igitur si tui compos fueris, possidebis quod nec tu
amittere umquam velis nec fortuna possit auferre.
Atque ut agnoscas in his fortuitis rebus beatitudinem
constare non posse, sic collige. Si beatitudo est sum-
80 mum naturae bonum ratione degentis nec est summum
bonum quod eripi ullo modo potest, quoniam prae-
cellit id quod nequeat auferri, manifestum est quoniam[1]
ad beatitudinem percipiendam fortunae instabilitas
adspirare non possit. Ad haec quem caduca ista
85 felicitas vehit vel scit eam vel nescit esse mutabilem.
Si nescit, quaenam beata sors esse potest ignorantiae
caecitate ? Si scit, metuat necesse est, ne amittat
quod amitti posse non dubitat ; quare continuus
timor non sinit esse felicem. An vel si amiserit,
90 neglegendum putat ? Sic quoque perexile bonum
est quod aequo animo feratur amissum. Et quoniam
tu idem es cui persuasum atque insitum permultis
demonstrationibus scio mentes hominum nullo modo
esse mortales cumque clarum sit fortuitam felicitatem
95 corporis morte finiri, dubitari nequit, si haec afferre
beatitudinem potest, quin omne mortalium genus in
miseriam mortis fine labatur. Quod si multos scimus
beatitudinis fructum non morte solum verum etiam
doloribus suppliciisque quaesisse, quonam modo prae-
100 sens facere beatos potest quae miseros transacta non
efficit ?

[1] quin *MSS.*

on what the greatest happiness really turns. Is anything more precious to you than yourself? Nothing, you will agree. If therefore you are in possession of yourself, you will possess that which you will never wish to lose, and which fortune cannot take away from you. Now to see that happiness cannot consist in the fortuitous things of this mortal life, look at it in this way. If happiness is the highest good of a rational nature, and that cannot be the highest good which can in any way be taken away—because clearly that which cannot be taken away is higher—then surely the instability of fortune cannot aspire to the attainment of happiness. Again, he who is borne up on this fallible happiness must either know or not know that it is changeable. If he does not know, can his state truly be a happy one in such blind ignorance? If he does know, he must fear that he may lose that which he knows can be lost, and his continual fear will prevent him being happy. Or does he think that when he does lose it, it does not matter? Then it must be an insignificant little good the loss of which he can bear so calmly! Now since you are still the same man who was deeply convinced by many proofs, as I know, that the minds of men are by no means mortal, and since it is obvious that the fortuitous happiness of the body is ended by death, you cannot now doubt that if such bodily pleasure can bring happiness, yet every kind of mortal thing falls into misery in the end, at death. But if we know that many have sought the enjoyment of happiness not simply through death but even through pain and suffering, how can this present life make them happy, when its being past does not make them miserable?

## IV

Quisquis volet perennem
 Cautus ponere sedem
Stabilisque nec sonori
 Sterni flatibus Euri
5 Et fluctibus minantem
 Curat spernere pontum,
Montis cacumen alti,
 Bibulas vitet harenas.
Illud protervus Auster
10 Totis viribus urget,
Hae pendulum solutae
 Pondus ferre recusant.
Fugiens periculosam
 Sortem sedis amoenae
15 Humili domum memento
 Certus figere saxo.
Quamvis tonet ruinis
 Miscens aequora ventus,
Tu conditus quieti
20 Felix robore valli
Duces serenus aevum
 Ridens aetheris iras.

## V

 Sed quoniam rationum iam in te mearum fomenta descendunt, paulo validioribus utendum puto. Age enim si iam caduca et momentaria fortunae dona non essent, quid in eis est quod aut vestrum umquam 5 fieri queat aut non perspectum consideratumque vilescat ? Divitiaene vel vestrae[1] vel sui natura pre-

---

 [1] vestrae *P, T*[1]*, V*[1] *(prob.)*: vestri *V*[2]: vestra *the other MSS.*

# CONSOLATION II

## IV

The prudent man
Intending to build a house to last
Stable, not to be tumbled down
By the south-east wind with its noisy blast,
Nor crumbled by the sea
With its threatening waves,
Will avoid the mountain top
And the thirsty desert sand ;
The one is buffeted
By all the force of the violent south wind ;
The other shifts
And will not bear the heavy-hanging weight.
Run from the risks of a beautiful place
That might be dangerous.
Be careful, certain :  build your house
On a low, rock base.
Then though the wind thunder and make
A ruinous turmoil of the troubled sea,
You, safe settled and content
Within your own strong walls,
Will quietly live your life
Smiling at all the anger of the skies.

*echo of Gospel*

## V

But since you are now well warmed by the poultices
of my arguments, I think it is now time to use rather
stronger medicines.  Come now, suppose that the
gifts of fortune were not transient and purely temporary, is there any among them which could ever
become truly yours or which on proper examination
is not seen to be worthless ?  Are riches either really

tiosae sunt ? Quid earum potius, aurumne an vis
congesta pecuniae ? Atqui haec effundendo magis
quam coacervando melius nitent, si quidem avaritia
10 semper odiosos, claros largitas facit. Quod si manere
apud quemque non potest quod transfertur in alterum,
tunc est pretiosa pecunia cum translata in alios
largiendi usu desinit possideri. At eadem si apud
unum quanta est ubique gentium congeratur, ceteros
15 sui inopes fecerit. Et vox quidem tota pariter
multorum replet auditum ; vestrae vero divitiae nisi
comminutae in plures transire non possunt. Quod
cum factum est, pauperes necesse est faciant quos
relinquunt. O igitur angustas inopesque divitias
20 quas nec habere totas pluribus licet et ad quemlibet
sine ceterorum paupertate non veniunt ! An gemmarum fulgor oculos trahit ? Sed si quid est in
hoc splendore praecipui, gemmarum est lux illa non
hominum, quas quidem mirari homines vehementer
25 admiror. Quid est enim carens animae motu atque
compage quod animatae rationabilique naturae pulchrum esse iure videatur ? Quae tametsi conditoris
opera suique distinctione postremae aliquid pulchritudinis trahunt, infra vestram tamen excellentiam
30 conlocatae admirationem vestram nullo modo mere-
bantur. An vos agrorum pulchritudo delectat ?
Quidni ? Est enim pulcherrimi operis pulchra portio.
Sic quondam sereni maris facie gaudemus ; sic caelum
200

yours or precious by their own nature ?  If so, what
part of them especially, the gold, or the piles of
money ?  But riches are more splendid in the spending than in the getting, since avarice makes men
hated, but liberality makes them famous.  Yet if that
cannot remain with a man which passes to another,
then money is precious just when it passes over to
others, and in being liberally given ceases to be possessed.  If all the money there is in the world were
heaped together in one man's possession, it would
make all the rest of men live in lack of it.  The voice
wholly fills the ears of many hearers simultaneously,
but your riches cannot pass to many unless they are
split into small parts first.  When that is done, those
who part with money must necessarily become
poorer.  Well then, O riches, how poor and mean
you are !  You can neither be wholly possessed by
many nor come to any man without impoverishing
others !

Are your eyes attracted by glittering jewels ?  But
even if their sparkling is in any way wonderful, the
light is the gems', not men's, and I am amazed that
men admire them so.  What is there, lacking the
structure and movement of the living spirit, which a
living, rational being could rightly think beautiful ?
Although through the work of the Creator and because of their own peculiarities they have something
of the lower kind of beauty, yet they are so far beneath your excellence as a man that they did not by
any means deserve your admiration.

Does the beauty of the countryside delight you ?
As why should it not ?  It is a beautiful part of the
whole creation, which is beautiful.  So we sometimes
take pleasure in the calm aspect of the sea, and so

sidera lunam solemque miramur. Num te horum
35 aliquid attingit ? Num audes alicuius talium splendore gloriari ? An vernis floribus ipse distingueris aut
tua in aestivos fructus intumescit ubertas ? Quid
inanibus gaudiis raperis ? Quid externa bona pro tuis
amplexaris ? Numquam tua faciet esse fortuna quae
40 a te natura rerum fecit aliena. Terrarum quidem
fructus animantium procul dubio debentur alimentis.
Sed si, quod naturae satis est, replere indigentiam
velis, nihil est quod fortunae affluentiam petas.
Paucis enim minimisque natura contenta est, cuius
45 satietatem si superfluis urgere velis, aut iniucundum
quod infuderis fiet aut noxium. Iam vero pulchrum
variis fulgere vestibus putas, quarum si grata intuitu
species est, aut materiae naturam aut ingenium
mirabor artificis. An vero te longus ordo famulorum
50 facit esse felicem ? Qui si vitiosi moribus sint, perniciosa domus sarcina et ipsi domino vehementer
inimica ; sin vero probi, quonam modo in tuis opibus
aliena probitas numerabitur ? Ex quibus omnibus
nihil horum quae tu in tuis conputas bonis tuum esse
55 bonum liquido monstratur. Quibus si nihil inest
appetendae pulchritudinis, quid est quod vel amissis
doleas vel laeteris retentis ? Quod si natura pulchra
sunt, quid id tua refert ? Nam haec per se a tuis
quoque opibus sequestrata placuissent. Neque enim
60 idcirco sunt pretiosa quod in tuas venere divitias,
202

also we admire the sky with its stars and the moon and the sun. Does any of these things belong to you ? Dare you boast of the splendour of any of them ? Are *you* adorned with flowers in spring ? Is it *your* plenteousness which grows big with summer fruits ? Why are you captivated by empty pleasures, why embrace external goods as though they were your own ? Fortune will never make yours what nature has made otherwise. The fruits of the earth are surely intended for the sustenance of living things. But if you want to satisfy your needs, which is enough for nature, there is no need to ask fortune for abundance. For nature is content with few things and small : if you want to overlay that satisfaction with superfluity, then what you add will be either unpleasant or positively harmful.

Perhaps now you think it fine to be admired in a variety of clothes ? If their appearance is pleasing to the eye, I admire either the material itself or the skill of the tailor. But perhaps a great household of servants makes you happy ? If they are wicked in their ways, they are a ruinous burden on the house and highly dangerous to the master himself ; but if they are honest, how can the honesty of others be counted among your own possessions ? So it is clearly shown by all this that, of what you count among your goods, none is a good of yours. And if they have no beauty in them which you should seek, why should you grieve when they are lost or rejoice when you hold on to them ? If they are beautiful by their own nature, what has that to do with you ? For they would have pleased of themselves quite separated from your possessions. It is not that they are precious because they form part of your riches, but

sed quoniam pretiosa videbantur, tuis ea divitiis
adnumerare maluisti.  Quid autem tanto fortunae
strepitu desideratis ?  Fugare credo indigentiam
copia quaeritis.  Atqui hoc vobis in contrarium cedit.
65 Pluribus quippe adminiculis opus est ad tuendam
pretiosae supellectilis varietatem, verumque illud
est permultis eos indigere qui permulta possideant
contraque minimum qui abundantiam suam naturae
necessitate non ambitus superfluitate metiantur.
70 Itane autem nullum est proprium vobis atque insitum bonum ut in externis ac sepositis rebus bona
vestra quaeratis ?  Sic rerum versa condicio est
ut divinum merito rationis animal non aliter sibi
splendere nisi inanimatae supellectilis possessione
75 videatur ?  Et alia quidem suis contenta sunt ; vos
autem deo mente consimiles ab rebus infimis excel-
lentis naturae ornamenta captatis nec intellegitis
quantum conditori vestro faciatis iniuriam.  Ille genus
humanum terrenis omnibus praestare voluit ; vos
80 dignitatem vestram infra infima quaeque detruditis.
Nam si omne cuiusque bonum eo cuius est constat
esse pretiosius, cum vilissima rerum vestra bona esse
iudicatis, eisdem vosmet ipsos vestra existimatione
submittitis, quod quidem haud immerito cadit.
85 Humanae quippe naturae ista condicio est ut tum
tantum ceteris rebus cum se cognoscit excellat,
eadem tamen infra bestias redigatur, si se nosse
desierit.  Nam ceteris animantibus sese ignorare
naturae est ; hominibus vitio venit.  Quam vero
90 late patet vester hic error qui ornari posse aliquid
ornamentis existimatis alienis ?  At id fieri nequit.
204

you preferred to count them among your riches because you thought them precious.

But what do you so noisily demand of fortune ? You want, I think, to banish need with plenty. But yet you achieve exactly the opposite. For you need a good many aids to help you guard your many kinds of precious furniture ! And it is true that they need very many things who have very great possessions, while they need least who measure their sufficiency by the requirements of nature, not by the excesses of ambitious vanity. Have you no personal good of your own within yourself, that you seek your goods in other things, externally ? Is the state of nature so upside-down that man, a living and rational—and therefore godlike—animal, can only appear splendid to himself by the possession of lifeless stuff ? Other things are content with what is their own ; but you men, like God in your minds, seek to bedeck your nature, excellent that it is, with lower things, and do not see how greatly you injure your maker. *He* wanted man to be above all earthly things ; *you men* reduce your worth to less than that of the lowest. For if it is agreed that the good of anything is of higher worth than that whose good it is, then when you judge the lowest things to be your goods, you put yourselves in your own estimation lower than them—and entirely deservedly ! For the nature of man is such that he is better than other things only when he knows himself, and yet if he ceases to know himself he is made lower than the brutes. For it is natural for other animals not to have this self-knowledge ; in man it is a fault. How far from your true state have you wandered when you think you can be at all improved by the addition of the beauties of other things ! That

Nam si quid ex appositis luceat, ipsa quidem quae
sunt apposita laudantur ; illud vero his tectum atque
velatum in sua nihilo minus foeditate perdurat.  Ego
95 vero nego ullum esse bonum quod noceat habenti.
Num id mentior ?  ' Minime,' inquis.  Atqui divitiae
possidentibus persaepe nocuerunt, cum pessimus
quisque eoque alieni magis avidus quidquid usquam
auri gemmarumque est se solum qui habeat dignissi-
100 mum putat.  Tu igitur qui nunc contum gladiumque
sollicitus pertimescis, si vitae huius callem vacuus
viator intrasses, coram latrone cantares.  O praeclara
opum mortalium beatitudo quam cum adeptus fueris
securus esse desistis !

## V

Felix nimium prior aetas
Contenta fidelibus arvis
Nec inerti perdita luxu,
Facili quae sera solebat
5    Ieiunia solvere glande.
Non Bacchica munera norant
Liquido confundere melle
Nec lucida vellera Serum
Tyrio miscere veneno.
10    Somnos dabat herba salubres,
Potum quoque lubricus amnis,
Umbras altissima pinus.
Nondum maris alta secabat
Nec mercibus undique lectis

---

[a] *Cf.* Juvenal, *Sat.* x. 20-22.  After the Civil War that
ended in Augustus' principate, the roads of Italy were beset
by highwaymen and brigands, and the Roman traveller, who

cannot be ; if something seem fine because of its wrappings, it is the wrappings that are praised, while what is covered and hidden by them persists no less foul and ugly underneath. Now I maintain that nothing is good which harms its possessor. Am I wrong ? Of course not, you answer. Yet riches have often harmed their possessors, since every man of base character, and therefore the more greedy for others' goods, thinks himself the only one really worthy to possess all the gold and jewels there are. So you who now anxiously fear to be attacked and murdered, had you entered on this life's road an empty-handed traveller, would laugh at robbers.[a]  O marvellous blessedness of mortal riches ! When you have gained that, you have lost your safety.

## V

How happy was that earlier age
When men content depended on the trusty land,
And not yet sunk in idle luxury
Sated their hunger only at their need
With acorns gathered with ease.
They had not learned to mix
Wine with clear honey ;
Nor to dye shining silken stuffs
With Tyrian purple.
The greensward gave them healthy sleep,
The gliding river water for their thirst,
And the tall pine a shadow from the sun.
Not yet did they cut deep waters with their ships,
Nor seeking trade abroad

*invokes Golden Age*

carried his plate with him, went in fear of the pikes and swords of robbers (*contum gladiumque*).

15 Nova litora viderat hospes.
Tunc classica saeva tacebant,
Odiis neque fusus acerbis
Cruor horrida tinxerat arva.
Quid enim furor hosticus ulla
20 Vellet prior arma movere,
Cum vulnera saeva viderent
Nec praemia sanguinis ulla ?
Utinam modo nostra redirent
In mores tempora priscos !
25 Sed saevior ignibus Aetnae
Fervens amor ardet habendi.
Heu primus quis fuit ille
Auri qui pondera tecti
Gemmasque latere volentes
30 Pretiosa pericula fodit ?

## VI

Quid autem de dignitatibus potentiaque disseram
quae vos verae dignitatis ac potestatis inscii caelo
exaequatis ?  Quae si in improbissimum quemque
ceciderunt, quae flammis Aetnae eructantibus, quod
5 diluvium tantas strages dederint ?  Certe, uti memi-
nisse te arbitror, consulare imperium, quod libertatis
principium fuerat, ob superbiam consulum vestri
veteres abolere cupiverunt, qui ob eandem superbiam
prius regium de civitate nomen abstulerant.  At si
10 quando, quod perrarum est, probis deferantur, quid

---

*a* The dual consulships traditionally date from the expulsion of the kings in about 509 B.C. ;  the power of the aristo-
cratic consuls was gradually limited during the " Struggle
between the Orders," which lasted some 150 years, beginning
with the institution of the tribunate in 495, when the
plebeians elected two officers of their own, the tribunes.

## CONSOLATION II

Stand strangers on an unknown shore.
There was no sound of savage bugle-calls,
Nor had men's blood been shed in bitter hate
Staining the scrubby fields.
For why should any man in furious enmity
Want to strike first
When he could see what cruel wounds would come
With no reward for blood ?
Would that our present times
Would now return to those good ancient ways !
But fiercer now than Etna's fires
Burns the hot lust for gain.
Ah who was he
Who first dug out those perilous precious things—
Nuggets of gold, which had lain concealed,
And gems, far better hid ?

## VI

But what shall I say of your worthy offices and
power, which you praise to high heaven, being ignorant of true worth and real power ? When such things
have fallen into the hands of the worst of men, what
Etnas with belching flames or what floods have caused
greater destruction ? Certainly your old Romans
once, as you remember, I expect, wanted to abolish
the power of the consuls, which had earlier been the
beginning of Roman liberty, because of the arrogance
of the consuls—those same Romans who because of
the same arrogance had formerly removed the power
and the name of kings from the state.[a] And whenever such offices and powers have—very rarely !—
been given to good men, surely the only acceptable
goodness seen in those powers and offices has been

209

in eis aliud quam probitas utentium placet ? Ita fit
ut non virtutibus ex dignitate sed ex virtute dignitatibus honor accedat. Quae vero est ista vestra
expetibilis ac praeclara potentia ? Nonne, o terrena
15 animalia, consideratis quibus qui praesidere videa-
mini ? Nunc si inter mures videres unum aliquem
ius sibi ac potestatem prae ceteris vindicantem,
quanto movereris cachinno ! Quid vero, si corpus
spectes, inbecillius homine reperire queas quos
20 saepe muscularum quoque vel morsus vel in secreta
quaeque reptantium necat introitus ? Quo vero
quisquam ius aliquod in quempiam nisi in solum
corpus et quod infra corpus est, fortunam loquor,
possit exserere ? Num quidquam libero imperabis
25 animo ? Num mentem firma sibi ratione cohaerentem
de statu propriae quietis amovebis ? Cum liberum
quendam virum suppliciis se tyrannus adacturum
putaret, ut adversum se factae coniurationis conscios
proderet, linguam ille momordit atque abscidit et in
30 os tyranni saevientis abiecit ; ita cruciatus, quos
putabat tyrannus materiam crudelitatis, vir sapiens
fecit esse virtutis. Quid autem est quod in alium
facere quisquam[1] possit, quod sustinere ab alio ipse
non possit ? Busiridem accipimus necare hospites so-
35 litum ab Hercule hospite fuisse mactatum. Regulus
plures Poenorum bello captos in vincla coniecerat, sed
mox ipse victorum catenis manus praebuit. Ullamne

---

[1] quisque *the best MSS.*

---

[a] The free man was the Democritean philosopher Anaxarchus, the tyrant Nicocreon ; Anaxarchus became for the
Romans the typical instance of indifference to pain, *cf.*

210

that of the men possessing them? So it comes about not that virtues are honoured because of office, but office because of the virtue of the holders.

Now what is this famous power of yours, so much sought after? Will you not consider, earthbound animals that you are, whom you think you command, and in what manner? If you saw one mouse among many claiming to have rightful power over the rest, how you would laugh! Now if you look at the body only, what can you find weaker than man, whom a little fly often kills with its bite or by crawling into some innermost part? How could anyone exert any power over anyone else except over his body, or over what is inferior to his body, that is, his fortune? Can you ever command a free mind in anything? Can you ever disturb the natural calm of a mind made whole and one by firm reason? When a tyrant thought he was going to drive a free man by torture to betray those conspiring against him, the man bit off his own tongue and spat it in the face of that raging tyrant.[a] So the very torture which the tyrant thought was the instrument of his cruelty the philosopher made the instrument of virtue. What is there that anyone can do to a man which he might not have done to himself by another? We read that Busiris used to murder his guests, and that he himself was killed by his guest Hercules.[b] Regulus had chained in prison many Carthaginians taken in war, but then he himself found his hands bound by the chains of his captors[c] Do you think that that man has any real

Cicero, *Tusc.* ii. 52 ; *De Nat. Deor.* iii. 82. The story is told by Valerius Maximus III. iii. 4, and Diogenes Laertius ix. 59.
[b] Hyginus, *Fabulae*, 31. 2.
[c] *Cf.* Cic. *De Off.* iii. 99, and esp. Aul. Gell. vii (vi). 4.

igitur eius hominis potentiam putas, qui quod ipse in
alio potest, ne id in se alter valeat efficere non possit ?
40 Ad haec si ipsis dignitatibus ac potestatibus inesset
aliquid naturalis ac proprii boni, numquam pessimis
provenirent. Neque enim sibi solent adversa sociari ;
natura respuit ut contraria quaeque iungantur. Ita
cum pessimos plerumque dignitatibus fungi dubium
45 non sit, illud etiam liquet natura sui bona non esse
quae se pessimis haerere patiantur. Quod quidem
de cunctis fortunae muneribus dignius existimari
potest, quae ad improbissimum quemque uberiora per-
veniunt. De quibus illud etiam considerandum puto,
50 quod nemo dubitat esse fortem, cui fortitudinem inesse conspexerit, et cuicumque velocitas adest manifestum est esse velocem. Sic musica quidem musi-
cos, medicina medicos, rhetorice rhetores facit. Agit
enim cuiusque rei natura quod proprium est nec
55 contrariarum rerum miscetur effectibus et ultro quae
sunt aversa depellit. Atqui nec opes inexpletam
restinguere avaritiam queunt nec potestas sui compotem fecerit quem vitiosae libidines insolubilibus
adstrictum retinent catenis, et collata improbis
60 dignitas non modo non efficit dignos, sed prodit
potius et ostentat indignos. Cur ita provenit ?
Gaudetis enim res sese aliter habentes falsis com-
pellare nominibus quae facile ipsarum rerum red-
arguuntur effectu ; itaque nec illae divitiae nec illa
65 potentia nec haec dignitas iure appellari potest.
Postremo idem de tota concludere fortuna licet in
qua nihil expetendum, nihil nativae bonitatis inesse

power who cannot prevent another from doing to
him what he himself can do to others ?

Consider also that if those offices and powers had
in them any natural and proper good they would
never be possessed by evil men ; for it is not usual
for opposites to be associated—nature rejects the
conjunction of contraries. Therefore since there is
no doubt that offices are often filled by evil men, this
also is clear, that they are not good in their nature,
since they allow themselves to be joined with evil in
this way. The same may be very rightly held true
of all the gifts of fortune which evil men all enjoy so
abundantly. Now we can also look at it in this way.
No one hesitates to call that man brave in whom he
sees bravery present, and clearly he is swift who
possesses swiftness ; so too art makes a man an
artist, medicine makes him a medical man, and
rhetoric makes him an orator. The nature of each
produces what is proper to it, and is not mixed with
contrary effects, but naturally rejects what is opposed
to it. Yet riches cannot get rid of avarice, for it is
insatiable, nor can power give a man self-control if
he is too firmly in the grip of sinful lusts ; and a high
office given to dishonest men not only does not make
them worthy of it, but rather betrays and publishes
their unworthiness. Why is this so ? Because you
delight to give to things which are really otherwise
names they should not bear and which are easily
shown to be false by the effects of the things themselves, so that this cannot rightly be called wealth,
nor that really power, nor the other truly an honour.
Lastly, we may draw the same conclusion in the
matter of a man's fortune as a whole, in which there
is obviously nothing really worth the seeking, no

manifestum est, quae nec se bonis semper adiungit
et bonos quibus fuerit adiuncta non efficit.

## VI

   Novimus quantas dederit ruinas
   Urbe flammata patribusque caesis
   Fratre qui quondam ferus interempto
   Matris effuso maduit cruore
5   Corpus et visu gelidum pererrans
   Ora non tinxit lacrimis, sed esse
   Censor extincti potuit decoris.
   Hic tamen sceptro populos regebat
   Quos videt condens radios sub undas
10   Phoebus extremo veniens ab ortu,
   Quos premunt septem gelidi triones,
   Quos Notus sicco violentus aestu
   Torret ardentes recoquens harenas.
   Celsa num tandem valuit potestas
15   Vertere pravi rabiem Neronis ?
   Heu gravem sortem, quotiens iniquus
   Additur saevo gladius veneno ! "

## VII

  Tum ego : " Scis," inquam, " ipsa minimum nobis
ambitionem mortalium rerum fuisse dominatam. Sed
materiam gerendis rebus optavimus quo ne virtus

---

  [a] Nero (A.D. 54–68) poisoned Britannicus, the son of his
step-father and predecessor as emperor, Claudius, when his
ambitious and scheming mother Agrippina, Claudius's
widow, seemed to be supporting Britannicus against him ;
Agrippina protected his wife Octavia, but under the influence

# CONSOLATION II

natural goodness, since it is not always conjoined with good men, nor does it make good those to whom it is joined.

## VI

*[handwritten note: classical example of tyrant in power]*

We know what great destruction that man caused
The city blazing, Senators killed,
His brother murdered, and his savage hand
Wet with the blood that from his mother flowed—
He could gaze on her cold corpse
And not shed tears
But coolly criticize her beauty dead.[a]
And yet beneath his sceptre's sway he held
Peoples the sun sees as he sinks in western waves
After his rising in the farthest east,
Those beneath the cold stare of the Bear
And those burnt by the harsh south wind
That bakes the hot dry sands.
Could not such power
Turn this perverted madness ? Alas, how many times
Both knife and poison served the dreadful state of
    Nero ! ''

## VII

*[handwritten note: True philosopher should be thinking about eternity anyway]*

    She finished, and I replied : '' You know yourself that ambition for mortal things governed me very little ; but I wanted the chance to take an active part

of his mistress Poppaea he first murdered Agrippina (Tacitus in *Annals*, xiv. 9, says that '' some say, and others deny, that Nero looked at his lifeless mother and praised the beauty of her body '') and then Octavia, making Poppaea empress. He was responsible also for the deaths of his counsellor Burrus, his old tutor and adviser Seneca, the poet Lucan, and many other nobles, as well as many Christians after the great fire in Rome in 64, before his own suicide in 68.

tacita consenesceret." Et illa : " Atqui hoc unum
5 est quod praestantes quidem natura mentes sed
nondum ad extremam manum virtutum perfectione
perductas allicere possit, gloriae scilicet cupido et
optimorum in rem publicam fama meritorum ; quae
quam sit exilis et totius vacua ponderis, sic considera.
10 Omnem terrae ambitum, sicuti astrologicis demonstrationibus accepisti, ad caeli spatium puncti constat
obtinere rationem, id est ut, si ad caelestis globi
magnitudinem conferatur, nihil spatii prorsus habere
iudicetur. Huius igitur tam exiguae in mundo
15 regionis quarta fere portio est, sicut Ptolomaeo pro-
bante didicisti, quae nobis cognitis animantibus in-
colatur. Huic quartae, si quantum maria paludesque
premunt quantumque siti vasta regio distenditur
cogitatione subtraxeris, vix angustissima inhabitandi
20 hominibus area relinquetur. In hoc igitur minimo
puncti quodam puncto circumsaepti atque conclusi de
pervulganda fama, de proferendo nomine cogitatis ?
Aut quid habeat amplum magnificumque gloria tam
angustis exiguisque limitibus artata ? Adde quod
25 hoc ipsum brevis habitaculi saeptum plures incolunt
nationes lingua, moribus, totius vitae ratione distantes,
ad quas tum difficultate itinerum tum loquendi diversitate tum commercii insolentia non modo fama
hominum singulorum sed ne urbium quidem pervenire

---

[a] Cf. Macrob. Somn. ii. 5-9, esp. 9, where Macrobius
says : " And the reason he so carefully stresses the smallness of the earth is so that a brave man may reckon little
of the desire for fame, which cannot be great in so small a
context."

[b] Ptolemy (Claudius Ptolemaeus, astronomer and geo-
grapher, who worked in Alexandria in the first half of the
second century A.D.) summed up Greek astronomical knowledge in his day in a work known as the Almagest, from one

in affairs of state, so that what powers for good I possess might not wither with age unused."

"Yet that is the only thing that could attract minds which are naturally outstanding, but not yet brought to the perfecting of their virtues to their finished condition : namely the desire for glory and the reputation of having deserved well of the state. How unsubstantial that glory is, how totally without weight, you may learn in this way. You have learned from astronomical proofs [a] that the whole circle of our earth is but a point in comparison with the extent of the whole heavens ; that is, if it is compared in size with the celestial sphere, it is judged to have no size at all. Of this very tiny part of the universe only a quarter, as you know from Ptolemy's [b] proofs, is inhabited by living things known to us. If in your imagination you subtract from that quarter all that is covered by seas and marshes and all the regions which extend in dried-up deserts, only a very narrow portion indeed is left for habitation by men. Now is it in this tightly-enclosed and tiny point, itself but part of a point, that you think of spreading your reputation, of glorifying your name ? What grandeur or magnificence can glory have, contracted within such small and narrow limits ? Consider also that in this little habitable enclosure there live many nations, different in language and customs and in their whole ways of life ; because of the difficulties of travel, and differences of language, and the rarity of trading contacts, the fame not merely of individual men but

of its late Greek titles, ἡ μεγίστη (σύνταξις) with the article ἡ translated into Arabic. The smallness of the part of our earth known to be inhabited was illustrated by Ptolemy in his γεωγραφικὴ σύνταξις. *Cf.* also pp. 136-137, note.

30 queat. Aetate denique Marci Tullii, sicut ipse
quodam loco significat, nondum Caucasum montem
Romanae rei publicae fama transcenderat, et erat tunc
adulta Parthis etiam ceterisque id locorum gentibus
formidolosa. Videsne igitur quam sit angusta, quam
35 compressa gloria quam dilatare ac propagare laboratis?
An ubi Romani nominis transire fama nequit, Romani
hominis gloria progredietur ? Quid quod diversarum
gentium mores inter se atque instituta discordant, ut
quod apud alios laude apud alios supplicio dignum
40 iudicetur. Quod fit ut si quem famae praedicatio
delectat, huic in plurimos populos nomen proferre
nullo modo conducat. Erit igitur pervagata inter
suos gloria quisque contentus et intra unius gentis
terminos praeclara illa famae immortalitas coarta-
45 bitur.

Sed quam multos clarissimos suis temporibus viros
scriptorum inops delevit oblivio ! Quamquam quid
ipsa scripta proficiant, quae cum suis auctoribus
premit longior atque obscura vetustas ? Vos vero
50 inmortalitatem vobis propagare videmini, cum futuri
famam temporis cogitatis. Quod si aeternitatis
infinita spatia pertractes, quid habes quod de nominis
tui diuturnitate laeteris ? Unius etenim mora momenti, si decem milibus conferatur annis, quoniam
55 utrumque spatium definitum est, minimam, licet,
habet tamen aliquam portionem. At hic ipse
numerus annorum eiusque quamlibet multiplex ad
interminabilem diuturnitatem ne comparari quidem
potest. Etenim finitis ad se invicem fuerit quaedam,

---

*a* Cic. *Rep.* vi. 22 ; but Boethius is quoting from Macrobius's Commentary on Cicero's *Republic*, ii. 10.

even of cities cannot reach them all. Lastly, in
Cicero's time, as he himself says somewhere,[a] the
fame of the Roman state had not yet gone beyond
the Caucasus, though Rome was then in her prime
and feared by Parthians and other peoples in that
region. Do you then see how narrow, how contracted
is that glory which you labour to increase and spread
abroad ? Or shall the glory of one Roman go where
the fame of Rome herself cannot ? Besides, the
customs and conventions of different peoples vary so
much that what is praised in one may be judged
deserving of punishment in another. This is why even
if a man is delighted to have his fame publicly proclaimed, it is by no means to his advantage to have
his name spread abroad among many nations. Each
man must therefore be content to have his glory
well-known among his own people, and the glorious
immortality of his fame must be restricted within the
bounds of one nation.

But how many men famous in their own time are
now completely forgotten, for want of written record ?
Though what is the value of such records themselves
when they and their writers arc lost in the obscurity
of long ages ? Yet *you* suppose that you provide for
your own immortality when you are concerned for
your future fame. But if you really consider the
infinite space of eternity, have you any reason to
rejoice in the long life of your own name ? For, one
moment compared with ten thousand years, since
each is a determinate length of time, is a certain
proportion, even if a very small fraction ; but even
that length of years, or any multiple of it, cannot be
compared at all with the infinite length of time. For
there can be a comparison between finite things, but

219

60 infiniti vero atque finiti nulla umquam poterit esse
collatio. Ita fit ut quamlibet prolixi temporis fama,
si cum inexhausta aeternitate cogitetur, non parva
sed plane nulla esse videatur. Vos autem nisi ad
populares auras inanesque rumores recte facere
65 nescitis et relicta conscientiae virtutisque praestantia
de alienis praemia sermunculis postulatis. Accipe in
huiusmodi arrogantiae levitate quam festive aliquis
inluserit. Nam cum quidam adortus esset hominem
contumeliis, qui non ad verae virtutis usum sed ad
70 superbam gloriam falsum sibi philosophi nomen
induerat, adiecissetque iam se sciturum, an ille philo-
sophus esset, si quidem illatas iniurias leniter patien-
terque tolerasset, ille patientiam paulisper adsumpsit
acceptaque contumelia velut insultans : ' Iam tan-
75 dem,' inquit, ' intellegis me esse philosophum ? '
Tum ille nimium mordaciter : ' Intellexeram,' inquit,
' si tacuisses.' Quid autem est quod ad praecipuos
viros, de his enim sermo est, qui virtute gloriam
petunt, quid, inquam, est quod ad hos de fama post
80 resolutum morte suprema corpus attineat ? Nam si,
quod nostrae rationes credi vetant, toti moriuntur
homines, nulla est omnino gloria, cum is cuius ea
esse dicitur non exstet omnino. Sin vero bene sibi
mens conscia terreno carcere resoluta caelum libera
85 petit, nonne omne terrenum negotium spernat quae
se caelo fruens terrenis gaudet exemptam ?

---

[a] That silence when necessary was a mark of the philosopher seems to have been a commonplace of antiquity

there can never be any proportion between the finite and the infinite. That is why however long a time fame last, if it is thought of in the context of boundless eternity, it is clearly seen to be, not small, but nothing at all. Yet *you* do not know how to act rightly unless you are favoured by the changing winds of popularity and empty rumour, and ignoring the excellence of the knowledge of your own virtue, you ask for the rewards of the common chatter of other men. Hear now how one man joked about the triviality of this kind of arrogance. He had insultingly attacked a man who had falsely assumed the title of philosopher, not for the practice of true virtue but simply from vanity, to increase his own glory ; and he added that he would know he was really a philosopher if he bore all the injuries heaped upon him calmly and patiently. The other adopted a patient manner for a time and bore the insults, and then said tauntingly : " Now do you recognize that I am a philosopher ? " To which the first very cuttingly replied : " I should have, had you kept silent." [a] But what has fame to offer men of the best sort—for these are the ones we are talking about, whose means to glory has been their virtue—what indeed, I ask, after death has finally destroyed the body ? If men wholly perish (which our arguments in fact forbid us to believe), glory is really nothing at all, since he to whom it is said to belong will no longer exist. If however a mind fully aware of its own nature, loosed from its earthly prison, is free to seek its heavenly home, will it not despise all earthly affairs, and in the joy of heaven rejoice to be freed from earthly things ?

(and *cf.* Proverbs 11. 12), but the origin of this story is unknown.

# BOETHIUS

## VII

Quicumque solam mente praecipiti petit
    Summumque credit gloriam,
Late patentes aetheris cernat plagas
    Artumque terrarum situm.
5    Brevem replere non valentis ambitum
    Pudebit aucti nominis.
Quid o superbi colla mortali iugo
    Frustra levare gestiunt ?
Licet remotos fama per populos means
10    Diffusa linguas explicet
Et magna titulis fulgeat claris domus,
    Mors spernit altam gloriam,
Involvit humile pariter et celsum caput
    Aequatque summis infima.
15    Ubi nunc fidelis ossa Fabricii manent,
    Quid Brutus aut rigidus Cato ?
Signat superstes fama tenuis pauculis
    Inane nomen litteris.
Sed quod decora novimus vocabula,
20    Num scire consumptos datur ?
Iacetis ergo prorsus ignorabiles
    Nec fama notos efficit.
Quod si putatis longius vitam trahi
    Mortalis aura nominis,
25    Cum sera vobis rapiet hoc etiam dies,
    Iam vos secunda mors manet.

## VIII

    Sed ne me inexorabile contra fortunam gerere
bellum putes, est aliquando cum de hominibus illa,

# CONSOLATION II

## VII

The man who rushes after glory
And nothing else, thinking it highest of all,
Let him compare the vastness of the heavens
With the narrowness of earth :
He'll blush for his proud name that cannot satisfy
Even his brief ambition.
Why do men in their pride—and yet in vain !—
Long to shake from their necks the yoke
Of their mortality ?
Though fame may spread abroad
Loosing the tongues of many different peoples,
And though a great house blaze with many a famous
  title,
Death despises the heights of glory,
Enfolds alike the humble and the proud,
Making the lowest equal to the highest.
Where now are the bones of good Fabricius ?
What is Brutus now, or stern old Cato ?
What little fame is left them—just their names
In a few old stories !
And if we read and learn their glorious names
Do we then know the dead ?
And so you too will all be quite forgotten,
Nor can fame make you known by any man.
And if you think you may live longer yet
At least as a name alive on the lips of men,
When your last day takes even *this* from you,
There's still to come
That second death.

## VIII

But in case you think I am inexorably hostile to
fortune, know that there is a time when she deserves

fallax illa nihil, bene mereatur, tum scilicet cum se
aperit, cum frontem detegit moresque profitetur.
5 Nondum forte quid loquar intellegis. Mirum est
quod dicere gestio, eoque sententiam verbis explicare
vix queo. Etenim plus hominibus reor adversam
quam prosperam prodesse fortunam. Illa enim
semper specie felicitatis cum videtur blanda,
10 mentitur ; haec semper vera est, cum se instabilem
mutatione demonstrat. Illa fallit, haec instruit, illa
mendacium specie bonorum mentes fruentium ligat,
haec cognitione fragilis felicitatis absolvit. Itaque
illam videas ventosam, fluentem suique semper
15 ignaram, hanc sobriam succinctamque et ipsius
adversitatis exercitatione prudentem. Postremo
felix a vero bono devios blanditiis trahit, adversa
plerumque ad vera bona reduces unco retrahit. An
hoc inter minima aestimandum putas quod amicorum
20 tibi fidelium mentes haec aspera, haec horribilis
fortuna detexit, haec tibi certos sodalium vultus
ambiguosque secrevit, discedens suos abstulit, tuos
reliquit ? Quanti hoc integer, ut videbaris tibi
fortunatus, emisses ! Nunc et amissas opes querere ;
25 quod pretiosissimum divitiarum genus est amicos
invenisti.

well of men, not deceiving them at all : when she
shows herself clearly, uncovering her face and declaring her ways. Perhaps you do not yet understand
what I am saying. What I want to tell you is something wonderful, which makes it very difficult for me
to put it into words. For I think that ill fortune is
better for men than good. Fortune always cheats
when she seems to smile, with the appearance of
happiness, but is always truthful when she shows
herself to be inconstant by changing. The first kind
of fortune deceives, the second instructs ; the one
binds the minds of those who enjoy goods that
cheatingly only seem to be good, the other frees them
with the knowledge of the fragility of mortal happiness. So you can see that the one is inconstant,
always running hither and thither, uncertain of herself ; and the other is steady, well prepared and—
with the practice of adversity itself—wise. Lastly
fortune when apparently happy leads men astray by
her blandishments, wandering from the true good ;
when she is adverse, she commonly draws them back,
as it were with a hook, towards it. Surely you do not
think it wholly unimportant that this rough and unpleasant fortune has discovered those friends who
are truly loyal to you, and has divided the honest
from the dishonest among your companions, by taking
her own kind with her when she left you, leaving your
sort with you ? How dearly would you have bought
such knowledge in your unaffected and—as you
thought— fortunate state ! As it is, you are even
complaining of your lost wealth ; but you have
found the most precious of all kinds of riches—true
friends.

## VIII

Quod mundus stabili fide
Concordes variat vices,
Quod pugnantia semina
Foedus perpetuum tenent,
5 Quod Phoebus roseum diem
Curru provehit aureo,
Ut quas duxerit Hesperos
Phoebe noctibus imperet,
Ut fluctus avidum mare
10 Certo fine coerceat,
Ne terris liceat vagis
Latos tendere terminos,
Hanc rerum seriem ligat
Terras ac pelagus regens
15 Et caelo imperitans amor.
Hic si frena remiserit,
Quidquid nunc amat invicem
Bellum continuo geret
Et quam nunc socia fide
20 Pulchris motibus incitant,
Certent solvere machinam.
Hic sancto populos quoque
Iunctos foedere continet,
Hic et coniugii sacrum
25 Castis nectit amoribus,
Hic fidis etiam sua
Dictat iura sodalibus.
O felix hominum genus,
Si vestros animos amor
30 Quo caelum regitur regat."

# CONSOLATION II

## VIII

In regular harmony
The world moves through its changes ;
Seeds in competition with each other
Are held in balance by eternal law ;
Phoebus brings rosy dawns
In his golden chariot
That his sister Phoebe may rule the nights
That Hesperus brings ;
The waves of the greedy sea
Are kept within fixed bounds,
Nor may the land move out
And extend its limits.
What binds all things to order,
Governing earth and sea and sky,
Is love.
If love's rein slackened
All things now held by mutual love
At once would fall to warring with each other
Striving to wreck that engine of the world
Which now they drive
In mutual trust with motion beautiful.
And love joins peoples too
By a sacred bond,
And ties the knot of holy matrimony
That binds chaste lovers,
Joins too with its law
All faithful comrades.
O happy race of men,
If the love that rules the stars
May also rule your hearts ! "

*love makes the world go round*

*love rules everything*

ANICII MANLII SEVERINI BOETHII

V.C. ET INL. EXCONS. ORD. PATRICII

# PHILOSOPHIAE CONSOLA-
# TIONIS

## LIBER SECUNDUS EXPLICIT

## INCIPIT LIBER III

### I

Iam cantum illa finiverat, cum me audiendi avidum
stupentemque arrectis adhuc auribus carminis mul-
cedo defixerat. Itaque paulo post : " O," inquam,
" summum lassorum solamen animorum quam tu me
5 vel sententiarum pondere vel canendi etiam iucunditate refovisti ! Adeo ut iam me post haec inparem
fortunae ictibus esse non arbitrer. Itaque remedia
quae paulo acriora esse dicebas, non modo non per-
horresco, sed audiendi avidus vehementer efflagito."
10 Tum illa : " Sensi," inquit, " cum verba nostra tacitus
attentusque rapiebas, eumque tuae mentis habitum
vel exspectavi vel, quod est verius, ipsa perfeci.
Talia sunt quippe quae restant, ut degustata quidem mordeant, interius autem recepta dulcescant.
15 Sed quod tu te audiendi cupidum dicis, quanto ar-
dore flagrares, si quonam te ducere aggrediamur
228

BOETHIUS

# THE CONSOLATION OF PHILOSOPHY

## BOOK III

### I

SHE had just finished singing, while the sweetness of her song held me with still attentive ears, struck silent, and eager to listen further. So after a little while I said : " O best of comforters of weary spirits, how well you have revived me with the weight of your arguments and also with the delights of your songs ! So well that now I no longer think myself unequal to the blows of fortune. So now I am not only not terrified of those remedies you described as somewhat more bitter, but I do most strongly urge you to administer them, since I am eager to listen further."

" I felt it was so," she said in reply, " when you were so absorbed, silent and attentive, by what I was saying, and I expected—or, more truly, I brought about —your present state of mind. Those remedies that are left now are like those that sting on the tongue, but sweeten once taken within. But you say you are desirous to hear more : with what desire you would burn if you knew where I am going to lead you ! "

agnosceres ! " " Quonam ? " inquam. " Ad veram, "
inquit, " felicitatem, quam tuus quoque somniat
animus, sed occupato ad imagines visu ipsam illam
20 non potest intueri." Tum ego : " Fac obsecro et
quae illa vera sit, sine cunctatione demonstra.''
" Faciam," inquit illa, " tui causa libenter. Sed quae
tibi causa notior est, eam prius designare verbis
atque informare conabor ut ea perspecta cum in
25 contrariam partem flexeris oculos, verae beatitudinis
speciem possis agnoscere.

### I

Qui serere ingenuum volet agrum,
Liberat arva prius fructibus,
Falce rubos filicemque resecat,
Ut nova fruge gravis Ceres eat.
5 Dulcior est apium mage labor,
Si malus ora prius sapor edat.
Gratius astra nitent ubi Notus
Desinit imbriferos dare sonos.
Lucifer ut tenebras pepulerit
10 Pulchra dies roseos agit equos.
Tu quoque falsa tuens bona prius
Incipe colla iugo retrahere.
Vera dehinc animum subierint."

### II

Tum defixo paululum visu et velut in augustam
suae mentis sedem recepta sic coepit : " Omnis

230

# CONSOLATION III

" Where ? " I asked.

" To that true happiness," said she, " which your spirit, too, dreams of, but cannot see as it really is because your sight is too occupied with images."

Then I said : " Tell me, show me without delay, I beg you, what that true happiness is."

" I shall willingly," she answered, " for your sake. But first I shall try to describe in words and delineate a subject better known to you, so that, when you have seen that clearly, you may, since you will then have turned your eyes on its opposite, recognize the appearance of true blessedness."

## I

Whoever wants to sow a virgin field,
First clears the ground of scrub,
And with his sickle cuts down fern and bramble,
That Ceres may come, heavy with new grain.
Bees' honey is sweeter far
If first a bitter flavour bites the mouth.
The stars shine brighter
When the south wind has ceased its noisy rain.
When the morning star has driven away the dark,
Fair the day drives its rosy steeds.
So must you too, who now have eyes
Only for false goods, first begin
To draw your neck from the yoke,
That then the true may slip into your mind.

## II

Then for a little her look was cast down and, as if withdrawn into the depths of her noble mind, she

mortalium cura quam multiplicium studiorum labor
exercet, diverso quidem calle procedit, sed ad unum
5 tamen beatitudinis finem nititur pervenire. Id autem
est bonum quo quis adepto nihil ulterius desiderare
queat. Quod quidem est omnium summum bonorum
cunctaque intra se bona continens, cui si quid aforet
summum esse non posset, quoniam relinqueretur
10 extrinsecus quod posset optari. Liquet igitur esse
beatitudinem statum bonorum omnium congregatione
perfectum. Hunc, uti diximus, diverso tramite
mortales omnes conantur adipisci. Est enim mentibus hominum veri boni naturaliter inserta cupiditas,
15 sed ad falsa devius error abducit. Quorum quidem
alii summum bonum esse nihilo indigere credentes
ut divitiis affluant elaborant ; alii vero bonum quod
sit dignissimum veneratione iudicantes adeptis
honoribus reverendi civibus suis esse nituntur. Sunt
20 qui summum bonum in summa potentia esse con-
stituant ; hi vel regnare ipsi volunt vel regnantibus
adhaerere conantur. At quibus optimum quiddam
claritas videtur, hi vel belli vel pacis artibus gloriosum
nomen propagare festinant. Plurimi vero boni fruc-
25 tum gaudio laetitiaque metiuntur ; hi felicissimum
putant voluptate diffluere. Sunt etiam qui horum
fines causasque alterutro permutent, ut qui divitias
ob potentiam voluptatesque desiderant vel qui
potentiam seu pecuniae causa seu proferendi nominis
30 appetunt. In his igitur ceterisque talibus humanorum
232

began : " The whole concern of men, which the effort of a multitude of pursuits keeps busy, moves by different roads, yet strives to arrive at one and the same end, that of happiness. Now that is the good which, once a man attains it, leaves no room for further desires. And it is the highest of all goods, containing in itself all that is good, for if there were anything lacking to it, it could not be the highest good, since there would remain something outside it which could be desired. So it is clear that happiness is that state which is perfect since all goods are gathered together in it. This it is, as I have said, that all men strive to obtain by various paths ; for the desire for the true good is naturally inborn in the minds of men, but they are led astray after false goods. Now some men believe that the highest good is to want nothing, so that they labour to abound in riches ; but others hold whatever is most worthy of honour to be the good, and strive to be honoured and respected by their fellow citizens for the distinctions they receive. There are some who think that the highest good lies in the greatest power ; these either wish themselves to rule, or try to attach themselves to those who rule. But those who think fame is something very good hasten to spread their names abroad, made glorious through some skill in war or peace. More, however, measure their enjoyment of the good in terms of joy and gladness, and think it most happy to abandon themselves to pleasure. And there are those too who interchange and intermingle these various aims and motives, such as those who desire riches for the sake of power or pleasure, or those who seek power for the sake of wealth or to advance their own fame. So, to these and to all

actuum votorumque versatur intentio, veluti nobilitas
favorque popularis quae videntur quandam claritudinem comparare, uxor ac liberi quae iucunditatis gratia
petuntur ; amicorum vero quod sanctissimum quidem
35 genus est, non in fortuna sed in virtute numeratur,
reliquum vero vel potentiae causa vel delectationis
assumitur. Iam vero corporis bona promptum est
ut ad superiora referantur. Robur enim magnitudo-
que videtur praestare valentiam, pulchritudo atque
40 velocitas celebritatem, salubritas voluptatem ; quibus
omnibus solam beatitudinem desiderari liquet. Nam
quod quisque prae ceteris petit, id summum esse
iudicat bonum. Sed summum bonum beatitudinem
esse definivimus ; quare beatum esse iudicat statum
45 quem prae ceteris quisque desiderat.

Habes igitur ante oculos propositam fere formam
felicitatis humanae—opes, honores, potentiam,
gloriam, voluptates. Quae quidem sola considerans
Epicurus[a] consequenter sibi summum bonum volup-
50 tatem esse constituit, quod cetera omnia iucunditatem
animo videantur afferre. Sed ad hominum studia
revertor, quorum animus etsi caligante memoria
tamen bonum suum repetit,[b] sed velut ebrius domum
quo tramite revertatur ignorat. Num enim videntur
55 errare hi qui nihilo indigere nituntur ? Atqui non
est aliud quod aeque perficere beatitudinem possit

---

[a] The founder of the Epicurean school of philosophers ;
born about 342 B.C. in Attica and brought up in Samos, he
adopted the physics of Democritus with its atomic theory to
make a mechanistic universe that would free men from fear
of the gods and life after death and enable them to live a life
of pleasure, which for him meant freedom from fear and
worry.

[b] The ideas of seeking the good again (*repetit*) and of the
memory of it being clouded both refer to the Platonic notion

other such things are the aims and purposes of men's
acts and prayers related : so noble rank and the
support of the populace are sought after because they
appear to acquire some sort of renown, or a wife and
children are sought after for the pleasure they give ;
but the most sacred kind of good is that of friendship,
a good reckoned not a matter of fortune but of virtue,
while any other kind is chosen for the sake of power
or delight.  Now all the goods connected with the
body can easily be related to the things mentioned
above :  physical strength and size seem to provide
influence ;  beauty and swiftness, fame ;  and health,
pleasure.  In all of these things it is obviously happiness alone that is desired ;  for whatever a man seeks
above all else, that he reckons the highest good.  But
we have defined the highest good as happiness ;
wherefore each man judges that state to be happy
which he desires above all others.

So now you have as it were set before your eyes
the delineaments of human happiness :  wealth,
honour, power, glory, pleasure.  Epicurus [a] looked
only at these things, and consequently decided that
for him the highest good was pleasure, since all the
others seemed to bring delight to the mind.  But I
turn back to the endeavours of men : for man's mind,
though the memory of it is clouded, yet does seek
again its proper good,[b] but like a drunken man cannot
find by what path it may return home.  For are they
really wrong, who strive to lack nothing ?  But
surely there is nothing else so conducive to perfect

that the soul is of one kind with Ideas, the perfect Forms,
including the Form of the Good, and is born with a knowledge of them, but forgets them on being imprisoned, as it
were, in the body.

quam copiosus bonorum omnium status nec alieni
egens sed sibi ipse sufficiens. Num vero labuntur hi
qui quod sit optimum, id etiam reverentiae cultu
60 dignissimum putent ? Minime. Neque enim vile
quiddam contemnendumque est quod adipisci omnium
fere mortalium laborat intentio. An in bonis non est
numeranda potentia ? Quid igitur ? Num imbecillum
ac sine viribus aestimandum est, quod omnibus rebus
65 constat esse praestantius ? An claritudo nihili
pendenda est ? Sed sequestrari nequit quin omne
quod excellentissimum sit id etiam videatur esse
clarissimum. Nam non esse anxiam tristemque
beatitudinem nec doloribus molestiisque subiectam
70 quid attinet dicere, quando in minimis quoque rebus
id appetitur quod habere fruique delectet ? Atqui
haec sunt quae adipisci homines volunt eaque de
causa divitias, dignitates, regna, gloriam voluptatesque
desiderant quod per haec sibi sufficientiam, reveren-
75 tiam, potentiam, celebritatem, laetitiam credunt esse
venturam. Bonum est igitur quod tam diversis
studiis homines petunt ; in quo quanta sit naturae
vis facile monstratur, cum licet variae dissidentesque
sententiae tamen in diligendo boni fine consentiunt.

## II

Quantas rerum flectat habenas
Natura potens, quibus immensum
Legibus orbem provida servet
Stringatque ligans inresoluto
5 Singula nexu, placet arguto
Fidibus lentis promere cantu.

happiness as a condition possessing plenty of all goods, needing no other's help, but being self-sufficient. Are they indeed mistaken, who think that whatever is best is also most worthy of reverence and respect ? Of course not : for that cannot be base and contemptible which the efforts and labour of almost all men strive to obtain. Is power not to be accounted a good ? Why, surely we are not to think that to be feeble and lacking in vigour which it is agreed is more excellent than all else ? Is fame to be rated as nothing ? Yet it cannot be set aside that all that is most excellent also seems to be most famous. Is there any point in saying that happiness is not worried or depressed, not subject to pain or vexation ? Since even in the least things men seek that which they delight to have and to enjoy. These surely are the things men want to gain, and for that reason they desire riches, high office, the rule of men, glory and pleasure, because they believe that through them they will achieve sufficiency, respect, power, celebrity and joy. The good is therefore that which men pursue in so many different endeavours ; and we can easily see how great is nature's power in this, since although opinions vary and differ so much, yet they agree in loving the same end, the good.

## II

I have decided now
In clear song, with my pliant strings, to show
What great control Nature in her power
Wields over all things, with what laws
She in her foresight keeps the vast universe
Tied fast, each single thing, in indissoluble bonds.

Quamvis Poeni pulchra leones
Vincula gestent manibusque datas
Captent escas metuantque trucem
10    Soliti verbera ferre magistrum,
Si cruor horrida tinxerit ora,
Resides olim redeunt animi
Fremituque gravi meminere sui ;
Laxant nodis colla solutis
15    Primusque lacer dente cruento
Domitor rabidas imbuit iras.
Quae canit altis garrula ramis
Ales caveae clauditur antro ;
Huic licet inlita pocula melle
20    Largasque dapes dulci studio
Ludens hominum cura ministret,
Si tamen arto saliens texto
Nemorum gratas viderit umbras,
Sparsas pedibus proterit escas,
25    Silvas tantum maesta requirit,
Silvas dulci voce susurrat.
Validis quondam viribus acta
Pronum flectit virga cacumen ;
Hanc si curvans dextra remisit,
30    Recto spectat vertice caelum.
Cadit Hesperias Phoebus in undas,
Sed secreto tramite rursus
Currum solitos vertit ad ortus.
Repetunt proprios quaeque recursus
35    Redituque suo singula gaudent
Nec manet ulli traditus ordo
Nisi quod fini iunxerit ortum
Stabilemque sui fecerit orbem.

# CONSOLATION III

Though lions from Carthage wear fine-fashioned
  chains
And eat out of a man's hand,
And fear—being used to beatings—their harsh master,
If blood once touch their bristling jaws
Their long inactive spirits straight revive,
With rumbling growls they are themselves again,
Shake their necks free from broken knots,
And the first to slake their rage, torn by their blood-
  stained teeth,
Is their trainer.
The tree-top loving, chirruping bird
Is shut in a coop like a cavern.
Men treat her as a toy and care for her
With kindliness putting in honeyed drink
And food in plenty :
Yet if she sees, hopping in her narrow cage,
The beloved shade of trees,
She scatters her food beneath her feet
And all she wants is her woods,
Sings sadly, softly, sweetly of her woods.
Bend now, with all your strength,
A sapling's top to the ground ;
But if the right hand bowing it let go
Its top again points straight up to the sky.
Phoebus sinks under western waves
But by a secret path again
He turns his car
To his accustomed rising.
Each thing seeks its own way back
And coming back is glad ,
None is consigned to any ordered course
Save that which links the end to the beginning
And makes its cycle firm.

### III

Vos quoque, o terrena animalia, tenui licet imagine
vestrum tamen principium somniatis verumque illum
beatitudinis finem licet minime perspicaci quali-
cumque tamen cogitatione prospicitis eoque vos et
5 ad verum bonum naturalis ducit intentio et ab eodem
multiplex error abducit. Considera namque an per
ea quibus se homines adepturos beatitudinem putant
ad destinatum finem valeant pervenire. Si enim
vel pecuniae vel honores ceteraque tale quid afferunt
10 cui nihil bonorum abesse videatur, nos quoque
fateamur fieri aliquos horum adeptione felices.
Quod si neque id valent efficere quod promittunt
bonisque pluribus carent, nonne liquido falsa in eis
beatitudinis species deprehenditur ? Primum igitur
15 te ipsum qui paulo ante divitiis affluebas, interrogo :
inter illas abundantissimas opes numquamne animum
tuum concepta ex qualibet iniuria confudit anxietas ? ”
“ Atqui,” inquam, “ libero me fuisse animo quin
aliquid semper angerer reminisci non queo.” “ Nonne
20 quia vel aberat quod abesse non velles vel aderat
quod adesse noluisses ? ” “ Ita est,” inquam. “ Illius
igitur praesentiam huius absentiam desiderabas ? ”
“ Confiteor,” inquam. “ Eget vero,” inquit, “ eo
quod quisque desiderat ? ” “ Eget,” inquam. “ Qui
240

## III

And you also, earthly creatures that you are, have some image, though hazy, in your dreams of your beginning ; you see, though with a far from clear imagination yet with some idea, that true end of your happiness. Your natural inclinations draw you towards that end, to the true good, though mistaken notions of many kinds lead you away from it. For consider, can men come to the end they set themselves through those things by which they think they will obtain happiness ? For if money or honours or the rest do produce any such thing, from which no good seems to be lacking, even we should admit that some men are made happy by getting them. But if they cannot perform what they promise, but lack many goods, is not the appearance of happiness that they produce clearly false ? First then, I ask you yourself, you who were not so long ago very wealthy, were you never, among all your vast riches, troubled in mind by some anxiety, arising from some wrong or other ? "

" I certainly cannot remember," I answered, " that my mind was so free that it was not always in some way tormented."

" Was it not either because something was missing that you wanted, or because something you did not want was present ? "

" Yes," I said.

" So you desired the presence of the one, and the absence of the other ? "

" That is so," I said,

" Now any man must lack that thing which he desires ? "

" Yes, he must," said I.

25 vero eget aliquo, non est usquequaque sibi ipse
sufficiens ? " " Minime," inquam. " Tu itaque hanc
insufficientiam plenus," inquit, " opibus sustinebas ? "
" Quidni ? " inquam. " Opes igitur nihilo indigentem
sufficientemque sibi facere nequeunt et hoc erat quod
30 promittere videbantur. Atqui hoc quoque maxime
considerandum puto quod nihil habeat suapte natura
pecunia ut his a quibus possidetur invitis nequeat
auferri." " Fateor," inquam. " Quidni fateare, cum
eam cotidie valentior aliquis eripiat invito ? Unde
35 enim forenses querimoniae nisi quod vel vi vel fraude
nolentibus pecuniae repetuntur ereptae ? " " Ita
est," inquam. " Egebit igitur," inquit, " extrinsecus
petito praesidio quo suam pecuniam quisque tueatur? "
" Quis id," inquam, " neget ? " " Atqui non egeret
40 eo, nisi possideret pecuniam quam posset amittere ? "
" Dubitari," inquam, " nequit." " In contrarium
igitur relapsa res est ; nam quae sufficientes sibi facere putabantur opes, alieno potius praesidio faciunt indigentes. Quis autem modus est quo pellatur
45 divitiis indigentia ? Num enim divites esurire nequeunt ? Num sitire non possunt ? Num frigus hi-
bernum pecuniosorum membra non sentiunt ? Sed
adest, inquies, opulentis quo famem satient, quo
sitim frigusque depellant. Sed hoc modo consolari

" But whoever lacks anything, is not completely self-sufficient ? "

" No, he is certainly not," I said.

" So, did *you*, loaded with wealth as you were," she said, " feel this insufficiency ? "

" Why not ? " I asked.

" Then wealth cannot make a man self-sufficient, lacking nothing, though this was what it seemed to promise. And I think that this also is specially worth considering, that there is nothing in the nature of money which prevents its being taken away from those who possess it, against their will."

" I grant that," I said.

" Why shouldn't you grant it, since every day someone who is stronger takes it from another against his will ? What else causes all the lawsuits, if not that someone is trying to get back money that has been taken against their will by force or by fraud ? "

" That is so," said I.

" So," said she, " a man will need some help sought from outside himself by which to keep his money safe ? "

" Who would deny it ? " I asked.

" But he would not need it, did he not possess money, which he could lose."

" There is no doubt of that," said I.

" So the very opposite is true to what was expected. Wealth, which was thought to make a man self-sufficient, actually makes him need another's help. And by what means does wealth get rid of need ? Can rich men not get hungry, can they not be thirsty, do the bodies of the moneyed men not feel the winter's cold ? But, you will argue, the wealthy have the means to satisfy their hunger, and to be rid of thirst

50 quidem divitiis indigentia potest, auferri penitus non
potest. Nam si haec hians semper atque aliquid
poscens opibus expletur, maneat necesse est quae
possit expleri. Taceo quod naturae minimum, quod
avaritiae nihil satis est. Quare si opes nec sub-
55 movere possunt indigentiam et ipsae suam faciunt,
quid est quod eas sufficientiam praestare credatis ?

## III

Quamvis fluente dives auri gurgite
    Non expleturas cogat avarus opes
Oneretque bacis colla rubri litoris
    Ruraque centeno scindat opima bove,
5    Nec cura mordax deseret superstitem,
    Defunctumque leves non comitantur opes.

## IV

Sed dignitates honorabilem reverendumque cui
provenerint reddunt. Num vis ea est magistratibus
ut utentium mentibus virtutes inserant vitia depellant ? Atqui non fugare sed illustrare potius
5 nequitiam solent ; quo fit ut indignemur eas saepe
nequissimis hominibus contigisse, unde Catullus licet
in curuli Nonium sedentem strumam tamen appellat.
Videsne quantum malis dedecus adiciant dignitates ?
Atqui minus eorum patebit indignitas, si nullis
10 honoribus inclarescant. Tu quoque num tandem tot

---

   *a* A *struma* is a " scrofulous tumour " (in *Cat.* lii. 2 it is a
proper name, as also in Pliny, *N.H.* xxxvii. 81) : the curule
chairs (*sellae curules*) in the Senate House were the official
seats of consuls and other magistrates.

or cold. But in that way need can be made easier to bear by riches, it cannot be removed altogether. For if need, always gasping for and demanding something, is satisfied by riches, there must remain a need still which could be satisfied. I pass over the fact that nature is satisfied with very little, while nothing satisfies avarice. So if riches not only cannot remove need, but even produce a need of their own, why should you believe that they can provide sufficiency?

### III

*[handwritten note: portrait of greedy man]*

Let the rich man in his avarice pile up his wealth
(Which is never enough!) with flowing streams of
    gold;
Let him load his neck with Red Sea pearls;
And plough his fat fields with hundreds of oxen!
Gnawing care will never leave him while he lives,
Nor does his insubstantial wealth go with him dead.

*[handwritten note: Horace's influence]*

### IV

But high offices bring to him who acquires them honour and respect. Yet is there really this power in offices, that they instil virtues into the minds of those who fill them, and drive away vices? Surely they do not usually drive off wickedness but rather make it notorious? That is why we are indignant that they are often bestowed on wicked men: so that Catullus called Nonius a ' growth ' although he was sitting in a curule chair.[a] Do you see how much dishonour high offices bring on bad men? Their baseness would surely be less obvious if they were not well known for any honours. And could you

245

periculis adduci potuisti ut cum Decorato gerere
magistratum putares, cum in eo mentem nequissimi
scurrae delatorisque respiceres ?  Non enim possumus
ob honores reverentia dignos iudicare quos ipsis
15 honoribus iudicamus indignos.  At si quem sapientia
praeditum videres, num posses eum vel reverentia
vel ea qua est praeditus sapientia non dignum putare ?
Minime.  Inest enim dignitas propria virtuti, quam
protinus in eos quibus fuerit adiuncta transfundit.
20 Quod quia populares facere nequeunt honores, liquet
eos propriam dignitatis pulchritudinem non habere.

In quo illud est animadvertendum magis.  Nam si
eo abiectior est quo magis a pluribus quisque con-
temnitur, cum reverendos facere nequeat quos
25 pluribus ostentat, despectiores potius improbos
dignitas facit.  Verum non impune ; reddunt namque
improbi parem dignitatibus vicem quas sua contagione
commaculant.  Atque ut agnoscas veram illam reverentiam per has umbratiles dignitates non posse con-
30 tingere, si qua multiplici consulatu functus in barbaras
nationes forte devenerit, venerandumne barbaris
honor faciet ?  Atqui si hoc naturale munus dignitatibus foret, ab officio suo quoquo gentium nullo
modo cessarent, sicut ignis ubique terrarum numquam
35 tamen calere desistit, sed quoniam id eis non propria
vis sed hominum fallax adnectit opinio, vanescunt

---

[a] Decoratus was a magistrate, possibly quaestor, about
A.D. 508 (cf. Cassiodorus, *Variae*, v. 3 and 4).

yourself ever have been induced by any number of
dangers to think of taking office with Decoratus,
since you perceived that he had the disposition of a
wicked clown and informer ? [a] For we cannot judge
those worthy of respect because of their offices whom
we judge unworthy of the offices themselves. But if
you saw someone endowed with wisdom, could you
think him unworthy of respect or of that wisdom with
which he is endowed ? Of course not. So there is
some worth proper to virtue which is immediately
transferred to those to whom virtue is joined. Now
since honours acclaimed by the mob cannot do this,
it is clear that they do not possess the beauty proper
to real worth. And in this matter you should further
consider this : if a man is the more abject the more
he is despised by the more people, high office, since
it cannot make dishonest men worthy of respect, for
it exposes them to the gaze of more people, makes
them rather the more despised. But the offices themselves do not escape without harm, for those dishonest
men do an equally bad turn to them by defiling them
with their own infection.

Now that you may recognize that that true respect
cannot be derived from these shadowy dignities,
suppose a man who has been consul many times
should happen to visit some barbarian nations outside
the Roman world, will his high rank make him respected by the barbarians ? If such dignities did
possess this ability naturally, they would not lose
their power among any peoples at all, just as fire
never ceases to be hot anywhere in the world. But
since it is not a power proper to them, but only attributed to them by the delusory opinion of men, they
at once became empty as soon as they come among

247

ilico, cum ad eos venerint qui dignitates eas esse non
aestimant.

Sed hoc apud exteras nationes. Inter eos vero
40 apud quos ortae sunt, num perpetuo perdurant ?
Atqui praetura magna olim potestas nunc inane
nomen et senatorii census gravis sarcina ; si quis
populi quondam curasset annonam, magnus habe-
batur, nunc ea praefectura quid abiectius ?  Ut
45 enim paulo ante diximus, quod nihil habet proprii
decoris, opinione utentium nunc splendorem accipit
nunc amittit.  Si igitur reverendos facere nequeunt
dignitates, si ultro improborum contagione sordescunt,
si mutatione temporum splendere desinunt, si gentium
50 aestimatione vilescunt, quid est quod in se expetendae
pulchritudinis habeant, nedum aliis praestent ?


IV

Quamvis se Tyrio superbus ostro
  Comeret et niveis lapillis,
Invisus tamen omnibus vigebat
  Luxuriae Nero saevientis.
5 Sed quondam dabat improbus verendis
  Patribus indecores curules.
Quis illos igitur putet beatos
  Quos miseri tribuunt honores ?


V

An vero regna regumque familiaritas efficere
potentem valet ?  Quidni, quando eorum felicitas

---

[a] There is possibly a reference here to Pompey the Great ;
*cf.* Cassiod. *Variae*, vi. 18 (*Formula Praefectus Annonae ;*
Migne, *P.L.* lxix. 699).

peoples who do not count them dignities at all. But this is of course so among foreigners. Yet do they last constant among those who created these high offices ? The praetorship was once an office of great power, now it is an empty name and a heavy burden on the resources of the Senatorial order. Once, when a man had charge of the public corn-dole, he was held to be great ; now, is there anything lower than that prefectship ? [a] For as I said just now, that which has no glory of its own nature, is in the estimation of those using it at one time splendid, at another, not. If, then, high offices cannot make a man worthy of respect ; if, what is more, they are readily sullied by being infected by dishonest men occupying them ; if they cease to be splendid as times change, and are cheapened in the judgement of different peoples, what beauty can they have in themselves which we should seek after or which, still less, they can confer on others ?

## IV

Though in his pride he decked himself
In Tyrian purple and in snowy pearls,
Nero for all his pomp was hated by all
For his self-indulgent cruelty.
Shamelessly once he gave the reverend Senators
Unworthy consuls to elect :
Who could then think such honours blessed
Granted by such miserable men ?

## V

But surely kingdoms and association with kings can make a man truly powerful ? Why not, when

249

perpetuo perdurat ? Atqui plena est exemplorum
vetustas, plena etiam praesens aetas, qui reges
5 felicitatem calamitate mutaverint. O praeclara
potentia quae ne ad conservationem quidem sui satis
efficax invenitur ! Quod si haec regnorum potestas
beatitudinis auctor est, nonne si qua parte defuerit,
felicitatem minuat, miseriam inportet ? Sed quamvis
10 late humana tendantur imperia, plures necesse est
gentes relinqui quibus regum quisque non imperet.
Qua vero parte beatos faciens desinit potestas, hac
inpotentia subintrat quae miseros facit ; hoc igitur
modo maiorem regibus inesse necesse est miseriae
15 portionem. Expertus sortis suae periculorum
tyrannus regni metus pendentis supra verticem gladii
terrore simulavit. Quae est igitur haec potestas
quae sollicitudinum morsus expellere, quae formi-
dinum aculeos vitare nequit ? Atqui vellent ipsi
20 vixisse securi, sed nequeunt ; dehinc de potestate
gloriantur. An tu potentem censes quem videas
velle quod non possit efficere ? Potentem censes
qui satellite latus ambit, qui quos terret ipse plus
metuit, qui ut potens esse videatur, in servientium
25 manu situm est ? Nam quid ego de regum familiari-
bus disseram, cum regna ipsa tantae inbecillitatis
plena demonstrem ? Quos quidem regia potestas
saepe incolumis saepe autem lapsa prosternit. Nero
Senecam familiarem praeceptoremque suum ad
30 eligendae mortis coegit arbitrium. Papinianum diu
inter aulicos potentem militum gladiis Antoninus

---

[a] Dionysius I of Syracuse (430–367 B.C.); the story is told
in Cic. *Tusc.* V. xxi. 61-62.

[b] Tac. *Ann.* xiv. 53-54 ; and *cf.* Book II, pp. 214-215:
the date was A.D. 65.

their happiness lasts for ever ? Yet ancient times are full—and the present times are full, too—of examples of kings whose happiness changed to misfortune. O a fine power indeed, that is discovered to be insufficient even for its own preservation ! If this power over kingdoms does produce happiness, would it not lessen that happiness and introduce misery if it were lacking in any respect ? But however widely any human empires may extend, there must always be many nations left which any particular king does not rule. Now wherever the power that makes kings happy ends, there their lack of power creeps in and makes them miserable ; in this way, then, kings must have a larger share of misery than happiness. Knowing by experience the dangers of his own position, one tyrant [a] likened his fears as king to the terror of the sword hanging over Damocles' head. What is this power, then, that cannot get rid of gnawing care or prevent the pricks of fear ? Surely kings would like to have lived out their lives without care, yet they cannot : and then they boast of their power ! If you see a man who wants to do what he cannot, do you think him powerful ? Do you think him powerful who goes everywhere with a bodyguard at his side ? Or him who himself is more afraid of others than they of him ? Or him whose show of power depends on a crowd of courtiers ? Well, need I say anything about the companions of kings, when I have shown that kingship itself is full of such weakness ? For courtiers are cast down often both when kingly power is secure and when it is overthrown. Nero forced Seneca, his old companion and teacher, to choose the manner of his own death [b] ; Papinian had long been powerful at court, but Antoninus threw him to his soldier's

251

obiecit. Atqui uterque potentiae suae renuntiare voluerunt, quorum Seneca opes etiam suas tradere Neroni seque in otium conferre conatus est ; sed
35 dum ruituros moles ipsa trahit, neuter quod voluit effecit. Quae est igitur ista potentia quam pertimescunt habentes, quam ne cum habere velis tutus sis et cum deponere cupias vitare non possis ? An praesidio sunt amici quos non virtus sed fortuna
40 conciliat ? Sed quem felicitas amicum fecit, infortunium faciet inimicum. Quae vero pestis efficacior ad nocendum quam familiaris inimicus ?

## V

Qui se volet esse potentem
Animos domet ille feroces
Nec victa libidine colla
Foedis submittat habenis.
5   Etenim licet Indica longe
Tellus tua iura tremescat
Et serviat ultima Thyle,
Tamen atras pellere curas
Miserasque fugare querelas
10  Non posse potentia non est.

## VI

Gloria vero quam fallax saepe, quam turpis est !

---

<sup>a</sup> Papinian, the greatest perhaps of the Roman jurists, and praetorian prefect under Severus (emperor from 192 to 211) was killed by Severus's son M. Antoninus Caracalla in about 212 (*cf.* Spartianus, *Caracalla*, 8 : *a militibus non solum permittente verum etiam suadente Antonino occisum*).

swords.[a]  Yet both wanted to renounce their power ;
Seneca even tried to hand his wealth over to Nero
and to retire.  But while they stood on the brink and
their very greatness drew them down, neither
achieved what he wished.  What is this power, then,
which those who have it greatly fear ?  While you
want to possess it, you are not safe, and when you
want to put it aside, you cannot get rid of it.  Are we
really helped by friends who are drawn to us not by
our virtue but by our fortune ?  But a man made a
friend by good fortune, misfortune will make an
enemy.  And what plague is more able to hurt a man
than an enemy who was once a familiar friend ?

## V

The man who wants to be powerful
Must tame his high spirits,
Must not submit his neck, conquered by lust,
To its stinking halter ;
For indeed though far-off Indian soil
Tremble under your sway,
And furthest Thule [b] serve you,
Yet not to be able to dispel black care
Or put complaining misery to flight
This is no power at all.

## VI

And glory—how deceptive that often is, how base !
That is why the tragic poet [c] was not wrong when

[b] *ultima Thule* : *cf*. Virg. *Georg*. i. 30 ; a land or island
of dubious identity (Iceland ? Norway ?) in the far north of
Europe.
[c] Eur. *Andr*. 319 f.

# BOETHIUS

Unde non iniuria tragicus exclamat :

*Ὦ δόξα δόξα μυρίοισι δὴ βροτῶν
οὐδὲν γεγῶσι βίοτον ὤγκωσας μέγαν.

5 Plures enim magnum saepe nomen falsis vulgi
opinionibus abstulerunt ; quo quid turpius excogitari
potest ?  Nam qui falso praedicantur, suis ipsi
necesse est laudibus erubescant. Quae si etiam
meritis conquisita sit, quid tamen sapientis adiecerit
10 conscientiae qui bonum suum non populari rumore,
sed conscientiae veritate metitur ?  Quod si hoc
ipsum propagasse nomen pulchrum videtur, consequens est ut foedum non extendisse iudicetur.
Sed cum, uti paulo ante disserui, plures gentes esse
15 necesse sit ad quas unius fama hominis nequeat
pervenire, fit ut quem tu aestimas esse gloriosum,
proxima[1] parte terrarum videatur inglorius. Inter
haec vero popularem gratiam ne commemoratione
quidem dignam puto, quae nec iudicio provenit nec
20 umquam firma perdurat. Iam vero quam sit inane
quam futtile nobilitatis nomen, quis non videat ?
Quae si ad claritudinem refertur, aliena est. Videtur
namque esse nobilitas quaedam de meritis veniens
laus parentum. Quod si claritudinem praedicatio
25 facit, illi sint clari necesse est qui praedicantur.
Quare splendidum te, si tuam non habes, aliena
claritudo non efficit. Quod si quid est in nobilitate
bonum, id esse arbitror solum, ut inposita nobilibus
necessitudo videatur ne a maiorum virtute degeneret.

[1] *var. lect.* pro maxima.

[a] Reading *proxima* with Weinberger and Bieler ; *pro
maxima* would presumably mean " in the greater part of the
earth," but I prefer *proxima* if only on the *difficilior lectio*
principle.

254

he exclaimed :

> O glory, glory, myriads of mortals,
> Born nothings, thou hast blown their lives up big.

For too many men have often acquired a great reputation because of the mistaken notions of the mob—and what can be imagined baser that that ?  For those who are much talked about, but mistakenly, must surely blush to hear their own praises.  Even if such praises are won by deserts, what will they have added to the self-knowledge of a wise man who measures his own good not by gossip of the populace but by the truth of that self-knowledge ?  But if to have had even one's reputation spread abroad seems fair, then it follows that for it not to have been so widely spread must be adjudged foul.  But since, as I showed just now, there must be many nations which the reputation of one man cannot reach, it happens that the man you think glorious may seem inglorious in the very next-door region of the earth.[a] But here I may say that I do not think popular favour even worth mentioning ;  it neither proceeds from judgement nor ever firmly endures.  But now who does not see how empty and vain a thing is a reputation for nobility ?  If it is related to fame, it belongs to another :  for nobility seems to be a kind of praise deriving from the deserts of one's parents.  Now if being talked about produces fame, then those must be famous who are talked about ;  wherefore the fame of others, if you have none of your own, does not make you renowned.  But if there is anything good in nobility, I think it is this only, that there seems to be an obligation imposed on the noble not to let it degenerate from the virtue of their ancestors.

# BOETHIUS

## VI

Omne hominum genus in terris simili surgit ab ortu.
Unus enim rerum pater est, unus cuncta ministrat.
Ille dedit Phoebo radios dedit et cornua lunae,
Ille homines etiam terris dedit ut sidera caelo,
5 Hic clausit membris animos celsa sede petitos.
Mortales igitur cunctos edit nobile germen.
Quid genus et proavos strepitis ? Si primordia vestra
Auctoremque deum spectes, nullus degener exstat,
Ni vitiis peiora fovens proprium deserat ortum.

## VII

Quid autem de corporis voluptatibus loquar
quarum appetentia quidem plena est anxietatis,
satietas vero poenitentiae ? Quantos illae morbos,
quam intolerabiles dolores quasi quendam fruc-
5 tum nequitiae fruentium solent referre corporibus !
Quarum motus quid habeat iucunditatis, ignoro.
Tristes vero esse voluptatum exitus, quisquis reminisci libidinum suarum volet, intelleget. Quae si
beatos explicare possunt, nihil causae est quin
10 pecudes quoque beatae esse dicantur quarum omnis
ad explendam corporalem lacunam festinat intentio.
Honestissima quidem coniugis foret liberorumque
iucunditas, sed nimis e natura dictum est nescio
quem filios invenisse tortores[1] ; quorum quam sit

[1] *var. lect.* tortorem.

# CONSOLATION III

## VI

All human kind on earth arises from the same origin ;
There is one Father of all things, one who looks after
  all.
He gave the sun his rays, the moon her horns,
He peopled too the earth with men as the sky with
  constellations ;
He locked into limbs spirits brought down from their
  high abode.
So did a noble seed produce all mortals.
Why shout about your lineage or your forbears ?   If
  you consider
Your beginnings and God your Author, no man is now
  degenerate
Save who embracing baser things in vice forsakes his
  proper origin.

## VII

What shall I say about the pleasures of the body,
the longing for which is full of anxiety, the satisfaction of which full of regret ?   What dreadful diseases,
what unbearable pains they generally cause in the
bodies of those enjoying them, as a kind of fruit of
their wickedness !   What pleasure there is in stirring
them up, I do not know ;   but that these pleasures
have a bitter end, anyone will understand who is
willing to recall his own lusts.   If bodily pleasures
can make men happy, there is no reason why beasts
should not be called happy too, since their whole
effort is directed to fulfilling their bodies' missing
needs.   The pleasure derived from wife and children
should surely be wholly good, but it was too well said,
too truly to nature, that someone invented children

15 mordax quaecumque condicio, neque alias expertum
te neque nunc anxium necesse est admonere. In
quo Euripidis mei sententiam probo, qui carentem
liberis infortunio dixit esse felicem.

## VII

Habet hoc voluptas omnis,
Stimulis agit fruentes
Apiumque par volantum
Ubi grata mella fudit,
5      Fugit et nimis tenaci
Ferit icta corda morsu.

## VIII

Nihil igitur dubium est quin hae ad beatitudinem
viae devia quaedam sint nec perducere quemquam
eo valeant ad quod se perducturas esse promittunt.
Quantis vero implicitae malis sint, brevissime mon-
5 strabo. Quid enim ? Pecuniamne congregare cona-
beris ? Sed eripies habenti. Dignitatibus fulgere
velis ? Danti supplicabis et qui praeire ceteros
honore cupis, poscendi humilitate vilesces. Poten-
tiamne desideras ? Subiectorum insidiis obnoxius
10 periculis subiacebis. Gloriam petas ? Sed per aspera
quaeque distractus securus esse desistis. Voluptariam
vitam degas ? Sed quis non spernat atque abiciat

---

<sup>a</sup> Reading *tortores*. If *tortorem* (which has better MSS.
authority) is retained, the translation should be : " that
some tormentor invented children."

to be tormentors.[a]   There is no need to warn you—
having experienced it before and even now being
anxious—how, whatever their condition is, it gnaws
at you with worry.   In this matter I agree with the
opinion of my Euripides, who said that one who lacks
children is happy in his misfortune.[b]

## VII

Such is every pleasure
Goading those enjoying it,
And like swarming bees
That have poured out their pleasing honey,
It flees, and strikes our hearts
With a too lasting sting.

## VIII

There is therefore no doubt but that these ways to
happiness are a kind of by-paths and cannot bring
anyone to that place to which they promise to lead
him.   Now I shall very briefly show with what great
evils they are bound up.   What then, will you try to
amass money ?   But you will have to take it from
him who has it.   Would you like to be illustrious for
your honours ?   You will have to beg them humbly
of their giver, and you who long to surpass others in
honour will become cheap through the baseness of
your begging.   Do you desire power ?   You will lie
exposed to dangers, prey to your subjects' treachery.
Do you seek glory ?   But pulled about through every
kind of difficulty you cease to be safe.   Would you
lead a life of pleasure ?   But who would not despise

[b] Eur. *Andr.* 420 : δυστυχῶν εὐδαιμονεῖ.

vilissimae fragilissimaeque rei corporis servum ? Iam
vero qui bona prae se corporis ferunt, quam exigua,
15 quam fragili possessione nituntur ! Num enim
elephantos mole, tauros robore superare poteritis,
num tigres velocitate praeibitis ? Respicite caeli
spatium firmitudinem celeritatem et aliquando
desinite vilia mirari. Quod quidem caelum non his
20 potius est quam sua qua regitur ratione mirandum.
Formae vero nitor ut rapidus est, ut velox et
vernalium florum mutabilitate fugacior ! Quod si, ut
Aristoteles ait, Lynceis oculis homines uterentur,
ut eorum visus obstantia penetraret, nonne intro-
25 spectis visceribus illud Alcibiadis superficie pulcherrimum corpus turpissimum videretur ? Igitur
te pulchrum videri non tua natura sed oculorum
spectantium reddit infirmitas. Sed aestimate quam
vultis nimio corporis bona, dum sciatis hoc quod-
30 cumque miramini triduanae febris igniculo posse
dissolvi ! Ex quibus omnibus illud redigere in
summam licet, quod haec quae nec praestare quae
pollicentur bona possunt nec omnium bonorum
congregatione perfecta sunt, ea nec ad beatitudinem
35 quasi quidem calles ferunt nec beatos ipsa perficiunt.


## VIII

Eheu quae miseros tramite devios
    Abducit ignorantia !
Non aurum in viridi quaeritis arbore
    Nec vite gemmas carpitis,

---

[a] Arist. fr. 59 ; and *cf. An. Post.* 1397 b 18. The sharp
sight of the Argonaut Lynceus became proverbial.

and reject the service of so very base and frail a
thing as the body ? Now indeed those indeed who
boast of the good qualities of their bodies—how mean
and how frail the possession on which they rely !
Could you exceed elephants in size, or bulls in
strength, could you outstrip tigers in speed ? Look
on the space and steadfastness and speed of the
heavens and cease hereafter to wonder at base things ;
though the heavens are rather to be wondered at not
for these things but for the order by which they are
governed. But how brief is the brightness of beauty,
how swiftly passing, more quickly fleeting than the
changing loveliness of spring flowers. And if, as
Aristotle says,[a] men enjoyed the use of Lynceus' eyes
so that their sight penetrated obstacles, would not
the superficially very beautiful body of Alcibiades
seem most vile when his inwards could be seen ? So
it is not your nature that makes you appear fair, but
the weakness of the eyes of those who look at you.
But you may over-esteem the body's good qualities
as much as you like, provided you realize that what
you admire can be destroyed by the burning of a
three-days fever. Out of all which we may gather
this in sum, that these things which can neither provide those goods they promise nor are perfect by
amassing all goods, neither lead to happiness like so
many roads, nor themselves make men happy.

## VIII

Alas, what ignorance
Leads wretched men astray on a devious path !
You seek not gold on a green tree,
Nor gather gems from the vine ;

5 Non altis laqueos montibus abditis
    Ut pisce ditetis dapes
Nec vobis capreas si libeat sequi,
    Tyrrhena captatis vada.
Ipsos quin etiam fluctibus abditos
10     Norunt recessus aequoris,
Quae gemmis niveis unda feracior
    Vel quae rubentis purpurae
Nec non quae tenero pisce vel asperis
    Praestent echinis litora.
15 Sed quonam lateat quod cupiunt bonum,
    Nescire caeci sustinent,
Et quod stelliferum trans abiit polum,
    Tellure demersi petunt.
Quid dignum stolidis mentibus inprecer ?
20     Opes honores ambiant ;
Et cum falsa gravi mole paraverint,
    Tum vera cognoscant bona.

## IX

Hactenus mendacis formam felicitatis ostendisse suffecerit, quam si perspicaciter intueris, ordo est deinceps quae sit vera monstrare." " Atqui video," inquam, " nec opibus sufficientiam nec regnis poten-
5 tiam nec reverentiam dignitatibus nec celebritatem gloria nec laetitiam voluptatibus posse contingere." " An etiam causas, cur id ita sit, deprehendisti ? " " Tenui quidem veluti rimula mihi videor intueri, sed ex te apertius cognoscere malim."

You do not spread your hidden nets on mountains high
To enrich your feast with fish,
Nor if it please you hunt roe-deer
Do you search Tyrrhenian seas.
Rather indeed men know the deep retreats
Hidden by the waves of the sea,
What waters more abound in snowy pearls,
Which in red murices,
As too which shores provide the tender fish
Or the prickly sea-urchin.
But where the good that they desire may hide,
They blindly ignorant remain,
And that which passes far beyond the starry pole
Sunk in the earth they seek.
What curse can I invoke on such stupid minds ?
Let them strive for wealth and honours, and then
When they have gained false goods with labour great,
Let them recognize true goods.

## IX

Now let what I have so far shown you of the shape
of false happiness suffice : if you look at that properly
and thoroughly, the right order now is to show you
what true happiness is."

"Indeed I see," I said, " that sufficiency cannot be
obtained through wealth, nor power through kingship, nor respect through office, nor fame through
glory, nor joy through pleasures."

"And have you also grasped the reasons why this
is so ? "

" I think I glimpse them as it were through a
narrow crack, but I should prefer to learn of them
more plainly from you."

10 " Atqui promptissima ratio est. Quod enim simplex est indivisumque natura, id error humanus separat et a vero atque perfecto ad falsum imperfectumque traducit. An tu arbitraris quod nihilo indigeat egere potentia ? " " Minime," inquam. " Recte tu
15 quidem. Nam si quid est quod in ulla re inbecillioris valentiae sit, in hac praesidio necesse est egeat alieno." " Ita est," inquam. " Igitur sufficientiae potentiaeque una est eademque natura." " Sic videtur." " Quod vero huiusmodi sit, spernendumne
20 esse censes an contra rerum omnium veneratione dignissimum ? " " At hoc," inquam, " ne dubitari quidem potest." " Addamus igitur sufficientiae potentiaeque reverentiam, ut haec tria unum esse iudicemus." " Addamus, si quidem vera volumus
25 confiteri."

" Quid vero," inquit, " obscurumne hoc atque ignobile censes esse an omni celebritate clarissimum ? Considera vero, ne quod nihilo indigere, quod potentissimum, quod honore dignissimum esse concessum est,
30 egere claritudine quam sibi praestare non possit atque ob id aliqua ex parte videatur abiectius." " Non possum," inquam, " quin hoc uti est ita etiam celeberrimum esse confitear." " Consequens igitur est ut claritudinem superioribus tribus nihil differre fatea-
35 mur." " Consequitur," inquam. " Quod igitur nullius

" The explanation is indeed very ready to hand, for that which is simple and undivided by nature, human error divides and perverts from the true and perfect to the false and imperfect. Do you think that that which needs nothing is in want of power ? "

" Certainly not," I said.

" You are quite right," she said, " for if there is something the power of which is in any respect too weak, there must be in that respect a need for others' help."

" That is so," I said.

" Therefore the nature of sufficiency and that of power are one and the same."

" So it seems."

" Now do you think that what is of this kind is to be despised or, on the contrary, to be of all things the most worthy of respect ? "

" The latter," I said ; " it cannot even be doubted."

" So let us add respect to sufficiency and power, so that we judge these three to be one."

" Let us so add it, since we wish indeed to acknowledge the truth."

" Well then," she said, " do you think it is obscure and undistinguished, or is it most famous, with all renown ? Now consider whether that which it is granted lacks nothing, which is most powerful and most worthy of honour, is in want of fame, and cannot provide it for itself, and for that reason seems in some respect to be lower."

" I cannot but acknowledge," I said, " that being what it is, it is also most renowned."

" Consequently, then, let us admit that fame differs not at all from the previous three."

" It follows," I said.

egeat alieni, quod suis cuncta viribus possit, quod sit
clarum atque reverendum, nonne hoc etiam constat
esse laetissimum ? " " Sed unde huic," inquam, " tali
maeror ullus obrepat ne cogitare quidem possum ; quare
40 plenum esse laetitiae, si quidem superiora manebunt,
necesse est confiteri." " Atqui illud quoque per
eadem necessarium est sufficientiae, potentiae, clari-
tudinis, reverentiae, iucunditatis nomina quidem esse
diversa, nullo modo vero discrepare substantiam."
45 " Necesse est," inquam. " Hoc igitur quod est unum
simplexque natura, pravitas humana dispertit et dum
rei quae partibus caret partem conatur adipisci, nec
portionem quae nulla est nec ipsam quam minime
affectat assequitur." " Quonam," inquam, " modo ? "
50 " Qui divitias," inquit, " petit penuriae fuga, de
potentia nihil laborat, vilis obscurusque esse mavult,
multas etiam sibi naturales quoque subtrahit voluptates, ne pecuniam quam paravit amittat. Sed hoc
modo ne sufficientia quidem contingit ei quem
55 valentia deserit, quem molestia pungit, quem vilitas
abicit, quem recondit obscuritas. Qui vero solum
posse desiderat, profligat opes, despicit voluptates
honoremque potentia carentem gloriam quoque nihili
pendit. Sed hunc quoque quam multa deficiant
60 vides. Fit enim ut aliquando necessariis egeat, ut
anxietatibus mordeatur cumque haec depellere
266

" Now that which needs no-one else, which can do all things by its own power, which is famous and worthy of respect—should we not agree that it is also most joyful ? "

" I cannot even conceive," I said, " whence any sadness might steal upon it, such as it is ; wherefore it must be acknowledged to be full of joy, if indeed what has been said before shall remain true."

" And this too is necessary according to those same arguments, that the *names* of sufficiency, power, fame, respect and pleasure are different, but their *substance* differs in no respect."

" That is necessary," I said.

" Now this, which is one and simple in its nature, man's perversity splits up, and while he tries to obtain a part of it, though in fact it has no parts, he gains neither a portion of it, for there are no portions, nor the thing itself, which he is not in the least trying to get."

" How is that ? " I asked.

" He who in flight from want seeks riches," she answered, " takes no pains over power, prefers to be base and obscure, and also deprives himself of many pleasures, even natural ones, in case he lose the money he has acquired. But in this way he does not even achieve sufficiency, since he is deserted by power, afflicted by trouble, made abject by baseness and hidden in obscurity. Now he who only desires power, squanders his wealth, despises pleasures, and all honour without power, as well as glory, he counts as worthless. But you see how many things are wanting to him too : for it happens that sometimes he lacks necessities, so that he is gnawed by worries, and since he cannot get rid of these worries, he loses

nequeat, etiam id quod maxime petebat potens esse
desistat. Similiter ratiocinari de honoribus, gloria,
voluptatibus licet. Nam cum unumquodque horum
65 idem quod cetera sit, quisquis horum aliquid sine
ceteris petit, ne illud quidem quod desiderat apprehendit." " Quid igitur," inquam, " si qui cuncta
simul cupiat adipisci, summam quidem ille beatudinis
velit ? " " Sed num in his eam reperiet, quae demon-
70 stravimus id quod pollicentur non posse conferre ? "
" Minime," inquam. " In his igitur quae singula
quaedam expetendorum praestare creduntur, beatitudo nullo modo vestiganda est." " Fateor," inquam, " et hoc nihil dici verius potest." " Habes
75 igitur," inquit, " et formam falsae felicitatis et causas.
Deflecte nunc in adversum mentis intuitum ; ibi
enim veram quam promisimus statim videbis."
" Atqui haec," inquam, " vel caeco perspicua est
eamque tu paulo ante monstrasti, dum falsae causas
80 aperire conaris. Nam nisi fallor ea vera est et perfecta felicitas quae sufficientem, potentem, reverendum, celebrem laetumque perficiat. Atque ut me
interius animadvertisse cognoscas, quae unum horum,
quoniam idem cuncta sunt, veraciter praestare potest
85 hanc esse plenam beatitudinem sine ambiguitate
cognosco." " O te alumne hac opinione felicem, si
quidem hoc," inquit, " adieceris." " Quidnam ? " inquam. " Essene aliquid in his mortalibus caducisque

even that which he most sought after, being powerful.
We may produce similar arguments about honours,
glory and pleasures ; for since each one of these is
essentially the same thing as the rest, whoever seeks
one of them apart from the others does not even grasp
that one he desires."

" Well then," I said, " suppose a man desire to
obtain them all together ; he would indeed be de-
siring the sum of happiness." " But surely he will
not find it in those things we have shown cannot
bestow what they promise ? "

" No indeed," I said.

" Therefore happiness is by no means to be sought
in these things, which are believed to provide each
desirable thing separately ? "

" I admit it," I said, " and nothing could be truer."

" You know, then," she said, " both the form of
false happiness, and its causes. Now turn your
mind's gaze in the opposite direction ; for there you
will at once see true happiness, as I promised."

" It is indeed clear," I said, " even to a blind man,
and you have shown it to me just now, while you
were seeking to display the causes of false happiness.
For unless I am wrong, that is true and perfect happiness which makes a man sufficient, powerful, respected, famous and joyful. And so that you may
know that I have inwardly understood this, that
which can truly provide one of these—since all are
really the same—that I recognize unequivocally as
full happiness."

" O my pupil," she said, " I should call you happy
in this opinion, if you but added this."

" What, please ? " I asked.

" Do you think that there is any among these

rebus putas quod huiusmodi statum possit afferre ? ”
90 “ Minime,” inquam, “ puto idque a te, nihil ut amplius
desideretur, ostensum est.” “ Haec igitur vel
imagines veri boni vel inperfecta quaedam bona dare
mortalibus videntur, verum autem atque perfectum
bonum conferre non possunt.” “ Assentior,” in-
95 quam. “ Quoniam igitur agnovisti quae vera illa sit,
quae autem beatitudinem mentiantur, nunc superest
ut unde veram hanc petere possis agnoscas.” “ Id
quidem,” inquam, “iam dudum vehementer exspecto.”
“ Sed cum, ut in Timaeo[1] Platoni,” inquit, “ nostro
100 placet, in minimis quoque rebus divinum praesidium
debeat implorari, quid nunc faciendum censes, ut
illius summi boni sedem reperire mereamur ? ”
“ Invocandum,” inquam, “ rerum omnium patrem,
quo praetermisso nullum rite fundatur exordium.”
105 “ Recte,” inquit, ac simul ita modulata est.

## IX

“ O qui perpetua mundum ratione gubernas
   Terrarum caelique sator qui tempus ab aevo
Ire iubes stabilisque manens das cuncta moveri,
   Quem non externae pepulerunt fingere causae

---

[1] uti Timaeo *the best* MSS.

---

[a] *Tim.* 27 c.

[b] This poem is largely derived from Plato's *Timaeus*
27 c—42 D, with much use of the Neo-platonist commentary
of Proclus (ed. Ernest Diehl, Teubner (3 vols.), 1903–1906).
It has been described by Courcelle as “ substantiel et concis,
obscur et presque intraduisable ”, and its difficulty, because
of the compression of so much thought in so few lines, has
called forth commentaries throughout medieval and modern
times. For a full account of sources and commentary see
F. Klingner, *De Boethii Consolatione*, in *Philologische Unter-*

mortal and impermanent things which could produce a condition of this kind ? "

" I most certainly think not," I replied, " and that has been so demonstrated by you that no further argument is desired."

" These things, therefore, seem to give mortals images of the true good, or certain imperfect goods, but they cannot confer the true and perfect good."

" I agree," I said.

" Then since you have recognized what is the true happiness, and what things counterfeit it, it now remains for you to recognize whence you can seek this true happiness."

" That indeed," I said, is what I have long been eagerly hoping for."

" But since," said she, " as is my Plato's opinion in the *Timaeus*,[a] we ought to implore God's help in even the least of matters, what do you think we should do now, that we may be worthy to discover the abode of that highest good ? "

" We must call upon the Father of all things," I said, " for if this is omitted no beginning can be rightly and properly based."

" You are right," she said, and at once began singing in this way :

## IX [b]

" O you who in perpetual order govern the universe,
Creator of heaven and earth, who bid time ever move,
And resting still, grant motion to all else ;
Whom no external causes drove to make

*suchungen*, xxvii (Berlin, 1921), pp. 38-67 and P. Courcelle, *La Consolation de Philosophie dans la tradition littéraire* (Paris, 1967), pp. 161 ff.

5    Materiae fluitantis opus, verum insita summi
     Forma boni livore carens, tu cuncta superno
     Ducis ab exemplo, pulchrum pulcherrimus ipse
     Mundum mente gerens similique in imagine formans
     Perfectasque iubens perfectum absolvere partes.
10   Tu numeris elementa ligas ut frigora flammis
     Arida conveniant liquidis, ne purior ignis
     Evolet aut mersas deducant pondera terras.
     Tu triplicis mediam naturae cuncta moventem
     Conectens animam per consona membra resolvis.
15   Quae cum secta duos motum glomeravit in orbes,
     In semet reditura meat mentemque profundam
     Circuit et simili convertit imagine caelum.
     Tu causis animas paribus vitasque minores
     Provehis et levibus sublimes curribus aptans
20   In caelum terramque seris quas lege benigna
     Ad te conversas reduci facis igne reverti.

---

   [a] Matter, all sensible things, is flowing, ever coming to be,
changing and passing away ; the only reason for God's
creation is the outpouring of good, since the Form of the
Good is in him, a Good lacking all grudging spirit (the
" envy of the gods," φθόνος θεῶν, their grudging nature, was
a commonplace among the Greeks). God creates on the
pattern of the eternal Forms, which for the Neo-platonists
and their Christian followers were in the mind of God.
   [b] Soul's nature is threefold : God took the eternal Same,
and the changing Other, and forced the two into union to
produce their harmony, Being ; and then of these three
fashioned Soul. All movement is caused by Soul, the only
self-mover, or by its parts, which are harmonious since they
too are formed of the same three elements, Same, Other and
Being.
   [c] The two circles into which the divided Soul is bent are
the celestial equator and the ecliptic ; the Mind is the

# CONSOLATION III

Your work of flowing matter,[a] but the form
Within yourself of the highest good, ungrudging ;
    from a heavenly pattern
*You* draw out all things, and being yourself most fair,
A fair world in your mind you bear, and forming it
In the same likeness, bid it being perfect to complete
    itself
In perfect parts.   *You* bind its elements with law, so
    that the cold
Come together with flames, the dry with liquids, lest
    the fire too pure
Fly off, or lest its weight pull down the overwhelmed
    earth.
*You*, binding soul together in its threefold nature's
    midst,[b]
Soul that moves all things, then divide it into har-
    monious parts ;
Soul thus divided has its motion gathered
Into two circles,[c] moves to return into itself, and the
    Mind deep within
Encircles, and makes the heaven turn, in likeness to
    itself.
*You* then bring forth, with the same bases, lesser
    living souls,[d]
And giving them light chariots fitting their heavenly
    nature,
Broadcast them in the heavens and on earth, and by
    your bounteous law
Make them, turned towards you, with returning fire
    come back.

moving soul in the outermost, invisible heaven, which turns
the visible heaven in its perfect motion.

    [d] The lesser souls are the souls of men, each assigned to a
star as its chariot, and each returning when purified after a
good life in the body to the heavens (see *Tim.* 41 D—42 D).

Da pater augustam menti conscendere sedem,
Da fontem lustrare boni, da luce reperta
In te conspicuos animi defigere visus.
25    Dissice terrenae nebulas et pondera molis
Atque tuo splendore mica ! Tu namque serenum,
Tu requies tranquilla piis, te cernere finis,
Principium, vector, dux, semita, terminus idem.

## X

Quoniam igitur quae sit imperfecti, quae etiam
perfecti boni forma vidisti, nunc demonstrandum
reor quonam haec felicitatis perfectio constituta sit.
In quo illud primum arbitror inquirendum, an aliquod
5 huiusmodi bonum quale paulo ante definisti in rerum
natura possit exsistere, ne nos praeter rei subiectae
veritatem cassa cogitationis imago decipiat. Sed
quin exsistat sitque hoc veluti quidam omnium
fons bonorum negari nequit. Omne enim quod
10 inperfectum esse dicitur, id inminutione perfecti
inperfectum esse perhibetur. Quo fit, ut si in
quolibet genere inperfectum quid esse videatur, in
eo perfectum quoque aliquid esse necesse sit.
Etenim perfectione sublata, unde illud quod inper-
15 fectum perhibetur exstiterit ne fingi quidem potest.
Neque enim ab deminutis inconsummatisque natura
rerum coepit exordium, sed ab integris absolutisque
procedens in haec extrema atque effeta dilabitur.
Quod si, uti paulo ante monstravimus, est quaedam
274

Grant, Father, to my mind to rise to your majestic
    seat,
Grant me to wander by the source of good, grant
    light to see,
To fix the clear sight of my mind on you.
Disperse the clouding heaviness of this earthly mass
And flash forth in your brightness. For, to the
    blessed, *you*
Are clear serenity, and quiet rest : to see *you* is their
    goal,
And you, alone and same,
Are their beginning, driver, leader, pathway, end.

## X

  " Now since you have seen what is the form both
of the imperfect and of perfect good, I think we must
now show where this perfection of happiness is set.
And in this I think we first have to inquire whether
any good of this kind, as you have just defined it, can
exist in the world, lest we are deceived by an empty
imagining going beyond the truth of the reality
before us. But that there exists this thing, as it were
a kind of fount of all goods, cannot be denied. For
everything which is called imperfect is held to be
imperfect because of some diminution of what is
perfect. Hence it happens that if in any class something seems to be imperfect, there must also be
something perfect of that class ; for if we take away
perfection altogether, it cannot even be imagined
how that which is held to be imperfect can exist. For
the universe did not take its origin from diminished
and unfinished beginnings, but proceeding from beginnings whole and completely finished it lapses into
this latest, exhausted state. But if, as we have just

20 boni fragilis inperfecta felicitas, esse aliquam solidam
perfectamque non potest dubitari." " Firmissime,"
inquam, " verissimeque conclusum est." " Quo vero,"
inquit, " habitet, ita considera. Deum rerum omnium
principem bonum esse communis humanorum con-
25 ceptio probat animorum. Nam cum nihil deo melius
excogitari queat, id quo melius nihil est bonum esse
quis dubitet ? Ita vero bonum esse deum ratio
demonstrat, ut perfectum quoque in eo bonum
esse convincat. Nam ni tale sit, rerum omnium
30 princeps esse non poterit. Erit enim eo praestantius aliquid perfectum possidens bonum, quod hoc
prius atque antiquius esse videatur ; omnia namque
perfecta minus integris priora esse claruerunt. Quare
ne in infinitum ratio prodeat, confitendum est sum-
35 mum deum summi perfectique boni esse plenissimum. Sed perfectum bonum veram esse beatitudinem
constituimus ; veram igitur beatitudinem in summo
deo sitam esse necesse est." " Accipio," inquam,
" nec est quod contradici ullo modo queat." " Sed
40 quaeso," inquit, " te vide quam id sancte atque
inviolabiliter probes quod boni summi summum deum
diximus esse plenissimum." " Quonam," inquam,
" modo ? " " Ne hunc rerum omnium patrem illud
summum bonum quo plenus esse perhibetur vel
45 extrinsecus accepisse vel ita naturaliter habere prae-

shown, there is a certain imperfect happiness in a good that perishes, it cannot be doubted that there is some enduring and perfect happiness."

" The conclusion is most firmly and truly drawn," I said.

" Now where that dwells," she said, " consider in this way. That God, the principle of all things, is good is proved by the common concept of all men's minds ; for since nothing better than God can be conceived of, who can doubt that that, than which nothing is better, is good ? But reason so much shows that God is good that it proves clearly that perfect good also is in him. For unless he were such, he could not be the principle of all things ; for there would be something possessing perfect good more excellent than he, which in this would seem to be prior and more ancient. For it has become clear that all perfect things are prior to the less perfect. There-fore, so that our argument does not fall into an in-finite regress, we must admit that the most high God is full of the most high and perfect good ; but we have decided that the perfect good is true happi-ness ; therefore true happiness must reside in the most high God."

" I accept that," I said, " nor can it in any way be contradicted."

" But now I ask you," said she, " see how solemnly and inviolably you approve what we said of the most high God being filled full of the highest good."

" How ? " I asked.

" So that you may not suppose that he, the Father of all things, has received that highest good, of which it is agreed he is filled, from outside, or in such a way naturally possesses it, as if you might think that the

sumas, quasi habentis dei habitaeque beatitudinis
diversam cogites esse substantiam. Nam si extrinsecus acceptum putes, praestantius id quod dederit
ab eo quod acceperit existimare possis. Sed hunc
50 esse rerum omnium praecellentissimum dignissime
confitemur. Quod si natura quidem inest, sed est
ratione diversum, cum de rerum principe loquamur
deo, fingat qui potest : quis haec diversa coniunxerit ?
Postremo quod a qualibet re diversum est, id non
55 est illud a quo intellegitur esse diversum. Quare
quod a summo bono diversum est sui natura, id
summum bonum non est—quod nefas est de eo
cogitare quo nihil constat esse praestantius. Omnino
enim nullius rei natura suo principio melior poterit
60 exsistere, quare quod omnium principium sit, id
etiam sui substantia summum esse bonum verissima
ratione concluserim." " Rectissime," inquam. " Sed
summum bonum beatitudinem esse concessum est."
" Ita est," inquam. " Igitur," inquit, " deum esse
65 ipsam beatitudinem necesse est confiteri." " Nec
propositis," inquam, " prioribus refragari queo et
illis hoc inlatum consequens esse perspicio."

   " Respice," inquit, " an hinc quoque idem firmius
approbetur, quod duo summa bona quae a se diversa
70 sint esse non possunt. Etenim quae discrepant
bona, non esse alterum quod sit alterum liquet ;
quare neutrum poterit esse perfectum, cum alterutri
278

substance of the happiness possessed is different from that of God the possessor. For if you thought it was received from outside, you could think that which gave it more excellent than that which received it : but we most rightly confess that he is the most excellent of all things. But if it is by nature that it is in him, but it is essentially different, then since we are speaking of God the Author of all things, let him imagine who can who it was joined these two different natures. Finally, that which is different from something is not that from which it is understood to be different ; therefore that which is different in its nature from the highest good is not itself the highest good, which it would be wicked to think of him than whom it is agreed there is nothing more excellent. For since there could exist no nature of anything at all better than its own principle, therefore I would conclude with the truest reasoning, that which is the principle of all things is also in its substance the highest good."

" Most rightly," I said.

" But we have granted that the highest good is happiness."

" That is so," I said.

" Therefore," she said, " it must be confessed that happiness is itself God."

" I both am unable to refute your previous propositions," I said, " and see that this inference follows from them."

" Consider," she said, " whether the same is not more firmly proved also from this, that two highest goods different from one another cannot exist. For it is clear that when two goods are different, the one is not the other ; and therefore neither could be

279

alterum deest. Sed quod perfectum non sit, id
summum non esse manifestum est ; nullo modo igitur
75 quae summa sunt bona ea possunt esse diversa.
Atqui et beatitudinem et deum summum bonum esse
collegimus ; quare ipsam necesse est summam esse
beatitudinem quae sit summa divinitas." " Nihil,"
inquam, " nec reapse verius[1] nec ratiocinatione firmius
80 nec deo dignius concludi potest." " Super haec,"
inquit, " igitur veluti geometrae solent demonstratis
propositis aliquid inferre quae porismata ipsi vocant,
ita ego quoque tibi veluti corollarium dabo. Nam
quoniam beatitudinis adeptione fiunt homines beati,
85 beatitudo vero est ipsa divinitas, divinitatis adeptione
beatos fieri manifestum est : sed uti iustitiae adeptione iusti, sapientiae sapientes fiunt, ita divinitatem
adeptos deos fieri simili ratione necesse est. Omnis
igitur beatus deus, sed natura quidem unus ; parti-
90 cipatione vero nihil prohibet esse quam plurimos."
" Et pulchrum," inquam, " hoc atque pretiosum, sive
porisma sive corollarium vocari mavis." " Atqui hoc
quoque pulchrius nihil est, quod his annectendum
esse ratio persuadet." " Quid ? " inquam.

95    " Cum multa," inquit, " beatitudo continere videatur, utrumne haec omnia unum veluti corpus beatitudinis quadam partium varietate coniungant an sit

[1] reapse verius *Schepss* : re ab severius *or* re ipsa verius
*the best* MSS.

perfect, since the one is lacking from the other ; but it is obvious that what is not perfect is not the highest ; and therefore in no way can those highest goods be different from one another. But we have concluded that both God and happiness are the highest good, so that that must be the highest happiness which is the highest divinity."

—" No conclusion could be drawn," I said, " more genuinely true, more firmly based on argument, or more worthy of God."

" Now in addition to these things," she said, " just as geometricians are used to draw from the theorems they have proved what they call *porismata* (corollaries), so I shall give you too a kind of corollary. For since men are made happy by the acquisition of happiness, but happiness is itself divinity, it is obvious that they are made happy by the acquisition of divinity. But as by the acquisition of justice they become just, or by the acquisition of wisdom, wise, so by the same argument they must, when they have acquired divinity, become gods. Therefore every happy man is a god, though by nature God is one only : but nothing prevents there being as many as you like by participation."

" That is both a beautiful and a precious thing," I said, " whether you prefer it to be called a *porisma* or a corollary."

" And yet there is nothing more beautiful than this, which reason persuades us should be added to what we have said."

" What ? " I asked.

" Since happiness," she said, " seems to include many things, do they all join, with a certain variability of parts, to make as it were one body of happiness

eorum aliquid quod beatitudinis substantiam compleat, ad hoc vero cetera referantur ? "  " Vellem,"
100 inquam, " id ipsarum rerum commemoratione pate-
faceres."  " Nonne," inquit, " beatitudinem bonum
esse censemus ? "  " Ac summum quidem," inquam.
" Addas," inquit, " hoc omnibus licet.  Nam eadem
sufficientia summa est, eadem summa potentia, reve-
105 rentia quoque, claritas ac voluptas beatitudo esse
iudicatur.  Quid igitur ?  Haecine omnia—bonum
sufficientia  potentia  ceteraque—veluti  quaedam
beatitudinis membra sunt an ad bonum veluti ad
verticem cuncta referuntur ? "  " Intellego," inquam,
110 " quid investigandum proponas, sed quid constituas
audire desidero."  " Cuius discretionem rei sic accipe.
Si haec omnia beatitudinis membra forent, a se
quoque invicem discreparent.  Haec est enim partium
natura ut unum corpus diversa componant.  Atqui
115 haec omnia idem esse monstrata sunt ; minime igitur
membra sunt.  Alioquin ex uno membro beatitudo
videbitur esse coniuncta—quod fieri nequit."  " Id
quidem," inquam, " dubium non est, sed id quod
restat exspecto."  " Ad bonum vero cetera referri
120 palam est.  Idcirco enim sufficientia petitur quoniam
bonum esse iudicatur, idcirco potentia quoniam id
quoque esse creditur bonum ; idem de reverentia,
claritudine, iucunditate coniectare licet.  Omnium
igitur expetendorum summa atque causa bonum
125 est.  Quod enim neque re neque similitudine ullum
282

or is there some one of them which completely makes
up the substance of happiness, and to which all the
rest are related ? "

" I should like you to make this clear," I said, " by
mentioning the things themselves."

" Now we think happiness is good, do we not ? "

" And indeed the highest good," I agreed.

" You may add that to each of them," she said,
" for happiness is also judged to be the highest sufficiency, the highest power, and the highest respect,
fame and pleasure. What, then ? Are all these—
good, sufficiency, power and so on—as it were members of the body, happiness, or do they all stand in
relation to the good as it were to their head ? "

" I understand what you are proposing for our
investigation," I said, " but I long to hear what your
conclusion is."

" Hear then how we distinguish in this matter. If
all these things were parts of happiness, they would
also differ from one another, for this is the nature of
parts, that being different they make up one body ;
yet all these things have been shown to be one and
the same ; therefore they are not parts. Otherwise
happiness will seem to be conjoined of one part,
which cannot be done."

" Well that, certainly, is beyond doubt," I said,
" but I am waiting for the rest."

" Clearly, then, the others are related to the good.
This is why sufficiency is sought after, because it is
adjudged to be good ; this is why power is sought
after, because it too is thought to be good ; and the
same may be inferred of respect, fame, and pleasure
The sum and cause of all things that are to be sought
after is the good : for that which holds no good in

in se retinet bonum, id expeti nullo modo potest.
Contraque etiam quae natura bona non sunt, tamen
si esse videantur, quasi vere bona sint appetuntur.
Quo fit uti summa, cardo atque causa expetendorum
130 omnium bonitas esse iure credatur. Cuius vero
causa quid expetitur, id maxime videtur optari,
veluti si salutis causa quispiam velit equitare, non
tam equitandi motum desiderat quam salutis effectum.
Cum igitur omnia boni gratia petantur, non illa
135 potius quam bonum ipsum desideratur ab omnibus.
Sed propter quod cetera optantur, beatitudinem esse
concessimus ; quare sic quoque sola quaeritur beatitudo. Ex quo liquido apparet ipsius boni et beatitudinis unam atque eandem esse substantiam."
140 " Nihil video cur dissentire quispiam possit." " Sed
deum veramque beatitudinem unum atque idem esse
monstravimus." " Ita," inquam. " Securo igitur
concludere licet dei quoque in ipso bono nec usquam
alio sitam esse substantiam.

## X

Huc omnes pariter venite capti
Quos fallax ligat improbis catenis
Terrenas habitans libido mentes,
Haec erit vobis requies laborum,
5      Hic portus placida manens quiete,

itself either in reality or by some resemblance cannot by any means be sought after. And on the other hand, those things which are not good by nature, provided they seem so, are sought as though they were really good. That is why it is rightly held that the chief or cardinal cause of all things sought after is goodness. Now the cause for which a thing is sought is seen to be most greatly desired, as for example if a man wanted to ride for the sake of his health, he does not so much desire the motion of riding, but the effect, health. Therefore, since all things are sought after for the sake of good, they are not so much desired by all as the good itself. But we have granted that that for which the rest are desired is happiness ; so in the same way, only happiness is sought after. From this it clearly appears that the substance of goodness and of happiness is one and the same."

" I see no reason why anyone could disagree," I said.

" But we have shown that God and true happiness are one and the same."

" Yes," I said.

" We may therefore safely conclude that the substance of God too is established in goodness itself and nowhere else.

## X

Come here together, all you prisoners, come,
You who are bound in shameful chains
By cheating lust that lives in your earthbound minds ;
Here will you find from all your labours rest,
Here is a haven of quiet abiding calm,

# BOETHIUS

Hoc patens unum miseris asylum.
Non quidquid Tagus aureis harenis
Donat aut Hermus rutilante ripa
Aut Indus calido propinquus orbi
10   Candidis miscens virides lapillos,
Inlustrent aciem magisque caecos
In suas condunt animos tenebras.
Hoc quidquid placet excitatque mentes,
Infimis tellus aluit cavernis ;
15   Splendor quo regitur vigetque caelum,
Vitat obscuras animae ruinas.
Hanc quisquis poterit notare lucem,
Candidos Phoebi radios negabit."

## XI

"Assentior," inquam, " cuncta enim firmissimis nexa rationibus constant." Tum illa, " Quanti," inquit, " aestimabis, si bonum ipsum quid sit agnoveris ? " " Infinito," inquam, " si quidem mihi pariter deum
5 quoque qui bonum est continget agnoscere." " Atqui hoc verissima," inquit, " ratione patefaciam, maneant modo quae paulo ante conclusa sunt." " Manebunt." " Nonne," inquit, " monstravimus ea quae appetuntur pluribus idcirco vera perfectaque bona non esse
10 quoniam a se invicem discreparent cumque alteri abesset alterum, plenum absolutumque bonum afferre non posse ? Tum autem verum bonum fieri cum in unam veluti formam atque efficientiam colliguntur,

---

ᵃ The rivers Tagus (in Spain and Portugal) and Hermus (in Aeolis in Asia Minor) were sources of alluvial gold.

286

Here lies the only refuge for unfortunates.
Neither whatever Tagus yields with its golden sands,
Nor Hermus with its ruddy-glowing bank,[a]
Nor Indus, next the torrid zone,
Mingling its emeralds and brilliant stones
Would clear men's sight ; but in their dark they all
Bury men's even blinder minds.
Whatever that is that stirs men's minds with pleasure
The earth has cherished in its deepest caves.
The brightness by which the lively heavens are ruled
Shuns the soul's ruin and obscurity ;
And any man who can observe this light
Will say the rays of Phoebus are not bright."


## XI

"I agree," I said, "for all is bound together by most firm reasoning." Then she said : "How highly will you value it, if you come to know what the good itself is ?"

"Infinitely highly," I replied, "since together with that I shall also come to know God, who is the good."

"I shall indeed make that clear too," she said, "with most valid reasoning, provided those conclusions stand which have just now been reached."

"They shall stand," I said.

"Have we not shown," said she, "that those things which are sought by many are not true and perfect goods for this reason, because they are different from one another, and since each one lacks the others, none can confer the full and absolute good ; but the true good is only produced when they are gathered as it were into one form which as efficient cause makes

ut quae sufficientia est, eadem sit potentia, reverentia,
15 claritas atque iucunditas, nisi vero unum atque idem
omnia sint, nihil habere quo inter expetenda nume-
rentur ? " " Demonstratum," inquam " nec dubitari
ullo modo potest." " Quae igitur cum discrepant
minime bona sunt, cum vero unum esse coeperint,
20 bona fiunt ; nonne haec ut bona sint, unitatis fieri
adeptione contingit ? " " Ita," inquam, " videtur."
" Sed omne quod bonum est boni participatione
bonum esse concedis an minime ? " " Ita est."
" Oportet igitur idem esse unum atque bonum simili
25 ratione concedas ; eadem namque substantia est
eorum quorum naturaliter non est diversus effectus."
" Negare," inquam, " nequeo." " Nostine igitur,"
inquit, " omne quod est tam diu manere atque subsistere quam diu sit unum, sed interire atque dissolvi
30 pariter atque unum destiterit ? " " Quonam modo ? "
" Ut in animalibus," inquit, " cum in unum coeunt
ac permanent anima corpusque, id animal vocatur ;
cum vero haec unitas utriusque separatione dissol-
vitur, interire nec iam esse animal liquet. Ipsum
35 quoque corpus cum in una forma membrorum con-
iunctione permanet, humana visitur species ; at si
distributae segregataeque partes corporis distraxerint
unitatem, desinit esse quod fuerat. Eoque modo
288

that which is sufficiency the same as power, respect, fame and pleasure ; but unless all are one and the same, they possess nothing to justify their inclusion among those things we should seek ? "

" That has been demonstrated," I said, " and it cannot by any means be doubted."

" Now those things which are not good, since they differ, but become good when they begin to be one, does it not happen that they become good by the acquisition of unity ? "

" So it appears," I said.

" But do you agree or not, that everything which is good is good by participation in the good ? "

" That is so."

" Then by the same argument you must agree that the one and the good are the same ; for those things have the same substance the effect of which, according to their nature, is not different."

" I cannot deny it," I said.

" Then you know," she said, " that everything that is, endures and subsists so long as it is one, and perishes and is destroyed as soon as it ceases to be one ? "

" How is that ? "

" For example, in living things," she replied, " while the body and soul come together and remain as one, the result is called a living thing ; but when this unity is dissolved by the separation of the two, clearly it perishes and is no longer a living thing. And the body itself, so long as by the conjunction of its members it remains in one form, is seen as a human shape ; but if the parts, being separated and scattered, tear apart the unity of the body, it ceases to be what it was. In the same way it will be obvious

L                                                        289

percurrenti cetera procul dubio patebit subsistere
40 unumquodque, dum unum est, cum vero unum esse
desinit, interire." " Consideranti," inquam, " mihi
plura minime aliud videtur." " Estne igitur," inquit,
" quod in quantum naturaliter agat relicta subsistendi
appetentia venire ad interitum corruptionemque
45 desideret ? " " Si animalia," inquam, " considerem
quae habent aliquam volendi nolendique naturam,
nihil invenio quod nullis extra cogentibus abiciant
manendi intentionem et ad interitum sponte festinent.
Omne namque animal tueri salutem laborat, mortem
50 vero perniciemque devitat. Sed quid de herbis
arboribusque, quid de inanimatis omnino consentiam
rebus prorsus dubito."

" Atqui non est quod de hoc quoque possis ambi-
gere, cum herbas atque arbores intuearis primum sibi
55 convenientibus innasci locis, ubi quantum earum
natura queat cito exarescere atque interire non
possint. Nam aliae quidem campis aliae montibus
oriuntur, alias ferunt paludes, aliae saxis haerent,
aliarum fecundae sunt steriles harenae, quas si in alia
60 quispiam loca transferre conetur, arescant. Sed dat
cuique natura quod convenit et ne, dum manere
possunt, intereant, elaborat. Quid quod omnes velut
in terras ore demerso trahunt alimenta radicibus ac
per medullas robur corticemque diffundunt ? Quid
65 quod mollissimum quidque, sicuti medulla est, in-

beyond doubt to anyone surveying other examples
that each thing subsists so long as it is one, but when
it ceases to be one, it perishes."

" If I consider many more things," I said, " it
seems not in the least different."

" Then is there anything," she asked, " that, so
far as it acts naturally, abandons the appetite for
subsistence and desires to come to its own corruption
and destruction ? "

" If I consider living things," I answered, " which
have some natural ability to want or not to want a
thing, I find nothing which with no forces working
from outside is such as to cast aside the effort to
remain alive, and hasten voluntarily to its own destruction. For every animal strives to guard its own
safety and avoids death and destruction. But what
I should think of plants and trees, or of things altogether without life, I am very much in doubt."

" But there is nothing that you could be in doubt
about in their case either, since you perceive first that
plants and trees grow in places suitable to them,
where, so far as their nature permits, they are able
to avoid withering swiftly and perishing. For some
spring up in the fields, others on mountains ; others
marshes bring forth, and others cling to stones, while
the barren sands are productive of others which would
wither if one tried to transplant them into other
places. But nature gives to each what is fitting for
it, and labours to prevent their dying for as long as
they can endure. Have you not noticed that they
all, with, as it were, their mouths buried in the
ground, draw nourishment through their roots and
diffuse strength through their pith and bark ? Have
you not noticed that all that is softest, like the pith,

teriore semper sede reconditur, extra vero quadam
ligni firmitate, ultimus autem cortex adversum caeli
intemperiem quasi mali patiens defensor opponitur ?
Iam vero quanta est naturae diligentia, ut cuncta
70 semine multiplicato propagentur ! Quae omnia non
modo ad tempus manendi verum generatim quoque
quasi in perpetuum permanendi veluti quasdam
machinas esse quis nesciat ? Ea etiam quae inani-
mata esse creduntur nonne quod suum est quaeque
75 simili ratione desiderant ? Cur enim flammas quidem
sursum levitas vehit, terras vero deorsum pondus
deprimit, nisi quod haec singulis loca motionesque
conveniunt ? Porro autem quod cuique consentaneum
est, id unumquodque conservat, sicuti ea quae sunt
80 inimica corrumpunt. Iam vero quae dura sunt ut
lapides, adhaerent tenacissime partibus suis et ne
facile dissolvantur resistunt. Quae vero liquentia
ut aer atque aqua, facile quidem dividentibus cedunt,
sed cito in ea rursus a quibus sunt abscisa relabuntur,
85 ignis vero omnem refugit sectionem. Neque nunc
nos de voluntariis animae cognoscentis motibus, sed
de naturali intentione tractamus, sicuti est quod
acceptas escas sine cogitatione transigimus, quod in
somno spiritum ducimus nescientes ; nam ne in
90 animalibus quidem manendi amor ex animae voluntatibus, verum ex naturae principiis venit. Nam
saepe mortem cogentibus causis quam natura re-
formidat voluntas amplectitur, contraque illud quo
solo mortalium rerum durat diuturnitas gignendi
95 opus, quod natura semper appetit, interdum coercet

is hidden always in an inside place, covered without by some woody hardness, and lastly the bark is set as a defence against the inclemency of the weather, as able to bear its ill-usage ? Again, how great indeed is nature's care that all are propagated by the multiplication of seed ! Who does not know that they are all as it were a kind of mechanism not only for enduring for a time, but also from one generation to another as if to last for ever ? And do not all those things which are believed to be without life in a similar way desire each what is fitting for itself ? For why else does their lightness bear flames upwards, or its weight press earth downwards, except because these directions and motions are fitting for each ? And further, whatever is suited to any thing preserves that thing, whatever it is ; just as those things injurious to it destroy it. Again, those things which are hard, like stones, cling most tenaciously to their parts and resist easy dissolution ; but those things which are flowing, as air or water, yield easily it is true to forces dividing them, but the parts so divided swiftly flow together as one again ; while fire shuns all division.

Nor are we now dealing with the voluntary motions of the intelligent soul, but with the exertion of nature, such as when we digest food we have taken in without any conscious thought, or when we draw breath in our sleep without knowing it. For not even in living things does the love of survival proceed from the acts of will of the soul, but from natural principles. For often for compelling reasons the will embraces death, which nature fears and avoids, and on the other hand, though nature always desires it, the will sometimes restrains that act of generation by which alone the

voluntas. Adeo haec sui caritas non ex animali motione sed ex naturali intentione procedit. Dedit enim providentia creatis a se rebus hanc vel maximam manendi causam ut quoad possunt naturaliter manere
100 desiderent ; quare nihil est quod ullo modo queas dubitare cuncta quae sunt appetere naturaliter constantiam permanendi, devitare perniciem."

" Confiteor," inquam, " nunc me indubitato cernere quae dudum incerta videbantur." " Quod autem,"
105 inquit, " subsistere ac permanere petit, id unum esse desiderat ; hoc enim sublato ne esse quidem cuiquam permanebit." " Verum est," inquam. " Omnia igitur," inquit, " unum desiderant." Consensi. " Sed unum id ipsum monstravimus esse quod bonum."
110 " Ita quidem." " Cuncta igitur bonum petunt, quod quidem ita describas licet : ipsum bonum esse quod desideretur ab omnibus." " Nihil," inquam, " verius excogitari potest. Nam vel ad nihil unum cuncta referuntur et uno veluti vertice destituta sine rectore
115 fluitabunt, aut si quid est ad quod universa festinent, id erit omnium summum bonorum." Et illa : " Nimium," inquit, " o alumne laetor, ipsam enim mediae veritatis notam mente fixisti. Sed in hoc patuit tibi quod ignorare te paulo ante dicebas."
120 " Quid ? " inquam. " Quis esset," inquit, " rerum

perpetuation of mortal things is assured. So this love of self proceeds not from a motion of the soul but from an exertion of nature ; for providence has given to her creatures this most important cause of enduring, that by their nature they desire to endure so far as they can. Therefore there is nothing that could in any way make you doubt that all things that are seek naturally the continuance of their own survival, and avoid destruction."

" I confess," I said, " that now I see without any doubt what previously seemed doubtful."

" Now that," said she, " which seeks to subsist and endure, desires to be one ; for if this unity is destroyed not even continued existence will be left to anything."

" That is true," I said.

" Therefore all things desire unity," she said. I agreed.

" But we have shown that unity is the very same as the good."

" That is so. "

" Therefore all things seek the good, which indeed you may describe in this way : the good is that which is desired by all things."

" Nothing truer can be conceived," I said ; " for either all things are unrelated to any one thing and, as it were left without one thing as head, flow about with no direction, or, if there is anything towards which all things swiftly move, that will be the highest good of all."

And she said : " I am so glad, dear pupil : you have fixed in your mind that mark which is at the very centre of truth. But now that has become clear to you which just now you said you did not know."

" What ? " I asked.

omnium finis. Is est enim profecto, quod desideratur
ab omnibus, quod quia bonum esse collegimus,
oportet rerum omnium finem bonum esse fateamur.

## XI

Quisquis profunda mente vestigat verum
Cupitque nullis ille deviis falli,
In se revolvat intimi lucem visus
Longosque in orbem cogat inflectens motus
5 Animumque doceat quidquid extra molitur
Suis retrusum possidere thesauris.
Dudum quod atra texit erroris nubes
Lucebit ipso perspicacius Phoebo.
Non omne namque mente depulit lumen
10 Obliviosam corpus invehens molem.
Haeret profecto semen introrsum veri
Quod excitatur ventilante doctrina.
Nam cur rogati sponte recta censetis,
Ni mersus alto viveret fomes corde ?
15 Quod si Platonis musa personat verum,
Quod quisque discit immemor recordatur."

## XII

Tum ego : " Platoni," inquam, " vehementer assentior, nam me horum iam secundo commemoras,
primum quod memoriam corporea contagione, dehinc

---

<sup>a</sup> According to Plato's doctrine of " reminiscence " (*ana-
mnesis*, for which see esp. *Meno*, 81-86 and *Phaedo*, 72-76)
the soul, when it is imprisoned in the body at birth, forgets all
it naturally knows of the eternal world of Ideas to which it

# CONSOLATION III

" What was the end of all things," she answered ;
" for surely that is the end, which is desired by all ;
and, since we have agreed that that is the good, we
must also admit the good is the end of all things.

## XI

Whoever with deep thought seeks out the truth
And wants not to go wrong down devious ways,
Must on himself turn back the light of his inward
    vision,
Bending and forcing his far-reaching movements
Into a circle, and must teach his mind,
Whatever she is striving for without,
Removed within her treasury to grasp ;
What the black cloud of error lately covered
Will shine then clearer than Phoebus himself.
For the body weighing upon the mind with bulky
    oblivion
Has not removed all light :
Assuredly there sticks within some seed of truth
Which is stirred to life by learning's breeze.
For why, being asked a question, do you rightly judge
Out of yourself, unless the kindling lived
Deep down in your heart ? If Plato's muse rings true,
What each man learns, forgetful he recalls." [a]

## XII

Then I said : " I strongly agree with Plato ; for
this is now the second time you have reminded me
of these things The first time was after I lost them
from my memory because the body contaminated it,

belongs, and all learning of the truth in this life is a recalling
of that forgotten knowledge.

cum maeroris mole pressus amisi." Tum illa : " Si
5 priora," inquit, " concessa respicias, ne illud quidem
longius aberit quin recorderis quod te dudum nescire
confessus es." " Quid ? " inquam. " Quibus," ait
illa, " gubernaculis mundus regatur." " Memini,"
inquam, " me inscitiam meam fuisse confessum, sed
10 quid afferas, licet iam prospiciam, planius tamen ex
te audire desidero." " Mundum," inquit, " hunc deo
regi paulo ante minime dubitandum putabas." " Ne
nunc quidem arbitror," inquam, " nec umquam dubitandum putabo quibusque in hoc rationibus accedam
15 breviter exponam. Mundus hic ex tam diversis
contrariisque partibus in unam formam minime con-
venisset, nisi unus esset qui tam diversa coniungeret.
Coniuncta vero naturarum ipsa diversitas invicem
discors dissociaret atque divelleret, nisi unus esset
20 qui quod nexuit contineret. Non tam vero certus
naturae ordo procederet nec tam dispositos motus
locis, temporibus, efficientia, spatiis, qualitatibus
explicarent, nisi unus esset qui has mutationum
varietates manens ipse disponeret. Hoc quidquid
25 est quo condita manent atque agitantur, usitato
cunctis vocabulo deum nomino."

Tum illa : " Cum haec," inquit, " ita sentias,
298

and the second when I was oppressed by the weight of grief."

"If you reflect on the things we have so far granted," she then said, "you will not be very far from remembering even that which lately you confessed to not knowing."

"What ?" I asked.

"By what governance the universe is ruled," she replied.

"I remember," I said, "that I did confess my ignorance, but what you are now bringing to light, though I can already glimpse it far off, yet I long to hear more clearly from you."

"A little while ago," she said, "you thought it not to be doubted that this universe is ruled by God."

"Nor do I even now think," I said, "nor shall I ever think that to be doubted, and I shall briefly set out by what arguments I come to this position. This universe is of such different and contrary parts that it would never have come together in one form were there not one to join such diverse elements together. And this very conjoined diversity of natures discordant among themselves would split and fall apart if there were not one to hold together what he has connected. Nor indeed would so certain an order of nature go on, nor would things work out such well-ordered motions in place and time, in their effects, their spaces and their qualities, unless there were one who himself enduring disposed and ordered this variety of changes. And whatever this is by which created things continue in being and move, I call by the name used by all, God."

Then she said : " Since this is how you feel, I think

299

parvam mihi restare operam puto ut felicitatis
compos patriam sospes revisas. Sed quae proposui-
30 mus intueamur. Nonne in beatitudine sufficientiam
numeravimus deumque beatitudinem ipsam esse consensimus ? " " Ita quidem." " Et ad mundum igitur,"
inquit, " regendum nullis extrinsecus adminiculis in-
digebit ; alioquin si quo egeat, plenam sufficientiam
35 non habebit." " Id," inquam, " ita est necessarium."
" Per se igitur solum cuncta disponit." " Negari,"
inquam, " nequit." " Atqui deus ipsum bonum esse
monstratus est." "Memini," inquam. " Per bonum
igitur cuncta disponit, si quidem per se regit omnia
40 quem bonum esse consensimus et hic est veluti
quidam clavus atque gubernaculum quo mundana
machina stabilis atque incorrupta servatur." " Vehementer assentior," inquam, " et id te paulo ante
dicturam tenui licet suspicione prospexi." " Credo ";
45 inquit, " iam enim ut arbitror vigilantius ad cernenda
vera oculos deducis. Sed quod dicam non minus
ad contuendum patet." " Quid ? " inquam. " Cum
deus," inquit, " omnia bonitatis clavo gubernare iure
credatur eademque omnia sicuti docui ad bonum
50 naturali intentione festinent, num dubitari potest
quin voluntaria regantur seque ad disponentis nutum
300

there is only a little more left for me to do for you to come back to your homeland safely, capable of grasping happiness. But let us look at what we have set out. Have we not included sufficiency under happiness, and granted that God is happiness itself ? "

" Yes indeed."

" And therefore," she said, " he will need no outside assistance in ruling the universe ; otherwise, if he need anything, he will not have full sufficiency."

" That is necessarily so," I said.

" Therefore he alone disposes all things, by himself ? "

" It cannot," I said, " be denied."

" And God has been shown to be the good itself."

" So I recall," I said.

" So he disposes all things by the good, since he rules all things by himself, and we have agreed that he is the good ; and this is as it were the tiller or helm by which the fabric of the universe is preserved stable and unharmed."

" I firmly agree," I said, " and I foresaw just now, although only with a vague suspicion, that that was what you would say."

" So I believe," she said, " for now, I think, you direct your gaze more watchfully to discern the truth ; but what I shall now say lies no less obviously before your eyes."

" What is that ? " I asked.

" Since God is rightly believed," she answered, " to govern all things with the helm of goodness, and all these same things, as I have taught you, hasten towards the good by their natural exertion, can it possibly be doubted that they are ruled voluntarily, and of their own accord give heed to the command

veluti convenientia contemperataque rectori sponte
convertant ? " " Ita," inquam, " necesse est ; nec
beatum regimen esse videretur, si quidem detrec-
55 tantium iugum foret, non obtemperantium salus."
" Nihil est igitur quod naturam servans deo contraire
conetur." " Nihil," inquam. " Quod si conetur,"
ait, " num tandem proficiet quidquam adversus eum
quem iure beatitudinis potentissimum esse con-
60 cessimus ? " " Prorsus," inquam, " nihil valeret."
" Non est igitur aliquid quod summo huic bono vel
velit vel possit obsistere." " Non," inquam, " arbitror." " Est igitur summum," inquit, " bonum
quod regit cuncta fortiter suaviterque disponit."
65 Tum ego : " Quam," inquam, " me non modo ea quae
conclusa est summa rationum, verum multo magis
haec ipsa quibus uteris verba delectant, ut tandem
aliquando stultitiam magna lacerantem sui pudeat."

" Accepisti," inquit, " in fabulis lacessentes caelum
70 Gigantas ; sed illos quoque, uti condignum fuit,
benigna fortitudo disposuit. Sed visne rationes
ipsas invicem collidamus ? Forsitan ex huiusmodi
conflictatione pulchra quaedam veritatis scintilla
dissiliat." " Tuo," inquam, " arbitratu." " Deum,"
75 inquit, " esse omnium potentem nemo dubitaverit."

---

[a] Cf. Wisdom 8. 1.

of their disposer, being as it were constitutionally accordant to their ruler ? "

" It must be so," I said ; " nor would his rule seem happy, if indeed it were a yoke on the necks of those who would reject it, and not the preservation of willing subjects."

" There is therefore nothing," she said, " which while remaining true to its nature would try to go against God ? "

" Nothing," I said.

" But if anything were to try," she said, " will it accomplish anything against him, whom we have justly agreed to be most powerful in his blessedness ? "

" Surely it would not be able to achieve anything," " I said.

Therefore there is nothing, which either would or could resist this, the highest good ? "

" I think not," I said.

" It is therefore the highest good," she said, " which rules all things firmly, and sweetly disposes them." *a*

" How much," I then said, " does not only the conclusion, the sum of your arguments, delight me, but much more the very words you use, so that at long last the folly which tortured me so cruelly is ashamed."

" You have read in stories," she said, " of the giants challenging heaven ; but those too, as was wholly right, a kindly strength put in their proper place. But would you like us to clash together our arguments, for perhaps out of a conflict of this kind some fair spark of truth will fly out ? "

" As it pleases you," I said.

" No one would doubt," she said, " that God has power over all things."

"Qui quidem," inquam, "mente consistat, nullus prorsus ambigat." "Qui vero est," inquit, "omnium potens, nihil est quod ille non possit." "Nihil," inquam. "Num igitur deus facere malum potest?"

80 "Minime," inquam. "Malum igitur," inquit, "nihil est, cum id facere ille non possit, qui nihil non potest." "Ludisne," inquam, "me inextricabilem labyrinthum rationibus texens, quae nunc quidem qua egrediaris introeas, nunc vero quo introieris

85 egrediare, an mirabilem quendam divinae simplicitatis orbem complicas? Etenim paulo ante beatitudine incipiens eam summum bonum esse dicebas quam in summo deo sitam loquebare. Ipsum quoque deum summum esse bonum plenamque beatitudinem

90 disserebas; ex quo neminem beatum fore nisi qui pariter deus esset quasi munusculum dabas. Rursus ipsam boni formam dei ac beatitudinis loquebaris esse substantiam ipsumque unum id ipsum esse bonum docebas quod ab omni rerum natura peteretur.

95 Deum quoque bonitatis gubernaculis universitatem regere disputabas volentiaque cuncta parere nec ullam mali esse naturam. Atque haec nullis extrinsecus sumptis sed ex altero altero fidem trahente insitis domesticisque probationibus explicabas."

100 Tum illa: "Minime," inquit, "ludimus remque omnium maximam dei munere quem dudum depre-

" No one indeed," I said, " who is in his right mind could possibly doubt it."

" But there is nothing," she said, " which he cannot do, who has power over all."

" Nothing," I said.

" Now God cannot do evil, can he ? " she asked.

" Not in the least," I said.

" Evil, then," she said, " is nothing, since he cannot do it, and there is nothing he cannot do."

" Are you playing a game with me," I said, " weaving an inextricable labyrinth with your arguments, since at one time you go in where you are going to come out again, and at another come out where you went in ? Or are you folding together as it were a wonderful circle of the simplicity of God ? For a little while ago, beginning with happiness, you said it was the highest good, and you said it was set in the most high God ; and you argued that God himself was the highest good and complete happiness, from which you gave me as a sort of little present the conclusion that no one would be happy unless he was also a god. Again, you spoke of that same form of the good being the substance of God and of happiness, and you taught me that unity itself was the same thing as the good, which was sought after by the whole natural world. Then too, you argued that God ruled the whole with the helm of goodness, that all things willingly obeyed, and that evil had no real nature. And these things you set out with proofs not fetched in from outside, but belonging within and native to our sphere, each one drawing its validity from another."

Then she said : " We are not in the least playing a game, but we have examined the most important

305

cabamur exegimus. Ea est enim divinae forma substantiae ut neque in externa dilabatur nec in se
externum aliquid ipsa suscipiat, sed, sicut de ea
105 Parmenides ait :

> Πάντοθεν εὐκύκλου σφαίρης ἐναλίγκιον ὄγκῳ,

rerum orbem mobilem rotat, dum se immobilem ipsa
conservat. Quod si rationes quoque non extra
petitas sed intra rei quam tractabamus ambitum
110 collocatas agitavimus, nihil est quod admirere, cum
Platone sanciente didiceris cognatos de quibus
loquuntur rebus oportere esse sermones.

## XII

    Felix qui potuit boni
    Fontem visere lucidum,
    Felix qui potuit gravis
    Terrae solvere vincula.
5    Quondam funera coniugis
    Vates Threicius gemens
    Postquam flebilibus modis
    Silvas currere mobiles,
    Amnes stare coegerat,
10    Iunxitque intrepidum latus
    Saevis cerva leonibus,
    Nec visum timuit lepus,
    Iam cantu placidum canem,
    Cum flagrantior intima
15    Fervor pectoris ureret,
    Nec qui cuncta subegerant
    Mulcerent dominum modi,

---

<sup>a</sup> Diels fr. 8. 43.    <sup>b</sup> *Tim.* 29 в.

of all matters, with the help of God, to whom we prayed at the beginning. For such is the form of the divine substance that it does not slip away into external things, nor does it receive anything external into itself, but as Parmenides says of it [a] :

> Like the body of a sphere well-rounded on all sides,

it turns the moving circle of the universe while it keeps itself unmoved. But if we have dealt in arguments not sought outside but set within the area we were working in, there is no reason for you to wonder, since you have learned under Plato's authority that words should be akin to the things spoken about.[b]

## XII

Happy was he who could look upon
The clear fount of the good ;
Happy who could loose the bonds
Of heavy earth.
Of old the Thracian poet mourned
His wife's sad death,
He who before had made the woods so nimbly run
And rivers stand
With his weeping measures,
And the hind's fearless flank
Lay beside savage lions,
Nor was the hare afraid to look upon
The hound, made peaceful by his song ;
When grief burned yet more fierce and hot
His inmost heart,
And measures that subdued all else
Soothed not their master,

|    |                              |
|----|------------------------------|
|    | Inmites superos querens      |
|    | Infernas adiit domos.        |
| 20 | Illic blanda sonantibus      |
|    | Chordis carmina temperans    |
|    | Quidquid praecipuis deae     |
|    | Matris fontibus hauserat,    |
|    | Quod luctus dabat impotens,  |
| 25 | Quod luctum geminans amor,   |
|    | Deflet Taenara commovens     |
|    | Et dulci veniam prece        |
|    | Umbrarum dominos rogat.      |
|    | Stupet tergeminus novo       |
| 30 | Captus carmine ianitor,      |
|    | Quae sontes agitant metu     |
|    | Ultrices scelerum deae       |
|    | Iam maestae lacrimis madent. |
|    | Non Ixionium caput           |
| 35 | Velox praecipitat rota       |
|    | Et longa site perditus       |
|    | Spernit flumina Tantalus.    |
|    | Vultur dum satur est modis,  |
|    | Non traxit Tityi iecur.      |
| 40 | Tandem, ' Vincimur,' arbiter |
|    | Umbrarum miserans ait,       |
|    | ' Donamus comitem viro       |
|    | Emptam carmine coniugem.     |
|    | Sed lex dona coerceat,       |
| 45 | Ne, dum Tartara liquerit,    |

---

<sup>a</sup> Orpheus's mother was Calliopê, the chief of the Muses and goddess of poetry (especially epic).

<sup>b</sup> Taenarus on Cape Matapan possessed a cavern which was one of the entrances to Hades.

<sup>c</sup> Ixion was bound to a turning wheel for having attempted to ravish Juno ; Tantalus was condemned, for betraying the

# CONSOLATION III

Complaining of inexorable gods above
He approached the halls below.
There modulating gentle songs
On the sounding lyre
All that he drew from the foremost springs
Of his goddess mother,[a]
All that his unquelled grief bestowed
And love, that doubles grief,
Make his laments ; he moves Taenarian hearts,[b]
And with sweet prayer
Asks pardon of the lords of Hades' shades.
Taken by his strange song the doorkeeper
Three-headed Cerberus stands benumbed ;
Goddess-avengers of men's crimes who make
The guilty quake with fear
Now full of sadness melt in tears ;
Ixion's swift wheel [c]
No longer spins his head,
And Tantalus tormented by long thirst
Scorns stooping to the water ;
The vulture, while he is filled with Orpheus' mea-
    sures,
Stops tearing at Tityus' liver.
At last ' We are overborne ' in pity says
The ruler of the shades ;
' We grant the man his wife to go with him,
Bought by his song ;
Yet let our law restrict the gift,
That, while he Tartarus quits,

secrets of the gods, to stand up to his neck in water under a
fruit tree, and water and fruit receded as he attempted to
drink or eat ; Tityus lay stretched over a space of nine acres,
as a punishment for his attempt on Leto's honour (the mother
of Apollo), with a vulture tearing at his ever-replenished
liver.

Fas sit lumina flectere.'
Quis legem det amantibus ?
Maior lex amor est sibi.
Heu, noctis prope terminos
50 Orpheus Eurydicen suam
Vidit, perdidit, occidit.
Vos haec fabula respicit
Quicumque in superum diem
Mentem ducere quaeritis.
55 Nam qui Tartareum in specus
Victus lumina flexerit,
Quidquid praecipuum trahit
Perdit, dum videt inferos."

He shall not turn his gaze.'
Who can give lovers laws ?
Love is a greater law unto itself.
Woe ! By the very boundaries of Night
Orpheus his Eurydice
Saw, lost, and killed.
To you this tale refers,
Who seek to lead your mind
Into the upper day ;
For he who overcome should turn back his gaze
Towards the Tartarean cave,
Whatever excellence he takes with him
He loses when he looks on those below.

# ANICII MANLII SEVERINI BOETHII

### V.C. ET INL. EXCONS. ORD. PATRICII

# PHILOSOPHIAE CONSOLA-
# TIONIS

## LIBER TERTIUS EXPLICIT

## INCIPIT LIBER IV

## I

Haec cum Philosophia dignitate vultus et oris
gravitate servata leniter suaviterque cecinisset, tum
ego nondum penitus insiti maeroris oblitus intentionem dicere adhuc aliquid parantis abrupi. Et :
5 " O," inquam, " veri praevia luminis quae usque
adhuc tua fudit oratio, cum sui speculatione divina
tum tuis rationibus invicta patuerunt, eaque mihi etsi
ob iniuriae dolorem nuper oblita non tamen antehac
prorsus ignorata dixisti. Sed ea ipsa est vel maxima
10 nostri causa maeroris, quod, cum rerum bonus rector
exsistat, vel esse omnino mala possint vel impunita
praetereant ; quod solum quanta dignum sit ad-
miratione profecto consideras. At huic aliud maius
adiungitur. Nam imperante florenteque nequitia
15 virtus non solum praemiis caret, verum etiam

312

BOETHIUS

# THE CONSOLATION OF PHILOSOPHY

## BOOK IV

### I

WHEN Philosophy had finished softly and sweetly singing these verses, while preserving the dignity and gravity of her face and visage, then I, not yet having completely forgotten my inward grief, interrupted her as she was just preparing to say something more, and said : " Lady, you who lead the way to the true light, what your speech has so far poured into my mind has clearly been both divine, contemplated on its own, and invincible because of your arguments, and you have told me things which, although lately forgotten because of the pain of my injuries, I was not previously totally ignorant of. But this itself is the very greatest cause of my grief, that, although there does exist a good ruler of the universe, evil can exist at all and even pass unpunished ; and I beg you consider now how much wonder this fact alone properly causes. And to this is added another thing, of greater import : for when wickedness flourishes and is in control, virtue not only lacks rewards, but

313

sceleratorum pedibus subiecta calcatur et in locum
facinorum supplicia luit. Quae fieri in regno scientis
omnia, potentis omnia sed bona tantummodo volentis
dei nemo satis potest nec admirari nec conqueri."

20 Tum illa : " Et esset," inquit, " infiniti stuporis
omnibusque horribilius monstris, si, uti tu aestimas,
in tanti velut patrisfamilias dispositissima domo vilia
vasa colerentur, pretiosa sordescerent. Sed non ita
est. Nam si ea quae paulo ante conclusa sunt incon-
25 vulsa servantur, ipso de cuius nunc regno loquimur
auctore cognosces semper quidem potentes esse
bonos, malos vero abiectos semper atque inbecillos
nec sine poena umquam esse vitia nec sine praemio
virtutes, bonis felicia, malis semper infortunata con-
30 tingere multaque id genus quae sopitis querelis firma
te soliditate corroborent. Et quoniam verae formam
beatitudinis me dudum monstrante vidisti, quo etiam
sita sit agnovisti, decursis omnibus quae praemittere
necessarium puto, viam tibi quae te domum revehat
35 ostendam. Pennas etiam tuae menti quibus se in
altum tollere possit adfigam, ut perturbatione depulsa
sospes in patriam meo ductu, mea semita, meis etiam
vehiculis revertaris.

I

Sunt etenim pennae volucres mihi
Quae celsa conscendant poli.

is even thrown down and trodden under the feet of wicked men and pays the penalty in place of vice. That this should happen in the kingdom of God who knows all, and is all-powerful, but only wills the good, no man can sufficiently wonder at or complain of."

Then she replied : " It would indeed be a matter of boundless wonder more dreadful than any evil omens if, as you think, as it were in the most well arranged house of so great a master the worthless vessels were cherished while the precious ones were allowed to get filthy. But it is not so ; for if those conclusions we have just now reached are preserved and not overthrown, by the help of that same God of whose kingdom we are now speaking you will learn that the good are always powerful, while the bad are always abject and weak, nor are vices ever without punishment, nor virtues without reward ; that success attends the good and misfortune the wicked, and many things of this kind, which will settle your complaints and strengthen you firmly and solidly. And since I have just shown you and you have seen the form of true blessedness, and also recognized wherein it is placed, when we have run through all those things I think it necessary to set out first, I shall show you the way which will bring you back home. And I shall affix to your mind wings, whereby it may raise itself aloft, so that with all disturbance dispelled, you may return safely to your homeland, under my guidance, on my path, and in my carriage.

## I

For I have wings swift flying
Which can ascend the heights of heaven ;

Quas sibi cum velox mens induit,
　　Terras perosa despicit,
5　Aeris inmensi superat globum,
　　Nubesque postergum videt,
Quique agili motu calet aetheris,
　　Transcendit ignis verticem,
Donec in astriferas surgat domos
10　　Phoeboque coniungat vias
Aut comitetur iter gelidi senis
　　Miles corusci sideris,
Vel quocumque micans nox pingitur,
　　Recurrat astri circulum
15　Atque ubi iam exhausti fuerit satis,
　　Polum relinquat extimum
Dorsaque velocis premat aetheris
　　Compos verendi luminis.
Hic regum sceptrum dominus tenet
20　　Orbisque habenas temperat
Et volucrem currum stabilis regit
　　Rerum coruscus arbiter.
Huc te si reducem referat via,
　　Quam nunc requiris immemor :
25　' Haec,' dices, ' memini, patria est mihi,
　　Hinc ortus, hic sistam gradum.'
Quod si terrarum placeat tibi
　　Noctem relictam visere,
Quos miseri torvos populi timent
30　　Cernes tyrannos exules.''

# CONSOLATION IV

When your quick mind has put them on,
It looks down on the hated earth,
Passes beyond the sphere of measureless air,
And looks back at the clouds
And climbs beyond the highest point of fire
That burns with the rapid motion of the upper air,[a]
Until it rise to the houses of the stars
And join its path to Phoebus',
Or go along the road with the cold old god,
Squire to his shining star,
Or where the glittering night is painted forth
Turn with the circling stars ;
Then when it is satisfied with all so far achieved,
It leaves the furthest pole,
And stands on the outside of the swift upper air,
Mastering its awful light.
Here the lord of kings his sceptre holds,
Controls the reins of the world,
And guides its swift chariot, though himself unmoved,
The shining master of the universe.
If the road bring you back, returning to this place,
Which you now seek, forgetful,
" This," you will say, " I remember, is my native land,
Here I was born, here shall I halt my step."
But if you like to look upon
Earth's night that you have left,
Those tyrants wretched peoples fear as fierce
You will see as exiles.

[a] The upper air, or ether, is the outermost sphere, that
moves the rest, and beyond which is the empyrean, the abode
of God  The " star-bearing houses " are the twelve mansions
of the zodiac, the twelve sections of the ecliptic through
which the sun moves in the year ; the " cold old god " is
Saturn, the furthest out of the five visible planets (*cf.* Virgil,
*Georg.* i. 336).

317

## II

Tum ego : " Papae," inquam, " ut magna promittis ! Nec dubito quin possis efficere ; tu modo quem excitaveris ne moreris." " Primum igitur," inquit, " bonis semper adesse potentiam, malos cunctis viribus esse
5 desertos agnoscas licebit, quorum quidem alterum demonstratur ex altero. Nam cum bonum malumque contraria sint, si bonum potens esse constiterit, liquet inbecillitas mali ; at si fragilitas clarescat mali, boni firmitas nota est. Sed uti nostrae sententiae fides
10 abundantior sit, alterutro calle procedam nunc hinc nunc inde proposita confirmans.

Duo sunt quibus omnis humanorum actuum constat effectus, voluntas scilicet ac potestas, quorum si alterutrum desit, nihil est quod explicari queat. Deficiente
15 etenim voluntate ne aggreditur quidem quisque quod non vult ; at si potestas absit, voluntas frustra sit. Quo fit ut si quem videas adipisci velle quod minime adipiscatur, huic obtinendi quod voluerit defuisse valentiam dubitare non possis." " Perspicuum est,"
20 inquam, " nec ullo modo negari potest." " Quem vero effecisse quod voluerit videas, num etiam potuisse dubitabis ? " " Minime." " Quod vero quisque potest, in eo validus, quod vero non potest, in hoc imbecillis esse censendus est." " Fateor," inquam.
318

# CONSOLATION IV

## II

Then I exclaimed, " Wonderful ! What great things you promise me ! Nor do I doubt that you can do them, but do not hold me back, whom you have now so aroused."

" First then," she said, " that good men always possess power, and that the wicked are deprived of all their strength, you may learn, since indeed the one is proved from the other. For since good and evil are contraries, if it is established that good is powerful, the weakness of evil is clear ; and if the frailty of evil is evident, the strength of good is known. But that the trustworthiness of our opinion may be the greater, I shall proceed by either path, confirming my propositions now from this side, now from that. There are two things, by which the effect of all human actions is achieved, will and ability. If either of these be lacking, there is nothing which can be completed. For the will being lacking, no man can even begin anything, because he does not will it ; but if the ability were to be wanting, the will would be frustrated. That is why, if you were to see any man wanting to obtain something which he was not in fact obtaining, you could not doubt that he lacked the ability to get what he wanted."

" That is obvious," I said, " nor can it by any means be denied."

" And the man you see has achieved what he desired, will you doubt that he was also able to do it ? "

" Not in the least."

" And every man should be reckoned strong in that point in which he is able, and weak in that in which he is not able."

25 " Meministine igitur," inquit, " superioribus rationibus esse collectum intentionem omnem voluntatis
humanae quae diversis studiis agitur ad beatitudinem
festinare ? " " Memini," inquam, " illud quoque
esse demonstratum." " Num recordaris beatitudinem
30 ipsum esse bonum eoque modo, cum beatitudo petitur,
ab omnibus desiderari bonum ? " " Minime," inquam
" recordor, quoniam id memoriae fixum teneo."
" Omnes igitur homines boni pariter ac mali indiscreta intentione ad bonum pervenire nituntur ? "
35 " Ita," inquam, " consequens est." " Sed certum est
adeptione boni bonos fieri." " Certum." " Adipiscuntur igitur boni quod appetunt ? " " Sic videtur."
" Mali vero si adipiscerentur quod appetunt bonum,
mali esse non possent." " Ita est." " Cum igitur
40 utrique bonum petant, sed hi quidem adipiscantur,
illi vero minime, num dubium est bonos quidem
potentes esse, qui vero mali sunt imbecillos ? "
" Quisquis," inquam, " dubitat, nec rerum naturam
nec consequentiam potest considerare rationum."
45 " Rursus," inquit, " si duo sint quibus idem secundum
naturam propositum sit eorumque unus naturali
officio id ipsum agat atque perficiat, alter vero naturale
320

" That I admit," I said.

" Do you then remember," she asked, " that it was concluded from our previous arguments that the whole effort of man's will, which is active in various pursuits, hastens towards happiness ? "

" I remember," I said, " that that also was proved."

" And do you not recall that happiness is the good itself, and that in that way, when happiness is sought, the good is desired by all men ? "

" I do not recall it at all," I said, " for I hold it fixed in my memory."

" All men, therefore, good and evil alike, strive with an effort not to be distinguished, to arrive at the good."

" So it follows," I said.

" But it is certain that men become good by obtaining the good."

" It is certain."

" The good, then, obtain what they seek ? "

" So it seems."

" And if evil men obtained what they seek, that is, the good, they could not be evil."

" That is so."

" Since then both seek the good, but the former obtain it and the latter do not, can there be any doubt that the good are powerful, and those who are evil, weak ? "

" Whoever doubts it," I said, " can be considering neither the nature of things nor what follows from the arguments."

" Again," she said, " suppose two men, to whom the same natural action is proposed, and one of them does that same action and completes it by exercising the proper natural function, but the other cannot

illud officium minime administrare queat, alio vero
modo quam naturae convenit non quidem impleat
50 propositum suum sed imitetur implentem, quemnam
horum valentiorem esse decernis ? " " Etsi coniecto,"
inquam, " quid velis, planius tamen audire desidero."
" Ambulandi," inquit, " motum secundum naturam
esse hominibus num negabis ? " " Minime," inquam.
55 " Eiusque rei pedum officium esse naturale num
dubitas ? " " Ne hoc quidem," inquam. " Si quis
igitur pedibus incedere valens ambulet aliusque cui
hoc naturale pedum desit officium, manibus nitens
ambulare conetur, quis horum iure valentior existimari
60 potest ? " " Contexe," inquam, " cetera ; nam quin
naturalis officii potens eo qui idem nequeat valentior
sit, nullus ambigat." " Sed summum bonum, quod
aeque malis bonisque propositum, boni quidem
naturali officio virtutum petunt, mali vero variam
65 per cupiditatem, quod adipiscendi boni naturale
officium non est, idem ipsum conantur adipisci. An
tu aliter existimas ? " " Minime," inquam, " nam
etiam quod est consequens patet. Ex his enim quae
concesserim, bonos quidem potentes, malos vero esse
70 necesse est imbecillos."

" Recte," inquit, " praecurris idque, uti medici
sperare solent, indicium est erectae iam resisten-
tisque naturae. Sed quoniam te ad intellegendum
322

manage that natural function, but in a manner different from that according to nature does not perform what was proposed to him but imitates the one who does perform it —which of these two would you decide was the stronger ? "

" Though I guess what you would like me to say," I said, " yet I desire to hear it more plainly."

" You will not deny," she said, " that the action of walking is natural to men ? "

" Not in the least," I replied.

" Nor do you doubt, surely, that the performing of that action is the natural function of the feet ? "

" I don't doubt that either," I said.

" Then if one man being able to move on his feet, walked, while another who lacked this natural function of the feet, tried to walk leaning on his hands, which of these can rightly be thought the stronger ? "

" Construct the rest of the argument," I said, " for no one would doubt that he who is able to use that natural function is stronger than the one who is unable to do the same thing."

" Now the highest good, which is proposed to good and evil men alike, the good seek by the natural function of their virtues, but the evil only try to obtain it through their fluctuating desire, which is not the natural function for obtaining the good ; or do you think otherwise ? "

" Not in the least," I said, " for what follows is also clear. For from these propositions, which I have granted, it follows necessarily that the good are powerful, but the evil weak."

" You run ahead rightly," she said, " and that is, as doctors usually hope, an indication of a nature now raised up and resistant. But since I see you very

promptissimum esse conspicio, crebras coacervabo
75 rationes. Vide enim quanta vitiosorum hominum
pateat infirmitas qui ne ad hoc quidem pervenire
queunt ad quod eos naturalis ducit ac paene compellit intentio. Et quid si hoc tam magno ac paene
invicto praeeuntis naturae desererentur auxilio ?
80 Considera vero quanta sceleratos homines habeat
impotentia. Neque enim levia aut ludicra praemia
petunt, quae consequi atque obtinere non possunt,
sed circa ipsam rerum summam verticemque deficiunt
nec in eo miseris contingit effectus quod solum
85 dies noctesque moliuntur ; in qua re bonorum vires
eminent. Sicut enim eum qui pedibus incedens
ad eum locum usque pervenire potuisset, quo nihil
ulterius pervium iaceret incessui, ambulandi potentissimum esse censeres, ita eum qui expetendorum
90 finem quo nihil ultra est apprehendit, potentissimum
necesse est iudices. Ex quo fit quod huic obiacet,
ut idem scelesti, idem viribus omnibus videantur
esse deserti. Cur enim relicta virtute vitia sectantur ?
Inscitiane bonorum ? Sed quid enervatius ignorantiae
95 caecitate ? An sectanda noverunt, sed transversos
eos libido praecipitat ? Sic quoque intemperantia
fragiles qui obluctari vitio nequeunt. An scientes
volentesque bonum deserunt, ad vitia deflectunt ?
Sed hoc modo non solum potentes esse sed omnino
100 esse desinunt. Nam qui communem omnium quae

---

*a* Virgil, *Aeneid*, xii. 764 f.

ready to learn, I shall heap up many arguments together. For see how plainly great is the weakness
of corrupt men, who cannot attain even to that
towards which their natural inclination draws and
almost compels them. And what would it be like if
they were deprived of this great and almost invincible aid, of nature leading the way ? And consider
also how great is the impotence that grips wicked
men. For those things they seek as rewards, which
they cannot acquire and possess, are not trifles or
playthings [a] ; they fail in what concerns the very
sum and summit of things, nor do the wretches
achieve the performance of that for which alone they
spend days and nights striving ; and it is in this
matter that the strength of good men is outstandingly
clear. For just as you would judge him most powerful in walking who, proceeding on foot, was able to
reach a place so distant that no further passable place
lay before his step, so you are bound to judge him
most powerful who attains the end of all things
desirable, beyond which is nothing. And hence we
have also the opposite to this, that those same men
who are wicked are those who appear destitute of
all power. For why do they abandon virtue and
pursue vices ? Is it because they do not know what
things are good— but what is more weakly than the
blindness of ignorance ? Or do they know what
should be pursued, but does inordinate desire lead
them headlong astray ? Then this way too they are
frail because of their lack of control, those who are
unable to struggle against vice. Or do they forsake
the good and turn aside to vice knowingly and wil
lingly ? But in this case they cease not merely to be
powerful, but simply to be : for those who leave aside

sunt finem relinquunt, pariter quoque esse desistunt.
Quod quidem cuipiam mirum forte videatur, ut malos,
qui plures hominum sunt, eosdem non esse dicamus ;
sed ita sese res habet.   Nam qui mali sunt eos malos
105 esse non abnuo ;  sed eosdem esse pure atque simpliciter nego.

Nam uti cadaver hominem mortuum dixeris,
simpliciter vero hominem appellare non possis, ita
vitiosos malos quidem esse concesserim, sed esse
110 absolute nequeam confiteri.   Est enim quod ordinem
retinet servatque naturam ;  quod vero ab hac deficit,
esse etiam, quod in sua natura situm est, derelinquit.
' Sed possunt,' inquies, ' mali.'   Ne ego quidem
negaverim, sed haec eorum potentia non a viribus
115 sed ab imbecillitate descendit.   Possunt enim mala
quae minime valerent, si in bonorum efficientia
manere potuissent.   Quae possibilitas eos evidentius
nihil posse demonstrat.   Nam si, uti paulo ante
collegimus, malum nihil est, cum mala tantummodo
120 possint, nihil posse improbos liquet."   " Perspicuum
est."   " Atque ut intellegas quaenam sit huius
potentiae vis, summo bono nihil potentius esse paulo
ante definivimus."   " Ita est," inquam.   " Sed idem,"
inquit, " facere malum nequit."   " Minime."   " Est

the common end of all things that are, at the same time also leave off being.

And this indeed may seem strange to some, that we should say of evil men, who are the majority of mankind, that they do not exist; but that is how things are. For of those who are evil I do not deny that they are evil; but that they are, purely and simply, I do deny. For as you would say that a corpse was a dead man, but you could not call it simply a man, so I concede of the vicious that they are indeed evil, but I cannot admit that they are, absolutely. For that *is*, which keeps its order and preserves its nature; and whatever falls from this, also abandons being, which is dependent on its nature. But evil men, you will say, are able to do things. Not even I would deny that, but this ability of theirs is derived not from their strength but from their weakness. For they can do evil things, which they would not be able to do, had they been able to persevere in the performance of good things. And that ability they do have shows more clearly that they can really do nothing; for if, as we concluded just now, evil is nothing, since they can only do evil, it is obvious that the wicked can do nothing."

" That is very clear."

" And that you may understand what the nature of this power of theirs is, remember we laid it down a little while ago that nothing was more powerful than the highest good."

" That is so," I said.

" But that, the highest good," she said, " cannot do evil."

" Not at all."

125 igitur," inquit, " aliquis qui omnia posse homines
putet ? " " Nisi quis insaniat, nemo." " Atqui idem
possunt mala." " Utinam quidem," inquam, " non
possent." " Cum igitur bonorum tantummodo potens
possit omnia, non vero queant omnia potentes etiam
130 malorum, eosdem qui mala possunt minus posse manifestum est. Huc accedit quod omnem potentiam
inter expetenda numerandam omniaque expetenda
referri ad bonum velut ad quoddam naturae suae
cacumen ostendimus. Sed patrandi sceleris possi-
135 bilitas referri ad bonum non potest ; expetenda
igitur non est. Atqui omnis potentia expetenda
est ; liquet igitur malorum possibilitatem non esse
potentiam. Ex quibus omnibus bonorum quidem
potentia, malorum vero minime dubitabilis apparet
140 infirmitas veramque illam Platonis esse sententiam
liquet solos quod desiderent facere posse sapientes,
improbos vero exercere quidem quod libeat, quod
vero desiderent explere non posse. Faciunt enim
quaelibet, dum per ea quibus delectantur id bonum
145 quod desiderant se adepturos putant ; sed minime
adipiscuntur, quoniam ad beatitudinem probra non
veniunt.

## II

Quos vides sedere celsos solii culmine reges
Purpura claros nitente saeptos tristibus armis
Ore torvo comminantes rabie cordis anhelos,

---

[a] Cf. Gorgias, 507 c ; the whole of this chapter and the
next are very similar to the Gorgias.

" Now is there anyone," she asked, " who thinks that men can do all things ? "

" No one, unless he is mad."

" Yet men can do evil."

" Would indeed," I exclaimed, " that they could not ! "

" Since then he who can only do good things can do all things, and they cannot do all things who *can* do evil, it is plain that those same men, who can do evil, can do less. And what is more, we have shown that all power is to be counted among desirable things, and all desirable things are related to the good as to the very summit of their nature. But it is impossible for the ability to commit evil to be related to the good, and therefore it is not to be desired. Yet all power is to be desired ; clearly therefore the ability to do evil is not a power. From all of which the power of good men and the quite undoubted weakness of evil men is plain, and clearly the opinion of Plato is true that only wise men can do what they desire and that wicked men can perform what pleases them but not achieve what they desire.[a] For they do anything you like thinking they will obtain through those things in which they take pleasure, that good which they desire ; but they do not obtain it, since shameful deeds are not conducive to happiness.

## II

Those lofty kings you see seated high on thrones,
Bright in their glowing purple, hedged in with brist-
    ling arms,
Threatening with visage stern, and gasping in the
    frenzy of their hearts—

Detrahat si quis superbis vani tegmina cultus,
5    Iam videbit intus artas dominos ferre catenas.
Hinc enim libido versat avidis corda venenis,
Hinc flagellat ira mentem fluctus turbida tollens
Maeror aut captus fatigat aut spes lubrica torquet.
Ergo cum caput tot unum cernas ferre tyrannos,
10   Non facit quod optat ipse dominis pressus iniquis.

### III

Videsne igitur quanto in caeno probra volvantur,
qua probitas luce resplendeat ?  In quo perspicuum
est numquam bonis praemia numquam sua sceleribus
deesse supplicia.  Rerum etenim quae geruntur illud
5 propter quod unaquaeque res geritur, eiusdem rei
praemium esse non iniuria videri potest, uti currendi
in stadio propter quam curritur iacet praemium
corona.  Sed beatitudinem esse idem ipsum bonum
propter quod omnia geruntur ostendimus.  Est igitur
10 humanis actibus ipsum bonum veluti praemium
commune propositum.  Atqui hoc a bonis non potest
separari neque enim bonus ultra iure vocabitur qui
careat bono ;  quare probos mores sua praemia non
relinquunt.  Quantumlibet igitur saeviant mali,
15 sapienti tamen corona non decidet, non arescet.
Neque enim probis animis proprium decus aliena
330

If a man strip from those proud kings the cloak of
    their empty splendour,
At once he will see these lords within bear close-
    bound chains ;
For there, lust stirs their hearts with poisonous greed,
There anger whips the mind as a whirlwind whips up
    waves,
And either close-confined sorrow plagues, or slippery
    hope torments.
Therefore since as you see one head so many tyrants
    bears,
He does not do what he himself would do, by these
    harsh masters pressed.

### III

Do you see, then, in what deep mire wickedness
wallows, with what brightness goodness shines ?
From which it is obvious that good deeds never lack
their rewards, nor wicked deeds their punishments.
For in all actions performed, that for which each
action is performed can rightly be seen as the reward
of that action, as for example, for running on the
racetrack, the crown, for which the race is run, is
clearly the reward. But we have shown that happiness is the good itself, that good for which all things
are done ; therefore the good itself is proposed as
the common reward for all human actions. But this
cannot be separated from good men—for he will no
longer rightly be called good who lacks goodness—
and therefore good behaviour is not left without its
rewards. However much, therefore, evil men may
rage, yet the wise man's laurels will not fall, nor
wither ; for neither does another's wickedness pluck

decerpit improbitas. Quod si extrinsecus accepto
laetaretur, poterat hoc vel alius quispiam vel ipse
etiam qui contulisset auferre ; sed quoniam id sua
20 cuique probitas confert, tum suo praemio carebit,
cum probus esse desierit. Postremo cum omne
praemium idcirco appetatur quoniam bonum esse
creditur, quis boni compotem praemii iudicet ex-
pertem ? At cuius praemii ? Omnium pulcherrimi
25 maximique. Memento etenim corollarii illius quod
paulo ante praecipuum dedi ac sic collige : cum ipsum
bonum beatitudo sit, bonos omnes eo ipso quod boni
sint fieri beatos liquet. Sed qui beati sint deos esse
convenit. Est igitur praemium bonorum quod nullus
30 deterat dies, nullius minuat potestas, nullius fuscet
improbitas, deos fieri. Quae cum ita sint, de malorum
quoque inseparabili poena dubitare sapiens nequeat.
Nam cum bonum malumque item poenae atque praemium adversa fronte dissideant, quae in boni praemio
35 videmus accedere eadem necesse est in mali poena
contraria parte respondeant. Sicut igitur probis
probitas ipsa fit praemium, ita improbis nequitia ipsa
supplicium est. Iam vero quisquis afficitur poena,
malo se affectum esse non dubitat. Si igitur sese
40 ipsi aestimare velint, possuntne sibi supplicii expertes
videri quos omnium malorum extrema nequitia non
affecit modo verum etiam vehementer infecit ? Vide
autem ex adversa parte bonorum, quae improbos

---

[a] Book III, pr. 10, p. 280.

their proper glory from good spirits. But should a man rejoice in what he received from someone else, some other man or even he who gave it would be able to take it away. But since his goodness confers on each man his reward, he will only lack it when he has ceased to be good. Lastly, since every reward is sought after because it is believed to be good, who will judge one who possesses the good to be without his reward ? But what reward ? The greatest and fairest of all : for remember that corollary *a* which I gave you a little time ago as an excellent present, and conclude thus : since the good itself is happiness, it is clear that all good men are made happy for this reason, that they are good. But those who are happy, it is agreed, are gods ; and therefore that is the reward of good men, which no time can lessen, no man's power diminish, no man's wickedness obscure, to become gods. These things being so for good men, no wise man can doubt either of the punishment inseparable from evil men ; for since good and evil, and also punishment and reward, are directly opposite to one another, what we see added in the case of the good man's reward must necessarily be reflected in an opposite manner in the case of the evil man's punishment. As therefore goodness is itself the reward for good men, so for wicked men wickedness is itself the punishment. Now whoever is punished is in no doubt that he is afflicted with evil. If therefore they were willing to appraise their own state, could those men think themselves without punishment whom wickedness—the worst of all evils ! —not only affects but even disastrously infects ?

But see, by comparing it with its opposite in the case of the good, what punishment attends the

poena comitetur. Omne namque quod sit unum
45 esse ipsumque unum bonum esse paulo ante didicisti,
cui consequens est ut omne quod sit id etiam bonum
esse videatur. Hoc igitur modo quidquid a bono
deficit esse desistit ; quo fit ut mali desinant esse
quod fuerant, sed fuisse homines adhuc ipsa humani
50 corporis reliqua species ostentat. Quare versi in
malitiam humanam quoque amisere naturam. Sed
cum ultra homines quemque provehere sola probitas
possit, necesse est ut quos ab humana condicione
deiecit, infra hominis meritum detrudat improbitas.
55 Evenit igitur, ut quem transformatum vitiis videas
hominem aestimare non possis. Avaritia fervet
alienarum opum violentus ereptor ? Lupi similem
dixeris. Ferox atque inquies linguam litigiis exercet ?
Cani comparabis. Insidiator occultus subripuisse
60 fraudibus gaudet ? Vulpeculis exaequetur. Irae in-
temperans fremit ? Leonis animum gestare credatur.
Pavidus ac fugax non metuenda formidat ? Cervis
similis habeatur. Segnis ac stupidus torpit ? Asinum
vivit. Levis atque inconstans studia permutat ?
65 Nihil avibus differt. Foedis inmundisque libidinibus
immergitur ? Sordidae suis voluptate detinetur.
Ita fit ut qui probitate deserta homo esse desierit,
cum in divinam condicionem transire non possit,
vertatur in beluam.

wicked. For you learned a little time ago that everything that is, is one, and that oneness itself is good ; and from this it follows that everything, since it is, is seen also to be good. In this way, then, whatever falls from goodness, ceases to be ; wherefore evil men cease to be what they were—but that they were men till now their still surviving form of the human body shows—and therefore by turning to wickedness they have by the same act lost their human nature. But since only goodness can raise anyone above mankind, it follows necessarily that wickedness thrusts down beneath deserving the name of men those whom it has cast down from the human condition. So it follows that you cannot adjudge him a man whom you see transformed by vices. The violent plunderer of others' wealth burns with avarice : you would say he was like a wolf. The wild and restless man exercises his tongue in disputes : you will compare him to a dog. The secret trickster rejoices that he succeeds in his frauds : let him be on a level with the little foxes. He that cannot govern his anger roars : let him be thought to have the spirit of a lion. The timorous and fugitive is afraid of things not fearful : let him be reckoned like a deer. The stupid sluggard is numb : he lives an ass's life. The fickle and inconstant changes his pursuits : he is no different from the birds. A man is drowned in foul and unclean lusts : he is gripped by the pleasure of a filthy sow. So he who having left goodness aside has ceased to be a man, since he cannot pass over into the divine state, turns into a beast.

## III

Vela Neritii ducis
Et vagas pelago rates
Eurus appulit insulae,
Pulchra qua residens dea

5    Solis edita semine
Miscet hospitibus novis
Tacta carmine pocula.
Quos ut in varios modos
Vertit herbipotens manus,

10   Hunc apri facies tegit,
Ille Marmaricus leo
Dente crescit et unguibus.
Hic lupis nuper additus,
Flere dum parat, ululat.

15   Ille tigris ut Indica
Tecta mitis obambulat.
Sed licet variis malis
Numen Arcadis alitis
Obsitum miserans ducem

20   Peste solverit hospitis,
Iam tamen mala remiges
Ore pocula traxerant,
Iam sues Cerealia
Glande pabula verterant

25   Et nihil manet integrum
Voce corpore perditis.
Sola mens stabilis super

---

[a] Lit. " the Neritian leader "—Ovid's phrase (*Fasti*, iv. 69) for Ulysses ; Neritos was a mountain in Ithaca, Ulysses's home.

[b] Circê was the daughter of the Sun and Persê, the daughter of Oceanus.

## III

The ship of Ulysses [a]
And his ocean-wandering fleet
The south-east wind drove to the isle
Where the fair goddess dwells
Sprung from the Sun's seed,[b]
Who mixes for each new guest
An enchanted cup.
Her herb-skilled hand
Thus changes them in various ways :
This one the shape of boar conceals,
That one a lion of Africa [c]
Grows fangs and claws ;
Another just becoming one with wolves,
While he essays to weep, but howls ;
Another like an Indian tiger
Prowls tame around the house.
But though the power of the Arcadian flyer [d]
Had pity on the captain
Beset by these different ills,
And freed him from the poison of his host,
Yet already his oarsmen's throats
Had drained the evil drinks,
Already as swine they had changed
Their bread for acorns,
And for them, lost,
Nothing, in voice or body, stays unchanged.
Alone the mind of each, surviving firm,

[c] " Marmaric," of Marmarica, to the west of Egypt ; so
generally, African, in late classical and early medieval
poetry, in imitation of Lucan, iii. 293.
  [d] Mercury, who was born on Mt. Cyllenê in Arcadia ; *cf.*
*Cyllenius ales*, Claudian xxxiii. 77.

Monstra quae patitur gemit.
O levem nimium manum
30      Nec potentia gramina,
Membra quae valeant licet,
Corda vertere non valent !
Intus est hominum vigor
Arce conditus abdita.
35      Haec venena potentius
Detrahunt hominem sibi
Dira quae penitus meant
Nec nocentia corpori
Mentis vulnere saeviunt."

## IV

Tum ego : " Fateor," inquam, " nec iniuria dici video vitiosos, tametsi humani corporis speciem servent, in beluas tamen animorum qualitate mutari ; sed quorum atrox scelerataque mens bonorum pernicie
5 saevit, id ipsum eis licere noluissem." " Nec licet," inquit, " uti convenienti monstrabitur loco. Sed tamen si id ipsum quod eis licere creditur auferatur, magna ex parte sceleratorum hominum poena relevetur. Etenim quod incredibile cuiquam forte
10 videatur, infeliciores esse necesse est malos, cum cupita perfecerint, quam si ea quae cupiunt implere non possint. Nam si miserum est voluisse prava, potuisse miserius est, sine quo voluntatis miserae langueret effectus. Itaque cum sua singulis miseria
15 sit, triplici infortunio necesse est urgeantur quos
338

Bemoans the monster it endures.
O too feeble hand,
And powerless herbs !
Though they have power over the limbs of men
They cannot change their hearts.
Within is the strength of men,
Kept close in a hidden citadel.
Those poisons do more powerfully
Drag down man from himself—
Dire they are !—that deep within do move,
And leaving the body unharmed
Cruelly wound the mind.

## IV

Then I said : " I admit, and I see that it is not wrongly said that the wicked, although they preserve the form of a human body, yet in the quality of their minds they are changed into beasts ; but I should have wished that those whose savage and wicked mind rages for the destruction of the good had not had that within their power."

" It is not," she said, " as will be shown in its proper place ; and yet, if that very power which is believed to be theirs were taken away, in great measure the punishment of these wicked men would also be relieved. For indeed, as may perhaps seem unbelievable to some, the wicked must necessarily be more unhappy when they achieve what they desire than if they are unable to carry out their desires. For if it is wretched to have the will to do evil things, it is more wretched to have the ability to do them, without which the effecting of the will wretchedly fails. So since each of these has its own proper wretchedness, those must be oppressed with

339

videas scelus velle, posse, perficere." "Accedo,"
inquam, " sed uti hoc infortunio cito careant patrandi
sceleris possibilitate deserti vehementer exopto."
" Carebunt," inquit, " ocius quam vel tu forsitan velis
20 vel illi sese aestiment esse carituros. Neque enim
est aliquid in tam brevibus vitae metis ita serum
quod exspectare longum immortalis praesertim animus
putet : quorum magna spes et excelsa facinorum
machina repentino atque insperato saepe fine de-
25 struitur, quod quidem illis miseriae modum statuit.

Nam si nequitia miseros facit, miserior sit necesse
est diuturnior nequam ; quos infelicissimos esse
iudicarem, si non eorum malitiam saltem mors
extrema finiret. Etenim si de pravitatis infortunio
30 vera conclusimus, infinitam liquet esse miseriam quam
esse constat aeternam." Tum ego : " Mira quidem,"
inquam, " et concessu difficilis inlatio, sed his eam
quae prius concessa sunt nimium convenire cognosco."
" Recte," inquit, " aestimas. Sed qui conclusioni
35 accedere durum putat, aequum est vel falsum aliquid
praecessisse demonstret vel collocationem proposi-
tionum non esse efficacem necessariae conclusionis
ostendat ; alioquin concessis praecedentibus nihil
prorsus est quod de inlatione causetur. Nam hoc
40 quoque quod dicam non minus mirum videatur, sed
ex his quae sumpta sunt aeque est necessarium."
340

a threefold misfortune whom you see wanting to do evil, able to do evil, and actually doing evil."

" That I grant," I said, " but I very strongly wish they might swiftly lose that misfortune by being deprived of the ability to commit evil."

" They will lose it," she said, " more swiftly than you desire, perhaps, or than they think that they will. For there is nothing within the brief limits of this life so late that man's mind, considering especially that it is immortal, should think it long to wait for. Their great expectation and the heights of their evil machinations are suddenly destroyed and brought to an end, often unexpectedly ; and that indeed sets a limit to their wretchedness. For if wickedness makes them wretched, your long-time miscreant is bound to be more wretched. And I should judge them the most unfortunate of men but that death at least, in the end, sets a term on their wickedness ; for indeed if we have come to a true conclusion about the misfortune attendant upon evil-doing, clearly that wretchedness is infinite which it is agreed is eternal."

" A wonderful conclusion," I then said, " and one hard to concede : but I acknowledge that it accords very well with what was granted earlier."

" Your thoughts are right," she said, " but it is proper for one who thinks it hard to accede to a conclusion either to demonstrate that something false has been premised or to show that the conjunction of the premises does not give a necessary conclusion. Otherwise, if the premises are granted, there is absolutely no reason why he should dispute the conclusion. For this also, which I am going to tell you, may seem no less wonderful, but it follows equally necessarily from those things already taken as true."

" Quidnam ? " inquam. " Feliciores," inquit, " esse improbos supplicia luentes quam si eos nulla iustitiae poena coerceat. Neque id nunc molior quod cuivis

45 veniat in mentem, corrigi ultione pravos mores et ad rectum supplicii terrore deduci, ceteris quoque exemplum esse culpanda fugiendi, sed alio quodam modo infeliciores esse improbos arbitror impunitos, tametsi nulla ratio correctionis, nullus respectus

50 habeatur exempli." " Et quis erit," inquam, " praeter hos alius modus ? " Et illa : " Bonos," inquit, " esse felices, malos vero miseros nonne concessimus ? " " Ita est," inquam. " Si igitur," inquit, " miseriae cuiuspiam bonum aliquid addatur, nonne felicior est

55 eo cuius pura ac solitaria sine cuiusquam boni admixtione miseria est ? " " Sic," inquam, " videtur." " Quid si eidem misero qui cunctis careat bonis, praeter ea quibus miser est malum aliud fuerit adnexum, nonne multo infelicior eo censendus est

60 cuius infortunium boni participatione relevatur ? " " Quidni ? " inquam. " Sed puniri improbos iustum, impunitos vero elabi iniquum esse manifestum est." " Quis id neget ? " " Sed ne illud quidem," ait, " quisquam negabit bonum esse omne quod iustum

65 est contraque quod iniustum est malum." Liquere,

" What is that ? " I asked.

" That the wicked," she answered, " are happier being punished than if the penalty required by justice did not constrain them. And I am not now labouring a point that might occur to anyone's mind, that wicked behaviour is corrected by retribution and brought back to the right way by fear of punishment, and that it is also an example to others that they should avoid anything blameworthy ; but that it is in another way, I think, that the wicked are more unhappy if unpunished, even if no account were to be taken of correction, no regard paid to example."

" And what will be that other way," I asked, " besides these ? "

And she answered : " Have we not granted that the good are happy, the wicked wretched ? "

" We have," I said.

" Now if," she said, " to the wretchedness of any man some good were added, is he not happier than the man whose wretchedness is uniquely pure with no admixture of good ? "

" So it seems," I said.

" Suppose to that same wretched man, who lacks every good, there should have been added another evil besides those because of which he is wretched, is he not to be considered far less happy than he whose misfortune is relieved by some share in the good ? "

" Surely," I said.

" But it is obviously just for the wicked to be punished, and unjust for them to escape unpunished."

" Who would deny it ? "

" But neither will anyone deny *this*," she said, " that everything that is just is good, and on the other hand whatever is unjust is evil."

respondi.[1] " Habent igitur improbi, cum puniuntur
quidem boni aliquid adnexum poenam ipsam scilicet
quae ratione iustitiae bona est, idemque cum supplicio
carent, inest eis aliquid ulterius mali ipsa impunitas
70 quam iniquitatis merito malum esse confessus es."
" Negare non possum." " Multo igitur infeliciores
improbi sunt iniusta impunitate donati quam iusta
ultione puniti." Tum ego : " Ista quidem con-
sequentia sunt eis quae paulo ante conclusa sunt.
75 Sed quaeso," inquam, " te, nullane animarum supplicia post defunctum morte corpus relinquis ? "
" Et magna quidem," inquit, " quorum alia poenali
acerbitate, alia vero purgatoria clementia exerceri
puto. Sed nunc de his disserere consilium non est.
80 Id vero hactenus egimus, ut quae indignissima tibi
videbatur malorum potestas eam nullam esse cogno-
sceres quosque impunitos querebare, videres numquam improbitatis suae carere suppliciis, licentiam
quam cito finiri precabaris nec longam esse disceres
85 infelicioremque fore, si diuturnior, infelicissimam
vero, si esset aeterna ; post haec miseriores esse
improbos iniusta impunitate dimissos quam iusta
ultione punitos. Cui sententiae consequens est
ut tum demum gravioribus suppliciis urgeantur, cum
90 impuniti esse creduntur."

---

[1] Sed puniri . . . respondi, *which MSS. have after* ultioni
puniti *below, was transferred here by Langen.*

---

[a] Or : " they have some further evil in them—their
impunity, which you have admitted. . . . "
[b] Nor, indeed, later ; there is no need to see here a reference to Purgatory (in that sense the word is not found until
six centuries later) but to the myths of Plato's dialogues,
especially, as H. F. Stewart says (*Boethius : an Essay*, 1891,
pp. 98 f.), to *Gorgias*, 525 B.

I replied that that was clear.

" The wicked, therefore, at the time when they are punished, have some good added to them, that is, the penalty itself, which by reason of its justice is good ; and in the same way, when they go without punishment, they have something further in them, the very impunity of their evil,[a] which you have admitted is evil because of its injustice."

" I cannot deny it."

" Therefore the wicked granted unjust impunity are much less happy than those punished with just retribution."

Then I said : " These things do indeed follow from those which were just now concluded. But I now ask you, do you keep no punishments for souls after the end of the body in death ? "

" Great punishments, indeed," she said ; " some of them I think are executed with penal harshness, but others with a purifying clemency. But it is not my design to discuss these now. [b]

But so far we have aimed to make you recognize that the power of the wicked, which appeared to you most intolerable, is really nothing, and to make you see that those who you complained were unpunished never lack the punishments due for their wickedness ; and to make you learn that the licence which you prayed might swiftly be ended is not long-lasting, but would be more unhappy if it lasted longer, and most unhappy if it were eternal ; and lastly, that the wicked are more wretched if they are allowed to escape in unjust impunity than if they are punished with just retribution. And it follows from this conclusion that they are oppressed by heavier punishments precisely when they are thought to be unpunished."

Tum ego : " Cum tuas," inquam, " rationes con-
sidero, nihil dici verius puto. At si ad hominum
iudicia revertar, quis ille est cui haec non credenda
modo sed saltem audienda videantur ? " " Ita est,"
95 inquit illa. " Nequeunt enim oculos tenebris assuetos
ad lucem perspicuae veritatis attollere, similesque
avibus sunt quarum intuitum nox inluminat dies
caecat. Dum enim non rerum ordinem, sed suos
intuentur affectus, vel licentiam vel impunitatem
100 scelerum putant esse felicem. Vide autem quid
aeterna lex sanciat. Melioribus animum confor-
maveris, nihil opus est iudice praemium deferente ;
tu te ipse excellentioribus addidisti. Studium ad
peiora deflexeris, extra ne quaesieris ultorem. Tu te
105 ipse in deteriora trusisti, veluti si vicibus sordidam
humum caelumque respicias, cunctis extra cessantibus
ipsa cernendi ratione nunc caeno nunc sideribus
interesse videaris. At vulgus ista non respicit.
Quid igitur ? Hisne accedamus quos beluis similes
110 esse monstravimus ? Quid si quis amisso penitus
visu ipsum etiam se habuisse oblivisceretur intuitum
nihilque sibi ad humanam perfectionem deesse arbi-
traretur, num videntes eadem caeco[1] putaremus ?
Nam ne illud quidem adquiescent quod aeque validis
115 rationum nititur firmamentis : infeliciores eos esse
qui faciant quam qui patiantur iniuriam." " Vellem,"

[1] caeco *Weinberger, Bieler, following Bases* (ΑΘΗΝΑ *IV*,
*1892, 341 ff.*) ; *cf. Planudes* ταὐτὰ τῷ τυφλῷ : caecos *MSS.*
*King Alfred seems to have read* caeco, *Queen Elizabeth I*
caecos (*and made little sense of it*) ; *Chaucer's text is doubtful.*

# CONSOLATION IV

Then I said : " When I consider your arguments, I think nothing is more truly stated, but if I were to turn again to the judgements of men, is there any-one to whom they would not seem unworthy not merely of belief but even of a hearing ? "

" That is so," she said. " For they cannot raise eyes accustomed to darkness to the light of manifest truth, and they are like birds whose sight night enlightens but day makes blind. For while they have regard not to the order of the world but their own desires, they think the freedom to commit evil and go unpunished for the evil done is a happy thing. But see what eternal law ordains. Suppose you have conformed your mind to better things : there is no need of a judge to confer rewards, you have yourself joined yourself to the more excellent things. Suppose you turn aside to worse things : look not without for one to punish you, you have yourself thrust yourself down among the baser things ; just as, if you were to look by turns now at the squalid ground, now at the sky, leaving aside all other out-ward signs, on the evidence of your sight itself you would seem now to be in the dirt, now among the stars. But the common herd does not look up at the stars : well then, shall we join them, who we have shown are like the beasts ? Suppose a man having completely lost his sight forgot even that he ever possessed sight at all, and thought he lacked nothing needed to make him perfectly a man, surely we who see would not have the same opinions as that blind man ? For not even this will they assent to, which rests on equally strong foundations, that those are more unhappy who commit injustice than those who suffer it."

347

inquam, " has ipsas audire rationes." " Omnem,"
inquit, " improbum num supplicio dignum negas ? "
" Minime." " Infelices vero esse qui sint improbi
120 multipliciter liquet." " Ita," inquam. " Qui igitur
supplicio digni sunt miseros esse non dubitas ? "
" Convenit," inquam. " Si igitur cognitor," ait,
" resideres, cui supplicium inferendum putares, eine
qui fecisset an qui pertulisset iniuriam ? " " Nec
125 ambigo," inquam, " quin perpesso satisfacerem dolore
facientis." " Miserior igitur tibi iniuriae inlator
quam acceptor esse videretur." " Consequitur,"
inquam. " Hinc igitur aliis de causis ea radice
nitentibus, quod turpitudo suapte natura miseros
130 faciat, apparet inlatam cuilibet iniuriam non accipien-
tis sed inferentis esse miseriam." " Atqui nunc,"
ait, " contra faciunt oratores. Pro his enim qui
grave quid acerbumque perpessi sunt miserationem
iudicum excitare conantur, cum magis admittentibus
135 iustior miseratio debeatur ; quos non ab iratis sed
a propitiis potius miserantibusque accusatoribus ad
iudicium veluti aegros ad medicum duci oportebat,

" Those are arguments," I said, " which I should like to hear."

" You do not deny," she said, " that every wicked man is worthy of punishment ? "

" Not at all."

" But it is in many ways obvious that those who are wicked are unhappy."

" Yes," I said.

" Therefore you do not doubt that those who are worthy of punishment are wretched ? "

" Agreed," I said.

" Now if you," she said, " were sitting as judge, which would you think should bear the punishment, the one who has committed the injustice or the one who suffered it ? "

" I am in no doubt," I said, " that I should give satisfaction to the sufferer by the pain of the perpetrator."

" So the committer of the injustice would seem to you more wretched than the receiver of it."

" That follows," I said. " And therefore for this and other causes resting on the same principle, that dishonesty makes men wretched by its very nature, it is clear that an injustice committed against any man means wretchedness not for the receiver but for the doer of the injustice."

" Yet now-a-days," she said, " orators take the opposite line. For they try to stir the judges to mercy for those who have suffered some severe and grievous injury, when the mercy is more justly owed rather to those perpetrating the injury, who ought, not by angry, but rather by kindly and merciful accusers to be brought to judgment like sick men to a doctor, that they might cut out their fault by being

ut culpae morbos supplicio resecarent. Quo pacto
defensorum opera vel tota frigeret, vel si prodesse
140 hominibus mallet, in accusationis habitum verteretur.
Ipsi quoque improbi, si eis aliqua rimula virtutem
relictam fas esset aspicere vitiorumque sordes
poenarum cruciatibus se deposituros viderent, com-
pensatione adipiscendae probitatis nec hos cruciatus
145 esse ducerent defensorumque operam repudiarent ac
se totos accusatoribus iudicibusque permitterent.
Quo fit ut apud sapientes nullus prorsus odio locus
relinquatur. Nam bonos quis nisi stultissimus
oderit ? Malos vero odisse ratione caret. Nam si,
150 uti corporum languor, ita vitiositas quidam est quasi
morbus animorum, cum aegros corpore minime dignos
odio sed potius miseratione iudicemus, multo magis
non insequendi sed miserandi sunt quorum mentes
omni languore atrocior urget improbitas.

## IV

Quid tantos iuvat excitare motus
 Et propria fatum sollicitare manu ?
Si mortem petitis, propinquat ipsa
 Sponte sua volucres nec remoratur equos.
5 Quos serpens leo tigris ursus aper
 Dente petunt, idem se tamen ense petunt.
An distant quia dissidentque mores,
 Iniustas acies et fera bella movent

punished. In this way, the work of defence-counsel would either languish altogether or, if they preferred to do men good, their role would be changed to that of prosecutors. And the wicked themselves, if it were allowable to glimpse through some small chink the virtue they had abandoned, and see that they would lay aside, through the torments of their punishment, the filth of their vices, they would not think them torments, weighing against them the benefit of acquiring goodness, and they would reject the efforts of defence lawyers and give themselves wholly over to their prosecutors and judges. Wherefore in wise men there would be left no place at all for hatred : for who except an utter fool would hate good men ? Yet to hate the wicked lacks all reason. For if, just as faintness is a disease of the body, so is any vice a sort of disease of the mind, since we should think those sick in body not at all deserving of hatred, but rather of pity, much more are those to be pitied, not persecuted, whose minds are oppressed by what is crueller than any bodily weakness, wickedness."

## IV

Why do you delight to stir up great commotion
And with your own hand to invite your fate ?
If you seek death, herself draws near
Of her own accord, and does not slow her flying steeds.
Those whom the serpent, lion, tiger, bear or boar
Hunt with their teeth, the same hunt one another
    with their swords.
Is it because they differ and their customs disagree,
That they unjustly wage such cruel wars

Alternisque volunt perire telis ?
10    Non est iusta satis saevitiae ratio.
Vis aptam meritis vicem referre ?
    Dilige iure bonos et miseresce malis."

## V

Hic ego : " Video," inquam, " quae sit vel felicitas
vel miseria in ipsis proborum atque improborum
meritis constituta.  Sed in hac ipsa fortuna populari
non nihil boni malive inesse perpendo.  Neque enim
5 sapientum quisquam exul inops ignominiosusque esse
malit, potius quam pollens opibus, honore reverendus,
potentia validus, in sua permanens urbe florere. Sic
enim clarius testatiusque sapientiae tractatur officium, cum in contingentes populos regentium quo-
10 dam modo beatitudo transfunditur, cum praesertim
carcer, nex[1] ceteraque legalium tormenta poenarum
perniciosis potius civibus propter quos etiam constituta
sunt debeantur.  Cur haec igitur versa vice mutentur
scelerumque supplicia bonos premant, praemia vir-
15 tutum mali rapiant, vehementer admiror, quaeque
tam iniustae confusionis ratio videatur ex te scire
desidero.  Minus etenim mirarer, si misceri omnia
fortuitis casibus crederem.  Nunc stuporem meum
deus rector exaggerat. Qui cum saepe bonis iucunda,
20 malis aspera contraque bonis dura tribuat, malis
optata concedat, nisi causa deprehenditur, quid est

----

[1] nex *Bieler* : lex *most* MSS. : *Weinberger omits.*

And by each others' weapons are willing to die ?
Not right enough is cruelty's reasoning ;
Would you give fair return for men's deserts ?
Rightly then love the good, and pity the evil.

## V

Then said I : " I see what happiness and what
wretchedness is implicit in the deserts of honest and
of dishonest men. Yet even in that popular idea of
fortune itself I consider there is some good or ill :
for none of those who are wise would prefer to be an
exile, poor and disgraced, rather than to flourish
staying in his own city, powerful because of his riches,
respected for his honours, and strong in his power.
For thus is the office of wisdom practised in a more
notable and manifest way, when the happiness of
the rulers is in some manner transferred to the peoples
under them, especially when prison, death and the
other torments of the punishments of the law are due
rather to wicked citizens, for whom indeed they were
established. Now why these things are changed
about, *vice versa*, and the punishments due to the
wicked oppress the good, while the wicked seize the
rewards due to virtue, I earnestly wonder, and I long
to learn from you what might appear to be the explanation of such iniquitous confusion. For I should
indeed wonder less, if I believed that all were jumbled
up by random chances. But as it is, my belief in God
as governor increases my astonishment. Since he
frequently grants delights to the good and unpleasant
things to the wicked, and on the other hand frequently
metes out harshness to the good and grants their
desires to the wicked, unless the cause is discovered,

quod a fortuitis casibus differre videatur ? "  " Nec
mirum," inquit, " si quid ordinis ignorata ratione
temerarium confusumque credatur.  Sed tu quamvis
25 causam tantae dispositionis ignores, tamen quoniam
bonus mundum rector temperat, recte fieri cuncta ne
dubites.

## V

Si quis Arcturi sidera nescit
    Propinqua summo cardine labi,
Cur legat tardus plaustra Bootes
    Mergatque seras aequore flammas,
5    Cum nimis celeres explicet ortus,
    Legem stupebit aetheris alti.
Palleant plenae cornua lunae
    Infecta metis noctis opacae
Quaeque fulgenti texerat ore
10    Confusa Phoebe detegat astra,
Commovet gentes publicus error
    Lassantque crebris pulsibus aera.
Nemo miratur flamina Cori
    Litus frementi tundere fluctu
15    Nec nivis duram frigore molem
    Fervente Phoebi solvier aestu.
Hic enim causas cernere promptum est,
    Illic latentes pectora turbant.
Cuncta quae rara provehit aetas
20    Stupetque subitis mobile vulgus,

---

[a] The reference is to an eclipse of the full moon, hidden
in the cone of the earth's shadow (*cf.* Ptolemy vi. 5 and
Macrobius, *In Somn. Scip.* i. 15. 10 ff.) ; at such times, the

why should his governance seem to be any different from that of random chances ? "

" It is no wonder," she said, " if a thing be thought random and confused, when the true ground of its order is unknown. But you, although you do not know the cause of this great ordering, yet, since a good governor does regulate the universe, do not doubt that all things are rightly done."

## V

If a man know not how Arcturus' stars
Glide next the pole of heaven,
Or why Boötes follows slow the Wain,
And sinks his fires so late into the sea,
While he so quickly rises,
He will be astounded at high heaven's law.
Let the full moon's horns grow pale,
Darkened by thick night's cone,
And the stars she hid with her shining face
Let Phoebe, thus obscured, discover :
The common people's error troubles the nations
And the bronze is worn with constant striking.[a]
No man wonders that the blowing of the north-west
    wind
Beats on the shore with rumbling wave,
Nor that the snow's hard weight of cold
Is loosed by the glowing warmth of Phoebus.
For to see the causes here is easy,
While there they are hidden and disturb men's hearts ;
All things that time brings forth but rarely,
And unexpected things, astound the excitable mob.

Romans, fearing the omen, made great noise of gongs and trumpets (*cf.* Livy xxvi. 5. 9 and Tacitus, *Ann.* i. 28).

# BOETHIUS

Cedat inscitiae nubilus error,
Cessent profecto mira videri."

## VI

" Ita est," inquam ; " sed cum tui muneris sit latentium rerum causas evolvere velatasque caligine explicare rationes, quaeso uti quae hinc decernas, quoniam hoc me miraculum maxime perturbat,
5 edisseras." Tum illa paulisper arridens : " Ad rem me," inquit, " omnium quaesitu maximam vocas, cui vix exhausti quicquam satis sit. Talis namque materia est ut una dubitatione succisa innumerabiles aliae velut hydrae capita succrescant, nec ullus fuerit
10 modus, nisi quis eas vivacissimo mentis igne coerceat. In hac enim de providentiae simplicitate, de fati serie, de repentinis casibus, de cognitione ac prae-destinatione divina, de arbitrii libertate quaeri solet, quae quanti oneris sint ipse perpendis. Sed quoniam
15 haec quoque te nosse quaedam medicinae tuae portio est, quamquam angusto limite temporis saepti tamen aliquid delibare[1] conabimur. Quod si te musici carminis oblectamenta delectant, hanc oportet paulisper differas voluptatem, dum nexas sibi ordine
20 contexo rationes." " Ut libet," inquam.

Tunc velut ab alio orsa principio ita disseruit : " Omnium generatio rerum cunctusque mutabilium naturarum progressus et quidquid aliquo movetur

---

[1] deliberare *MSS.*; delibare *Pulman.*

---

[a] The seven-headed water-serpent slain by Hercules ; when one head was cut off, two grew in its place.

Let the clouded error of ignorance give place,
And straightway let them cease to seem astonishing.

## VI

" That is so," I said. " Yet since it is your office to
unfurl the causes of hidden things and to unfold
explanations veiled in mist, I beseech you to explain
what conclusions you draw from this, for that wonder
I mentioned disturbs me very greatly."

Then she said, smiling a little, " You invite me to
discuss a matter greatest of all in the seeking, and
such that almost no discourse, however exhaustive, is
sufficient for it. It is such a kind of matter that, when
one doubt is cut away, innumerable others grow in
its place, like the heads of the Hydra [a] ; nor would
there be any limit to them, if one did not repress
them with the most lively fire of one's mind. For
under this head enquiry is made concerning the
singleness of providence, the course of fate, the
suddenness of chance, the knowledge and predestina-
tion of God, and the freedom of the will—and you are
well aware what weighty questions these are. But
since that you should know these things too is some
part of your medicine, although we are constrained
within a narrowly limited time, we shall try to have
some discussion of them. But if the delights of music
and song please you, for a little while you must post-
pone that pleasure, while I weave arguments for you
bound to each other in due order."

" As it pleases you," I said

Then as if beginning from a new starting-point, she
discoursed in this way : " The generation of all things,
and the whole development of changeable natures,

modo, causas, ordinem, formas ex divinae mentis
25 stabilitate sortitur. Haec in suae simplicitatis arce
composita multiplicem rebus[1] regendis modum statuit. Qui modus cum in ipsa divinae intellegentiae
puritate conspicitur, providentia nominatur ; cum
vero ad ea quae movet atque disponit refertur, fatum
30 a veteribus appellatum est. Quae diversa esse facile
liquebit, si quis utriusque vim mente conspexerit.
Nam providentia est ipsa illa divina ratio in summo
omnium principe constituta quae cuncta disponit ;
fatum vero inhaerens rebus mobilibus dispositio per
35 quam providentia suis quaeque nectit ordinibus.
Providentia namque cuncta pariter quamvis diversa
quamvis infinita complectitur ; fatum vero singula
digerit in motum locis formis ac temporibus dis-
tributa, ut haec temporalis ordinis explicatio in
40 divinae mentis adunata prospectum providentia sit,
eadem vero adunatio digesta atque explicata temporibus fatum vocetur. Quae licet diversa sint,
alterum tamen pendet ex altero. Ordo namque
fatalis ex providentiae simplicitate procedit. Sicut
45 enim artifex faciendae rei formam mente praecipiens
movet operis effectum, et quod simpliciter prae-
sentarieque prospexerat, per temporales ordines
ducit, ita deus providentia quidem singulariter

---

[1] rebus *cod. Emmeramensis s. x/xi* ; *the rest omit.*

---

[a] *moveri* gives great trouble to translators of Latin philosophical and scientific works : it is both middle and passive,
and can mean " to move " (intransitive : *the moon moves*)
and " to be moved " (passive : *furniture is moved*) ; and it
is used by Latin writers for the Greek κινεῖσθαι, which is used
by Aristotle and others of all kinds of " motion " or change

and whatever moves in any manner,[a] are given their causes, order and forms from the stability of the divine mind. That mind, firmly placed in the citadel of its own simplicity of nature, established the manifold manner in which all things behave. And this manner, when it is contemplated in the utter purity of the divine intelligence, is called providence ; but when related to those things it moves and disposes, it was by the ancients called fate. And that these are different will easily be seen, if one mentally examine the nature of each : for providence is the divine reason itself, established in the highest ruler of all things, the reason which disposes all things that exist ; but fate is a disposition inherent in movable things, through which providence binds all things together, each in its own proper ordering. For providence embraces all things together, though they are different, though they are infinite ; but fate arranges as to their motion separate things, distributed in place, form and time ; so that this unfolding of temporal order being united in the foresight of the divine mind is providence, and the same unity when distributed and unfolded in time is called fate.

Now although these are different, yet the one depends on the other ; for the order of fate proceeds from the simplicity of providence. For in the same way as a craftsman first conceives in his mind the form of the thing he is to make and then puts the work into effect, and produces by stages in temporal order what he had previously envisaged in a simple and instantaneous manner, just so God by providence disposes what is to be done in a single and unchanging

of state. " Move " in this version should be read with this in mind.

stabiliterque facienda disponit, fato vero haec ipsa
50 quae disposuit multipliciter ac temporaliter adminis-
trat. Sive igitur famulantibus quibusdam providentiae divinis spiritibus fatum exercetur seu anima
seu tota inserviente natura seu caelestibus siderum
motibus seu angelica virtute seu daemonum varia
55 sollertia seu aliquibus horum seu omnibus fatalis
series texitur, illud certe manifestum est immobilem
simplicemque gerendarum formam rerum esse providentiam, fatum vero eorum quae divina simplicitas
gerenda disposuit mobilem nexum atque ordinem
60 temporalem. Quo fit ut omnia quae fato subsunt
providentiae quoque subiecta sint cui ipsum etiam
subiacet fatum, quaedam vero quae sub providentia
locata sunt fati seriem superent. Ea vero sunt
quae primae propinqua divinitati stabiliter fixa fatalis
65 ordinem mobilitatis execedunt. Nam ut orbium
circa eundem cardinem sese vertentium qui est
intimus ad simplicitatem medietatis accedit ceterorumque extra locatorum veluti cardo quidam circa
quem versentur exsistit, extimus vero maiore ambitu
70 rotatus quanto a puncti media individuitate discedit
tanto amplioribus spatiis explicatur, si quid vero illi
se medio conectat et societ, in simplicitatem cogitur
diffundique ac diffluere cessat, simili ratione quod
longius a prima mente discedit maioribus fati nexibus
75 implicatur ac tanto aliquid fato liberum est quanto
illum rerum cardinem vicinius petit. Quod si
supernae mentis haeserit firmitati, motu carens fati
360

way, but by fate accomplishes those same things he
has disposed in a manifold and temporal way. Now
whether fate works by certain divine spirits acting
as servants of providence, or whether the course of
fate is woven by the service of the soul or of the whole
of nature, or by the celestial motions of the stars, or
by angelic power or demons' ingenuity, or by any or
all of these, this surely is clear, that the unmoving
and simple form of the way things are done is providence, and fate is the movable interlacing and
temporal ordering of those things which the divine
simplicity has disposed to be done.

So it is that all things that are under fate are also
subject to providence, to which even fate itself is
subordinate ; but that some things, which are placed
under providence, are above the course of fate.
These are the things which are immovably fixed close
to the principal divinity and so are beyond the
ordering of fate's moving nature. For just as, of a
number of spheres turning about the same centre, the
innermost one approaches the simplicity of middle-
ness and is a sort of pivot for the rest, which are placed
outside it, about which they turn ; but the outermost
one, turning with a greater circumference, the further
it is separated from the indivisibility of the central
point, the wider the spaces it spreads over ; and if
anything is joined or associated with that centre, it
is gathered into its simplicity and ceases to spread
and diffuse itself : in a similar manner, that which is
furthest separated from the principal mind is en-
tangled in the tighter meshes of fate, and a thing is
the more free from fate the more closely it moves
towards that centre of all things. And if it should
cling fast to the firmness of the supernal mind, then

quoque supergreditur necessitatem. Igitur uti est
ad intellectum ratiocinatio, ad id quod est id quod
80 gignitur, ad aeternitatem tempus, ad punctum
medium circulus, ita est fati series mobilis ad providentiae stabilem simplicitatem. Ea series caelum ac
sidera movet, elementa in se invicem temperat et
alterna commutatione transformat ; eadem nascentia
85 occidentiaque omnia per similes fetuum seminumque
renovat progressus. Haec actus etiam fortunasque
hominum indissolubili causarum conexione constringit,
quae cum ab immobilis providentiae proficiscatur
exordiis, ipsas quoque immutabiles esse necesse est.
90 Ita enim res optime reguntur, si manens in divina
mente simplicitas indeclinabilem causarum ordinem
promat. Hic vero ordo res mutabiles et alioquin
temere fluituras propria incommutabilitate coerceat.
Quo fit ut tametsi vobis hunc ordinem minime con-
95 siderare valentibus confusa omnia perturbataque
videantur, nihilo minus tamen suus modus ad bonum
dirigens cuncta disponat. Nihil est enim quod mali
causa ne ab ipsis quidem improbis fiat ; quos, ut
uberrime demonstratum est, bonum quaerentes pravus
100 error avertit, nedum ordo de summi boni cardine
proficiscens a suo quoquam deflectat exordio.

Quae vero, inquies, potest ulla iniquior esse confusio, quam ut bonis tum adversa tum prospera, malis
etiam tum optata tum odiosa contingant ? Num
105 igitur ea mentis integritate homines degunt, ut quos
362

being without motion it is also superior to the necessity of fate. Therefore as reasoning is to understanding, as that which becomes is to that which is, as time is to eternity, as the circle is to its centre, so is the moving course of fate to the unmoving simplicity of providence. That course moves the heaven and the stars, it mingles the elements with one another in proportion and transforms them by changing one with another ; it renews all things that are born and die through the growth of their young and their seedlings in their likeness ; and it also binds the acts and fortunes of men in an unbreakable chain of causes, which since they start from beginnings in immovable providence must also be themselves immutable. For things are governed in the best way if the simplicity which rests in the divine mind produces an inflexible order of causes, and this order constrains with its own immutability things which are mutable and would otherwise be in random flux.

So it is that although all things may seem confused and disordered to you, unable as you are to contemplate this order, nevertheless their own measure directing them towards the good disposes them all. For there is nothing which is done for the sake of evil, even by the wicked themselves ; they, as has been very fully demonstrated, are turned aside by perverse error as they seek the good, far from it being that order, proceeding from the centre of the highest good, which turns them aside in any direction from the beginning. But, you will say, what confusion could possibly be more unfair than that for the good, things turn out both ill and well, and to the bad also both desired and detestable things happen ? Do men, then, really live with such soundness of

363

probos improbosve censuerunt eos quoque uti existimant esse necesse sit ? Atqui in hoc hominum iudicia
depugnant, et quos alii praemio alii supplicio dignos
arbitrantur. Sed concedamus ut aliquis possit bonos
110 malosque discernere ; num igitur poterit intueri illam
intimam temperiem, velut in corporibus dici solet,
animorum ? Non enim dissimile est miraculum
nescienti cur sanis corporibus his quidem dulcia illis
vero amara conveniant, cur aegri etiam quidam lenibus
115 quidam vero acribus adiuventur. At hoc medicus,
qui sanitatis ipsius atque aegritudinis modum tem-
peramentumque dinoscit, minime miratur. Quid
vero aliud animorum salus videtur esse quam probitas ? Quid aegritudo quam vitia ? Quis autem alius
120 vel servator bonorum vel malorum depulsor quam
rector ac medicator mentium deus ? Qui cum ex alta
providentiae specula respexit, quid unicuique conveniat agnoscit et quod convenire novit accommodat.
Hic iam fit illud fatalis ordinis insigne miraculum,
125 cum ab sciente geritur quod stupeant ignorantes.
Nam ut pauca quae ratio valet humana de divina
profunditate perstringam, de hoc quem tu iustissimum
et aequi servantissimum putas omnia scienti providentiae diversum videtur ; et victricem quidem
130 causam dis, victam vero Catoni placuisse familiaris
noster Lucanus admonuit. Hic igitur quidquid citra
spem videas geri, rebus quidem rectus ordo est,

---

*a* Lucan, *Pharsalia*, i. 128 ; *victrix cau*⌐ *deis placuit, sed
victa Catoni.*

understanding that those they have judged to be good or bad must necessarily also be as they think ? Yet in this matter the judgements of men conflict, and there are those whom some judge worthy of reward, others deserving of punishment.

But let us concede that there is someone who can discern good men from evil. Will he really therefore be able to see that inward temper—as one says of the body—of men's minds ? For the case is not unlike that which is a wonder to an ignorant man, why with some healthy bodies sweet things agree, with others bitter, or why, again, of the sick, some are helped by mild medicines, others by sharp ones. But this the doctor, who distinguishes the manner and temper of health itself and of sickness, does not wonder at. Now what else, think you, is the health of minds but goodness, what their sickness but vices, and who else is both the preserver of good things and the remover of evils besides the ruler and healer of minds, God ? He, when he has looked out from the lofty watch-tower of his providence, sees what is fitting for each individual, and arranges what he knows is fitting. Here now happens that remarkable wonder of the ordering of fate, when by him who knows, such things are done as the ignorant are amazed at.

For to glance at a few examples, which human reason can grasp, of the depth of God, in the case of that man whom you think to be most just and the greatest preserver of justice, to providence that knows all, the opposite seems true. And our school-fellow Lucan suggests that the conqueror's cause pleased the gods, the conquered's, Cato.[a] Therefore whatever you see happen here contrary to your

365

opinioni vero tuae perversa confusio. Sed sit aliquis
ita bene moratus ut de eo divinum iudicium pariter
135 et humanum consentiat, sed est animi viribus in-
firmus ; cui si quid eveniat adversi, desinet colere
forsitan innocentiam per quam non potuit retinere
fortunam. Parcit itaque sapiens dispensatio ei quem
deteriorem facere possit adversitas, ne cui non con-
140 venit, laborare patiatur. Est alius cunctis virtutibus
absolutus sanctusque ac deo proximus ; hunc con-
tingi quibuslibet adversis nefas providentia iudicat
adeo ut ne corporeis quidem morbis agitari sinat.
Nam ut quidam me quoque excellentior :

145     Ἀνδρὸς δὴ ἱεροῦ δέμας αἰθέρες ᾠκοδόμησαν.

Fit autem saepe, uti bonis summa rerum regenda
deferatur, ut exuberans retundatur improbitas. Aliis
mixta quaedam pro animorum qualitate distribuit ;
quosdam remordet ne longa felicitate luxurient, alios
150 duris agitari[1] ut virtutes animi patientiae usu atque
exercitatione confirment. Alii plus aequo metuunt
quod ferre possunt, alii plus aequo despiciunt quod
ferre non possunt ; hos in experimentum sui tristibus
ducit. Nonnulli venerandum saeculi nomen gloriosae
155 pretio mortis emerunt : quidam suppliciis inexpugna-
biles exemplum ceteris praetulerunt invictam malis

---

[1] agitat *Warmington*. *Perhaps* duris ⟨sinit⟩ agitari.

---

[a] The Greek text is uncertain and otherwise unknown ;
an early variant produced " virtues " in place of αἰθέρες (so
not only Chaucer and Elizabeth but even Notker in the ninth
century). The plural αἰθέρες means it is very late, and not
Parmenides, as Peiper suggested. It is probably from some
late " Orphic " source, and undoubtedly culled by Boethius
from a Neo-platonist commentary, possibly on Plato's
*Epinomis*, 984 E. " Orpheus " would surely be acceptable
as " one more excellent even than " Philosophy.

expectation, is indeed right order in fact, though in your opinion it is perverse confusion. Yet suppose there be someone so well constituted that about him the judgement of God and man agree together, yet he is weak in strength of mind ; if anything adverse happen to him he will perhaps cease to preserve his innocence, because he has not been able to keep his good fortune by its means. So a wise dispensation spares him whom adversity could make worse, lest it allow him to be afflicted for whom it is not fitting. There is another perfect in all virtues, a holy man and near to God ; that he should be affected by any adversity at all providence so far judges monstrous that it does not allow him to be troubled even by bodily illnesses. For as one more excellent even than myself said :

The body of a holy man the heavens did build.[a]

But it often happens that the highest direction of affairs is given to good men, that luxuriating wickedness may be beaten back. To some providence metes out a fitting mixture of good and ill fortune according to the quality of their minds ; some it vexes, lest they run to excess with long prosperity ; others it allows to be troubled with hardships, that the virtues of their minds may be strengthened by the use and practice of patience. Some are over afraid of what they can bear, others are over contemptuous of what they can not—these it leads with harsh treatment to test themselves. Some have bought a name respected in this world at the price of a glorious death ; others by remaining unbeaten by their torments have shown the rest of men an example, that virtue is unconquered by evils. And

esse virtutem. Quae quam recte atque disposite et
ex eorum bono quibus accedere videntur fiant, nulla
dubitatio est. Nam illud quoque, quod improbis
160 nunc tristia nunc optata proveniunt, ex eisdem
ducitur causis ; ac de tristibus quidem nemo miratur,
quod eos male meritos omnes existimant. Quorum
quidem supplicia tum ceteros ab sceleribus deterrent,
tum ipsos quibus invehuntur emendant ; laeta vero
165 magnum bonis argumentum loquuntur, quid de
huiusmodi felicitate debeant iudicare quam famulari
saepe improbis cernant. In qua re illud etiam dis-
pensari credo, quod est forsitan alicuius tam praeceps
atque inportuna natura ut eum in scelera potius
170 exacerbare possit rei familiaris inopia ; huius morbo
providentia collatae pecuniae remedio medetur.
Hic foedatam probris conscientiam exspectans et se
cum fortuna sua comparans, forsitan pertimescit ne
cuius ei iucundus usus est, sit tristis amissio.
175 Mutabit igitur mores ac dum fortunam metuit
amittere, nequitiam derelinquit. Alios in cladem
meritam praecipitavit indigne acta felicitas ; quibusdam permissum puniendi ius, ut exercitii bonis et
malis esset causa supplicii. Nam ut probis atque
180 improbis nullum foedus est, ita ipsi inter se improbi
nequeunt convenire. Quidni, cum a semet ipsis
discerpentibus conscientiam vitiis quisque dissentiat
faciantque saepe, quae cum gesserint non fuisse
368

there is no doubting how rightly and in what good order these things are done, and how much in accord with the good of those to whom they come. For this too, that the wicked are sometimes harshly treated and sometimes gain their desires, proceeds from the same causes. Their harsh treatment no-one wonders at, since all think they deserve ill—and their torments indeed both deter the rest from crime and correct those they fall upon—but their joyful fortune speaks a great argument for the good to hear, how they ought to judge this kind of prosperity, which they see often attendant upon the wicked. And in this matter I think it is also arranged, that there is some man whose nature is so headstrong and rude, that the want of property could very likely provoke him to crime ; and his sickness providence cures with this remedy, the provision of money. One man, regarding his own conscience soiled by his misdeeds, and comparing his own character with his fortune, is afraid perhaps lest it should be hard for him to lose that the enjoyment of which he finds pleasant ; therefore he will change his behaviour and, while he is afraid of losing his fortune, he leaves his wickedness. Others prosperity unworthily used has hurled to well-deserved disaster. To some the right to punish others is granted, that it may be the cause of the employment of the good and the chastisement of the bad. For just as there is no compact between honest and dishonest men, so too the dishonest cannot agree among themselves. How can they, when each differs even with himself, their vices tearing their consciences apart, and when they often do things which, once they have done them, they see ought not to have been done ?

gerenda decernant ?  Ex quo saepe summa illa
185 providentia protulit insigne miraculum, ut malos
mali bonos facerent.  Nam dum iniqua sibi a pessimis
quidam perpeti videntur, noxiorum odio flagrantes
ad virtutis frugem rediere, dum se eis dissimiles
student esse quos oderant.  Sola est enim divina vis
190 cui mala quoque bona sint, cum eis competenter
utendo alicuius boni elicit effectum.  Ordo enim
quidam cuncta complectitur, ut quod adsignata
ordinis ratione decesserit, hoc licet in alium, tamen
ordinem relabatur, ne quid in regno providentiae
195 liceat temeritati.

’Αργαλέον δέ με ταῦτα θεὸν ὣς πάντ’ ἀγορεύειν.

Neque enim fas est homini cunctas divinae operae
machinas vel ingenio comprehendere vel explicare
sermone.  Hoc tantum perspexisse sufficiat, quod
200 naturarum omnium proditor deus idem ad bonum
dirigens cuncta disponat, dumque ea quae protulit in
sui similitudinem retinere festinat, malum omne de
reipublicae suae terminis per fatalis seriem necessitatis eliminet.  Quo fit ut quae in terris abundare
205 creduntur, si disponentem providentiam spectes,
nihil usquam mali esse perpendas.  Sed video te
iam dudum et pondere quaestionis oneratum et
rationis prolixitate fatigatum aliquam carminis exspectare dulcedinem.  Accipe igitur haustum quo
210 refectus firmior in ulteriora contendas.

---

[a] Homer, *Il.* xii. 176.

# CONSOLATION IV

And often that highest providence produces from all this a remarkable wonder, that evil men make evil men good. For some of them, while they think they are suffering injustices at the hands of men much worse than they, being inflamed with hatred of those injuring them, have come back to virtue's harvest, striving to be unlike those whom they hated. For only the divine nature is such that to it even evils are good, since by suitable use of them God draws out as a result some good. For a certain order embraces all things, so that that which has departed from the rule of this order appointed to it, although it slips into another condition yet that too is order, so that nothing in the realm of providence may be left to chance.

" But it is grievous that I should talk of all this as if I were a god." [a] For it is not allowed to a man either to comprehend with his natural powers or to express in words all the devices of the work of God. Let it suffice to have perceived only this, that God the author of all natures himself directing them towards the good disposes all things, and while he is swift to retain those things he has made in his own likeness, he removes all evil from within the bounds of his commonwealth by the course of the necessity of fate. Thus it happens that if you were to have regard to providence's disposing, looking at those things which are thought so widespread on earth, you would judge that there was no evil anywhere in them. But I see that you are long since burdened with the weight of this enquiry and tired by the length of the argument, and are waiting for some sweetness in verse ; therefore take a draught, that you may be refreshed by it and go more firmly further on.

# BOETHIUS

## VI

Si vis celsi iura tonantis
Pura sollers cernere mente,
Aspice summi culmina caeli.
Illic iusto foedere rerum
5    Veterem servant sidera pacem.
Non sol rutilo concitus igne
Gelidum Phoebes impedit axem
Nec quae summo vertice mundi
Flectit rapidos Ursa meatus,
10    Numquam occiduo lota profundo
Cetera cernens sidera mergi
Cupit oceano tingere flammas.
Semper vicibus temporis aequis
Vesper seras nuntiat umbras
15    Revehitque diem Lucifer almum.
Sic aeternos reficit cursus
Alternus amor, sic astrigeris
Bellum discors exulat oris.
Haec concordia temperat aequis
20    Elementa modis, ut pugnantia
Vicibus cedant umida siccis
Iungantque fidem frigora flammis,
Pendulus ignis surgat in altum
Terraeque graves pondere sidant.
25    Isdem causis vere tepenti
Spirat florifer annus odores,
Aestas Cererem fervida siccat,
Remeat pomis gravis autumnus,
Hiemem defluus inrigat imber.
30    Haec temperies alit ac profert
Quidquid vitam spirat in orbe.

## CONSOLATION IV

### VI

If you would see, with pure discerning mind,
The lofty Thunderer's laws,
Look up to the heights of the topmost heaven ;
There the stars keep their ancient peace
In the just compact of the universe.
The sun with his red fire roused does not detain
Phoebe's cold chariot,
Nor does the Bear, who turns his rapid course
About the highest pole of the universe,
Ever in western deeps submerged—
Although he sees the other stars sink down—
Desire to plunge his flames in Ocean's waves.
Always with fair exchange of time
Vesper announces late the shades of night
And Lucifer brings back the kindly day.
So mutual love renews eternal motions,
So from those star-strewn regions
Discordant war is banished.
Concord these elements regulates
In equal measures, that the warring wet
In turn yield place to dry,
And cold joins faith with flames.
The hanging fire rises on high
And heavy earth sinks down beneath its weight.
These are the causes why in the warmth of spring
The year in flower breathes out its lovely scents,
Hot summer dries the corn,
Autumn heavy with fruits returns,
And falling rain waters the winter earth.
This due proportion nourishes and brings forth
All things that breathe their life on earth,

Eadem rapiens condit et aufert
Obitu mergens orta supremo.
Sedet interea conditor altus
35 Rerumque regens flectit habenas
Rex et dominus fons et origo
Lex et sapiens arbiter aequi
Et quae motu concitat ire,
Sistit retrahens ac vaga firmat.
40 Nam nisi rectos revocans itus
Flexos iterum cogat in orbes,
Quae nunc stabilis continet ordo
Dissaepta suo fonte fatiscant.
Hic est cunctis communis amor
45 Repetuntque boni fine teneri,
Quia non aliter durare queant,
Nisi converso rursus amore
Refluant causae quae dedit esse.

## VII

Iamne igitur vides quid haec omnia quae diximus
consequatur ? " " Quidnam ? "inquam. " Omnem,"
inquit, " bonam prorsus esse fortunam." " Et qui id,"
inquam, " fieri potest ? " " Attende," inquit. " Cum
5 omnis fortuna vel iucunda vel aspera tum remunerandi
exercendive bonos tum puniendi corrigendive improbos causa deferatur, omnis bona quam vel iustam
constat esse vel utilem." " Nimis quidem," inquam,
" vera ratio et si quam paulo ante docuisti providentiam

---

*a i.e.* the planets ; *cf.* Cic. *Rep.* i. 14. 22 : *stellae quae errantes et quasi vagae nominantur.*

## CONSOLATION IV

And the same order seizing them, bears and hides
    them away,
Burying all that was born in its final end.
While the Creator sits on high,
And ruling the universe guides its reins,
Their king and lord, fount and beginning,
Their law, and judge in wisdom of their right,
And those he stirs to motion, drawing back
He halts and stays their wanderings [a] ;
For if he did not call them back to their right paths,
Forcing them run their circles once again,
All things now stable order holds so fast
Would tear apart, and from their origin in pieces fall.
This is the love common to all things,
And they seek to be bound by their end, the good,
Since in no other way could they endure,
If the causes that gave them being did not flow back
Under the power of returning love.

### VII

"And now do you see what follows from all these
things we have been saying ? "

" What ? " I asked.

" That every kind of fortune," she replied, " is
good."

" But how can that be ? " I asked.

" Attend to this," she said, " Since every kind of
fortune, whether pleasing or hard, is granted for the
purpose either of rewarding or exercising good men,
or of punishing or correcting the bad, every kind is
good, since it is agreed to be just or useful."

" Now that is indeed very true reasoning," I said,
" and if I considered providence, about which you

10 fatumve considerem, firmis viribus nixa sententia.
Sed eam si placet inter eas quas inopinabiles paulo
ante posuisti numeremus." " Qui ? "inquit. " Quia
id hominum sermo communis usurpat et quidem
crebro quorundam malam esse fortunam." " Visne
15 igitur," inquit, " paulisper vulgi sermonibus accedamus, ne nimium velut ab humanitatis usu recessisse
videamur ? " " Ut placet," inquam. " Nonne igitur
bonum censes esse quod prodest ? " " Ita est,"
inquam. " Quae vero aut exercet aut corrigit,
20 prodest ? " " Fateor," inquam. " Bona igitur ? "
" Quidni ? " " Sed haec eorum est qui vel in virtute
positi contra aspera bellum gerunt, vel a vitiis
declinantes virtutis iter arripiunt." " Negare,"
inquam, " nequeo." " Quid vero iucunda, quae in
25 praemium tribuitur bonis, num vulgus malam esse
decernit ? " " Nequaquam ; verum uti est ita quoque
esse optimam censet." " Quid reliqua, quae cum sit
aspera, iusto supplicio malos coercet, num bonam
populus putat ? " " Immo omnium,"inquam, " quae
30 excogitari possunt, iudicat esse miserrimam." " Vide

taught me just now, or fate, I should see that it was an opinion strongly and firmly founded. But if you agree, let us count it among those things you just now posited as unthinkable."

" How so ? " she asked.

" Because the common talk of men usually says, and indeed often, that some men have ill fortune."

" Then do you want us," she asked, " to have recourse for a while to terms like those of the common people, in case we seem to have withdrawn too far, as it were, from the practice of men ? "

" As you think best," I said.

" Then do you not judge that which is profitable to be good ? "

" That is so," I said.

" But that which either exercises or corrects is profitable ? "

" I agree," I said.

" And therefore good ? "

" How could it not be ? "

" But this is the case with those who, either being established in virtue wage war against adversity, or turning aside from their vices take the path of virtue."

" I cannot deny it," I said.

" Now what about the pleasant fortune which is granted as a reward to the good : do the common people judge that to be bad ? "

" By no means, but as indeed it is, so also they judge it to be, very good."

" What of the other, which although it is hard, constrains the wicked with just punishment ; the people do not think that good, do they ? "

" Indeed not," I said, " they judge it to be the most wretched of all conceivable things."

igitur ne opinionem populi sequentes quiddam valde
inopinabile confecerimus." " Quid ? " inquam. " Ex
his enim," ait, " quae concessa sunt, evenit eorum
quidem qui vel sunt vel in possessione vel in pro-
35 vectu vel in adeptione virtutis, omnem quaecumque
sit bonam, in improbitate vero manentibus omnem
pessimam esse fortunam." " Hoc," inquam, " verum
est, tametsi nemo audeat confiteri." " Quare,"
inquit, " ita vir sapiens moleste ferre non debet,
40 quotiens in fortunae certamen adducitur, ut virum
fortem non decet indignari, quotiens increpuit
bellicus tumultus ; utrique enim, huic quidem gloriae
propagandae illi vero conformandae sapientiae, diffi-
cultas ipsa materia est. Ex quo etiam virtus vocatur
45 quod suis viribus nitens non superetur adversis.
Neque enim vos in provectu positi virtutis diffluere
deliciis et emarcescere voluptate venistis. Proelium
cum omni fortuna animis[1] acre conseritis, ne vos aut
tristis opprimat aut iucunda corrumpat. Firmis
50 medium viribus occupate ! Quidquid aut infra subsistit aut ultra progreditur, habet contemptum
felicitatis, non habet praemium laboris. In vestra
enim situm manu qualem vobis fortunam formare
malitis ; omnis enim quae videtur aspera nisi aut
55 exercet aut corrigit punit.

---

[1] animis *the better* MSS. : *var. reading* nimis.

---

[a] Boethius here derives *virtus* from *vires* ; and *virtus* can
also mean " strength " or " vigour "—*cf.* Cic. *de Or.* ii. 27.
120 : *oratoris vis divina virtusque. . . . Virtus* is properly
derived, as Cicero elsewhere says (*Tusc.* ii. 18. 43), from
*vir*, a man.

378

# CONSOLATION IV

" See then whether we have not reached a most surprising conclusion by following the opinion of common folk."

" What ? " I asked.

" Because from those things that have been granted," she said, " it has followed that the fortune of those who indeed are either in possession of virtue, or making progress in it, or attaining to it, whatever that fortune may be, is all good, but for those who persevere in wickedness every kind of fortune is very bad."

" That," I said, " is true, though no-one would dare to admit it."

" And therefore," she said, " a wise man ought not to take it ill, every time he is brought into conflict with fortune, just as it would not be fitting for a brave man to be vexed every time the sound of war crashed out. Since for each of these the difficulty is itself the occasion, for the latter of increasing his glory, for the former of further fashioning his wisdom. And this is indeed why virtue is so called, because relying on its own powers it is not overcome by adversity.[a] For neither have you, who are set on the road to virtue, come here to wallow in luxury or swoon with pleasure. You are engaged in bitter mental strife with every kind of fortune, lest ill fortune oppress you or pleasant fortune corrupt. Hold to the mean with firm strength ; whatever either remains below the mean or passes beyond it has contempt for good fortune, but not the reward for labour. For it is placed in your own hands, what kind of fortune you prefer to shape for yourselves ; for all fortune that seems adverse, if it does not exercise or correct, punishes.

379

# BOETHIUS

## VII

Bella bis quinis operatus annis
Ultor Atrides Phrygiae ruinis
Fratris amissos thalamos piavit ;
Ille dum Graiae dare vela classi
Optat et ventos redimit cruore,
Exuit patrem miserumque tristis
Foederat[1] natae iugulum sacerdos.
Flevit amissos Ithacus sodales
Quos ferus vasto recubans in antro
Mersit inmani Polyphemus alvo ;
Sed tamen caeco furibundus ore
Gaudium maestis lacrimis rependit.
Herculem duri celebrant labores.
Ille Centauros domuit superbos,
Abstulit saevo spolium leoni
Fixit et certis volucres sagittis,
Poma cernenti rapuit draconi
Aureo laevam gravior metallo,
Cerberum traxit triplici catena.
Victor immitem posuisse fertur
Pabulum saevis dominum quadrigis.
Hydra combusto periit veneno,
Fronte turpatus Achelous amnis
Ora demersit pudibunda ripis.
Stravit Antaeum Libycis harenis,
Cacus Evandri satiavit iras
Quosque pressurus foret altus orbis
Saetiger spumis umeros notavit.

5

10

15

20

25

---

[1] foderat *early versions,* σφαγίασσε *Planudes.*

---

[a] Agamemnon, who waged the war against Troy, a
Phrygian city, for ten years, to avenge the abduction of
Helen, his brother Menelaus's wife, by Paris ; the Greek

## CONSOLATION IV

### VII

Having warred a decade
The vengeful son of Atreus [a] with Phrygia's fall
Avenged his brother's violated bed.
He when he wants the fleet of Greece to sail
And buys a wind with blood,
Puts off the father and sternly as a priest
Makes a pact of his daughter's throat—poor girl.
Odysseus of Ithaca wept for his comrades lost,
Whom savage Polyphemus, lying in his vast cave,
Engulfed in his monstrous belly ;
But when the Cyclops raged with his one eye blinded
Then were his bitter tears with joy requited.
Harsh labours make the fame of Hercules :
He tamed the arrogant Centaurs,
Stole the spoil from the savage lion,
Pierced the Stymphalian birds with arrows sure ;
He seized the fruits from the watching dragon,
His hand the heavier for the golden ball,
And with triple chain led Cerberus.
The tale is told how he beat and gave as fodder
That cruel master to his own savage steeds.
Its poison burnt, the Hydra died ;
The river Achelous, in shame for his hornless brow,
Disgraced, did bury in his banks his face.
Hercules stretched Antaeus' length on Libyan sands,
And Cacus dead sated Evander's wrath.
Those shoulders which the high sphere of heaven was
　　to press
The bristled boar did fleck with foam.

fleet was becalmed after sailing for Troy from Mycenae, at
Aulis, and to get a wind Agamemnon had to sacrifice his
daughter Iphigenia.

Ultimus caelum[1] labor inreflexo
30     Sustulit collo pretiumque rursus
Ultimi caelum meruit laboris.
Ite nunc fortes ubi celsa magni
Ducit exempli via !   Cur inertes
Terga nudatis ?   Superata tellus
35           Sidera donat.''

[1] caelo *the better* MSS.

## CONSOLATION IV

As his last labour he with unbended neck
Bore up the heavens, and as his reward
For that last labour, heaven deserved.
Go then, you brave, where leads the lofty path
Of this great example.  Why in indolence
Do you turn your backs in flight ?  Earth overcome
Grants you the stars.

# ANICII MANLII SEVERINI BOETHII

V.C. ET INL. EXCONS. ORD. EX MAG. OFF. PATRICII

# PHILOSOPHIAE CONSOLA-TIONIS

## LIBER QUARTUS EXPLICIT

## INCIPIT LIBER V

## I

Dixerat orationisque cursum ad alia quaedam tractanda atque expedienda vertebat. Tum ego : " Recta quidem," inquam, " exhortatio tuaque prorsus auctoritate dignissima, sed quod tu dudum de providentia
5 quaestionem pluribus aliis implicitam esse dixisti, re experior. Quaero enim an esse aliquid omnino et quidnam esse casum arbitrere." Tum illa : " Festino," inquit, " debitum promissionis absolvere viamque tibi qua patriam reveharis aperire. Haec autem etsi
10 perutilia cognitu tamen a proposti nostri tramite paulisper aversa sunt, verendumque est ne deviis fatigatus ad emetiendum rectum iter sufficere non possis." " Ne id, " inquam, " prorsus vereare. Nam quietus mihi loco fuerit ea quibus maxime delector

384

## BOETHIUS

# THE CONSOLATION OF PHILOSOPHY

### BOOK V

### I

SHE finished speaking, and was going to turn the course of her speech to deal with and explain some other questions ; then I said : " Your exhortation is right indeed and very worthy of your authority, but what you said just now about providence, that it was a question involving many others, I know from experience. For I want to know whether you think chance is anything at all, and if so, what ? "

" I am hastening," she replied, " to make good my promise and open the way to you by which you may be brought back to your homeland. But these things, though they are very useful to know, are yet a little aside from the path we have set ourselves, and it is to be feared you may not be able to last out to the end of the direct road if you are tired by going down by-paths."

" There is really no need," I said, " for you to be afraid of that. For I shall find it a resting-place, to

15 agnoscere, simul cum omne disputationis tuae latus
indubitata fide constiterit, nihil de sequentibus
ambigatur." Tum illa : " Morem," inquit, " geram
tibi," simulque sic orsa est : " Si quidem," inquit,
" aliquis eventum temerario motu nullaque causarum
20 conexione productum casum esse definiat, nihil
omnino casum esse confirmo et praeter subiectae rei
significationem inanem prorsus vocem esse decerno.
Quis enim coercente in ordinem cuncta deo locus
esse ullus temeritati reliquus potest ? Nam nihil ex
25 nihilo exsistere vera sententia est cui nemo umquam
veterum refragatus est, quamquam id illi non de
operante principio, sed de materiali subiecto hoc
omnium de natura rationum quasi quoddam iecerint
fundamentum. At si nullis ex causis aliquid oriatur,
30 id de nihilo ortum esse videbitur. Quod si hoc fieri
nequit, ne casum quidem huiusmodi esse possibile
est qualem paulo ante definivimus." " Quid igitur,"
inquam, " nihilne est quod vel casus vel fortuitum
iure appellari queat ? An est aliquid, tametsi vulgus
35 lateat, cui vocabula ista conveniant ? " " Aristoteles
meus id," inquit, " in Physicis et brevi et veri
propinqua ratione definivit." " Quonam," inquam
" modo ? " " Quotiens," ait, " aliquid cuiuspiam rei
gratia geritur aliudque quibusdam de causis quam
40 quod intendebatur obtingit, casus vocatur, ut si quis
colendi agri causa fodiens humum defossi auri pondus

---

<sup>a</sup> *Physics*, ii. 4-5.

understand these things, which I most delight in. At the same time, since every side of your argument would be set up in undoubted credibility, nothing that follows from it would be doubted."

" I will grant your wish," she said then ; and at once began thus : " If indeed someone were to define chance as an event produced by random motion and not by any chain of causes, then I assert that chance is nothing at all, and I judge that apart from signifying the subject-event it refers to, it is a sound entirely empty of meaning. For what place can be left for randomness where God constrains all things into his order ? For that nothing comes from nothing is a true opinion, which none of the ancients ever contested, but they laid it as it were as a foundation of all arguments about nature, though they applied it not to the creative principle but to the material subject to it. But if something were to arise from no causes, that will seem to have arisen from nothing ; and if this cannot be, then even chance cannot even possibly exist, of such a kind as we have just now defined."

" Why then," I said, " is there nothing which can rightly be called chance or fortuitousness ? Or is there something, although it is hidden from common men, to which these names belong ? "

" My Aristotle," she said, " defined it in his *Physics* [a] in an argument brief and close to the truth."

" How ? " I asked.

" Whenever," she said, " something is done for the sake of some given end, and another thing occurs, for some reason or other, different from what was intended, it is called chance : as, for example, if a man digging in the ground in order to till his field were

387

inveniat. Hoc igitur fortuito quidem creditur acci-
disse, verum non de nihilo est ; nam proprias causas
habet quarum inprovisus inopinatusque concursus
45 casum videtur operatus. Nam nisi cultor agri
humum foderet, nisi eo loci pecuniam suam de-
positor obruisset, aurum non esset inventum. Haec
sunt igitur fortuiti causa compendii, quod ex obviis
sibi et confluentibus causis, non ex gerentis inten-
50 tione provenit. Neque enim vel qui aurum obruit
vel qui agrum exercuit ut ea pecunia reperiretur
intendit ; sed uti dixi, quo ille obruit hunc fodisse
convenit atque concurrit. Licet igitur definire
casum esse inopinatum ex confluentibus causis in his
55 quae ob aliquid geruntur eventum ; concurrere vero
atque confluere causas facit ordo ille inevitabili
conexione procedens, qui de providentiae fonte
descendens cuncta suis locis temporibusque disponit.

I

Rupis Achaemeniae scopulis ubi versa sequentum
Pectoribus figit spicula pugna fugax,
Tigris et Euphrates uno se fonte resolvunt
Et mox abiunctis dissociantur aquis.

---

[a] Achaemenes was the grandfather of Cyrus, king of
Persia, and the adjective *Achaemenius* is used to mean simply
" Persian," as by Horace and Ovid. As to the notion that
the Tigris and Euphrates rise from the same source (false, as

to find he had dug up a quantity of gold. Now this
is indeed believed to have happened by chance, but
it does not come from nothing ; for it has its proper
causes, and their unforeseen and unexpected coming
together appears to have produced a chance event.
For if the man tilling his field were not digging the
ground, and if the man who put it there had not
hidden his money in that particular spot, the gold
would not have been found. These are therefore the
causes of that fortuitous profit, which is produced by
causes meeting one another and coming together,
not by the intention of the doer of the action. For
neither he who hid the gold, nor he who worked the
field, intended that money to be found, but as I said,
where the one buried it the other happens and
chances to have dug. We may therefore define
chance as the unexpected event of concurring causes
among things done for some purpose. Now causes
are made to concur and flow together by that order
which, proceeding with inevitable connexion, and
coming down from its source in providence, disposes
all things in their proper places and times."

1

Among the crags of the Achaemenian cliffs, where
    turned in flight [a]
The fighting Parthian's arrows pierce his pursuers'
    breast,
The Tigris and Euphrates rise from one spring,
Next they separate and their waters divide ;

Herodotus, Strabo and Pliny knew) *cf.* Isidore, *Etym.* XII.
xxi. 10 : *Sallustius autem, auctor certissimus, asserit Tigrim
et Euphraten uno fonte manare in Armenia.*

5    Si coeant cursumque iterum revocentur in unum,
         Confluat alterni quod trahit unda vadi ;
     Convenient puppes et vulsi flumine trunci
         Mixtaque fortuitos implicet unda modos,
     Quos tamen ipsa vagos terrae declivia casus
10        Gurgitis et lapsi defluus ordo regit.
     Sic quae permissis fluitare videtur habenis
         Fors patitur frenos ipsaque lege meat."


## II

    " Animadverto," inquam, " idque, uti tu dicis, ita
esse consentio.   Sed in hac haerentium sibi serie
causarum estne ulla nostri arbitrii libertas an ipsos
quoque humanorum motus animorum fatalis catena
5 constringit ? "   " Est," inquit, " neque enim fuerit
ulla rationalis natura quin eidem libertas adsit arbitrii.
Nam quod ratione uti naturaliter potest id habet
iudicium  quo  quidque  discernat ;   per se igitur
fugienda  optandave  dinoscit.   Quod  vero  quis
10 optandum esse iudicat petit ;   refugit vero quod
aestimat esse fugiendum.   Quare quibus in ipsis
inest ratio, inest etiam volendi nolendique libertas.
Sed hanc non in omnibus aequam esse constituo.
Nam supernis divinisque substantiis et perspicax

If they should come together, into one course brought
    back again,
If all that the water of each stream bears should flow
    into one,
Their ships would meet, as will treetrunks torn up by
    the river,
And their mingled waters in chance paths will twist
    and turn.
Yet these chance wanderings the very slopes of the
    land
And the downflowing nature of the slipping stream
    control.
So too that chance which seems slack-reined to roam
Endures its own bridle, and itself moves by law.

## II

" I see that," I said, " and I agree it is as you say.
But in this close-linked series of causes, is there any
freedom of our will, or does this chain of fate also bind
even the motions of men's minds ? "

" Freedom there is," she said, " for there could
not be any nature rational, did not that same nature
possess freedom of the will. For that which can by
its nature use reason, has the faculty of judgement,
by which it determines everything ; of itself, therefore, it distinguishes those things which are to be
avoided, and those things that are to be desired.
Now what a man judges is to be desired, that he seeks ;
but he runs away from what he thinks is to be
avoided. And therefore those who have in themselves reason have also in them freedom to will or not
to will, but this freedom is not, I am sure, equal in
all of them. For heavenly, divine substances possess

15 iudicium et incorrupta voluntas et efficax optatorum
praesto est potestas. Humanas vero animas liberiores
quidem esse necesse est cum se in mentis divinae
speculatione conservant, minus vero cum dilabuntur
ad corpora, minusque etiam, cum terrenis artubus
20 colligantur. Extrema vero est servitus, cum vitiis
deditae rationis propriae possessione ceciderunt.
Nam ubi oculos a summae luce veritatis ad inferiora
et tenebrosa deiecerint, mox inscitiae nube caligant,
perniciosis turbantur affectibus quibus accedendo
25 consentiendoque quam invexere sibi adiuvant servi-
tutem et sunt quodam modo propria libertate
captivae. Quae tamen ille ab aeterno cuncta prospiciens providentiae cernit intuitus et suis quaeque
meritis praedestinata disponit.


## II

Πάντ᾽ ἐφορᾶν καὶ πάντ᾽ ἐπακούειν[1]
Puro clarum lumine Phoebum
Melliflui canit oris Homerus ;
Qui tamen intima viscera terrae
5      Non valet aut pelagi radiorum
Infirma perrumpere luce.
Haud sic magni conditor orbis ;
Huic ex alto cuncta tuenti
Nulla terrae mole resistunt,
10    Non nox atris nubibus obstat.
Quae sint, quae fuerint veniantque
Uno mentis cernit in ictu ;

[1] *The reconstruction of verse the and the right disposal of
the words are due to Engelbrecht.*

---

<sup>a</sup> *Il.* iii. 277 *et alibi.*

penetrating judgement, an uncorrupted will, and the ability to achieve what they desire. But human souls must indeed be more free when they preserve themselves in the contemplation of the divine mind ; less free, however, when they slip down to the corporeal, and still less free when they are bound into earthly limbs. But their ultimate servitude is when, given over to vice, they have lapsed from the possession of the reason proper to them. For when from the light of the highest truth they have lowered their eyes to inferior, darkling things, at once they are befogged by the cloud of unknowing, they are disturbed by destructive affections, by giving in and by consenting to which they strengthen that servitude which they have brought upon themselves, and are in a way made captive by their freedom. Yet that regard of providence which looks forth on all things from eternity, sees this and disposes all that is predestined to each according to his deserts."

## II

That Phoebus shining with pure light
" Sees all and all things hears, "
So Homer sings, he of the honeyed voice [a] ;
Yet even he, with the light of his rays, too weak,
Cannot burst through
To the inmost depths of earth or ocean.
Not thus the Maker of this great universe :
Him, viewing all things from his height,
No mass of earth obstructs,
No night with black clouds thwarts.
What is, what has been, and what is to come,
In one swift mental stab he sees ;

Quem, quia respicit omnia solus,
Verum possis dicere solem."

## III

Tum ego : " En," inquam, " difficiliore rursus
ambiguitate confundor." " Quaenam," inquit, " ista
est ? Iam enim quibus perturbere coniecto."
" Nimium," inquam, " adversari ac repugnare videtur
5 praenoscere universa deum et esse ullum libertatis
arbitrium. Nam si cuncta prospicit deus neque falli
ullo modo potest, evenire necesse est quod providentia futurum esse praeviderit. Quare si ab aeterno
non facta hominum modo sed etiam consilia volun-
10 tatesque praenoscit, nulla erit arbitrii libertas ; neque
enim vel factum aliud ullum vel quaelibet exsistere
poterit voluntas nisi quam nescia falli providentia
divina praesenserit. Nam si aliorsum quam provisae
sunt detorqueri valent, non iam erit futuri firma
15 praescientia, sed opinio potius incerta, quod de deo
credere nefas iudico. Neque enim illam probo
rationem qua se quidam credunt hunc quaestionis
nodum posse dissolvere. Aiunt enim non ideo quid
esse eventurum, quoniam id providentia futurum
20 esse prospexerit, sed e contrario potius, quoniam quid
futurum est, id divinam providentiam latere non
posse eoque modo necessarium hoc in contrariam
relabi partem, neque enim necesse esse contingere
quae providentur, sed necesse esse quae futura sunt
25 provideri—quasi vero quae cuius rei causa sit prae-
394

Him, since he only all things sees,
The true sun could you call.

### III

Then I said : " See, I am again confused, with a
still more difficult doubt."

" What is that ? " she asked. " Tell me, for I
already guess what troubles you."

" It seems," I said, " much too conflicting and
contradictory that God foreknows all things *and* that
there is any free will. For if God foresees all and
cannot in any way be mistaken, then that must necessarily happen which in his providence he foresees will
be. And therefore if he foreknows from all eternity
not only the deeds of men but even their plans and
desires, there will be no free will ; for it will be
impossible for there to be any deed at all or any
desire whatever except that which divine providence,
which cannot be mistaken, perceives beforehand. For
if they can be turned aside into a different way from
that foreseen, then there will no longer be firm foreknowledge of the future, but rather uncertain opinion,
which I judge impious to believe of God.

For neither do I agree with that argument according to which some believe that they can solve this
knotty question. For they say that a thing is not
going to happen because providence has foreseen
that it will be, but rather to the contrary, that since
something is going to be, it cannot be hidden from
divine providence, and in this way the necessity slips
over to the opposite side. For, they say, it is not
necessary that those things happen which are foreseen, but it is necessary that those things that will
happen are foreseen ; as if indeed our work were to

395

scientiane futurorum necessitatis an futurorum necessitas providentiae laboretur, ac non illud demonstrare
nitamur, quoquo modo sese habeat ordo causarum,
necessarium esse eventum praescitarum rerum, etiam
30 si praescientia futuris rebus eveniendi necessitatem
non videatur inferre.  Etenim si quispiam sedeat,
opinionem quae eum sedere coniectat veram esse
necesse est ; atque e converso rursus, si de quopiam
vera sit opinio quoniam sedet, eum sedere necesse
35 est.  In utroque igitur necessitas inest, in hoc quidem
sedendi, at vero in altero veritatis.  Sed non idcirco
quisque sedet quoniam vera est opinio, sed haec
potius vera est quoniam quempiam sedere praecessit.
Ita cum causa veritatis ex altera parte procedat,
40 inest tamen communis in utraque necessitas.

Similia de providentia futurisque rebus ratiocinari
patet.  Nam etiam si idcirco quoniam futura sunt,
providentur, non vero ideo quoniam providentur eveniunt, nihilo minus tamen ab deo vel ventura provideri
45 vel provisa necesse est evenire,[1] quod ad perimendam
arbitrii libertatem solum satis est.  Iam vero quam
praeposterum est ut aeternae praescientiae temporalium rerum eventus causa esse dicatur !  Quid
est autem aliud arbitrari ideo deum futura quoniam
50 sunt eventura providere, quam putare quae olim
acciderunt causam summae illius esse providentiae ?
Ad haec sicuti cum quid esse scio, id ipsum esse
necesse est, ita cum quid futurum novi, id ipsum

[1] evenire provisa *the better* MSS.

_____

[a] The argument is that God *does* foresee all, and therefore . . .

396

discover which is the cause of which, foreknowledge of future things' necessity, or future things' necessity of providence, and as if we were not striving to show this, that whatever the state of the ordering of causes, the outcome of things foreknown is necessary, even if that foreknowledge were not to seem to confer on future things the necessity of occurring.

For indeed, if anyone sit, then the opinion that thinks that he sits must be true ; and conversely also, if the opinion about any man be true, that he sits, then he must be sitting. There is thus a necessity in both cases : in the latter, he must be sitting, but in the former, the opinion must be true. But a man does not sit because the opinion about him is true, but rather that opinion is true because that someone is sitting happened first. So that although the cause of truth proceeds from the one part, yet there is in both a common necessity.

Obviously the same reasoning holds with regard to providence and future events : for even if the reason they are foreseen is that they *are* future events, yet they do not happen simply because they are foreseen ; and yet nevertheless things either must be foreseen by God because they are coming or happen because they are foreseen,[a] and that alone is enough to destroy the freedom of the will. But now how upside down it is that it should be said that the cause of eternal foreknowledge is the occurrence of temporal things ! But what else is it, to think that God foresees future things because they are going to happen, than to think that those things, once they have happened, are the cause of his highest providence ? Furthermore, just as when I know that something is, then that necessarily is so, so when I

397

futurum esse necesse est. Sic fit igitur ut eventus
55 praescitae rei nequeat evitari. Postremo si quid
aliquis aliorsum atque sese res habet existimet, id
non modo scientia non est, sed est opinio fallax ab
scientiae veritate longe diversa. Quare si quid ita
futurum est ut eius certus ac necessarius non sit
60 eventus, id eventurum esse praesciri qui poterit ?
Sicut enim scientia ipsa impermixta est falsitati, ita
id quod ab ea concipitur esse aliter atque concipitur
nequit. Ea namque causa est cur mendacio scientia
careat, quod se ita rem quamque habere necesse est
65 uti eam sese habere scientia comprehendit. Quid
igitur ?  Quonam modo deus haec incerta futura
praenoscit ?  Nam si inevitabiliter eventura censet
quae etiam non evenire possibile est, fallitur ;  quod
non sentire modo nefas est, sed etiam voce proferre.
70 At si ita uti sunt, ita ea futura esse decernit, ut
aeque vel fieri ea vel non fieri posse cognoscat, quae
est haec praescientia quae nihil certum nihil stabile
comprehendit ?  Aut quid hoc refert vaticinio illo
ridiculo Tiresiae ?

75                  Quidquid dicam, aut erit aut non.[a]

Quid etiam divina providentia humana opinione
praestiterit, si uti homines incerta iudicat quorum
est incertus eventus ?  Quod si apud illum rerum
omnium certissimum fontem nihil incerti esse potest,
80 certus eorum est eventus quae futura firmiter ille
praescierit. Quare nulla est humanis consiliis actioni-

---

[a] Hor. *Sat.* ii. 5. 59 ; *cf.* Cic. *N.D.* i. 70.

know something will be, then that necessarily will be so ; and so it happens that the occurrence of a thing foreknown cannot be avoided. Lastly, if a man think a thing to be otherwise than it is, that is not only not knowledge, but it is a mistaken opinion very different indeed from the truth of knowledge. And therefore if something is future in such a way that its occurrence is not certain or necessary, how will it be possible for it to be foreknown that it will occur ? For just as real knowledge is unmixed with falsity, so that which is grasped by knowledge cannot be otherwise than as it is grasped. For the real reason why knowledge lacks any falsehood is that every single thing must necessarily be just as knowledge comprehends it to be.

Well then, how does God foreknow that these uncertain things shall be ? For if he thinks those things will inevitably occur which it is yet possible may not occur, he is mistaken, which it is not only impious to think but still more impious to say aloud. But if he sees that those future things are just as indeed they are, so that he knows that they can equally either happen or not happen, what sort of foreknowledge is this, that grasps nothing certain, nothing stable ? Or how does it compare with that ridiculous prophecy of Tiresias?—" Whatever I say will either happen or not ? " [a] And in what will divine providence be better than the opinions of men, if it judges in the way men do those things to be uncertain the occurrence of which is uncertain ? But if in him, the most certain fount of all things, there can be nothing uncertain, then the occurrence is certain of those things which he firmly foreknows will be.

And therefore there is no freedom in human inten-

busque libertas quas divina mens sine falsitatis errore
cuncta prospiciens ad unum alligat et constringit
eventum.  Quo semel recepto quantus occasus
85 humanarum rerum consequatur liquet.  Frustra enim
bonis malisque praemia poenaeve proponuntur quae
nullus meruit liber ac voluntarius motus animorum.
Idque omnium videbitur iniquissimum quod nunc
aequissimum iudicatur vel puniri improbos vel
90 remunerari probos quos ad alterutrum non propria
mittit voluntas, sed futuri cogit certa necessitas.
Nec vitia igitur nec virtutes quidquam fuerint, sed
omnium meritorum potius mixta atque indiscreta
confusio.  Quoque nihil sceleratius excogitari potest,
95 cum ex providentia rerum omnis ordo ducatur nihilque consiliis liceat humanis, fit ut vitia quoque nostra
ad bonorum omnium referantur auctorem.  Igitur
nec sperandi aliquid nec deprecandi ulla ratio est.
Quid enim vel speret quisque vel etiam deprecetur,
100 quando optanda omnia series indeflexa conectit ?
Auferetur igitur unicum illud inter homines deumque
commercium sperandi scilicet ac deprecandi.  Si
quidem iustae humilitatis pretio inaestimabilem
vicem divinae gratiae promeremur, qui solus modus
105 est quo cum deo colloqui homines posse videantur
illique inaccessae luci prius quoque quam impetrent
ipsa supplicandi ratione coniungi.  Quae si recepta
futurorum necessitate nihil virium habere credantur,
quid erit quo summo illi rerum principi conecti atque

---

[a] It is assumed that Boethius here uses *deprecari* in the
usual sense of " to pray against, " not simply " to pray " or
" to pray for, " and that by *optanda* he means things to be
desired, whether positive or negative.

tions or actions, which the divine mind, foreseeing all without mistaken error, binds and constrains to one actual occurrence. This once accepted, it is clear what a great collapse of human affairs follows ! For it is vain to propose for good and evil men rewards or punishments which no free and voluntary act of their minds has deserved. And that very thing will seem most unjust of all which now is judged most just, that either the wicked are punished or the good rewarded, since they have not been brought by their own wills but driven by the certain necessity of what shall be to one or other end. And therefore there would be no vices nor virtues, but rather a mixed-up and indistinguishable confusion of all deserts, and— than which nothing more wicked can be conceived ! —since the whole ordering of things proceeds from providence and nothing is really possible to human intentions, it follows that even our vices are to be referred to the author of all things good. And therefore there is no sense in hoping for anything or in praying that anything may be averted [a] ; for what even should any man hope for or pray to be averted when an inflexible course links all that can be desired ? And so that sole intercourse between men and God will be removed, that is, hope and prayer for aversion (if indeed at the price of a proper humility we deserve the inestimable return of God's grace), and that is the only way in which men seem able to converse with God and to be joined by the very manner of their supplication to that inaccessible light, even before they receive what they seek. Now if these things, once the necessity of what shall be is admitted, be thought to have no power, how should we be able to be joined and cleave to him, the highest principle of

*of what use is ? prayer*

110 adhaerere possimus ?   Quare necesse erit humanum
genus, uti paulo ante cantabas, dissaeptum atque
disiunctum suo fonte fatiscere.

### III

Quaenam discors foedera rerum
Causa resolvit ?   Quis tanta deus
Veris statuit bella duobus,
Ut quae carptim singula constent
5    Eadem nolint mixta iugari ?
An nulla est discordia veris
Semperque sibi certa cohaerent,
Sed mens caecis obruta membris
Nequit oppressi luminis igne
10   Rerum tenues noscere nexus ?
Sed cur tanto flagrat amore
Veri tectas reperire notas ?
Scitne quod appetit anxia nosse ?
Sed quis nota scire laborat ?
15   At si nescit, quid caeca petit ?
Quis enim quidquam nescius optet
Aut quis valeat nescita sequi ?
Quove inveniat, quisque[1] repertam
Queat ignarus noscere formam ?
20   An cum mentem cerneret altam,
Pariter summam et singula norat ?
Nunc membrorum condita nube
Non in totum est oblita sui
Summamque tenet singula perdens.
25   Igitur quisquis vera requirit,

[1] quisque *codex Bambergensis s. xi* :   quis *the better* MSS.

---

*a* Book IV, m. VI. 43, pp. 374-375.

all things ? So it will necessarily follow, as you sang
a little while ago,[a] that human kind would, torn
apart and disjoined, in pieces fall from their origin.

### III

What cause discordant breaks the world's compact ?
What god sets strife so great
Between two truths,
That those same things which stand, alone and
    separate,
Together mixed, refuse to be so yoked ?
Or is there no such discord between truths,
And do they ever each to other firmly cleave,
But is it the mind, eclipsed by the body's unseeing
    parts,
That cannot recognize, by its suppressed light's fire,
The world's fine fastenings ?
But why does it blaze with so great love
To find the hidden characters of truth ?
Does it know what it anxiously seeks to know ?
But who is there labours to know known things ?
Yet if it does not know, why then in blindness seek ?
For who would long for anything he knows not of,
Or who could follow after things unknown,
Or how discover them ? Who could in ignorance
    recognize
The form of what he found ?
Or, when it perceived the highest mind,
Did it know at once the whole and the separate parts ?
Now, clouded and hidden by the body's parts,
It is not totally forgetful of itself,
And the whole it keeps, losing the separate parts.
Therefore whoever seeks the truth

Neutro est habitu ; nam neque novit
Nec penitus tamen omnia nescit,
Sed quam retinens meminit summam
Consulit alte visa retractans,
30     Ut servatis queat oblitas
       Addere partes."

## IV

Tum illa : " Vetus," inquit, " haec est de providentia querela Marcoque Tullio, cum divinationem
distribuit, vehementer agitata tibique ipsi res diu
prorsus multumque quaesita, sed haud quaquam ab
5 ullo vestrum hactenus satis diligenter ac firmiter
expedita. Cuius caliginis causa est, quod humanae
ratiocinationis motus ad divinae praescientiae simplicitatem non potest admoveri, quae si ullo modo
cogitari queat, nihil prorsus relinquetur ambigui.
10 Quod ita demum patefacere atque expedire temptabo,
si prius ea quibus moveris expendero. Quaero enim,
cur illam solventium rationem minus efficacem putes,
quae quia praescientiam non esse futuris rebus
causam necessitatis existimat, nihil impediri prae-
15 scientia arbitrii libertatem putat. Num enim tu
aliunde argumentum futurorum necessitatis trahis,
nisi quod ea quae praesciuntur non evenire non
possunt ? Si igitur praenotio nullam futuris rebus
adicit necessitatem, quod tu etiam paulo ante fate-
20 bare, quid est quod voluntarii exitus rerum ad certum
cogantur eventum ? Etenim positionis gratia, ut

---

<sup>a</sup> *De Divin.* ii. 8 ff.

# CONSOLATION V

Is of neither class : for he neither knows
Nor is altogether ignorant of all,
But the whole he keeps, remembers and reflects on,
All from that height perceived goes over once again,
That he might to those things he has preserved
Add the forgotten parts."

## IV

Then she said : " That is the old complaint about
providence, one powerfully dealt with by Cicero when
he was classifying kinds of divination,[a] and a matter
for a very long time and deeply investigated by
yourself ; but it has so far been by no means sufficiently carefully or steadfastly developed by any of
you. The cause of this obscurity is that the movement of human reasoning cannot approach the simplicity of divine foreknowledge ; if that could by any
means be conceived, no doubt whatever will remain.
And I shall try to make clear and explain this only
when I have first considered those things by which
you are now troubled. For I ask, why do you think
that explanation of those solving the problem less
than effectual which, since it considers that foreknowledge is not the cause of any necessity for future
events, thinks the freedom of the will not at all
restricted by foreknowledge ? For you, surely, do
not produce proof of the necessity of future things
other than from the fact that those things that are
foreknown cannot not happen ? Then if foreknowledge imposes no necessity on future things, which
you did indeed admit a little while ago, what is the
reason why the outcome of those things dependent
on the will should be forced to end in a certain result ?

quid consequatur advertas, statuamus nullam esse
praescientiam. Num igitur quantum ad hoc attinet,
quae ex arbitrio eveniunt ad necessitatem cogantur ? "

25 " Minime." " Statuamus iterum esse, sed nihil rebus
necessitatis iniungere ; manebit ut opinor eadem
voluntatis integra atque absoluta libertas.

Sed praescientia, inquies, tametsi futuris eveniendi
necessitas non est, signum tamen est necessario ea

30 esse ventura. Hoc igitur modo, etiam si praecognitio
non fuisset, necessarios futurorum exitus esse con-
staret. Omne etenim signum tantum quid sit
ostendit, non vero efficit quod designat. Quare
demonstrandum prius est nihil non ex necessitate

35 contingere, ut praenotionem signum esse huius
necessitatis appareat. Alioquin si haec nulla est, ne
illa quidem eius rei signum poterit esse quae non est.
Iam vero probationem firma ratione subnixam constat
non ex signis neque petitis extrinsecus argumentis

40 sed ex convenientibus necessariisque causis esse
ducendam. Sed qui fieri potest ut ea non proveniant
quae futura esse providentur ? Quasi vero nos ea
quae providentia futura esse praenoscit non esse
eventura credamus ac non illud potius arbitremur,

45 licet eveniant, nihil tamen ut evenirent sui natura
necessitatis habuisse ; quod hinc facile perpendas
licebit. Plura etenim dum fiunt subiecta oculis
406

# CONSOLATION V

Now for the sake of argument, that you may see what follows, let us suppose that there is no fore-knowledge. In such a case, those things that depend upon the will would not be forced into any necessity, would they ? "

" Not at all."

" Again, let us suppose that there is foreknowledge, but that it enjoins no necessity on things ; there will remain, I think, that same freedom of the will, whole and absolute. But foreknowledge, you will say, although it does not constitute a necessity for future things, of their happening, yet it is a sign that they will necessarily come to be. In this way, then, even had there been no foreknowledge, it would be agreed that the outcome of future things is necessary ; for every sign only points to what is, but does not cause to be what it signifies. Wherefore it must first be demonstrated that nothing happens except of neces-sity, that foreknowledge may be seen to be the sign of that necessity ; otherwise, if there is no necessity, nor then will foreknowledge be able to be a sign for that which does not exist. But it is agreed that a proof supported by firm reasoning must be drawn not from signs nor from arguments fetched from outside the subject, but from relevant and necessary causes.

But how could it be that those things should not happen which are foreseen to be future ? Just as if we were to believe that those things which providence foreknows will happen were not going to happen, and did not rather think that although they do happen, yet they have of their nature no necessity that they must happen. Which you may easily gather from this : for many things, while they are happening, we

407

intuemur, ut ea quae in quadrigis moderandis atque
flectendis facere spectantur aurigae, atque ad hunc
50 modum cetera.   Num igitur quidquam illorum ita
fieri necessitas ulla compellit ? "   " Minime.   Frustra
enim esset artis effectus, si omnia coacta moverentur."
" Quae igitur cum fiunt carent exsistendi necessitate,
eadem prius quam fiant sine necessitate futura sunt.
55 Quare sunt quaedam eventura quorum exitus ab
omni necessitate sit absolutus.   Nam illud quidem
nullum arbitror esse dicturum, quod quae nunc fiunt,
prius quam fierent, eventura non fuerint.   Haec
igitur etiam praecognita liberos habent eventus.
60 Nam sicut scientia praesentium rerum nihil his quae
fiunt, ita praescientia futurorum nihil his quae
ventura sunt necessitatis importat.   Sed hoc, inquis,
ipsum dubitatur, an earum rerum quae necessarios
exitus non habent ulla possit esse praenotio.   Dis-
65 sonare etenim videntur putasque si praevideantur
consequi necessitatem, si necessitas desit minime
praesciri nihilque scientia comprehendi posse nisi
certum ;   quod si quae incerti sunt exitus ea quasi
certa providentur, opinionis id esse caliginem non
70 scientiae veritatem.   Aliter enim ac sese res habeat
arbitrari ab integritate scientiae credis esse diversum.
Cuius erroris causa est, quod omnia quae quisque
408

look at set out before our eyes, as for example those things which charioteers are watched doing in guiding and turning their teams, and other things of a similar kind. Now surely no necessity compels any of these things to happen as it does ? "

" Not at all ; for the exercise of skill would be useless if all things moved under compulsion."

" Therefore things which, while they are happening, lack any necessity of being so, these same things, before they happen, are future without any necessity. And therefore there are some things going to happen the occurrence of which is free from all necessity. For I do not think that any man would say this, that those things which are happening now were not " going to happen " before they happened ; therefore of these, even foreknown, the occurrence is free. For just as knowledge of present things introduces no necessity into those things which are happening, so the foreknowledge of future things introduces none into those things which are to come. But this, you say, is exactly what is in doubt, whether there can be any foreknowledge of those things which do not have necessary outcomes. For these two (foreknowledge and not-necessary outcomes) seem to be incompatible, and you think that if things are foreseen, necessity is a consequence, and if there is no necessity, they cannot be foreknown at all, and nothing can be grasped by knowledge except what is certain. But if those things which are of uncertain outcome are foreseen as if they were certain, that is really the obscurity of opinion, not the truth of knowledge ; for you believe thinking things to be other than as they are to be alien to the integrity of knowledge. The cause of this mistake is that each

409

novit ex ipsorum tantum vi atque natura cognosci
aestimat quae sciuntur ; quod totum contra est.
75 Omne enim quod cognoscitur non secundum sui vim
sed secundum cognoscentium potius comprehenditur
facultatem. Nam ut hoc brevi liqueat exemplo,
eandem corporis rotunditatem aliter visus aliter
tactus agnoscit. Ille eminus manens totum simul
80 iactis radiis intuetur ; hic vero cohaerens orbi atque
coniunctus circa ipsum motus ambitum rotunditatem
partibus comprehendit. Ipsum quoque hominem
aliter sensus, aliter imaginatio, aliter ratio, aliter
intellegentia contuetur. Sensus enim figuram in
85 subiecta materia constitutam, imaginatio vero solam
sine materia iudicat figuram. Ratio vero hanc
quoque transcendit speciemque ipsam quae singularibus inest universali consideratione perpendit. Intellegentiae vero celsior oculus exsistit ; supergressa
90 namque universitatis ambitum ipsam illam simplicem
formam pura mentis acie contuetur.

In quo illud maxime considerandum est : nam
superior comprehendendi vis amplectitur inferiorem,
inferior vero ad superiorem nullo modo consurgit.
95 Neque enim sensus aliquid extra materiam valet vel
universales species imaginatio contuetur vel ratio capit
simplicem formam, sed intellegentia quasi desuper
spectans concepta forma quae subsunt etiam cuncta
diiudicat, sed eo modo quo formam ipsam, quae nulli
100 alii nota esse poterat, comprehendit. Nam et rationis

---

[a] This principle, which is stated again later, is virtually to
be found—though not in this formulation—in the commentary
of Ammonius on Aristotle's *De Interpretatione* (*Comm. Arist.
Graeca*, iv. 5. 12 ff., where Ammonius claims to be following
Iamblichus) to which Boethius owes a good deal in this part
of his work.

thinks that all that he knows is known simply by the power and nature of those things that are known. Which is altogether otherwise : for everything which is known is grasped not according to its own power but rather according to the capability of those who know it.[a] For—that this may become clear by a brief example—the same roundness of a body sight recognizes in one way and touch in another ; the former sense remaining at a distance looks at the whole at once by the light of its emitted rays, while the latter, being united and conjoined to the round body, going right round its circuit, grasps the roundness by parts.

Man himself also, sense, imagination, reason and intelligence look at in different ways. For sense examines the shape set in the underlying matter, imagination the shape alone without the matter ; while reason surpasses this too, and examines with a universal consideration the specific form itself, which is present in single individuals. But the eye of intelligence is set higher still ; for passing beyond the process of going round the one whole, it looks with the pure sight of the mind at the simple Form itself. And herein the greatest consideration is to be given to this : for the higher power of comprehension embraces the lower, while the lower in no way rises to the higher. For neither can sense attain to anything outside matter, nor does imagination look at universal specific forms, nor does reason grasp the simple Form : but the intelligence, as it were looking down from above, by conceiving the Form distinguishes all the things subject to that Form, but only because of the way it comprehends the Form itself, which could not be known to anything else. For it knows

universum et imaginationis figuram et materiale sensibile cognoscit nec ratione utens nec imaginatione nec
sensibus, sed illo uno ictu mentis formaliter, ut ita
dicam, cuncta prospiciens. Ratio quoque cum quid
105 universale respicit, nec imaginatione nec sensibus
utens imaginabilia vel sensibilia comprehendit.
Haec est enim quae conceptionis suae universale ita
definivit : homo est animal bipes rationale. Quae
cum universalis notio sit, tum imaginabilem sensi-
110 bilemque esse rem nullus ignorat, quod illa non
imaginatione vel sensu sed in rationali conceptione
considerat. Imaginatio quoque tametsi ex sensibus
visendi formandique figuras sumpsit exordium, sensu
tamen absente sensibilia quacque conlustrat non
115 sensibili sed imaginaria ratione iudicandi. Videsne
igitur ut in cognoscendo cuncta sua potius facultate
quam eorum quae cognoscuntur utantur ? Neque id
iniuria ; nam cum omne iudicium iudicantis actus
exsistat, necesse est ut suam quisque operam non ex
120 aliena sed ex propria potestate perficiat.

## IV

Quondam porticus attulit
Obscuros nimium senes
Qui sensus et imagines
E corporibus extimis
5     Credant mentibus imprimi,
Ut quondam celeri stilo
Mos est aequore paginae,
Quae nullas habeat notas,

---

<sup>a</sup> The Porch refers to the *Stoa Poikilê*, or Painted Porch,
in Athens, used as a lecture-hall by Zeno, the founder of the
Stoic school of philosophers.

the reason's universal, and the imagination's shape, and what is materially sensible, but without using reason, imagination or the senses, but by the one stroke of the mind, Formally, so to speak, looking forth on all these things together. Reason, too, when it regards some universal, without using imagination or the senses grasps the imaginable and sensible aspects. For reason it is which defines the universal it has conceived thus : man is a rational, bipedal animal. And although this is a universal idea, at the same time no-one is ignorant that it is an imaginable and sensible thing which the reason is considering, not by means of imagination or sense, but in its rational conceiving. Imagination also, although it has taken its beginning of seeing and forming shapes from the senses, yet with sense removed surveys all sensible things not by a sensible manner of examining them but by an imaginative one. Do you therefore see that in knowing, all these use their own capability rather than that of those things which are known ? Nor is this wrong : for since every judgement is the act of one judging, it must be that each performs his task not from some other's power but from his own.

## IV

Sometimes the Porch [a] has brought into the world
Some very obscure old philosophers,
Such as think sensible images
From bodies outside themselves
Are impressed upon men's minds ;
As at times with swiftly-moving stylus
Men are used to print the blank space of a page
Which has no marks

Pressas figere litteras.
10 Sed mens si propriis vigens
Nihil motibus explicat,
Sed tantum patiens iacet
Notis subdita corporum
Cassasque in speculi vicem
15 Rerum reddit imagines,
Unde haec sic animis viget
Cernens omnia notio ?
Quae vis singula perspicit
Aut quae cognita dividit ?
20 Quae divisa recolligit
Alternumque legens iter
Nunc summis caput inserit,
Nunc decedit in infima,
Tum sese referens sibi
25 Veris falsa redarguit ?
Haec est efficiens magis
Longe causa potentior
Quam quae materiae modo
Impressas patitur notas.
30 Praecedit tamen excitans
Ac vires animi movens
Vivo in corpore passio.
Cum vel lux oculos ferit
Vel vox auribus instrepit,
35 Tum mentis vigor excitus
Quas intus species tenet
Ad motus similes vocans
Notis applicat exteris
Introrsumque reconditis
40 Formis miscet imagines.

414

# CONSOLATION V

With impressed letters.
But if the mind, with the strength of its proper
    motions,
Nothing unfolds,
But merely passive lies
Subject to other bodies' marks,
And like a mirror but reflects
The empty images of things,
Whence then this all-discerning common concept's
    strength
In the minds of men ?
What power singulars perceives,
Or what power all things known divides ?
Things thus divided what collects again,
And taking either way in turn
Now lifts its head to highest things
And now to lowest things descends,
Then to itself returning
Falsehood refutes with truth ?
This is an efficient cause
More powerful by far
Than that which passively receives
Only the impressed marks on things material.
Yet there precedes,
To stir and move the powers of the mind,
Emotive movement in the living body,
As when light strikes the eyes,
Or a cry in the ears resounds.
Then the mind's wakened power,
Calling upon these forms it holds within
To similar motions,
Applies them to the marks received from without
And joins those images
To the forms hidden within.

## V

Quod si in corporibus sentiendis, quamvis afficiant
instrumenta sensuum forinsecus obiectae qualitates
animique agentis vigorem passio corporis antecedat
quae in se actum mentis provocet excitetque interim
5 quiescentes intrinsecus formas, si in sentiendis,
inquam, corporibus animus non passione insignitur,
sed ex sua vi subiectam corpori iudicat passionem,
quanto magis ea quae cunctis corporum affectionibus
absoluta sunt, in discernendo non obiecta extrinsecus
10 sequuntur, sed actum suae mentis expediunt ? Hac
itaque ratione multiplices cognitiones diversis ac
differentibus cessere substantiis. Sensus enim solus
cunctis aliis cognitionibus destitutus immobilibus
animantibus cessit quales sunt conchae maris quaeque
15 alia saxis haerentia nutriuntur, imaginatio vero
mobilibus beluis quibus iam inesse fugiendi appe-
tendive aliquis videtur affectus, ratio vero humani
tantum generis est sicut intellegentia sola divini.
Quo fit ut ea notitia ceteris praestet quae suapte
20 natura non modo proprium sed ceterarum quoque
notitiarum subiecta cognoscit. Quid igitur, si ratio-
cinationi sensus imaginatioque refragentur, nihil esse
illud universale dicentes quod sese intueri ratio
putet ? Quod enim sensibile vel imaginabile est, id
25 universum esse non posse ; aut igitur rationis verum
esse iudicium nec quidquam esse sensibile, aut
416

## V

Now if in perceiving corporeal things, although qualities presented from without affect the apparatus of the senses, and the emotive movement of the body precedes the activity of the active mind, a movement which calls forth upon itself the action of the mind and stirs up the forms previously lying at rest within ; if, I say, in perceiving corporeal things, the mind is not marked by that movement, but of its own power judges that movement, which is a quality of the body, then how much the more do those things which are quite separate from all bodily affections, in the act of judgement not follow things presented from without, but set in motion the action of the mind to which they belong ! And so on this principle many kinds of knowledge belong to different and diverse substances. For sense alone without any other kind of knowledge belongs to living things that do not move, such as are sea shells and such other things as feed clinging to rocks ; but imagination belongs to beasts that move, which seem already to have in them some disposition to flee or to seek out things. But reason belongs only to human kind, as intelligence only to the divine. So it is that that kind of knowledge is better than the rest which of its own nature knows not only its own object but the subjects of other kinds of knowledge also.

What, then, if sense and imagination gainsay reasoning, saying that that universal which reason thinks she perceives, is nothing at all ? For that which is the object of sense and imagination cannot, they say, be universal ; therefore either the judgement of reason is true, and there is nothing sensible,

quoniam sibi notum sit plura sensibus et imaginationi
esse subiecta, inanem conceptionem esse rationis quae
quod sensibile sit ac singulare quasi quiddam univer-
30 sale consideret. Ad haec, si ratio contra respondeat
se quidem et quod sensibile et quod imaginabile sit
in universitatis ratione conspicere, illa vero ad universitatis cognitionem adspirare non posse, quoniam
eorum notio corporales figuras non possit excedere, de
35 rerum vero cognitione firmiori potius perfectiorique
iudicio esse credendum, in huiusmodi igitur lite nos
quibus tam ratiocinandi quam imaginandi etiam
sentiendique vis inest nonne rationis potius causam
probaremus ? Simile est quod humana ratio divinam
40 intellegentiam futura, nisi ut ipsa cognoscit, non
putat intueri. Nam ita disseris: Si qua certos ac
necessarios habere non videantur eventus, ea certo
eventura praesciri nequeunt. Harum igitur rerum
nulla est praescientia, quam si etiam in his esse
45 credamus, nihil erit quod non ex necessitate proveniat. Si igitur uti rationis participes sumus, ita
divinae iudicium mentis habere possemus, sicut
imaginationem sensumque rationi cedere oportere
iudicavimus, sic divinae sese menti humanam sub-
50 mittere rationem iustissimum censeremus. Quare in
illius summae intellegentiae cacumen, si possumus,
erigamur ; illic enim ratio videbit quod in se non
potest intueri, id autem est, quonam modo etiam
quae certos exitus non habent, certa tamen videat
418

or, since they know that many things are objects of
the senses and imagination, reason's concept is empty,
since she thinks of that which is sensible and singular
as if it were some kind of universal. Further, if
reason rejoins to this that she does indeed see both
the object of sense and the object of imagination
under the aspect of their universality, but that they
cannot aspire to the knowledge of universality since
their knowledge cannot go beyond corporeal shapes,
but we must give credence rather to the more firm
and perfect judgement concerning the knowledge of
things : in this sort of argument, then, should we
not, we who have in us the power of reasoning as well
as those of imagination and sense, should we not
rather judge in favour of reason's case ? It is similar
when human reason thinks that the divine intelligence does not see future things except in the same
manner as she herself knows them. For this is how
you argue : if any things seem not to have certain
and necessary occurrences, those things cannot be
certainly foreknown as going to occur. Therefore
of these things there is no foreknowledge, and if we
think there is foreknowledge in these matters, there
will be nothing which does not happen from necessity.
Now if just as we have a share in reason, so we could
possess the judgement belonging to the divine mind,
then just as we have judged that imagination and
sense ought to give way to reason, so we should think
it most just that human reason should submit to the
divine mind. Wherefore let us be raised up, if we
can, to the height of that highest intelligence ; for
there reason will see that which she cannot look at
in herself, and that is, in what way even those things
which have no certain occurrence a certain and

55 ac definita praenotio neque id sit opinio sed summae
   potius scientiae nullis terminis inclusa simplicitas.

V

Quam variis terras animalia permeant figuris !

Namque  alia  extento  sunt  corpore  pulveremque
   verrunt

Continuumque trahunt vi pectoris incitata sulcum,

Sunt quibus alarum levitas vaga verberetque ventos

5 Et liquido longi spatia aetheris enatet volatu,

Haec pressisse solo vestigia gressibusque gaudent

Vel virides campos transmittere vel subire silvas.

Quae variis videas licet omnia discrepare formis,

Prona tamen facies hebetes valet ingravare sensus.

10 Unica gens hominum celsum levat altius cacumen

Atque levis recto stat corpore despicitque terras.

Haec nisi terrenus male desipis, admonet figura,

Qui recto caelum vultu petis exserisque frontem,

In sublime feras animum quoque, ne gravata pessum

15 Inferior sidat mens corpore celsius levato.

definite foreknowledge yet does see, neither is that opinion, but rather the simplicity, shut in by no bounds, of the highest knowledge.

## V

In what diversity of shapes do living things traverse
    the lands !
For some are long in body and sweep the dust
And draw a continuous furrow, moved by their belly's
    power ;
There are those the lightness of whose wandering
    wings beats on the winds
And floats in the spaces of the ether far with flight
    so smooth ;
These others delight to press their footprints in the
    ground, and with their steps
To cross green fields, or pass beneath the woods.
And all these, though you see they differ in their
    various forms,
Yet their downturned faces make their senses heavy
    grow and dull.
Only the race of men lift high their lofty heads
And lightly stand with upright bodies, looking down
    so on the earth.
And (unless, being earthly, you are stupidly wrong)
    this shape tells you,
You who with upright face do seek the sky, and
    thrust your forehead out,
You should also bear your mind aloft, lest weighted
    down
The mind sink lower than the body raised above.

## VI

Quoniam igitur, uti paulo ante monstratum est, omne quod scitur non ex sua sed ex conprehendentium natura cognoscitur, intueamur nunc quantum fas est, quis sit divinae substantiae status, ut quaenam
5 etiam scientia eius sit, possimus agnoscere. Deum igitur aeternum esse cunctorum ratione degentium commune iudicium est. Quid sit igitur aeternitas consideremus ; haec enim nobis naturam pariter divinam scientiamque patefacit. Aeternitas igitur
10 est interminabilis vitae tota simul et perfecta possessio, quod ex collatione temporalium clarius liquet. Nam quidquid vivit in tempore id praesens a praeteritis in futura procedit nihilque est in tempore constitutum quod totum vitae suae spatium pariter
15 possit amplecti. Sed crastinum quidem nondum adprehendit, hesternum vero iam perdidit ; in hodierna quoque vita non amplius vivitis quam in illo mobili transitorioque momento. Quod igitur temporis patitur condicionem, licet illud, sicuti de mundo censuit
20 Aristoteles, nec coeperit umquam esse nec desinat vitaque eius cum temporis infinitate tendatur, nondum tamen tale est ut aeternum esse iure credatur. Non enim totum simul infinitae licet vitae spatium comprehendit atque complectitur, sed futura nondum,
25 transacta iam non habet. Quod igitur interminabilis vitae plenitudinem totam pariter comprehendit ac possidet, cui neque futuri quidquam absit nec praeteriti fluxerit, id aeternum esse iure perhibetur, idque

## VI

Since, then, as was shown a little while ago, everything which is known is known not according to its own nature but according to the nature of those comprehending it, let us now examine, so far as is allowable, what is the nature of the divine substance, so that we may be able to recognize what kind of knowledge his is. Now that God is eternal is the common judgement of all who live by reason. Therefore let us consider, what is eternity; for this makes plain to us both the divine nature and the divine knowledge. Eternity, then, is the whole, simultaneous and perfect possession of boundless life, which becomes clearer by comparison with temporal things. For whatever lives in time proceeds in the present from the past into the future, and there is nothing established in time which can embrace the whole space of its life equally, but tomorrow surely it does not yet grasp, while yesterday it has already lost. And in this day to day life you live no more than in that moving and transitory moment. Therefore whatever endures the condition of time, although, as Aristotle thought concerning the world, it neither began ever to be nor ceases to be, and although its life is drawn out with the infinity of time, yet it is not yet such that it may rightly be believed to be eternal. For it does not simultaneously comprehend and embrace the whole space of its life, though it be infinite, but it possesses the future not yet, the past no longer. Whatever therefore comprehends and possesses at once the whole fullness of boundless life, and is such that neither is anything future lacking from it, nor has anything past flowed away, that is

necesse est et sui compos praesens sibi semper ad-
30 sistere et infinitatem mobilis temporis habere praesentem. Unde non recte quidam, qui cum audiunt
visum Platoni mundum hunc nec habuisse initium
temporis nec habiturum esse defectum, hoc modo
conditori conditum mundum fieri coaeternum putant.
35 Aliud est enim per interminabilem duci vitam, quod
mundo Plato tribuit, aliud interminabilis vitae totam
pariter complexum esse praesentiam, quod divinae
mentis proprium esse manifestum est. Neque deus
conditis rebus antiquior videri debet temporis quan-
40 titate sed simplicis potius proprietate naturae. Hunc
enim vitae immobilis praesentarium statum infinitus
ille temporalium rerum motus imitatur cumque eum
effingere atque aequare non possit, ex immobilitate
deficit in motum, ex simplicitate praesentiae decrescit
45 in infinitam futuri ac praeteriti quantitatem ; et
cum totam pariter vitae suae plenitudinem nequeat
possidere, hoc ipso quod aliquo modo numquam esse
desinit, illud quod implere atque exprimere non
potest, aliquatenus videtur aemulari alligans se ad
50 qualemcumque praesentiam huius exigui volucrisque
momenti, quae, quoniam manentis illius praesentiae
quandam gestat imaginem, quibuscumque contigerit
id praestat ut esse videantur. Quoniam vero manere
non potuit, infinitum temporis iter arripuit eoque
55 modo factum est ut continuaret eundo vitam cuius
plenitudinem complecti non valuit permanendo.
Itaque si digna rebus nomina velimus imponere,
424

rightly held to be eternal, and that must necessarily both always be present to itself, possessing itself in the present, and hold as present the infinity of moving time.

And therefore those are not right who, when they hear that Plato thought this world neither had a beginning in time nor would have an end, think that in this way the created world is made co-eternal with the Creator. For it is one thing to be drawn out through a life without bounds, which is what Plato attributes to the world, but it is a different thing to have embraced at once the whole presence of boundless life, which it is clear is the property of the divine mind. Nor should God seem to be more ancient than created things by some amount of time, but rather by his own simplicity of nature. For this present nature of unmoving life that infinite movement of temporal things imitates, and since it cannot fully represent and equal it, it fails from immobility into motion, it shrinks from the simplicity of that present into the infinite quantity of the future and the past and, since it cannot possess at once the whole fullness of its life, in this very respect, that it in some way never ceases to be, it seems to emulate to some degree which it cannot fully express, by binding itself to the sort of present of this brief and fleeting moment, a present which since it wears a kind of likeness of that permanent present, grants to whatsoever things it touches that they should seem to be. But since it could not be permanent, it seized on the infinite journeying of time, and in that way became such that it should continue by going on a life the fullness of which it could not embrace by being permanent. And so if we should wish to give things

425

Platonem sequentes deum quidem aeternum, mundum vero dicamus esse perpetuum. Quoniam igitur
60 omne iudicium secundum sui naturam quae sibi subiecta sunt comprehendit, est autem deo semper
aeternus ac praesentarius status ; scientia quoque
eius omnem temporis supergressa motionem in suae
manet simplicitate praesentiae infinitaque praeteriti
65 ac futuri spatia complectens omnia quasi iam gerantur
in sua simplici cognitione considerat. Itaque si praescientiam[1] pensare velis qua cuncta dinoscit, non esse
praescientiam quasi futuri sed scientiam numquam
deficientis instantiae rectius aestimabis ; unde non
70 praevidentia sed providentia potius dicitur, quod
porro ab rebus infimis constituta quasi ab excelso
rerum cacumine cuncta prospiciat. Quid igitur
postulas ut necessaria fiant quae divino lumine lus-
trentur, cum ne homines quidem necessaria faciant
75 esse quae videant ? Num enim quae praesentia
cernis, aliquam eis necessitatem tuus addit intuitus ? "
" Minime." " Atqui si est divini humanique praesentis digna collatio, uti vos vestro hoc temporario
praesenti quaedam videtis, ita ille omnia suo cernit
80 aeterno. Quare haec divina praenotio naturam rerum
proprietatemque non mutat taliaque apud se praesentia spectat qualia in tempore olim futura pro-
venient. Nec rerum iudicia confundit unoque suae
mentis intuitu tam necessarie quam non necessarie

---

[1] praescientian $V^2$ *Land* : praevidentiam $V^1$ : praesentiam
*the other MSS.*

426

names befitting them, then following Plato we should say that God indeed is eternal, but that the world is perpetual.

Since then every judgement comprehends those things subject to it according to its own nature, and God has an always eternal and present nature, then his knowledge too, surpassing all movement of time, is permanent in the simplicity of his present, and embracing all the infinite spaces of the future and the past, considers them in his simple act of knowledge as though they were now going on. So if you should wish to consider his foreknowledge, by which he discerns all things, you will more rightly judge it to be not foreknowledge as it were of the future but knowledge of a never-passing instant. And therefore it is called not prevision (*praevidentia*) but providence (*providentia*), because set far from the lowest of things it looks forward on all things as though from the highest peak of the world. Why then do you require those things to be made necessary which are scanned by the light of God's sight, when not even men make necessary those things they see? After all, your looking at them does not confer any necessity on those things you presently see, does it?"

"Not at all."

"But if the comparison of the divine and the human present is a proper one, just as you see certain things in this your temporal present, so he perceives all things in his eternal one. And therefore this divine foreknowledge does not alter the proper nature of things, but sees them present to him just such as in time they will at some future point come to be. Nor does he confuse the ways things are to be judged, but with one glance of his mind distinguishes both

427

85 ventura dinoscit ; sicuti vos cum pariter ambulare in
terra hominem et oriri in caelo solem videtis, quamquam simul utrumque conspectum tamen discernitis
et hoc voluntarium illud esse necessarium iudicatis,
ita igitur cuncta despiciens divinus intuitus quali-
90 tatem rerum minime perturbat apud se quidem praesentium, ad condicionem vero temporis futurarum.
Quo fit ut hoc non sit opinio sed veritate potius nixa
cognitio, cum exstaturum quid esse cognoscit quod
idem exsistendi necessitate carere non nesciat. Hic
95 si dicas quod eventurum deus videt id non evenire
non posse, quod autem non potest non evenire id ex
necessitate contingere, meque ad hoc nomen necessitatis adstringas, fatebor rem quidem solidissimae
veritatis sed cui vix aliquis nisi divini speculator
100 accesserit. Respondebo namque idem futurum, cum
ad divinam notionem refertur, necessarium, cum vero
in sua natura perpenditur, liberum prorsus atque
absolutum videri. Duae sunt etenim necessitates,
simplex una, veluti quod necesse est omnes homines
105 esse mortales, altera condicionis, ut si aliquem
ambulare scias, eum ambulare necesse est ; quod
enim quisque novit, id esse aliter ac notum est
nequit, sed haec condicio minime secum illam simplicem trahit. Hanc enim necessitatem non propria
110 facit natura sed condicionis adiectio ; nulla enim
necessitas cogit incedere voluntate gradientem,
428

those things necessarily coming to be and those not necessarily coming to be, just as you, when you see at one and the same time that a man is walking on the ground and that the sun is rising in the sky, although the two things are seen simultaneously, yet you distinguish them, and judge the first to be voluntary, the second necessary. So then the divine perception looking down on all things does not disturb at all the quality of things that are present indeed to him but future with reference to imposed conditions of time. So it is that it is not opinion but a knowledge grounded rather upon truth, when he knows that something is going to happen, something which he is also aware lacks all necessity of happening. If at this point you were to say that what God sees is going to occur cannot not occur, and that what cannot not occur happens from necessity, and so bind me to this word " necessity," I will admit that this is a matter indeed of the firmest truth, but one which scarcely anyone except a theologian could tackle. For I shall say in answer that the same future event, when it is related to divine knowledge, is necessary, but when it is considered in its own nature it seems to be utterly and absolutely free. For there are really two necessities, the one simple, as that it is necessary that all men are mortal ; the other conditional, as for example, if you know that someone is walking, it is necessary that he is walking. Whatever anyone knows cannot be otherwise than as it is known, but this conditional necessity by no means carries with it that other simple kind. For this sort of necessity is not caused by a thing's proper nature but by the addition of the condition ; for no necessity forces him to go who walks of his own will, even

quamvis eum tum cum graditur incedere necessarium
sit. Eodem igitur modo, si quid providentia praesens
videt, id esse necesse est, tametsi nullam naturae
115 habeat necessitatem. Atqui deus ea futura quae ex
arbitrii libertate proveniunt praesentia contuetur.
Haec igitur ad intuitum relata divinum necessaria
fiunt per condicionem divinae notionis ; per se vero
considerata ab absoluta naturae suae libertate non
120 desinunt. Fient igitur procul dubio cuncta quae
futura deus esse praenoscit, sed eorum quaedam de
libero proficiscuntur arbitrio ; quae quamvis eveniant,
exsistendo tamen naturam propriam non amittunt,
qua priusquam fierent non evenire potuissent.
125 Quid igitur refert non esse necessaria, cum propter
divinae scientiae condicionem modis omnibus necessitatis instar eveniet ? Hoc scilicet quod ea quae
paulo ante proposui, sol oriens et gradiens homo.
Quae dum fiunt, non fieri non possunt ; eorum tamen
130 unum prius quoque quam fieret, necesse erat exsistere,
alterum vero minime. Ita etiam quae praesentia
deus habet, dubio procul exsistent, sed eorum hoc
quidem de rerum necessitate descendit, illud vero
de potestate facientium. Haud igitur iniuria diximus
135 haec si ad divinam notitiam referantur necessaria,
si per se considerentur necessitatis esse nexibus
absoluta ; sicuti omne quod sensibus patet, si ad
rationem referas, universale est, si ad se ipsa respicias,
singulare. ' Sed si in mea,' inquies, ' potestate situm
430

though it is necessary that he is going at the time
when he is walking. Now in the same way, if providence sees anything as present, that must necessarily
be, even if it possesses no necessity of its nature. But
God beholds those future events which happen because of the freedom of the will, as present; they
therefore, related to the divine perception, become
necessary through the condition of the divine knowledge, but considered in themselves do not lose the
absolute freedom of their nature. Therefore all those
things which God foreknows will come to be, will
without doubt come to be, but certain of them proceed from free will, and although they do come to be,
yet in happening they do not lose their proper nature,
according to which, before they happened, they
might also not have happened. What then does it
matter that they are not necessary, since on account
of the condition of the divine knowledge it will turn
out in all respects like necessity? Surely as much as
those things I put before you a moment ago, the
rising sun and the walking man: while these things
are happening, they cannot not happen, but of the
two one, even before it happened, was bound to
happen, while the other was not. So also, those
things God possesses as present, beyond doubt will
happen, but of them the one kind is consequent upon
the necessity of things, the other upon the power of
those doing them. So therefore we were not wrong
in saying that these, if related to the divine knowledge,
are necessary, if considered in themselves, are free
from the bonds of necessity, just as everything which
lies open to the senses, if you relate it to the reason,
is universal, if you look at it by itself, is singular.

But if, you will say, it lies in my power to change

140 est mutare propositum, evacuabo providentiam, cum
quae illa praenoscit forte mutavero.' Respondebo :
propositum te quidem tuum posse deflectere, sed
quoniam et id te posse et an facias quove convertas
praesens providentiae veritas intuetur, divinam te
145 praescientiam non posse vitare, sicuti praesentis oculi
effugere non possis intuitum, quamvis te in varias
actiones libera voluntate converteris. Quid igitur
inquies ? Ex meane dispositione scientia divina muta-
bitur, ut cum ego nunc hoc nunc aliud velim, illa
150 quoque noscendi vices alternare videatur ? Minime.
Omne namque futurum divinus praecurrit intuitus
et ad praesentiam propriae cognitionis retorquet ac
revocat nec alternat, ut aestimas, nunc hoc nunc
illud praenoscendi vice, sed uno ictu mutationes tuas
155 manens praevenit atque complectitur. Quam comprehendendi omnia visendique praesentiam non ex
futurarum proventu rerum, sed ex propria deus
simplicitate sortitus est. Ex quo illud quoque re-
solvitur quod paulo ante posuisti indignum esse, si
160 scientiae dei causam futura nostra praestare dicantur.
Haec enim scientiae vis praesentaria notione cuncta
complectens rebus modum omnibus ipsa constituit,
nihil vero posterioribus debet. Quae cum ita sint,
manet intemerata mortalibus arbitrii libertas nec
165 iniquae leges solutis omni necessitate voluntatibus
praemia poenasque proponunt. Manet etiam spec-
tator desuper cunctorum praescius deus visionisque
eius praesens semper aeternitas cum nostrorum actuum
432

my intention, I shall make nonsense of providence, since what providence foreknows, I shall perhaps have changed. I shall reply that you can indeed alter your intention, but since the truth of providence sees in its present both that you can do so, and whether you will do so and in what direction you will change, you cannot avoid the divine prescience, just as you could not escape the sight of an eye that was present, even though of your own free will you changed to different courses of action. What then will you say? Will the divine knowledge be changed by my disposition, so that, since I want to do this at one time and that at another, it too alternates from this kind of knowledge to that? Not at all. For the divine perception runs ahead over every future event and turns it back and recalls it to the present of its own knowledge, and does not alternate, as you suggest, foreknowing now this, now that, but itself remaining still anticipates and embraces your changes at one stroke. And God possesses this present instant of comprehension and sight of all things not from the issuing of future events but from his own simplicity. In this way that too is resolved which you suggested a little while ago, that it is not right that our future actions should be said to provide the cause of the knowledge of God. For the nature of his knowledge as we have described it, embracing all things in a present act of knowing, establishes a measure for everything, but owes nothing to later events. These things being so, the freedom of the will remains to mortals, inviolate, nor are laws proposing rewards and punishments for wills free from all necessity unjust. There remains also as an observer from on high foreknowing all things, God, and the always present

futura qualitate concurrit bonis praemia malis sup-
170 plicia dispensans. Nec frustra sunt in deo positae
spes precesque ; quae cum rectae sunt, inefficaces esse
non possunt. Aversamini igitur vitia, colite virtutes,
ad rectas spes animum sublevate, humiles preces in
excelsa porrigite. Magna vobis est, si dissimulare
175 non vultis, necessitas indicta probitatis, cum ante
oculos agitis iudicis cuncta cernentis."

eternity of his sight runs along with the future quality of our actions dispensing rewards for the good and punishments for the wicked. Nor vainly are our hopes placed in God, nor our prayers, which when they are right cannot be ineffectual. Turn away then from vices, cultivate virtues, lift up your mind to righteous hopes, offer up humble prayers to heaven. A great necessity is solemnly ordained for you if you do not want to deceive yourselves, to do good, when you act before the eyes of a judge who sees all things.

# INDEX

437

# INDEX

divine nature, eternal, 57 ;
  substance, 9, 305
*divisio*, 82 n.

EGYPT, 63, 65
Εἰσαγωγή, Porphyry's, xi ;
  Boethius' Commentary, xi,
  6 n., 8 n., 10 n., 82 n., 96 n.
Eleatic studies, 135
elements, 273
Epicureans, 143, 234 n. ;
  Epicurus, 152 n., 235
*esse*, 40 n.
*essentia*, 89 ff.
eternity, *see aeternitas*
Etna, 209
Eudoxus, 136 n.
Euphrates, 389
Euripides, 253, 259
Euripus, 178
Eurus, 198, 336
Eurydice, 311
Eutyches, 67, 73 ff. ; Euty-
  chians, 113
Evander, 381
Eve, 59
evil is nothing, 305

FABRICIUS, 223
faith, xiv
fame, 3, 219 ; *see* glory
Fate, 59 ff.
fire, 293
Flood, 61 ff.
form, 9 ff., 13, 15
Fortune, 175 ff., 375, 379
free-will, 391 ff.
Furies, 309

GAIUS CALIGULA, 153
Gaudentius, 151
geometricians, 41, 281

giants, 303
glory, 253 ff.
God, categories applied to,
  17 ff., 23 ff. ; without
  difference, 13 ; is what He
  is, 19, 51 ; is Pure Form,
  15 ; is οὐσία, οὐσίωσις,
  ὑφίστασθαι, 91 ; One, 7,
  29, 33 ; Triune, 7, 29,
  33 ; is good, 277 ff., 301,
  305 ; happiness, 277, 301,
  305 ; eternal, 21, 423 ff. ;
  omnipresent, 21 ; incom-
  prehensible, 371 ; one
  Father, 257 ; true Sun,
  395 ; Creator, 57, 71, 159,
  271 ff. ; Ruler, 271 ff.,
  299 ff., 365 ; Mover, 299 ;
  Judge, 433, 435 ; sees all
  things, 427 ff. ; foresees
  all things, 397 ff., 427 ;
  His knowledge, 427 ff. ;
  His providence, 359 ff. ;
  cannot do evil, 305 ; wills
  only good, 315, 371 ;
  prayer to Him not in
  vain, 307, 435. *See* Trinity
good, 39-51 ; the prime,
  45 ff., 49 ff., 272 ff. ; all
  seek the good, 233 ff., 291,
  295, 331 ; goodness is
  happiness, is God, 275,
  277, 301, 305, 331 ff.
grace, 401
Greek, 87, 89

HAPPINESS is God, 277, 301,
  305
*Hebdomads*, 39
Hecuba, 87
Hercules, 211, 381, 383
heresy, *see* Arius, Eutyches,

439

# INDEX

# INDEX

# INDEX

Stoics, 143, 412 n.
Stymphalian birds, 381
*subsistentia, subsistere*, 89 ff.
substance, divine, 9, 23, 29,
    33, 307, 423 ; substances,
    39 ff.
*substantia, substare*, 39, 83 ff.,
    89 ff.
sun, *see* Phoebus
Symmachus, Q. Aurel., xi ;
    Q. Aur. Memmius, father-
    in-law of Boethius, xi n.,
    3 ; cp. 74, 187 ; son of
    Boethius, xi, 193 (his
    other son was Anicius, xi,
    193) ; Symmachus, Pope,
    72 n.

TAENARUS, 309
Tagus, 287
Tantalus, 309
Tartarus, 309, 311
Testament, Old and New, 53,
    55, 57, 99 ; *see* scripture
Θ, 133
Theodoric, xi, 148 n., 155
Theology, xiii, 9
Thomas, St., xii, xiv, xv,
    85 n.
Thrace, 141, 307
Thule, 253
Tigris, 389

*Timaeus, see* Plato
Tiresias, 399
Tityus, 309
triangle, 45
Trigguilla, 149
Trinity, the unity of, 7,
    13 ff., 29 ff., 33 ff., 53 ff.,
    91
Tyrian, 207, 249
Tyrrhenian, 263

ΥΛΗ ἄποιος, 10
Ulysses, 337, 381 (Odysseus)
unity, 13
unity of the Trinity, 7, 29,
    33 ff.
ὑπόστασις, 85 ff., 89
ὑποστῆναι, 40 n.

VENUS, planet, 159, 226 (Hes-
    perus), 230, 373 (Lucifer)
Verona, 155
Vesuvius, 145
*via media*, 100 n., 121
Virgin Mary, the, *see* Mary
*virtus*, 378 n.

WILL, free-will, 391 ff.

ZENO, 134 n., 143
Zephyrus, 160, 188

*Printed in Great Britain by* R. & R. CLARK, LIMITED, *Edinburgh*

(74)